T0360401

Firms and Workers in a Globalized World
Larger Markets, Tougher Competition

World Scientific Studies in International Economics
(ISSN: 1793-3641)

World Scientific Studies in International Economics includes works dealing with the theory, empirical analysis, and evaluation of international economic policies and institutions, with topics covering international macroeconomics and finance, international trade theory and policy, as well as international legal and political economy. Monographs and edited volumes will comprise the core of the publications.

The complete list of the published volumes in the series can be found at
https://www.worldscientific.com/series/wssie

79 World Scientific
Studies in
International
Economics

Firms and Workers in a Globalized World
Larger Markets, Tougher Competition

Gianmarco I P Ottaviano
Bocconi University, Italy

World Scientific

NEW JERSEY · LONDON · SINGAPORE · BEIJING · SHANGHAI · HONG KONG · TAIPEI · CHENNAI · TOKYO

Published by

World Scientific Publishing Co. Pte. Ltd.
5 Toh Tuck Link, Singapore 596224
USA office: 27 Warren Street, Suite 401-402, Hackensack, NJ 07601
UK office: 57 Shelton Street, Covent Garden, London WC2H 9HE

Library of Congress Cataloging-in-Publication Data
Names: Ottaviano, Gianmarco I. P., author.
Title: Firms and workers in a globalized world : larger markets, tougher competition /
    Gianmarco IP Ottaviano, Bocconi University, Italy.
Description: Singapore ; Hackensack, NJ : World Scientific Publishing Co. Pte. Ltd., [2021] |
    Series: World scientific studies in international economics, 1793-3641 ; vol. 79 |
    Includes bibliographical references.
Identifiers: LCCN 2021008790 | ISBN 9789811233388 (hardcover) |
    ISBN 9789811233395 (ebook) | ISBN 9789811233401 (ebook other)
Subjects: LCSH: Foreign trade and employment | Globalization--Economic aspects.
Classification: LCC HD5710.7 .O88 2021 | DDC 331.12--dc23
LC record available at https://lccn.loc.gov/2021008790

British Library Cataloguing-in-Publication Data
A catalogue record for this book is available from the British Library.

For any available supplementary material, please visit
https://www.worldscientific.com/worldscibooks/10.1142/12184#t=suppl

Desk Editors: Priyanka Murugan/Natalie Wee/Karimah Samsudin

Typeset by Stallion Press
Email: enquiries@stallionpress.com

Printed in Singapore

To Paola

About the Author

 **Gianmarco I.P. Ottaviano** is Professor of Economics and Boroli Chair in European Studies at Bocconi University, having previously taught at the London School of Economics and the University of Bologna. He received his BA in Economics from Bocconi University, his MSc in Economics from the London School of Economics, and his PhD in Economics from the Université Catholique de Louvain. He is the co-author of many works in international trade, urban economics, and economic geography. His recent publications focus on the competitiveness of firms in the global economy as well as the economic effects of immigration and offshoring on employment and wages.

Acknowledgments

I would like to thank all my co-authors of the articles in this volume for what I have learned from them. I would also like to thank the following publishers and journals for granting their permissions to reproduce the articles in this volume:

Publishers
American Economic Association
Elsevier Science
John Wiley & Sons
Oxford University Press
Springer Nature

Journals
American Economic Review
European Economic Review
International Economic Review
Journal of Economic Geography
Journal of Economic Growth
Journal of the European Economic Association
Journal of Urban Economics
The Review of Economic Studies

Contents

Introduction

Globalization is a complex phenomenon involving the mobility of goods, capital, labor, and ideas across country borders. From an economic point of view, two clear waves of globalization have been identified so far. The first wave materialized between the second half of the Nineteenth century and WWI; the second wave rose after WWII and gained momentum at the end of the Twentieth century before slowing down in the aftermath of the global financial crisis due to renewed protectionist pressures.

This collection of essays studies the implications of this second wave of globalization for national economic performance. In doing so, it takes a bottom-up approach, building up the macroeconomic trajectories from the microeconomic effects of globalization on firms and workers. The collected essays highlight the asymmetry of responses across firms and workers between and within industries as well as between and within territories, thus explaining the forces behind the emergence of "winners" and "losers" from globalization.

The collection shows how state-of-the-art models of international economics and economic geography can be brought to life by addressing several topical issues in the public debate, ranging from regional growth and regional decline to international competition and creative destruction, from innovation patterns to cultural diversity, from immigration to offshoring.

Part I of the book is devoted to firms. It contains two sets of essays. The first set investigates the conditions under which lower trade barriers, more integrated value chains, and easier mobility of people and ideas can lead to the endogenous emergence of uneven economic development by affecting, sometimes dramatically, the geographical distribution of economic activities across countries and regions.

Chapter 1, co-authored with Philippe Martin, constructs a model of endogenous growth and endogenous industry location where the two interact. We show that with global spillovers in R&D, a high growth rate and a high level of transaction costs are associated with foreign direct investment to the South (the location with a low initial wealth). With local spillovers in R&D, this activity is agglomerated in the North and the rate of innovation increases with the concentration of firms in the North. This in turn implies that a decrease of transaction costs, through its impact on economic geography, will increase the growth rate. We show that industrial concentration can be beneficial for both regions if its impact on the rate of innovation is large enough to compensate the South for the loss of industry. This will be the case only for low enough transaction costs and high enough spillovers.

Chapter 2, co-authored with Richard Baldwin and Philippe Martin, formalizes the theoretical interconnections among four post-industrial revolution phenomena — the industrialization and growth take-off of rich northern nations, massive global income divergence, and rapid trade expansion. In the proposed stages-of-growth model, the four phenomena are jointly endogenous and are triggered by falling trade costs. In the first growth stage (with high trade costs), industry is dispersed internationally, and growth is low. In the second (medium trade costs), the North industrializes rapidly, growth takes off, and the South diverges. In the third (low trade costs), high growth and global divergence become self-sustaining. In the fourth stage, when the cases of "trading" ideas decrease, the South quickly industrializes and converges.

Chapter 3, co-authored with Takatoshi Tabuchi and Jacques-François Thisse, has two objectives. First, we present an alternative model of agglomeration and trade that displays the main features of the acclaimed core-periphery model by Paul Krugman while allowing for the derivation of analytical results by means of simple algebra. Second, we show how this framework can be used to permit (i) a welfare analysis of the agglomeration process, (ii) a full-fledged forward-looking analysis of the role of history and expectations in the emergence of economic clusters, and (iii) a simple analysis of the impact of urban costs on the spatial distribution of economic activities.

The second set of essays dedicated to firms investigates the conditions under which trade liberalization leads to diverging destinies between more and less efficient firms in the wake of the celebrated selection model by Marc Melitz. The most important implication of this model is that trade liberalization induces the reallocation of resources from less to more productive firms, thereby increasing aggregate productivity and national welfare through an industry composition effect. This happens without any adjustment in markups due to isoelastic demand.

Chapter 4, co-authored with Marc Melitz, shows that replacing isoelastic demand with linear demand brings additional action into the picture in terms of markup and intensive margin adjustments. In particular, we develop a monopolistically competitive model of trade with firm heterogeneity — in terms of productivity differences — and endogenous differences in the "toughness" of competition across markets — in terms of the number and average productivity of competing firms. We analyze how these features vary across markets of different sizes that are not perfectly integrated through trade; we then study the effects of different trade liberalization policies. In our model, market size and trade affect the toughness of competition, which then feeds back into the selection of heterogeneous producers and exporters in that market. Aggregate productivity and average markups thus respond to both the size of a market and the extent of its integration through trade (larger, more integrated markets exhibit higher productivity and lower markups). Our model remains highly tractable, even when extended to a general framework with multiple asymmetric countries integrated to different extents through asymmetric trade costs. We believe this provides a useful modeling framework that is particularly well suited to the analysis of trade and regional integration policy scenarios in an environment with heterogeneous firms and endogenous markups.

Chapter 5, co-authored with Thierry Mayer and Marc Melitz, builds a theoretical model of multi-product firms that highlights how competition across market destinations affects both a firm's exported product range and product mix. We show how tougher competition in an export market induces a firm to skew its export sales toward its best performing products. We find very strong confirmation of this competitive effect for French exporters across export market destinations. Theoretically, this within-firm change in product mix driven by the trading environment has important repercussions on firm productivity. A calibrated fit to our theoretical model reveals that these productivity effects are potentially quite large.

Part II of the book is devoted to workers. It contains two sets of essays. The first set studies the effects of immigration and diversity on the labor market performance of native workers at the local level with an emphasis on cities.

Chapter 6, co-authored with Giovanni Peri, investigates whether cultural diversity across US cities (measured as the variety of native languages spoken by city residents) is associated with any effect on their productivity. Diversity of cultures may imply diversity of production skills, of abilities, and of occupations that enhance the productive performance of a city. On the contrary, transaction costs and frictions across groups may hurt productivity. Similarly, diversity in available goods and services can increase utility, but distaste for (or hostility to) different cultural groups may decrease it. Using census data from 1970 to 1990, we find that wages and employment density of US-born workers were systematically higher, ceteris paribus, in cities with richer linguistic diversity. These positive correlations reveal a net positive effect of diversity on productivity that survives robustness checks and instrumental variable estimation. This effect is found to be stronger for highly educated workers and for white workers. We also show that better "assimilated" nonnative speakers, i.e. those who speak English well and have been in the US for more than five years, are most beneficial to the productivity of US-born workers.

Chapter 7, co-authored with Giovanni Peri, addressed two questions. What are the economic consequences to US natives of the growing diversity of American cities? Is their productivity or utility affected by cultural diversity as measured by the diversity of the countries of birth of US residents? We document in this paper a very robust correlation: US-born citizens living in metropolitan areas where the share of foreign-born increased between 1970 and 1990 experienced a significant increase in their wage and in the rental price of their housing. Such a finding is economically significant and survives omitted variable bias and endogeneity bias. As people and firms are mobile across cities in the long run, we argue that, in equilibrium, these correlations are consistent with a net positive effect of cultural diversity on the productivity of natives.

The second set of essays dedicated to workers studies the effects of immigration and diversity on the labor market performance of native workers at the national level.

Chapter 8, co-authored with Francesco D'Amuri and Giovanni Peri, estimates the wage and employment effects of immigration in Western Germany. Using administrative data for the period 1987–2001 and a labor-market equilibrium model, we find that the substantial immigration of the 1990s had very little adverse effects on native wages and on their employment levels. Instead, it had a sizeable adverse employment effect on previous immigrants as well as a small adverse effect on their wages. These asymmetric results are partly driven by a higher degree of substitution between old and new immigrants in the labor market and in part by the rigidity of wages in less than flexible labor markets. In a simple counterfactual experiment, we show that in a world of perfect wage flexibility and no unemployment insurance the wage-bill loss of old immigrants would be much smaller.

Chapter 9, co-authored with Giovanni Peri, calculates the effects of immigration on the wages of native US workers of various skill levels in two steps. In the first step, we use labor demand functions to estimate the elasticity of substitution across different groups of workers. Second, we use the underlying production structure and the estimated elasticities to calculate the total wage effects of immigration in the long run. We emphasize that a production function framework is needed to combine own-group effects with cross-group effects in order to obtain the total wage effects for each native group. In order to obtain a parsimonious representation of elasticities that can be estimated with available data, we adopt alternative nested models and let the data select the preferred specification. New to this paper is the estimate of the substitutability between natives and immigrants of similar education and experience levels.

In the data-preferred model, there is a small but significant degree of imperfect substitutability between natives and immigrants which, when combined with the other estimated elasticities, implies that in the period from 1990 to 2006 immigration had a small effect on the wages of native workers with no high school degree. It also had a small positive effect on average native wages and a substantial negative effect on wages of previous immigrants in the long run.

Chapter 10, co-authored with Giovanni Peri and Greg Wright, estimates a trade-in-tasks model in which tasks of varying complexity are matched to workers of varying skill in order to develop and test predictions regarding the effects of immigration and offshoring on US native-born workers. We find that immigrant and native-born workers do not compete much due to the fact that they tend to perform tasks at opposite ends of the task complexity spectrum, with offshore workers performing the tasks in the middle. An effect of offshoring and a positive effect of immigration on native-born employment suggest that immigration and offshoring improve industry efficiency.

Part I
Firms

Chapter 1

Growing locations: Industry location in a model of endogenous growth[†]

Philippe Martin[a,b,c,*], Gianmarco I.P. Ottaviano[c,d,e]

[a] Graduate Institute of International Studies, Geneva, Switzerland
[b] CERAS, 28 rue des Saints-Pères, 75343 Paris Cedex 7, France
[c] CEPR, London, UK
[d] Università di Bologna, Bologna, Italy
[e] CORE, Université Catholique de Louvain, Louvain-la-Neuve, Belgium

Received 1 July 1996; accepted 1 December 1997

Abstract

This paper constructs a model of endogenous growth and endogenous industry location where the two interact. We show that with global spillovers in R&D, a high growth rate and a high level of transaction costs are associated with foreign direct investment to the South (the location with a low initial wealth). With local spillovers in R&D, this activity is agglomerated in the North and the rate of innovation increases with the concentration of firms in the North. This in turn implies that a decrease of transaction costs, through its impact on economic geography, will increase the growth rate. We show that industrial concentration can be beneficial for both regions if its impact on the rate of innovation is large enough to compensate the South for the loss of industry. This will be the case only for low enough transaction costs and high enough spillovers. © 1999 Elsevier Science B.V. All rights reserved.

JEL classification: F43; O30; R12

Keywords: Endogenous growth; Geography; Spillovers; Welfare

* Correspondence address: CERAS, 28 rue des Saints-Pères, 75343 Paris Cedex 7, France.
E-mail: martin@enpc.fr.

†This article originally appeared in European Economic Review, **43** 281–302 © 1999
Elsevier Science Publishers B.V.

282   *P. Martin, G.I.P. Ottaviano / European Economic Review 43 (1999) 281–302*

1. Introduction

Until recently, the theoretical research on endogenous growth and on new 'economic geography' have mostly been kept separate. In most economic geography models, location dynamics are based on the redistribution of a given amount of resources and in most new growth models, the geographical dimension is absent. An exception is Bertola (1993) who develops a model of growth driven by capital accumulation to analyse how the move from autarky to capital and labour mobility affects the location of activity. The result – with increasing returns and mobile factors, one of the two regions will 'disappear' – does not however tell us what is the relation between location and growth in less dramatic scenarios. Walz (1996) constructs a R&D model of growth and location based on aggregate returns to scale at the local level and migration. Trade liberalisation is shown to lead to agglomeration and faster growth. However, his focus on aggregate rather than firm-level increasing returns to scale makes the model distant from one of the main themes of the "new economic geography". The separation between the two fields is unfortunate because they ask related questions. Endogenous growth theory, especially in its most recent direction (Romer, 1990; Grossman and Helpman, 1991) asks the question of how new firms or new goods are created through technological change. The new economic geography asks where firms are located and why they tend to concentrate in a few regions. The absence of a geographical dimension in growth models also contradicts a point stressed by Lucas (1988), that is that the economic mechanism at the origin of endogenous growth requires social interactions or external effects which, precisely, are mostly local in nature.

The separation between the two fields is also surprising. First, from a methodological point of view some of the models used in the two literatures often share a common assumption on the structure of the industry, namely monopolistic competition. This implies that technically the models are not very far apart. Second, the link between growth and location has been studied extensively at the empirical level. A large literature using industrial data at the level of cities and regions has shown the essential role of economic concentration and geography in explaining growth, innovation and the level of productivity.[1]

Hence, we believe that the process of creation of new firms and the process of location should be thought as joint processes. When the external effects which are at the source of endogenous growth are local in nature because they involve localized interactions between economic agents, then the location of firms and of R&D activities will affect the process of technological change. Technological change, when it materializes in the creation of new goods and new firms, will in

---

[1] For such evidence see Arthur (1989), Glaeser et al. (1992), Jaffe et al. (1993), Henderson (1994), Henderson et al. (1995), and Ciccone and Hall (1996).

P. Martin, G.I.P. Ottaviano / European Economic Review 43 (1999) 281–302   283

turn have an impact on the extent and the direction of foreign direct investment and, more generally, capital flows.

This paper presents a model that integrates the features of endogenous growth and endogenous industry location. We analyse how the dynamics of growth (the creation of new firms) and the dynamics of industrial location interact and show that the introduction of explicit dynamics in a location model changes some of the results of the "new geography" literature. We examine how growth affects the location decisions of firms and hence how it affects geography and the dynamics of spatial distribution of economic activities. We also analyse how the rate of technological progress, at the origin of growth, is determined by the location decision of firms and economic geography.

To answer these questions we construct a model where firms can choose to locate between two trading locations, that we call North and South. New firms, each requiring a new "idea", are continuously created through R&D so that growth comes into the form of an expansion in the variety of products consumed. Hence, our model puts together a growth framework à la Romer (1990) and Grossman and Helpman (1991) and a location framework based on Martin and Rogers (1995) itself a variant of Helpman and Krugman (1985) and Krugman (1991). This location framework is different from the "new economic geography" because cumulative causation mechanisms such as migration or vertical linkages are excluded so that we do not model a catastrophic agglomeration phenomenon.

We analyse the relation between location and growth in two different contexts. In the first one, the spillovers in R&D are global: the invention of a new good affects negatively the future cost of R&D in both locations. In this equilibrium, economic geography has no influence on the growth rate. However, determinants of growth such as the cost of R&D and the discount rate have an impact on income differentials between North and South and therefore on the location of firms. We show that in this case high growth rates and high transaction costs are associated with foreign direct investment from North to South. In the second specification, R&D spillovers between industries are local, that is the R&D cost is lowest in the location with the highest number of firms producing differentiated products. In this case, all R&D activities agglomerate in the North where firms are more numerous and the growth rate is higher the more concentrated the industry. This induces an interesting link between trade costs, location and growth. A decrease of transaction costs, for example through trade integration, leads firms to concentrate, but not always entirely, in the location with the R&D activity, and because of local spillovers, it also induces an increase in the growth rate. This positive link between trade integration and growth is different from the ones identified by Rivera-Batiz and Romer (1991), Baldwin (1992), Baldwin and Seghezza (1995) and Baldwin and Forslid (1995). Also, in contrast to the literature in new geography, and due to the introduction of endogenous growth we show that welfare in the South can improve when industrial concentration in the North increases if transaction costs are low

284   *P. Martin, G.I.P. Ottaviano / European Economic Review 43 (1999) 281–302*

enough. This is because the increase in the rate of innovation which comes from spatial concentration also benefits the South.

The next section presents the general framework of the model. Section 3 describes the location decision of firms. Section 4 analyses the related dynamics of growth and location when spillovers are global. Section 5 does the same exercise when the spillovers are local. Section 6 analyses the welfare impact of industrial concentration.

2. The general framework

We study two locations which trade with each other and which we will call North and South. The two are identical except for their initial level of non-labour wealth, K_0 in the North and K_0^* in the South. We assume that the North is initially richer than the South so that $K_0 > K_0^*$. We therefore describe the economy only in the North as the South is almost symmetric. An asterisk refers to variables of the South. Both locations are inhabited by representative households who perform the tasks of consumers, workers and researchers. There are L households in the North and in the South. The utility of a representative household in the North is

$$U = \int_0^\infty \log[D(t)^\alpha Y(t)^{1-\alpha}]e^{-\rho t}\, dt. \tag{1}$$

The intertemporal elasticity of substitution has been chosen at unity for simplicity. Y is the numeraire good and D is a composite good which, following the framework of Dixit and Stiglitz (1977) is made up of a large number of differentiated products:

$$D(t) = \left[\int_{i=0}^{N(t)} D_i(t)^{1-1/\sigma}\, di\right]^{1/(1-1/\sigma)}, \quad \sigma > 1, \tag{2}$$

where N is the total number of differentiated goods produced both in the North and in the South. Growth will come from an increase in the number of the differentiated goods.

The value of total expenditures E is

$$\int_{i\in n} p_i D_i\, di + \int_{j\in n^*} \tau p_j^* D_j\, dj + Y = E. \tag{3}$$

In what follows we leave implicit the dependence of variables on time except for initial variables subscripted by 0. The set of firms in each region is endogenous and denoted n and n^*, with $n + n^* = N$. p_i and p_j^* are, respectively, the producer prices in the North and the South. As in Samuelson (1954) and in common with recent work in economic geography, transaction costs τ on the differentiated

P. Martin, G.I.P. Ottaviano / European Economic Review 43 (1999) 281–302   285

goods in the form of iceberg costs have been introduced. We can interpret them as both transport costs and transaction costs due to various trade impeding policies. As is usual in the new geography models, no transaction cost exists on the numeraire good which serves to tie down the wage rate w.

The differentiated goods are produced with identical technologies. One patent is required to start producing one variety of good and this requirement is the source of increasing returns in this sector. As in Helpman (1984) and Flam and Helpman (1987), this input is firm specific but does not require to be developed in the location where production actually takes place because there is free trade in patents. Each good also has a unit labour cost of β. The choice of p_i that maximizes profits obeys the standard rule in monopolistic competition: $p_i = w\beta\sigma/(\sigma - 1)$.

The operating profits of each firm in the increasing returns sector equal the difference between revenues and labour costs:

$$\pi_{IRS} = p_i x_i (p_i) - w\beta x_i (p_i) = \frac{w\beta x}{(\sigma - 1)}, \tag{4}$$

where x is the size of production.

Good Y is produced under constant returns to scale, using only labor as an input. Labor is intersectorally mobile so that the introduction of the constant returns to scale sector ties down the wage rate in each location at each instant. We will assume throughout the paper that the parameters of the model are such that both locations produce the constant returns to scale good so that constant identical wages hold. The restriction on parameters for this condition to hold is given in Appendix A. It takes one unit of labour to produce one unit of Y. Since Y is the numeraire, profit maximization implies that $w = 1$ at any time and $p = p^* = \beta\sigma/(\sigma - 1)$.

Finally, in contrast to firms, households (workers/researchers/consumers) are immobile so that their incomes are geographically fixed even though firms are not. This implies that no cumulative agglomeration process will be generated in this way when capital movements occur. This will enable us to focus on equilibria other than core–periphery ones. Solving the first order conditions for the consumers, we get the usual consumer demands:

$$D_i = \frac{\sigma - 1}{\beta\sigma} \frac{\alpha E}{n + n^*\delta}, \tag{5a}$$

$$D_j = \frac{\sigma - 1}{\beta\sigma} \frac{\alpha E \tau^{-\sigma}}{n + n^*\delta}, \tag{5b}$$

$$Y = (1 - \alpha)E, \tag{5c}$$

where $\delta = \tau^{1-\sigma}$ measures the freeness of trade.

Saving takes place in the form of a riskless asset that pays an interest rate r or in the form of investment in shares of firms on a world stock market. K is the number of firms owned by the North and K^* is the number of firms owned by the South. Because of the infinitely lived patent required to start production of a new variety, a firm that has bought a patent has a perpetual monopoly for that particular good. The value of a firm on the stock market is the present discounted value of all future operating profits. These operating profits will have to be the same in both locations as long as there are no capital movement restrictions. This also implies that the value of any firm in the world is

$$v(t) = \int_t^\infty e^{-[R(s)-R(t)]} \frac{\beta x(s)}{\sigma - 1}\, ds, \tag{6}$$

where $R(t)$ represents the cumulative discount factor applicable to profits earned at time t. Differentiating with respect to time, we get the arbitrage condition on capital markets:

$$\frac{\beta x}{\sigma - 1} + \dot{v} = rv, \tag{7}$$

which says that the returns on the different riskless assets must be equalized. On an investment of size v in a firm, the return is equal to the operating profits (or the dividends paid to the shareholders) plus the change in the value of the firm (the capital gains or losses). From the intertemporal optimization problem we also know that with log preferences, expenditures E must grow at an instantaneous rate equal to the difference between the interest rate r (paid in units of the numeraire) on a safe asset and the subjective discount rate. Because of free capital movements between the South and the North, the same condition applies in the South:

$$\frac{\dot{E}}{E} = \frac{\dot{E}^*}{E^*} = r - \rho. \tag{8}$$

It will turn out in equilibrium that nominal expenditures are constant so that $r = \rho$.

3. The equilibrium location of firms

The location of firms is free and we assume no relocation costs. For example, if a firm owned by an agent of the North locates in the South, then the operating profits of this firm are repatriated to the North.

Four equilibrium conditions determine firms' size (x, x^*) and location (n, n^*). First, when differentiated goods are produced in both locations,

P. Martin, G.I.P. Ottaviano / European Economic Review 43 (1999) 281–302   287

demands (inclusive of transport costs) must equal supplies at home and abroad:

$$x = \frac{\alpha L(\sigma - 1)}{\beta \sigma} \left(\frac{E}{n + n^*\delta} + \frac{E^*\delta}{n^* + n\delta} \right), \tag{9a}$$

$$x^* = \frac{\alpha L(\sigma - 1)}{\beta \sigma} \left(\frac{E\delta}{n + n^*\delta} + \frac{E^*}{n^* + n\delta} \right). \tag{9b}$$

Next, when capital flows are unrestricted, neither location can offer higher operating profits. In equilibrium, when n and n^* are positive, these must be equalized, which implies

$$\pi_{\mathrm{IRS}} = \pi_{\mathrm{IRS}}^* \tag{9c}$$

so that $x = x^*$. Finally, the total number of firms is fixed by the world number of patents N and also by the world number of firms owned by private agents on the stock market so

$$n + n^* = K + K^* = N. \tag{9d}$$

Solving (9a)–(9d), we get that, for a given level of expenditures, the optimal size of each firm is

$$x = \alpha L \frac{\sigma - 1}{\beta \sigma} \frac{E + E^*}{N}. \tag{10}$$

The proportion of firms in the North which we call γ is

$$\gamma = \frac{n}{N} = \frac{E - E^*\delta}{(1 - \delta)(E + E^*)}. \tag{11}$$

This says that the location with the largest market size or the highest expenditure level will get the majority of the firms. Because of transaction costs and increasing returns, firms want to be located next to the largest markets. This result is the 'home market effect' analysed by Krugman (1980) in the context of the 'new trade theory'. When transaction costs are low, i.e. δ is large, the sensitivity of the location decision to market size differentials increases because it makes it easier for firms to locate in the largest market and then export to the other location.

4. The case of global spillovers

We now want to analyse how the stock of patents is growing. We introduce the R&D sector which works as in Grossman and Helpman (1991): to invent a new variety, a researcher must employ η/N units of labor. This is also the cost

288   *P. Martin, G.I.P. Ottaviano / European Economic Review 43 (1999) 281–302*

of R&D as the wage rate is 1. This specification says that the invention of a new good in one country decreases the future R&D cost in both countries so that the spillovers are global and the cost of R&D is the same in the North and in the South.[2] This compensates for the decrease in the operating profits as the number of varieties increases so that an incentive to engage in R&D remains in steady state.

Researchers enter freely into R&D so that, as long as new patented goods are continuously created, the profits in the R&D sector are driven to zero. As the R&D sector is perfectly competitive, the marginal cost of inventing a new variety is equal to the value of the patent. In equilibrium, the value of each firm is itself equal to the value of the patent it owns so that $v = \eta/N$. Note that this is the same in both locations because of the assumption of global spillovers.

In equilibrium, the world labor market must clear. We know that workers will either be working in the R&D sector ($\eta \hat{N}$ of them) or in the two manufacturing sectors for which we know the demands and the unit labor requirements. Hence, at the world level this implies

$$\eta\hat{N} + \frac{\sigma - \alpha}{\sigma} L(E + E^*) = 2L. \tag{12}$$

We can already see that if a balanced growth path with a constant growth rate $g = \dot{N}/N = \hat{N}$ exists, then it must be that world aggregate expenditures are constant which then implies that $r = \rho$. We also know that in equilibrium $v = \eta/N$ which implies that v decreases at the same rate as N increases, that is $\hat{v} = -g$. Then, using the equilibrium volume of production per firm, x, and the arbitrage condition, we get

$$\frac{\alpha L(E + E^*)}{\eta\sigma} = \rho + g. \tag{13}$$

Using Eqs. (12) and (13), the constant growth rate of K, K^* and N is

$$g = \frac{2L}{\eta}\frac{\alpha}{\sigma} - \left(\frac{\sigma - \alpha}{\sigma}\right)\rho. \tag{14}$$

The growth rate of D can be checked to be $g/(\sigma - 1)$ and as in Grossman and Helpman (1991) there is no transition. Note that with global spillovers, the growth rate is independent of the location of firms and of the level of transaction

---

[2] Irwin and Klenow (1994) give evidence on such international spillovers in the semiconductor industry. They argue that in this industry spillovers are quantitatively similar between firms in different countries as between firms within a given country. Coe and Helpman (1995), and Coe et al. (1997) also provide evidence for strong international knowledge spillovers.

P. Martin, G.I.P. Ottaviano / European Economic Review 43 (1999) 281–302   289

costs. The constant level of per capita expenditures at the world level is then

$$E + E^* = 2 + \frac{\eta\rho}{L}. \tag{15}$$

This is consistent with the budget constraints in each location as the per capita incomes are equal to the per capita labor incomes (the wage rate 1) plus the income from investment which is just the value of the firms owned in each location ($\eta K/N$ in the North and $\eta K^*/N$ in the South) multiplied by the equilibrium return ρ. This implies that incomes rise at the same rate in both locations (in fact they are constant). Per capita expenditures in the North and in the South are always equal to per capita incomes:

$$E = 1 + \frac{\rho\eta k}{L}, \quad E^* = 1 + \frac{\rho\eta(1 - k)}{L}, \tag{16}$$

where $k = K/N$ is the constant share of firms owned by Northerners and is more than 1/2 as we assume that the North is initially wealthier.

Using the equilibrium per capita expenditures, we get that the proportion of firms located in the North is

$$\gamma = \frac{n}{N} = \frac{(1 - \delta)L + \rho\eta[k - \delta(1 - k)]}{(1 - \delta)(2L + \rho\eta)}, \quad \gamma \le 1, \tag{17}$$

with a possible corner solution at $\gamma = 1$. n, n^* and N grow at the same rate g. Eq. (17) also implies that $\gamma > 1/2$. There are more firms of the increasing returns sector in the North than in the South because the Northerners have a higher wealth and a higher level of expenditure. They therefore represent a larger market size. More labor will be employed in the increasing returns sector in the North than in the South ($\beta n x$ in the North and $\beta n^* x$ in the South).

We can analyse the relation between industrial location, growth and foreign direct investment. Foreign direct investment or more generally capital flows take place in the interval dt if the increase in the number of firms producing in a location (dn/dt) is different from the number of firms bought by residents in that same location (dK/dt). We can measure the extent of net foreign direct investment as

$$\frac{dn}{dt} - \frac{dK}{dt} = g(n - K) \tag{18}$$

which can be positive or negative. Note first that, not surprisingly, net foreign direct investment increases with the growth rate, that is, as more firms are being created in the world. The direction of the net flow depends on the sign of $(n - K)$, so that

$$\frac{dn}{dt} - \frac{dK}{dt} = \frac{g(K - K^*)}{(1 - \delta)(2L + \rho\eta)}[\eta\rho\delta - L(1 - \delta)]. \tag{19}$$

290   *P. Martin, G.I.P. Ottaviano / European Economic Review 43 (1999) 281–302*

As the North has an initial larger endowment of wealth than the South and we have seen that wealth in the form of firms' ownership grows at the same rate in both locations so that $K > K^*$, the extent of net foreign direct investment, for a given direction, grows with time. Eq. (19) also implies that some of the firms owned by the Northerners will locate in the South, generating constant net capital flows from North to South over time, if the last expression in bracket in Eq. (19) is negative. On the contrary, net capital flows will take place from South to North in the case where the last expression in this equation is positive. There are two opposite effects that explain why the direction of net capital flows is ambiguous. First, the poor capital location will tend to attract firms because its low capital base implies that firms installed in that location face less competition. This competition effect contradicts the capital income effect which implies that the North, owning a larger number of firms, has a larger income and therefore will attract firms which want to take advantage of returns to scale by locating near the rich markets. The inequality above illustrates the relative impact of these two effects. The capital income effect will be smaller when L is large because the income from capital is, in this case, small relative to the income from labor which we assume equal in the two locations.[3] When δ is small, that is transaction costs are large, firms will prefer to be close to their different markets rather than being concentrated in the rich location. This is the usual result from the new geography literature. Here, it is less dramatic because we have excluded mechanisms that could generate cumulative agglomeration of economic activities in the North such as migration or the presence of vertically linked industries. Therefore, in general, no core–periphery pattern will emerge.

Hence, an interesting feature of our model which comes from the introduction of endogenous dynamics is that industrial concentration in the North – the richer location has a higher proportion of firms – is compatible with net capital flows from North to South. This comes from the fact that a larger number of the new economic activities are owned by the North than by the South.

It is also interesting to note that, for a given value of transaction costs, values of the parameters (η and ρ) that induce a high world growth rate are associated to net capital flows from North to South. This is because these capital flows depend on the differential in capital income levels which themselves are inversely related to the incentives to engage in accumulating capital or to create new

---

[3] When labour supplies differ in the two locations, it can be shown that a location with a small L and with a high capital labour ratio (a high K/L) will export capital so that firms owned by the agents of that location will produce in the other location. The intuition is simply that such a location continuously buys more firms than its small market can 'absorb'. This fits well with the importance of multinationals in small rich countries such as Switzerland, Netherlands and Sweden.

P. Martin, G.I.P. Ottaviano / European Economic Review 43 (1999) 281–302 291

firms. For example, a decrease in the R&D cost, η, increases the growth rate, i.e. the creation of new firms. This in turn reduces the monopoly power of existing firms (a larger proportion of which is owned by the North than by the South) and therefore leads to a reduction of the differential in incomes and market size between North and South and net capital flows from North to South.

Note also that a decrease in transaction costs can reverse the direction of capital flows. Suppose that history is such that transaction costs are initially very large and then decreasing with time. In this case, the model predicts that when growth is strong enough and transaction costs high enough firms owned by the Northerners will locate in the South. Then, as transaction costs decrease, capital flows may decrease and may then change direction for some critical value of the transaction costs.

5. The case of local spillovers

We now look at the case of localized spillovers in R&D. These spillovers, between different industries at the level of a city or a region, have been documented by Glaeser et al. (1992), Henderson et al. (1995) and also Jacobs (1969). In line with these studies, we assume that the cost of R&D in a certain location depends negatively on the number of firms located in that location such that: η/n in the North and η/n^* in the South. These are different spillovers from the ones assumed by Grossman and Helpman (1991) because in our framework, what decreases the R&D cost is not the presence of other researchers but the presence of producers of different goods. From that perspective, our formalization of external effects is closer to the Jacobs' type of knowledge spillovers than to the so-called Marshall–Arrow–Romer (MAR) ones. In our model, the mechanism for agglomeration of R&D activities in one location will come from the benefit of interactions with producers of other goods, the Jacobs type of external effect, rather than producers in the same industry as in the MAR theories. These benefits come for example from the direct observation of the production process: researchers observe the production process and find it easier to invent how new goods can be produced. In this sense, our model with local spillovers can be thought of as a model of the Silicon Valley.

The fact that it is less costly to engage in R&D in the location where there are more firms immediately implies that all the R&D activity will take place in the location with an initial higher stock of capital and therefore an initial higher number of firms. This is due to the fact that, if the cost of R&D is lower in one location (because of a higher concentration of firms), no researcher will have interest to do R&D in the other location. As the shares of these firms which are perfect substitutes to each other can be traded internationally with no transaction cost, their price must be the same so that no R&D activity will take place in the South.[4] As R&D is located where most of the producers are, the growth rate of the world is determined entirely by the level of R&D done in the North which itself now depends on the location of industry.

We first have to determine the expenditure levels. Free capital movements insure that the growth rates of consumption are equal in both locations: $\hat{E} = \hat{E}^* = r - \rho$. Eq. (11) then tells us that if the growth rate of expenditures is the same in both locations, it must be that $\gamma = n/N$, the ratio of firms producing in the North, is also constant over time. The value of shares v is still determined by the zero profit condition in the R&D sector: $v = \eta/(N\gamma)$. It decreases at rate g, the rate of innovation. The world resource constraint, $E + E^* = 2 + (r\eta)/(L\gamma)$, in turn implies that expenditures are constant ove time[5] so that we can again use the same method to find the growth rate. The world labour market equilibrium is now

$$\eta \frac{\hat{N}}{\gamma} + \frac{\sigma - \alpha}{\sigma} L(E + E^*) = 2L. \tag{20}$$

Using the same methodology as in the previous section we find that the growth rate is then

$$g = \frac{2L}{\eta} \frac{\alpha}{\sigma} \gamma - \left(\frac{\sigma - \alpha}{\sigma}\right)\rho. \tag{21}$$

Because of the local spillovers, concentration of industries in the North measured by γ has a positive effect on the world growth rate.

The equilibrium location of firms is still given by Eq. (11) because firms, when they choose where to produce, only compare the expenditures levels of the two locations. The levels of per capita expenditures in the North and the South are the total respective wealth multiplied by the propensity to consume which, in our log utility case, is just ρ:

$$E = \rho \left[\frac{1}{\rho} + \frac{K(0)v(0)}{L}\right] = 1 + \frac{\rho\eta k}{\gamma L}, \tag{22a}$$

$$E^* = \rho \left[\frac{1}{\rho} + \frac{K^*(0)v(0)}{L}\right] = 1 + \frac{\rho\eta(1 - k)}{\gamma L}, \tag{22b}$$

where $v(0)$ is the value of shares owned by agents at time 0. Note that the income from capital decreases with the level of industrial concentration in the North.

---

[4] When spillovers are partially local, i.e. the cost of R&D in a given location depends more on the number of firms located in that location than on the number of firms located in the other location, the same agglomeration of R&D activities takes place. This would be so if, for example, the R&D cost in the North was $\eta/(n + \varepsilon n^*)$ with $0 < \varepsilon < 1$.

[5] The interest rate must be constant over time and equal to ρ so that it does not diverge.

P. Martin, G.I.P. Ottaviano / European Economic Review 43 (1999) 281–302 293

Using the equilibrium levels of expenditures and Eq. (11), the ratio of firms located in the North to the total number of firms is given by

$$\gamma = \frac{(1 - \delta)L + (\rho\eta)/\gamma[k - \delta(1 - k)]}{(1 - \delta)(2L + (\rho\eta/\gamma))}, \quad 0 \le \gamma \le 1. \tag{23}$$

The proportion of firms in the North γ depends on the differential in expenditures which itself now depends, through the differential in incomes, on the location of firms. The quadratic equation that determines the proportion of firms located in the North to the total stock of capital γ is

$$2L(1 - \delta)\gamma^2 + (1 - \delta)(\rho\eta - L)\gamma - \eta\rho[k - \delta(1 - k)] = 0. \tag{24}$$

One of the roots of this equation can be ruled out because it would imply $\gamma < 0$ and a negative growth rate. The other root is

$$\gamma = \frac{(L - \eta\rho) + \sqrt{(L - \eta\rho)^2 + 8L[\eta\rho/(1 - \delta)][k - \delta(1 - k)]}}{4L}. \tag{25}$$

It can be shown that this expression is more than $1/2$ as long as k itself is more than $1/2$ as we have assumed: as income is lower in the South than in the North, there will always be less firms in the South than in the North. However, there can still be firms located in the South (i.e. $\gamma < 1$) if

$$\rho\eta[(1 + \delta)k - 1] < L(1 - \delta).$$

We assume in the rest of the paper that indeed we are not at a corner solution. The parameters (ρ, η and L) that generate high growth rates are associated with foreign direct investment from North to South. This time, because all firms are created in the North, some of the newly created firms in the North will relocate to the South (if $\gamma < 1$).

We can also analyse the factors that determine location of firms:

$$\frac{\partial\gamma}{\partial\delta} > 0, \quad \frac{\partial\gamma}{\partial\eta} > 0, \quad \frac{\partial\gamma}{\partial\rho} > 0, \quad \frac{\partial\gamma}{\partial k} > 0.$$

Note in particular the first of these partial derivatives. It says that lower transaction costs will be associated with more concentration of firms in the North: when transaction costs are low, firms can locate near the largest markets (in the North) and still export to the South. This has the important implication that, with local spillovers in R&D, lower transactions costs through a decrease of transportation costs or through trade liberalization will increase the growth rate. This positive impact of a decrease of transaction costs on growth works through a location effect as it implies a stronger concentration of firms in the location where the R&D activity is entirely agglomerated and through the localized spillovers, a decrease of the effective cost of R&D. Hence, our model predicts a positive impact of trade integration on the world growth rate through its impact on geography. Note also that, through this impact on geography (γ increases), our model predicts that trade integration leads to a decrease in income differentials between the North and the South (see Eqs. (22a) and (22b)).

We can also analyse the impact of trade integration between the North and the South on the extent to which new firms created in the North decide to locate production in the South. The number of new firms locating South in each period is

$$S = \frac{dK}{dt} - \frac{dn}{dt} = g(1 - \gamma)N. \tag{26}$$

We can analyse the impact of an increase in δ on the quantity of new firms owned by the North that decide to locate in the South at a given period, i.e. for a given number of firms N at the world level. The differential of expression (26) with respect to δ keeping N constant is given by:

$$\frac{\partial S}{\partial \delta} = N\left[(1 - \gamma)\frac{\partial g}{\partial \gamma} - g\right]\frac{\partial \gamma}{\partial \delta} = N\left[\frac{\sigma - \alpha}{\sigma}\rho - (2\gamma - 1)\frac{2L\alpha}{\eta\sigma}\right]\frac{\partial \gamma}{\partial \delta}. \tag{27}$$

This expression can be negative (γ is more than 1/2) or positive.[6] It will be positive – meaning that relocation to the South will be increased by trade integration – when γ is low enough, i.e. when countries are similar enough in their industrial structure. In this case, even if γ, the proportion of firms which are located in the North, increases, the number of firms which relocate to the South is larger because of trade integration. This is due to the fact that trade integration leads to an increase in the creation of new firms, of which a certain proportion will locate to the South. This second effect explains why the absolute number of firms locating in the South can increase following trade integration between North and South. However, integration does not generate an increase in the relative size of industry in the South as in the latter stage of integration in the model developed by Krugman and Venables (1990) when higher wages in the North push firms to relocate in the South. This mechanism is absent from our model because nominal wages are equalized across countries.

---

[6] The restriction that growth is positive is not enough to sign this expression.

P. Martin, G.I.P. Ottaviano / European Economic Review 43 (1999) 281–302   295

The impact of the R&D cost and of the subjective discount factor on location have the same interpretation as with global spillovers. However, they now also have an impact on the growth rate through location. This impact is the opposite to the usual one. That is, an increase in the R&D cost or of the discount factor tends to foster concentration of industrial activities in the North which itself is favourable to growth. However, it can be checked that this positive location effect on growth of an increase in the R&D cost is always less than the negative direct effect on the incentive to engage in R&D. The impact of an increase of the R&D cost or of the discount factor on the growth rate is less than in the case where location has no impact on growth but it is still negative.

6. Welfare analysis

We now want to ask whether the concentration of firms in the market equilibrium described above is too low or too high from a welfare point of view when spillovers are local. In particular, starting from the market equilibrium, we ask whether a Pareto improvement can be obtained by a marginal change in economic geography as described by γ. The model exhibits several externalities which, in general, will make the market equilibrium different from the one chosen by a planner.

First of all, there is the standard distortion due to spillovers in innovation. Because current research has a positive spillover on the productivity of future research, a planner would engage in more R&D activity than the decentralized economy (Romer, 1990; Grossman and Helpman, 1991).

Second, because firms have zero mass, investors do not take into account the positive impact of spatial concentration on the world growth rate in their decision about where to invest their capital. From the point of view of this externality, γ, which measures the concentration of firms in the North, is too low as an increase in γ will increase the growth rate in the world.

Third, the location decision of investment also has a welfare impact on consumers that investors do not internalize. This happens for two reasons. On the one hand, when capital flows increase spatial concentration of firms, the cost of innovation goes down due to local spillovers. This in turn reduces the value of capital and thus of nominal wealth. Having a larger initial stock of capital, the North suffers more than the South. On the other hand, the consumers in the location of destination of capital flows gain because they save the transport cost on the additional goods produced locally. In this case, the real wealth of these consumers increases. Symmetrically, the consumers in the location of origin now have to pay the transport cost on a larger number of foreign goods and therefore see their real wealth decrease. The existence of these two effects implies that the welfare impact of an increase in γ will differ for the North and for the South.

Call V and V^* the indirect utilities in the North and in the South, respectively. Then we have

$$
V = \frac{1}{\rho} \ln \left\{ \alpha^\alpha (1 - \alpha)^{1-\alpha} \left(1 + \frac{\rho \eta k}{\gamma L} \right) \right.
$$

$$
\left. \times \left(\frac{\sigma - 1}{\beta \sigma} \right)^\alpha N_0^{\alpha/(\sigma-1)} [(1 - \delta)\gamma + \delta]^{\alpha/(\sigma-1)} e^{\alpha g/(\rho(\sigma-1))} \right\}, \tag{28a}
$$

$$
V^* = \frac{1}{\rho} \ln \left\{ \alpha^\alpha (1-\alpha)^{1-\alpha} \left(1 + \frac{\rho \eta (1-k)}{\gamma L} \right) \right.
$$

$$
\left. \times \left(\frac{\sigma - 1}{\beta \sigma} \right)^\alpha N_0^{\alpha/(\sigma-1)} [1 - (1 - \delta)\gamma]^{\alpha/(\sigma-1)} e^{\alpha g/(\rho(\sigma-1))} \right\}. \tag{28b}
$$

We first look at the impact of an increase in industrial concentration in the North. Differentiating the indirect utility for the North with respect to γ, we get the following expression:

$$
\frac{\partial V}{\partial \gamma} = - \frac{\eta k}{L\gamma^2 + \rho \eta \gamma k} + \frac{2L\alpha^2}{\rho^2 \eta \sigma(\sigma-1)} + \frac{\alpha}{\rho(\sigma-1)} \frac{1-\delta}{(1-\delta)\gamma + \delta}. \tag{29}
$$

The first element of this expression is the negative impact that an increase of γ has on Northerners' wealth. The second element represents the positive impact on the growth rate. The last element represents the welfare improvement due to the decrease in transport costs for consumers in the North when γ increases. For Northerners, the sum of the first two effects (the income and the growth effects) is ambiguous in welfare terms. This is due to the fact that some of the income of Northerners comes from monopolistic profits extracted from consumers in the South. An increase of the concentration of firms in the North will in effect increase the pace of innovation and lower the value of firms owned by Northerners.

For the South, an increase in concentration of firms has the following welfare impact:

$$
\frac{\partial V^*}{\partial \gamma} = - \frac{\eta(1-k)}{L\gamma^2 + \rho \eta \gamma(1-k)} + \frac{2L\alpha^2}{\rho^2 \eta \sigma(\sigma-1)} - \frac{\alpha}{\rho(\sigma-1)} \frac{1-\delta}{1 - \gamma(1-\delta)}. \tag{30}
$$

The first and second terms again represent the negative wealth and the positive growth effect of spatial concentration in the North. It can be shown (see technical Appendix B) that, as long as growth is positive and k is more than $1/2$, which is our characterization of the South, the positive growth effect is more than the negative wealth effect of concentration. The third element represents the transaction cost effect and is negative as concentration in the North

P. Martin, G.I.P. Ottaviano / European Economic Review 43 (1999) 281–302   297

Table 1

σ	α	τ	η	k	L	ρ	γ (market equilibrium)	g (in %)	dV/dγ	dV*/dγ
3	0.8	1.2	10	0.8	2	0.05	0.74	4.2	21.3	4.2 base case
4	–	–	–	–	–	–	0.67	1.4	14.8	– 7.4
–	0.5	–	–	–	–	–	0.74	0.8	10.9	– 6.2
–	–	1.5	–	–	–	–	0.63	3.0	30.4	– 5.2
–	–	–	20	–	–	–	0.87	1.0	10.8	– 3.9
–	–	–	–	0.6	–	–	0.60	2.7	20.8	– 0.5
–	–	–	–	–	3	–	0.68	7.2	30.9	12.5
–	–	–	–	–	–	0.03	0.67	4.9	56.8	24.4

increases the price index in the South.[7] This marginal welfare loss of the Southerners from industrial concentration in the North is always more than the marginal welfare gain for the Northeners. This is because the Northerners already have a majority of the firms in their location, and therefore, a lower price index.

To compare the market determined geography to the optimal geography, we need to evaluate the sign of expressions (29) and (30) at the market equilibrium γ given in Eq. (25). The expressions are too complex to be evaluated analytically so we look at numerical examples. We can establish that both countries can gain from more concentration of firms in the North. Even though the existing literature of the new economic geography does not analyse explicitly welfare in the way we do, it is clear, in Krugman (1991) or Krugman and Venables (1995) for example, that the South systematically loses because of industrial concentration in the North. Our model shows that the introduction of endogenous growth can reverse this result. The first line in Table 1, which we call the base case, presents a numerical example where both countries would gain from more concentration in the North compared to the market determined geography. The other lines in the table illustrate how the results are sensitive to parameters.

Quite intuitively, both countries gain from more concentration in the North if the welfare gain from higher growth is large enough. This is the case when the elasticity of substitution between goods σ is low, the share of manufactured goods α is high, the cost of R&D η is low, the market size L is large, and the rate of time preference ρ is low. Transaction costs, τ, need to be low enough also for both countries to gain from concentration in the North. In this case, the

---

[7] The price index corresponding to the nested CES utility function is defined as: $P^\alpha = (\beta\sigma/(\sigma - 1))^\alpha (n + \delta n^*)^{\alpha/(1-\sigma)}$ in the North and $P^{\alpha*} = (\beta\sigma/(\sigma - 1))^\alpha (n^* + \delta n)^{\alpha/(1-\sigma)}$ in the South.

relocation of industries to the North does not penalize too much the South because the increase in the transaction cost of goods now produced in the North is not too large. Finally, if initial wealth is very unequally distributed (k is high), the North gains less from concentration because of the loss in the value of its firms due to higher growth. The reverse is true for the South.

We can also ask whether a monetary transfer exists such that one of the two locations is left indifferent by the change in γ and the other one better off. Suppose that the transfer (positive or negative) from the North to the South is such that utility is left unchanged in the North by the change in γ. The change in utility in the South, when this transfer is taken into account, is given by

$$\frac{\partial V_T^*}{\partial \gamma} = \frac{\partial V^*}{\partial \gamma} + \frac{L\gamma + \rho\eta k}{L\gamma + \rho\eta(1-k)} \frac{\partial V}{\partial \gamma}, \tag{31}$$

where the subscript T means that the change in utility takes the transfer into account. The term multiplying the change in utility of the North is more than 1 as marginal utility is larger for the South than for the North which is richer. The sign of this expression is ambiguous as the positive effect on growth may not compensate the fact that the Southerners lose more in terms of transport costs from industrial concentration than what the Northerners gain from it.

As in the previous case, we can not give an analytical answer to the question whether a transfer exists such that a world planner could, by increasing industrial concentration, improve welfare for both locations compared to the market equilibrium. However, we can answer this question for some specific market equilibrium outcomes. First, with this welfare criterium, the optimal γ is always more than 1/2. Suppose that $k = 1/2$ so that the market equilibrium is $\gamma = 1/2$ (see Eq. (25)). It can be checked (see Appendix C) that, when evaluated at $\gamma = 1/2$, the expression in Eq. (31) is unambiguously positive. This is stems from the fact that, in this case, Southerners lose in terms of transport costs exactly as much as the Northeners gain in transport cost. Because of the positive growth effect of an increase in industrial concentration, a transfer can always be found such that the South is made better off with higher industrial concentration while the North welfare is left unchanged.

Suppose now that full industrial concentration ($\gamma = 1$) is the market equilibrium outcome. Would a world planner choose a different geography in this case? We can answer this question by evaluating the sign of Eq. (31) at $\gamma = 1$ for parameters such that the market equilibrium is indeed $\gamma = 1$. Using Eq. (25), we find that $\gamma = 1$ for the employment level:

$$L = \frac{\eta\rho}{1-\delta}(k + \delta k - 1). \tag{32}$$

P. Martin, G.I.P. Ottaviano / European Economic Review 43 (1999) 281–302   299

Substituting this level for L in expression in Eq. (31) evaluated at $\gamma = 1$, we get

$$\frac{\partial V_T^*}{\partial \gamma} = \frac{\partial V^*}{\partial \gamma} + \frac{1}{\delta}\frac{\partial V}{\partial \gamma}. \tag{33}$$

Using Eqs. (29) and (30) evaluated at $\gamma = 1$, with L given by Eq. (32), we get

$$\left.\frac{\partial V_T^*}{\partial \gamma}\right|_{\gamma=1} = -\frac{1-\delta}{\delta(2k-1)\rho} + \frac{4\alpha^2(k+\delta k-1)}{(1-\delta)\rho\sigma(\sigma-1)\delta}. \tag{34}$$

This expression can be positive or negative so that a market equilibrium of full concentration may not be optimal. It may be negative so that the market equilibrium displays too much industrial concentration if δ is low, so that transport costs are high. In this case, the growth gains of a spatially concentrated geography will be lower than the welfare loss due to the higher transaction costs effect in the South than in the North. This will also be the case if the elasticity of substitution σ is high. In this case, the increase in the diversity of goods consumed due to higher growth has a small welfare impact.

7. Conclusion

The model we have presented is an attempt to merge the theory of endogenous growth and the theory of endogenous location. Through this exercise, we have been able to learn both on growth and on location:

(1) When spillovers are global, economic geography does not influence the growth rate. However, high growth rates are associated with capital flows to the South because the factors that increase the growth rate (such as a decrease in the R&D cost) also decrease the differential in income between North and South. In this case, the creation of new firms is the driving force behind capital flows.

(2) When spillovers are local, spatial concentration of activities is beneficial to growth. This in turn implies that a decrease in transaction costs, through its geography effect, favours the rate of innovation and growth.

(3) When spillovers are local, industrial concentration brings an interesting welfare tradeoff between aggregate growth and regional equity which has not been analysed in the literature. On the one hand, an increase in industrial concentration in the location where R&D is performed increases growth, an effect not internalized in the location choice of firms. On the other hand, the welfare cost of transportation between the two locations is minimized when the

300 *P. Martin, G.I.P. Ottaviano / European Economic Review 43 (1999) 281–302*

industry is perfectly split between the two locations. This implies that a decrease of transport costs and of R&D costs increase, at the world level, the welfare gains of spatial concentration. Also, in contrast to other geography models, we show that the South can gain from more concentration in the North if the growth benefits are large enough.

We believe that one benefit of our model is its simplicity: the introduction of endogenous growth in the static location model does not make the exercise intractable. This suggests that we can use this model, and make it more complicated, to answer a certain number of questions. We can use it to look at the dynamic effects of preferential trading agreements on growth and location. We could also analyse a circular relation between growth and location. In the model presented here industrial concentration fosters growth due to the local spillovers. If the R&D sector also uses the differentiated goods, then an increase in growth will increase the market size of the innovative location and lead to industrial relocation to that location. This interaction between growth and location would give rise to an agglomeration process that we analyse in another recent paper (Martin and Ottaviano, 1996).

Acknowledgements

We thank Richard Baldwin, Vincenzo Denicolo, Elhanan Helpman, Diego Puga, Jacques Thisse, Tony Venables and two anonymous referees for their comments on a previous version. We are also grateful for comments from participants at the CEPR/CUSO conference on "Trade, Location and Technology" in Champéry, the CEP/CEPR workshop in London, the CEPR/NBER conference International Seminar in International Trade in Royaumont and at seminars at Universities of Bologna, Lausanne, Ancona, Base and CORE (Louvain). Ottaviano gratefully acknowledges financial support from the Consiglio Nazionale delle Ricerche (pos. 140.2, prot. 065855) and the European Commission. Martin thanks the Swiss National Science Foundation (grant no. 1214-050783.97) for financial support.

Appendix A: Restriction on parameters for the constant returns to scale sector to exist in both regions

We need to look for conditions under which, at $\gamma = 1$, the South is not able to satisfy the world demand for the homogeneous good so that: $(1 - \alpha)(E + E^*)L > L$. World income is the same with global or local spillovers at $\gamma = 1$ (see Eqs. (15), (22a) and (22b) in the text): $E + E^* = 2 + \eta\rho/L$. Hence, the condition on parameters is $(1 - \alpha)(2L + \eta\rho) > L$.

P. Martin, G.I.P. Ottaviano / European Economic Review 43 (1999) 281–302   301

Appendix B: The positive growth effect is larger than the negative wealth effect for the South

We need to show that the sum of the first two terms in Eq. (30) is positive. For growth to be positive (see Eq. (21)), the minimum L has to be greater than

$$\frac{(\sigma - \alpha)\rho\eta}{2\alpha\gamma}.$$

Substituting this expression for L in the first two terms of Eq. (30) we get the following expression:

$$\frac{(\sigma - \alpha)\alpha}{(\sigma - 1)\sigma\rho\gamma} - \frac{2\alpha(1 - k)}{(\sigma - \alpha)\rho\gamma + 2\alpha\rho\gamma(1 - k)}.$$

If this expression is positive then we will have shown that the growth effect of industrial concentration is always more than its wealth effect. Transforming this expression, we find that it will be positive if

$$(\sigma - \alpha)^2 + 2\alpha(\sigma - \alpha)(1 - k) - 2\sigma(\sigma - 1)(1 - k)$$

is positive. This is true as long as $k \geq 1/2$.

Appendix C: At $k = \gamma = 1/2$, more industrial concentration is welfare improving

Evaluated at this market equilibrium, Eq. (31) is

$$\frac{\partial V_T^*}{\partial \gamma} = \frac{\partial V^*}{\partial \gamma} + \frac{\partial V}{\partial \gamma}.$$

This expression is positive as long as growth is positive. The proof is identical to the one given in Appendix B.

References

Arthur, B., 1989. Silicon valley locational clusters: When do increasing returns imply monopoly? Working Paper, Santa Fe Institute, Santa Fe.

Baldwin, R., 1992. Measurable dynamic gains from trade. Journal of Political Economy 100 (1), 162–174.

Baldwin, R., Forslid, R., 1995. Trade liberalization and endogenous growth: A q-theory approach. Mimeo., The Graduate Institute of International Studies, Geneva.

Baldwin, R., Seghezza, E., 1995. An empirical investigation of the trade, investment and growth relationship. Mimeo., The Graduate Institute of International Studies, Geneva.

Bertola, G., 1993. Models of economic integration and localized growth. In: Torres, F., Giavazzi, F. (Eds.), Adjustment and Growth in the European Monetary Union. CEPR and Cambridge University Press, Cambridge.

302　　　*P. Martin, G.I.P. Ottaviano / European Economic Review 43 (1999) 281–302*

Ciccone, A., Hall, R., 1996. Productivity and the density of economic activity. American Economic Review 87 (1), 54–70.

Coe, D., Helpman, E., 1995. International R&D spillovers. European Economic Review 39, 859–887.

Coe, D., Helpman, E., Hoffmaister, A., 1997. North–south R&D spillovers. The Economic Journal 107 (440), 134–149.

Dixit, A.K., Stiglitz, J.E., 1977. Monopolistic competition and optimum product diversity. American Economic Review 67 (3), 297–308.

Flam, H., Helpman, E., 1987. Industrial policy under monopolistic competition. Journal of International Economics 22, 79–102.

Glaeser, E., Kallal, H.D., Sheinkman, J.A., Shleifer, A., 1992. Growth in cities. Journal of Political Economy 100 (6), 1126–1152.

Grossman, G.M., Helpman, E., 1991. Innovation and Growth in the Global Economy. MIT Press, Cambridge, MA.

Helpman, E., 1984. A simple theory of international trade with multinational corporations. Journal of Political Economy 92 (3), 451–471.

Helpman, E., Krugman, P., 1985. Market Structure and Foreign Trade. MIT Press, Cambridge, MA.

Henderson, V., 1994. Externalities and industrial development. Working Paper No. 4730. NBER, Cambridge, MA.

Henderson, V., Kuncoro, A., Turner, M., 1995. Industrial development in cities. Journal of Political Economy 103 (5), 1067–1090.

Irwin, D., Klenow, P., 1994. Learning by doing in the semiconductor industry. Journal of Political Economy 102 (6), 1200–1227.

Jacobs, J., 1969. The Economy of Cities. Vintage, New York.

Jaffe A., Trajtenberg, M., Henderson, R., 1993. Geographic localization of knowledge spillovers as evidenced by patent citations. Quarterly Journal of Economics 108.

Krugman, P., 1980. Scale economies, product differentiation, and the patten of trade. American Economic Review 70, 950–959.

Krugman, P., 1991a. Increasing returns and economic geography. Journal of Political Economy 99, 483–499.

Krugman, P., Venables, A., 1990. Integration and the competitiveness of peripheral industry. In: Bliss, C., de Macedo, J.B. (Eds.), Unity with Diversity in the European Community. Cambridge University Press, Cambridge, pp. 56–75.

Krugman, P., Venables, A., 1995. Globalization and the inequality of nations. Quarterly Journal of Economics 110 (2), 857–880.

Lucas, R.E., 1988. On the mechanics of economic development. Journal of Monetary Economics 22, 3–42.

Martin, P., Rogers, C.A., 1995. Industrial location and public infrastructure. Journal of International Economics 39, 335–351.

Martin, P., Ottaviano, G.I.P., 1996. Growth and agglomeration. CEPR Papers No. 1529, CEPR, London.

Rivera-Batiz, L.A., Romer, P., 1991. Economic integration and endogenous growth. Quarterly Journal of Economics 106 (2), 531–555.

Romer, P.M., 1990. Endogenous technological change. Journal of Political Economy, Part II 98 (5), S71–S102.

Samuelson, P., 1954. The transfer problem and transport costs, II: Analysis of effects of trade impediments. Economic Journal LXIV, 264–289.

Walz, U., 1996. Transport costs, intermediate goods, and localized growth. Regional Science and Urban Economics 26, 671–695.

Chapter 2

Global Income Divergence, Trade, and Industrialization: The Geography of Growth Take-Offs[†]

RICHARD E. BALDWIN

Graduate Institute of International Studies, 11a Ave de la Paix, 1202 Geneva, Switzerland, and CEPR

PHILIPPE MARTIN

CERAS-ENPC, Paris, and CEPR

GIANMARCO I. P. OTTAVIANO

Bocconi University and CEPR

This article formalizes the theoretical interconnections among four post–industrial revolution phenomena—the industrialization and growth take-off of rich northern nations, massive global income divergence, and rapid trade expansion. In stages-of-growth model, the four phenomena are jointly endogenous and are triggered by falling trade costs. In the first growth stage (with high trade costs) industry is dispersed internationally, and growth is low. In the second (medium trade costs), the North industrializes rapidly, growth take-off, and the South diverges. In the third (low trade costs), high growth and global divergence become self-sustaining. In the fourth stage, when the cases of "trading" ideas decreases, the South quickly industrializes and converges.

Keywords: growth, take-off, industrial revolution, economic geography, endogenous growth, trade and development

JEL classification: F43, F01, O19, N13

1. Introduction

In 1990 the world's richest nation was 4500 percent richer than the poorest; in 1870 the figure was 900 percent, and before the first industrial revolution (mid-eighteenth century) West European per capita incomes were only 30 percent above those of China and India (Maddison, 1983; Bairoch, 1993). While some scholars disagree with Bairoch's estimate of eighteenth century income gaps, none disputes the conclusion. Authors as diverse as Braudel (1984), Kuznets (1965, 1966), Baumol (1994), and Maddison (1983, 1991) assert that the big North-South income divergence appeared with the first industrial revolution. For example, Kuznets (1965, p. 20) says: "Before the nineteenth century and perhaps not much before it, some presently underdeveloped countries, notably China and parts of India, were believed by Europeans to be more highly developed than Europe, and at that earlier

---

[†]This article originally appeared in *Journal of Economic Growth*, **6** 5–37 © 2001 Springer Nature.

6   BALDWIN, MARTIN, AND OTTAVIANO

time their per capita incomes may have been higher than the then per capita incomes of the presently developed countries." Thus, by the timeframe of human history, "the current wide disparities—between rich and poor countries—are recent" (Kuznets, 1966, p. 393).

The industrial revolution caused this rapid income divergence by triggering industrialization and growth in Europe while incomes stagnated in the now poor nations. At the same time, the world experienced a rapid expansion of international trade.

We present a stages-of-growth model in which these four phenomena—northern industrialization and growth take-off, income divergence, and trade expansion—are jointly endogenous. They are triggered by a gradual, exogenous fall in the cost of international trade driven by lower transportation cost as well as by market opening initiatives. In the first stage—while trade costs are still high—falling trade costs have the usual static effects on prices, trade, and welfare but no growth effects. Growth in this stage may be positive or zero, but in any case it proceeds at a fairly low rate since growth-driving externalities, which are localized, are dampened by geographical dispersion of industry. In the second stage—when trade costs have just crossed a certain threshold—industrial agglomeration occurs very rapidly and, to be specific, say it occurs in the North. Agglomeration triggers a take-off in northern growth because the geographic concentration if industry amplifies the exploitation of localized technological externalities. In our model, agglomeration implies that the South has no incentive to invest and innovate while the incentive to innovate in the North increases. Therefore, it not only generates industrialization and a growth take-off, but it also produces income divergence. In fact, in our model, global divergence is both the cause and the consequence of growth take-off in the North. Yet despite this, the South may still benefit in welfare terms. In the third stage, high growth becomes stable and self-sustaining.

The fact that externalities are localized—or to put it another way, that the cost of transporting ideas is high—is one element that makes the agglomeration phenomenon sustainable. We show that, when the cost of transporting goods asymptotes toward some natural limit but that the cost of trading ideas decreases, then the model can generate a fourth stage. This entails rapid industrialization in the South driven by heightened access to northern technologies. The emergence of southern industry slows global growth somewhat and forces a relative deindustrialization in the North.

1.1.   Relation to Early Literature

Our model captures some elements of the informal analyses of the classic growth scholars such as Kuznets and Rostow. Despite their disagreements on important points, both think of the industrial revolution as a structural break. Kuznets (1966) divides growth into two types: traditional growth (pre-1750) and modern economic growth (post-1750). The distinctive feature of modern growth, according to Kuznets, is the rapidity of the shifts in industrial structure (he talks of sweeping structural changes) and their magnitude when cumulated over decades. Rostow (1990) goes further, identifying five stages in economic growth: the traditional society, the preconditions for takeoff, the takeoff, the drive to maturity, and the age of high mass consumptions. Finally, both Kuznets and Rostow view modern economic growth as a sustained and nonreversible process.

GLOBAL INCOME DIVERGENCE, TRADE, AND INDUSTRIALIZATION 7

1.2. Relation to Recent Literature

The existing formal endogenous-growth models deal with modern economic growth, to use Kuznet's phrase. Models such as Romer (1990), Aghion and Howitt (1992), and Grossman and Helpman (1991) do not model the emergence of growth preconditions, nor do these models consider the forces that initiate the transition to an endogenous, sustained growth process (see Crafts, 1995, however, for an analysis of the British industrial revolution in the light of endogenous-growth models). Lucas (1988, 1993) insists on the role of localized social interactions and positive spillovers, which are essential for growth, but does not model growth stages.

The "big push" literature of Murphy, Shleifer, and Vishny (1989a, 1989b) points out that due to pecuniary externalities, an economy may be marked by two growth equilibria: one in which investment and therefore growth is nil, since the economy is too small, and one in which agents invest in anticipation of growth. The jump from one equilibrium to the other generates sudden industrialization. These models do not, however, imply that one of the equilibria must precede the other and as such are not models of growth stages. There is also no clear reason why the economy could not jump back (because of a war, for example) to the zero-growth equilibrium. Furthermore, as made clear by Matsuyama (1991) and Krugman (1991a), differences in initial conditions (history) or in self-fulfilling expectations explain why an economy experiences take-off or stays in a poverty trap. Hence, the difference in the path taken by poor and rich economies, the divergence phenomenon, lies out of the model.

Other models of take-off include Goodfriend and McDeremott (1995), Acemoglu and Zilibotti (1997), and Galor and Weil (1999, 2000). The first paper shows that industrialization can be driven by increased population and market size. In the second one, accumulation of capital is facilitated by financial development. Galor and Weil show that at a certain level of population, a virtuous circle develops for which higher human capital raises technological progress, which in turn raises the value of human capital. The focus of these papers, as well as other models of take-off, such as Azariadis and Drazen (1990) and Zilibotti (1995), is quite different from ours, and in particular they do not relate the take-off to the divergence phenomenon.

The literatures on uneven development (formalized by Krugman, 1981, and Faini, 1984) and on economic geography (see Krugman and Venables, 1995) analyze trade and global income divergence. None of these papers endogenizes growth, so the long-run growth rate is never affected, and growth stages are not modeled. In Krugman (1981) the divergence is driven by technological externalities; in Krugman and Venables (1995) it arises due to pecuniary externalities. The interesting contribution of Kelly (1997) is the closest to ours as it shows that the expansion of market size through a gradual improvement of transport linkages can lead to a sudden take-off of the economy. This model does not, however, explain why certain economies have experienced such a take-off and others have not—that is, the divergence phenomenon. Furthermore, Kelly's take-off is only temporary (the long-run growth rate is exogenous) despite the importance of the sustainability of growth in the transition from traditional to modern growth identified by early growth scholars. Also close to our model are Goodfriend and McDermott (1998), who show that the extent to which technological spillovers are localized is key to the divergence phenomenon, a theme that is also present in our article. However, their model does not feature an endogenous take-off—that is, an abrupt jump in northern growth—which is both the consequence and the cause of global income divergence. More generally, while aware of the possible relevance of multiple equilibria, Goodfriend and McDermott do not investigate their implications in terms of catastrophic outcomes.

The remainder of this article is in five parts. Section 2, reviews the historical evidence on the four phenomena that we want to model and on the diminution of transaction costs that triggers them. Section 3 introduces the model, determines its steady states, and studies their stability. The fourth section describes the fundamental logic of the model, explaining why the gradual reduction of trade costs eventually produces a catastrophic agglomeration of industry. Section 5 studies the growth and divergence implications. The sixth section discusses the conditions under which the South can rapidly converge, and the last section presents our concluding remarks.

2.   Motivation and Historical Evidence

Since it would be too ambitious to try to capture the richness of history within a single analytical framework, we coherently model one of the possible forces at work during the industrial revolution. While it might not be the single most important force at work, we develop an intuitive argument in favor of its existence.

2.1.   Growth, Technological Innovation, and Divergence

Perhaps the most striking feature of the industrial revolution concerns the increase in growth rates. For example, Great Britain's per capita income rose by 14 percent between 1700 and 1760, by 34 percent between 1760 and 1820, and by 100 percent between 1820 and 1870 (Maddison, 1983). Population growth also increased sharply during this period (due chiefly to better economic conditions), so Britain's GDP rose even faster than the per capita figures. in their recent reanalysis of growth in this period, Crafts and Harley (1992) and Crafts (1995) have revised downward Maddison's growth figures. Nevertheless, they confirm Maddison's basic message by finding a structural break in the trend growth of industrial production in Great Britain around 1776 (see Figure 1). Additionally, economic historians (Crafts, 1995) argue that the growth take-off was accompanied by a rapid increase in innovation seen as a profit-seeking activity. Sullivan (1989), for example, finds that the growth rate of patenting was 0.5 percent before 1754 and 3.6 percent thereafter. Ashton (1971), in his memorable phrase on the industrial revolution, sums it up in this way: "About 1760 a wave of gadgets swept over England.... It was not only gadgets, however but innovations of various kinds—in agriculture, transport, manufacture, trade and finance—that surged up with a suddenness for which it is difficult to find a parallel at any other time or place."

Economic historians have different views about the role of technological progress in the industrial revolution in Britain. On the one hand, Crafts and Harley (1992) view the industrial revolution as the result of mostly exogenous technical change in a few industries

GLOBAL INCOME DIVERGENCE, TRADE, AND INDUSTRIALIZATION   9

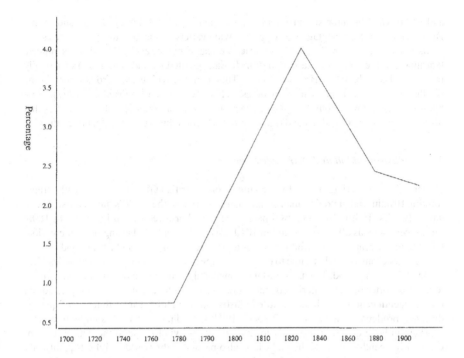

Figure 1. Trend growth in industrial production (Craft, 1995).

(cotton and iron). On the other hand, the more traditional and broad view of the industrial revolution, as illustrated by the above quote of Ashton and the image of the unbound Prometheus of Landes (1969), is that of widespread change and technical progress in many industries. Even though this view gives an important role to a few macro inventions, it also insists on the role played by the many small technological innovations and improvements that took place in many industries during this period and on the importance of learning by doing. Rosenberg (1994) and Crafts (1995) explicitly stress the importance of localized cumulative learning processes in their accounts of the industrial revolution. The pervasiveness of technological change across many sectors makes this broad view inconsistent with an explanation of the industrial revolution solely based on a few big exogenous technological shocks limited to a few industries. Perhaps paradoxically, the traditional broad view is therefore more consistent with a theoretical framework where innovation is not solely the result of a few exogenous shocks but the endogenous product of economic incentives, such as in some models of the new growth theory.

The broad view is corroborated by the work of Mokyr (1990) and Temin (1997). Using British trade data, Temin discriminates between the two views. The narrow view implies that Britain should have had a growing comparative advantage in a few industries (cotton and iron), which is inconsistent with the trade data. On the contrary, Temin shows that British comparative advantage was clear in a wide variety of manufacturing industries.

Historical data on growth in other countries are scarce, but the available estimates indicate that nineteenth-century per capita GDP in India stagnated (Maddison, 1971) or actually regressed (Bairoch, 1993; Braudel, 1984). This, coupled with higher growth rates in the North, explains the divergence in incomes. This is confirmed by Pritchett (1997), who, by calculating a lower bound for income per capita in poor countries, also concludes that divergence was a very sudden and dramatic phenomenon during the nineteenth century.

2.2.   Industrialization and Deindustrialization

During this same period, the sectoral composition of British GDP shifted radically, trans-forming Britain from a predominantly agrarian country into the world's most industrialized nation (Crafts, 1989). In 1700, 18.5 percent of the labor force was in industry. In 1800, this percentage was 29.5 percent and in 1840 it was 47.3 percent. During the same period, Great Britain became a large food importer and a large exporter of industrial goods.

Structural changes in what came to be known as the developing countries were no less dra-matic during this period. India, for instance, switched from a net exporter of manufactures to a net exporter of raw materials (Chaudhuri, 1966). To take a specific example, during the eighteenth century the Indian textile industry was the global leader in terms of quality, diversity, production, and exports (Braudel, 1984; Chaudhuri, 1991). Indian textiles were exported in huge quantities not only to Europe but also via Europe to the American con-tinent. Eighteenth-century India and China also produced the world's highest-quality silk and porcelain. These manufactured goods were exchanged for silver since many European manufactures were uncompetitive in the East (Barraclough, 1978).

Yet at the end of the nineteenth century, more than 70 percent of Indian textile consumption was imported, mainly from Great Britain (Bairoch, 1993). A similar but less dramatic story can be told for the Indian shipbuilding and steel industries. Until the mid-nineteenth century, on Asian seas, only Indian-built boats were used, in particular by the British merchants. They were, however, forbidden in English harbors (Braudel, 1984). Similar cases can be found across Latin America and the Middle East (Batou, 1990; Braudel, 1984).

These dramatic shifts in specialization suggest that the massive industrialization in the now rich North may have been accompanied by a deindustrialization in the now poor South. Bairoch (1982) has attempted to quantify these trends in industrialization and deindustrialization. Table 1 reports the evolution of per capita industry levels. There are several striking features. First, in the mid-eighteenth century, there was practically no difference in industrialization between Europe and the developing countries. All European nations were at levels between 6 and 10 (with the United Kingdom's level in 1900 being 100). India and China were at levels 7 and 8, respectively. The performance of the United Kingdom starting in 1750 and later on in the rest of Europe is spectacular. On the other hand, the parallel process of deindustrialization in China and India is dramatic as China drops from 8 to about 3 at the end of the nineteenth century. These estimates also suggest that the combination of basic equality of industry per capita levels in the eighteenth century with Europe's small population meant that the developing countries' industry dominated world

GLOBAL INCOME DIVERGENCE, TRADE, AND INDUSTRIALIZATION   11

Table 1. Per capita industrialization levels, 1750–1913 (United Kingdom in 1900 = 100).

	1750	1800	1830	1860	1880	1900	1913
United Kingdom	10	16	25	64	87	100	115
Europe (excluding the United Kingdom)	7	8	9	14	21	36	57
China	8	6	6	4	4	3	3
India-Pakistan	7	6	6	3	2	1	2

Source: Bairoch (1982).

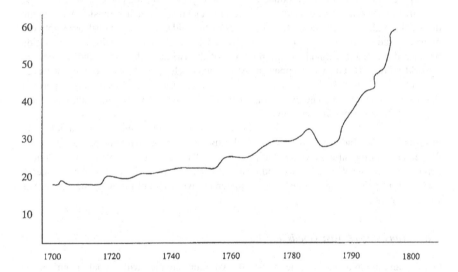

Figure 2. English foreign trade (eighteenth century).

production. Bairoch asserts that in 1750 it accounted for 73 percent of world manufacturing but that in 1913 it had dropped to a mere 7.5 percent.

2.3. Trade

Historians disagree on trade's exact role in the industrial revolution (on this debate see Engermann, 1996; O'Brien and Engermann, 1991). None, however, disputes its rapid increase during this period (Figure 2, from Deane, 1979, illustrates this rapid increase in English foreign trade during the period of the first industrial revolution). At least part of this rise was due to the decrease in trade costs during the eighteenth century (see next subsection).

On one side of the debate, the fact that exports accounted for a modest fraction of GNP suggests a limited role for trade. On the other side, it is important to note that, during the nineteenth century, Britain (which industrialized first) exported an unusually high proportion of its total output, around 25 percent compared with 10 to 12 percent for France (Crafts, 1984, 1989). Also, even before the industrial revolution, Britain's economy was more open than the economy of any continental country, exporting close to 15 percent of its GNP. The role of trade was especially important for several leading industries that exported a third of their output product in 1800 (Mokyr, 1993). The cotton sector depended for more than half of its sales on foreign markets. Cotton was also cheap to transport at a time where most goods were not (Crafts, 1989). Braudel (1984) takes trade to be a key factor, noting that between 1700 and 1800 British industries that focused on domestic sales increased output by 50 percent while those that produced for export expanded by 500 percent. Deane (1979) also stresses the role of trade speaking of a commercial revolution that transformed London during the eighteenth century into "the center of the wide, intricate, multilateral network of world trade." According to her, trade helped to precipitate the industrial revolution because it created a demand for the products of the British industry: without access to a world market, Britain was trapped in the vicious circle of a closed economy in which it is not possible to "obtain economies of scale and experience.... Increasing exports of British manufactures encouraged new industrial investment and innovation and generated increased domestic purchasing power."

Deane also noted that British trade during this period expanded much more rapidly with the West and East Indies and Africa than with Europe, its traditional trade partner. In 1700, 85 percent of English exports (excluding reexports) were directed toward Europe, and 9 percent toward the West and East Indies and Africa. Thus, at the end of the nineteenth century, Europe's share amounted to only 30 percent while that of the West and East Indies was 38 percent.

2.4. Transaction Costs: Goods and Ideas

Our explanation of a take-off (the industrial revolution) coupled with global income divergence, depends crucially on a gradual exogenous decrease in transaction costs on goods. The possibility of later rapid convergence and industrialization of the South is conditioned by a subsequent exogenous decrease in the cost of transacting ideas. Because there is a threshold effect in the level of transaction costs that triggers the take-off and then the rapid convergence, the decrease in transaction costs (first on trading goods and then on trading ideas) does not need to be large.

North (1968) offers precise evidence of the decrease of the cost of shipping during the period between 1600 and 1850. He shows that this decrease was gradual and that, prior to 1800, it was the decline of piracy "permitting ships to reduce both manpower and armament, which contributed to most of the fall." Moreover, this decrease was more important on "routes still infested by pirates (East Indies, Mediteranean, West Indies) than on routes free of pirates (Baltic, North Europe, North Atlantic)." As a result of this increased security of shipping, insurance costs also declined, and by 1770 they "had fallen to approximately two-thirds of the 1635 rate and continued to drop throughout the first half of the nineteenth century." Since most of the dramatic drop of shipping costs had already taken place before the "wave of gadgets and innovations" that Ashton (1971) associates with the industrial

GLOBAL INCOME DIVERGENCE, TRADE, AND INDUSTRIALIZATION   13

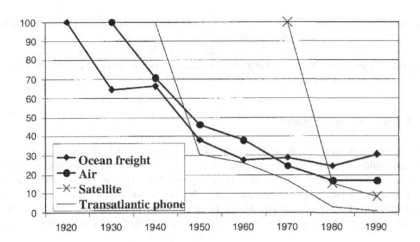

Figure 3. Transportation and communication costs, 1920–1950. Source: World Bank (1995).

revolution, and since increased shipping speed was not a very important factor in the decrease of the shipping cost during the whole period, a significant part of the decrease of transaction costs prior and during the first industrial revolution can be thought of as an exogenous phenomenon.

The gradual decrease in the cost of trading goods continued during the nineteenth century. For example, Bairoch (1989) estimates that the transport cost as a percentage of production costs for a 800 kilometer trade shipment of manufactured iron goods was 27 percent in 1830, 21 percent in 1850, 10 percent in 1880, and 6 percent in 1910. As illustrated in Figure 3, in the twentieth century, transport costs on goods continued to decrease until 1960 (for oceanic shipping costs) and until 1980 for airfreight. Communication costs, however, continued to plunge. Caincross (1997) further documents the decrease in the cost of trading ideas internationally. The cost of a three-minute call from New York to London fell from about $250 in 1940 to a few pennies today.

3. The Model

The basic logic of our growth take-off story is that, at some point, decreasing transportation costs cause a process of catastrophic agglomeration that speeds growth in the presence of localized externalities. Even though, we conjecture, the same logic would make sense in a very broad class of models,[1] for concreteness we choose to build our model on new economic geography and new growth theory. The former (see, e.g., Fujita, Krugman, and Venables, 2000) consists mainly of essentially static models in which, due to localized pecuniary externalities, a given amount of productive resources tends to agglomerate in space as transport costs fall. The latter (see, e.g., Grossman and Helpman, 1991) proposes dynamic models of endogenous growth in which localized technological externalities lead to different speeds of innovation across locations. Since, in the light of the historical evidence discussed above, both types of externalities seem to be relevant, we follow Baldwin (1999) as well as Martin and Ottaviano (1999) and adopt a unified analytical framework that merges the crucial features of both strands of literature.

3.1. Structure of the Model

Consider a world economy with two regions (North and South), each with two factors (labor L and capital K) and three sectors: manufactures M, traditional goods T, and a capital-producing sector I. Regions are symmetric in terms of preferences, technology, trade costs, and labor endowments. Things pertaining to the North bear no label, while those pertaining to the South are labeled by an asterisk (*). For conciseness of exposition, we focus on the North. The corresponding expressions for the South can be derived by symmetry.

3.1.1. Technology The M-sector output is a horizontally differentiated good that is supplied under increasing returns to scale and Dixit-Stiglitz monopolistic competition. Specificly, the production of each variety of the manufacturing good entails a fixed cost (one unit of K) and a variable cost (a_M units of labor per unit of output). Its cost function, therefore, is $(\pi + wa_M m_i)$, where π is K's rental rate, w is the wage rate, and m_i is total output of a typical firm. The T-sector supplies a homogenous good, which is produced under constant returns and perfect competition. By choice of units, one unit of T is made with one unit of L.

While regional labor stocks are fixed, each region's K is accumulated by its I-sector, which is perfectly competitive and produces one unit of K with a_I units of L. To individual I-firms, a_I is a parameter; however, following Romer (1990) and Grossman and Helpman (1991), we assume a sector-wide learning curve. That is, the marginal cost of producing new capital declines (that is, a_I falls) as the sector's cumulative output rises. many justifications of this learning are possible. Romer (1990), for instance, rationalizes it by referring to the nonrival nature of knowledge.

The specific production and marginal cost functions assumed are

$$\dot{K} = Q_K = \frac{L_I}{a_I}, \quad F = wa_I; \quad a_I \equiv \frac{1}{K^w A}, \quad A \equiv \theta_K + \lambda(1 - \theta_K), \quad \theta_K \equiv \frac{K}{K^W}, \quad (1)$$

where Q_K and L_I are I-sector output and employment, F is I-sector marginal cost (in equilibrium F is the M-sector's fixed cost), $K^W = K + K^*$, where K and K^* are the northern and southern cumulative I-sector production levels, and λ is a parameter governing the internationalization of learning effects. Southern technology is isomorphic. In particular, $A^* = \lambda\theta_K + 1 - \theta_K$. Finally, following Romer (1990) and Grossman and Helpman (1991), depreciation of knowledge capital is ignored, so $\dot{K} = Q_K$. The regional K's therefore represents three quantities: region-specific capital stocks, region-specific cumulative I-sector production (learning), and region-specific numbers of varieties (recall that there is one unit of K per variety). To ease notation, the dependence of variables on time is left implicit.

The early trade-and-endogenous-growth literature (e.g., Grossman and Helpman, 1991; Rivera-Batiz and Romer, 1991) considered only the extreme cases of $\lambda = 1$ and $\lambda = 0$. However, recent empirical studies—such as Caballero and Jaffe (1993), Eaton and Kortum (1996), and Ciccone (1997)—indicate that international learning spillovers are neither perfect nor nonexistant. We therefore assume partially localized learning externalities—that is, $0 < \lambda < 1$. When $\lambda < 1$, regional I-sector labor productivities, $1/a_I$ and $1/a_I^*$, depend on a common global element K^W and a regional element—namely, $A = \theta_K + \lambda(1 - \theta_K)$ for the North and $A^* \equiv \lambda\theta_K + 1 - \theta_K$ for the South.[2]

Given (1), the growth rate of North's K is related to L_I, λ and θ_K according to

$$g \equiv \frac{\dot{K}}{K} = \frac{L_I A}{\theta_K}. \tag{2}$$

The corresponding expression for K^*'s growth is $g^* = L_I^* A^*/(1 - \theta_k)$.

3.1.2. Preferences

On the demand side, we model preferences in terms of an infinitely lived representative consumer (in each region) with utility function:

$$U = \int_{t=0}^{\infty} e^{-\rho t} \ln Q dt, \; Q \equiv C_T^{1-\alpha} C_M^{\alpha}, \quad C_M \equiv \left(\int_{i=0}^{K+K^*} c_i^{1-1/\sigma} di \right)^{\frac{1}{1-1/\sigma}} \sigma > 1, \tag{3}$$

where ρ is the rate of time preference, Q is a consumption composite of C_T and C_M (respectively, consumption of T and a CES composite of M-varieties), and c_i is consumption of variety i.

3.1.3. Goods and Factor Mobility

While goods (M and T) are traded, factors (L and K) are not. We view K as knowledge capital and note that while some aspects of knowledge are easily transferred internationally, others are not. Some easily transferred aspects of knowledge are captured by $\lambda > 0$ in our model, but we also assume that important aspects of variety-specific knowledge are tacit in the sense that they are embodied in the skill and knowhow of workers. This component makes K difficult to trade. To keep our results as sharp as possible, we make the simplifying assumption that K is nontraded.[3] For goods, we adopt the standard simplifying assumptions (Krugman, 1991b; Krugman and Venables, 1995) that T-trade is costless but trade in M is impeded by frictional (that is, iceberg) import barriers (see Fujita, Krugman, and Venables, 2000, for a detailed discussion of this assumption). Specifically, $\tau \geq 1$ units of M must be exported to sell one unit abroad. τ is viewed as reflecting all costs of doing business abroad. These include everything from the mundane—shipping costs and trade policy barriers (tariffs, and so on)—to more exotic factors such as the cost of providing after-sales services.

3.2. Short-Run Equilibrium

In an instantaneous equilibrium, for given capital endowments K and K^*, the consumer maximizes utility, firms maximize profits, and all goods and factors markets clear.

3.2.1. Consumer's Choice Due to the chosen functional forms, utility optimization can be thought of as a multiple-staged decision in which the consumer first allocates her income between consumption and savings, then allocates consumption between the manufacturing and traditional goods, and finally distributes manufacturing consumption across varieties.

In the first stage, the consumer decides how much consumption to postpone to take advantage of investment opportunities in the I-sector. However, for expository purposes it is useful to follow Grossman and Helpman (1991) and introduce an additional asset bearing a risk-free interest rate r. Since the aim of this asset is only to clarify the intertemporal decision of the consumer, its tradability must mirror capital mobility—that is, the asset is not traded between regions.

As a result intertemporal optimization implies that the time path of consumption expenditures E is driven by the standard Euler equation:

$$\frac{\dot{E}}{E} = r - \rho, \tag{4}$$

with the interest rate r satisfying the no-arbitrage-opportunity condition between investments in the safe asset in capital accumulation:

$$r = \frac{\pi}{F} + \frac{\dot{F}}{F}, \tag{5}$$

where π is the rental rate of capital and F is its asset value, which, due to perfect competition in the I-sector, is equal to its marginal cost of production.

In the second stage, utility maximization implies that a constant fraction α of expenditure E falls on M with the rest spent on T.

Finally, in the third stage, the amount of M expenditures αE is allocated across varieties, which yields the following CES demand function for a typical M variety:

$$c_j = \frac{s_j \alpha E}{P_j}; \quad s_j \equiv \frac{p_j^{1\sigma}}{\int_{i=0}^{K+K^*} p_i^{1-\sigma} di}, \tag{6}$$

where s_j is variety j's share of expenditure on all M-varieties, and p_j is variety j's consumer price.

3.2.2. Firm's Choice On the supply side, free trade in T equalizes its price across regions, $p_T = p_T^*$, as long as both regions produce some T—that is, if α is not too large, which we assume from now on.[4] Due to perfect competition in the T-sector, price equalization implies also wage equalization, $w = w^*$. It is therefore convenient to choose home labor as numeraire so that $p_T = p_T^* = w = w^* = 1$.

As to the M-sector, since wages are the same everywhere and, by (6), all varieties' demands have the same constant price elasticity σ, firms' profit maximization yields local and export market prices that are identical for all varieties no matter where they are produced—that is, we have optimal mark-up pricing $p = a_M \sigma/(\sigma - 1)$ and $p' = \tau p$, respectively. For simplicity we follow the standard convention of choosing units such that $a_M = 1 - 1/\sigma$ so that $p = 1$. Southern M-firms have analogous pricing rules.

With monopolistic competition, equilibrium operating profit is the value of sales divided by σ. Due to free entry, this profit is entirely absorbed by the fixed cost of production—that is, by the rental rate of capital π. Using the M-good market clearing condition by variety together with (6) and optimal pricing, this implies

$$\pi = B \left(\frac{\alpha E^w}{\sigma K^w} \right); \quad B \equiv \left[\frac{\theta_E}{\theta_K + \phi(1 - \theta_K)} + \frac{\phi(1 - \theta_E)}{\phi \theta_K + 1 - \theta_K} \right], \quad \theta_E \equiv \frac{E}{E^w}, \quad (7)$$

where $E^w = E + E^*$ is world expenditure, θ_E is North's share of E_w, and $\phi \equiv \tau^{1-\sigma}$ measures the freeness of trade since trade gets freer as ϕ rises from 0 (prohibitive costs) to 1 (costless trade). Also, B measures the bias in favor of northern M-sector sales since it measures the extent to which the value of sales of a northern variety exceeds average sales per variety worldwide (namely, $\alpha E^w/K^w$). Note that the definition of B permits a decomposition of π changes into global developments (measured by $\dot{\theta}_K$ and $\dot{\theta}_E$).

3.2.3. M-Good- and T-Good-Market Clearing   When we consider the CES composite as one good, its world markets clear whenever world M-good expenditures αE^w equal the value of world M-good output $a_M(L_M + L_M^*)$, where L_M is labor employed in sector M. Analogously, in the case of the T-good its world market clears whenever world expenditures $(1 - \alpha)E^w$ equal the value of world supply $(L_T + L_T^*)$, where L_T is labor employed in sector T and we have used the fact that one unit of labor produces one unit of T.

3.2.4. Labor-Market Clearing   To simplify notation, we have already used the capital-market clearing condition implying that the number of active firms and varieties in each region is equal to the local capital stock. Thus, to complete the characterization of the instantaneous equilibrium, all we need is to state the labor-market condition. At world level, it is $2L = (L_T + L_T^*) + (L_M + L_M^*) + (L_I + L_I^*)$. Using M-good and T-good market clearing, that can be rewritten as

$$E^w = \frac{\sigma}{\sigma - \alpha}(2L - L_I - L_I^*), \quad (8)$$

where, by definition, labor employed in capital accumulation is equal to investment (that is, income minus consumption):

$$L_I = L + \pi K - E. \quad (9)$$

We can thus summarize the evolution of the economy by a system of three differential equations in E, E^*—using $\theta_E = E/(E + E^*)$—and θ_K plus transversality conditions. Two of them, one for each region, are derived by substituting for r from (5) into (6). After using (1) and (7) in the resulting expression to get rid of π and F, respectively, for the North we have

$$\frac{\dot{E}}{E} = \frac{\alpha}{\sigma} \left[AB - \theta_K B - \lambda(1 - \theta_K)B^* \right] (E + E^*) + (E + \lambda E^*)$$
$$- (1 - \lambda)L - \rho, \tag{10a}$$

with a symmetric expression holding for the South:

$$\frac{\dot{E}^*}{E^*} = \frac{\alpha}{\sigma} \left[A^* B^* - (1 - \theta_K)B^* - \lambda \theta_K B \right] (E + E^*)$$
$$+ (E^* + \lambda E) - (1 - \lambda)L - \rho. \tag{10b}$$

Finally, the third and last equations come from differentiating the definition of θ_K with respect to time. This gives

$$\dot{\theta}_K = \theta_K(1 - \theta_K) \left(\frac{\dot{K}}{K} - \frac{\dot{K}^*}{K^*} \right), \tag{11}$$

which, given (1), (2), (7), and (9), can be written as

$$\dot{\theta}_K = (1 - \theta_K)AL_I - \theta_K A^* L_I^*$$
$$= (1 - \theta_K)A \left[L + \frac{\alpha}{\sigma}\theta_K B(E + E^*) - E \right]$$
$$- \theta_K A^* \left[L + \frac{\alpha}{\sigma}(1 - \theta_K)B^*(E + E^*) - E^* \right]. \tag{12}$$

The two subsections that follow are devoted, respectively, to the steady-state and stability analyses of the three-dimensional dynamic system (10a)-(10b)-(12).

3.3. Long-Run Equilibrium

A steady state of the system(10a)-(10b)-(12) is a triple $(\bar{E}, \bar{E}^*, \bar{\theta}_K)$ such that $\dot{E} - \dot{E}^* = \dot{\theta}_K = 0$ (from now on upper bars label steady-state values). Inspection of (11) simplifies the search of such steady states. Since $\dot{\theta}_K = 0$ in steady state, the model has only two types of long-run equilibria: those in which regions accumulate capital at the same constant rate (say, $\bar{g}$) and those in which θ_K equals either unity or zero and only one region accumulates capital. We refer to these two types as, respectively, the interior and core-periphery outcomes. Exploiting the symmetry of the model to avoid repetition, we will consider only the core-in-North case: $\theta_K = 1$.

3.3.1. Expenditures   In steady state, (4) implies $\bar{r} = \bar{r}^* = \rho$. Straightforward calculations reveal that steady-state expenditures are set at the permanent income levels.

That is, expenditures equal labor income plus the annuity value of steady-state wealth: $\bar{E} = L + \rho \bar{F} K = L + \bar{\theta}_K / \bar{A}$, and $\bar{E}^* = L + \rho \bar{F}^* K^* = L + (1 - \bar{\theta}_K)/\bar{A}^*$. Thus, by (1), we get

$$\bar{E} = L + \rho \frac{\bar{\theta}_K}{\bar{A}}, \quad \bar{E}^* = L + \rho \frac{1 - \bar{\theta}_K}{\bar{A}^*}. \tag{13}$$

3.3.2. Interregional Distribution of Capital   Associated with (13) there are three alternative steady state values of θ_K:

$$\bar{\theta}_K = \frac{1}{2}, \quad \bar{\theta}_K = \frac{1}{2}\left[1 \pm \sqrt{\left(\frac{1+\lambda}{1-\lambda}\right)\left(\frac{1+\lambda\Lambda}{1-\lambda\Lambda}\right)}\right];$$

$$\Lambda \equiv \left\{1 - \frac{2\rho\phi(1 - \lambda\phi)}{[(\lambda(1 + \phi^2) - 2\phi]L}\right\}. \tag{14}$$

In (14) the first value is the symmetric case in which capital is evenly distributed across regions. The second and third values—which correspond to interior, nonsymmetric steady states—are economically relevant only for a narrow rang of ϕ. In particular, the second and third solutions converge to $1/2$ as ϕ approaches the value

$$\phi^{\mathrm{cat}} = \frac{[L(1 + \lambda) + \rho] - \sqrt{(1 - \lambda^2)[(1 + \lambda) + \rho]^2 + \lambda^2 \rho^2}}{\lambda[L(1 + \lambda) + 2\rho]} \tag{15}$$

from above. For levels of ϕ below ϕ^{cat}, the second and third solutions are imaginary and so are irrelevant.

In addition, for levels of ϕ above another critical value—

$$\phi^{CP} = \frac{2L + \rho - \sqrt{(2L + \rho)^2 - 4\lambda^2 L(L + \rho)}}{2\lambda(L + \rho)} \tag{16}$$

—the second solution is negative, and the third solution exceeds unity. Since both violate boundary conditions on θ_K, the corresponding steady-state outcomes are to be found at the corners $\theta_K = 0$ and $\theta_K = 1$.

For $\bar{E}$, $\bar{E}^*$, and $\bar{\theta}_K$ given by (13) and (14), the remaining aspects of the steady states can be calculated. In particular, labor employed in the northern I-sector is

$$\bar{L}_I = \frac{\bar{\theta}_K}{\bar{A}} \left\{\frac{\alpha}{\sigma}\left[2L + \rho\left(\frac{\bar{\theta}_K}{\bar{A}} + \frac{1 - \bar{\theta}_K}{\bar{A}^*}\right)\right]\bar{A}\bar{B} - \rho\right\}, \tag{17}$$

with a symmetric expression for $\bar{L}_I^*$. While the expression for a generic interior steady states are too cumbersome to be revealing, for the symmetric case ($\bar{\theta}_K = 1/2$) it is readily established that

$$\bar{L}_I = \bar{L}_I^* = \frac{\alpha(1 + \lambda)L - \rho(\sigma - \alpha)}{\sigma(1 + \lambda)}, \tag{18}$$

while for the core-in-north case ($\bar{\theta}_K = 1$) we get

$$\bar{L}_I = \frac{\alpha 2L - \rho(\sigma - \alpha)}{\sigma}, \quad \bar{L}_I^* = 0. \tag{19}$$

Finally, by (1) and (2) the steady-state growth rate of capital is

$$\bar{g} = \frac{\bar{L}_I[\bar{\theta}K + \lambda(1 - \bar{\theta}_K)]}{\bar{\theta}_K}. \tag{20}$$

3.4. Stability of Long-Run Equilibria

In the previous section we showed that, for any parameter configuration, the model exhibits a persistent steady state at $\bar{\theta}_K = 1/2$. In addition, when they exist, other steady-state values of θ_K are symmetric around $1/2$. These are typical features of pitchfork bifurcations.

In this section we show that indeed the three-dimensional family of dynamical systems (11), (10a), and (10b) parameterized by ϕ undergoes a pitchfork bifurcation as ϕ crosses ϕ^{cat}. In so doing, we exploit the differentiability of the corresponding vector fields, which entails that the qualitative results of the local stability analysis around the symmetric steady state $\theta_K = 1/2$ map into global stability results (see, e.g., Guckenheimer and Holmes, 1990).

Local stability is studied in terms of the eigenvalues of the Jacobian matrix associated with the system. These eigenvalues are

$$e_1 - L(1 + \lambda) + \rho; , \quad e_{2,3} = \frac{b \pm \sqrt{b^2 - 4c\sigma(1 + \lambda)}}{2\sigma(1 + \lambda)};$$

$$b \equiv \sigma[e_1(1 - \lambda) + 2\lambda\rho] + 4\frac{\alpha\phi(1 - \lambda\phi)e_1}{(1 + \phi)^2},$$

$$c \equiv -2\alpha e_1 \left(e_1 \left[\lambda - 2\frac{\phi(1 + \lambda)}{(1 + \phi)^2} \right] - \frac{\lambda\rho(1 - \phi)}{1 + \phi} \right). \tag{21}$$

While the first eigenvalue is plainly real and positive, the second and third give rise to different cases. By inspection, when $b^2 - 4c\sigma(1 + \lambda) > 0$—that is, at sufficiently low levels of ϕ, eigenvalues are all real. In this case, given that the positive radicals in e_2 and e_3 are positive, it follows that the eigenvalue that adds the radical—call these e_2—is always positive. The third eigenvalue changes sign at the point were $c = 0$. Solving this for ϕ, we get exactly ϕ^{cat}. Thus, for $\phi < \phi^{\text{cat}}$, since we have one negative and two positive eigenvalues, the symmetric steady state is a saddle point (stable). Differently, for $\phi > \phi^{\text{cat}}$, since we have three positive eigenvalues, the symmetric steady state is a source (unstable).

The crucial thing to notice is that, as pointed out in the previous section, while for $\phi < \phi^{\text{cat}}$ only the symmetric steady state exists, for $\phi > \phi^{\text{cat}}$ two additional steady states appear. In other words, when ϕ rises from below to above ϕ^{cat}, the symmetric steady state loses its stability to the two new neighboring interior steady states, which, by continuity, are thus saddle points (supercritical pitchfork bifurcation). These results are summarized in Figure 4.

GLOBAL INCOME DIVERGENCE, TRADE, AND INDUSTRIALIZATION 21

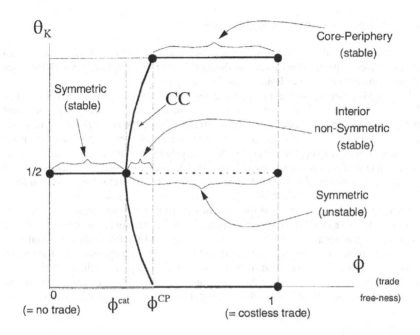

Figure 4. Map of long-run equilibria.

When $\phi > \phi^{\text{cat}}$, whether or not the second and third eigenvalues are real makes a fundamental difference in terms of equilibrium selection. When they are real, the initial condition on θ_K—say, θ_K^0—determines the long-run equilibrium. If $\theta_K^0 > 1/2(\theta_K^0 < 1/2)$, the system will asymptotically reach a steady state with $\theta_K > 1/2(\theta_K < 1/2)$. On the contrary, when they are complex numbers (that is, $b^2 - 4c\sigma(1 + \lambda) < 0$), we have multiple equilibrium trajectories that spiral out of $\theta_K = 1/2$. In this case, self-fulfilling expectations may choose the long-run equilibrium that is eventually reached.

In any case, whether initial conditions or expectations dominate, it is decided outside the model which interior nonsymmetric steady state becomes the long-run outcome once the symmetric steady state loses its stability. Hence, which zone becomes industrialized and which zone becomes deindustrialized are indeterminate in the model. However, this indeterminacy can be partly reconciled with historical evidence. Many historians (see, for example, Braudel, 1984) believe that Europe, and especially the United Kingdom, had, just before the first industrial revolution, a technological advance over the rest of the world. However, they insist that this advance was relatively small (in particular relative to China nd India) especially compared to what followed. This is consistent with a someway generous reading of our model, suggesting that the small European technological advance that existed at the time the transaction costs reached the critical level was sufficient to put in place the virtuous circle at the origin of the take-off.

4.   The Logic of Catastrophic Agglomeration

To convey the economic logic of our model, we find it useful to reinterpret the formal results derived in the previous section in the light of the more intuitive approach proposed by Baldwin (1999) as well as Baldwin and Forslid (2000a).

The starting point is to realize that L_I indicates labor devoted to creating new K—that is, the levels of real investment. While there may be many ways of determining investment in a general equilibrium model, Tobin's q-approach (Tobin, 1969) is a powerful, intuitive, and well-known method for doing just that. The essence of Tobin's approach is to assert that the equilibrium level of investment is characterized by the equality of the stock-market value of a unit of capital—which we denote with the symbol V—and the replacement cost of capital, P_K. Tobin takes the ratio of these, so what the M-sector free-entry condition (namely, $V = P_K$) becomes Tobin's famous condition $q = V/P_K = 1$.

The denominator of Tobin's q is the price of new capital that, as already argued, is the I-sector marginal cost F. In steady-state calculating the numerator of Tobin's q (the present value of introducing a new variety) requires us to discount the future flow of rental rates (operating profits) $\bar{\pi}$ at the steady-state interest rate ρ. In addition, from (7), the present value of a new variety also depends (through K^w) on the rate $\bar{g}$ at which new varieties are created: either the common growth rate (in the interior case) or North's growth rate (in the core-periphery case). In both cases, the steady-state values of investing in new units of k are

$$\bar{V} - \frac{\pi}{\rho + \bar{g}}, \quad \bar{V}^* = \frac{\bar{\pi}^*}{\rho + \bar{g}}. \tag{22}$$

Given this, steady-state qs are

$$\bar{q} = \frac{\bar{\pi}/(\rho + \bar{g})}{\bar{F}}, \quad \bar{q}^* = \frac{\bar{\pi}^*/(\rho + \bar{g})}{\bar{F}^*}. \tag{23}$$

As we have seen, although an equal division of M-varieties is always an equilibrium, it need not be stable. Indeed, in our model two cycles of circular causality tend to destabilize the symmetric equilibrium. The first is the well-known demand-linked cycle in which production shifting leads to expenditure shifting and vice versa. The particular variant present in our model is based on the mechanism introduced by Baldwin (1999). To see the logic of this linkage, consider a perturbation that exogenously shifts one M-sector firm from the South to the North. Firms are associated with a unit of capital and capital-earnings are spent with a local bias because of transaction costs, so production shifting leads to expenditure shifting.[5] Other things equal, this expenditure shifting raises northern operating profits and lowers southern operating profits due to a market-size effect (home-market effect).[6] This tends to raise the value of an extra unit of capital in the North. Therefore, it raises q and lowers q^*, thereby speeding the North's accumulation and retarding the South's. The initial exogenous shift thus leads to another round of production shifting, and the cycle repeats. As we shall see, if trade costs are sufficiently low, demand-linked circular causality alone can destabilize the symmetric equilibrium.

The second link is the growth-linked circular causality introduced by Martin and Otta-viano (1999). When I-sector technological externalities are transmitted imperfectly across borders, production shifting leads to cost shifting in the I-sector. For instance, suppose an

GLOBAL INCOME DIVERGENCE, TRADE, AND INDUSTRIALIZATION 23

exogenous perturbation increased θ_K slightly. Given localized knowledge spillovers, this shock lowers the marginal cost of the northern I-sector while raising that of the South. Other things equal, this raises q and lowers q^*, so the initial production shifting raises the North's rate of investment and lowers the South's. Of course, this growth shifting further increases θ_K, and the cycle repeats. Again, if trade costs are low enough, growth-linked circular causality alone can yield to total agglomeration.

The sole force opposing agglomeration here is the local competition effect. Namely, raising θ_K (North's share of varieties) tends to raise local competition in the North and lower it in the South. Since competition is bad for profits, raising θ_K tends to lower q and raise q^*.[7]

These forces can be singled out if one exogenously increases θ^K by a small amount and then checks the impact of this perturbation on the regional $\bar{q}$'s. In particular, using (1), (2), (7), (9), (13), and (18), the steady-state q can be expressed as a function of θ_K and L_I. Holding L_I constant for the moment, the partial derivative of interest is $\partial \bar{q}/\partial \theta_K$ from $\bar{q} = [\bar{\theta}_K, \bar{L}_I, \bar{\theta}_E[\bar{\theta}_K]; \phi]$. The symmetric equilibrium is stable if and only if $\partial \bar{q}/\partial \theta_K$ is negative for a simple reason. If a unit of capital accidentally disturbs symmetry, the accident lowers Tobin's q in the North and raises it in the South (by symmetry $\partial \bar{q}^*/\partial \theta_K$ and $\partial \bar{q}/\partial \theta_K$ have opposite signs). Moreover, these incipient changes in Tobin's q are sufficient statistics for changes in regional investment levels (see Baldwin and Forslid, 2000b, Proposition 1 for details). Thus, when $\partial \bar{q}/\partial \theta_K < 0$, the perturbation generates self-correcting forces in the sense that L_I falls and L_I^* rises. If the derivative is positive, the accident boosts L_I and lowers L_I^*, thus amplifying the initial shock to θ_K. Plainly the symmetric equilibrium is unstable in this case. We turn now to signing $\partial \bar{q}/\partial \theta_K$.

Differentiating the definition of q with respect to θ_K, we have

$$\left(\frac{\partial \bar{q}/\bar{q}}{\partial \theta_K} \right)_{|\bar{\theta}_K = 1/2} = 2 \left(\frac{1-\phi}{1+\phi} \right) \left(\frac{d\bar{\theta}_E}{d\theta_K} \right)_{|\bar{\theta}_K = 1/2}$$

$$+ \frac{4}{1+\lambda} \frac{1+\phi^2}{(1+\phi^2)} \left[\frac{-(1-\phi)^2}{1+\phi^2} + 1 - \lambda \right]. \tag{24}$$

Using (13) to find $d\bar{\theta}_E/d\theta_K = 2\rho\lambda/[L(1+\lambda)+\rho](1+\lambda)$, we see that the system is unstable for sufficiently low trade costs (that is, $\phi \approx 1$). And, under weak regulatory conditions, the system is stable—that is, (24) is negative, for sufficiently high trade costs $\phi \approx 0$.[8]

Expression (24) illustrates the three forces affecting stability. The first and third terms are positive, so they represent the destabilizing forces—namely, the demand-linked and growth-linked circular causalities, respectively. The negative second term reflects the stabilizing local-competition effect. Clearly, reducing trade costs ($d\phi > 0$) erodes the stabilizing force more quickly than it erodes the destabilizing demand-linkage.

To isolate the two distinct cycles of circular causality, suppose, for the sake of argument, that the demand-linkage is cut so that $d\bar{\theta}_E/d\theta_K = 0$. In this case, $\partial \bar{q}/\partial \theta_K$ is positive, and the system is unstable when $\lambda < 2\phi/(1+\phi^2)$. This shows that growth-linked circular causality can by itself produce total agglomeration when trade costs are low enough. (Recall that $0 \le \phi \le 1$ is a measure of the freeness of trade, so $\phi = 1$ indicates costless trade). To see the dependence of growth-linked circular causality on localized knowledge spillovers, note that with $\lambda = 1$ and $d\bar{\theta}_E/d\theta_K = 0$, the symmetric equilibrium is always stable. Hence, divergence would not occur in a set of countries for which technological spillovers are sufficiently strong. This is reminiscent of Goodfriend and McDermott (1998). At the other extreme, when spillovers are purely local ($\lambda = 0$), the symmetric equilibrium is never stable even without the demand linkage.

Finally, the critical level of ϕ at which the symmetric equilibrium becomes unstable is defined by the point where (24) switches sign—namely, $\partial \bar{q}/\partial \theta_K = 0$. This expression is quadratic in ϕ, so it has two roots. The economically relevant one is ϕ^{cat} as defined in (15), Observe that the range of unstable ϕ's, (ϕ^{cat}, 1], gets smaller as the internationalization of learning effects (as measured by λ) increases. Since the growth-linkage becomes weaker as λ rises, it is easy to understand why the range of trade costs that leads to instability shrinks as λ rises. We come back in Section 6 to the role of rising λ for possible convergence in the South. Additionally, the instability set expands as the discount rate ρ rises since this amplifies the demand linkage. That is, the equilibrium return to capital rises with ρ, so a higher ρ amplifies the expenditure shifting that accompanies production shifting.

5. Three Stages of Growth

The cost of doing business internationally has declined sharply since the eighteenth century. While this trend seems obvious and irreversible with hindsight, it was not obviously pre-dictable in advance, nor was it monotonic. For example, as shown in Section 2, just before the industrial revolution this decrease was mostly exogenous and not primarily related to technical progress. During many periods and sometimes for decades at a time, the trend was reversed. From 1929 to 1945, for example, international trade became increasingly difficult. Restoration of peace and the founding of GATT allowed the trend to resume, but this was not a foregone conclusion in, say, 1938. Hence, even though we think of transaction costs as decreasing with time, we assume that agents take the level of the transaction cost to be given to their private decisions. If we were to take into account forward expectations on future lower transaction costs, we would need to specify an exogenous rate of decrease of τ with time. This would greatly complicate this analysis and would introduce addi-tional expectation-driven equilibria. Following Krugman and Venables (1995), this section considers the implications of lowering the cost of trade (as captured by the parameter τ).

In particular, rather than tackling the very ambitious task of fully characterizing the off steady-state dynamics of the three-dimensional system (10a)-(10b)-(11), we prefer to focus on the long-run response of our economy through comparative statics across steady states.

5.1. Location and Trade Costs: A Punctuated Equilibrium

When trade costs are high, the symmetric steady state is stable, and gradually reducing trade costs ($d\phi > 0$) produces standard, static effects—more trade, lower prices for im-ported foods, and higher welfare (more on this below). There is, however, no impact on industrial location, so during an initial phase, the global distribution of industry appears unaffected by ϕ.

As trade freeness moves beyond ϕ^{cat}, however, the world enters a qualitatively distinct phase. The symmetric distribution of industry becomes unstable, and northern as well as southern industrial structures begin to diverge; to be concrete, as done so far, assume industry agglomerates in the North. If θ_K could jump, it would be on the interior-nonsymmetric equilibrium (shown as the CC locus in Figure 4). Since CC is vertical at ϕ^{cat}, the impact on location would be catastrophic. That is to say, an infinitesimal change in trade costs would produce a discrete change in the steady-state global distribution of industry.

Since θ_K cannot jump, crossing ϕ^{cat} triggers transitional dynamics in which northern industrial output and investment rise and southern industrial output and investment fall. Moreover, in a very well-defined sense, the South would appear to be in the midst of a vicious circle driven by backward (demand) linkages and forward (cost) linkages. The demand linkages would have southern firms lowering employment and abstaining from investment because southern wealth is falling, and southern wealth is falling since southern firms are failing to invest. The cost linkages would lead to an increase in the cost of southern investment/innovation relative to the North as θ_K rises (due to localized learning externalities) and to an increase in θ_K since the cost of southern investment/innovation rises relative to the North. By the same logic, the North would appear to be in the midst of a virtuous circle. Rising θ_K would expand the North's relative market size and reduce its relative cost of investment/innovation.

Although we cannot analytically characterize the transitional dynamics of a system with three nonlinear differential equations, we can say that a continuing rise in trade freeness would raise θ_K until the core-periphery outcome is the only stable long-run equilibrium. of course, southern knowledge never disappears entirely, so the core-periphery outcome is only reached asymptotically (the number of southern varieties remains fixed, but the value of these drops forever toward zero due to the ceaseless introduction of new northern varieties).

Once the core-periphery outcome is reached—or more precisely, once we can approximate θ_K as unity—the world economy enters a third distinct phase. For trade costs lower than this point, the world economy behaves as it did in the first phase. That is to say, making trade less costly has the usual static effects but no location effects.

Plainly, the location equilibrium in this world would appear as a punctuated equilibrium. In the first and third phases, lower trade costs have no impact on the distribution of world industry, but in the second phase, the North's share of world industry increases rapidly.

We can also note that catastrophic agglomeration will not occur for countries for which international technological spillovers are important (high λ). This may be the case because of physical, political, linguistic, and cultural proximity ('familiarity' according to Goodfriend and McDermott, 1998). Our model is therefore consistent with a process of divergence between North and South while no divergence occurs among countries in the North (Europe and North America), a group for which technological spillovers were certainly quite high even in the eighteenth and nineteenth centuries.

5.2. Growth Stages

Long-run growth in this model is driven by the ceaseless accumulation of knowledge capital resulting in an ever greater range of M-varieties. Given preferences, this ceaseless expansion of variety raises real consumption continually. While technology and output in the traditional sector are stagnant, the expansion of M-varieties decreases the CES price indices of the manufacturing composite C_M in the two regions:

$$P_M = K^{w\frac{1}{1-\sigma}} [\theta_K + \phi(1 - \theta_K)]^{\frac{(1)}{(1-\sigma)}}, \quad P_M^* = K^{w\frac{1}{1-\sigma}} [\phi\theta_K + 1 - \theta_K]^{\frac{1}{1-\sigma}}. \quad (25)$$

This forces up the value of good T in terms of the composite good C_M so that the values of the two sectoral outputs grow in tandem.

5.2.1. Stage-One Growth and Investment Rates   By definition, the initial interior solution entails symmetry—that is, $\bar{\theta}_E = \bar{\theta}_K = 1/2$—and, as long as $\phi < \phi^{\text{cat}}$, this outcome is stable. The steady-state rate of K accumulation during this phase is found using the expression for $\bar{L}_1$ from (18) in (2), to get

$$Stage\ I : \bar{g} = \bar{g}^* = \frac{\alpha(1 + \lambda)L - \rho(\sigma - \alpha)}{\sigma}. \quad (26)$$

this common rate of K-accumulation is unaffected by the level of trade costs, ϕ.

   Steady-state growth in real income is nominal Y divided by the perfect consumption price index, P. Given preferences (3) and price normalization, the perfect price index is P_M^α. In steady state, nominal Y and θ_K are time-invariant, yet P falls along the steady-state growth path since K^w rises at the common rate of $\bar{g}$. Thus P_M falls at $\bar{g}/(\sigma - 1)$ and real income grows at $\alpha\bar{g}/(\sigma - 1)$. using (26):

$$Stage\ I: \bar{g}_{income} = \bar{g}_{income}^* = \frac{\alpha^2(1 + \lambda)L - \rho\alpha(\sigma - \alpha)}{\sigma(\sigma - 1)}, \quad (27)$$

where g_{income} is the real income-growth rate. By inspection, the growth rate rises with λ and α but falls with ρ and σ (all of which are standard results in the trade and endogenous growth literature) (see, e.g., Grossman and Helpman, 1991). Again trade costs do not play any role as long as the economy remains at the symmetric equilibrium.

   Consider next the rate of investment in innovation. With labor as numeraire, the rate of investment in steady states is $\bar{L}_I/\bar{Y}$. Using (18) and the definition of $\bar{Y}$, we have

$$Stage\ I: \frac{\bar{L}_I}{\bar{Y}} = \frac{\alpha(1 + \lambda)L - \rho(\sigma - \alpha)}{(\sigma + \alpha)(1 + \lambda)L + \alpha\rho}. \quad (28)$$

Again, the ratio is rising in λ and α, falling in ρ and σ, and unaffected by ϕ.

5.2.2. Stage-Three Growth and Investment Rates   Once the stage-three steady state is reached (or at least when θ_K is close enough to unity to approximate the steady-state θ_K as equal to unity), (2) and (19) imply

$$Stage \ III: \bar{g} = \frac{\alpha 2L - \rho(\sigma - \alpha)}{\sigma} \tag{29}$$

This $\bar{g}$ exceeds the stage-one $\bar{g}$ only to the extent that spillovers are localized—that is, $\lambda < 1$—the gap being $\alpha(1 - \lambda)L/\sigma$. The common real income growth rate—$\bar{g}\alpha/(\sigma - 1)$, where $\bar{g}$ is given by (29)—is thus also higher than the stage-one growth rates (as longs as $\lambda < 1$) with a gap equal to $\alpha^2(1 - \lambda)L/\sigma$. Observe that the South—which is completely specialized in the traditional sector—engages in no innovation and indeed makes no investment of any kind. Nevertheless, the South experiences the same rate of growth as the North due to continual terms-of-trade gains: as already argued, the price of T (which South exports) is time-invariant, but the price index of the composite good C_M (which South imports) falls as the number of varieties is growing.

The stage-three northern investment ratio is

$$Stage \ III: \frac{\bar{L}_I}{\bar{Y}} = \frac{\alpha 2L - \rho(\sigma - \alpha)}{(\sigma + 2\alpha)L + \alpha\rho}. \tag{30}$$

As long as growth is positive in the third stage, this is greater than that of the first stage even with $\lambda = 1$ since all investment/innovation occurs in the North.

Finally, notice that while further reduction of ϕ raises both nations' real income trajectories (via one-off drops in the perfect price index), liberalization has no effect on the common slope of their growth paths.

5.2.3. Stage-Two: Growth and Investment During the Take-off As soon as ϕ rises from below to above ϕ^{cat}, the symmetric steady state becomes unstable and the economy starts moving toward one of the interior asymmetric steady state in (14). In our discussion where the North becomes the leader, the steady state satisfies $\theta_K > 1/2$. While the exact path cannot be found analytically, the pitchfork bifurcation properties of the system entail that the economy leaves a neighborhood of the symmetric steady state (source) to reach a neighborhood of the asymmetric steady state (saddle point) in finite time ('take-off'). Once there, it reaches the new steady state only asymptotically with a speed of convergence equal to the negative eigenvalue of the Jacobian of the system evaluated at the asymmetric steady state. When this coincides with the core-periphery outcome ($\theta_K = 1$), the negative eigenvalue is identical to the opposite of (29) as one should expect. After the take-off the third phase of our model is marked by a high and stable rate of economic growth as well as by a more stable sectoral composition of output.

5.3. Income Divergence

Figure 5 shows how the ratio of steady-state real income levels (North's divided by South's) varies with trade costs. There are clearly three phases in the figure. In the first phase, trade-cost reductions have no impact on this ratio. Per capita income levels are identical since $\bar{\theta}_E = \bar{\theta}_K = 1/2$, and, by symmetry, northern and southern price indices are identical. In the

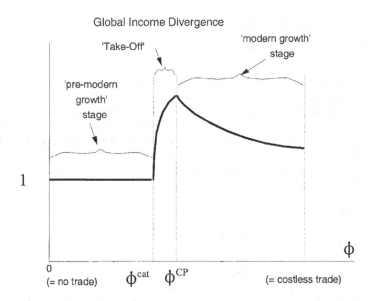

Figure 5. Global income divergence.

second phase, where $\phi > \phi^{cat}$, industry begins to agglomerate in the North. This has two effects, both promoting income divergence. First, as $\bar{\theta}_K$ rises, northern steady-state wealth rises while southern steady-state wealth falls. Second, due the home-market effect, the shift in industry location has a favorable impact on the northern price index and a dilatory impact on the South's price index. That is, as long as trade is not costless, southern consumers face higher consumer prices since all trade costs are passed on to consumers. In the final phase, some of the divergence is reversed. The reason is that although the North's wealth is higher than the South's, lowering trade costs reduces the differences in North and South price indices up to the point $\phi = 1$, where the two price indices are identical.

5.4.   Welfare

As pointed out above, our model is an example of uneven development in the sense that the agglomeration of industry in the North produces immediate divergence with respect to the South. However, because agglomeration generates a take-off that materializes itself into an acceleration of the world rate of innovation, the take-off also produces benefits for the South. The tension between the negative effect of agglomeration and the positive effect of the increase in the rate of innovation is what makes the long-run welfare effect of the take-off ambiguous for the South. Northern and southern steady-state welfare (that is, the

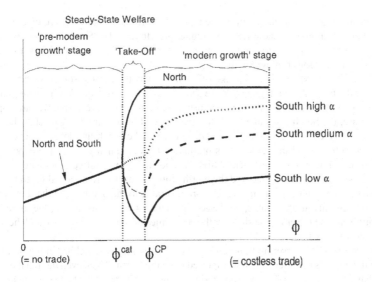

Figure 6. Steady-state welfare.

present value of the utility flows) as functions of ϕ are, respectively,

$$U = \frac{c_0 \alpha \bar{g}}{\rho^2 (\sigma - 1)} \ln \left\{ \left(L + \frac{\rho \bar{\theta}_K}{\bar{A}} \right) [\bar{\theta}_K + \phi (1 - \bar{\theta}_K)]^{\frac{\alpha}{\alpha - 1}} \right\},$$

$$U^* = \frac{c_0 \alpha \bar{g}}{\rho^2 (\sigma - 1)} \ln \left\{ \left(L + \frac{\rho (1 - \bar{\theta}_k)}{\bar{A}^*} \right) (\phi \bar{\theta}_K + 1 - \bar{\theta}_K)^{\frac{\alpha}{\alpha - 1}} \right\}, \qquad (31)$$

where $\bar{g}$ and $\bar{\theta}_K$ depend on ϕ as described above, and c_0 captures terms that do not depend on ϕ. Notice that while a rise in $\bar{g}$ is welfare enhancing in both regions, raising $\bar{\theta}_K$ raises northern welfare but lowers that of the South. As discussed above, the impact of raising the steady-state θ_K is twofold: it shifts wealth from South to North and it lowers the northern price index relative to the southern price index, as along as $\phi < 1$.

Figure 6 plots the levels of welfare corresponding to the higher arm of the pitchfork represented in Figure 4. We have simulated these levels of welfare as a function of trade costs and found three generic cases (again considering only steady states). Two elements are constant in all cases. First, both regional welfare levels rise as ϕ rises (imports get cheaper) during stage-one (the premodern growth phase), and second, the North's welfare is insensitive to ϕ in the final stage. Symmetry explains the first element and the fact that $\bar{\theta}_K = 1$ in the final phase accounts for the second element. The cases differ only in the South's welfare level in the third phase.

Note first that when transaction costs are sufficiently high (ϕ is below the threshold level), a decrease in transaction costs has the usual static effects in both the South and the North. It raises welfare because it lowers the effective (inclusive of transaction costs) price of traded manufactured goods. At the point of the take-off, North and South welfare diverge. The North benefits from agglomeration and a higher growth rate. The South benefits only from higher growth; agglomeration actually harms the South. This explains why post-take-off welfare is always lower in the South.

The positive growth effect of the take-off explains why the comparison of welfare before and after the take-off is ambiguous. If the share of manufacturing goods is low enough, the increase in the growth rate of the manufacturing sector does not have a large welfare impact. In this case, the South loses due to agglomeration, and its welfare never reaches the level it had before the take-off. In the intermediate α case, the South first loses but eventually attains a welfare level that exceeds its pre-take-off level. Finally, when the expenditure share of manufacturing is sufficiently high, the positive-growth effect dominates and the take-off benefits both the South and the North. Similar results are obtained when we vary other parameters: the welfare impact is more favorable to the South the higher the growth effect of agglomeration—that is, the larger the market size (the higher L), the more local the spillovers (the lower λ), the stronger the economies of scale (the lower σ), and the lower the subjective discount rate ρ.

After the take-off, lowering transaction costs always improves welfare in the South because it decreases the price of goods imported from the North. Thus, even though the South may have been worse off by agglomeration in the North, resisting further reductions in transaction costs is not welfare improving.

5.5. Trade

At the symmetric steady state, North and South engage in pure intraindustry trade in differentiated products only. When $1/2 < \theta_K < 1$, the regions have different relative factor stocks, and some Heckscher-Ohlin interindustry trade occurs (North is the net exporter of capital-intensive M-good). The last case is when θ_K equals unity, and only interindustry trade occurs; the North exports M-varieties in exchange for T from the South. While through time the greater bulk of trade flows has become intraindustry trade between northern countries, the prediction of the model seems to fit the essentially interindustry nature of North-South trade.

Because factors are not traded, goods trade balance each period. The global volume of exports is thus twice the North's exports of manufactures. From (6), the steady-state volume of manufactures exports to the South (exclusive of transport costs) is

$$V_T = \frac{1}{\tau}\alpha\theta_K \frac{E^w \phi(1 - \theta_E)}{\phi\theta_K + 1 - \theta_K}. \tag{32}$$

We can now study the expansion of trade during the three phases. The global trade volume is graphed in Figure 7 (using the same parameters as in the previous figure with $\alpha = 0.3$). Again there are three distinct phases. In the initial phase, the level of trade is fairly low, and all trade is intraindustry trade: $(1/\tau)\alpha\phi/(1 + \phi)[L + \rho/(1 + \lambda)]$. Furthermore, lowering trade costs promotes trade in a smooth, gradual fashion. Once $\phi > \phi^{cat}$, agglomeration occurs rapidly in the North, so the nature of trade shifts. The North becomes a net exporter of industrial goods and a net importer of traditional goods. Once

GLOBAL INCOME DIVERGENCE, TRADE, AND INDUSTRIALIZATION   31

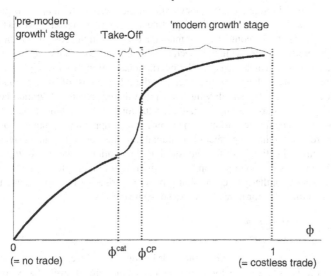

Figure 7. Steady-state world trade.

all industry is in the North, the South must satisfy all its demand for industrial goods via imports, and exports of manufactures from the North (exclusive of trade costs) are $(1/\tau)\alpha L$. It can be shown that indeed trade is larger after the take-off than just before (when $\phi = \phi^{\text{cat}}$).

Furthermore, trade does not need to be large before the take-off to be at the origin of the take-off. As a ratio of income in the North, exports just before the take-off are $(1\tau^{\text{cat}})\alpha\phi^{\text{cat}}/(1 + \phi^{\text{cat}})$. Because $\alpha < 1$, $\phi^{\text{cat}} < 1$ and $\tau^{\text{cat}} > 1$, this ratio can actually be very small. Just after the take-off this ratio becomes $(\alpha/\tau^{\text{cp}})(1 + \rho)$. The reason that trade before the take-off does not need to be quantitatively large to cause the take-off is that at the threshold level of transaction costs, catastrophic agglomeration just requires that the demand and growth linkages outweigh the local-competition effect so as to put into motion the circular mechanism that produces the take-off.

6. Globalization and Industrialization of the South

While the radical income disparity between poor and rich countries is still a dominant feature, the decades since WWII have also seen some spectacular examples of rapid convergence—what Lucas (1993) calls "miracle." Here we show that our model can produce a miracle in the South (with a two-region model, a miracle in the South produces full income convergence). The key is to take a broader view of international integration.

Up to this point, we have viewed integration as nothing more than the lowering of trade costs. As discussed in Section 2, the postwar integration, especially that of the past two or three decades, has lowered the cost of transporting ideas more than it has lowered the cost of transporting goods. In the context of our model, a decrease in the cost of communications and more generally an increase in the speed of international diffusion of ideas is translated into an increase in λ, which measures the internationalization of knowledge spillovers in the I-sector. To focus sharply on this trend in the relative cost of trading goods and of trading ideas, we make the simplifying assumption that all recent integration consists of rising λ. That is, we start from the stage-three situation of full agglomeration in the North and suppose that trade freeness ϕ has risen to some natural upper bound, but in a fourth stage λ rises toward unity—that is, perfect international transmission of learning externalities.

Starting from a situation with full industrial agglomeration in the North ($\bar{\theta}_K = 1$), the increase in λ initially has no impact on southern industry or on the global growth rate given by (29). However, southern I-sector labor productivity rises with λ, so at some threshold level of λ (call this λ^{mir}, for miracle), the steady-state q^*

$$\bar{q}^* = \lambda \frac{(1 + \phi^2)L + \phi^2 \rho}{(2L + \rho)\phi} \tag{33}$$

exceeds unity. Beyond this, also the South finds it profitable to invest in new ideas/varieties. The value of λ that sets $\bar{q}^* = 1$ for a given ϕ defines the critical level of λ beyond which the core-periphery outcome is not longer stable. Using (33) this level is

$$\lambda^{\text{mir}} = \frac{\phi(2L + \rho)}{L(1 + \phi^2) + \rho\phi^2}. \tag{34}$$

Clearly λ^{mir} rises with the freeness of trade.

As in the case of falling trade barriers, there is a second critical value of λ where the symmetric equilibrium becomes stable. This value, denoted as $\lambda^{\text{mir}'}$, is the level of λ where $\partial \bar{q}/\partial \theta_K$ evaluated at $\theta_K = 1/2$—that is, (24)—becomes negative. Expression (24) is quadratic in λ, and the economically relevant solution defines $\lambda^{\text{mir}'}$. The different phases of the miracle are described in Figure 8.

As with the North's take-off, the miracle in the South would appear to be driven by two virtuous circles. When the South invests, its capital stock and therefore permanent income begins to rise, triggering demand-linked circular causality. Rising local expenditures boosts southern profits, and this in turn gives a new incentive to innovate/invest. Moreover, as K^* rises, the southern I-sector begins to benefit from localized learning externalities, and this triggers cost-linked circular causality. The net effect is a drastic structural change as the South industrializes. During the transitional phase North and South real incomes converge.

The miracle in the South, however, differs from the initial Northern take-off in three ways. First, the southern industrialization does not shut down northern innovation. It merely forces a shift of some northern resources from the M-sector to the T-sector (here we think of the T-sector as including services as well as agriculture). Second, the source of the South's take-off is quite different. The miracle occurs due to the South's ability to learn from the North's experience in innovation rather than trade openness per se. As in Goodfriend and McDermott (1998), for this convergence process to occur, openness to

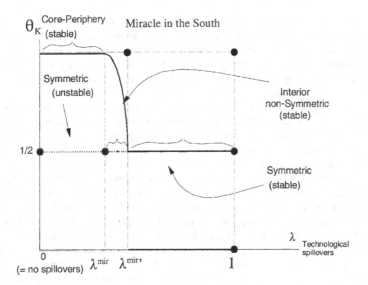

Figure 8. Miracle in the South.

foreign ideas and technologies is key. This is consistent with the Japanese experience at the end of the nineteenth century and the account of Rodrick (1995) on the success of the Asian dragons.

Finally, the convergence of the South pushes the global steady-state growth rate to a level that is between the stage-one (pre-industrial revolution) rate and the stage-three (rich-North-poor-South) rate. In particular, defining stage four as the phase where $\bar\theta_K$ has returned to 1/2, the stage-four rate of innovation is

$$\bar g = \bar g^* = \frac{\alpha(1 + \lambda^{mir'})L - \rho(\sigma - \alpha)}{\sigma}. \tag{35}$$

By inspection this is higher that the stage-one rate since $\lambda^{mir'}$ exceeds the λ in (26). But it is lower than the stage-three rate in (29) since $\lambda^{mir'} < 1$ assuming that some barriers prevent λ from reaching unity.

7. Concluding Remarks

Our model has some interesting and intriguing political-economy implications. The most obvious one would, at first glance, appear to support notions of inequalizing trade. In our model, the big divergence between rich and poor countries is a necessary implication of Europe's industrial revolution, and the expansion of international trade triggered both. Indeed, the creation of a global core-periphery situation is a necessary condition for the growth take-off. Moreover, our article describes a purely economic mechanism (that is, other than cultural or political) that explains why the industrial revolution did not spread to what we now call the developing countries. The traumatic experience of massive deindustrialization in India during the nineteenth century is consistent with our model, and it also suggests one reason that India, along with most other developing countries, kept an attitude of distrust toward international trade.

Our model, however, departs sharply from the inequalizing-trade paradigm on several key points. First, we showed that the present value of the South's welfare could have been increased by the industrial-revolution-*cum*-income-divergence. That is, the South could be even poorer than it is today had the industrial revolution not occurred. Second, our model posits that income divergence was caused by lower trade costs, not only by plunder or imperialism. Third, in our model, trade liberalization and more generally the reduction in transaction costs first generates massive divergence of real incomes but then is conducive to a process of relative convergence. Fourth, we show that to the extent that the recent decades of international integration have lowered the cost of trading ideas more than they have lowered the cost of trading goods, integration can be the key to southern industrialization.

Finally, our model may also be taken as providing a long-term perspective on the convergence literature (see Barro and Sala-i-Martin, 1992, *inter alia*). That literature essentially takes the nineteenth-century global income disparity as given and seeks to measure whether this gap has narrowed in the postwar period. Our model attempts to analyze the long-term origin of the divergence between North and South by linking it explicitly to the growth take-off of the industrial revolution.

Acknowledgments

We thank Raquel Rernandez, Jim Brander, Barbara Spencer, Bob Staiger, Jim Markusen, Jacques Thisse, Jonathon Eaton, Giorga Giovanetti, Ramon Marimon, Steve Parente, and seminar participants at Berkeley, Birbeck Bocconi, Bonn, Georgetown, IMF, Louivain, LSE, Lund, MIT, Northwestern, NYU, Paris, Princeton, Stockholm, Vancouver, and Wisconsin for comments and suggestions. Comments by the editor and the anonymous referees helped us to improve the article. The Swiss National Science Foundation Grant 12-50783.97 provided support for this research. Ottaviano also thanks the TMR of the European Commission for financial support.

Notes

1. In the working paper version of this article (Baldwin, Martin, and Ottaviano, 1998), we show that we can use forward and backward linkages as in Martin and Ottaviano (2000) as the source of localized spillovers. Even though there are no local technological externalities but only localized pecuniary externalities in the I-sector (via traded inputs into capital production), the results, in particular on growth stages, are very similar.
2. This formulation of imperfect interregional spillovers is reminiscent of Goodfriend and McDermott (1998), who connect such an imperfection to a lack of familiarity between technologically leading and following regions.
3. See, however, Martin and Ottaviano (1999, 2000) for analyses of the impact of free capital flows in related situations.

GLOBAL INCOME DIVERGENCE, TRADE, AND INDUSTRIALIZATION 35

4. This assumption is made here for two reasons. First, in Section 6 we discuss North-South reconvergence after the divergence induced by the take-off. In Krugman and Venables (1995) reconvergence of industrial structure takes place due to factor price differences that arise when, for very low trade costs, the traditional good ends up being produced by one country only (here, it would be by the South). Since we want to focus on international spillovers as a source of convergence, we want to rule out the factor-price-difference scenario. Second, this also allows us to keep the model as simple as possible by avoiding an additional differential equation driving relative factor prices.

5. Production does not literally shift since factors are internationally immobile. Nevertheless, θ_K rises since capital accumulation is encouraged in the North and discouraged in the South.

6. Specifically, the home-market effect is, by definition, the impact of $d\theta_E$ on π and π^*. By inspection of (7), π is increasing and π^* is decreasing in θ_E, as long as trade is less than perfectly free—that is, $\phi < 1$.

7. Specifically, the local competition effect is, by definition, the impact of $d\theta_K$ on π and π^*. By inspection of (7), π is decreasing and π^* is increasing in in θ_K, as long as trade is less than perfectly free—that is, $\phi < 1$.

8. In particular, we need that $\lambda\rho < (1 + \lambda)L$.

References

Acemoglu, D., and F. Zilibotti. (1997). "Was Prometheus Unbound by Chance? Risk, Diversification and Growth." *Journal of Political Economy* 105, 709–751.

Aghion, P., and P. Howitt. (1992). "A Model of Growth Through Creative Destruction." *Econometrica* 60, 323–351.

Ashton, T. S. (1971). *The Industrial Revolution.* Oxford University Press.

Azariadis, C., and A. Drazen (1990). "Threshold Externalities in Economic Development." *Quarterly Journal of Economics* 105, 501–526.

Bairoch, P. (1982). "International Industrialization Levels from 1750 to 1980." *Journal of European Economic History* 2, 268–333.

Bairoch, P. (1989). "European Trade Policy, 1815–1914." In P. Mathias and S. Pollard (eds.), *The Cambridge Economic History of Europe* (vol. 8). Cambridge: Cambridge University Press.

Bairoch, P. (1993). *Economics and World History: Myths and Paradoxes.* Chicago: University of Chicago Press.

Baldwin, R. (1999). "Agglomeration and Endogenous Capital." *European Economic Review* 43, 253—280.

Baldwin, R., P. Martin, and G. Ottaviano. (1998). "Global Income Divergence, Trade and Industrialization: The Geography of Growth Take-Off." NBER Working Paper No. 6458.

Baldwin, R., and R. Forslid. (2000a). "The Core-Periphery Model and Endogenous Growth." *Economica* 67, 307–324.

Baldwin, R., and R. Forslid. (2000b). "Trade Liberalization and Endogenous Growth: A q-Theory Approach." *Journal of International Economics* 50, 497–517.

Barraclough, G. (1978). *The Times Atlas of World History.* London: Times Books.

Barro, R, and X. Sala-i-Martin. (1992)."Convergence." *Journal of Political Economy* 100, 223–251.

Batou, F. (1990). *Cent ans de Résistance du Sous Dévelopemente,* Geneva: University of Geneva Press.

Baumol, W. (1994). "Multivariate Growth Patterns: Contagion and Common Forces as Possible Sources of Convergence." In W. Baumol, R. Nelson, and E. Wolf (eds.), *Convergence of Productivity, Cross-national Studies and Historical Evidence.* New York: Oxford University Press.

Braudel, F. (1984). *Civilization and Capitalism, Fifteenth–Eighteenth Century, The Perspective of the World* (vol. 3). New York: Harper and Row.

Caballero, R., and A. Jaffe. (1993). "How High Are the Giants' Shoulders? An Empirical Assessment of Knowledge Spillovers and Creative Destruction in a Model of Economic Growth." In O. Blanchard and S. Fischer (eds.), *NBER Macroeconomics Annual.* Cambridge, MA: MIT Press.

Caincross, F. (1997). *The Death of Distance.* London: Orion.

Chaudhuri, K. N. (1966). "India's Foreign Trade and the cessation of the East India Company's Trading Activities, 1828–40." *Economic History Review* 19, 345–363.

Chaudhuri, K. N. (1991). *Asia Before Europe: Economy and Civilization of the Indian Ocean from the Rise of Islam to 1750.* Cambridge: Cambridge University Press.

Ciccone, A. (1997). "Externalities and Interdependent Growth: Theory and Evidence." Mimeo, University of California, Berkeley.

Crafts, N. (1984). "Patterns of Development in Nineteenth Century Europe." *Oxford Economic Paper* XXXVI, 438–458.

Crafts, N. (1989). "British Industrialization in an International Context." *Journal of Interdisciplinary History* 19, 415–428.

Crafts, N. (1995). "Exogenous or Endogenous Growth? The Industrial Revolution Reconsidered." *The Journal of Economic History* 55, n. 4.

Crafts, N., and C. Harley. (1992). "Output Growth and the British Industrial Revolution: A Restatement of the Crafts-Harley View." *Economic History Review* 45, 703–730.

Deane, P. (1979). *The First Industrial Revolution.* Cambridge: Cambridge University Press.

Eaton, J., and S. Kortum. (1996). "Trade in Ideas: productivity and patenting in the OECD." *Journal of International Economics* 40, 251–278.

Engerman, S. (1996). "Trade and the Industrial Revolution, 1700–1850." Brookfield, UK: Edward Elgar.

Faini, R. (1984). "Increasing Returns, Nontraded Inputs and Regional Developments." *Economic Journal* 94, 308–323.

Fujita, M., P. Krugman, and A. Venables. (2000). *The Spatial Economy: Cities, Regions and International Trade.* Cambridge, MA: MIT Press.

Galor, O., and D. Weil. (2000). "Population, Technology and Growth: From the Malthusian Regime to the Demographic Transition." *American Economic Review,* 90, 806–828.

Galor, O., and D. Weil. (1999). "From Malthusian Stagnation to Modern Growth." *American Economic Review* 89, 150–155.

Goodfriend, M., and J. McDermott. (1995). "Early Development." *American Economic Review* 85, 116–133.

Goodfriend, M., and J. McDermott. (1998). "Industrial Development and the Convergence Question." *American Economic Review* 88, 1277–1289.

Grossman, G., and E. Helpman. (1991). *Innovation and Growth in the World Economy.* Cambridge, MA: MIT Press.

Guckenheimer, J., and P. J. Holmes. (1990). *Nonlinear Oscillations, Dynamical Systems and Bifurcations of Vector Fields* (corrected 3rd printing). New York: Springer-Verlag.

Kelly, M. (1997). "The Dynamics of Smithian Growth." *Quarterly Journal of Economics* 112, 939–964.

Krugman, P. (1981). "Trade, Accumulation and Uneven Development." *Journal of Development Economics* 8, 149–161.

Krugman, P. (1991a). "History Versus Expectations." *Quarterly Journal of Economics* 106, 651–667.

Krugman, P. (1991b). "Increasing Returns and Economic Geography." *Journal of Political Economy* 99, 483–499.

Krugman, P, and A. Venables. (1995). "Globalization and the Inequality of Nations." *Quarterly Journal of Economics* 110, 857–880.

Kuznets, S. (1965). *Economic Growth and Structure, Selected Essays.* London: Heinemann.

Kuznets, S. (1966). *Modern Economic Growth, Rate Structure and Spread.* New Haven: Yale University Press.

Landes, D. (1969). *The Unbound Prometheus, Technological Change and Industrial Development in Western Europe from 1750 to the Present.* Cambridge: Cambridge University press.

Lucas, R. (1988). "On the Process of Economic Development." *Journal of Monetary Economics* 22, 3–42.

Lucas, R. (1993). "Making a Miracle." *Econometrica* 61, 251–272.

Maddison, A. (1971). *Class Structure and Economic Growth: India and Pakistan Since the Moguls.* London: Allen and Unwin.

Maddison, A. (1983). "A Comparison of Levels of GDP per capita in Developed and Developing Countries, 1700–1980." *Journal of Economic History* XLIII, n. 1.

Maddison, A. (1991). *Dynamic Forces in Capitalistic Development: A Long-Run Comparative View.* New York: Oxford University Press.

Martin, P., and G. Ottaviano. (1999). "Growing Locations: Industry Location in a Model of Endogenous Growth." *European Economic Review* 43, 281–302.

Martin, P., and G. Ottaviano. (2000). "Growth and Agglomeration." *International Economic Review,* 41, 315–343.

Matsuyama, K. (1991). "Increasing Returns, Industrialization, and Indeterminacy of Equilibrium." *Quarterly Journal of Economics* 106, 617–650.

Mokyr, J. (1990). *The Lever of Riches: Technological Creativity and Economic Progress.* Oxford: Oxford University Press.

GLOBAL INCOME DIVERGENCE, TRADE, AND INDUSTRIALIZATION   37

Mokyr, J. (1993). "Introduction: The New Economic history and the Industrial Revolution." In Joel Mokyr (ed.), *The British Industrial Revolution: An Economic Perspective*. Oxford: Westview Press.

Murphy, K., A. Shleifer, and R. Vishny. (1989a). "Income Distribution, Market Size and Industrialization." *Quarterly Journal of Economics* 104, 537–564.

Murphy, K., A. Shleifer, and R. Vishny. (1989b). "Industrialization and the Big Push." *Journal of Political Economy* 97, 1023–1026.

North, D. (1968). "Sources of Productivity Change in Ocean Shipping, 1600–1850." *Journal of Political Economy* 76, 953–970.

O'Brien, P., and S. Engerman. (1991). "Exports and the Growth of the British Economy from the Glorious Revolution to the Peace of Amiens." In Barbara Solow (ed.), *Slavery and the Rise of the Atlantic System*. Cambridge: Cambridge University Press.

Pritchett, L. (1997). "Divergence, Bit Time." *Journal of Economic Perspectives* 11, 3–18.

Rivera-Batiz, L., and P. Romer. (1991). "Economic Integration and Endogenous Growth." *Quarterly Journal of Economics* 106, 531–555.

Rodrick, D. (1995). "Getting Interventions Right: how South Korea and Taiwan Grew Rich." *Economic Policy* 20, 55–97.

Romer, P. (1990). "Endogenous Technological Change." *Journal of Political Economy* 98, S71–S102.

Rosenberg, N. (1994). *Exploring the Black Box: Technology, Economics and History*. Cambridge: Cambridge University Press.

Rostow, W. W. (1990). *The Stages of Economic Growth: Anti-communist Manifesto* (3rd ed.). Cambridge: Cambridge University Press. Originally published in 1960.

Sullivan, R. (1989). "England's Age of Invention: The Acceleration of Patents and Patentable Invention During the Industrial Revolution." *Explorations in Economic History* 26, 424–452.

Temin, P. (1997). "Two Views of the British Industrial Revolution." *Journal of Economic History* 57, 63–82.

Tobin, J. (1969). "A General Equilibrium Approach to Monetary Theory." *Journal of Money, Credit and Banking* 1, 15–29.

World Bank. (1995). *The World Development Report*. Washington, DC: World Bank.

Young, A. (1991). "Learning by Doing and the Dynamic Effects of International Trade." *Quarterly Journal of Economics* 106, 369–406.

Zilibotti, F. (1995). "A Rostovian Model of Endogenous Growth and underdevelopment Traps." *European Economic Review* 39, 156–163.

Chapter 3

AGGLOMERATION AND TRADE REVISITED*,†

By Gianmarco Ottaviano, Takatoshi Tabuchi,
and Jacques-François Thisse[1]

*Università "L. Bocconi", Italy; University of Tokyo, Japan; CORE, Université
Catholique de Louvain, Belgium, CERAS, Ecole Nationale des Ponts et
Chaussées, France*

The purpose of this article is twofold. First, we present an alternative model
of agglomeration and trade that displays the main features of the recent
economic geography literature while allowing for the derivation of analytical
results by means of simple algebra. Second, we show how this framework can be
used to permit (i) a welfare analysis of the agglomeration process, (ii) a full-
fledged forward-looking analysis of the role of history and expectations in the
emergence of economic clusters, and (iii) a simple analysis of the impact of
urban costs on the spatial distribution of economic activities.

1. INTRODUCTION

The agglomeration of activities in a few locations is probably the most distinctive
feature of the economic space. Despite some valuable early contributions made by
Hirschman, Perroux, or Myrdal, this fact remained unexplained by mainstream
economic theory for a long time. It is only recently that economists have become
able to provide an analytical framework explaining the emergence of economic
agglomerations in an otherwise homogenous space. As argued by Krugman (1995),
this is probably because economists lacked a model embracing both increasing
returns and imperfect competition, the two basic ingredients of the formation of the
economic space, as shown by the pioneering work of Hotelling (1929), Lösch (1940),
and Koopmans (1957).

However, even though several modeling strategies are available to study the
emergence of economic agglomerations (Fujita and Thisse, 1996), their potential has
not been really explored, as recognized by Krugman (1998) himself:

* Manuscript received December 1999; revised February 2000.
[1] We should like to thank four referees for their comments as well as R. Baldwin, G. Duranton,
M. Fujita, P. Jehiel, A. Linbeck, K. Middelfart-Knarvik, T. Mori, D. Peeters, P. Picard, D. Pines,
K. Stahl, D.-Z. Zeng, participants of seminars at University of Colorado, Kyoto University, IUI
in Stockholm, CEPR ERWIT in Rotterdam, SITE in Stanford, ASSET in Bologna, and Kagawa
University. The first author is grateful to the EU TMR programme, the second author to the Japan
Society for the Promotion of Science through the Future Program, and the first and third authors to
FNRS (Belgium) for funding. The revision was made when the first author was Jean Monnet Fellow
at EUI Florence (Italy). E-mail: *thisse@core.ucl.ac.be*.

409

†This article originally appeared in *International Economic Review*, **43** 409–436 ©
2002 John Wiley & Sons.

To date, the new economic geography has depended heavily on the tricks summarized in Fujita et al. (1999) with the slogan "Dixit–Stiglitz, icebergs, evolution, and the computer" (p. 164).

The slogan of the new economic geography is explained by the following methodology (see Fujita et al., 1999): First, the main tool used in the new economic geography is a particular version of the Chamberlinian model of monopolistic competition developed by Dixit and Stiglitz (1977) in which consumers love variety and firms have fixed requirements for limited productive resources (hence, "Dixit–Stiglitz"). Love of variety is captured by a CES utility function that is symmetric in a bundle of differentiated products. Each firm is assumed to be a negligible actor in that it has no impact on overall market conditions. Second, transportation is modeled as a costly activity that uses the transported good itself: In other words, a certain fraction of the good melts on the way (hence, "icebergs"). Taken together, these assumptions yield a demand system in which the own-price elasticities of demands are constant, identical to the elasticities of substitutions, and equal to each other across all differentiated products. This entails equilibrium prices that are independent of the spatial distribution of firms and consumers. Though convenient from an analytical point of view, such a result conflicts with research in spatial pricing theory that shows that demand elasticity varies with distance while prices change with the level of demand and the intensity of competition. Moreover, the iceberg assumption also implies that any increase in the price of the transported good is accompanied by a proportional increase in its trade cost, which is unrealistic. Third, the stability analysis used to select spatial equilibria rests on myopic adjustment processes in which the location of mobile factors is driven by differences in current returns. Despite some analogy with evolutionary game theory (hence, "evolution"), this approach neglects the role of expectations (Krugman, 1991a; Matsuyama, 1991), which may be crucial for locational decisions since they are often made once and for all.[2] Last, notwithstanding their simplifying assumptions, the models of the new economic geography are often beyond the reach of analytical resolution, so that authors have to appeal to numerical investigations (hence, "the computer").[3]

The purpose of this article is to propose a complementary modeling strategy that allows us to go beyond some of the current limits of the new economic geography. In particular, we do that by presenting a model of agglomeration and trade that, while displaying the main features of the core-periphery model by Krugman (1991b), differs under several major respects. First, preferences are not CES in that we adopt an alternative specification of the preference for variety, namely, the *quadratic utility* model, which is also popular in industrial organization (Dixit, 1979; Vives, 1990), in international trade (Krugman and Venables, 1990; Anderson et al., 1995), as well as in demand analysis (Phlips, 1983). Moreover, while firms are still considered as negligible actors, we adopt a broader concept of equilibrium than the one in Dixit

---

[2] See, however, Ottaviano (1999) for the analysis of a special case.

[3] The most that can be obtained within this framework without resorting to numerical solutions has probably been achieved by Puga (1999). See also some chapters of Fujita et al. (1999).

AGGLOMERATION AND TRADE REVISITED 411

and Stiglitz (1977). Second, trade costs are assumed to absorb resources that are different from the transported good itself. Taken together, our specifications allow us to disentangle the economic meanings of the various parameters, thus leading to clear-cut comparative static results that are likely to be easier to test than those based on Dixit and Stiglitz (1977).[4] They also entail elasticities of demand and substitution that vary with prices, while equilibrium prices now depend on all the fundamentals of the market.

Using this framework, we are able to derive analytically the results obtained by Krugman (1991b). Going beyond them, our setting allows us to provide a neat welfare analysis of agglomeration. While natural due to the many market imperfections that are present in new economic geography models, such an analysis is seldom touched due to the limits of the standard approach.[5] What we show is that the market yields agglomeration for values of the trade costs for which it is socially desirable to keep activities dispersed. Hence, while they coincide for high and low values of the trade costs, *the equilibrium and the optimum differ for a domain of intermediate values.* In this case, there is room for regional policy interventions grounded on both efficiency and equity considerations.

In addition, our framework allows us to study forward-looking location decisions and to determine the exact domain in which expectations matter for agglomeration to arise. Specifically, we show that expectations influence the agglomeration process in a totally unsuspected way in that they have an influence on the emergence of a particular agglomeration for intermediate values of the trade cost only. For such values, and only for them, *if* (for whatever reason) *workers expect the lagging region to become the leading one, their expectations will reverse the dynamics of the economy provided that the difference in initial endowments between the two regions is not too large.*

Finally, our model is sufficiently flexible to establish a bridge between the new economic geography and urban economics. We show that it can be easily extended to accommodate urban costs (Fujita, 1989). This trade-off leads to a set of results richer than the core-periphery model. When the manufactured goods' trade costs decrease, *the economy now displays a scheme given by dispersion, agglomeration, and redispersion* (Alonso, 1980).[6] Such a result confirms and extends preliminary explorations undertaken by Helpman (1998), Tabuchi (1998), and Puga (1999). It also agrees with the observations according to which some developed economies

---

[4] As an additional example, in Krugman (1991b) the same parameter turns out to measure not only the elasticities of demand and substitution but also (inversely) the returns to scale that remain unexploited in equilibrium.

[5] The utilitarian approach is difficult to justify in the CES case because farmers and workers have different incomes, hence a different marginal utility for the numéraire. See, however, Krugman and Venables (1995) and Helpman (1998) for some numerical developments about the welfare implications of agglomeration in related models. See also Trionfetti (2001) for a particular example of a more general insight we will develop in the present article, namely, that in some cases market forces may lead to inefficient agglomeration.

[6] Other reasons leading to a similar scheme are discussed in Ottaviano and Puga (1998) and Fujita et al. (1999).

(especially the United Kingdom) would experience redispersion (Geyer and Kontuly, 1996).

The organization of the article reflects what we have said earlier. The model is presented in the next section, while the equilibrium prices and wages are determined in Section 3 for any given distribution of firms and workers. The process of agglomeration is analyzed in Section 4 by using the standard myopic approach in selecting the stable equilibria. In Section 5, we compare the optimum and market outcomes. In Section 6, we introduce forward-looking behavior and show how our model can be used to compare history (in the sense of initial endowments) and expectations in the emergence of an agglomeration. The impact of urban costs associated with the formation of an agglomeration is investigated in Section 7. Section 8 concludes.

2. THE MODEL

The economic space is made of two regions, called H and F. There are two factors, called A and L. Factor A is evenly distributed across regions and is spatially immobile. Factor L is mobile between the two regions, and $\lambda \in [0,1]$ denotes the share of this factor located in region H. For expositional purposes, we refer to sector A as "agriculture" and sector L as "manufacturing." Accordingly, we call "farmers" the immobile factor A and "workers" the mobile factor L. We want to stress the fact, however, that *the role of factor A is to capture the idea that some inputs* (such as land or some services) *are nontradeable while some others have a very low spatial mobility* (such as low-skilled workers). Hence our model, as Krugman's one, should not necessarily be interpreted as an agriculture-oriented model.

There are two goods in the economy. The first good is homogenous. Consumers have a positive initial endowment of this good that is also produced using factor A as the only input under constant returns to scale and perfect competition. This good can be traded freely between regions and is chosen as the numéraire. The other good is a horizontally differentiated product; it is supplied by using L as the only input under increasing returns to scale and imperfect competition.

Each firm in the manufacturing sector has a negligible impact on the market outcome in the sense that it can ignore its influence on, and hence reactions from, other firms. To this end, we assume that there is a continuum N of potential firms, so that all the unknowns are described by density functions. There are no scope economies so that, due to increasing returns to scale, there is a one-to-one relationship between firms and varieties. Since each firm sells a differentiated variety, it faces a downward-sloping demand.

Since there is a continuum of firms, each firm is negligible and the interaction between any two firms is zero. However, aggregate market conditions of some kind (here average price across firms) affect any single firm. This provides a setting in which individual firms are not competitive (in the classic economic sense of having infinite demand elasticity) but, at the same time, they have no strategic interactions with one another.

AGGLOMERATION AND TRADE REVISITED 413

Each variety can be traded at a positive cost of τ units of the numéraire for each unit transported from one region to the other, regardless of the variety, where τ accounts for all the impediments to trade.

Preferences are identical across individuals and described by a *quasi-linear utility with a quadratic subutility* that is supposed to be symmetric in all varieties (see the Appendix for more details):

$$
(1) \qquad U(q_0; q(i), i \in [0,N]) = \alpha \int_0^N q(i)\,di - \frac{\beta - \gamma}{2} \int_0^N [q(i)]^2\,di - \frac{\gamma}{2} \left[\int_0^N q(i)\,di \right]^2 + q_0
$$

where $q(i)$ is the quantity of variety $i \in [0, N]$, and q_0 the quantity of the numéraire. The parameters in (1) are such that $\alpha > 0$ and $\beta > \gamma > 0$. In this expression, α expresses the intensity of preferences for the differentiated product, whereas $\beta > \gamma$ means that consumers are biased toward a dispersed consumption of varieties. Suppose, indeed, that an individual consumes a total mass of Nq of the differentiated product. If consumption is uniform on $[0,x]$ and zero on $(x,N]$, then the density on $[0,x]$ is Nq/x. Equation (1) evaluated for this consumption pattern is

$$
(2) \qquad U = \alpha \int_0^x \frac{Nq}{x}\,di - \frac{\beta - \gamma}{2} \int_0^x \left(\frac{Nq}{x}\right)^2 di - \frac{\gamma}{2} \left[\int_0^x \left(\frac{Nq}{x}\right)di \right]^2 + q_0
$$

$$
= \alpha Nq - \frac{\beta - \gamma}{2x} N^2 q^2 - \frac{\gamma}{2} N^2 q^2 + q_0
$$

which is strictly increasing in x since $\beta > \gamma$. Hence, regardless of the values of q and N, (2) is maximized at $x = N$ where variety consumption is maximal. We may then conclude that *the quadratic utility function exhibits love of variety as long as $\beta > \gamma$.* Finally, for a given value of β, the parameter γ expresses the substitutability between varieties: The higher γ, the closer substitutes the varieties.[7]

We use a quasi-linear utility that abstracts from general equilibrium income effects for analytical convenience. Although this modeling strategy gives our framework a fairly strong partial equilibrium flavor, it does not remove the interaction between product and labor markets, thus allowing us to develop a full-fledged model of agglomeration formation, independently of the relative size of the manufacturing sector.

Any individual is endowed with one unit of labor (of type A or L) and $\bar{q}_0 > 0$ units of the numéraire. His budget constraint can then be written as follows:

$$
\int_0^N p(i)q(i)\,di + q_0 = y + \bar{q}_0
$$

---

[7] When $\beta = \gamma$, substitutability is perfect. Indeed, (1) degenerates into a utility function that is quadratic in total consumption $\int_0^N q(i)\,di$, which is exactly what one would expect with a homogeneous product.

where y is the individual's labor income, $p(i)$ is the price of variety i, and the price of the agricultural good is normalized to one. The initial endowment $\bar{q}_0$ is supposed to be sufficiently large for the equilibrium consumption of the numéraire to be positive for each individual. By this assumption we want to focus on interior solutions only. This has some costs in terms of generality but, as we will see, larger benefits in terms of simpler analysis. It is also consistent with the idea that each individual is interested in consuming both types of goods. Note that this assumption does not imply that the share of the manufacturing sector must be small. It only requires that the equilibrium expenditure share on the differentiated product is smaller than one.

Solving the budget constraint for the numéraire consumption, plugging the corresponding expression into (1), and solving the first-order conditions with respect to $q(i)$ yields

$$\alpha - (\beta - \gamma)q(i) - \gamma \int_0^N q(j)\,dj = p(i) \qquad i \in [0, N]$$

Therefore, the demand for variety $i \in [0, N]$ is

(3) $$q(i) = a - bp(i) + c \int_0^N [p(j) - p(i)]\,dj$$

where $a \equiv \alpha/[(\beta + (N-1)\gamma]$, $b \equiv 1/[\beta + (N-1)\gamma]$, and $c \equiv \gamma/(\beta - \gamma)[\beta + (N-1)\gamma]$.[8] Increasing the degree of product differentiation among a given set of varieties amounts to decreasing c. However, assuming that all prices are identical and equal to p, we see that the aggregate demand for the differentiated product equals $aN - bpN$, which is independent of c. Hence, (3) has the desirable property that the market size in the industry does not change when the substitutability parameter c varies. More generally, it is possible to decrease (increase) c through a decrease (increase) in the parameter γ in the utility U while keeping the other structural parameters a and b of the demand system unchanged. The own-price effect is stronger (as measured by $b + cN$) than each cross-price effect (as measured by c) as well as the sum of all cross-price effects (cN), thus allowing for different elasticities of substitution between pairs of varieties as well as for different own elasticities at different prices.

The indirect utility corresponding to the demand system (3) is as follows:

(4) $$V(y; p(i), i \in [0, N]) = \frac{a^2 N}{2b} - a \int_0^N p(i)\,di + \frac{b + cN}{2} \int_0^N [p(i)]^2\,di$$

$$- \frac{c}{2} \left[\int_0^N p(i)\,di \right]^2 + y + \bar{q}_0$$

---

[8] Notice that when $\gamma = \beta$, the indirect demand cannot be inverted in terms of each variety's quantity $q(i)$ but only in terms of total quantity $\int_0^N q(i)\,di$. Once more, this is what one would expect with homogeneous products and explains why parameter c degenerates to infinity as γ tends to β.

AGGLOMERATION AND TRADE REVISITED   415

Turning to the supply side, technology in agriculture requires one unit of A in order to produce one unit of output. With free trade in agriculture, the choice of this good as the numéraire implies that in equilibrium the wage of the farmers is equal to one in both regions, that is, $w_H^A = w_F^A = 1$. Technology in manufacturing requires ϕ units of L in order to produce any amount of a variety; that is, the marginal cost of production of a variety is set equal to zero. This simplifying assumption, which is standard in many models of industrial organization, entails no loss of generality when firms' marginal costs are incurred in the numéraire. Clearly, ϕ is a measure of the degree of increasing returns in the manufacturing sector.

Let n_H and n_F be the mass of firms in regions H and F, respectively. Labor market clearing implies that

(5) $$n_H = \lambda L / \phi$$

and

(6) $$n_F = (1 - \lambda)L / \phi$$

Consequently, the total mass of firms (varieties) in the economy is fixed and equal to $N = L/\phi$. This means that, in equilibrium, ϕ can also be interpreted as an inverse measure of the mass of firms. As $\phi \to 0$ (or $L \to \infty$), the mass of varieties becomes arbitrarily large. In addition, (5) and (6) show that the region with the larger labor market is also the region accommodating the larger proportion of firms. In addition, (5) and (6) imply that any change in the population of workers located in one region must be accompanied by a corresponding change in the mass of firms.

As to equilibrium wages, they are determined as follows: Due to free entry and exit, profits are zero in equilibrium. As in Krugman (1991b), the equilibrium wages corresponding to (5) and (6) are determined by a bidding process between firms for workers, which ends when no firm can earn a strictly positive profit at the equilibrium market prices. In other words, all operating profits are absorbed by the wage bills.

Since trade costs are positive, firms have the ability to segment markets; that is, each firm is able to set a price specific to the market in which its product is sold. Indeed, even for very low trade costs, empirical work shows that firms succeed in price discriminating among spatially separated markets (McCallum, 1995; Wei, 1996; Head and Mayer, 2000).

In the sequel, we focus on region H. Things pertaining to region F can be derived by symmetry. Using the assumption of symmetry between varieties and (3), demands faced by a representative firm located in H in region H (q_{HH}) and region F (q_{HF}) are given respectively by

(7) $$q_{HH} = a - (b + cN)p_{HH} + cP_H$$

and

(8) $$q_{HF} = a - (b + cN)p_{HF} + cP_F$$

where

$$P_H \equiv n_H p_{HH} + n_F p_{FH}$$

$$P_F \equiv n_H p_{HF} + n_F p_{FF}$$

Clearly, P_H/N and P_F/N are the average prices prevailing in regions H and F, so that P_H and P_F can be interpreted as the corresponding price indices since N is fixed. Finally, the profits made by a firm in H are defined as follows:

(9) $\Pi_H = p_{HH} q_{HH}(p_{HH})(A/2 + \lambda L) + (p_{HF} - \tau)q_{HF}(p_{HF})[A/2 + (1 - \lambda)L] - \phi w_H$

where $A/2$ stands for the number of farmers in each region, and w_H for the wage prevailing in region H.

3.   SHORT-RUN PRICE EQUILIBRIA

In this section, we study the process of competition between firms for a given spatial distribution of workers. Prices are obtained by maximizing profits, while wages are determined as described above by equating the resulting profits to zero. Since we have a continuum of firms, each one is negligible in the sense that its action has no impact on the market. Hence, when choosing its prices, a firm in H accurately neglects the impact of its decision over the two price indices P_H and P_F. In addition, because firms sell differentiated varieties, each one has some monopoly power in that it faces a demand function with finite elasticity.

When Dixit and Stiglitz use the CES, the same assumption implies that each firm is able to determine its price independently of the others because the price index enters the demand function as a multiplicative term. This no longer holds in our model because the price index now enters the demand function as an additive term (see (7) and (8)). Stated differently, a firm must account for the distribution of the firms' prices through some aggregate statistics, given here by the price index, in order to find its equilibrium price. As a consequence, our market solution is given by a Nash equilibrium with a continuum of players in which prices are interdependent: *Each firm neglects its impact on the market but is aware that the market as a whole has a nonnegligible impact on its behavior.* As a result, the equilibrium prices will depend on key aspects of the market instead of being given by a simple relative markup rule.

Since profit functions are concave in own price, solving the first-order conditions for profit maximization with respect to prices yields the equilibrium prices (denoted by *). In order to illustrate the type of interaction that characterizes our model of monopolistic competition, we describe how the equilibrium prices are determined. First, each firm i in region H maximizes its profit Π_H, assuming accurately that its price choice has no impact on the regional price indices P_H and P_F. By symmetry, the prices selected by the firms located within the same region are identical; hence, they are, respectively, given by two linear expressions $p^*_{HH}(P_H)$ and $p^*_{HF}(P_F)$. Second, these prices must be consistent; that is, they must satisfy the following relations:

$$n_H p^*_{HH}(P_H) + n_F p^*_{FH}(P_H) = P_H$$
$$n_H p^*_{HF}(P_F) + n_F p^*_{FF}(P_F) = P_F$$

Given (5) and (6), it is then readily verified that

(10) $p^*_{HH} = \dfrac{1}{2} \dfrac{2a + \tau c(1 - \lambda)N}{2b + cN}$

AGGLOMERATION AND TRADE REVISITED 417

$$(11) \qquad p^*_{FF} = \frac{1}{2}\frac{2a + \tau c \lambda N}{2b + cN}$$

$$(12) \qquad p^*_{HF} = p^*_{FF} + \frac{\tau}{2}$$

$$(13) \qquad p^*_{FH} = p^*_{HH} + \frac{\tau}{2}$$

Consequently, *the equilibrium prices under monopolistic competition depend on the demand and firm distributions between regions.* In particular, the prices charged by both local and foreign firms fall when the mass of local firms increases (because price competition is fiercer), but the impact is weaker when τ is smaller. In the limit, when τ is negligible, the relocation of firms in say, H, has almost no impact on market prices. In this case, prices are "independent" of the way firms are distributed between the two regions.

Equilibrium prices also rise when the relative desirability of the differentiated product with respect to the numéraire, evaluated by a, gets larger or when the degree of product differentiation, inversely measured by c, increases provided that trade occurs (see (14)). All these results are in accordance with what is known in industrial organization and spatial pricing theory.

Furthermore, *there is freight absorption since only a fraction of the trade cost is passed on to the consumers.* Indeed, we have

$$p^*_{HF} - p^*_{HH} = \tau\frac{b + c\lambda N}{2b + cN} < \tau \qquad \text{which is equal to } \frac{\tau}{2} \text{ when } \lambda = 1/2$$

$$p^*_{FH} - p^*_{FF} = \tau\frac{b + c(1 - \lambda)N}{2b + cN} < \tau \qquad \text{which is equal to } \frac{\tau}{2} \text{ when } \lambda = 1/2$$

It is well known that a monopolist facing a linear demand absorbs exactly one-half of the trade cost. By contrast, we see that monopolistic competition leads to less (more) freight absorption than monopoly when the foreign market is the small (large) one: In an attempt to penetrate the distant market, competition leads firms to a price gap that varies with the relative size of the home and foreign markets.

By inspection, it is readily verified that p^*_{HH} (p^*_{FF}) is increasing in τ because the local firms in H (F) are more protected against foreign competition, while $p^*_{HF} - \tau$ $(p^*_{FH} - \tau)$ is decreasing because it is now more difficult for these firms to sell on the foreign market. Observe also that arbitrage is never profitable since price differentials are always lower than trade costs. Finally, our demand side happens to be consistent with identical demand functions at different locations but different price levels, as in standard spatial pricing theory.

Deducting the unit trade cost τ from the prices set on the distant markets, that is, (12) and (13), we see that firms' prices net of trade costs are positive regardless of the workers' distribution if and only if

$$(14) \qquad \tau < \tau_{\text{trade}} \equiv \frac{2a\phi}{2b\phi + cL}$$

which depends only upon the primitives $(A, L, \alpha, \beta, \gamma, \phi)$ once a, b, c, and N are replaced by their values. The same condition must hold for consumers in F (H) to buy from firms in H (F), that is, for the demand (8) evaluated at the prices (10) and (11) to be positive for all λ. From now on, condition (14) is assumed to hold. Consequently, there is intra-industry trade and reciprocal dumping, as in Anderson et al. (1995). However, *there must be increasing returns for trade to occur.* Indeed, when $\phi = 0$, all potential varieties are produced in each region that becomes autarkic. More generally, it is readily verified that

$$\frac{d\tau_{\text{trade}}}{d\phi} > 0 \qquad \frac{d\tau_{\text{trade}}}{d\gamma} < 0$$

so that trade is more likely the higher are the intensity of increasing returns and the degree of product differentiation.

It is easy to check that the equilibrium gross profits earned by a firm established in H on each separated market are as follows:

(15) $$\Pi^*_{HH} = (b + cN)(p^*_{HH})^2 (A/2 + \lambda L)$$

where Π^*_{HH} denotes the profits earned in H, while the profits made from selling in F are

(16) $$\Pi^*_{HF} = (b + cN)(p^*_{HF} - \tau)^2 [A/2 + (1 - \lambda)L]$$

Increasing λ has two opposite effects on Π^*_{HH}. First, due to tougher competition, the equilibrium price (10) falls as well as the quantity of each variety bought by each consumer living in region H. At the same time, the total population of consumers residing in this region increases, so that the profits made by a firm located in H on local sales might rise. What is at work here is *an aggregate local demand effect due to the increase in the local population that may compensate firms for the adverse price effect as well as for the individual demand effect generated by a wider array of local varieties.*

The individual consumer surplus S_H in region H associated with the equilibrium prices (10) and (13) is then as follows (a symmetric expression holds in region F):

$$S_H(\lambda) = \frac{a^2 L}{2b\phi} - \frac{aL}{\phi} \left[\lambda p^*_{HH} + (1 - \lambda)p^*_{FH} \right]$$
$$+ \frac{(b\phi + cL)L}{2\phi^2} \left[\lambda(p^*_{HH})^2 + (1 - \lambda)(p^*_{FH})^2 \right]$$
$$- \frac{cL^2}{2\phi^2} \left[\lambda p^*_{HH} + (1 - \lambda)p^*_{FH} \right]^2$$

Differentiating twice this expression with respect to λ shows that $S_H(\lambda)$ is concave. Furthermore, (14) implies that $S_H(\lambda)$ is always increasing in λ over the interval $[0, 1]$.

The equilibrium wage prevailing in region H may be obtained by evaluating $w^*_H(\lambda)(\Pi^*_{HH} + \Pi^*_{HF})/\phi$, thus yielding the following expression:

AGGLOMERATION AND TRADE REVISITED 419

$$w_H^*(\lambda) = \frac{b\phi + cL}{4(2b\phi + cL)^2\phi^2} \left\{ [2a\phi + \tau cL(1 - \lambda)]^2 \left(\frac{A}{2} + \lambda L \right) \right.$$
$$\left. + [2a\phi - 2\tau b\phi - \tau cL(1 - \lambda)]^2 \left[\frac{A}{2} + (1 - \lambda)L \right] \right\}$$

which, after simplifying, turns out to be quadratic in λ. Standard, but cumbersome, investigations reveal that $w_H^*(\lambda)$ is concave and increasing (convex and decreasing) in λ when ϕ is large (small) as well as when τ, c, A, and L are small (large). This implies that both $S_H(\lambda)$ and $w_H^*(\lambda)$ increase with λ when τ is small, while they go in opposite directions when τ is large.

4. WHEN DO WE OBSERVE AGGLOMERATION?

The distribution $\lambda \in [0, 1]$ is a *spatial equilibrium* when no worker may get a higher utility level by changing location. Given that the indirect utility in region H is as follows:

$$V_H(\lambda) = S_H(\lambda) + w_H^*(\lambda) + \bar{q}_0$$

a spatial equilibrium arises at $\lambda \in (0, 1)$ when

$$\Delta V(\lambda) \equiv V_H(\lambda) - V_F(\lambda) = 0$$

or at $\lambda = 0$ when $\Delta V(0) \leq 0$, or at $\lambda = 1$ when $\Delta V(1) \geq 0$.

In order to study the stability of a spatial equilibrium, we assume that local labor markets adjust instantaneously when some workers move from one region to the other. More precisely, the number of firms in each region must be such that the labor market clearing conditions (5) and (6) remain valid for the new distribution of workers. Wages are then adjusted in each region for each firm to earn zero profits everywhere. For now, we assume a myopic adjustment process; that is, the driving force in the migration process is workers' current utility differential between H and F:

$$(17) \qquad \dot{\lambda} \equiv d\lambda/dt = \begin{cases} \Delta V(\lambda) & \text{if } 0 < \lambda < 1 \\ \min\{0, \Delta V(\lambda)\} & \text{if } \lambda = 1 \\ \max\{0, \Delta V(\lambda)\} & \text{if } \lambda = 0 \end{cases}$$

when t is time. Clearly, a spatial equilibrium implies $\dot{\lambda} = 0$. If $\Delta V(\lambda)$ is positive, some workers will move from F to H; if it is negative, some will go in the opposite direction. In the sequel, we assume that individual consumption of the numéraire is positive during the adjustment process. This assumption is made to capture the idea that individuals need both types of goods.[9]

A spatial equilibrium is *stable* for (17) if, for any marginal deviation from the equilibrium, this equation of motion brings the distribution of workers back to the original one. Therefore, the agglomerated configuration is always stable when it is an equilibrium, while the dispersed configuration is stable if and only if the slope of $\Delta V(\lambda)$ is nonpositive in a neighborhood of this point.

---

[9] An analytically convenient way to achieve that is to assume that each consumer receives the same endowment $\bar{q}_0$ at each point in time.

The forces at work are similar to those found in the core-periphery model. First, the immobility of the farmers is a centrifugal force, at least as long as there is trade between the two regions. The centripetal force finds its origin in a demand effect generated by the preference for variety. If a larger number of firms are located in region H, there are two effects at work. First, less varieties are imported. Second, (10) and (13) imply that the equilibrium prices of all varieties sold in H are lower. (Observe that the latter effect does not appear in Krugman's model.) This, in turn, induces some consumers to migrate toward this region. The resulting increase in the number of consumers creates a larger demand for the industrial good in the corresponding region, which therefore increases operating profits (hence, wages) and leads to more firms to move there. In other words, both backward and forward linkages are present in our model.

It is readily verified that the indirect utility differential can be written as follows:

(18) $$\Delta V(\lambda) \equiv V_H(\lambda) - V_F(\lambda) \equiv S_H(\lambda) - S_F(\lambda) + w_H^*(\lambda) - w_F^*(\lambda)$$
$$= C\tau(\tau^* - \tau)(\lambda - 1/2)$$

where

$$C \equiv [2b\phi(3b\phi + 3cL + cA) + c^2L(A + L)]\frac{L(b\phi + cL)}{2\phi^2(2b\phi + cL)^2} > 0$$

and

$$\tau^* \equiv \frac{4a\phi(3b\phi + 2cL)}{2b\phi(3b\phi + 3cL + cA) + c^2L(A + L)} > 0$$

which can also be restated in terms of the primitives of the economy.

It follows immediately from (18) that $\lambda = 1/2$ is always an equilibrium. Since $C > 0$, for $\lambda \neq 1/2$ the indirect utility differential has always the same sign as $\lambda - 1/2$ if and only if $\tau < \tau^*$; otherwise it has the opposite sign. In particular, *when there are no increasing returns in the manufacturing sector* ($\phi = 0$), the coefficient of ($\lambda - 1/2$) is always negative since $\tau^* = 0$, so that *dispersion is the only* (*stable*) *equilibrium*. This shows once more the importance of increasing returns for the possible emergence of an agglomeration.

It remains to determine when τ^* is lower than τ_{trade}. This is so if and only if

(19) $$A/L > \frac{6b^2\phi^2 + 8bc\phi L + 3c^2L^2}{cL(2b\phi + cL)} > 3$$

where the second inequality holds because $b/c = \beta/\gamma - 1 \in (0, +\infty)$. This inequality means that the population of farmers is large relative to the population of workers. When (19) does not hold, the coefficient of ($\lambda - 1/2$) in (18) is always positive for all $\tau < \tau_{\text{trade}}$.

When $\tau < \tau^*$, the symmetric equilibrium is unstable and workers agglomerate in region $H(F)$ provided that the initial fraction of workers residing in this region exceeds $1/2$. In other words, *agglomeration arises when the trade cost is low enough*, as in Krugman (1991b) and for similar reasons. In contrast, for large trade costs, that

AGGLOMERATION AND TRADE REVISITED   421

is, when $\tau > \tau^*$, it is straightforward to see that the symmetric configuration is the only stable equilibrium. Hence, the threshold τ^* corresponds to both the critical value of τ at which symmetry ceases to be stable (the "break point") and the value below which agglomeration is stable (the "sustain point"); this follows from the fact that (18) is linear in λ.

PROPOSITION 1. *Assume that $\tau < \tau_{\text{trade}}$. Two cases may arise:*

(i) *When* (19) *holds, we have the following: If $\tau > \tau^*$, then the symmetric configuration is the only stable spatial equilibrium with trade; if $\tau < \tau^*$, there are two stable spatial equilibria corresponding to the agglomerated configurations with trade; if $\tau = \tau^*$, then any configuration is a spatial equilibrium.*

(ii) *When* (19) *does not hold, any stable spatial equilibrium involves agglomeration.*

The reverse of (19) plays a role similar to the "black hole" condition in Krugman and Venables (1995) and Fujita et al. (1999): Regardless of the value of the trade costs, the region with the larger initial share of the manufacturing sector always attracts the whole sector. As in their case, more product differentiation (lower c) and stronger increasing returns (higher ϕ) make the black hole condition more likely. Although the size of the industrial sector is captured here through the relative population size A/L and not through its share in consumption, the intuition is similar: The ratio A/L must be sufficiently large for the economy to display different types of equilibria according to the value of τ. Our result does not depend on the expenditure share on the manufacturing sector because of the absence of general equilibrium income effects: Either small or large sectors in terms of expenditure share may be agglomerated when τ is small enough. This does not strike us as being implausible.

Furthermore, when $\tau_{\text{trade}} > \tau^*$, trade occurs regardless of the type of equilibrium that is stable. However, the nature of trade varies with the type of configuration emerging in equilibrium. In the dispersed configuration, there is only intra-industry trade in the differentiated product; in the agglomerated equilibrium, the region accommodating the manufacturing sector only imports the homogenous good from the other region.

When increasing returns are stronger, as expressed by higher values of ϕ, τ^* rises since $d\tau^*/d\phi > 0$. This means that *the agglomeration of the manufacturing sector is more likely, the stronger are the increasing returns at the firm's level.* In addition, τ^* increases with product differentiation since $d\tau^*/d\gamma < 0$. In other words, *more product differentiation fosters agglomeration.* In particular, γ very small implies that $\tau_{\text{trade}} < \tau^*$, so that agglomeration always arises under trade.

The best way to convey the economic intuition behind Proposition 1 is probably to make use of a graphical analysis.[10] Figure 1 depicts the aggregate inverse demand in region H for a typical local firm after choosing, for simplicity, the units of L so that $b + cN = 1$:

---

[10] For illustrative purposes, we neglect the impact of relocation on the firm's profit in F since this one is typically smaller than the impact on its profit in H.

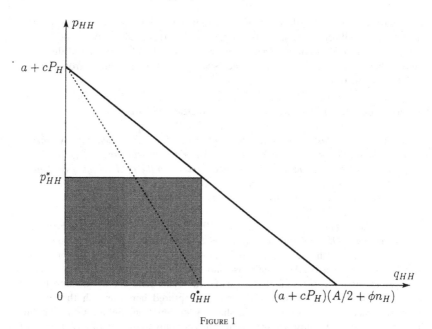

FIGURE 1

DETERMINATION OF THE EQUILIBRIUM OUTCOME

(20) $$p_{HH} = a + cP_H(n_H, \tau) - \frac{q_{HH}}{A/2 + \phi n_H}$$

Since $p_{FH} > p_{HH}$ and the total number of firms is fixed by labor market clearing, the price index P_H is a decreasing function of n_H at a rate that increases with τ:

(21) $$\frac{\partial P_H(n_H, \tau)}{\partial n_H} < 0 \quad \text{and} \quad \left| \frac{\partial^2 P_H(n_H, \tau)}{\partial n_H \partial \tau} \right| > 0$$

The horizontal and vertical intercepts of (20) are, respectively, $[a + cP_H(n_H, \tau)]$ $(A/2 + \phi n_H)$ and $[a + cP_H(n_H, \tau)]$. The equilibrium values of q_{HH} and p_{HH} are shown as q_{HH}^* and p_{HH}^*. They are found by setting marginal revenue equal to marginal cost. The operating profits are shown by the shaded rectangle and accrue to the workers while, as usual, the triangle in Figure 1 represents the consumer surplus enjoyed by both types of workers.

Although it depicts a partial equilibrium argument, Figure 1 is a powerful learning device to understand the forces at work in our model. To see why, start from an initial situation where regions are identical ($n_H = n_F$). Suppose that some firms move from the foreign to the home region, so that n_H rises and n_F falls. For these firms to want to stay in the home region, operating profits, thus wages, have to increase. Indeed, were this not the case, the firms would rather go back to the foreign region.

As revealed by Figure 1, an increase in n_H has two opposite effects on operating profits, hence on wages. First, as new firms enter the home region, the price index

$P_H(n_H, \tau)$ decreases. Ceteris paribus, this would shift the inverse demand (20) toward the origin of the axes, and operating profits, hence wages, would shrink. This effect is due to increased competition in the home market and stems from the fact that fewer firms now face trade costs when supplying the home market. But this negative competition effect is not the only effect. For some firms to move to the home region, some workers have to follow, since $n_H = \lambda L/\phi$. This means that, as n_H increases, λ also goes up, so that the market of the home region expands. Ceteris paribus, the horizontal intercept of the inverse demand would move away from the origin, and operating profits, thus wages, would expand. This is a positive demand effect that is induced by the linkage between the locations of firms and workers' expenditures.

Since the two effects oppose each other, the net result is a priori ambiguous. But we can say more than that. In particular, we can assess which effect prevails depending on parameter values. Start with the competition effect that goes through $[a + cP_H(n_H, \tau)]$. This effect is strong if c is large, that is, if varieties are good substitutes. It is also strong if $|\partial P_H(n_H, \tau)/\partial n_H|$ is large. As shown in (21), this happens if τ is large, because, when obstacles to trade are high, competition from the other region is weak and home firms care a lot about their competitors' being close rather than distant. As to the demand effect, it will be strong if ϕ is large because each new firm brings along many workers, and if A is small because immigrants have a large impact on the local market size.

We can therefore conclude that the demand effect dominates the competition effect when goods are bad substitutes (c small), increasing returns are intense (ϕ large), the farmers are unimportant (A small), and trade costs are low (τ small). Under such circumstances, the entry of new firms in one region would raise the operating profits of all firms, hence wages. *Higher operating profits and wages would attract more firms and workers, thus generating circular causation among locational decisions.* Agglomeration would then be sustainable as a spatial equilibrium.

This argument establishes a sufficient condition for agglomeration. Since the impact of firms' relocation on consumer surplus is always positive, agglomeration could still arise even when operating profits, hence wages, decrease with the size of the local market, because the demand effect is dominated by the competition effect. Furthermore, the same argument is likely to hold for most downward-sloping demand functions.

5. OPTIMALITY VERSUS EQUILIBRIUM

We now wish to determine whether or not such an agglomeration is socially optimal. To this end, we assume that the planner is able (i) to assign any number of workers (or, equivalently, of firms) to a specific region and (ii) to use lump-sum transfers from all workers to pay for the loss may incur while pricing at marginal cost. Observe that no distortion arises in the total number of varieties since N is determined by the factor endowment (L) and technology (ϕ) in the manufacturing sector and is, therefore, the same at both the equilibrium and optimum outcomes. Because our setting assumes transferable utility, the planner chooses λ in order to maximize the sum of individual indirect utilities:

(22) $$W(\lambda) \equiv \frac{A}{2}[S_H(\lambda) + 1] + \lambda L[S_H(\lambda) + w_H(\lambda)] + \frac{A}{2}[S_F(\lambda) + 1]$$
$$+ (1 - \lambda)L[S_F(\lambda) + w_F(\lambda)]$$

in which all prices have been set equal to marginal cost:

$$p_{HH}^o = p_{FF}^o = 0 \qquad \text{and} \qquad p_{HF}^o = p_{FH}^o = \tau$$

thus implying by (15) and (16) that operating profits are zero, and hence $w_H^o(\lambda) = w_F^o(\lambda) = 0$ for every λ, so that firms do not incur any loss. Hence, (22) becomes

(23) $$W(\lambda) = C^o\tau(\tau^o - \tau)\lambda(\lambda - 1)L + \text{constant}$$

where

$$C^o \equiv \frac{L}{2\phi^2}[2b\phi + c(A + L)]$$

and

$$\tau^o \equiv \frac{4a\phi}{2b\phi + c(A + L)}$$

The function (23) is strictly concave in λ if $\tau > \tau^o$, and strictly convex if $\tau < \tau^o$. Furthermore, since the coefficients of λ^2 and of λ are the same (up to their sign), this expression has always an interior extremum at $\lambda = 1/2$. As a result, the optimal choice of the planner is determined by the sign of the coefficient of λ^2, that is, by the value of τ with respect to τ^o.

Hence, we have the following proposition:

PROPOSITION 2. *If $\tau > \tau^o$, then the symmetric configuration is the optimum; if $\tau < \tau^o$, any agglomerated configuration is the optimum; if $\tau = \tau^o$, any configuration is an optimum.*

In accordance with intuition, it is socially desirable to agglomerate the manufacturing sector into a single region once trade costs are low, increasing returns in the manufacturing sector are strong enough ($d\tau^o/d\phi > 0$), and/or the output of this sector is sufficiently differentiated ($d\tau^o/d\gamma < 0$). In particular, the optimum is always dispersed when increasing returns vanish ($\phi = 0$).

A simple calculation shows that $\tau^o < \tau^*$. This means that *the market yields an agglomerated configuration for a whole range ($\tau^o < \tau < \tau^*$) of trade cost values for which it is socially desirable to have a dispersed pattern of activities.* Accordingly, when trade costs are low ($\tau < \tau^o$) or high ($\tau > \tau^*$), no regional policy is required from the efficiency point of view, although equity considerations might justify such a policy when agglomeration arises. On the contrary, for intermediate values of trade costs ($\tau^o < \tau < \tau^*$), the market provides excessive agglomeration, thus justifying the need for an active regional policy in order to foster the dispersion of the modern sector on both the efficiency and equity grounds.

This discrepancy may be explained as follows: First, workers do not internalize the negative external effects they impose on the farmers who stay put in the workers'

AGGLOMERATION AND TRADE REVISITED 425

region of origin, nor do they account for the impact of their migration decisions on the residents in their region of destination. Hence, even though the workers have individual incentives to move, these incentives do not reflect the social value of their move. This explains why equilibrium and optimum do not necessarily coincide. Second, the individual demand elasticity is much lower at the optimum (marginal cost pricing) than at the equilibrium (Nash equilibrium pricing), so that regional price indices are less sensitive to a decrease in τ. As a result, the fall in trade costs must be sufficiently large to make the agglomeration of workers socially desirable, which tells us why $\tau^0 < \tau^*$.

We will return to the debate of spatial equilibrium versus optimum in Section 7.

6. THE IMPACT OF WORKERS' EXPECTATIONS ON THE AGGLOMERATION PROCESS

The adjustment process (17) is often used in new economic geography. Yet, the underlying dynamics are myopic because workers care only about their current utility level, thus implying that only history matters. This is a fairly restrictive assumption to the extent that *migration decisions are typically made on the grounds of current and future utility flows*. In addition, this approach has been criticized because it is not consistent with fully rational forward-looking behavior (Matsuyama, 1991). In this section, we want to see how the model presented above can be used to shed more light on the interplay between history and expectations in the formation of the economic space when migrants maximize the intertemporal value of their utility flows. In particular, we are interested in identifying the conditions under which, when initially regions host different numbers of workers, the common belief that workers will eventually agglomerate in the smaller region can reverse the historically inherited advantage of the larger region. Formally, we are interested in determining *the parameter domains for which there exists an equilibrium path consistent with this belief*, assuming that workers have perfect foresight *(self-fulfilling prophecy)*.

For concreteness, let us consider the case in which initially region F is larger than H. The opposite case can be studied in a symmetric way. Therefore, we want to test the consistency of the belief that, starting from $t = 0$, all workers will end up being concentrated in H at some future date $t = T$; that is, there exists $T \geq 0$ such that, given $\lambda_0 < 1/2$,

(24) $\dot{\lambda}(t) \neq 0$ and $\lambda(t) < 1$ for $t \in [0, T)$

$\dot{\lambda}(t) = 0$ and $\lambda(t) = 1$ for $t \geq T$

Let $V_H(t)$ and $V_F(t)$ be the instantaneous utility levels of a worker currently in regions H and F, respectively, at time $t \geq 0$.[11] Furthermore, let V^C be the instantaneous utility level in region H at $\lambda = 1$. Then, under (24),

---

[11] To ease notation, when variables depend on time t through $\lambda(t)$, we only report their dependence on time as long as this does not lead to any ambiguity. Moreover, throughout this section, we keep on assuming that the consumption of the numéraire is always positive in both regions at any time. Formally, this implies that we assume away any form of intertemporal trade.

$$V_H(t) = V^C \qquad \text{for all } t \geq T$$

Since workers have perfect foresight, the easiest way to generate a non-bang-bang migration behavior is to assume that, when moving from one region to the other, workers incur a utility loss that depends on the rate of migration (Mussa, 1978). In other words, a migrant imposes a negative externality on the others by congesting the migration process. Specifically, we follow Krugman (1991a) and assume that the utility loss for a migrant at time t is equal to $|\dot{\lambda}(t)|/\delta$, where $\delta > 0$ is the speed of adjustment. Thus, under (24), the intertemporal utility of a worker who moves from F to H at time $t \in [0, T)$ is given by

$$(25) \qquad u(t) = \int_0^t e^{-\rho s} V_F(s)\,ds + \int_t^T e^{-\rho s} V_H(s)\,ds + e^{-\rho T} V^C / \rho - e^{-\rho t} \dot{\lambda}(t)/\delta$$

where $\rho > 0$ is the rate of time preference.

We are now ready to characterize the equilibrium migration process. At the initial time 0, each worker residing in F decides at which date $t \geq 0$ to migrate from F to H. In so doing, she believes that at date T all workers will end up being in H. As argued by Fukao and Bénabou (1993) and Ottaviano (1999), for this belief to be consistent with the equilibrium outcome, a worker must be indifferent between moving at any date $t \geq 0$ or at the final expected date T. In the former case, she expects to receive (25). In the latter, she forecasts

$$(26) \qquad u(T) = \int_0^T e^{-\rho s} V_F(s)\,ds + e^{-\rho T} V^C / \rho$$

that is, the limit of (25) as t approaches T where the moving cost disappears since migration stops. Notice that, since the assumed belief has all workers in H from T onwards, in both cases the worker expects a utility flow $V_H(t)$ for all $t \geq T$.

Subtracting (26) from (25), for each $t \geq 0$, we get

$$(27) \qquad u(t) - u(T) = \int_t^T e^{-\rho s}[V_H(s) - V_F(s)]\,ds - e^{-\rho t}\dot{\lambda}(t)/\delta$$

$$= e^{-\rho t}[v_H(t) - v_F(t)] - e^{-\rho t}\dot{\lambda}(t)/\delta$$

$$= e^{-\rho t}\Delta v(t) - e^{-\rho t}\dot{\lambda}(t)/\delta$$

where

$$v_r(t) \equiv \int_t^T e^{-\rho(s-t)} V_r(s)\,ds + e^{-\rho(T-t)} V^C / \rho \quad r = H, F$$

is what residence in r buys to a worker who stays in $H (r = H)$ or to a worker in F who plans to move to H at $T (r = F)$ from t onwards, while $\Delta v(t) \equiv v_H(t) - v_F(t)$ and $\Delta v(T) = 0$.

Since in equilibrium a worker moving at t must be indifferent between migrating at that date or at any other date, until the final expected date T, along an equilibrium path it must be that $u(t) = u(T)$ for all $t \in [0, T)$, which, using (27), implies

(28) $$\dot{\lambda}(t) = \delta \Delta v(t) \quad \text{for all } t \in [0, T)$$

with $\lambda(T) = 1$.

Furthermore, differentiating $\Delta v(t)$ with respect to time yields

(29) $$\dot{\Delta v}(t) = \rho \Delta v(t) - \Delta V(t)$$

where $\Delta V(t) \equiv V_H(t) - V_F(t)$ stands for the expected instantaneous indirect utility differential flow given by (18). Hence, we obtain a system of two linear differential equations, instead of the first-order differential equation (17), with the terminal conditions $\lambda(T) = 1$, $\Delta v(T) = 0$.

Since $\lambda = 1/2$ implies $\Delta V = 0$, the systems (28) and (29) have always an interior steady state at $(\lambda, \Delta v) = (1/2, 0)$ that corresponds to the dispersed configuration. While for $\tau > \tau^*$ it is the only steady state; for $\tau < \tau^*$ two other steady states exist at $(\lambda, \Delta v) = (0, 0)$ and $(\lambda, \Delta v) = (1, 0)$. In the latter case, as in Fukao and Bénabou (1993), since all workers are concentrated within the same region, there is no reason to hold that

$$\dot{\Delta v}(T) = 0$$

in (29). In fact, by the terminal conditions, we have

$$\dot{\Delta v}(T) = -\Delta V(T) = -C\tau(\tau^* - \tau)/2 < 0$$

which ensures that the spatial equilibrium involves no worker in F. Therefore, the assumed belief (24) can be consistent only in the latter case, on which we concentrate from now on.

In order to identify the conditions under which the belief that workers will eventually agglomerate in the initially smaller region H can reverse the historically inherited advantage of the larger region F, we have to study the global stability of systems (28) and (29). In so doing, we exploit the fact that, since the system is linear, local and global stability properties coincide, and we focus on the former. The eigenvalues of the Jacobian matrix of the systems (28) and (29) are given by

(30) $$\frac{\rho \pm \sqrt{\rho^2 - 4\delta C\tau(\tau^* - \tau)}}{2}$$

When $\tau < \tau^*$, two scenarios may arise. In the first one, $\rho > 2\sqrt{C\delta\tau(\tau^* - \tau)}$ so that the two eigenvalues are real and both positive. The steady state $(1/2, 0)$ is an unstable node, and there are two trajectories that steadily go to the endpoints, $(0, 0)$ or $(1, 0)$, depending on the initial spatial distribution of workers, say, λ_0. In this case, *only history matters*: From any initial $\lambda_0 \neq 1/2$, there is a single trajectory that goes toward the closer endpoint as in the case where the dynamics are given by (17). This means that belief (24) is inconsistent with the equilibrium path, whence the myopic adjustment process studied in the previous section provides a good approximation of the qualitative evolution of the economy under forward-looking behavior.

Things turn out to be quite different in the second scenario in which $\rho < 2\sqrt{C\delta\tau(\tau^* - \tau)}$. Since $C\tau(\tau^* - \tau) = 0$ at both $\tau = 0$ and $\tau = \tau^*$, the equation $C\tau(\tau^* - \tau) - \rho^2/4\delta = 0$ has two positive real roots in τ, denoted τ_1^e and τ_2^e, that are smaller than τ^*:

$$\tau_1^e \equiv \frac{\tau^* - D}{2} \quad \text{and} \quad \tau_2^e \equiv \frac{\tau^* + D}{2}$$

where

$$D \equiv \sqrt{(\tau^*)^2 - \rho^2/C\delta}$$

stands for the size of the domain of values of τ for which expectations matter; it shrinks as the discount rate ρ increases or as the speed of adjustment δ decreases. Indeed, for $\tau \in (0, \tau_1^e)$ as well as for $\tau \in (\tau_2^e, \tau^*)$, both eigenvalues are real positive numbers and the steady state $(1/2, 0)$ is an unstable node as before. However, for $\tau \in (\tau_1^e, \tau_2^e)$, they become complex numbers with a positive real part, so that the steady state is an unstable focus. The two trajectories spiral out from $(1/2, 0)$. Therefore, for any λ_0 close enough to, but different from, $1/2$, there are two alternative trajectories going in opposite directions. It is in such a case that expectations decide along which trajectory the system moves, so that belief (24) is self-fulfilling. In other words, *expectations matter for λ close enough to $1/2$, while history matters otherwise.* The corresponding domains are now described.

The range of values for which expectations matter, called the *overlap* by Krugman (1991a), can be obtained as follows: As observed by Fukao and Bénabou (1993), the system must be solved backwards in time starting from the terminal points $(0, 0)$ and $(1, 0)$. The first time the backward trajectories intersect the locus $\Delta v = 0$ allows for the identifications of the endpoints of the overlap:

$$\lambda^L \equiv \frac{1}{2}(1 - \Lambda) \qquad \lambda^H \equiv \frac{1}{2}(1 + \Lambda)$$

where

$$\Lambda \equiv \exp\left(-\frac{\rho\pi}{\sqrt{4\delta C\tau(\tau^* - \tau) - \rho^2}}\right)$$

is the width of the overlap, which is an interval centered around $\lambda = 1/2$.

The overlap is nonempty as long as $\tau \in (\tau_1^e, \tau_2^e)$. Thus, the width of the overlap is increasing in δ, C, and τ^*, while it decreases in ρ. Moreover, it is $\cap$-shaped with respect to τ, reaching a maximum at $\tau = \tau^*/2$. Since $C\tau(\tau^* - \tau) > 0$ is the slope of ΔV and since this one measures the strength of the forward and backward linkages pushing towards agglomeration, we see that expectations matter more when such linkages are stronger. Consequently, we have shown the following result:

PROPOSITION 3.   *Let λ_0 be the initial spatial distribution of workers. If $\tau < \tau^*$ and $\rho < 2\sqrt{C\delta\tau(\tau^* - \tau)}$, there exist $\tau_1^e \in (0, \tau^*/2)$, $\tau_2^e \in (\tau^*/2, \tau^*)$, $\lambda^L \in (0, 1/2)$, and*

AGGLOMERATION AND TRADE REVISITED 429

$\lambda^H \in (1/2, 1)$ *such that workers' beliefs about their future earnings influence the process of agglomeration if and only if* $\tau \in (\tau_1^e, \tau_2^e)$ *and* $\lambda_0 \in [\lambda^L, \lambda^H]$.

Hence, history alone matters when τ and λ are large enough or small enough. In other words, the agglomeration process evolves as if workers were shortsighted when obstacles to trade are high or low and when regions are initially quite different. Instead, as long as obstacles to trade take intermediate values and regions are not initially too different, *the equilibrium is determined by workers' expectations and not by history.*[12]

The existence of the range (τ_1^e, τ_2^e) may be explained as follows: Suppose, indeed, that the economy is such that $\lambda_0 < 1/2$, and ask what is needed to reverse an ongoing agglomeration process currently leading towards $\lambda = 0$. If the evolution of the economy were to change direction, workers would experience falling instantaneous indirect utility flows for some time period as long as $\lambda < 1/2$. The instantaneous indirect utility flows would start growing only after λ becomes larger than $1/2$. Accordingly, workers would first experience utility losses followed by utility gains. Since the losses would come before the gains, they would be less discounted. This provides the root for the intuition behind Proposition 3. When the forward and backward linkages lead to substantial wage rises (that is, for intermediate values of τ), the benefits of agglomerating at $\lambda = 1$ can compensate workers for the losses they incur during the transition phase, thus making the reversal of migration possible. On the contrary, when these linkages get weaker (that is, for low or high values of τ), the benefits of agglomerating at $\lambda = 1$ do not compensate workers for the losses. As a consequence, *the reversal in the migration process may occur only for intermediate values of* τ.

As to the remaining comparative static properties of the overlap, they are explained by the fact that proximity to $\lambda = 0$ increases the time period over which workers bear losses, a large rate of time preference gives more weight to them, and a slow speed of adjustment extends the time period over which workers' well-being is reduced.

7. THE IMPACT OF URBAN COSTS

So far, we have assumed that the agglomeration of workers into a single region does not involve any agglomeration costs. Yet, it is reasonable to believe that a growing settlement in a given region will often take the form of an urban area, typically a city. In order to deal with such an aspect of the process of agglomeration, we extend the core-periphery model by adding the central variables suggested by urban economics (Fujita, 1989). In order to keep the analysis short, we go back to the myopic adjustment process of Section 4.

---

[12] When $\tau > \tau^*$, we know that the equilibrium path is inconsistent with workers' expectations under (24). And, indeed, the two eigenvalues are real and have opposite signs, so that the steady state is a saddle point. Under the assumption of perfect foresights, regardless of the initial distribution λ_0, the system moves along a single stable trajectory toward the symmetric steady state. In other words, the system converges toward the dispersed configuration, thus implying that neither expectations nor history matter for the final outcome.

Space is now continuous and one-dimensional. Each region has a spatial extension and involves a linear city whose center is given but with a variable size. The city center stands for a central business district (CBD) in which all firms locate once they have chosen to set up in the corresponding region (see Fujita and Thisse, 1996, for various arguments explaining why firms want to be agglomerated in a CBD). The two CBDs are two remote points of the location space. Interregional trade flows go from one CBD to the other.

Housing is a new good in our economy and is described by the amount of land used by workers. While firms are assumed not to consume land, workers, when they live in a certain region, are urban residents who consume land and commute to the regional CBD in which manufacturing firms are located. Hence, unlike Krugman (1991b) but like Alonso (1964), Helpman (1998), and Tabuchi (1998), *each agglomeration has a spatial extension that imposes commuting and land costs on the corresponding workers.* For simplicity, workers consume a fixed lot size normalized to unity, while commuting costs are linear in distance, the commuting cost per unit of distance being given by $\theta > 0$ units of the numéraire. Without loss of generality, the opportunity cost of land is normalized to zero.

When λL workers live in H, they are equally distributed around the H-CBD. In equilibrium, since all workers residing in region H earn the same wage, they reach the same utility level. Furthermore, since they all consume one unit of land, the equilibrium land rent at distance $x < \lambda L/2$ from the H-CBD is given by

$$R^*(x) = \theta(\lambda L/2 - x)$$

Hence, a worker located at the average distance $\lambda L/4$ from the H-CBD bears a commuting cost equal to $\theta \lambda L/4$ and pays the average land rent $\theta \lambda L/4$ (Fujita, 1989; Papageorgiou and Pines, 1999). When the land rents go to absentee landlords, individual urban costs, defined by commuting cost plus land rent at each residence x, are given by $\theta \lambda L/2.$ In order to avoid working with absentee landlords, we assume that all the land rents are collected and equally redistributed among the H-city workers.[13] Consequently, the individual urban costs after redistribution are equal to $\theta \lambda L/4.$

Since the urban costs prevailing in regions H and F are not equal, the incentives to move from one region to the other are no longer given by (18). Indeed, we must account for the difference in urban costs between H and F, namely,

$$\lambda \theta L/4 - (1 - \lambda)\theta L/4 = (\lambda - 1/2)\theta L/2$$

which must be subtracted from (18) to obtain the actual utility differential:

$$\Delta V_u(\lambda) = [C\tau(\tau^* - \tau) - \theta L/2][\lambda - 1/2]$$

---

[13] Assuming, as in Helpman (1998), that the total land rent across regions is equally redistributed among workers (hence controlling for the resulting fiscal externality) does not affect the utility differential, whereas the difference in urban costs becomes twice as large. Hence, θ is to be replaced by 2θ in the foregoing developments. This reduces the value of E and shrinks the interval (τ_1^u, τ_2^u). As a result, Proposition 4 shows that agglomeration is less likely to occur.

AGGLOMERATION AND TRADE REVISITED 431

As in Section 4, agglomeration is a spatial equilibrium when the slope of $\Delta V_u(\lambda)$ is positive. This is the case as long as τ falls within the two values

$$\tau_1^u \equiv \frac{\tau^* - E}{2} \quad \text{and} \quad \tau_2^u \equiv \frac{\tau^* + E}{2}$$

where $\tau_1^u, \tau_2^u \in (0, \tau^*)$, and

$$E \equiv \sqrt{(\tau^*)^2 - 2\theta L/C}$$

measures the domain of values of τ for which $\Delta V_u(\lambda) > 0$. Notice that such domain shrinks as the commuting cost per unit of distance θ increases. Consequently, we have the following proposition:

PROPOSITION 4. *If $2\theta L < C(\tau^*)^2$, there exist $\tau_1^u \in (0, \tau^*/2)$ and $\tau_2^u \in (\tau^*/2, \tau^*)$ such that agglomeration (dispersion) is the only stable equilibrium if and only if $\tau \in (\tau_1^u, \tau_2^u)$ ($\tau \notin (\tau_1^u, \tau_2^u)$). For $\tau = \tau_1^u$ or $\tau = \tau_2^u$, any distribution of workers is a spatial equilibrium. If $2\theta L > C(\tau^*)^2$, dispersion is the only spatial equilibrium.*

Thus, *the existence of positive commuting costs within the regional centers is sufficient to yield dispersion when the trade costs are sufficiently low.* This implies that, as trade costs fall, the economy involves dispersion, agglomeration, and redispersion. An increase (decrease) in the commuting costs fosters dispersion (agglomeration) by widening (shrinking) the left range of τ-values for which dispersion is the only spatial equilibrium. Also, sufficiently high commuting costs always yield dispersion.

It is interesting to point out that while dispersion arises for both high and low trade costs, this happens for very different reasons. In the former case, firms are dispersed as a response to the high trade costs they would incur by supplying farmers from a single agglomeration. In the latter, firms are dispersed as a response to the high urban costs workers would bear within a single agglomeration.

In the present context, we may assume that there are no farmers without annihilating the dispersion force. If $A = 0$, it is readily verified that $\tau_{\text{trade}} < \tau^*/2 < \tau_2^u$, so that dispersion does not arise when trade costs are high. Consequently, *the economy moves from agglomeration to dispersion when trade costs fall*, thus confirming the numerical results obtained by Helpman (1998).

Finally, it is worth revisiting the debate about the social desirability of the market outcome once we account for urban costs. Computing the first-order condition for the social optimum as in Section 5 in which we now account for the urban costs $\theta \lambda L/4$ in region H and $\theta(1 - \lambda)L/4$ in region F, we obtain the new critical values:

$$\tau_1^{uo} \equiv \frac{\tau^o - F}{2} \quad \text{and} \quad \tau_2^{uo} \equiv \frac{\tau^o + F}{2}$$

where $\tau_1^{uo}, \tau_2^{uo} \in (0, \tau^o)$, and

$$F \equiv \sqrt{(\tau^o)^2 - 2\theta L/C^o}$$

and we fall back on the condition obtained in Section 5 when $\theta = 0$. As a result, we have the following proposition:

PROPOSITION 5. *Assume* $(\tau^o)^2 > 2\theta L/C^o$. *Then, there exist* $\tau_1^{uo} \in (0, \tau^o/2)$ *and* $\tau_2^{uo} \in (\tau^o/2, \tau^o)$ *such that the agglomerated configuration is the optimum when* $\tau \in (\tau_1^{uo}, \tau_2^{uo})$. *When* $\tau = \tau_1^{uo}, \tau_2^{uo}$, *any configuration is an optimum. Otherwise, the symmetric configuration is the optimum.*

Observe that the domain for which agglomeration is optimal shrinks as the commuting cost θ increases.

The comparison between the optimum and equilibrium outcomes is less straightforward than it was in Section 5, with Figure 2 showing the different possible patterns. First, as in Section 5, it is readily verified that excessive agglomeration arises for intermediate values of the trade costs. Second, when urban costs are positive, the equilibrium may yield either suboptimal agglomeration or suboptimal dispersion, depending on the parameter values of the economy. In particular, if we set $A = 0$, the interval I_2 in Figure 2 disappears, so that inefficiency arises only a range of low trade costs for which "market forces do not generate enough agglomeration" (Helpman, 1998, p. 46).[14]

8. CONCLUDING REMARKS

Recent years have seen the proliferation of applications of the "Dixit–Stiglitz, iceberg, evolution, and the computer" framework for studying the impact of trade costs on the spatial distribution of economic activities. While these applications have produced valuable insights, they have often been criticized because they rely on a very particular research strategy.

We have proposed *a different framework that is able not only to confirm those insights but also to produce new results that could barely be obtained within the standard one.* Specifically, we have used this framework to deal with the following issues: (i) the welfare properties of the core-periphery model, (ii) the impact of expectations in shaping the economic space, and (iii) the effects of urban costs on the interregional distribution of activities. This suggests that our framework is versatile enough to accommodate other extensions.

So, we have shown that the main results in the literature do not depend on the specific modeling choices made, as often argued by their critics. In particular, the robustness of the results obtained in the core-periphery model against an alternative formulation of preferences and transportation seems to point to the existence of a whole class of models for which similar results would hold. However, we have also shown that those modeling choices can be fruitfully reconsidered once the aim is to shed light on different issues.

---

[14] These results are a novel example of the ambiguous welfare properties of agglomerations that have been pointed out especially in urban economics. As argued recently by Papageorgiou and Pines (2000), such an ambiguity finds its origin in the simultaneous working of many potential sources of distortions such as various kinds of external (dis)economies, indivisibilities, and nonreplicabilities.

AGGLOMERATION AND TRADE REVISITED 433

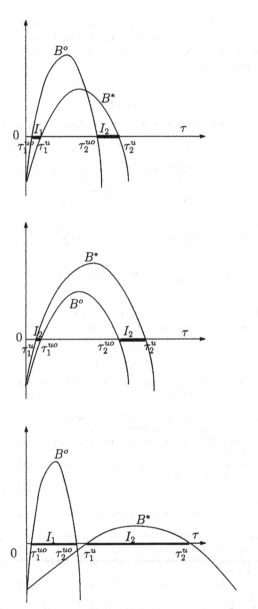

FIGURE 2

DIVERGENCE BETWEEN EQUILIBRIUM AND OPTIMUM: THE THREE CASES

The model used in this article still displays some undesirable features that should be remedied in future research. First, there is a fixed mass of firms regardless of the consumer distribution. Furthermore, by ignoring income effects, our setting has a strong partial equilibrium flavor.

APPENDIX

In the case of two varieties, the symmetric quadratic utility is given by

$$U(q_1, q_2) = \alpha(q_1 + q_2) - (\beta/2)(q_1^2 + q_2^2) - \gamma q_1 q_2 + q_0$$

In the case of $n > 2$ varieties, this expression is extended as follows:

$$U(q) = \alpha \sum_{i=1}^{n} q_i - (\beta/2) \sum_{i=1}^{n} q_i^2 - (\gamma/2) \sum_{i=1}^{n} \sum_{j \neq i}^{n} q_i q_j + q_0$$

$$= \alpha \sum_{i=1}^{n} q_i - [(\beta - \gamma)/2] \sum_{i=1}^{n} q_i^2 - (\gamma/2) \sum_{i=1}^{n} \left(q_i \sum_{j=1}^{n} q_j \right) + q_0$$

$$= \alpha \sum_{i=1}^{n} q_i - [(\beta - \gamma)/2] \sum_{i=1}^{n} q_i^2 - (\gamma/2) \left(\sum_{i=1}^{n} q_i \right)^2 + q_0$$

When $\gamma \to \beta$, this utility boils to a standard quadratic utility for a homogenous good. Letting $n \to \infty$ and $q_i \to 0$, we obtain (1), in which N stands for the mass of varieties.

REFERENCES

ALONSO, W., *Location and Land Use* (Cambridge, MA: Harvard University Press, 1964).
———, "Five Bell Shapes in Development," *Papers of the Regional Science Association* 45 (1980), 5–16.
ANDERSON, S. P., N. SCHMITT, AND J.-F. THISSE, "Who Benefits from Antidumping Legislation?," *Journal of International Economics* 38 (1995), 321–37.
DIXIT, A. K., "A Model of Duopoly Suggesting a Theory of Entry Barriers," *Bell Journal of Economics* 10 (1979), 20–32.
———, AND J. E. STIGLITZ, "Monopolistic Competition and Optimum Product Diversity," *American Economic Review* 67 (1977), 297–308.
FUJITA, M., *Urban Economic Theory: Land Use and City Size* (Cambridge: Cambridge University Press, 1989).
———, AND J.-F. THISSE, "Economics of Agglomeration," *Journal of the Japanese and International Economies* 10 (1996), 339–78.
———, P. KRUGMAN, AND A. VENABLES, *The Spatial Economy: Cities, Regions, and International Trade* (Cambridge, MA: MIT Press, 1999).
FUKAO, K., AND R. BÉNABOU, "History versus Expectations: A Comment," *Quarterly Journal of Economics* 108 (1993), 535–42.
GEYER, H. S., AND T. M. KONTULY, *Differential Urbanization: Integrating Spatial Models* (London: Arnold, 1996).
HEAD, K., AND T. MAYER, "Non-Europe: The Magnitude and Causes of Market Fragmentation in the EU," *Weltwirtschaftliches Archiv* 136 (2000), 284–314.
HELPMAN, E., "The Size of Regions," in D. Pines, E. Sadka, and I. Zilcha, eds., *Topics in Public Economics. Theoretical and Applied Analysis* (Cambridge: Cambridge University Press, 1998), 33–54.
HOTELLING, H., "Stability in Competition," *Economic Journal* 39 (1929), 41–57.

AGGLOMERATION AND TRADE REVISITED   435

KOOPMANS, T. C., *Three Essays on the State of Economic Science* (New York: McGraw-Hill, 1957).

KRUGMAN, P., "History versus Expectations," *Quarterly Journal of Economics* 106 (1991a), 651–67.

———, "Increasing Returns and Economic Geography," *Journal of Political Economy* 99 (1991b), 483–99.

———, *Development, Geography, and Economic Theory* (Cambridge, MA: MIT Press, 1995).

———, "Urban Concentration: The Role of Increasing Returns and Transport Costs," *International Regional Science Review* 19 (1996), 5–30.

———, "Space: The Final Frontier," *Journal of Economic Perspectives* 12 (1998), 161–74.

———, AND A. J. VENABLES, "Integration and the Competitiveness of Peripheral Industry," in C. Bliss and J. Braga de Macedo, eds., *Unity with Diversity in the European Community* (Cambridge: Cambridge University Press, 1990), 56–75.

——— AND ———, "Globalization and the Inequality of Nations," *Quarterly Journal of Economics* 110 (1995), 857–80.

LÖSCH, A., *Die Räumliche Ordnung der Wirtschaft* (Jena: Gustav Fischer Verlag, 1940). English translation: *The Economics of Location* (New Haven, CT: Yale University Press, 1954).

MATSUYAMA, K., "Increasing Returns, Industrialization, and Indeterminacy of Equilibrium," *Quarterly Journal of Economics* 106 (1991), 617–50.

McCALLUM, J., "National Borders Matter: Canada–US Regional Trade Patterns," *American Economic Review* 85 (1995), 615–23.

MUSSA, M., "Dynamic Adjustment in the Heckscher–Ohlin–Samuelson Model," *Journal of Political Economy* 86 (1978), 775–91.

OTTAVIANO, G. I. P., "Integration, Geography and the Burden of History," *Regional Science and Urban Economics* 29 (1999), 245–56.

———, AND D. PUGA, "Agglomeration in the Global Economy: A Survey of the 'New Economic Geography,'" *World Economy* 21 (1998), 707–31.

PAPAGEORGIOU, Y. Y., AND D. PINES, *An Essay in Urban Economic Theory* (Dordrecht: Kluwer Academic Publishers, 1999).

———, AND ———, "Externalities, Indivisibility, Nonreplicability and Agglomeration," *Journal of Urban Economics* 48 (2000), 509–35.

PHLIPS, L., *Applied Consumption Analysis* (Amsterdam: North-Holland, 1983).

PUGA, D., "The Rise and Fall of Regional Inequalities," *European Economic Review* 43 (1999), 303–34.

TABUCHI, T., "Agglomeration and Dispersion: A Synthesis of Alonso and Krugman," *Journal of Urban Economics* 44 (1998), 333–51.

TRIONFETTI, F., "Public Procurement, Market Integration, and Income Inequalities," *Review of International Economics* 9 (2001), 29–41.

VIVES, X., "Trade Association Disclosure Rules, Incentives to Share Information, and Welfare," *Rand Journal of Economics* 21 (1990), 409–30.

WEI, S.-J., "Intra-national versus International Trade: How Stubborn Are Nations in Global Integration," National Bureau of Economic Research Working Paper No. 5531, 1996.

Chapter 4

Market Size, Trade, and Productivity[†]

MARC J. MELITZ

Princeton University, NBER, and CEPR

and

GIANCARLO I. P. OTTAVIANO

University of Bologna, FEEM and CEPR

First version received May 2006; final version accepted May 2007 (Eds.)

We develop a monopolistically competitive model of trade with firm heterogeneity—in terms of productivity differences—and endogenous differences in the "toughness" of competition across markets—in terms of the number and average productivity of competing firms. We analyse how these features vary across markets of different size that are not perfectly integrated through trade; we then study the effects of different trade liberalization policies. In our model, market size and trade affect the toughness of competition, which then feeds back into the selection of heterogeneous producers and exporters in that market. Aggregate productivity and average mark-ups thus respond to both the size of a market and the extent of its integration through trade (larger, more integrated markets exhibit higher productivity and lower mark-ups). Our model remains highly tractable, even when extended to a general framework with multiple asymmetric countries integrated to different extents through asymmetric trade costs. We believe this provides a useful modelling framework that is particularly well suited to the analysis of trade and regional integration policy scenarios in an environment with heterogeneous firms and endogenous mark-ups.

1. INTRODUCTION

We develop a monopolistically competitive model of trade with heterogeneous firms and endogenous differences in the "toughness" of competition across countries. Firm heterogeneity—in the form of productivity differences—is introduced in a similar way to Melitz (2003): firms face some initial uncertainty concerning their future productivity when making a costly and irreversible investment decision prior to entry. However, we further incorporate endogenous mark-ups using the linear demand system with horizontal product differentiation developed by Ottaviano, Tabuchi and Thisse (2002). This generates an endogenous distribution of mark-ups across firms that responds to the toughness of competition in a market—the number and average productivity of competing firms in that market. We analyse how these features vary across markets of different size that are not perfectly integrated through trade and then study the effects of different trade liberalization policies.

In our model, market size and trade affect the toughness of competition in a market, which then feeds back into the selection of heterogeneous producers and exporters in that market. Aggregate productivity and average mark-ups thus respond to both the size of a market and the extent of its integration through trade (larger, more integrated markets exhibit higher productivity and lower mark-ups). Our model remains highly tractable, even when extended to a general framework with multiple asymmetric countries integrated to different extents through asymmetric trade costs. We believe this provides a useful modelling framework that is particularly well suited to the analysis of trade and regional integration policy scenarios in an environment with heterogeneous firms and endogenous mark-ups.

295

[†] This article originally appeared in *The review of economic studies*, **75** 295–316 © 2008 Oxford University Press.

We first introduce a closed-economy version of our model. In a key distinction from Melitz (2003), market size induces important changes in the equilibrium distribution of firms and their performance measures. Bigger markets exhibit higher levels of product variety and host more productive firms that set lower mark-ups (hence lower prices). These firms are bigger (in terms of both output and sales) and earn higher profits (although average mark-ups are lower), but face a lower probability of survival at entry.[1] We discuss how our comparative statics results for the effects of market size on the distribution of firm-level performance measures accord well with the evidence for U.S. establishments across regions. We then present the open-economy version of the model. We focus on a two-country case but show in the Appendix how this set-up can be extended to multiple asymmetric countries. We show how costly trade does not completely integrate markets and thus does not obviate the effects of market size differences across trading partners: the bigger market still exhibits larger and more productive firms as well as more product variety, lower prices, and lower mark-ups.

Our model's predictions for the effects of bilateral trade liberalization are very similar to those emphasized in Melitz (2003): trade forces the least productive firms to exit and reallocates market shares towards more productive exporting firms (lower productivity firms only serve their domestic market).[2] Our model also explains other empirical patterns linking the extent of trade barriers to the distribution of productivity, prices, and mark-ups across firms. In an important departure from Melitz (2003), our model exhibits a link between bilateral trade liberalization and reductions in mark-ups, thus highlighting the potential pro-competitive effects often associated with episodes of trade liberalization. We then analyse the effects of asymmetric liberalization. We consider the case of unilateral liberalization in a two-country world and that of preferential liberalization in a three-country world. Although the liberalizing countries always gain from the pro-competitive effects of increased import competition in the short run, we show that these gains may be overturned in the long run due to shifts in the pattern of entry.

The channels for all these welfare effects, stemming from both multilateral and unilateral liberalization, have all been previously identified in the early "new trade theory" literature emphasizing imperfect competition with representative firms. However, these contributions used very different modelling structures (monopolistic competition with product differentiation vs. oligopoly with a homogeneous good, free entry vs. a fixed number of firms) in order to isolate one particular welfare channel. The main contribution of our modelling approach is that it integrates all of these welfare channels into a single, unified (yet highly tractable) framework, while simultaneously incorporating the important selection and reallocation effects among heterogeneous firms that were previously emphasized. Krugman (1979) showed how trade can induce pro-competitive effects in a model with monopolistic competition and endogenous mark-ups while Markusen (1981) formalized and highlighted the pro-competitive effects from trade due to the reduction in market power of a domestic monopolist. This latter modelling framework was then extended by Venables (1985) and Horstmann and Markusen (1986) to the case of oligopoly with free entry (while maintaining the assumption of a homogeneous traded good). These papers emphasized, among other things, how free entry could generate welfare losses for a country unilaterally liberalizing imports—by "reallocating" firms towards the country's trading partners. Venables (1987) showed how this effect also can be generated in a model with monopolistic

---

1. This closed-economy version of our model is related to Asplund and Nocke (2006), which analyses firm dynamics in a closed economy. They obtain similar results linking higher firm churning rates with larger markets—and provide supporting empirical evidence. On the other hand, the increased tractability afforded by our model yields additional important comparative static predictions for this closed-economy case.

2. Microeconometric studies strongly confirm these selection effects of trade (both according to firm export status, and for the effects of trade liberalization). See, among others, Clerides, Lach and Tybout (1998), Bernard and Jensen (1999), Aw, Chung and Roberts (2000), Pavcnik (2002), Bernard, Jensen and Schott (2006), and the survey in Tybout (2002).

MELITZ & OTTAVIANO   MARKET SIZE, TRADE, AND PRODUCTIVITY   297

competition and product differentiation with exogenous mark-ups. Our model isolates this asymmetric effect of unilateral trade liberalization induced by entry by also considering a short-run response to liberalization, where the additional entry of firms is restricted. Of course, our model also features the now-standard welfare gains from additional product variety as well as the asymmetric welfare gains of trade induced by differences in country size and trade costs highlighted by Krugman (1980). Again, we emphasize that our contribution is not to highlight a new welfare channel but rather to show how all of these welfare channels can jointly be analysed within a single framework that additionally captures the welfare effects stemming from changes in average productivity based on the selection of heterogeneous firms into domestic and export markets.

Our paper is also related to a much more recent literature emphasizing heterogeneous firms and endogenous mark-ups, resulting in a non-degenerate distribution of mark-ups across firms. These models all generate the equilibrium property that more productive firms charge higher mark-ups. Bernard, Eaton, Jensen and Kortum (2003) also incorporate firm heterogeneity and endogenous mark-ups into an open-economy model. However, in their model, the distribution of mark-ups is invariant to country characteristics and to geographic barriers. Asplund and Nocke (2006) investigate the effect of market size on the entry and exit rates of heterogeneous firms. They analyse a stochastic dynamic model of a monopolistically competitive industry with linear demand and hence variable mark-ups. They consider, however, a closed economy, so they do not provide any results concerning the role of geography and partial trade liberalization. In this paper, we focus instead on the response of the mark-ups to country characteristics and to geographic barriers and their feedback effects on firm selection. Most importantly, we show how our model can be extended to an open-economy equilibrium with multiple countries, including the analysis of asymmetric trade liberalization scenarios.

The paper is organized in four additional sections after the introduction. The first presents and solves the closed-economy model. The second derives the two-country model and studies the effects of international market size differences. The third investigates the impacts of trade liberalization considering both bilateral and unilateral experiments. This includes a three-country version of the model that highlights the effects of preferential trade agreements. The last section concludes.

2. CLOSED ECONOMY

Consider an economy with L consumers, each supplying one unit of labour.

2.1. *Preferences and demand*

Preferences are defined over a continuum of differentiated varieties indexed by $i \in \Omega$, and a homogenous good chosen as numeraire. All consumers share the same utility function given by

$$U = q_0^c + \alpha \int_{i \in \Omega} q_i^c di - \frac{1}{2} \gamma \int_{i \in \Omega} (q_i^c)^2 di - \frac{1}{2} \eta \left(\int_{i \in \Omega} q_i^c di \right)^2, \tag{1}$$

where q_0^c and q_i^c represent the individual consumption levels of the numeraire good and each variety i. The demand parameters α, η, and γ are all positive. The parameters α and η index the substitution pattern between the differentiated varieties and the numeraire: increases in α and decreases in η both shift out the demand for the differentiated varieties relative to the numeraire. The parameter γ indexes the degree of product differentiation between the varieties. In the limit when $\gamma = 0$, consumers only care about their consumption level over all varieties, $Q^c = \int_{i \in \Omega} q_i^c di$. The varieties are then perfect substitutes. The degree of product differentiation increases with γ as consumers give increasing weight to the distribution of consumption levels across varieties.

The marginal utilities for all goods are bounded, and a consumer may thus not have positive demand for any particular good. We assume that consumers have positive demands for the numeraire good ($q_0^c > 0$). The inverse demand for each variety i is then given by

$$p_i = \alpha - \gamma q_i^c - \eta Q^c, \tag{2}$$

whenever $q_i^c > 0$. Let $\Omega^* \subset \Omega$ be the subset of varieties that are consumed ($q_i^c > 0$). Equation (2) can then be inverted to yield the linear market demand system for these varieties:

$$q_i \equiv L q_i^c = \frac{\alpha L}{\eta N + \gamma} - \frac{L}{\gamma} p_i + \frac{\eta N}{\eta N + \gamma} \frac{L}{\gamma} \bar{p}, \qquad \forall i \in \Omega^*, \tag{3}$$

where N is the measure of consumed varieties in Ω^* and $\bar{p} = (1/N) \int_{i \in \Omega^*} p_i di$ is their average price. The set Ω^* is the largest subset of Ω that satisfies

$$p_i \leq \frac{1}{\eta N + \gamma} (\gamma \alpha + \eta N \bar{p}) \equiv p_{\max}, \tag{4}$$

where the R.H.S. price bound $p_{\max}$ represents the price at which demand for a variety is driven to 0. Note that (2) implies $p_{\max} \leq \alpha$. In contrast to the case of Constant Elasticity of Substitution (CES) demand, the price elasticity of demand, $\varepsilon_i \equiv |(\partial q_i / \partial p_i)(p_i / q_i)| = [(p_{\max}/p_i) - 1]^{-1}$, is not uniquely determined by the level of product differentiation γ. Given the latter, lower average prices $\bar{p}$ or a larger number of competing varieties N induce a decrease in the price bound $p_{\max}$ and an increase in the price elasticity of demand ε_i at any given p_i. We characterize this as a "tougher" competitive environment.[3]

Welfare can be evaluated using the indirect utility function associated with (1):

$$U = I^c + \frac{1}{2}\left(\eta + \frac{\gamma}{N}\right)^{-1}(\alpha - \bar{p})^2 + \frac{1}{2}\frac{N}{\gamma}\sigma_p^2, \tag{5}$$

where I^c is the consumer's income and $\sigma_p^2 = (1/N) \int_{i \in \Omega^*} (p_i - \bar{p})^2 di$ represents the variance of prices. To ensure positive demand levels for the numeraire, we assume that $I^c > \int_{i \in \Omega^*} p_i q_i^c di = \bar{p} Q^c - N \sigma_p^2 / \gamma$. Welfare naturally rises with decreases in average prices $\bar{p}$. It also rises with increases in the variance of prices σ_p^2 (holding the mean price $\bar{p}$ constant), as consumers then re-optimize their purchases by shifting expenditures towards lower priced varieties as well as the numeraire good. Finally, the demand system exhibits "love of variety": holding the distribution of prices constant (namely holding the mean $\bar{p}$ and variance σ_p^2 of prices constant), welfare rises with increases in product variety N.

2.2. *Production and firm behaviour*

Labour is the only factor of production and is inelastically supplied in a competitive market. The numeraire good is produced under constant returns to scale at unit cost; its market is also competitive. These assumptions imply a unit wage. Entry in the differentiated product sector is costly as each firm incurs product development and production start-up costs. Subsequent production exhibits constant returns to scale at marginal cost c (equal to unit labour requirement).[4]

---

3. We also note that, given this competitive environment (given N and $\bar{p}$), the price elasticity ε_i monotonically increases with the price p_i along the demand curve.

4. For simplicity, we do not model any overhead production costs. This would significantly degrade the tractability of our model without adding any new insights. In our model with bounded marginal utility, high-cost firms will not survive, even without such fixed costs.

Research and development yield uncertain outcomes for c, and firms learn about this cost level only after making the irreversible investment f_E required for entry. We model this as a draw from a common (and known) distribution $G(c)$ with support on $[0, c_M]$. Since the entry cost is sunk, firms that can cover their marginal cost survive and produce. All other firms exit the industry. Surviving firms maximize their profits using the residual demand function (3). In so doing, given the continuum of competitors, a firm takes the average price level $\bar{p}$ and number of firms N as given. This is the monopolistic competition outcome.

The profit maximizing price $p(c)$ and output level $q(c)$ of a firm with cost c must then satisfy

$$q(c) = \frac{L}{\gamma}[p(c) - c]. \tag{6}$$

The profit maximizing price $p(c)$ may be above the price bound $p_{\max}$ from (4), in which case the firm exits. Let c_D reference the cost of the firm who is just indifferent about remaining in the industry. This firm earns zero profit as its price is driven down to its marginal cost, $p(c_D) = c_D = p_{\max}$, and its demand level $q(c_D)$ is driven to 0. We assume that c_M is high enough to be above c_D, so that some firms with cost draws between these two levels exit. All firms with cost $c < c_D$ earn positive profits (gross of the entry cost) and remain in the industry. The threshold cost c_D summarizes the effects of both the average price and number of firms on the performance measures of all firms. Let $r(c) = p(c)q(c)$, $\pi(c) = r(c) - q(c)c$, $\mu(c) = p(c) - c$ denote the revenue, profit, and (absolute) mark-up of a firm with cost c. All these performance measures can then be written as functions of c and c_D only:

$$p(c) = \frac{1}{2}(c_D + c), \tag{7}$$

$$\mu(c) = \frac{1}{2}(c_D - c), \tag{8}$$

$$q(c) = \frac{L}{2\gamma}(c_D - c), \tag{9}$$

$$r(c) = \frac{L}{4\gamma}[(c_D)^2 - c^2], \tag{10}$$

$$\pi(c) = \frac{L}{4\gamma}(c_D - c)^2. \tag{11}$$

As expected, lower cost firms set lower prices and earn higher revenues and profits than firms with higher costs. However, lower cost firms do not pass on all of the cost differential to consumers in the form of lower prices: they also set higher mark-ups (in both absolute and relative terms) than firms with higher costs.

2.3. *Free entry equilibrium*

Prior to entry, the expected firm profit is $\int_0^{c_D} \pi(c)dG(c) - f_E$. If this profit were negative, no firms would enter the industry. As long as some firms produce, the expected profit is driven to 0 by the unrestricted entry of new firms. Using (11), this yields the equilibrium free entry condition

$$\int_0^{c_D} \pi(c)dG(c) = \frac{L}{4\gamma} \int_0^{c_D} (c_D - c)^2 dG(c) = f_E, \tag{12}$$

which determines the cost cut-off c_D. This cut-off, in turn, determines the number of surviving firms, since $c_D = p(c_D)$ must also be equal to the zero demand price threshold in (4):

$$c_D = \frac{1}{\eta N + \gamma}(\gamma \alpha + \eta N \bar{p}).$$

This yields the zero cut-off profit condition

$$N = \frac{2\gamma}{\eta}\frac{\alpha - c_D}{c_D - \bar{c}}, \tag{13}$$

where $\bar{c} = \left[\int_0^{c_D} c\, dG(c) \right] / G(c_D)$ is the average cost of surviving firms.[5] The number of entrants is then given by $N_E = N/G(c_D)$.

Given a production technology referenced by $G(c)$, average productivity will be higher (lower $\bar{c}$) when sunk costs are lower, when varieties are closer substitutes (lower γ), and in bigger markets (more consumers L). In all these cases, firm exit rates are also higher (the pre-entry probability of survival $G(c_D)$ is lower). The demand parameters α and η that index the overall level of demand for the differentiated varieties (relative to the numeraire) do not affect the selection of firms and industry productivity—they only affect the equilibrium number of firms. Competition is "tougher" in larger markets as more firms compete and average prices $\bar{p} = (c_D + \bar{c})/2$ are lower. A firm with cost c responds to this tougher competition by setting a lower mark-up (relative to the mark-up it would set in a smaller market—see (8)).

2.4. Parametrization of technology

All the results derived so far hold for any distribution of cost draws $G(c)$. However, in order to simplify some of the ensuing analysis, we use a specific parametrization for this distribution. In particular, we assume that productivity draws $1/c$ follow a Pareto distribution with lower productivity bound $1/c_M$ and shape parameter $k \geq 1$.[6] This implies a distribution of cost draws c given by

$$G(c) = \left(\frac{c}{c_M} \right)^k, \quad c \in [0, c_M]. \tag{14}$$

The shape parameter k indexes the dispersion of cost draws. When $k = 1$, the cost distribution is uniform on $[0, c_M]$. As k increases, the relative number of high-cost firms increases, and the cost distribution is more concentrated at these higher cost levels. As k goes to infinity, the distribution becomes degenerate at c_M. Any truncation of the cost distribution from above will retain the same distribution function and shape parameter k. The productivity distribution of surviving firms will therefore also be Pareto with shape k, and the truncated cost distribution will be given by $G_D(c) = (c/c_D)^k$, $c \in [0, c_D]$.

Given this parametrization, the cut-off cost level c_D determined by (12) is then

$$c_D = \left[\frac{2(k+1)(k+2)\gamma (c_M)^k f_E}{L} \right]^{1/(k+2)}, \tag{15}$$

---

5. Given (7), it is readily verified that $\bar{p} = (c_D + \bar{c})/2$.
6. Del Gatto, Mion and Ottaviano (2006) estimate the distribution of total factor productivity using firm-level data for a panel of 11 EU countries and 18 manufacturing sectors. They find that the Pareto distribution provides a very good fit for firm productivity across sectors and countries. The average k is estimated to be close to 2. Combes, Duranton, Gobillon, Puga and Roux (2007) extend our model and consider general cost/productivity distributions. They show how our main comparative static results do not depend on our choice of parametrization.

where we assume that $c_M > \sqrt{[2(k+1)(k+2)\gamma f_E]/L}$ in order to ensure that $c_D < c_M$ as was previously anticipated. The number of surviving firms, determined by (13), is then

$$N = \frac{2(k+1)\gamma}{\eta} \frac{a - c_D}{c_D}. \tag{16}$$

This parametrization also yields simple derivations for the averages of all the firm-level performance measures described in (7)–(11):[7]

$$\bar{c} = \frac{k}{k+1}c_D, \qquad \bar{q} = \frac{L}{2\gamma}\frac{1}{k+1}c_D = \frac{(k+2)(c_M)^k}{(c_D)^{k+1}}f_E,$$

$$\bar{p} = \frac{2k+1}{2k+2}c_D, \qquad \bar{r} = \frac{L}{2\gamma}\frac{1}{k+2}(c_D)^2 = \frac{(k+1)(c_M)^k}{(c_D)^k}f_E,$$

$$\bar{\mu} = \frac{1}{2}\frac{1}{k+1}c_D, \qquad \bar{\pi} = f_E\frac{(c_M)^k}{(c_D)^k}.$$

As with the cost average $\bar{c}$, the average for a performance measure $z(c)$ is given by $\bar{z} = \left[\int_0^{c_D} z(c)dG(c)\right]/G(c_D)$. Although $\bar{c}$ is computed as the unweighted average of firm cost, it provides an index to a much broader set of inverse productivity measures. The average of firm productivity $1/c$—whether unweighted, weighted by revenue $r(c)$, or weighted by output $q(c)$— is proportional to $1/\bar{c}$ (and hence to $1/c_D$). In the Appendix, we further show how the variances of all the firm performance measures can be written as simple functions of the variance of the cost draws. Since the cut-off level completely summarizes the distribution of prices as well as all the other performance measures, it also uniquely determines welfare from (5):

$$U = 1 + \frac{1}{2\eta}(a - c_D)\left(a - \frac{k+1}{k+2}c_D\right). \tag{17}$$

Welfare increases with decreases in the cut-off c_D, as the latter induces increases in product variety N as well as decreases in the average price $\bar{p}$ (these effects dominate the negative impact of the lower price variance).[8]

We previously mentioned that bigger markets induced tougher selection (lower cut-off c_D), leading to higher average productivity (lower $\bar{c}$) and lower average prices. In addition, under our assumed parametrization of cost draws, average firm size (both in terms of output and sales) and profits are higher in larger markets: the direct market size effect outweighs its indirect effect through lower prices and mark-ups. Similarly, average mark-ups are lower as the direct effect of increased competition on firm-level mark-ups ($\mu(c)$ shifts down) outweighs the selection effect on firms with lower cost (and relatively higher mark-ups). We also note that average profits and sales increase by the same proportion when market size increases. Thus, average industry profitability $\bar{\pi}/\bar{r}$ does not vary with market size. Finally, we note that our technology parametrization also allows us to unambiguously sign the effects of market size on the dispersion of the firm performance measures: the variance of cost, prices, and mark-ups are lower in bigger markets (the selection effect decreases the support of these distributions for any distribution $G(c)$); on the

---

7. All derivations are based on the assumption that consumers have positive demands for the numeraire good. Consumers derive all of their income from their labour: there are no redistributed firm profits as industry profits (net of the entry costs) are 0. We therefore need to ensure that each consumer spends less than this unit income on the differentiated varieties. Spending per consumer on the varieties is $N\bar{r}/L = (a - c_D)c_D(k+1)/[\eta(k+2)]$. A sufficient condition for this to be less than 1 is $a < 2\sqrt{\eta(k+2)/(k+1)}$.

8. This welfare measure reflects the reduced consumption of the numeraire to account for the labour resources used to cover the entry costs.

other hand, the variance of firm size (in terms of either output or revenue) is larger in bigger markets due to the direct magnifying effect of market size on these variables.

These comparative statics for the effects of market size on the mean and variance of firm performance measures accord well with the empirical evidence for U.S. establishments/plants (across regions) reported by Syverson (2004, forthcoming) and Campbell and Hopenhayn (2005). These studies focus on sectors (retail, concrete, cement) where U.S. regional markets are relatively closed—and focus on the effects of U.S. market size (across regions) on the distribution of U.S. establishments. Campbell and Hopenhayn (2005) report that retail establishments in larger markets exhibit higher sales and employment and find weaker evidence that these distributions are more disperse. Syverson (2004, forthcoming) focuses on sectors where physical output can be measured along with sales (and hence prices recovered). He finds similar evidence of larger average plant size in larger markets along with higher average plant productivity. He finds further support for the tougher selection effect in the larger markets: the distribution of productivity is less disperse, with a higher lower bound for the productivity distribution. These effects also show up in the distribution of plant level prices: average prices are lower in bigger markets, while the dispersion is reduced.

2.5. A short-run equilibrium

In the following sections, we introduce an open-economy version of our model and analyse the consequences of various trade liberalization scenarios. The asymmetric liberalization scenarios induce a well-known relocation of firms (entrants in our model) across countries. We will then want to separate these "long-run" effects from the direct "short-run" effects of liberalization on competition and selection across markets. Towards this goal, we introduce a short-run version of our model. For now, we describe its main features and equilibrium characteristics in the closed economy.

Up to this point, we have considered a long-run scenario where entry and exit decisions were endogenously determined. In contrast, the short run is characterized by a fixed number and distribution of incumbents. In this time frame, these incumbents decide whether they should operate and produce—or shut down. If so, they can restart production without incurring the entry cost again. No entry is possible in the short run.

Let $\bar{N}$ denote the fixed number of incumbents and $\bar{G}(c)$ their cost distribution with support $[0, \bar{c}_M]$. We maintain our Pareto parametrization assumption for productivity $1/c$, implying $\bar{G}(c) = (c/\bar{c}_M)^k$. As was the case in the long run, only firms earning non-negative profits produce. This leads to the same determination of the cost cut-off c_D. Firms with cost $c > c_D$ shut down and the remaining $N = \bar{N}\bar{G}(c_D) = \bar{N}(c_D/\bar{c}_M)^k$ firms produce. If the least productive firm with cost $\bar{c}_M$ earns non-negative profits, then $c_D = \bar{c}_M$ and all firms produce in the short run. Otherwise, the cut-off c_D is determined by the zero cut-off profit condition (13):

$$N = \frac{2\gamma}{\eta}\frac{a - c_D}{c_D - \bar{c}} = \frac{2(k+1)\gamma}{\eta}\frac{a - c_D}{c_D}, \quad \text{whenever } c_D < \bar{c}_M,$$

since the average cost of producing firms is still $\bar{c} = [k/(k+1)]c_D$ as in the long-run equilibrium. Using the new condition for the number of firms $N = \bar{N}(c_D/\bar{c}_M)^k$, the zero cut-off profit condition yields

$$\frac{(c_D)^{k+1}}{a - c_D} = \frac{2(k+1)\gamma\,(\bar{c}_M)^k}{\eta\bar{N}}, \quad \text{whenever } c_D < \bar{c}_M,$$

which uniquely identifies the short-run cut-off c_D and the number of producing firms N.

MELITZ & OTTAVIANO   MARKET SIZE, TRADE, AND PRODUCTIVITY   303

In this short-run equilibrium, changes in market size do not induce any changes in the distribution of producing firms (c_D remains constant), nor in the distribution of prices and mark-ups (see (7) and (8)). All firms adjust their output levels in proportion to the market size change.[9] Only entry in the long run induces inter-firm reallocations (and the associated change in the cut-off c_D).

3. OPEN ECONOMY

In the previous section we used a closed-economy model to assess the effects of market size on various performance measures at the industry level. This closed-economy model could be immediately applied to a set of open economies that are perfectly integrated through trade. In this case, the transition from autarky to free trade is equivalent to an increase in market size—which would induce increases in average productivity and product variety, and decreases in average mark-ups. However, the closed-economy scenario cannot be readily extended to the case of goods that are not freely traded. Furthermore, although trade is costly, it nevertheless connects markets in ways that preclude the analysis of each market in isolation. To understand these inter-market linkages, we now extend our model to a two-country setting. In the Appendix, we show how our framework can be extended to an arbitrary number of countries and trade cost patterns (including arbitrary asymmetric costs).

Consider two countries, H and F, with L^H and L^F consumers in each country. Consumers in both countries share the same preferences, leading to the inverse demand function (2). The two markets are segmented, although firms can produce in one market and sell in the other, incurring a per-unit trade cost.[10] Specifically, the delivered cost of a unit with cost c to country l ($l = H, F$) is $\tau^l c$ where $\tau^l > 1$. Thus, we allow countries to differ along two dimensions: market size L^l and barriers to imports τ^l.

Let p_{max}^l denote the price threshold for positive demand in market l. Then (4) implies

$$p^l = \frac{1}{\eta N^l + \gamma}(\gamma \alpha + \eta N^l \bar{p}^l), \quad l = H, F, \tag{18}$$

where N^l is the total number of firms selling in country l (the total number of domestic firms and foreign exporters) and $\bar{p}^l$ is the average price (across both local and exporting firms) in country l. Let $p_D^l(c)$ and $q_D^l(c)$ represent the domestic levels of the profit maximizing price and quantity sold for a firm producing in country l with cost c. Such a firm may also decide to produce some output $q_X^l(c)$ that it exports at a delivered price $p_X^l(c)$.

Since the markets are segmented and firms produce under constant returns to scale, they independently maximize the profits earned from domestic and exports sales. Let $\pi_D^l(c) = [p_D^l(c) - c]q_D^l(c)$ and $\pi_X^l(c) = [p_X^l(c) - \tau^h c]q_X^l(c)$ denote the maximized value of these profits as a function of the firm's marginal cost c (where $h \neq l$).[11] Analogously to (6), the profit maximizing prices and output levels must satisfy: $q_D^l(c) = (L^l/\gamma)[p_D^l(c) - c]$ and $q_X^l(c) = (L^h/\gamma)[p_X^l(c) - \tau^h c]$. As was the case in the closed economy, only firms earning non-negative profits in a market (domestic or export) will choose to sell in that market. This leads to similar

---

9. When market size changes, the residual inverse demand curve rotates around the same price bound p_{max}. With linear demand curves, the marginal revenue curve rotates in such a way that the profit maximizing price for any given marginal cost remains unchanged.

10. We later show how our equilibrium conditions rule out any profitable arbitrage opportunities. For simplicity, we do not model any fixed export costs. This would significantly degrade the tractability of our model without adding any new insights. In our model with bounded marginal utility, per-unit costs alone are enough to induce selection into export markets.

11. Throughout this analysis, all derivations involving l and h hold for $l = H, F$, and $h \neq l$.

cost cut-off rules for firms selling in either market. Let c_D^l denote the upper bound cost for firms selling in their domestic market, and let c_X^l denote the upper bound cost for exporters from l to h. These cut-offs must then satisfy

$$c_D^l = \sup\{c : \pi_D^l(c) > 0\} = p_{\max}^l,$$
$$c_X^l = \sup\{c : \pi_X^l(c) > 0\} = \frac{p_{\max}^h}{\tau^h}. \tag{19}$$

This implies $c_X^h = c_D^l / \tau^l$: trade barriers make it harder for exporters to break even relative to domestic producers.

As was the case in the closed economy, the cut-offs summarize all the effects of market conditions relevant for firm performance. In particular, the optimal prices and output levels can be written as functions of the cut-offs:

$$p_D^l(c) = \tfrac{1}{2}(c_D^l + c), \quad q_D^l(c) = \tfrac{L^l}{2\gamma}(c_D^l - c),$$
$$p_X^l(c) = \tfrac{\tau^h}{2}(c_X^l + c), \quad q_X^l(c) = \tfrac{L^h}{2\gamma}\tau^h(c_X^l - c), \tag{20}$$

which yield the following maximized profit levels:

$$\pi_D^l(c) = \tfrac{L^l}{4\gamma}(c_D^l - c)^2,$$
$$\pi_X^l(c) = \tfrac{L^h}{4\gamma}(\tau^h)^2(c_X^l - c)^2. \tag{21}$$

3.1. *Free entry condition*

Entry is unrestricted in both countries. Firms choose a production location prior to entry and paying the sunk entry cost. In order to focus our analysis on the effects of market size and trade costs differences, we assume that countries share the same technology—referenced by the entry cost f_E and cost distribution $G(c)$.[12] Free entry of domestic firms in country l implies zero expected profits in equilibrium, hence

$$\int_0^{c_D^l} \pi_D^l(c) dG(c) + \int_0^{c_X^l} \pi_X^l(c) dG(c) = f_E.$$

We also assume the same Pareto parametrization (14) for the cost draws $G(c)$ in both countries. Given (21), the free entry condition can be re-written:

$$L^l(c_D^l)^{k+2} + L^h(\tau^h)^2(c_X^l)^{k+2} = \gamma\phi, \tag{22}$$

where $\phi \equiv 2(k+1)(k+2)(c_M)^k f_E$ is a technology index that combines the effects of better distribution of cost draws (lower c_M) and lower entry costs f_E.

This free entry condition will hold so long as there is a positive mass of domestic entrants $N_E^l > 0$ in country l.[13] In this paper, we focus on the case where both countries produce the differentiated good and $N_E^l > 0$ for $l = H, F$. Then, since $c_X^h = c_D^l / \tau^l$, the free entry condition

---

12. We relax this assumption in the Appendix and investigate the implications of Ricardian comparative advantage.

13. Otherwise, $\int_0^{c_D} \pi_D^l(c)dG(c) + \int_0^{c_X} \pi_X^l(c)dG(c) < f_E$, $N_E^l = 0$, and country l specializes in the numeraire. For the sake of parsimony, we rule out this case by assuming that α is large enough.

(22) can be re-written

$$L^l(c_D^l)^{k+2} + L^h \rho^h (c_D^h)^{k+2} = \gamma \phi,$$

where $\rho^l \equiv (\tau^l)^{-k} \in (0, 1)$ is an inverse measure of trade costs (the "freeness" of trade). This system (for $l = H, F$) can then be solved for the cut-offs in both countries:

$$c_D^l = \left[\frac{\gamma \phi}{L^l} \frac{1 - \rho^h}{1 - \rho^l \rho^h} \right]^{1/(k+2)}. \tag{23}$$

3.2. Prices, product variety, and welfare

The prices in country l reflect both the domestic prices of country-l firms, $p_D^l(c)$, and the prices of exporters from h, $p_X^h(c)$. Using (19) and (20), these prices can be written:

$$p_D^l(c) = \frac{1}{2}(p_{\max}^l + c), \ c \in [0, c_D^l],$$

$$p_X^h(c) = \frac{1}{2}(p_{\max}^l + \tau^l c), \ c \in [0, c_D^l / \tau^l],$$

where $p_{\max}^l$ is the price threshold defined in (18). In addition, the cost of domestic firms $c \in [0, c_D^l]$ and the delivered cost of exporters $\tau^l c \in [0, c_D^l]$ have identical distributions over this support, given by $G^l(c) = (c/c_D^l)^k$. The price distribution in country l of domestic firms producing in l, $p_D^l(c)$, and exporters producing in h, $p_X^h(c)$, are therefore also identical. The average price in country l is thus given by

$$\bar{p}^l = \frac{2k+1}{2k+2} c_D^l.$$

Combining this with the threshold price in (18) determines the number of firms selling in country l:

$$N^l = \frac{2(k+1)\gamma}{\eta} \frac{a - c_D^l}{c_D^l}. \tag{24}$$

These results for product variety and average prices are identical to the closed-economy case. This is driven by the matching price distributions of domestic firms and exporters in that market. Thus, welfare in country l can be written in an identical way to (17) as

$$U^l = 1 + \frac{1}{2\eta}(a - c_D^l)\left(a - \frac{k+1}{k+2} c_D^l\right). \tag{25}$$

Once again, welfare changes monotonically with the domestic cost cut-off, which captures the dominant effects of product variety and average prices.[14]

3.3. Number of entrants, producers, and exporters

The number of sellers (also indexing product variety) in country l is comprised of domestic producers and exporters from h. Given a positive mass of entrants N_E^l in both countries, there are $G(c_D^l)N_E^l$ domestic producers and $G(c_X^h)N_E^h$ exporters selling in l satisfying

---

14. The previously derived condition for the demand parameters α and η, and k again ensure that $q_0^l > 0$ as has been assumed.

$G(c_D^l)N_E^l + G(c_X^h)N_E^h = N^l$. This condition (holding for each country) can be solved for the number of entrants in each country:

$$N_E^l = \frac{(c_M)^k}{1 - \rho^l \rho^h} \left[\frac{N^l}{(c_D^l)^k} - \rho^l \frac{N^h}{(c_D^h)^k} \right]$$

$$= \frac{2(c_M)^k (k+1)\gamma}{\eta(1 - \rho^l \rho^h)} \left[\frac{\alpha - c_D^l}{(c_D^l)^{k+1}} - \rho^l \frac{\alpha - c_D^h}{(c_D^h)^{k+1}} \right]. \tag{26}$$

In the Appendix, we show that (26) further implies that $c_X^l < c_D^l$ in this non-specialized equilibrium ($N_E^l > 0$), so that only a subset of relatively more productive firms export. The remaining higher cost firms (with cost between c_X^l and c_D^l) only serve their domestic market. $G(c_D^l)N_E^l$ thus also represents the total number of firms producing in l (no firm produces in l without also serving its domestic market).

3.4. *Reciprocal dumping and arbitrage opportunities*

Brander and Krugman (1983) have shown that reciprocal dumping must occur in intra-industry trade equilibria under Cournot competition where representative firms produce a single homogeneous good in two countries. Ottaviano *et al.* (2002) show that dumping can also occur with differentiated products under monopolistic competition with representative firms. We extend this result to our current framework, where firms with heterogeneous costs produce differentiated varieties and face different residual demand elasticities.[15] Given the optimal price functions $p_D^l(c) = (c_D^l + c)/2$ and $p_X^l(c) = \tau^h(c_X^l + c)/2$ from (20), $c_X^l < c_D^l$ implies that $p_X^l(c)/\tau^h < p_D^l(c)$, $\forall c \geq c_X^l$. Therefore, all exporters set Free on Board (FOB) export prices (net of incurred trade costs) strictly below their prices in the domestic market. Thus, as emphasized by Weinstein (1992), dumping does not imply predatory pricing. Furthermore, as shown by Ottaviano *et al.* (2002), dumping need not be the outcome of oligopoly and strategic interactions between firms, which are absent in our model.

As described by Feenstra, Markusen and Rose (2001), dumping behaviour is closely linked to arbitrage conditions for the re-sale of goods across markets. This same link holds in our model, where dumping by exporters from country l ($p_X^l(c)/\tau^h < p_D^l(c)$) is equivalent to a no-arbitrage condition precluding the profitable export resale by a third party of a good produced and sold in country l. The dumping condition also precludes profitable resale of a good exported to country l, back in its origin country h ($p_D^h(c)/\tau^h < p_X^h(c)$).[16]

3.5. *The impact of trade*

We previously described how the distribution of the exporters' delivered cost $\tau^l c$ to country l matched the distribution of the domestic firms' cost c in country l. We then argued that this would lead to matching price distributions for both domestic firms in a country and exporters to that country. This argument extends to the distribution of all the other firm-level variables (markups, output, revenue, and profit). Thus, the distribution of all these firm performance measures in the open-economy equilibrium are identical to those in a closed-economy case with a matching

---

15. In related work, Holmes and Stevens (2004) show that the assumption of lower mark-ups in non-local markets, along with differences in transport costs across sectors, can explain cross-market differences in the size distribution of firms.

16. Since $p_X^h(c) = p_D^l(c\tau^l) > p_X^l(c\tau^l)/\tau^l = p_D^l(c\tau^l\tau^h)/\tau^h > p_D^h(c)/\tau^h$.

cost cut-off c_D. When analysing the impact of trade, we can therefore focus on the determination of the cost cut-off governed by (23).

Comparing this new cut-off condition to the one derived for the closed economy (15) immediately reveals that the cost cut-off is lower in the open economy: trade increases aggregate productivity by forcing the least productive firms to exit. This effect is similar to that analysed in Melitz (2003) but works through a different economic channel. In Melitz (2003), trade induces increased competition for scarce labour resources as real wages are bid up by the relatively more productive firms who expand production to serve the export markets. The increase in real wages forces the least productive firms to exit. In that model, import competition does not play a role in the reallocation process due to the CES specification for demand (residual demand price elasticities are exogenously fixed and unaffected by import competition). In the current model, the impact of these two channels—via increased factor market or product market competition—is reversed: increased product market competition is the only operative channel. Increased factor market competition plays no role in the current model, as the supply of labour to the differentiated goods sector is perfectly elastic. On the other hand, import competition increases competition in the domestic product market, shifting up residual demand price elasticities for all firms at any given demand level. This forces the least productive firms to exit. This effect is very similar to an increase in market size in the closed economy: the increased competition induces a downward shift in the distribution of mark-ups across firms. Although only relatively more productive firms survive (with higher mark-ups than the less productive firms who exit), the average mark-up is reduced. The distribution of prices shifts down due to the combined effect of selection and lower mark-ups. Again, as in the case of larger market size in a closed economy, average firm size and profits increase—as does product variety.[17] In this model, welfare gains from trade thus come from a combination of productivity gains (via selection), lower mark-ups (pro-competitive effect), and increased product variety.

3.6. Market size effects

We now focus on the consequences of market size differences for cross-country characteristics in the open-economy equilibrium. Once again, these cross-country differences in firm performance measures will be determined by the differences in the cost cut-offs c_D^l, as shown in (23). This immediately highlights how costly trade does not completely integrate markets as respective country size plays an important role in determining all firm performance measures and welfare in each country: When trade costs are symmetric ($\rho^l = \rho^h$), the larger country will have a lower cut-off, and thus higher average productivity and product variety, along with lower mark-ups and prices (relative to the smaller country). Welfare levels are thus higher in the larger country. Moreover, the latter will attract relatively more entrants and local producers. In short, all of the size-induced differences across countries in autarky persist (although not to the same extent). It is in this sense that costly trade does not completely integrate markets.

Surprisingly, (23) also indicates that the size of a country's trading partner does not affect the cost cut-off (and hence all firm performance measures and welfare). This highlights some important offsetting effects of trading partner size—although the exact outcome of these trade-offs are naturally influenced by our functional form assumptions. On the export side, a larger trading partner represents increased export market opportunities. However, this increased export market size is offset by its increased "competitiveness" (a greater number of more productive firms are competing in that market, driving down mark-ups). On the import side, a larger trading

17. Comparisons of changes in the variance of all performance measures are also identical to the case of increased market size.

partner represents an increased level of import competition. In the long run, this is offset by a smaller proportion of entrants, and hence less competition in the smaller market.[18]

3.7. *The open economy in the short run*

We now introduce the parallel version of the economy in the short run when it is open to trade. We will use this to separately identify the short- and long-run effects of liberalization in the following section. As was the case for the closed economy, no entry and exit is possible in the short run; incumbent firms decide whether to produce or shut-down. Each country l is thus characterized by a fixed number of incumbents $\bar{N}_D^l$ with cost distribution $\bar{G}^l(c)$ on $[0, \bar{c}_M^l]$. We continue to assume that productivity $1/c$ is distributed Pareto with shape k, implying $\bar{G}^l(c) = (c/\bar{c}_M^l)^k$. A firm produces if it can earn non-negative profits from sales to either its domestic or export market. This leads to cost cut-off conditions for sales in either market: $c_D^l = \sup\{c : \pi_D^l(c) \ge 0$ and $c \le \bar{c}_M^l\}$ and $c_X^l = \sup\{c : \pi_X^l(c) \ge 0$ and $c \le \bar{c}_M^l\}$.[19] Either of these cut-offs can reach their upper bound at $\bar{c}_M^l$, in which case all incumbent firms produce. So long as this is not the case, the cut-offs must satisfy the threshold price conditions in (24):

$$N^l = \frac{2(k+1)\gamma}{\eta} \frac{a - c_D^l}{c_D^l}, \quad \text{whenever } c_D^l < \bar{c}_M^l, \tag{27}$$

$$N^h = \frac{2(k+1)\gamma}{\eta} \frac{a - \tau^h c_X^l}{\tau^h c_X^l}, \quad \text{whenever } c_X^l < \bar{c}_M^l,$$

where N^l represents the endogenous number of sellers in country l in the short run. Note that $c_X^h = c_D^l/\tau^l$ as in the long run whenever both cut-offs are below their respective upper bounds $\bar{c}_M^h$ and $\bar{c}_M^l$.

There are $\bar{N}_D^l \bar{G}^l(c_D^l)$ producers from country l who sell in their domestic market and $\bar{N}_D^h \bar{G}^h(c_X^h)$ exporters from h to l. These numbers must add up to the total number of sellers in country l: $N^l = \bar{N}_D^l \bar{G}^l(c_D^l) + \bar{N}_D^h \bar{G}^h(c_X^h)$. Combining this with the threshold price conditions yield expressions for the cost cut-offs in both countries:

$$\frac{a - c_D^l}{(c_D^l)^{k+1}} = \frac{\eta}{2(k+1)\gamma} \left[\frac{\bar{N}_D^l}{(\bar{c}_M^l)^k} + \rho^l \frac{\bar{N}_D^h}{(\bar{c}_M^h)^k} \right], \quad \text{whenever } c_D^l < \bar{c}_M^l \text{ and } c_X^l < \bar{c}_M^l. \tag{28}$$

This condition clearly highlights the important role played by trading partner industrial size and import competition in the short run. An increase in the number of incumbents in country h increases import competition in country l and generates a decreases in the cost cut-off c_D^l, forcing some of the less productive firms in country l to shut down.[20] This effect is only offset with entry in the long run.

4. TRADE LIBERALIZATION

We have just shown how the firm location decision (driven by free entry in the long run) plays an important role in determining the extent of competition across markets in the open economy.

18. As highlighted by (26), differences in country size induce a larger proportion of entrants into the larger market. Equation (26) also indicates that country size differences must be bounded to maintain an equilibrium with incomplete specialization in the differentiated good sector. As country size differences become arbitrarily large, the number of entrants in the smaller country is driven to 0.

19. In the short run, it is possible for $c_X^l > c_D^l$, in which case firms with cost c in between these two cut-offs produce and export, but do not sell on their domestic market.

20. The overall number of sellers in country l (and hence product variety) increases as the increase in exporters from h dominates the decrease in domestic producers in l.

© 2008 The Review of Economic Studies Limited

MELITZ & OTTAVIANO   MARKET SIZE, TRADE, AND PRODUCTIVITY   309

This location decision also crucially affects the long-run consequences of trade liberalization—especially in situations where the decreases in trade barriers are asymmetric.

4.1. *Bilateral liberalization*

Before illustrating the consequences of asymmetric liberalization, we first quickly describe the case of symmetric liberalization. Here, we assume that trade costs are symmetric, $\tau^H = \tau^F = \tau$, and analyse the effects of decreases in τ (increases in $\rho^H = \rho^F = \rho$). In this case, the equilibrium cut-off condition (23) can be written:

$$c_D^l = \left[\frac{\gamma \phi}{L^l(1+\rho)} \right]^{1/(k+2)}. \tag{29}$$

Bilateral liberalization thus increases competition in both markets, leading to proportional changes in the cut-offs (and hence proportional increases in aggregate productivity) in both countries.[21] The effects of such liberalization are thus qualitatively identical to those described for the transition from autarky to the open economy: Product variety increases as a result of the increased competition, which also induces a decrease in mark-ups and prices. Again, welfare rises from a combination of higher productivity, lower mark-ups, and increased product variety.

Symmetric trade liberalization induces all of the same qualitative results in the short run. Although these effects do not depend on relative country size (so long as the differentiated good is produced in both countries), differences in country size nevertheless induce important changes in the relative pattern of entry in the long run following liberalization. Assuming $L^l > L^h$, the positive entry differential $N_E^l - N_E^h$ widens with liberalization as entry in the bigger market becomes relatively more attractive. This also induces a growing differential in the number of domestic producers $N_D^l - N_D^h$ (see Appendix for proofs).

4.2. *Unilateral liberalization*

We now describe the effects of a unilateral liberalization by country l (an increase in ρ^l, holding ρ^h constant). Given the cut-off condition (23), this leads to an increase in the cost cut-off c_D^l (less competition in the liberalizing country)—whereas the cut-off c_D^h in the country's trading partner decreases, indicating an increase in competition there. The liberalizing country thus experiences a welfare loss while its trading partner experiences a welfare gain.[22] As previously mentioned, these results are driven by the change in firm location induced by entry in the long run. Equation (26) indicates that the number of entrants N_E^l in the liberalizing country decreases, while the number of entrants in the other country, N_E^h, increases.

In order to isolate the direct impact of liberalization from the long-run effects generated by entry, we now turn to the short-run responses to unilateral liberalization by country l. The equilibrium condition (28) for the short-run cut-offs clearly shows that the cost cut-off c_D^l decreases in response to this liberalization—while the cost cut-off in h, c_D^h, remains unchanged. This highlights the pro-competitive effects of unilateral liberalization in the short run. Although the increase in import competition in l forces some of the least productive firms there to exit, product variety N^l nevertheless increases as the increased number of exporters to l dominates the decrease in domestic producers N_D^l (see (27)). Welfare in the liberalizing country (in the short

---

21. As indicated by (26), the number of entrants in the smaller economy is driven to 0 when trade costs drop below a threshold level—and the smaller economy no longer produces the differentiated good. We assume that trade costs remain above this threshold level.

22. Once again, the response of the cut-offs determines the response in all the other country level variables.

run) therefore rises from a combination of higher productivity, lower mark-ups, and increased product variety (welfare in the trading partner remains unchanged in the short run). These results clearly underline how the welfare loss associated with unilateral liberalization is driven by the shift in the pattern of entry (favouring the non-liberalizing trading partner) in the long run.

These long-run effects of liberalization on firm "de-location" have been extensively studied in previous work (see, for example, Venables, 1985, 1987; Horstmann and Markusen, 1986; and the synthesis in Helpman and Krugman, 1989, ch. 7; and Baldwin *et al.*, 2003, ch. 12). The novel features in our work show how this type of liberalization also affects firm selection, aggregate productivity, product variety, and mark-ups within a single model.[23]

4.3. Preferential liberalization

So far, our analysis has been restricted to two countries. This has generated a rich set of insights on the combined impact of market size and trade liberalization on industry performance and welfare. However, focusing on two countries in isolation neglects the effects of a country's position within an international trading network (which is determined by the whole matrix of bilateral trade barriers). When all trade barriers are symmetric, the insights of a multicountry model are a straightforward extension of the two-country case. However, new insights arise when bilateral barriers are allowed to differ.

While our model can easily deal with any number of countries of any size along with an arbitrary matrix of trade costs (see Appendix), considering three countries of equal size is enough to recover some of these related insights. We therefore introduce a third trading partner T, with $L^T = L^H = L^F = L$. Countries differ in terms of trade barriers that are assumed to be pairwise symmetric, with $\rho^{lh} = (\tau^{lh})^{-k} = (\tau^{hl})^{-k}$ measuring the "freeness" of trade between countries $l = \{H, F, T\}$ and $h \neq l$. Similarly, ρ^{lt} and ρ^{ht} measure the "freeness" of trade between l and h, and the third country $t \neq l \neq h$. As with the case of unilateral liberalization, preferential trade liberalization (non-proportional changes in these three bilateral trade barriers) induces important shifts in the pattern of entry across countries in the long run. Once again, we analyse both the long-run and short-run effects of such liberalization.

4.3.1. Long-run equilibrium. With three countries of equal size, the free entry condition (22) in country l becomes

$$(c_D^l)^{k+2} + \rho^{lh}(c_D^h)^{k+2} + \rho^{ht}(c_D^t)^{k+2} = \frac{\gamma \phi}{L} \quad l = \{H, F, T\}, \ t \neq l \neq h.$$

This provides a system of three linear equations in the three domestic cut-offs. When pairwise trade barriers are symmetric, the long-run cut-offs are given by

$$c_D^l = \left[\frac{\gamma \phi}{L} \frac{(1 - \rho^{ht})[1 + \rho^{ht} - (\rho^{lh} + \rho^{lt})]}{1 + 2\rho^{lh}\rho^{lt}\rho^{ht} - (\rho^{lh})^2 - (\rho^{lt})^2 - (\rho^{ht})^2} \right]^{1/(k+2)}. \tag{30}$$

The corresponding number of sellers N^l in country l is still given by (24), while the number of entrants solve $N_E^l + \rho^{lh}N_E^h + \rho^{lt}N_E^t = N^l(c_M/c_D^l)^k$.

In (30), international differences in cut-offs stem from the relative freeness measure $(1 - \rho^{ht})[1 + \rho^{ht} - (\rho^{lh} + \rho^{lt})]$, which implies that the cut-off is lowest in a country l with

---

23. Since most of the previous literature assumes representative firms, the link between trade policy and aggregate productivity (via firm selection into the domestic market) and product variety (via firm selection into export markets) is absent.

the lowest sum of bilateral barriers (highest $\rho^{lh} + \rho^{lt}$). In effect, this country is the best export base or "hub". Moreover, since ρ^{ht} enters the expression of the cut-off for country l, any change in bilateral trade costs affects all three countries. This has important implications for preferential trade agreements.[24] To see this as clearly as possible, consider three countries with initially symmetric trade barriers ($\rho^{lt} = \rho$). The initial cut-offs are then identical and equal to (see (30))

$$c_D = \left[\frac{\gamma\phi}{L} \frac{1}{1+2\rho} \right]^{1/(k+2)}. \tag{31}$$

A preferential trade agreement is then introduced between H and F, inducing $\rho^{HF} = \rho' > \rho = \rho^{FT} = \rho^{HT}$. The new trade regime affects the cut-offs for all countries. From (30), the cut-offs in the liberalizing countries are then

$$c_D^H = c_D^F = \left[\frac{\gamma\phi}{L} \frac{1-\rho}{1-2\rho^2+\rho'} \right]^{1/(k+2)}, \tag{32}$$

while the cut-off in the third country is given by

$$c_D^T = \left[\frac{\gamma\phi}{L} \frac{(1-\rho)+(\rho'-\rho)}{1-2\rho^2+\rho'} \right]^{1/(k+2)}. \tag{33}$$

The number of entrants in all three countries are given by (recall that $c_D^H = c_D^F$)

$$N_E^H = N_E^F = \frac{2(c_M)^k(k+1)\gamma}{\eta(1-2\rho^2+\rho')} \left[\frac{\alpha-c_D^H}{(c_D^H)^{k+1}} - \rho \frac{\alpha-c_D^T}{(c_D^T)^{k+1}} \right],$$

$$N_E^T = \frac{2(c_M)^k(k+1)\gamma}{\eta(1-2\rho^2+\rho')} \left[(1+\rho') \frac{\alpha-c_D^T}{(c_D^T)^{k+1}} - 2\rho \frac{\alpha-c_D^H}{(c_D^H)^{k+1}} \right].$$

Comparing (31)–(33), it is easily verified that preferential liberalization leads to lower cut-offs in the liberalizing countries and a higher cut-off in the third country. Thus, average costs, prices, and mark-ups also decrease in the liberalizing countries while they rise in the third country. The liberalizing countries become better "export bases": they gain better access to each other's market while maintaining the same ease of access to the third country's market. Thus, preferential liberalization leads to long-run welfare gains for the liberalizing countries, along with a welfare loss for the excluded country.

4.3.2. Short run. In order to highlight how the welfare loss in the third country is driven by the long-run shift in the pattern of entry, we briefly characterize the short-run response to the liberalization agreement between H and F. The short-run equilibrium in country l solves

$$\frac{\alpha-c_D^l}{(c_D^l)^{k+1}} = \frac{\eta}{2(k+1)\gamma} \left[\frac{\bar{N}_D^l}{(\bar{c}_M^l)^k} + \rho^{lh} \frac{\bar{N}_D^h}{(\bar{c}_M^h)^k} + \rho^{lt} \frac{\bar{N}_D^t}{(\bar{c}_M^t)^k} \right],$$

where the number of incumbents $\bar{N}_D^l$ and their productivity distribution on $[0, \bar{c}_M^l]$ are fixed in all countries, as in the previous short-run examples. When these numbers and distributions are symmetric (same $\bar{N}$ and $\bar{c}_M$), the country with the best accessibility (highest $\rho^{hl} + \rho^{lt}$) will have the lowest cut-off c_D^l. This country will have the lowest number of operating firms

---

24. In the Appendix, we show how such "third-country effect" can also be integrated in a gravity equation.

$N_D^l = \bar{N}_D^l G(c_D^l)$, but the highest number of sellers N^l (see (27)). Since the preferential liberalization between H and F does not affect accessibility to the third country ($\rho = \rho^{FT} = \rho^{HT}$), the cut-off in the latter is unaffected by the preferential liberalization in the short run. As in the case of unilateral liberalization, it is the long-run change in entry behaviour that is responsible for reduced competition and lower welfare in the excluded third country. On the other hand, the liberalizing countries gain in both the short run (via the direct pro-competitive effect) and the long run, when the pro-competitive effect is reinforced by the beneficial impact of increased entry.

5. CONCLUSION

We have presented a rich, though tractable, model that predicts how a wide set of industry performance measures (productivity, size, price, mark-up) respond to changes in the world trading environment. Our model incorporates heterogeneous firms and endogenous mark-ups that respond to the toughness of competition in a market. In such a setting, we show how market size induces important changes in industry performance measures: larger markets exhibit tougher competition resulting in lower average mark-ups and higher aggregate productivity. We also show how costly trade does not completely integrate markets and thus does not obviate these important consequences of market size differences across trading partners.

We then analyse several different trade liberalization scenarios. Our model highlights the pro-competitive effects of increased import competition and its effect on mark-ups, productivity, and product variety in the liberalized import market. Our model also echoes the findings in previous work that show how the short-run gains of asymmetric liberalization can be reversed by shifts in the pattern of entry in the long run. However, our model additionally incorporates the important feedbacks between entry and firm selection into domestic and export markets.

Although each of these individual channels for trade-induced gains have been previously analysed in models with different structures, we believe it is important to show how all of these channels can be captured within a single unified framework. This framework develops a new and very tractable way of describing how differences in market size and trade costs across trading partners affect the distribution of key firm-level performance measures across markets. We hope that this provides a useful foundation for future empirical investigations.

APPENDIX

A.1. Variance of firm performance measures

Let $\sigma_c^2 = \left[\int_0^{c_D} (c - \bar{c})^2 dG(c) \right] / G(c_D)$ denote the variance of the firm cost draws. As was mentioned earlier in the main text, the variance of all the firm performance measures can be written as simple expressions of this variance:

$$\sigma_p^2 = \tfrac{1}{4}\sigma_c^2, \; \sigma_q^2 = \tfrac{L^2}{4\gamma^2}\sigma_c^2,$$

$$\sigma_\mu^2 = \tfrac{1}{4}\sigma_c^2, \; \sigma_r^2 = \tfrac{L^2}{16\gamma^2}\sigma_{c^2}^2,$$

where $\sigma_z^2 = \left[\int_0^{c_D} [z(c) - \bar{z}]^2 dG(c) \right] / G(c_D)$ and $\bar{z}$ denote the variance and mean of a firm performance measure $z(c)$. Given the chosen parametrization for the cost draws, $\sigma_c^2 = [k/(k+1)^2(k+2)]c_D^2$.

A.2. Multiple countries, asymmetric trade costs, and comparative advantage

Our model can be readily extended to a setting with an arbitrary number of countries, asymmetric trade costs, and comparative advantage. Let M denote the number of countries, indexed by $l = 1, \ldots, M$. As in the main text $\rho^{lh} = (\tau^{lh})^{-k} \in (0, 1]$ measures the "freeness" of trade for exports from l to h. When trade costs are interpreted in a wide sense as all distance-related barriers, then within country trade may not be costless, and we allow for any $\rho^{ll} \in (0, 1]$. We introduce comparative advantage as technology differences that affect the distribution of the firm-level productivity

MELITZ & OTTAVIANO   MARKET SIZE, TRADE, AND PRODUCTIVITY   313

draws. For tractability, we assume that firm productivity $1/c$ is distributed Pareto with shape k in all countries, but allow for differences in the support of the distributions via differences in the upper-bound cost c_M^l. The cost draws in country l thus have a distribution $G^l(c) = (c/c_M^l)^k$. Whenever $c_M^l < c_M^h$, country l will have a comparative advantage with respect to country h in the differentiated good sector: entrants in country l have a better chance of getting higher productivity draws.[25]

In this extended model, the free entry condition (22) in country l becomes

$$\sum_{h=1}^{M} \rho^{lh} L^h (c_D^h)^{k+2} = \frac{2\gamma (k+1)(k+2) f_E}{\psi^l}, \quad l = 1, \ldots, M,$$

where $\psi^l = (c_M^l)^{-k}$ is an index of comparative advantage. This yields a system of M equations that can be solved for the M equilibrium domestic cut-offs using Cramer's rule:

$$c_D^l = \left(\frac{2(k+1)(k+2) f_E \gamma}{|P|} \frac{\sum_{h=1}^{M} |C_{hl}|/\psi^h}{L^l} \right)^{1/(k+2)}, \tag{A.1}$$

where $|P|$ is the determinant of the trade freeness matrix

$$P \equiv \begin{pmatrix} \rho_{11} & \rho_{12} & \cdots & \rho_{1M} \\ \rho_{21} & \rho_{22} & \cdots & \rho_{2M} \\ \vdots & \vdots & \ddots & \vdots \\ \rho_{M1} & \rho_{M2} & \cdots & \rho_{MM} \end{pmatrix},$$

and $|C_{hl}|$ is the cofactor of its ρ_{hl} element. Cross-country differences in cut-offs now arise from three sources: own country size (L^l), as well as a combination of market access and comparative advantage ($\sum_{h=1}^{M} |C_{hl}|/\psi^h$). Countries benefiting from a larger local market, a better distribution of productivity draws, and better market accessibility have lower cut-offs.

The mass of sellers N^l in each country l (including domestic producers in l and exporters to l) is still given by (24). Given a positive mass of entrants N_E^l in all countries, there are $G^l(c_D^l) N_E^l$ domestic producers and $\sum_{h \neq l} G^l(c_X^{hl}) N_E^h$ exporters selling in l, where c_X^{hl} is the export cut-off from h to l. This implies

$$\sum_{h=1}^{M} \rho^{hl} \psi^h N_E^h = \frac{N^l}{(c_D^l)^k}.$$

The latter provides a system of M linear equations that can be solved for the number of entrants in the M countries using Cramer's rule:[26]

$$N_E^l = \frac{2(k+1)\gamma}{\eta |P| \psi^l} \sum_{h=1}^{M} \frac{(\alpha - c_D^h)|C_{lh}|}{(c_D^h)^{k+1}}. \tag{A.2}$$

Given N_E^l entrants in country l, $N_E^l G^l(c_D^l)$ firms survive and produce for the local market. Among the latter, $N_E^l G^l(c_X^l)$ export to country h.

A.3. A gravity equation

Our multilateral model with heterogeneous firms, asymmetric trade costs, and comparative advantage also yields a gravity equation for aggregate bilateral trade flows. An exporter with cost c from country h generates export sales $r_X^{lh}(c) = p_X^{lh}(c) q_X^{lh}(c)$ where (see (19) and (20))

$$p_X^{lh}(c) = \frac{\tau^{lh}}{2} (c_X^h + c) = \frac{1}{2}(c_D^h + \tau^{lh} c),$$

$$q_X^{lh}(c) = \frac{L^h \tau^{lh}}{2\gamma} (c_X^h - c) = \frac{L^h}{2\gamma} (c_D^h - \tau^{lh} c).$$

25. The distribution of productivity draws in l stochastically dominates that in h.
26. We use the properties that relate the freeness matrix P and its transpose in terms of determinants and cofactors.

Aggregating these export sales $r_X^{lh}(c)$ over all exporters from l to h (with cost $c \le c_X^{lh}$) yields the aggregate bilateral exports from l to h:[27]

$$\mathrm{EXP}^{lh} = N_E^l \int_0^{c_X^{lh}} r_X^{lh}(c) dG^l(c)$$

$$= N_E^l \frac{L^h}{4\gamma} \int_0^{c_D^h/\tau^{lh}} [(c_D^h)^2 - (\tau^{lh}c)^2] dG^l(c)$$

$$= \frac{1}{2\gamma(k+2)} N_E^l \psi^l L^h (c_D^h)^{k+2} (\tau^{lh})^{-k}. \tag{A.3}$$

This gravity equation determines bilateral exports as a log-linear function of bilateral trade barriers and country characteristics. As in Eaton and Kortum (2002) and Helpman, Melitz and Rubinstein (2007), (A.3) reflects the joint effects of country size, technology (comparative advantage), and geography on both the extensive (number of traded goods) and intensive (amount traded per good) margins of trade flows. Similarly, (A.3) highlights how—holding the importing country size fixed—tougher competition in that country (lower average prices, reflected by a lower c_D^l) dampens exports by making it harder for potential exporters to break into that market.

A.4. *Selection into export markets*

In this section, we show that the assumption of a non-specialized equilibrium where both countries produce the differentiated good ($N_E^l > 0$, $l = H, F$) implies that only a subset of relatively more productive firms choose to export in either country ($c_X^l < c_D^l$, $l = H, F$). In the text, we showed that the number of entrants N_E^l satisfied (26). Thus,

$$N_E^l > 0 \iff \frac{a - c_D^l}{(c_D^l)^{k+1}} > \rho^l \frac{a - c_D^h}{(c_D^h)^{k+1}}$$

$$\iff \frac{a - c_D^l}{a - c_D^h} \left(\frac{c_D^h}{c_D^l} \right)^{k+1} > \rho^l$$

$$\iff \frac{\frac{a}{\tau^l} - c_X^h}{a - c_D^h} \left(\frac{c_D^h}{c_X^h} \right)^{k+1} > 1,$$

which is incompatible with $c_X^h \ge c_D^h$. Therefore, $c_X^h < c_D^h$ for $h = H, F$.

A.5. *Bilateral liberalization*

In this section, we prove a set of results for the two country model with different country sizes and symmetric trade barriers. Some results are already mentioned in the main text, while others complement the latter and provide a more detailed characterization of the effects of bilateral liberalization.

When trade barriers are symmetric, $\rho^l = \rho^h = \rho$, the number of entrants from (26) can be simplified to

$$N_E^l = \frac{(c_M)^k}{1 - \rho^2} \left[\frac{N^l}{(c_D^l)^k} - \rho \frac{N^h}{(c_D^h)^k} \right]. \tag{A.4}$$

Among these entrants, only

$$N_D^l = G(c_D^l) N_E^l = \left(\frac{c_D^l}{c_M} \right)^k N_E^l, \tag{A.5}$$

firms survive and produce. Without loss of generality, we assume $L^l > L^h$. The following results then apply:

1. The domestic cut-off is lower in the larger country: $c_D^l < c_D^h$.
   Proof. Follows directly from (29).

27. The integration measure $G^l(c_X^{lh})$ represents the proportion of entrants N_E^l in l that export to h.

2. There are more sellers in the larger country: $N^l > N^h$.
   Proof. Given 1, follows directly from (24).
3. There are more entrants in the larger country: $N^l_E > N^h_E$.
   Proof. Given 1 and 2, follows directly from (A.4).
4. There are more local producers in the larger country: $N^l_D > N^h_D$.
   Proof. Given (A.4) and (A.5),

$$N^l_D = \frac{1}{1-\rho^2}\left[N^l - \rho N^h \left(\frac{c^l_D}{c^h_D}\right)^k \right]. \tag{A.6}$$

The result then follows directly from 1 and 2.

5. Trade liberalization reduces the domestic cut-off differential: $d(c^h_D - c^l_D)/d\rho < 0$.
   Proof. Given (29), the result follows directly from

$$c^h_D - c^l_D = \left[\frac{\gamma\phi}{1+\rho}\left(\frac{1}{L^h} - \frac{1}{L^l}\right) \right]^{1/(k+2)} > 0.$$

6. Trade liberalization increases the cross-country difference in the number of sellers: $d(N^l - N^h)/d\rho > 0$.
   Proof. Given (29) and (27), the result follows directly from

$$N^l - N^h = \frac{2(k+1)\gamma\alpha}{\eta}\left(\frac{1}{c^l_D} - \frac{1}{c^h_D}\right)$$

$$= \frac{2(k+1)\gamma\alpha}{\eta}\left(\frac{1+\rho}{\gamma\phi}\right)^{1/(k+2)}\left[(L^l)^{1/(k+2)} - (L^h)^{1/(k+2)}\right] > 0.$$

7. Trade liberalization increases the cross-country difference in the number of entrants: $d(N^l_E - N^h_E)/d\rho > 0$.
   Proof. Given (29), (24), and (A.4),

$$N^l_E - N^h_E = \frac{(c_M)^k}{1-\rho}\left[\frac{N^l}{(c^l_D)^k} - \frac{N^h}{(c^h_D)^k} \right]$$

$$= \frac{2(k+1)\gamma}{\eta}\frac{(c_M)^k}{1-\rho}\left[\frac{\alpha-c^l_D}{(c^l_D)^{k+1}} - \frac{\alpha-c^h_D}{(c^h_D)^{k+1}} \right] > 0.$$

Then,

$$\frac{d(N^l_E - N^h_E)}{d\rho} = \frac{2(k+1)\gamma(c_M)^k}{\eta}\frac{1}{(1-\rho)^2}\left[\frac{\alpha-c^l_D}{(c^l_D)^{k+1}} - \frac{\alpha-c^h_D}{(c^h_D)^{k+1}} \right]$$

$$+ \frac{2(k+1)\gamma(c_M)^k}{\eta(k+2)}\frac{1}{(1+\rho)(1-\rho)}\left[\frac{\alpha(k+1)-kc^l_D}{(c^l_D)^{k+1}} - \frac{\alpha(k+1)-kc^h_D}{(c^h_D)^{k+1}} \right]$$

$$> 0.$$

8. Trade liberalization increases the cross-country difference in the number of producers: $d(N^l_D - N^h_D)/d\rho > 0$.
   Proof. Given (29) and (A.6),

$$N^l_D - N^h_D = \frac{1}{1-\rho^2}\left\{ N^l\left[1+\rho\left(\frac{c^h_D}{c^l_D}\right)^k\right] - N^h\left[1+\rho\left(\frac{c^l_D}{c^h_D}\right)^k\right] \right\}$$

$$= \frac{1}{1-\rho^2}\left\{ N^l\left[1+\rho\left(\frac{L^l}{L^h}\right)^{k/(k+2)}\right] - N^h\left[1+\rho\left(\frac{L^h}{L^l}\right)^{k/(k+2)}\right] \right\}.$$

Furthermore,

$$\frac{dN^l}{d\rho} = \frac{dN^l}{dc^l_D}\frac{dc^l_D}{d\rho} = \frac{2(k+1)\gamma\alpha}{\eta(k+2)}\frac{1}{c^l_D}\frac{1}{1+\rho},$$

$$\frac{dN^h}{d\rho} = \frac{dN^h}{dc^h_D}\frac{dc^h_D}{d\rho} = \frac{2(k+1)\gamma\alpha}{\eta(k+2)}\frac{1}{c^h_D}\frac{1}{1+\rho} < \frac{dN^l}{d\rho}.$$

Given $(L^l/L^h)^{k/(k+2)} > (L^h/L^l)^{k/(k+2)}$, then $d(N^l_D - N^h_D)/d\rho > 0$.

316   REVIEW OF ECONOMIC STUDIES

Acknowledgements.   We are grateful to Richard Baldwin, Alejandro Cunat, Gilles Duranton, Rob Feenstra, Elhanan Helpman, Tom Holmes, Alireza Naghavi, Diego Puga, Jacques Thisse, Jim Tybout, Alessandro Turrini, Tony Venables, and Zhihong Yu for helpful comments and discussions. The final draft also greatly benefited from three anonymous referee reports and comments from the editor. Ottaviano thanks MIUR and the European Commission for financial support. Melitz thanks the NSF and the Sloan Foundation for financial support.

REFERENCES

ASPLUND, M. and NOCKE, V. (2006), "Firm Turnover in Imperfectly Competitive Markets", *Review of Economic Studies*, **73**, 295–327.
AW, B. Y., CHUNG, S. and ROBERTS, M. J. (2000), "Productivity and Turnover in the Export Market: Micro-level Evidence from the Republic of Korea and Taiwan (China)", *World Bank Economic Review*, **14**, 65–90.
BALDWIN, R. E., MARTIN, P., OTTAVIANO, G. and ROBERT-NICOUD, F. (2003), *Economic Geography and Public Policy* (Princeton, NJ: Princeton University Press).
BERNARD, A. B., EATON, J., JENSEN, J. B. and KORTUM, S. (2003), "Plants and Productivity in International Trade", *American Economic Review*, **93**, 1268–1290.
BERNARD, A. and JENSEN, B. (1999), "Exceptional Exporter Performance: Cause, Effect, or Both?", *Journal of International Economics*, **47**, 1–25.
BERNARD, A. B., JENSEN, J. B. and SCHOTT, P. K. (2006), "Trade Costs, Firms and Productivity", *Journal of Monetary Economics*, **53**, 917–937.
BRANDER, J. and KRUGMAN, P. (1983), "A 'Reciprocal Dumping' Model of International Trade", *Journal of International Economics*, **15**, 313–321.
CAMPBELL, J. and HOPENHAYN, H. (2005), "Market Size Matters", *Journal of Industrial Economics*, **53**, 1–25.
CLERIDES, S. K., LACH, S. and TYBOUT, J. R. (1998), "Is Learning by Exporting Important? Micro-dynamic Evidence from Colombia, Mexico, and Morocco", *The Quarterly Journal of Economics*, **113**, 903–947.
COMBES, P., DURANTON, G., GOBILLON, L., PUGA, D. and ROUX, S. (2007), "The Productivity Advantage of Large Markets: Distinguishing Agglomeration from Firm Selection" (Mimeo, University of Toronto).
DEL GATTO, M., MION, G. and OTTAVIANO, G. I. P. (2006), "Trade Integration, Firm Selection and the Costs of Non-Europe" (Mimeo, University of Bologna).
EATON, J. and KORTUM, S. (2002), "Technology, Geography, and Trade", *Econometrica*, **70**, 1741–1779.
FEENSTRA, R., MARKUSEN, J. and ROSE, A. (2001), "Using the Gravity Equation to Differentiate Among Alternative Theories of Trade", *Canadian Journal of Economics*, **34**, 430–447.
HELPMAN, E. and KRUGMAN, P. (1989), *Trade Policy and Market Structure* (Cambridge, MA: MIT Press).
HELPMAN, E., MELITZ, M. J. and RUBINSTEIN, Y. (2007), "Estimating Trade Flows: Trading Partners and Trading Volumes" (NBER Working Paper No. 12927, National Bureau of Economic Research).
HOLMES, T. and STEVENS, J. (2004), "Geographic Concentration and Establishment Size: Analysis in an Alternative Economic Geography Model", *Journal of Economic Geography*, **4**, 227–250.
HORSTMANN, I. J. and MARKUSEN, J. R. (1986), "Up the Average Cost Curve: Inefficient Entry and the New Protectionism", *Journal of International Economics*, **20**, 225–247.
KRUGMAN, P. R. (1979), "Increasing Returns, Monopolistic Competition, and International Trade", *Journal of International Economics*, **9**, 469–479.
KRUGMAN, P. R. (1980), "Scale Economies, Product Differentiation, and the Pattern of Trade", *American Economic Review*, **70**, 950–959.
MARKUSEN, J. R. (1981), "Trade and the Gains from Trade with International Competition", *Journal of International Economics*, **11**, 531–551.
MELITZ, M. J. (2003), "The Impact of Trade on Intra-Industry Reallocations and Aggregate Industry Productivity", *Econometrica*, **71**, 1695–1725.
OTTAVIANO, G. I. P., TABUCHI, T. and THISSE, J.-F. (2002), "Agglomeration and Trade Revisited", *International Economic Review*, **43**, 409–436.
PAVCNIK, N. (2002), "Trade Liberalization, Exit, and Productivity Improvements: Evidence from Chilean Plants", *Review of Economic Studies*, **69**, 245–276.
SYVERSON, C. (2004), "Market Structure and Productivity: A Concrete Example", *Journal of Political Economy*, **112**, 1181–1222.
SYVERSON, C. "Prices, Spatial Competition, and Heterogeneous Producers: An Empirical Test" (forthcoming in *Journal of Industrial Economics*).
TYBOUT, J. (2002), "Plant and Firm-Level Evidence on New Trade Theories", in J. Harrigan (ed.) *Handbook of International Economics*, Vol. 38 (Oxford: Basil-Blackwell) 388–415.
VENABLES, A. J. (1985), "Trade and Trade Policy with Imperfect Competition: The Case of Identical Products and Free Entry", *Journal of International Economics*, **19**, 1–19.
VENABLES, A. J. (1987), "Trade and Trade Policy with Differentiated Products: A Chamberlinian-Ricardian Model", *Economic Journal*, **97**, 700–717.
WEINSTEIN, D. (1992), "Competition and Unilateral Dumping", *Journal of International Economics*, **32**, 379–388.

Chapter 5

Market Size, Competition, and
the Product Mix of Exporters[†,§]

By THIERRY MAYER, MARC J. MELITZ, AND GIANMARCO I. P. OTTAVIANO*

We build a theoretical model of multi-product firms that highlights how competition across market destinations affects both a firm's exported product range and product mix. We show how tougher competition in an export market induces a firm to skew its export sales toward its best performing products. We find very strong confirmation of this competitive effect for French exporters across export market destinations. Theoretically, this within-firm change in product mix driven by the trading environment has important repercussions on firm productivity. A calibrated fit to our theoretical model reveals that these productivity effects are potentially quite large. (JEL D21, D24, F13, F14, F41, L11)

Exports by multi-product firms dominate world trade flows. Variations in these trade flows across destinations reflect in part the decisions by multi-product firms to vary the range of their exported products across destinations with different market conditions.[1] In this paper, we further analyze the effects of those export market conditions on the *relative* export sales of those goods: we refer to this as the firm's product mix choice. We build a theoretical model of multi-product firms that highlights how market size and geography (the market sizes of, and bilateral economic distances to, trading partners) affect both a firm's exported product range and its exported product mix across market destinations. Differences in market sizes and geography generate differences in the toughness of competition across markets. Tougher competition shifts down the entire distribution of markups across products and induces firms to skew their export sales toward their better performing products. We find very strong confirmation of this competitive effect for French exporters

*Mayer: Sciences-Po, 28 rue des Saints-Pères, 75007 Paris, France, CEPII, and CEPR (e-mail: thierry.mayer@sciences-po.fr); Melitz: Department of Economics, Harvard University, Cambridge, MA 02138, CEPR, and NBER (e-mail: mmelitz@harvard.edu); Ottaviano: London School of Economics, Houghton Street, London WC2A 2AE, United Kingdom, CEP, and CEPR (e-mail: g.i.ottaviano@lse.ac.uk). This paper is produced as part of the project "European firms in a global economy: Internal policies for external competitiveness" (EFIGE), a collaborative project funded by the European Commission's Seventh Research Framework Programme, Contract #225551. The views expressed in this publication are the sole responsibility of the authors and do not necessarily reflect the views of the European Commission. We thank the French customs administration and CNIS for making the exports data available at CEPII. We thank two anonymous referees, Philippe Martin, Giordano Mion, Peter Neary, Steve Redding, and Dan Trefler for helpful comments and suggestions. We are also grateful to seminar participants for all the useful feedback we received. Ottaviano thanks Bocconi University, CEP, MIUR, and the European Commission for financial support. Melitz thanks the Sloan Foundation for financial support. Melitz and Ottaviano thank Sciences Po and CEPII for their hospitality while part of this paper was written.

†Go to http://dx.doi.org/10.1257/aer.104.2.495 to visit the article page for additional materials and author disclosure statement(s).

[1] See Mayer and Ottaviano (2008) for Europe, Bernard et al. (2007) for the United States, and Arkolakis and Muendler (2010) for Brazil.

495

across export market destinations. Our theoretical model shows how this effect of export market competition on a firm's product mix then translates into differences in measured firm productivity: when a firm skews its production toward better performing products, it also allocates relatively more workers to the production of those goods and raises its overall output (and sales) per worker. Thus, a firm producing a given set of products with given unit input requirements will produce relatively more output and sales per worker (across products) when it exports to markets with tougher competition. To our knowledge, this is a new channel through which competition (both in export markets and at home) affects firm-level productivity. This effect of competition on firm-level productivity is compounded by another channel that operates through the endogenous response of the firm's product range: firms respond to increased competition by dropping their worst performing products.[2]

Feenstra and Ma (2008) and Eckel and Neary (2010) also build theoretical models of multi-product firms that highlight the effect of competition on the distribution of firm product sales. Both models incorporate the cannibalization effect that occurs as large firms expand their product range. In our model, we rely on the competition effects from the demand side, which are driven by variations in the number of sellers and their average prices across export markets. The cannibalization effect does not occur as a continuum of firms each produce a discrete number of products and thus never attain finite mass. The benefits of this simplification is that we can consider an open economy equilibrium with multiple asymmetric countries and asymmetric trade barriers whereas Feenstra and Ma (2008) and Eckel and Neary (2010) restrict their analysis to a single globalized world with no trade barriers. Thus, our model is able to capture the key role of geography in shaping differences in competition across export market destinations.[3]

Another approach to the modeling of multi-product firms relies on a nested CES structure for preferences, where a continuum of firms produce a continuum of products. The cannibalization effect is ruled out by restricting the nests in which firms can introduce new products. Allanson and Montagna (2005) consider such a model in a closed economy, while Arkolakis and Muendler (2010) and Bernard, Redding, and Schott (2011) develop extensions to open economies. Given the CES structure of preferences and the continuum assumptions, markups across all firms and products are exogenously fixed. Thus, differences in market conditions or proportional reductions in trade costs have no effect on a firm's product mix choice (the relative distribution of export sales across products). In contrast, variations in markups across destinations (driven by differences in competition) generate differences in relative exports across destinations in our model: a given firm selling the same two products across different markets will export relatively more of the better performing product in markets where competition is tougher. In our comprehensive data

---

[2] Bernard, Redding, and Schott (2011) and Eckel and Neary (2010) emphasize this second channel. They show how trade liberalization between symmetric countries induces firms to drop their worst performing products (a focus on core competencies) leading to intra-firm productivity gains. We discuss those papers in further detail below.

[3] Nocke and Yeaple (2006) and Baldwin and Gu (2009) also develop models with multi-product firms and a pro-competitive effect coming from the demand side. These models investigate the effects of globalization on a firm's product scope and average production levels per product. However, those models consider the case of firms producing symmetric products whereas we focus on the effects of competition on the within-firm distribution of product sales.

VOL. 104 NO. 2   *MAYER ET AL.: MARKET SIZE, COMPETITION, AND PRODUCT MIX*   *497*

covering nearly all French exports, we find that there is substantial variation in this relative export ratio across French export destinations, and that this variation is consistently related to differences in market size and geography across those destinations (market size and geography both affect the toughness of competition across destinations). French exporters substantially skew their export sales toward their better performing products in markets where they face tougher competition.

Theoretically, we show how this effect of tougher competition in an export market on the exported product mix is also associated with an increase in productivity for the set of exported products to that market. We show how firm-level measures of exported output per worker as well as deflated sales per worker for a given export destination (counting only the exported units to a given destination and the associated labor used to produce those units) increase with tougher competition in that destination. This effect of competition on firm productivity holds even when one fixes the set of products exported, thus eliminating any potential effects from the extensive (product) margin of trade. Then, the firm-level productivity increase is entirely driven by the response of the firm's product mix: producing relatively more of the better performing products raises measured firm productivity. We use our theoretical model to calibrate the relationship between the skewness of the French exporters' product mix and a productivity average for those exporters. We find that our measured variation in product mix skewness across destinations corresponds to large differences in productivity. The effect of a doubling of destination country GDP on the French exporters' product mix corresponds to a measured productivity differential between 4 percent and 7 percent.

Our model also features a response of the extensive margin of trade: tougher competition in the domestic market induces firms to reduce the set of produced products, and tougher competition in an export market induces exporters to reduce the set of exported products. We do not emphasize these results for the extensive margin because they are quite sensitive to the specification of fixed production and export costs. In order to maintain the tractability of our multi-country asymmetric open economy, we abstract from those fixed costs (increasing returns are generated uniquely from the fixed/sunk entry cost). Conditional on the production and export of given sets of products, such fixed costs would not affect the relative production or export levels of those products. These are the product mix outcomes that we emphasize (and for which we find strong empirical support).

Although we focus our empirical analysis on these novel cross-sectional predictions, our model also predicts extensive and intensive margin responses over time to multilateral trade liberalization. Such liberalization induces an increase in the toughness of competition in each country. In response, firms reduce the number of products they produce and skew production and sales (in each destination) toward their better performing products. These firm-level responses have all been documented in recent empirical work on the effects of trade liberalization in North America. Baldwin and Gu (2009); Bernard, Redding, and Schott (2011), and Iacovone and Javorcik (2008) all report that (respectively) Canadian, US, and Mexican firms have reduced the number of products they produce during these trade-liberalization episodes. Baldwin and Gu (2009) and Bernard, Redding, and Schott (2011) further report that the Canada-United States Free Trade Agreement (CUSFTA) induced a significant increase in the skewness of production across products (an increase

498 *THE AMERICAN ECONOMIC REVIEW* FEBRUARY 2014

in entropy). Iacovone and Javorcik (2008) separately measure the skewness of Mexican firms' export sales to the United States. They report an increase in this skewness following NAFTA: they show that Mexican firms expanded their exports of their better performing products (higher market shares) significantly more than those for their worse performing exported products during the period of trade expansion from 1994–2003.

Our paper proceeds as follows. We first develop a closed economy version of our model in order to focus on the endogenous responses of a firm's product scope and product mix to market conditions. We highlight how competition affects the skewness of a firm's product mix, and how this translates into differences in firm productivity. Thus, even in a closed economy, increases in market size lead to increases in within-firm productivity via this product mix response. We then develop the open economy version of our model with multiple asymmetric countries and an arbitrary matrix of bilateral trade costs. The equilibrium connects differences in market size and geography to the toughness of competition in every market, and how the latter shapes a firm's exported product mix to that destination. We then move on to our empirical test for this exported product mix response for French firms. We show how destination market size as well as its geography induce increased skewness in the firms' exported product mix to that destination. In the last section before concluding we quantify the economic significance of those measured differences in export skewness for productivity.

I. Closed Economy

Our model is based on an extension of Melitz and Ottaviano (2008) that allows firms to endogenously determine the set of products that they produce. We start with a closed economy version of this model where L consumers each supply one unit of labor.

A. Preferences and Demand

Preferences are defined over a continuum of differentiated varieties indexed by $i \in \Omega$, and a homogenous good chosen as numeraire. All consumers share the same utility function given by

$$(1) \quad U = q_0^c + \alpha \int_{i \in \Omega} q_i^c \, di - \frac{1}{2} \gamma \int_{i \in \Omega} (q_i^c)^2 \, di - \frac{1}{2} \eta \left(\int_{i \in \Omega} q_i^c \, di \right)^2,$$

where q_0^c and q_i^c represent the individual consumption levels of the numeraire good and each variety i. The demand parameters α, η, and γ are all positive. The parameters α and η index the substitution pattern between the differentiated varieties and the numeraire: increases in α and decreases in η both shift out the demand for the differentiated varieties relative to the numeraire. The parameter γ indexes the degree of product differentiation between the varieties. In the limit when $\gamma = 0$, consumers only care about their consumption level over all varieties, $Q^c = \int_{i \in \Omega} q_i^c \, di$, and the varieties are then perfect substitutes. The degree of product differentiation increases with γ as consumers give increasing weight to smoothing consumption levels across varieties.

VOL. 104 NO. 2 *MAYER ET AL.: MARKET SIZE, COMPETITION, AND PRODUCT MIX* *499*

Our specification of preferences intentionally does not distinguish between the varieties produced by the same firm relative to varieties produced by other firms. We do not see any clear reason to enforce that varieties produced by a firm be closer substitutes than varieties produced by different firms—or vice-versa. Of course, some firms operate across sectors, in which case the varieties produced in different sectors would be more differentiated than varieties produced by other firms within the same sector. We eliminate those cross-sector, within-firm, varieties in our empirical work by restricting our analysis to the range of varieties produced by a firm within a sector classification.

The marginal utilities for all varieties are bounded, and a consumer may not have positive demand for any particular variety. We assume that consumers have positive demand for the numeraire good ($q_0^c > 0$). The inverse demand for each variety i is then given by

$$(2) \qquad p_i = \alpha - \gamma q_i^c - \eta Q^c,$$

whenever $q_i^c > 0$. Let $\Omega^* \subset \Omega$ be the subset of varieties that are consumed (such that $q_i^c > 0$). Equation (2) can then be inverted to yield the linear market demand system for these varieties:

$$(3) \qquad q_i \equiv L q_i^c = \frac{\alpha L}{\eta M + \gamma} - \frac{L}{\gamma} p_i + \frac{\eta M}{\eta M + \gamma} \frac{L}{\gamma} \bar{p}, \qquad \forall i \in \Omega^*,$$

where M is the measure of consumed varieties in Ω^* and $\bar{p} = (1/M) \int_{i\in\Omega^*} p_i di$ is their average price. The set Ω^* is the largest subset of Ω that satisfies

$$(4) \qquad p_i \leq \frac{1}{\eta M + \gamma} (\gamma \alpha + \eta M \bar{p}) \equiv p^{\text{max}},$$

where the right-hand-side price bound p^{max} represents the price at which demand for a variety is driven to zero. Note that (2) implies $p^{\text{max}} \leq \alpha$. In contrast to the case of CES demand, the price elasticity of demand, $\varepsilon_i \equiv |(\partial q_i/\partial p_i)(p_i/q_i)| = [(p^{\text{max}}/p_i) - 1]^{-1}$, is not uniquely determined by the level of product differentiation γ. Given the latter, lower average prices $\bar{p}$ or a larger number of competing varieties M induce a decrease in the price bound p^{max} and an increase in the price elasticity of demand ε_i at any given p_i. We characterize this as a "tougher" competitive environment.[4]

Welfare can be evaluated using the indirect utility function associated with (1):

$$(5) \qquad U = I^c + \frac{1}{2}\left(\eta + \frac{\gamma}{M}\right)^{-1}(\alpha - \bar{p})^2 + \frac{1}{2}\frac{M}{\gamma}\sigma_p^2,$$

where I^c is the consumer's income and $\sigma_p^2 = (1/M) \int_{i\in\Omega^*} (p_i - \bar{p})^2 di$ represents the variance of prices. To ensure positive demand levels for the numeraire,

---

[4] We also note that, given this competitive environment (given N and $\bar{p}$), the price elasticity ε_i monotonically increases with the price p_i along the demand curve.

we assume that $I^c > \int_{i\in\Omega^*} p_i\, q_i^c\, di = \overline{p}\, Q^c - M\sigma_p^2/\gamma$. Welfare naturally rises with decreases in average prices $\overline{p}$. It also rises with increases in the variance of prices σ_p^2 (holding the mean price $\overline{p}$ constant), as consumers then re-optimize their purchases by shifting expenditures toward lower priced varieties as well as the numeraire good.[5] Finally, the demand system exhibits "love of variety": holding the distribution of prices constant (namely holding the mean $\overline{p}$ and variance σ_p^2 of prices constant), welfare rises with increases in product variety M.

B. *Production and Firm Behavior*

Labor is the only factor of production and is inelastically supplied in a competitive market. The numeraire good is produced under constant returns to scale at unit cost; its market is also competitive. These assumptions imply a unit wage. Entry in the differentiated product sector is costly as each firm incurs product development and production startup costs. Subsequent production of each variety exhibits constant returns to scale. While it may decide to produce more than one variety, each firm has one key variety corresponding to its "core competency." This is associated with a core marginal cost c (equal to unit labor requirement).[6] Research and development yield uncertain outcomes for c, and firms learn about this cost level only after making the irreversible investment f_E required for entry. We model this as a draw from a common (and known) distribution $G(c)$ with support on $[0, c_M]$.

A firm can introduce any number of new varieties, but each additional variety entails an additional customization cost as it pulls a firm away from its core competency. This entails incrementally higher marginal costs of production for those varieties. The divergence from a firm's core competency may also be reflected in diminished product quality/appeal. For simplicity, we maintain product symmetry on the demand side and capture any decrease in product appeal as an increased production cost. We refer to this incremental production cost as a customization cost.

We index by m the varieties produced by the same firm in increasing order of distance from their core competency $m = 0$ (the firm's core variety). We then denote $v(m, c)$ the marginal cost for variety m produced by a firm with core marginal cost c and assume $v(m, c) = \omega^{-m}c$ with $\omega \in (0, 1)$. This defines a firm-level "competence ladder" with geometrically increasing customization costs. This modeling approach is isomorphic to one where we label the product ladder as reflecting decreasing quality/product appeal and insert the geometric term as a preference parameter multiplying quantities in the utility function (1). Our modeling approach also nests the case of single-product firms as the geometric step size becomes arbitrarily large (ω goes to zero); firms will then only be able to produce their core variety.

Since the entry cost is sunk, firms that can cover the marginal cost of their core variety survive and produce. All other firms exit the industry. Surviving firms maximize their profits using the residual demand function (3). In so doing, those firms take the average price level $\overline{p}$ and total number of varieties M as given.

---

[5] This welfare measure reflects the reduced consumption of the numeraire to account for the labor resources used to cover the entry costs.

[6] We use the same concept of a firm's core competency as Eckel and Neary (2010). For simplicity, we do not model any fixed production costs. This would significantly increase the complexity of our model without yielding much new insight.

VOL. 104 NO. 2   *MAYER ET AL.: MARKET SIZE, COMPETITION, AND PRODUCT MIX*   *501*

This monopolistic competition outcome is maintained with multi-product firms as any firm can only produce a countable number of products, which is a subset of measure zero of the total mass of varieties M.

The profit maximizing price $p(v)$ and output level $q(v)$ of a variety with cost v must then satisfy

$$(6) \qquad q(v) = \frac{L}{\gamma}[p(v) - v].$$

The profit maximizing price $p(v)$ may be above the price bound $p^{\max}$ from (4), in which case the variety is not supplied. Let v_D reference the cutoff cost for a variety to be profitably produced. This variety earns zero profit as its price is driven down to its marginal cost, $p(v_D) = v_D = p^{\max}$, and its demand level $q(v_D)$ is driven to zero. Let $r(v) = p(v)q(v)$, $\pi(v) = r(v) - q(v)v$, $\lambda(v) = p(v) - v$ denote the revenue, profit, and (absolute) markup of a variety with cost v. All these performance measures can then be written as functions of v and v_D only:[7]

$$(7) \qquad p(v) = \frac{1}{2}(v_D + v),$$

$$\lambda(v) = \frac{1}{2}(v_D - v),$$

$$q(v) = \frac{L}{2\gamma}(v_D - v),$$

$$r(v) = \frac{L}{4\gamma}[(v_D)^2 - v^2],$$

$$\pi(v) = \frac{L}{4\gamma}(v_D - v)^2.$$

The threshold cost v_D thus summarizes the competitive environment for the performance measures of all produced varieties. As expected, lower cost varieties have lower prices and earn higher revenues and profits than varieties with higher costs. However, lower cost varieties do not pass on all of the cost differential to consumers in the form of lower prices: they also have higher markups (in both absolute and relative terms) than varieties with higher costs.[8]

Firms with core competency $v > v_D$ cannot profitably produce their core variety and exit. Hence, $c_D = v_D$ is also the cutoff for firm survival and measures the "toughness" of competition in the market: it is a sufficient statistic for all

---

[7] Given the absence of cannibalization motive, these variety level performance measures are identical to the single product case studied in Melitz and Ottaviano (2008). This tractability allows us to analytically solve the closed and open equilibria with heterogenous firms (and asymmetric countries in the open economy).

[8] De Loecker et al. (2012) find empirical support for these properties, both across and within firms, in the case of Indian multi-product firms.

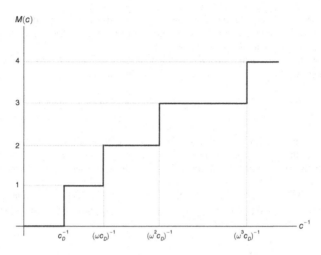

FIGURE 1. NUMBER OF VARIETIES PRODUCED AS A FUNCTION OF FIRM PRODUCTIVITY

performance measures across varieties and firms.[9] We assume that c_M is high enough that it is always above c_D, so exit rates are always positive. All firms with core cost $c < c_D$ earn positive profits (gross of the entry cost) on their core varieties and remain in the industry. Some firms will also earn positive profits from the introduction of additional varieties. In particular, firms with cost c such that $v(m, c) \leq v_D \Leftrightarrow c \leq \omega^m c_D$ earn positive profits on their mth *additional* variety and thus produce at least $m + 1$ varieties. The total number of varieties produced by a firm with cost c is

$$
(8) \qquad M(c) = \begin{cases} 0 & \text{if } c > c_D, \\ \max\{m \,|\, c \leq \omega^m c_D\} + 1 & \text{if } c \leq c_D, \end{cases}
$$

which is (weakly) decreasing for all $c \in [0, c_M]$. Accordingly, the number of varieties produced by a firm with cost c is indeed an integer number (and not a mass with positive measure). This number is an increasing step function of the firm's productivity $1/c$, as depicted in Figure 1. Firms with higher core productivity thus produce (weakly) more varieties.

Given a mass of entrants N_E, the distribution of costs across all varieties is determined by the optimal firm product range choice $M(c)$ as well as the distribution of core competencies $G(c)$. Let $M_v(v)$ denote the measure function for varieties (the measure of varieties produced at cost v or lower, given N_E entrants). Further define $H(v) \equiv M_v(v)/N_E$ as the normalized measure of varieties per unit mass of

---

[9] We will see shortly how the average price of all varieties and the number of varieties is uniquely pinned-down by this cutoff.

VOL. 104 NO. 2   *MAYER ET AL.: MARKET SIZE, COMPETITION, AND PRODUCT MIX*   503

entrants. Then $H(v) = \sum_{m=0}^{\infty} G(\omega^m v)$ and is exogenously determined from $G(\cdot)$ and ω. Given a unit mass of entrants, there will be a mass $G(v)$ of varieties with cost v or less; a mass $G(\omega v)$ of first additional varieties (with cost v or less); a mass $G(\omega^2 v)$ of second additional varieties; and so forth. The measure $H(v)$ sums over all these varieties.

C. *Free Entry and Equilibrium*

Prior to entry, the expected firm profit is $\int_0^{c_D} \Pi(c) \, dG(c) - f_E$ where

$$(9) \qquad \Pi(c) \equiv \sum_{m=0}^{M(c)-1} \pi(v(m, c))$$

denotes the profit of a firm with cost c. If this profit were negative for all cs, no firms would enter the industry. As long as some firms produce, the expected profit is driven to zero by the unrestricted entry of new firms. This yields the equilibrium free entry condition:

$$(10) \qquad \int_0^{c_D} \Pi(c) \, dG(c) = \int_0^{c_D} \left[\sum_{\{m \mid \omega^{-m} c \leq c_D\}} \pi(\omega^{-m} c) \right] dG(c)$$

$$= \sum_{m=0}^{\infty} \left[\int_0^{\omega^m c_D} \pi(\omega^{-m} c) \, dG(c) \right] = f_E,$$

where the second equality first averages over the mth produced variety by all firms, then sums over m.

The free entry condition (10) determines the cost cutoff $c_D = v_D$. This cutoff, in turn, determines the aggregate mass of varieties, since $v_D = p(v_D)$ must also be equal to the zero demand price threshold in (4):

$$v_D = \frac{1}{\eta M + \gamma} (\gamma \alpha + \eta M \bar{p}).$$

The aggregate mass of varieties is then

$$M = \frac{2\gamma}{\eta} \frac{\alpha - v_D}{v_D - \bar{v}},$$

where the average cost of all varieties,

$$\bar{v} = \frac{1}{M} \int_0^{v_D} v \, dM_v(v) = \frac{1}{N_E H(v_D)} \int_0^{v_D} v N_E \, dH(v) = \frac{1}{H(v_D)} \int_0^{v_D} v \, dH(v),$$

504   THE AMERICAN ECONOMIC REVIEW   FEBRUARY 2014

depends only on v_D.[10] Similarly, this cutoff also uniquely pins down the average price across all varieties:

$$\bar{p} = \frac{1}{M} \int_0^{v_D} p(v) \, dM_v(v) = \frac{1}{H(v_D)} \int_0^{v_D} p(v) \, dH(v).$$

Finally, the mass of entrants is given by $N_E = M/H(v_D)$, which can in turn be used to obtain the mass of producing firms $N = N_E G(c_D)$.

D. Parametrization of Technology

All the results derived so far hold for any distribution of core cost draws $G(c)$. However, in order to simplify some of the ensuing analysis, we use a specific parametrization for this distribution. In particular, we assume that core productivity draws $1/c$ follow a Pareto distribution with lower productivity bound $1/c_M$ and shape parameter $k \geq 1$. This implies a distribution of cost draws c given by

(11) $$G(c) = \left(\frac{c}{c_M}\right)^k, \quad c \in [0, c_M].$$

The shape parameter k indexes the dispersion of cost draws. When $k = 1$, the cost distribution is uniform on $[0, c_M]$. As k increases, the relative number of high cost firms increases, and the cost distribution is more concentrated at these higher cost levels. As k goes to infinity, the distribution becomes degenerate at c_M. Any truncation of the cost distribution from above will retain the same distribution function and shape parameter k. The productivity distribution of surviving firms will therefore also be Pareto with shape k, and the truncated cost distribution will be given by $G_D(c) = (c/c_D)^k$, $c \in [0, c_D]$.

When core competencies are distributed Pareto, then all produced varieties will share the same Pareto distribution:

(12) $$H(c) = \sum_{m=0}^{\infty} G(\omega^m c) = \Omega G(c),$$

where $\Omega = \left(1 - \omega^k\right)^{-1} > 1$ is an index of multi-product flexibility (which varies monotonically with ω). In equilibrium, this index will also be equal to the average number of products produced across all surviving firms:

$$\frac{M}{N} = \frac{H(v_D)N_E}{G(c_D)N_E} = \Omega.$$

---

[10] We also use the relationship between average cost and price $\bar{v} = 2\bar{p} - v_D$, which is obtained from (7).

VOL. 104 NO. 2   *MAYER ET AL.: MARKET SIZE, COMPETITION, AND PRODUCT MIX*   *505*

The Pareto parametrization also yields a simple closed-form solution for the cost cutoff c_D from the free entry condition (10):

$$(13) \qquad c_D = \left[\frac{\gamma \phi}{L\Omega} \right]^{\frac{1}{k+2}},$$

where $\phi \equiv 2(k + 1)(k + 2)(c_M)^k f_E$ is a technology index that combines the effects of better distribution of cost draws (lower c_M) and lower entry costs f_E. We assume that $c_M > \sqrt{[2(k + 1)(k + 2)\gamma f_E]/(L\Omega)}$ in order to ensure $c_D < c_M$ as was previously anticipated. We also note that, as the customization cost for non-core varieties becomes infinitely large ($\omega \to 0$), multi-product flexibility Ω goes to 1, and (13) then boils down to the single-product case studied by Melitz and Ottaviano (2008).

E. *Equilibrium with Multi-Product Firms*

Equation (13) summarizes how technology (referenced by the distribution of cost draws and the sunk entry cost), market size, product differentiation, and multi-product flexibility affect the toughness of competition in the market equilibrium. Increases in market size, technology improvements (a fall in c_M or f_E), and increases in product substitutability (a rise in γ) all lead to tougher competition in the market and thus to an equilibrium with a lower cost cutoff c_D. As multi-product flexibility Ω increases, firms respond by introducing more products. This additional production is skewed toward the better performing firms and also leads to tougher competition and a lower c_D cutoff.

A market with tougher competition (lower c_D) also features more product variety M and a lower average price $\bar{p}$ (due to the combined effect of product selection toward lower cost varieties and of lower markups). Both of these contribute to higher welfare U. Given our Pareto parametrization, we can write all of these variables as simple closed form functions of the cost cutoff c_D:

$$(14) \qquad M = \frac{2(k + 1)\gamma}{\eta} \frac{\alpha - c_D}{c_D},$$

$$\bar{p} = \frac{2k + 1}{2k + 2} c_D,$$

$$U = 1 + \frac{1}{2\eta} (\alpha - c_D) \left(\alpha - \frac{k + 1}{k + 2} c_D \right).$$

Increases in the toughness of competition do not affect the average number of varieties produced per firm $M/N = \Omega$ because the mass of surviving firms N rises by the same proportion as the mass of produced varieties M.[11] However, each firm

---

[11] This exact offsetting effect between the number of firms and the number of products is driven by our functional form assumptions. However, the downward shift in $M(c)$ in response to competition (described next) holds for a much more general set of parameterizations.

506   *THE AMERICAN ECONOMIC REVIEW*   *FEBRUARY 2014*

responds to tougher competition by dropping its worst performing varieties (highest m) and reducing the number of varieties produced $M(c)$.[12] The selection of firms with respect to exit explains how the average number of products produced per firm can remain constant: exiting firms are those with the highest cost c who produce the fewest number of products.

II. Competition, Product Mix, and Productivity

We now investigate the link between toughness of competition and productivity at both the firm and aggregate level. We just described how tougher competition affects the selection of both firms in a market, and of the products they produce: high cost firms exit, and firms drop their high cost products. These selection effects induce productivity improvements at both the firm and the aggregate level.[13]

However, our model features an important additional channel that links tougher competition to higher firm and aggregate productivity. This new channel operates through the effect of competition on a firm's product mix. Tougher competition induces multi-product firms to skew production toward their better performing varieties (closer to their core competency). Thus, holding a multi-product firm's product range fixed, an increase in competition leads to an increase in that firm's productivity. Aggregating across firms, this product mix response also generates an aggregate productivity gain from tougher competition, over and above the effects from firm and product selection.

We have not yet defined how firm and aggregate productivity are measured. We start with the aggregation of output, revenue, and cost (employment) at the firm level. For any firm c, this is simply the sum of output, revenue, and cost over all varieties produced:

$$(15) \qquad Q(c) \equiv \sum_{m=0}^{M(c)-1} q(v(m, c)),$$

$$R(c) \equiv \sum_{m=0}^{M(c)-1} r(v(m, c)),$$

$$C(c) \equiv \sum_{m=0}^{M(c)-1} v(m, c) \, q(v(m, c)).$$

One measure of firm productivity is simply output per worker $\Phi(c) \equiv Q(c)/C(c)$. This productivity measure does not have a clear empirical counterpart for multi-product firms, as output units for each product are normalized so that one

---

[12] To be precise, the number of produced varieties $M(c)$ weakly decreases: if the change in the cutoff c_D is small enough, then some firms may still produce the same number of varieties. For other firms with high cost c, $M(c)$ drops to zero which implies firm exit.
[13] This effect of product scope on firm productivity is emphasized by Bernard, Redding, and Schott (2011) and Eckel and Neary (2010).

VOL. 104 NO. 2   *MAYER ET AL.: MARKET SIZE, COMPETITION, AND PRODUCT MIX*   *507*

unit of each product generates the same utility for the consumer (this is the implicit normalization behind the product symmetry in the utility function). A firm's deflated sales per worker $\Phi_R(c) \equiv [R(c)/\overline{P}]/C(c)$ provides another productivity measure that has a clear empirical counterpart. For this productivity measure, we need to define the price deflator $\overline{P}$. We choose

$$\overline{P} \equiv \frac{\int_0^{c_D} R(c)\, dG(c)}{\int_0^{c_D} Q(c)\, dG(c)} = \frac{k+1}{k+2} c_D.$$

This is the average of all the variety prices $p(v)$ weighted by their output share. We could also have used the unweighted price average $\overline{p}$ that we previously defined, or an average weighted by a variety's revenue share (i.e., its market share) instead of output share. In our model, all of these price averages only differ by a multiplicative constant, so the effects of competition (changes in the cutoff c_D) on productivity will not depend on this choice of price averages.[14] We define the aggregate counterparts to our two firm productivity measures as industry output per worker and industry deflated sales per worker:

$$\overline{\Phi} \equiv \frac{\int_0^{c_D} Q(c)\, dG(c)}{\int_0^{c_D} C(c)\, dG(c)}, \qquad \overline{\Phi}_R = \frac{\left[\int_0^{c_D} R(c)\, dG(c)\right]/\overline{P}}{\int_0^{c_D} C(c)\, dG(c)}.$$

Our choice of the price deflator $\overline{P}$ then implies that these two aggregate productivity measures coincide:[15]

$$(16) \qquad \overline{\Phi} = \overline{\Phi}_R = \frac{k+2}{k} \frac{1}{c_D}.$$

Equation (16) summarizes the overall effect of tougher competition on aggregate productivity gains. This aggregate response of productivity combines the effects of competition on both firm productivity and inter-firm reallocations (including entry and exit). We now detail how tougher competition induces improvements in firm productivity through its impact on a firm's product mix. In Appendix B, we show that both firm productivity measures, $\Phi(c)$ and $\Phi_R(c)$, increase for all multi-product firms when competition increases (c_D decreases). The key component of this proof is that, holding a firm's product scope constant (a given number $M > 1$ of non-core varieties produced), firm productivity over that product scope (output or deflated sales of those M products per worker producing those products) increases whenever competition increases. This effect of competition on firm productivity, by construction, is entirely driven by the response of the firm's product mix.

---

[14] As we previously reported in equation (14), the unweighted price average is $\overline{p} = [(2k+1)/(2k+2)]c_D$; and the average weighted by market share is $[(6k+2k^2+3)/(2k^2+8k+6)]c_D$.

[15] If we had picked one of the other price averages, the two aggregate productivity measures would differ by a multiplicative constant.

To isolate this product mix response to competition, consider two varieties m and m' produced by a firm with cost c. Assume that $m < m'$ so that variety m is closer to the core. The ratio of the firm's output of the two varieties is given by

$$\frac{q(v(m, c))}{q(v(m', c))} = \frac{c_D - \omega^{-m}c}{c_D - \omega^{-m'}c}.$$

As competition increases (c_D decreases), this ratio increases, implying that the firm skews its production toward its core varieties. This happens because the increased competition increases the price elasticity of demand for all products. At a constant relative price $p(v(m, c))/p(v(m', c))$, the higher price elasticity translates into higher relative demand $q(v(m,c))/q(v(m', c))$ and sales $r(v(m, c))/r(v(m', c))$ for good m (relative to m').[16] In our specific demand parametrization, there is a further increase in relative demand and sales, because markups drop more for good m than m', which implies that the relative price $p(v(m, c))/p(v(m', c))$ decreases.[17] It is this reallocation of output toward better performing products (also mirrored by a reallocation of production labor toward those products) that generates the productivity increases within the firm. In other words, tougher competition skews the distribution of employment, output, and sales toward the better performing varieties (closer to the core), while it flattens the firm's distribution of prices.

In the open economy version of our model that we develop in the next section, we show how firms respond to tougher competition in export markets in very similar ways by skewing their exported product mix toward their better performing products. Our empirical results confirm a strong effect of such a link between competition and product mix.

III. Open Economy

We now turn to the open economy in order to examine how market size and geography determine differences in the toughness of competition across markets—and how the latter translates into differences in the exporters' product mix. We allow for an arbitrary number of countries and asymmetric trade costs. Let J denote the number of countries, indexed by $l = 1, \ldots, J$. The markets are segmented, although any produced variety can be exported from country l to country h subject to an iceberg trade cost $\tau_{lh} > 1$. Thus, the delivered cost for variety m exported to country h by a firm with core competency c in country l is $\tau_{lh} v(m, c) = \tau_{lh} \omega^{-m} c$.

A. *Equilibrium with Asymmetric Countries*

Let $p_l^{\max}$ denote the price threshold for positive demand in market l. Then (4) implies

(17) $$p_l^{\max} = \frac{1}{\eta M_l + \gamma} (\gamma \alpha + \eta M_l \bar{p}_l),$$

---

[16]For the result on relative sales, we are assuming that the price elasticity of demand (ε) is larger than one.
[17]Good m closer to the core initially has a higher markup than good m'; see (7).

VOL. 104 NO. 2 *MAYER ET AL.: MARKET SIZE, COMPETITION, AND PRODUCT MIX* *509*

where M_l is the total number of products selling in country l (the total number of domestic and exported varieties) and $\bar{p}_l$ is their average price. Let $\pi_{ll}(v)$ and $\pi_{lh}(v)$ represent the maximized value of profits from domestic and export sales to country h for a variety with cost v produced in country l. (We use the subscript ll to denote domestic variables, pertaining to firms located in l.) The cost cutoffs for profitable domestic production and for profitable exports must satisfy

$$(18) \qquad v_{ll} = \sup\{c : \pi_{ll}(v) > 0\} = p_l^{\max},$$

$$v_{lh} = \sup\{c : \pi_{lh}(v) > 0\} = \frac{p_h^{\max}}{\tau_{lh}},$$

and thus $v_{lh} = v_{hh}/\tau_{lh}$. As was the case in the closed economy, the cutoff v_{ll}, $l = 1, \ldots, J$, summarizes all the effects of market conditions in country l relevant for all firm performance measures. The profit functions can then be written as a function of these cutoffs (assuming that markets are segmented, as in Melitz and Ottaviano, 2008):

$$(19) \qquad \pi_{ll}(v) = \frac{L_l}{4\gamma}(v_{ll} - v)^2,$$

$$\pi_{lh}(v) = \frac{L_h}{4\gamma}\tau_{lh}^2(v_{lh} - v)^2 = \frac{L_h}{4\gamma}(v_{hh} - \tau_{lh}v)^2.$$

As in the closed economy, $c_{ll} = v_{ll}$ will be the cutoff for firm survival in country l (cutoff for domestic sales of firms producing in l). Similarly, $c_{lh} = v_{lh}$ will be the firm export cutoff from l to h (no firm with $c > c_{lh}$ can profitably export any varieties from l to h). A firm with core competency c will produce all varieties m such that $\pi_{ll}(v(m, c)) \geq 0$; it will export to h the subset of varieties m such that $\pi_{lh}(v(m, c)) \geq 0$. The total number of varieties produced and exported to h by a firm with cost c in country l are thus

$$M_{ll}(c) = \begin{cases} 0 & \text{if } c > c_{ll}, \\ \max\{m \,|\, c \leq \omega^m c_{ll}\} + 1 & \text{if } c \leq c_{ll}, \end{cases}$$

$$M_{lh}(c) = \begin{cases} 0 & \text{if } c > c_{lh}, \\ \max\{m \,|\, c \leq \omega^m c_{lh}\} + 1 & \text{if } c \leq c_{lh}. \end{cases}$$

We can then define a firm's total domestic and export profits by aggregating over these varieties:

$$\Pi_{ll}(c) = \sum_{m=0}^{M_{ll}(c)-1} \pi_{ll}(v(m, c)), \qquad \Pi_{lh}(c) = \sum_{m=0}^{M_{lh}(c)-1} \pi_{lh}(v(m, c)).$$

510   THE AMERICAN ECONOMIC REVIEW   FEBRUARY 2014

Entry is unrestricted in all countries. Firms choose a production location prior to entry and paying the sunk entry cost. We assume that the entry cost f_E and cost distribution $G(c)$ are common across countries (although this can be relaxed).[18] We maintain our Pareto parametrization (11) for this distribution. A prospective entrant's expected profits will then be given by

$$\int_0^{c_{ll}} \Pi_{ll}(c)\, dG(c) \;+\; \sum_{h \neq l} \int_0^{c_{lh}} \Pi_{lh}(c)\, dG(c)$$

$$= \sum_{m=0}^{\infty} \left[\int_0^{\omega^{-m} c_{ll}} \pi_{ll}(\omega^{-m} c)\, dG(c) \right] + \sum_{h \neq l} \sum_{m=0}^{\infty} \left[\int_0^{\omega^{-m} c_{lh}} \pi_{lh}(\omega^{-m} c)\, dG(c) \right]$$

$$= \frac{1}{2\gamma(k+1)(k+2)c_M^k} \left[L_l \Omega c_{ll}^{k+2} + \sum_{h \neq l} L_h \, \Omega \, \tau_{lh}^2 \, c_{lh}^{k+2} \right]$$

$$= \frac{\Omega}{2\gamma(k+1)(k+2)c_M^k} \left[L_l \, c_{ll}^{k+2} + \sum_{h \neq l} L_h \, \tau_{lh}^{-k} \, c_{hh}^{k+2} \right].$$

Setting the expected profit equal to the entry cost yields the free entry conditions:

$$(20) \qquad \sum_{h=1}^{J} \rho_{lh} L_h \, c_{hh}^{k+2} = \frac{\gamma \phi}{\Omega} \qquad l = 1, \ldots, J,$$

where $\rho_{lh} \equiv \tau_{lh}^{-k} < 1$ is a measure of "freeness" of trade from country l to country h that varies inversely with the trade costs τ_{lh}. The technology index ϕ is the same as in the closed economy case.

The free entry conditions (20) yield a system of J equations that can be solved for the J equilibrium domestic cutoffs using Cramer's rule:

$$(21) \qquad c_{hh} = \left(\frac{\gamma \phi}{\Omega} \frac{\sum_{l=1}^{J} |C_{lh}|}{|\mathbf{P}|} \frac{1}{L_h} \right)^{\frac{1}{k+2}},$$

---

[18] Differences in the support for this distribution could also be introduced as in Melitz and Ottaviano (2008).

where $|\mathbf{P}|$ is the determinant of the trade freeness matrix

$$
\mathbf{P} \equiv \begin{pmatrix} 1 & \rho_{12} & \cdots & \rho_{1M} \\ \rho_{21} & 1 & \cdots & \rho_{2M} \\ \vdots & \vdots & \ddots & \vdots \\ \rho_{M1} & \rho_{M2} & \cdots & 1 \end{pmatrix},
$$

and $|C_{lh}|$ is the cofactor of its ρ_{lh} element. Cross-country differences in cutoffs now arise from two sources: own country size (L_h) and geographical remoteness, captured by $\sum_{l=1}^{J} |C_{lh}| / |\mathbf{P}|$. Central countries benefiting from a large local market have lower cutoffs, and exhibit tougher competition than peripheral countries with a small local market.

As in the closed economy, the threshold price condition in country h (17), along with the resulting Pareto distribution of all prices for varieties sold in h (domestic prices and export prices have an identical distribution in country h) yield a zero-cutoff profit condition linking the variety cutoff $v_{hh} = c_{hh}$ to the mass of varieties sold in country h:

$$
(22) \qquad M_h = \frac{2(k+1)\gamma}{\eta} \frac{\alpha - c_{hh}}{c_{hh}}.
$$

Given a positive mass of entrants $N_{E,l}$ in country l, there will be $G(c_{lh})N_{E,l}$ firms exporting $\Omega \rho_{lh} G(c_{lh}) N_{E,l}$ varieties to country h. Summing over all these varieties (including those produced and sold in h) yields[19]

$$
\sum_{l=1}^{J} \rho_{lh} N_{E,l} = \frac{M_h}{\Omega c_{hh}^k}.
$$

The latter provides a system of J linear equations that can be solved for the number of entrants in the J countries using Cramer's rule:[20]

$$
(23) \qquad N_{E,l} = \frac{\phi \gamma}{\Omega \eta (k+2) f_E} \sum_{h=1}^{J} \frac{(\alpha - c_{hh})}{c_{hh}^{k+1}} \frac{|C_{lh}|}{|\mathbf{P}|}.
$$

As in the closed economy, the cutoff level completely summarizes the distribution of prices as well as all the other performance measures. Hence, the cutoff in each country also uniquely determines welfare in that country. The relationship between welfare and the cutoff is the same as in the closed economy (see (14)).

---

[19] Recall that $c_{hh} = \tau_{lh} c_{lh}$.

[20] We use the properties that relate the freeness matrix $\mathbf{P}$ and its transpose in terms of determinants and cofactors.

B. *Bilateral Trade Patterns with Firm and Product Selection*

We have now completely characterized the multi-country open economy equilibrium. Selection operates at many different margins: a subset of firms survive in each country, and a smaller subset of those export to any given destination. Within a firm, there is an endogenous selection of its product range (the range of product produced); those products are all sold on the firm's domestic market, but only a subset of those products are sold in each export market. In order to keep our multi-country open economy model as tractable as possible, we have assumed a single bilateral trade cost τ_{lh} that does not vary across firms or products. This simplification implies some predictions regarding the ordering of the selection process across countries and products that is overly rigid. Since τ_{lh} does not vary across firms in l contemplating exports to h, then all those firms would face the same ranking of export market destinations based on the toughness of competition in that market, c_{hh}, and the trade cost to that market τ_{lh}. All exporters would then export to the country with the highest c_{hh}/τ_{lh}, and then move down the country destination list in decreasing order of this ratio until exports to the next destination were no longer profitable. This generates a "pecking order" of export destinations for exporters from a given country l. Eaton, Kortum, and Kramarz (2011) show that there is such a stable ranking of export destinations for French exporters. Needless to say, the empirical prediction for the ordered set of export destinations is not strictly adhered to by every French exporter (some export to a given destination without also exporting to all the other higher ranked destinations). Eaton, Kortum, and Kramarz (2011) formally show how some idiosyncratic noise in the bilateral trading cost can explain those departures from the dominant ranking of export destinations. They also show that the empirical regularities for the ranking of export destinations are so strong that one can easily reject the notion of independent export destination choices by firms.

Our model features a similar rigid ordering within a firm regarding the products exported across destinations. Without any variation in the bilateral trade cost τ_{lh} across products, an exporter from l would always exactly follow its domestic core competency ladder when determining the range of products exported across destinations: an exporter would never export variety $m' > m$ unless it also exported variety m to any given destination. Just as we described for the prediction of country rankings, we clearly do not expect the empirical prediction for product rankings to hold exactly for all firms. Nevertheless, a similar empirical pattern emerges highlighting a stable ranking of products for each exporter across export destinations.[21] We empirically describe the substantial extent of this ranking stability for French exporters in our next section.

Putting together all the different margins of trade, we can use our model to generate predictions for aggregate bilateral trade. An exporter in country l with core competency c generates export sales of variety m to country h equal to (assuming that this variety is exported):

$$(24) \qquad r_{lh}(v(m, c)) = \frac{L_h}{4\gamma} \left[v_{hh}^2 - \left(\tau_{lh} v(m, c) \right)^2 \right].$$

---

[21] Bernard, Redding, and Schott (2011) and Arkolakis and Muendler (2010) report that there is such a stable ordering of a firm's product line for US and Brazilian firms.

VOL. 104 NO. 2   *MAYER ET AL.: MARKET SIZE, COMPETITION, AND PRODUCT MIX*   *513*

Aggregate bilateral trade from l to h is then:

$$(25) \qquad \text{EXP}_{lh} = N_{E,l} \, \Omega \, \rho^{lh} \int_0^{c_{lh}} r_{lh}(v(m,c)) \, dG(v)$$

$$= \frac{\Omega}{2\gamma(k+2)c_M^k} \cdot N_{E,l} \cdot c_{hh}^{k+2} \, L_h \cdot \rho_{lh}.$$

Thus, aggregate bilateral trade follows a standard gravity specification based on country fixed effects (separate fixed effects for the exporter and importer) and a bilateral term that captures the effects of all bilateral barriers/enhancers to trade.[22]

IV. Exporters' Product Mix across Destinations

We previously described how, in the closed economy, firms respond to increases in competition in their market by skewing their product mix toward their core products. We also analyzed how this product mix response generated increases in firm productivity. We now show how differences in competition across export market destinations induce exporters to those markets to respond in very similar ways: when exporting to markets with tougher competition, exporters skew their product level exports toward their core products. We proceed in a similar way as we did for the closed economy by examining a given firm's ratio of exports of two products m' and m, where m is closer to the core. In anticipation of our empirical work, we write the ratio of export sales (revenue not output), but the ratio of export quantities responds to competition in identical ways. Using (24), we can write this sales ratio:

$$(26) \qquad \frac{r_{lh}(v(m,c))}{r_{lh}(v(m',c))} = \frac{c_{hh}^2 - (\tau_{lh}\,\omega^{-m}c)^2}{c_{hh}^2 - (\tau_{lh}\,\omega^{-m'}c)^2}.$$

Tougher competition in an export market (lower c_{hh}) increases this ratio, which captures how firms skew their exports toward their core varieties (recall that $m' > m$ so variety m is closer to the core). The intuition behind this result is very similar to the one we described for the closed economy. Tougher competition in a market increases the price elasticity of demand for all goods exported to that market. As in the closed economy, this skews relative demand and relative export sales toward the goods closer to the core. In our empirical work, we focus on measuring this effect of tougher competition across export market destinations on a firm's exported product mix.

We could also use (26) to make predictions regarding the impact of the bilateral trade cost τ_{lh} on a firm's exported product mix: Higher trade costs raise the firm's delivered cost and lead to a higher export ratio. The higher delivered cost increase

---

[22] This type of structural gravity specification with country fixed-effects is generated by a large set of different modeling frameworks. See Feenstra (2004) for further discussion of this topic. In (25), we do not further substitute out the endogenous number of entrants and cost cutoff based on (21) and (23). This would lead to just a different functional form for the country fixed effects.

514   THE AMERICAN ECONOMIC REVIEW   FEBRUARY 2014

the competition faced by an exporting firm, as it then competes against domestic firms that benefit from a greater cost advantage. However, this comparative static is very sensitive to the specification for the trade cost across a firm's product ladder. If trade barriers induce disproportionately higher trade costs on products further away from the core, then the direction of this comparative static would be reversed. Furthermore, identifying the independent effect of trade barriers on the exporters' product mix would also require micro-level data for exporters located in many different countries (to generate variation across both origin and destination of export sales). Our data "only" covers the export patterns for French exporters, and does not give us this variation in origin country. For these reasons, we do not emphasize the effect of trade barriers on the product mix of exporters. In our empirical work, we will only seek to control for a potential correlation between bilateral trade barriers with respect to France and the level of competition in destination countries served by French exporters.[23]

As was the case for the closed economy, the skewing of a firm's product mix toward core varieties also entails increases in firm productivity. Empirically, we cannot separately measure a firm's productivity with respect to its production for each export market. However, we can theoretically define such a productivity measure in an analogous way to $\Phi(c) \equiv Q(c)/C(c)$ for the closed economy. We thus define the productivity of firm c in l for its exports to destination h as $\Phi_{lh}(c) \equiv Q_{lh}(c)/C_{lh}(c)$, where $Q_{lh}(c)$ are the total units of output that firm c exports to h, and $C_{lh}(c)$ are the total labor costs incurred by firm c to produce those units.[24] In Appendix B, we show that this export market-specific productivity measure (as well as the associated measure $\Phi_{R, lh}(c)$ based on deflated sales) increases with the toughness of competition in that export market. In other words, $\Phi_{lh}(c)$ and $\Phi_{R, lh}(c)$ both increase when c_{hh} decreases. Thus, changes in exported product mix also have important repercussions for firm productivity.

V. Empirical Analysis

A. *Skewness of Exported Product Mix*

We now test the main prediction of our model regarding the impact of competition across export market destinations on a firm's exported product mix. Our model predicts that tougher competition in an export market will induce firms to lower markups on all their exported products and therefore skew their export sales toward their best performing products. We thus need data on a firm's exports across products and destinations. We use comprehensive firm-level data on annual shipments by all French exporters to all countries in the world for a set of more than 10,000 goods. Firm-level exports are collected by French customs and include export sales for each

---

[23] The theoretical implications of our model for trade liberalization are discussed in Appendix A.

[24] In order for this productivity measure to aggregate up to overall country productivity, we incorporate the productivity of the transportation/trade cost sector into this productivity measure. This implies that firm c employs the labor units that are used to produce the "melted" units of output that cover the trade cost; those labor units are thus included in $C_{lh}(c)$. The output of firm c is measured as valued-added, which implies that those "melted" units are not included in $Q_{lh}(c)$ (the latter are the number of units produced by firm c that are consumed in h). Separating out the productivity of the transportation sector would not affect our main comparative static with respect to toughness of competition in the export market.

VOL. 104 NO. 2 *MAYER ET AL.: MARKET SIZE, COMPETITION, AND PRODUCT MIX* *515*

8-digit (combined nomenclature) product by destination country.[25] Since we are interested in the cross section of firm-product exports across destinations, we restrict our sample to a single year, for 2003 (this is the last year of our available data; results obtained from other years are very similar). The reporting criteria for all firms operating in the French metropolitan territory are as follows: for within EU exports, the firm's annual trade value exceeds 100,000 euros;[26] and for exports outside the EU, the exported value to a destination exceeds 1,000 euros or a weight of a ton. Despite these limitations, the database is nearly comprehensive. In 2003, 100,033 firms report exports across 229 destination countries (or territories) for 10,072 products. This represents data on over 2 million shipments. We restrict our analysis to export data in manufacturing industries, mostly eliminating firms in the service and wholesale/distribution sector to ensure that firms take part in the production of the goods they export.[27] This leaves us with data on over a million shipments by firms in the whole range of manufacturing sectors. We also drop observations for firms that the French national statistical institute reports as having an affiliate abroad. This avoids the issue that multinational firms may substitute exports of some of their best performing products with affiliate production in the destination country (following the export versus FDI trade-off described in Helpman, Melitz, and Yeaple 2004). We therefore limit our analysis to firms that do not have this possibility, in order to reduce noise in the product export rankings.

In order to measure the skewness of a firm's exported product mix across destinations, we first need to make some assumptions regarding the empirical measurement of a firm's product ladder. We start with the most direct counterpart to our theoretical model, which assumes that the firm's product ladder does *not* vary across destinations. For this measure, we rank all the products exported by a firm according to the value of exports to the world, and use this ranking as an indicator for the product rank m.[28] We call this the firm's *global* product rank. An alternative is to measure a firm's product rank for each destination based on the firm's exports sales to that destination. We call this the firm's *local* product rank. Empirically, this local product ranking can vary across destinations. However, as we alluded to earlier, this local product ranking is remarkably stable across destinations.

The Spearman rank correlation between a firm's local and global rankings (in each export market destination) is 0.68.[29] Naturally, this correlation might be partly driven by firms that export only one product to one market, for which the global rank has to be equal to the local rank. In Table 1, we therefore report the rank correlation as we gradually restrict the sample to firms that export many products to many markets. The bottom line is that this correlation remains quite stable: for firms exporting more than 50 products to more than 50 destinations, the correlation is still larger

---

[25] We thank the French customs administration and CNIS for making this data available to researchers at CEPII. Since this product-level data is collected by customs at the border, we unfortunately do not have access to data on a firm's sales by product on the French domestic market.

[26] If that threshold is not met, firms can choose to report under a simplified scheme without supplying export destinations. However, in practice, many firms under that threshold report the detailed export destination information.

[27] Some large distributors such as Carrefour account for a disproportionate number of annual shipments.

[28] We experimented ranking products for each firm based on the number of export destinations; and obtained very similar results to the ranking based on global export sales.

[29] Arkolakis and Muendler (2010) also report a huge amount of stability in the local rankings across destinations. The Spearman rank coefficient they report is 0.837. Iacovone and Javorcik (2008) report a rank correlation of 0.76 between home and export sales of Mexican firms.

516 THE AMERICAN ECONOMIC REVIEW FEBRUARY 2014

TABLE 1—SPEARMAN CORRELATIONS BETWEEN GLOBAL AND LOCAL RANKINGS

Firms exporting at least:	Number of products (percent)				
To number of countries	1	2	5	10	50
1	67.61	67.47	66.93	65.92	59.39
2	67.58	67.45	66.93	65.93	59.39
5	67.47	67.39	66.93	65.95	59.40
10	67.27	67.22	66.88	65.99	59.46
50	64.48	64.48	64.41	64.12	59.30

than 0.59. Another possibility is that this correlation is different across destination income levels. Restricting the sample to the top 50 or 20 percent richest importers hardly changes this correlation (0.69 and 0.71 respectively).[30] Table 1 does not directly control for product selection, whereby any product that is not exported to a destination is dropped from the local ranking. Although we do not use this extensive margin response, we show in Appendix E that this product selection into the local ranking is also strongly correlated with the product's global ranking for the firm: products with lower global ranking are exported to fewer destinations (on average, the second ranked product is exported to around five fewer destinations; see Appendix E for details).

Although high, this correlation still highlights substantial departures from a steady global product ladder. A natural alternative is therefore to use the local product rank when measuring the skewness of a firm's exported product mix. In this interpretation, the identity of the core (or other rank number) product can change across destinations. We thus use both the firm's global and local product rank to construct the firm's destination-specific export sales ratio $r_{lh}(v(m, c))/r_{lh}(v(m', c))$ for $m < m'$. Since many firms export few products to many destinations, increasing the higher product rank m' disproportionately reduces the number of available firm/destination observations. For most of our analysis, we pick $m = 0$ (core product) and $m' = 1$, but also report results for $m' = 2$.[31] Thus, we construct the ratio of a firm's export sales to every destination for its best performing product (either globally, or in each destination) relative to its next best performing product (again, either globally, or in each destination). The local ratios can be computed so long as a firm exports at least two products to a destination (or three when $m' = 2$). The global ratios can be computed so long as a firm exports its top (in terms of world exports) two products to a destination. We thus obtain these measures that are firm c and destination h specific, so long as those criteria are met (there is no variation in origin $l =$ France). We use those ratios in logs, so that they represent percentage differences in export sales. We refer to the ratios as either local or global, based on the ranking method used to compute them. Lastly, we also constrain the sample so that the two products considered belong to the same 2-digit product category (there are

---

[30] We nevertheless separately report our regression results for those restricted sample of countries based on income.

[31] We also obtain very similar results for $m = 1$ and $m' = 2$.

VOL. 104 NO. 2   *MAYER ET AL.: MARKET SIZE, COMPETITION, AND PRODUCT MIX*   *517*

97 such categories). This eliminates ratios based on products that are in completely different sectors; however, this restriction hardly impacts our reported results. We construct a third set of measures that seeks to capture changes in skewness of a firm's exported product mix over the entire range of exported products (instead of being confined to the top two or three products). We use several different skewness statistics for the distribution of firm export sales to a destination: the standard deviation of log export sales, a Herfindhal index, and a Theil index (a measure of entropy). Since these statistics are independent of the identity of the products exported to a destination, they are "local" by nature, and do not have any global ranking counterpart. These statistics can be computed for every firm-destination combination where the firm exports two or more products.

As we discussed in the introduction, we focus our empirical analysis on the response of the exported product mix (intensive margin) and do not investigate our model's prediction for the extensive margin across destinations. Empirically, the number of products exported is under-reported due to a minimum sales reporting threshold. Theoretically, the predictions for the response of the extensive margin is quite sensitive to the specification of fixed exporting costs (which could be either destination-specific, or product-destination-specific, or some combination of both). We abstract from these fixed costs in order to maintain the tractability of our model in an asymmetric multi-country setting.[32] As we previously noted, fixed export costs affect the extensive margin responses; but conditional on a firm's decision to export a given set of products, those costs would not affect our skewness measures for the firms' exported product mix. Our main novel prediction concerns how this skewness varies across export market destinations.

B. *Toughness of Competition across Destinations and Bilateral Controls*

Our theoretical model predicts that the toughness of competition in a destination is determined by that destination's size, and by its geography (proximity to other big countries). We control for country size using GDP expressed in a common currency at market exchange rates. We now seek a control for the geography of a destination that does not rely on country-level data for that destination. We use the *supply potential* concept introduced by Redding and Venables (2004) as such a control. In words, the supply potential is the aggregate predicted exports to a destination based on a bilateral trade gravity equation (in logs) with both exporter and importer fixed effects and the standard bilateral measures of trade barriers/enhancers. We construct a related measure of a destination's *foreign* supply potential that does not use the importer's fixed effect when predicting aggregate exports to that destination. By construction, foreign supply potential is thus uncorrelated with the importer's fixed-effect. It is closely related to the construction of a country's market potential (which seeks to capture a measure of predicted import demand for a country).

---

[32] Absent fixed exporting costs, our theoretical model predicts that a given firm exports fewer products to destinations where competition is tougher. However, a given firm would still export more products *above a given sales threshold* to larger destinations, even though competition is tougher there. Empirically, we observe that French firms report exporting more products to larger destinations (higher GDP). This could be due in part to the reporting threshold for exports, but is also a likely indication that destination-specific fixed export costs play an important role in determining the extensive margin of trade.

518   THE AMERICAN ECONOMIC REVIEW   FEBRUARY 2014

The construction of the supply potential measures is discussed in greater detail in Redding and Venables (2004); we use the foreign supply measure for the year 2003 from Head and Mayer (2011) who extend the analysis to many more countries and more years of data.[33] Since we only work with the foreign supply potential measure, we drop the qualifier "foreign" when we subsequently refer to this variable. There are likely several other country characteristics that affect competition in a destination. As a robustness check, we also use the number of French exporters to a destination as a measure of competition for French firms in that market; this measure combines the effects of both destination size and geography as well as other destination characteristics that impact the extent of competition for French exporters. Those robustness results are reported in Appendix D.

We also use a set of controls for bilateral trade barriers/enhancers (τ in our model) between France and the destination country: distance, contiguity, colonial links, common-language, and dummies for membership of Regional Trading Agreements, GATT/WTO, and a common currency area (the euro zone in this case).[34]

C. Results

Before reporting the regression results of the skewness measures on the destination country measures, we first show some scatter plots for the global ratio against both destination country GDP and our measure of supply potential. These are displayed in Figures 2 and 3. For each destination, we use the mean global ratio across exporting firms. Since the firm-level measure is very noisy, the precision of the mean increases with the number of available firm data points (for each destination). We first show the scatter plots using all available destinations, with symbol weights proportional to the number of available firm observations, and then again dropping any destination with fewer than 250 exporting firms.[35] Those scatter plots show a very strong positive correlation between the export share ratios and the measures of toughness of competition in the destination. Absent any variation in the toughness of competition across destinations—such as in a world with monopolistic competition and CES preferences where markups are exogenously fixed—the variation in the relative export shares should be white noise. The data clearly show that variations in competition (at least as proxied by country size and supplier potential) are strong enough to induce large variations in the firms' relative export sales across destinations. Scatter plots for the local ratio and Theil index look very similar.

We now turn to our regression analysis using the three skewness measures. Each observation summarizes the skewness of export sales for a given firm to a given destination. Since we seek to uncover variation in that skewness for a given firm, we include firm fixed effects throughout. Our remaining independent variables are destination specific: our two measures of competition (GDP and supplier potential, both in logs) as well as any bilateral measures of trade barriers/enhancers since

---

[33] As is the case with market potential, a country's supplier potential is strongly correlated with that country's GDP: big trading economies tend to be located near one-another. The supply potential data is available online at http://www.cepii.fr/anglaisgraph/bdd/marketpotentials.htm.

[34] All those variables are available at http://www.cepii.fr/anglaisgraph/bdd/gravity.htm.

[35] Increasing that threshold level for the number of exporters slightly increases the fit and slope of the regression line through the scatter plot.

VOL. 104 NO. 2   *MAYER ET AL.: MARKET SIZE, COMPETITION, AND PRODUCT MIX*   *519*

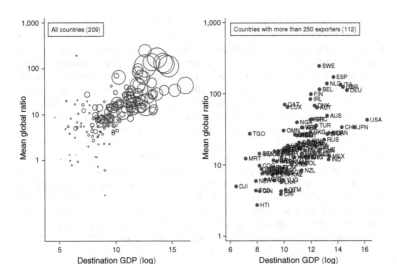

FIGURE 2. MEAN GLOBAL RATIO AND DESTINATION COUNTRY GDP IN 2003

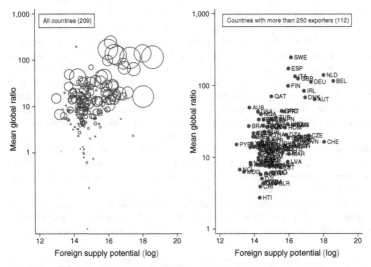

FIGURE 3. MEAN GLOBAL RATIO AND DESTINATION SUPPLY POTENTIAL IN 2003

there is no variation in country origin (we discuss how we specify those bilateral controls in further detail in the next paragraph). There are undoubtedly other unobserved characteristics of countries that affect our dependent skewness variables. These unobserved country characteristics are common to firms exporting to that destination and hence generate a correlated error-term structure, potentially biasing

520   *THE AMERICAN ECONOMIC REVIEW*   *FEBRUARY 2014*

downward the standard error of our variables of interest. The standard clustering procedure does not apply well here for two reasons: (i) the level of clustering is not nested within the level of fixed effects, and (ii) the number of clusters is quite small with respect to the size of each cluster. Harrigan and Deng (2010) encounter a similar problem and use the solution proposed by Wooldridge (2006), who recommends to run country-specific random effects on firm-demeaned data, with a robust covariance matrix estimation. This procedure allows to account for firm fixed effects, as well as country-level correlation patterns in the error term. We follow this estimation strategy here and apply it to all of the reported results below.[36]

Our first set of results regresses our two main skewness measures (log export ratio of best to next best product for global and local product rankings) on destination GDP and foreign supply potential. The coefficients, reported in columns 1 and 4 of Table 2, show a very significant impact of both country size and geography on the skewness of a firm's export sales to that destination (we discuss the economic magnitude in further detail below). This initial specification does not control for any independent effect of bilateral trade barriers on the skewness of a firm's exported product mix. Here, we suffer from the limitation inherent in our data that we do not observe any variation in the country of origin for all the export flows. This makes it difficult to separately identify the effects of those bilateral trade barriers from the destination's supply potential. France is located very near to the center of the biggest regional trading group in the world. Thus, distance from France is highly correlated with good geography and hence a high supply potential for that destination: the correlation between log distance and log supply potential is 78 percent. Therefore, when we introduce all the controls for bilateral trade barriers to our specification, it is not surprising that there is too much co-linearity with the destination's supply potential to separately identify the independent effect of the latter.[37] These results are reported in columns 2 and 5 of Table 2. Although the coefficient for supply potential is no longer significant due to this co-linearity problem, the effect of country size on the skewness of export sales remain highly significant. Other than country size, the only other variable that is significant (at 5 percent or below) is the effect of a common currency: export sales to countries in the euro zone display vastly higher skewness. However, we must exercise caution when interpreting this effect. Due to the lack of variation in origin country, we cannot say whether this captures the effect of a common currency between the destination and France, or whether this is an independent effect of the euro.[38]

Although we do not have firm-product-destination data for countries other than France, bilateral aggregate data is available for the full matrix of origins-destinations in the world. Our theoretical model predicts a bilateral gravity relationship (25) that

---

[36]We have experimented with several other estimation procedures to control for the correlated error structure: firm-level fixed effects with/without country clustering and demeaned data run with simple OLS. Those procedures highlight that it is important to account for the country-level error-term correlation. This affects the significance of the supply potential variable (as we highlight with our preferred estimation procedure). However, the p-values for the GDP variable are always substantially lower, and none of those procedures come close to overturning the significance of that variable.

[37]As we mentioned, distance by itself introduces a huge amount of co-linearity with supply potential. The other bilateral trade controls then further exacerbate this problem (membership in the European Union is also strongly correlated with good geography and hence supply potential).

[38]If this is a destination euro effect, then this would fit well with our theoretical prediction for the effect of tougher competition in euro markets on the skewness of export sales.

VOL. 104 NO. 2   *MAYER ET AL.: MARKET SIZE, COMPETITION, AND PRODUCT MIX*   *521*

TABLE 2—GLOBAL AND LOCAL EXPORT SALES RATIO: CORE $(m = 0)$ PRODUCT TO SECOND BEST $(m' = 1)$ PRODUCT

	Ratio of core to second product sales' regressions					
	Global ratio			Local ratio		
	(1)	(2)	(3)	(4)	(5)	(6)
ln GDP	0.092***	0.083***	0.107***	0.073***	0.057***	0.077***
	(0.013)	(0.012)	(0.010)	(0.008)	(0.005)	(0.006)
ln supply potential	0.067***	−0.017	0.044***	0.080***	0.018	0.068 ***
	(0.016)	(0.024)	(0.014)	(0.016)	(0.016)	(0.013)
ln distance		−0.063			−0.046*	
		(0.043)			(0.023)	
Contiguity		0.013			−0.108	
		(0.051)			(0.081)	
Colonial link		−0.060			−0.041	
		(0.051)			(0.043)	
Common language		0.023			−0.048	
		(0.050)			(0.038)	
RTA		0.066			0.004	
		(0.059)			(0.033)	
Common currency		0.182***			0.335***	
		(0.047)			(0.036)	
Both in GATT		0.006			−0.033	
		(0.046)			(0.026)	
ln freeness of trade			0.096***			0.028
			(0.026)			(0.017)
Constant	−0.000	0.000	−0.000	0.003	0.002	0.002
	(0.016)	(0.012)	(0.014)	(0.012)	(0.011)	(0.013)
Observations	56,097	56,097	56,093	96,891	96,891	96,878
Within R^2	0.004	0.006	0.005	0.007	0.011	0.007

Notes: All columns use Wooldridge's (2006) procedure: country-specific random effects on firm-demeaned data, with a robust covariance matrix estimation. Standard errors in parentheses.
   *** Significant at the 1 percent level.
    ** Significant at the 5 percent level.
     * Significant at the 10 percent level.

can be exploited to recover the combined effect of bilateral trade barriers as a single parameter (τ_{lh} in our model). The only property of our gravity relationship that we exploit is that bilateral trade can be decomposed into exporter and importer fixed effects, and a bilateral component that captures the joint effect of trade barriers.[39] We use the same bilateral gravity specification that we previously used to construct supply potential (again, in logs). We purge bilateral flows from both origin and destination fixed effects, to keep only the contribution of bilateral barriers to trade. This gives us an estimate for the bilateral log freeness of trade between all country pairs (ln ρ_{lh}).[40] We use the subset of this predicted data where France is the exporting country. Looking across destinations, this freeness of trade variable is still highly correlated

---

[39] This property of gravity equations is not specific to our model. It can be generated by a very large class of models. Head and Mayer (2011) discuss all the different models that lead to a similar gravity decomposition.
[40] Again, we emphasize that there is a very large class of models that would generate the same procedure for recovering bilateral freeness of trade.

522   *THE AMERICAN ECONOMIC REVIEW*   *FEBRUARY 2014*

with distance from France (the correlation with log distance is 60 percent); but it is substantially less correlated with the destination's supply potential than distance from France (the correlation between freeness of trade and log supply potential is 40 percent, much lower than the 78 percent correlation between log distance and log supply potential). This greatly alleviates the co-linearity problem while allowing us to control for the relevant variation induced by bilateral trade barriers (i.e., calculated based upon their impact on bilateral trade flows).

Columns 3 and 6 of Table 2 report the results using this constructed freeness of trade measure as our control for the independent effect of bilateral trade barriers on export skewness. The results are very similar to our initial ones without any bilateral controls: country size and supply potential both have a strong and highly significant effect on the skewness of export sales. These effects are also economically significant. The coefficient on country size can be directly interpreted as an elasticity for the sales ratio with respect to country GDP. The 0.107 elasticity for the global ratio implies that an increase in destination GDP from that of the Czech Republic to German GDP (an increase from the seventy-ninth to ninety-ninth percentile in the world's GDP distribution in 2003) would induce French firms to increase their relative exports of their best product (relative to their next best global product) by 42.1 percent: from an observed mean ratio of 20 in 2003 to 28.4.

We now investigate the robustness of this result to different skewness measures, to the sample of destination countries, and to an additional control for destination GDP per capita. From here on out, we use our constructed freeness of trade measure to control for bilateral trade barriers.

We report the same set of results for the global sales ratio in Table 3 and for the local ratio in Table 4. The first column reproduces baseline estimation reported in columns 3 and 6 with the freeness of trade control. In column 2, we use the sales ratio of the best to third best product as our dependent skewness variable.[41] We then return to sales ratio based on best to next best for the remaining columns. In order to show that our results are not driven by unmeasured quality differences between the products shipped to developed and developing countries, we progressively restrict our sample of country destinations to a subset of richer countries. In column 3 we restrict destinations to those above the median country income, and in column 4, we only keep the top 20 percent of countries ranked by income (GDP per capita).[42] In the fifth and last column, we keep the full sample of country destinations and add destination GDP per capita as a regressor in order to directly control for differences in preferences across countries (outside the scope of our theoretical model) tied to product quality and consumer income.[43] All of these different specifications in

---

[41] We also experimented with the ratio for the second best to third best product, and obtained very similar results.
[42] Since French firms ship disproportionately more goods to countries with higher incomes, the number of observations drops very slowly with the number of excluded country destinations.
[43] In particular, we want to allow consumer income to bias consumption toward higher quality varieties. If within-firm product quality is negatively related to its distance from the core product, then this would induce a positive correlation between consumer income and the within-firm skewness of expenditure shares. This is the sign of the coefficient on GDP per capita that we obtain; that coefficient is statistically significant for the regressions based on the local product ranking.

TABLE 3—GLOBAL EXPORT SALES RATIO: CORE PRODUCT ($m = 0$) TO PRODUCT m'

	(1)	(2)	(3)	(4)	(5)
ln GDP	0.107***	0.131***	0.110***	0.096***	0.098***
	(0.010)	(0.010)	(0.011)	(0.012)	(0.011)
ln supply potential	0.044***	0.038**	0.038***	0.022*	0.036**
	(0.014)	(0.016)	(0.014)	(0.012)	(0.016)
ln freeness of trade	0.096***	0.085**	0.113***	0.137***	0.092***
	(0.026)	(0.033)	(0.032)	(0.038)	(0.026)
ln GDP per cap					0.025
					(0.018)
$m' =$	1	2	1	1	1
Destination GDP/cap	all	all	top 50%	top 20%	all
Observations	56,093	22,576	50,623	40,964	56,093
Within R^2	0.005	0.006	0.004	0.002	0.005

Notes: All columns use Wooldridge's (2006) procedure: country-specific random effects on firm-demeaned data, with a robust covariance matrix estimation. Standard errors in parentheses.
*** Significant at the 1 percent level.
** Significant at the 5 percent level.
* Significant at the 10 percent level.

TABLE 4—LOCAL EXPORT SALES RATIO: CORE PRODUCT ($m = 0$) TO PRODUCT m'

	(1)	(2)	(3)	(4)	(5)
ln GDP	0.077***	0.100***	0.083***	0.061***	0.066***
	(0.006)	(0.012)	(0.011)	(0.016)	(0.008)
ln supply potential	0.068***	0.064***	0.051***	0.028*	0.057***
	(0.013)	(0.022)	(0.018)	(0.016)	(0.014)
ln freeness of trade	0.028	0.013	0.059	0.092*	0.025
	(0.017)	(0.042)	(0.039)	(0.052)	(0.017)
ln GDP per cap					0.029**
					(0.013)
$m' =$	1	2	1	1	1
Destination GDP/cap	all	all	top 50%	top 20%	all
Observations	96,878	49,554	84,708	64,653	96,878
Within R^2	0.007	0.009	0.005	0.002	0.007

Notes: All columns use Wooldridge's (2006) procedure: country-specific random effects on firm-demeaned data, with a robust covariance matrix estimation. Standard errors in parentheses.
*** Significant at the 1 percent level.
** Significant at the 5 percent level.
* Significant at the 10 percent level.

Tables 3 and 4 confirm the robustness of our baseline results regarding the strong impact of both country size and geography on the firms' export ratios.[44]

Lastly, we show that this effect of country size and geography on export skewness is not limited to the top 2–3 products exported by a firm to a destination. We now use our different statistics that measure the skewness of a firm's export sales over the entire range of exported products. The first three columns of Table 5 use the standard

---

[44] When we restrict the sample of destinations to the top 20 percent of richest countries, then our co-linearity problem resurfaces between the supply potential and freeness of trade measures, and the coefficient on supply potential is no longer statistically significant at the 5 percent level (only at the 10 percent level).

524   *THE AMERICAN ECONOMIC REVIEW*   *FEBRUARY 2014*

TABLE 5—SKEWNESS MEASURES FOR EXPORT SALES OF ALL PRODUCTS

	(1)	(2)	(3)	(4)	(5)	(6)
ln GDP	0.141***	0.019***	0.047***	0.052***	0.047***	0.041***
	(0.010)	(0.001)	(0.002)	(0.002)	(0.003)	(0.003)
ln supply potential	0.125***	0.016***	0.037***	0.033***	0.023***	0.031***
	(0.023)	(0.002)	(0.004)	(0.004)	(0.004)	(0.004)
ln freeness of trade	0.096***	0.007**	0.021**	0.032**	0.045**	0.021**
	(0.036)	(0.004)	(0.009)	(0.013)	(0.022)	(0.009)
ln GDP per cap						0.013**
						(0.005)
Dependent variable	s.d. ln x	herf	theil	theil	theil	theil
Destination GDP/cap	all	all	all	top 50%	top 20%	all
Observations	82,090	82,090	82,090	73,029	57,076	82,090
Within R^2	0.107	0.164	0.359	0.356	0.341	0.359

Notes: All columns use Wooldridge's (2006) procedure: country-specific random effects on firm-demeaned data, with a robust covariance matrix estimation. All columns include a cubic polynomial of the number of products exported by the firm to the country (also included in the within R^2). Standard errors in parentheses.
*** Significant at the 1 percent level.
** Significant at the 5 percent level.
* Significant at the 10 percent level.

deviation, Herfindahl index, and Theil index for the distribution of the firm's export sales to each destination with our baseline specification (freeness of trade control for bilateral trade barriers and the full sample of destination countries). In the last three columns, we stick with the Theil index and report the same robustness specifications as we reported for the local and global sales ratio: We reduce the sample of destinations by country income, and add GDP per capita as an independent control with the full sample of countries. Throughout Table 5, we add a cubic polynomial in the number of exported products by the firm to the destination (those coefficients are not reported). This controls for any mechanical effect of the number of exported products on the skewness statistic when the number of exported products is low. These results show how country size and geography increase the skewness of the firms' entire exported product mix. Using information on the entire distribution of exported sales increases the statistical precision of our estimates. The coefficients on country size and supply potential are significant well beyond the 1 percent threshold throughout all our different specifications.

In Appendix D, we report versions of Tables 3–5 using the number of French exporters to a destination as a combined measure of competition for French firms in a destination. This measure of competition across destinations is also very strongly associated with increased export skewness in all of our specifications.

VI. Economic Significance: Relationship Between Skewness and Productivity

We now quantitatively assess the economic significance of our main results. We have identified significant differences in skewness across destinations, and want to relate those differences in skewness to differences in competition across destinations—via the lens of our theoretical model. These differences in competition are important because tougher competition induces an aggregate increase in productivity—holding technology fixed. In a closed economy, we showed in Appendix B how firm productivity—measured either as output per worker $\Phi(c)$ or deflated sales per worker $\Phi_R(c)$—increases when competition increases (the cutoff c_D decreases). This effect holds even when the firm's product range $M(c)$ does not change, as it is driven by the increased skewness in the product mix (toward the best performing products). In the same Appendix, we also define parallel measures of firm productivity $\Phi_{lh}(c)$ and $\Phi_{R,lh}(c)$ for the bundle of products exported by firm c from l to h. Similarly, these productivity measures increase with competition in that destination (lower c_{hh}) due to the same intra-firm reallocations across products driven by the increase in skewness. Since our available data does not include measures of firm productivity, we must rely on the functional forms of our theoretical model to quantitatively relate export skewness to competition and productivity. This represents a significant departure from our empirical approach up to this point, which has avoided relying on those functional forms.

In Section II, we defined aggregate productivity $\overline{\Phi}$ and $\overline{\Phi}_R$ as the aggregate counterparts to $\Phi(c)$ and $\Phi_R(c)$, and showed that both aggregate measured were identical, and inversely related to the cost cutoff. This describes the overall response of productivity to changes in the toughness of competition in the closed economy. We define the aggregate productivity for all products exported from l to h in a similar way: $\overline{\Phi}_{lh}$ and $\overline{\Phi}_{R,lh}$ are the aggregate counterparts to the firm productivity measures $\Phi_{lh}(c)$ and $\Phi_{R,lh}(c)$. In Appendix C, we show that these two alternate measures coincide (just like they do for aggregate productivity in the closed economy) and are inversely proportional to the cost cutoff c_{hh} (the toughness of competition in the export destination). Thus, our theoretical model predicts that increases in the toughness of competition in a destination—measured as percentage decreases in the destination cutoff—lead to proportional increases in aggregate productivity (same percentage change as the cutoff). This aggregate productivity response combines the effects of skewness on firm productivity, holding the product range fixed, as well as reallocation effects across products when the number of products changes, and reallocation effects across firms. However, because product market shares continuously drop to zero as competition toughens, the contribution of the product extensive margin (adding/dropping products) to productivity changes is second order, while the contribution of product skewness to productivity changes is first order. Thus, the unit elasticity between productivity and toughness of competition is driven by the effects of competition on product skewness. This is the key new channel that we emphasize in this paper.

Our main results in the previous section have quantified the link between observable country characteristics and export skewness. In particular, we have shown how differences in GDP induce significant differences in skewness for French exporters. We now quantitatively determine what differences in competition (across countries) would yield those same observed differences in export skewness. This allows us to associate differences in competition with the differences in GDP, in terms of their effect on the skewness of exports. In our theoretical model, the relationship between competition in a destination (the cutoff c_{hh}) and export skewness for firm c from l (measured as the ratio of a firm's exports of its core product, $m = 0$, to its next best performing product, $m' = 1$) is given by (26):

$$(27) \qquad rr_{lh}(c) = \frac{r_{lh}(v(m, c))}{r_{lh}(v(m', c))} = \frac{(c_{hh})^2 - (\tau_{lh}c)^2}{(c_{hh})^2 - (\tau_{lh}c/\omega)^2}.$$

Our results in Tables 3 and 4 measure the average elasticity of this skewness measure with respect to destination h GDP—across all French exporters that export their top two products (global or local definition) to h. Using (27), we compute the average elasticity of this skewness measure with respect to competition in h (the cutoff c_{hh}):

$$\frac{d \ln rr_{lh}}{d \ln c_{hh}} = -2k \frac{1 - \omega^2}{\omega^2} \frac{(c_{hh}\tau_{lh})^2}{(\omega^2 c_{hh}/\tau_{lh})^k} \int_0^{\omega^2 c_{hh}/\tau_{lh}} \frac{c^{k+1}}{[c_{hh}^2 - (\tau_{lh}c)^2][c_{hh}^2 - (\tau_{lh}c/\omega)^2]} dc$$

$$= -2k \frac{1 - \omega^2}{\omega^{2k}} \int_0^{\omega^2} \frac{x^{k+1}}{(1 - x^2)(\omega^2 - x^2)} dx, \quad \text{where } x \equiv (\tau_{lh}/c_{hh})c \in [0, \omega^2]$$

$$\equiv f(\omega, k).$$

Here, we have averaged over all firms in l selling *at least* three products to h as the elasticity is not defined for some firms exporting two products, who become single product exporters when the cutoff c_{hh} decreases. We note that this average elasticity can be written as a function of just two model parameters: ω (the ladder step size), and k (the shape of the Pareto distribution for cost/productivity). We thus need empirical estimates of just those two coefficients. Several papers have estimated the Pareto shape coefficients k. Crozet and Koenig (2010) estimate a range for $\hat{k}$ between 1.34 and 4.43 for French exporters (by sector) while Eaton, Kortum, and Kramarz (2011) estimate $\hat{k} = 4.87$ for all French firms. This range coincides well with estimates from other countries: Corcos et al. (2012) estimate $\hat{k} = 1.79$ across European firms, and Bernard et al. (2003) estimate $\hat{k} = 3.6$ for US firms. We report estimates of $f(\hat{\omega}, \hat{k})$ for $\hat{k}$ between 1.34 and 4.87.

In order to estimate $\hat{\omega}$, we use our theoretical model to derive an estimation equation for $\vartheta \equiv k \ln \omega$ based on our product-destination export data (see Appendix C). This yields a very precise estimate for ϑ, $\hat{\vartheta} = -0.13$, which we use to recover $\hat{\omega}$, given a choice for $\hat{k}$. Given the small standard error for $\hat{\vartheta}$, differences in $\hat{\omega}$ will be driven by our choice of $\hat{k}$; however, any alternate assumption for $\hat{\vartheta}$ will have the same effect on $\hat{\omega}$ as a proportional change in $\hat{k}$. This completes our empirical derivation for the average elasticity of skewness with respect to competition, $d \ln rr_{lh}/d \ln c_{hh} \equiv f(\omega, k)$. This elasticity ranges from 0.635 for $\hat{k} = 1.34$ to 2.34 for $\hat{k} = 4.87$; it is 1.52 at the midpoint for $\hat{k} = 3.11$.

With estimates of this elasticity in hand, we can evaluate the economic significance of our previous results from Tables 3 and 4. In those tables, we reported an average elasticity of skewness to country GDP between 0.06 and 0.11. Dividing those elasticities by our estimate for $d \ln rr_{lh}/d \ln c_{hh}$ yields the change in competition that would induce the same change in skewness as a doubling of country GDP. In our theoretical model, those changes in competition are proportional to

VOL. 104 NO. 2   *MAYER ET AL.: MARKET SIZE, COMPETITION, AND PRODUCT MIX*   *527*

changes in aggregate productivity for the bundle of goods sold in that destination. Viewed through this lens, the economic impact of the changes in skewness are quite large. For a doubling of country GDP, they imply changes in productivity between 2.56 percent and 17.3 percent. At our midpoint for $\hat{k}$, the implied productivity changes are between 3.95 percent and 7.24 percent.

VII. Conclusion

In this paper, we have developed a model of multi-product firms that highlights how differences in market size and geography affect the within-firm distribution of export sales across destinations. This effect on the firms' product mix choice is driven by variations in the toughness of competition across markets. Tougher competition induces a downward shift in the distribution of markups across all products, and increases the relative market share of the better performing products. We test these predictions for a comprehensive set of French exporters, and find that market size and geography indeed have a very strong impact on their exported product mix across world destinations: French firms skew their export sales toward their better performing products in big destination markets, and markets where many exporters from around the world compete (high foreign supply potential markets). We have obtained these results without imposing the specific functional forms (for demand, for the geometric product ladder, and for the Pareto inverse cost draws) that we used in our theoretical model. We therefore view our results as giving a strong indication of substantial differences in competition across export markets—rather than providing goodness of fit test to our specific model (and its functional forms). We cannot measure markups directly but the strong link between tougher competition and a more skewed product mix is suggestive of substantial markup adjustments by exporters across destinations. In any event, trade models based on exogenous markups cannot explain this strong significant link between destination market characteristics and the within-firm skewness of export sales (after controlling for bilateral trade costs).

Theoretically, we showed how such an increase in skewness toward better performing products (driven by tougher competition) would also be reflected in higher firm productivity. We cannot directly test this link without productivity data. Instead, we have leaned more heavily on the functional forms of our theoretical model. A calibrated fit to that model reveals that these productivity effects are potentially quite large.

APPENDIX

A. *Trade Liberalization*

In this Appendix, we briefly discuss the predictions of our model regarding trade liberalization (unilateral and multilateral) in the context of a two country version of our model. The main message is that the effects of trade liberalization on aggregate variables (competition, productivity, welfare) are identical to those analyzed in Melitz and Ottaviano (2008) in the context of single-product firms. However, our current model allows us to translate those aggregate changes into predictions for the responses of multi-product firms. The main link is the one we have emphasized (both theoretically and empirically) in the cross section of destinations: how changes in competition lead to associated changes in the multi-product firms' product mix and hence to changes in their productivity. In this respect, the predictions are starkly different than the case of single-product firms where productivity (output per worker) is exogenously fixed independently of the competitive environment.

Equation (21) summarizes the effect of trade costs on competition in every market (the resulting cost cutoff c_{hh}) via the matrix of trade freeness $\mathbf{P} = [\rho_{lh}]$ where $\rho_{lh} \equiv \tau_{lh}^{-k} < 1$. In a two country world, this simplifies to:

$$(A1) \qquad c_{hh} = \left(\frac{1 - \rho_{hl}}{1 - \rho_{hl}\,\rho_{lh}} \frac{\gamma\phi}{\Omega L_h} \right)^{\frac{1}{k+2}}, \qquad l \neq h.$$

Equation (22) then expresses the resulting product variety in country h as a function of that cutoff. The determination of the cutoff in (A1) is very similar to the case of single-product firms: this is the case where $\Omega = 1$. Trade liberalization thus induces a similar response as in the single-product case. Bilateral trade liberalization (higher ρ_{lh} and ρ_{hl}) increases competition in both countries (lower cutoffs c_{hh} and c_{ll}). On the other hand, unilateral trade liberalization in country h (higher ρ_{lh} with ρ_{hl} remaining unchanged) results in weaker competition in h (higher c_{hh}) and tougher competition in its trading partner l (lower c_{ll}). This divergence is due to the impact of the asymmetric liberalization on the firms' entry decisions: unilateral trade liberalization by h increases the incentives for entry in its trading partner l; entry in h is reduced, while entry in l increases. We can also define a short-run equilibrium in a similar way to the one defined for single-product firms in Melitz and Ottaviano (2008). With entry fixed in the short run, unilateral trade liberalization will then increase competition in the liberalizing country, due to the increase in import competition (in the long run, the increase in import competition is more than offset by the effects of exit). An analysis of preferential trade liberalization would also lead to similar results on competition as those described in Melitz and Ottaviano (2008).

B. *Tougher Competition and Firm Productivity*

In Section II we argued that tougher competition induces improvements in firm productivity through its impact on a firm's product mix. Here we show that both firm productivity measures, output per worker $\Phi(c)$ and deflated sales per worker $\Phi_R(c)$, increase for all multi-product firms when competition increases (c_D decreases). We provide proofs for the closed as well as the open economy. In both cases we proceed in two steps. First, we show that, holding a firm's product scope constant, firm productivity over that product scope increases whenever competition increases. Then, we extend the argument by continuity to cover the case where tougher competition induces a change in product scope.

Closed Economy.—Consider a firm with cost c producing $M(c)$ varieties. Output per worker is given by

$$\Phi(c) = \frac{Q(c)}{C(c)} = \frac{\sum_{m=0}^{M(c)-1} q(v(m,c))}{\sum_{m=0}^{M(c)-1} v(m,c)\,q(v(m,c))} = \frac{\frac{L}{2\gamma} \sum_{m=0}^{M(c)-1} (c_D - \omega^{-m} c)}{\frac{L}{2\gamma} \sum_{m=0}^{M(c)-1} \omega^{-m}(c_D - \omega^{-m} c)}.$$

VOL. 104 NO. 2   MAYER ET AL.: MARKET SIZE, COMPETITION, AND PRODUCT MIX   529

For a fixed product scope M with $1 < M \leq M(c)$, this can be written as

(B1)
$$\Phi(c) = \frac{\omega^M(1 - \omega)}{\omega(1 - \omega^M)} \frac{M}{c} \frac{c_D - \dfrac{c}{M} \dfrac{\omega(1 - \omega^M)}{\omega^M(1 - \omega)}}{c_D - c \dfrac{\omega(1 + \omega^M)}{\omega^M(1 + \omega)}},$$

subject to $c \in [c_D \omega^M, c_D \omega^{M-1}]$. Differentiating (B1) with respect to c_D implies that

$$\frac{d\Phi(c)}{dc_D} < 0 \quad \Leftrightarrow \quad c \frac{\omega(1 + \omega^M)}{\omega^M(1 + \omega)} > \frac{c}{M} \frac{\omega(1 - \omega^M)}{\omega^M(1 - \omega)}$$

or, equivalently, if and only if

(B2)
$$M > \frac{(1 + \omega)(1 - \omega^M)}{(1 + \omega^M)(1 - \omega)}.$$

This is always the case for $M > 1$: the left- and right-hand sides are identical for $M = 0$ and $M = 1$, and the right-hand side is increasing and concave in M. This proves that, holding $M > 1$ constant, a firm's output per worker is larger in a market where competition is tougher (lower c_D).

Even when product scope M drops due to the decrease in c_D, output per worker must still increase due to the continuity of $\Phi(c)$ with respect to c_D (both $Q(c)$ and $C(c)$ are continuous in c_D as the firm produces zero units of a variety right before it is dropped when competition gets tougher). To see this, consider a large downward change in the cutoff c_D. The result for given M tells us that output per worker for a firm with given c increases on all ranges of c_D where the number of varieties produced does not change. This just leaves a discrete number of c_Ds where the firm changes the number of products produced. Since $\Phi(c)$ is continuous at those c_Ds, and increasing everywhere else, it must be increasing everywhere.

The unavailability of data on physical output often leads to a measure of productivity in terms of deflated sales per worker. Over the fixed product scope M with $1 < M \leq M(c)$, this alternate productivity measure is defined as

(B3) $\Phi_R(c) = \dfrac{R(c)/\overline{P}}{C(c)} = \dfrac{1}{2} \dfrac{k+2}{k+1} \dfrac{1}{c_D} \dfrac{M(c_D)^2 - c^2\omega^2 \dfrac{1 - \omega^{2M}}{\omega^{2M}(1 - \omega)(1 + \omega)}}{c_D c\omega \dfrac{1 - \omega^M}{\omega^M(1 - \omega)} - c^2\omega^2 \dfrac{1 - \omega^{2M}}{\omega^{2M}(1 - \omega)(1 + \omega)}},$

subject to $c \in [c_D \omega^M, c_D \omega^{M-1}]$. Differentiating (B3) with respect to c_D then yields

$$\frac{d\left(\dfrac{R(c)/\overline{P}}{C(c)}\right)}{dc_D} = -\frac{1}{2} \frac{k+2}{k+1} \frac{1 + \omega^M}{1 - \omega^M}.$$

$$\frac{M\omega^{2M}(1 - \omega^2)(c_D)^2 - 2c\omega^{M+1}(1 + \omega)(1 - \omega^M)c_D + c^2\omega^2(1 - \omega^{2M})}{(c_D)^2[\omega^M(1 + \omega)c_D - c\omega(1 + \omega^M)]^2} < 0.$$

530   *THE AMERICAN ECONOMIC REVIEW*   *FEBRUARY 2014*

Here, we have used the fact that $c \in [c_D \omega^M, c_D \omega^{M-1}]$ implies

$$M \omega^{2M}(1 - \omega^2)(c/\omega^M)^2 - 2c\omega^{M+1}(1 + \omega)(1 - \omega^M)(c/\omega^M) > 0.$$

This proves that, holding $M > 1$ constant, this alternative productivity measure $\Phi_R(c)$ also increases when competition is tougher (lower c_D). The same reasoning applies to the case where tougher competition induces a reduction in product scope M. Note that, in the special case of $M = 1$, we have

$$\Phi_R(c) = \frac{1}{2} \frac{k+2}{k+1} \left(\frac{1}{c} + \frac{1}{c_D} \right).$$

Hence, whereas tougher competition (lower c_D) has no impact on the output per worker $\Phi(c)$ of a single-product firm, it still raises deflated sales per worker $\Phi_R(c)$. This is due to the fact that deflated sales per worker are also affected by markup changes when the toughness of competition changes.

Open Economy.—Consider a firm with cost c selling $M_{lh}(c)$ varieties from country l to country h. Exported output per worker is given by

$$\Phi_{lh}(c) \equiv \frac{Q_{lh}(c)}{C_{lh}(c)} = \frac{\sum_{m=0}^{M_{lh}(c)-1} c_{hh} - \tau_{lh} \, \omega^{-m} c}{\sum_{m=0}^{M_{lh}(c)-1} (\tau_{lh} \omega^{-m} c)(c_{hh} - \tau^{lh} \, \omega^{-m} c)}.$$

For a fixed product scope M with $1 < M \leq M_{lh}(c)$, this can be written as

$$\text{(B4)} \qquad \Phi_{lh}(c) = \frac{\omega^M(1 - \omega)}{\omega(1 - \omega^M)} \frac{M}{c\tau_{lh}} \frac{c_{hh} - \frac{c\tau_{lh}}{M} \frac{\omega(1 - \omega^M)}{\omega^M(1 - \omega)}}{c_{hh} - c\tau_{lh} \frac{\omega(1 + \omega^M)}{\omega^M(1 + \omega)}},$$

subject to $c\tau_{lh} \in [c_{hh} \, \omega^M, c_{hh} \, \omega^{M-1}]$. Differentiating (B4) with respect to c_{hh} yields

$$\frac{d\Phi_{lh}(c)}{dc_{hh}} < 0 \quad \Leftrightarrow \quad c\tau_{lh} \frac{\omega(1 + \omega^M)}{\omega^M(1 + \omega)} > \frac{c\tau_{lh}}{M} \frac{\omega(1 - \omega^M)}{\omega^M(1 - \omega)}.$$

This must hold for $M > 1$ (see (B2)). Hence, tougher competition (lower c_{hh}) in the destination market increases exported output per worker. As in the closed economy, the fact that output per worker is continuous at a discrete number of c_{hh}s and decreasing in c_{hh} everywhere else implies that it is decreasing in c_{hh} everywhere.

We now turn to productivity measured as deflated export sales per worker. Over the fixed product scope M with $1 < M \leq M(c)$, this is defined as

$$\text{(B5)} \quad \Phi_{R,lh}(c) = \frac{R_{lh}(c)/\overline{P}_h}{C_{lh}(c)}$$

$$= \frac{1}{2} \frac{k+2}{k+1} \frac{1}{c_{hh}} \frac{M(c_{hh})^2 - c^2(\tau_{lh})^2 \omega^2 \frac{1 - \omega^{2M}}{\omega^{2M}(1 - \omega)(1 + \omega)}}{c_{hh} c\tau_{lh} \omega \frac{1 - \omega^M}{\omega^M(1 - \omega)} - c^2(\tau_{lh})^2 \omega^2 \frac{1 - \omega^{2M}}{\omega^{2M}(1 - \omega)(1 + \omega)}},$$

VOL. 104 NO. 2   *MAYER ET AL.: MARKET SIZE, COMPETITION, AND PRODUCT MIX*   531

subject to $c_{Th} \in [c_{hh}\omega^M, c_{hh}\omega^{M-1}]$. Differentiating (B5) with respect to c_{hh} yields

$$\frac{d\Phi_{R,lh}(c)}{dc_{hh}} = -\frac{1}{2}\frac{k+2}{k+1}\frac{1+\omega^M}{1-\omega^M}.$$

$$\frac{M\omega^{2M}(1-\omega^2)(c_{hh})^2 - 2c_T{}^{lh}\omega^{M+1}(1+\omega)(1-\omega^M)c_{hh} + c^2(\tau_{lh})^2\omega^2(1-\omega^{2M})}{(c_{hh})^2[\omega^M(1+\omega)c_{hh} - c_{Th}\omega(1+\omega^M)]^2} < 0.$$

The last inequality holds since $c_{Th} \in [c_{hh}\omega^M, c_{hh}\omega^{M-1}]$ implies

$$M\omega^{2M}(1-\omega^2)(c_{Th}/\omega^M)^2 - 2c_{Th}\omega^{M+1}(1+\omega)(1-\omega^M)(c_{Th}/\omega^M) > 0.$$

This proves that, holding $M > 1$ constant, productivity measured as deflated export sales per worker increases with tougher competition in the export market (lower c_{hh}). The same applies to the case where the tougher competition induces a response in the exported product scope M, as $\Phi_{R,lh}(c)$ is continuous in c_{hh}.

C. *Calibration of Relationship between Skewness and Productivity*

Aggregate Productivity Index for Bundle of Exported Goods.—In the previous Appendix section, we defined productivity indices for firm's c bundle of exported goods from l to h as the output per worker associated with that bundle of exports:

$$\Phi_{lh}(c) \equiv \frac{Q_{lh}(c)}{C_{lh}(c)} \quad \text{and} \quad \Phi_{R,lh}(c) = \frac{R_{lh}(c)/\overline{P}_h}{C_{lh}(c)},$$

where the R subscript are productivity measures based on deflated sales as a measure of firm output. The aggregate counterparts for all bilateral exports from l to h are just the same measures of output per worker computed for the aggregate bundle of exported goods:

$$\overline{\Phi}_{lh} \equiv \frac{\int_0^{\omega^m c_{hh}/\tau_{lh}} Q_{lh}(c)\,dG(c)}{\int_0^{\omega^m c_{hh}/\tau_{lh}} C_{lh}(c)\,dG(c)} = \frac{k+2}{k}\frac{1}{c_{hh}},$$

$$\overline{\Phi}_{R,lh} \equiv \frac{\left[\int_0^{\omega^m c_{hh}/\tau_{lh}} R_{lh}(c)\,dG(c)\right]/\overline{P}_h}{\int_0^{\omega^m c_{hh}/\tau_{lh}} C_{lh}(c)\,dG(c)} = \frac{k+2}{k}\frac{1}{c_{hh}}.$$

Just like the case of aggregate productivity in the closed economy, our two aggregate productivity measures overlap and are inversely proportional to the cutoff c_{hh} in the export destination h.

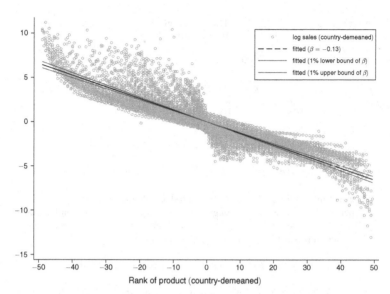

FIGURE C1. REGRESSION YIELDING ESTIMATE OF $\hat{\vartheta}$

Estimating the Product Ladder Step Size ω.—We obtain an estimating equation for the ladder step size ω by aggregating all the product export sales across firms (for bilateral exports from l to h) that are at the same ladder step m:

$$R_{lh}(m) = \int_0^{c_{hh}/(\tau_{lh}\omega^{-m})} R_{lh}(c, m)\, d\left(\frac{c}{c_M}\right)^k = \left[\frac{L}{\gamma(k+2)}\frac{(c_{hh})^{k+2}}{(\tau_{lh}c_M)^k}\right]\omega^{km}.$$

Thus, $R_{lh}(0)$ represents aggregate exports of core products from l to h; $R_{lh}(1)$ for the second best performing product, and so forth for the product that is m steps from the core product. This implies a linear relationship between the log of product export sales $\ln R_{lh}(m)$ and its associated ladder step m, with a slope given by $\vartheta \equiv k \ln \omega$ and an intercept that varies across bilateral country pairs. We can easily compute $R_{lh}(m)$ from our data by aggregating firm-product export sales from France to any destination h—across all products at the same ladder step m. A linear regression of $\ln R_{lh}(m)$ on m with destination h fixed effects (capturing the term in the brackets) will then yield our estimate for $\hat{\vartheta}$ (origin country l is held fixed for France).

We visually summarize this regression in Figure C1, where we have eliminated the destination fixed-effects by demeaning the export sales $\ln R_{lh}(m)$ and the associated product m by destination h. By construction, this regression must deliver a negative fitted line. However, Figure C1 also clearly reveals that the linear relationship provides an excellent fit. The figure also reveals that our slope coefficient $\hat{\vartheta} = -0.13$ is very tightly estimated, with no appreciable slope variation within a 99 percent confidence interval.

VOL. 104 NO. 2   *MAYER ET AL.: MARKET SIZE, COMPETITION, AND PRODUCT MIX*   533

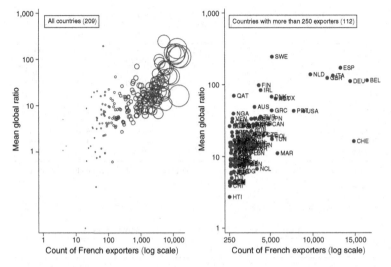

FIGURE D1. MEAN GLOBAL RATIO AND NUMBER OF FRENCH EXPLORERS IN DESTINATION COUNTRY IN 2003

TABLE D1—GLOBAL EXPORT SALES RATIO: CORE PRODUCT ($m = 0$) TO PRODUCT m'

	(1)	(2)	(3)	(4)	(5)
ln number of French exporters	0.226***	0.263***	0.233***	0.200***	0.200***
	(0.020)	(0.032)	(0.025)	(0.031)	(0.024)
ln freeness of trade	−0.034	−0.078***	−0.019	0.018	−0.029
	(0.032)	(0.029)	(0.037)	(0.043)	(0.033)
ln GDP per cap					0.031*
					(0.019)
$m' =$	1	2	1	1	1
Destination GDP/cap	all	all	top 50%	top 20%	all
Observations	56,093	22,576	50,623	40,964	56,093
Within R^2	0.005	0.005	0.004	0.002	0.005

Notes: All columns use Wooldridge's (2006) procedure: country-specific random effects on firm-demeaned data, with a robust covariance matrix estimation. All columns include a cubic polynomial of the number of products exported by the firm to the country (also included in the within R^2). Standard errors in parentheses.
  *** Significant at the 1 percent level.
  ** Significant at the 5 percent level.
  * Significant at the 10 percent level.

D. Robustness to Alternate Measure of Toughness of Competition

As we mentioned in the main text, we repeat our main estimation procedures using the number of French exporters to a destination as a combined measure of the toughness of competition (for French firms) in a destination. We begin by showing the scatter plots of the mean global ratio plotted against this alternate competition measure (direct parallel to Figures 2 and 3). Figure D1 clearly shows that there is also a very strong increasing relationship between the global ratio and this alternate measure of competition.

534   THE AMERICAN ECONOMIC REVIEW   FEBRUARY 2014

TABLE D2—LOCAL EXPORT SALES RATIO: CORE PRODUCT ($m = 0$) TO PRODUCT m'

	(1)	(2)	(3)	(4)	(5)
ln number French exporters	0.178***	0.210***	0.178***	0.119***	0.129***
	(0.012)	(0.027)	(0.026)	(0.035)	(0.018)
ln freeness of trade	−0.056**	−0.096*	−0.026	0.027	−0.040
	(0.026)	(0.050)	(0.045)	(0.058)	(0.026)
ln GDP per cap					0.049***
					(0.013)
$m' =$	1	2	1	1	1
Destination GDP/cap	all	all	top 50%	top 20%	all
Observations	96,878	49,554	84,708	64,653	96,878
Within R^2	0.007	0.008	0.005	0.001	0.007

Notes: All columns use Wooldridge's (2006) procedure: country-specific random effects on firm-demeaned data, with a robust covariance matrix estimation. Standard errors in parentheses.
*** Significant at the 1 percent level.
** Significant at the 5 percent level.
* Significant at the 10 percent level.

TABLE D3—SKEWNESS MEASURES FOR EXPORT SALES OF ALL PRODUCTS

	(1)	(2)	(3)	(4)	(5)	(6)
ln number French exporters	0.348***	0.045***	0.111***	0.118***	0.102***	0.086***
	(0.025)	(0.002)	(0.004)	(0.006)	(0.010)	(0.006)
ln freeness of trade	−0.065	−0.014***	−0.034***	−0.027*	−0.007	−0.024*
	(0.048)	(0.005)	(0.012)	(0.016)	(0.020)	(0.012)
ln GDP per cap						0.022***
						(0.006)
Dependent variable	s.d. ln x	herf	theil	theil	theil	theil
Destination GDP/cap	all	all	all	top 50%	top 20%	all
Observations	82,090	82,090	82,090	73,029	57,076	82,090
Within R^2	0.106	0.163	0.358	0.356	0.341	0.359

Notes: All columns use Wooldridge's (2006) procedure: country-specific random effects on firm-demeaned data, with a robust covariance matrix estimation. All columns include a cubic polynomial of the number of products exported by the firm to the country (also included in the within R^2). Standard errors in parentheses.
*** Significant at the 1 percent level.
** Significant at the 5 percent level.
* Significant at the 10 percent level.

We next replicate Tables 3–5 replacing country GDP and supply potential with the number of French exporters to the destination (in logs). Those tables clearly show that all our results are robust to this alternate measure of competition across destinations.[45]

---

[45] We have also constructed a sector-level competition proxy by counting the French exporters in a destination only within a 2-digit HS sector. Using this alternate measure of competition does not materially affect any of the specifications in those three tables. We also ran some specifications using all three competition measures jointly (GDP, supply potential, and number of exporters). Adding the third competition regressor does not affect the impact of the our first two baseline competition measures. The independent effect of the third measure remained significant for the global and overall skewness specifications.

VOL. 104 NO. 2   *MAYER ET AL.: MARKET SIZE, COMPETITION, AND PRODUCT MIX*   535

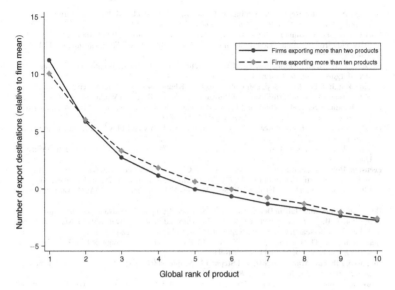

FIGURE E1. NUMBER OF EXPORT DESTINATIONS AS A FUNCTION OF A PRODUCT'S GLOBAL RANK

E. Selection of Products into the Local Ranking

Figure E1 plots changes in the average number of export destinations for a product as a function of its global ranking. The number of destinations is measured relative to the firm-mean number of destinations (across products). We restrict the plots to the firms' top ten products (according to their global ranking). In one of the plots, we also restrict the sample of firms to those that export at least ten products, so that there is no change in the sample of firms for the entire plot. We also show a plot for all firms in our analysis sample (that export at least two products). Here, there is attrition of firms along the plot as the global rank increases—but the plot is surprisingly similar to the one without any change in firm selection.

REFERENCES

▶ **Allanson, Paul, and Catia Montagna.** 2005. "Multiproduct Firms and Market Structure: An Explorative Application to the Product Life Cycle." *International Journal of Industrial Organization* 23 (7–8): 587–97.

Arkolakis, Costas, and Marc-Andreas Muendler. 2010. "The Extensive Margin of Exporting Products: A Firm-level Analysis." National Bureau of Economic Research Working Paper 16641.

Baldwin, John R., and Wulong Gu. 2009. "The Impact of Trade on Plant Scale, Production-Run Length and Diversification." In *Producer Dynamics: New Evidence from Micro Data*, edited by Timothy Dunne, J. Bradford Jensen, and Mark J. Roberts, 557–96. Chicago: University of Chicago Press.

▶ **Bernard, Andrew B., Jonathan Eaton, Brad Jensen, and Samuel Kortum.** 2003. "Plants and Productivity in International Trade." *American Economic Review* 93 (4): 1268–90.

▶ **Bernard, Andrew B., J. Bradford Jensen, Stephen J. Redding, and Peter K. Schott.** 2007. "Firms in International Trade." *Journal of Economic Perspectives* 21 (3): 105–30.

▶ **Bernard, Andrew B., Stephen J. Redding, and Peter K. Schott.** 2011. "Multiproduct Firms and Trade Liberalization." *Quarterly Journal of Economics* 126 (3): 1271–318.

▶ **Corcos, Gregory, Massimo Del Gatto, Giordano Mion, and Gianmarco I. P. Ottaviano.** 2012. "Productivity and Firm Selection: Quantifying the 'New' Gains from Trade." *Economic Journal* 122 (561): 754–98.

▶ **Crozet, Matthieu, and Pamina Koenig.** 2010. "Structural Gravity Equations with Intensive and Extensive Margins." *Canadian Journal of Economics* 43 (1): 41–62.

De Loecker, Jan, Pinelopi Koujianou Goldberg, Amit Khandelwal, and Nina Pavcnik. 2012. "Prices, Markups and Trade Reform." National Bureau of Economic Research Working Paper 17925.

▶ **Eaton, Jonathan, Samuel Kortum, and Francis Kramarz.** 2011. "An Anatomy of International Trade: Evidence from French Firms." *Econometrica* 79 (5): 1453–98.

▶ **Eckel, Carsten, and J. Peter Neary.** 2010. "Multi-product Firms and Flexible Manufacturing in the Global Economy." *Review of Economic Studies* 77 (1): 188–217.

Feenstra, Robert C. 2004. *Advanced International Trade: Theory and Evidence.* Princeton: Princeton University Press.

Feenstra, Robert C., and Hong Ma. 2008. "Optimal Choice of Product Scope for Multiproduct Firms under Monopolistic Competition." In *The Organization of Firms in a Global Economy,* edited by Elhanan Helpman, Dalia Marin, and Thierry Verdier, 173–99. Cambridge MA: Harvard University Press.

Harrigan, James, and Haiyan Deng. 2010. "China's Local Comparative Advantage." In *China's Growing Role in World Trade,* edited by Robert C. Feenstra and Shang-Jin Wei, 109–36. National Bureau of Economic Research Conference Report. Chicago: Chicago University Press.

▶ **Head, Keith, and Thierry Mayer.** 2011. "Gravity, Market Potential and Economic Development." *Journal of Economic Geography* 11 (2): 281–94.

▶ **Helpman, Elhanan, Marc J. Melitz, and Stephen R. Yeaple.** 2004. "Export versus FDI with Heterogeneous Firms." *American Economic Review* 94 (1): 300–16.

Iacovone, Leonardo, and Beata S. Javorcik. 2008. "Multi-product Exporters: Diversification and Micro-level Dynamics." The World Bank, Policy Research Working Paper 4723.

Mayer, Thierry, Marc J. Melitz, and Gianmarco I. P. Ottaviano. 2014. "Market Size, Competition, and the Product Mix of Exporters: Dataset." *American Economic Review.* http://dx.doi.org/10.1257/aer.104.2.495.

▶ **Mayer, Thierry, and Gianmarco I. P. Ottaviano.** 2008. "The Happy Few: The Internationalisation of European Firms: New Facts Based on Firm-Level Evidence." *Intereconomics/Review of European Economic Policy* 43 (3): 135–48.

▶ **Melitz, Marc J., and Giancarlo I. P. Ottaviano.** 2008. "Market Size, Trade, and Productivity." *Review of Economic Studies* 75 (1): 295–316.

Nocke, Volker, and Stephen Yeaple. 2006. "Globalization and Endogenous Firm Scope." National Bureau of Economic Research Working Paper 12322.

▶ **Redding, Stephen, and Anthony J. Venables.** 2004. "Economic Geography and International Inequality." *Journal of International Economics* 62 (1): 53–82.

Wooldridge, Jeffrey M. 2006. "Cluster-Sample Methods in Applied Econometrics: An Extended Analysis." Unpublished.

Part II
Workers

Chapter 6

Cities and cultures[†]

Gianmarco I.P. Ottaviano [a,b], Giovanni Peri [c,d,*]

[a] *Department of Economics, University of Bologna, Strada Maggiore 45, 40126 Bologna, Italy*
[b] *FEEM and CEPR*
[c] *Department of Economics, University of California, Davis, One Shield Avenue, Davis, CA 95616, USA*
[d] *UCLA and NBER*

Received 23 April 2004; revised 17 June 2005

Available online 18 August 2005

Abstract

We investigate whether cultural diversity across US cities (measured as the variety of native languages spoken by city residents) is associated with any effect on their productivity. Diversity of cultures may imply diversity of production skills, of abilities and of occupations that enhances the productive performance of a city. On the other hand transaction costs and frictions across groups may hurt productivity. Similarly, diversity in available goods and services can increase utility but distaste for (or hostility to) different cultural groups may decrease it. Using census data from 1970 to 1990, we find that wages and employment density of US-born workers were systematically higher, ceteris paribus, in cities with richer linguistic diversity. These positive correlations reveal a net positive effect of diversity on productivity that survives robustness checks and instrumental variable estimation. This effect is found to be stronger for highly educated workers and for white workers. We also show that better 'assimilated' non-native speakers, i.e. those who speak English well and have been in the US for more than five years, are most beneficial to the productivity of US-born workers.
© 2005 Elsevier Inc. All rights reserved.

JEL classification: O4; R0; F1

Keywords: Cultural diversity; Productivity; Wages; Employment; Cities

*   Corresponding author.
    E-mail addresses: ottavian@economia.unibo.it (G.I.P. Ottaviano), gperi@ucdavis.edu (G. Peri).

[†] This article originally appeared in *Journal of Urban Economics*, **58** 304–337 © 2005 Elsevier Science Publishers B.V.

G.I.P. Ottaviano, G. Peri / Journal of Urban Economics 58 (2005) 304–337   305

1. Introduction

"Global civilization could never be anything other than the coalition at global levels of cultures, each of them retaining its originality." (Claude Lévi-Strauss)

Recent world developments are bringing the issue of cultural diversity to the forefront. Indeed, as argued by Alesina and La Ferrara [1]: "In a more integrated world, the question of how different people can peacefully interact is the critical problem for the next many decades" (p. 29). From an economic perspective, the most salient question is whether a culturally homogeneous society can be more productive and affluent than a culturally diversified one. The answer is not obvious. On the one hand, cultural diversity can generate costs from potential conflicts of preferences, hurdles to communication, or outright racism, prejudice or fear of other groups, leading to a sub-optimal provision of private and public goods (Alesina et al. [2]; Alesina et al. [3]). On the other hand, cultural diversity can create potential benefits by increasing the variety of goods, services and skills available for consumption and production (Lazear [25,26]; O'Reilly et al. [29]). Moreover, by bringing together complementary skills, different abilities and alternative approaches to problem solving, diversity may also boost creativity, innovation and ultimately growth (Berliant and Fujita [6], Florida [20,21]).

The aim of the present article is to investigate the impact of cultural diversity on the economic life of US cities. Specifically, we tackle the following questions: Is there a *wage premium for diversity* in US cities? Do identical workers earn higher or lower wages in urban environments that are identical to others in all respects except their cultural diversity? And by qualifying the first question, a second question arises: Is such a wage premium a consequence of a *positive effect of diversity on productivity* (accompanied therefore by higher productive density), or a compensation for a *distaste of workers for diversity* (accompanied therefore by lower productive density)?

We first present a simple theoretical framework to think about effects of diversity in production and consumption and then we use data from 160 US metropolitan areas for three census years, 1970, 1980 and 1990 to discriminate between a net positive or negative effect of diversity on wages and employment. US metropolitan areas represent natural laboratories for investigating cultural diversity in many respects. First, the US has a long standing tradition of being a favorite destination for migrants from both developed and developing countries. During this period most immigrants have settled in urban rather than rural areas. This has made US cities 'melting pots' of different cultures. Second, the US is arguably both the most advanced market economy and the largest fully integrated marketplace in the world. As such, wages and prices reflect preferences and costs better than any other place. Moreover, people are highly mobile within the US. For instance, census data reveal that 36 percent of the population moved from one state to another between 1985 and 1990. As people respond to changes in their local working and living environments, we may expect them to 'vote with their feet,' thus seizing (and revealing) consumption and wage gains wherever they arise (Blanchard and Katz [7]). Last but not least, the availability and quality of data are better in the US than anywhere else.

We focus on different linguistic groups as the carriers of cultural identity, and use US-born individuals as our reference group. In other words, we investigate whether linguistic

306   *G.I.P. Ottaviano, G. Peri / Journal of Urban Economics 58 (2005) 304–337*

diversity affects the wage of the average US-born, and we also qualify the effect on particular sub-groups of the US population (black workers versus white workers, more educated versus less educated). Linguistic diversity, identified as the index of fractionalization of the mother tongues of workers, serves as a proxy for cultural diversity. We choose linguistic diversity as our central explanatory variable because it captures particularly well the culture of reference of individuals, and it is associated with traditions, values and habits that may affect individual productivity. Language allows us to capture cultural identity beyond merely the first generation of immigrants. At the same time linguistic diversity has a clear "communication" cost, due to the imperfect communication between groups.[1] While ethnicity is of course another important component of diversity, we do not focus on it in our work. One reason for this is that ethnicity is self-assessed, and therefore is more subject to endogeneity and measurement errors. Another reason is that the impact of ethnic diversity is likely to be dominated by the discrimination, segregation and disadvantages experienced by the African American community. These issues are important and deserve a more specific and separate analysis.[2]

The effects of diversity on aggregate economic performance have been previously studied mainly through cross-countries growth regressions that use racial fragmentation as the key explanatory variable. At the cross country level, Easterly and Levine [19] find that, ceteris paribus, income grows less in countries characterized by more racial fragmentation than in more homogeneous ones. Collier and Gunning [17] explain such behavior in terms of mutual distrust among ethnic groups, which makes it difficult to build social capital and share productive public goods. However, when comparing countries, institutions will also play a role. Collier [16] for example finds that democracies are better at coping with ethnic diversity. More generally, Easterly [18] stresses the importance of good institutions in mitigating the negative impact of diversity on growth.

Growth regressions have also been used at the city level. In those regressions population growth takes the place of income growth as dependent variable, because people are much more mobile across cities within the same country so that migration tends to arbitrage out income differences. Glaeser et al. [22] use this approach, and find that racial fragmentation has a positive impact on population growth only when accompanied by segregation. According to Alesina and La Ferrara [1], this may be due to the possibility that segregation can produce the benefits of diversity in production without any costly social conflicts over public goods provision. On the other hand, Florida [20,21] argues that segregation is not the only way to fence off social unrest arising from diversity. He shows that tolerant cities (where tolerance is instrumented by the presence of artists, bohemians, and other creative people) consist of the most innovative and educated people. Several authors, along similar lines, have argued that the functioning and thriving of urban clusters relies on the variety of people, factors, goods and services within them. Examples abound in the urban studies literature. Jacobs [24] views economic diversity as the key factor of a city's success. Sassen [33] studies 'global cities' and their strategic role in the development of activities

---

[1] Within the US, however, the overwhelming majority of non-native speakers report to understand English well (90% according to the 1990 census); thus problems of verbal communication, which would increase the cost of diversity, are, in general, not extremely severe.

[2] See Alesina and La Ferrara [1] for a review of this literature and Sparber [34] for a recent contribution.

G.I.P. Ottaviano, G. Peri / Journal of Urban Economics 58 (2005) 304–337   307

that are central to world economic growth and innovation. A key feature of these cities is the cultural diversity of their populations. Similarly, Bairoch [5] sees cities and their diversity as the engines of economic growth. Such diversity, however, has been seen mainly in terms of the diversified provision of consumer goods and services, as well as productive inputs (see, e.g., Quigley [31]; Glaeser et al. [23]). The positive 'production value' of diversity has also been stressed in the literature on the organization and management of teams. Here the standard assumption is that higher diversity can lead to more innovation and creativity by increasing the number of ways groups frame problems, thus producing a richer set of alternative solutions and consequently better decisions. Lazear [25] provides an attempt to model team interactions. He defines the 'global firm' as a team whose members come from different cultures or countries. Combining workers whose countries of origin have different cultures, legal systems, and languages imposes costs on the firm that would not be present if all the workers had similar backgrounds. However, complementarity between workers, in terms of skills, can more than offset the costs of cross-cultural interaction. Finally, several contributions have focussed on the issue of new immigrants into the US and their effects on native workers. For example, Borjas [8,9], Card [13,15] analyze the effects of immigration on the locations and wages of native workers. These works reveal a small negative impact of immigration on the wages of natives, especially the low-skilled ones.

A different approach to the study of diversity within cities is adopted by Ottaviano and Peri [30] and further developed in this article. Following Roback [32] our previous work developed a model of a multicultural system of open cities implying that we could use the observed variations in wages and rents of US-born workers to identify the nature of the effects associated with cultural diversity. Our main finding was that, on average, there is a positive production value of cultural diversity to US-born citizens. The present paper complements and expands that work in two main respects. First, we propose a more detailed model of the production and consumption side of the economy. We provide some explanation and formalization of how (and through which channels) diversity affects utility and productivity. Second, we use a different identification strategy in the empirical analysis. Specifically, we adapt the set-up by Alesina et al. [4] to design a theoretical model of aggregate production where the diversity of the workforce contributes different services (skills) but hampers worker exchange because of transaction costs. We complement the production side of the model with agents' utility functions that also exhibit a positive effect of diversity, through taste for variety in consumption, as well as a negative effect of diversity on utility, potentially created by aversion to different cultures. Allowing agents to move across cities in order to equate their utility and allowing firms to locate across cities in order to eliminate profit differentials, we obtain the equilibrium conditions on wages and employment. In particular, as we are interested in the effect of diversity on productivity and utility, the equilibrium conditions of the model provide the relationship between diversity, employment and wages that we can estimate empirically. The identification strategy produced by the model relies on the estimation of a wage and an employment (density) equation. This is close to the approach followed by the literature assessing the effects of immigration on US natives (such as Card [15]). In our empirical implementation we assume that we may identify an exogenous shifter of the amount of diversity across cities, which is based on different immigration rates across cities. Migration alters the linguis-

308   *G.I.P. Ottaviano, G. Peri / Journal of Urban Economics 58 (2005) 304–337*

tic diversity of cities and, by analyzing jointly the net employment changes and net wage (productivity) changes of natives, we infer the net effect of linguistic diversity. Implementing this strategy we find evidence in support of a *diversity wage premium*: richer diversity is associated with higher wages for natives. This positive effect seems strongest for highly skilled workers, although it is present for the unskilled as well. This association, which is both economically and statistically significant, can be interpreted in terms of higher productivity, for we also find a positive association between linguistic diversity and the employment of natives in a city. Moreover the benefits do not fall exclusively to the highly skilled. These results are compatible with the idea that different cultures provide different skills to production, beyond the formal schooling of their members (a 'horizontal' type of skill diversity). This is confirmed by the fact that the positive effect remains even after controlling for the years of schooling of non-native speakers.

Some of our findings may seem at odds with some of the previous literature. We investigate in greater detail this apparent incompatibility. This allows us to qualify our results in three respects. First, we highlight the importance of the adoption of a core of shared norms ('assimilation') for fruitful multicultural interactions, by showing that the impact of recent immigration on productivity is mildly negative, consistent with what is suggested by Borjas [8,9], while overall diversity has a positive effect. This fact is consistent with the idea that assimilation and the benefits of diversity may take some time to emerge. Second, differently from most of the labor literature that has looked at the shift of relative wages across different skill groups (e.g. Borjas [10,11], Card [15]) we focus on the average (overall) effect of diversity on wages of US-natives. Finally we clarify the different effects of diversity on the private and public sectors, by showing that the impact of diversity on the provision of public goods is indeed negative as argued in Alesina et al. [2,3].[3]

The paper is organized in five sections after the introduction. Section 2 presents the data set and some descriptive statistics. Section 3 derives the theoretical model that will be used to guide the empirical analysis. This is implemented in Section 4, which describes the main wage and employment regressions, along with a battery of robustness checks, and proposes an instrumental variable strategy to reduce the endogeneity problem. Section 5 compares our findings with related studies focussing on the impact of recent immigration and the provision of public goods. Section 6 concludes.

2. Descriptive statistics: cultures in US cities

We begin our analysis of the effects of cultural diversity on wages and employment in US cities by presenting the data set and some descriptive statistics.

2.1. Data on US cities

Our unit of observation is the Metropolitan Statistical Area (MSA). Data at the MSA level for the US are available from different sources. We use mostly the Census Public

---

[3] Specifically, in the provision of public goods ethnic diversity seems to play a significant negative role while linguistic diversity has no significant impact. Alesina et al. [2,3] analyze only the effect of ethnic diversity.

G.I.P. Ottaviano, G. Peri / Journal of Urban Economics 58 (2005) 304–337   309

Use Microdata Sample (PUMS) data (the 5% Form the Metro sample for 1970 and the 1% Metro Samples for 1980 and 1990) that allow for the most detailed analysis when calculating average values and shares across groups. We also include data from the 'County and City Data Book' from several years in order to obtain some aggregate variables such as aggregate employment, income, population, spending for local public goods, and some indices of cultural composition. We consider 160 MSAs that are identified in each of the three census years considered. From the PUMS we have around 1,200,000 individual observations for 1990, 900,000 for 1980, and 500,000 for 1970. We use these to construct aggregate variables and indices at the MSA level. The reason for focussing on MSAs is twofold. First, MSAs constitute closely connected economic units within which interactions are intense. Thus, they fit the theoretical model presented in Section 3, in which local services are used to produce final output. Second, they exhibit a higher degree of linguistic diversity than the rest of the country, as new immigrants and their offspring traditionally settle down in larger cities.

We measure average labor productivity as hourly wage. This is calculated as yearly salary divided by weeks worked in the year, and then by hours worked during the week.[4] Such a measure is not contaminated by the variations in individual labor supply. We select working individuals between 16 and 65 years of age as our workforce. In order to identify the average city-specific wage and estimate its dependence on cultural diversity, we select only US-born workers in a MSA and then control for their composition. In particular, we control for average schooling, average experience (and its square), the share of women, the share of blacks and the share of native Americans in the city. The residual variation of average wages of US-born workers in city c in year t, $\bar{w}_{ct}$, is therefore not affected by the demographic composition of the city. Its correlation with linguistic diversity can be used to capture co-movements between a city's productivity and its diversity.

Cultural diversity is a multi-dimensional concept. It could stem not just from groups with different languages or ethnicities, but also from groups with different skills or regional origins. Nonetheless, 'cultural diversity,' as it is commonly referred to, mostly involves ethno-linguistic differences. Ethnicity and language (with religion a possible third candidate) are probably the most important characteristics for the identification of a sub-group (or sub-culture) within the US. Indeed, especially in the US, apart from black-white issues, most debates about diversity are strongly related to issues such as the 'Latino identity' or the 'Chinese-American community,' which are identifiable with linguistic groupings. In this paper we choose to focus on the concept of linguistic diversity as a crucial and measurable dimension of the broader concept of cultural diversity.[5] Measures of diversity based on ancestry, race and regional origins will be used as controls in order to verify the robustness of our results.

The theoretical model of Section 3 suggests a specific index of diversity, stemming from the 'taste of variety' embedded in the aggregate production function (5) and utility function (3): the sum of the population shares of the different groups raised to the power of α. Since in (5) α represents the wage share of aggregate income, we follow common

---

[4] As hours worked in a week and weeks worked in a year are coded as categorical variables for 1970 we choose the median point of the range to impute the hours of a single individual.

[5] Recently, Sparber [34] analyzes the impact of racial diversity on productivity.

practice by setting $\alpha = 0.66$ for the US economy. Formally, we define our own index of linguistic diversity of city c in year t as:

$$div Lang_{ct} = \sum_j (l_j^c)_t^{0.66} \tag{1}$$

where $Lang$ labels the variable 'language' and $(l_j^c)_t$ is the share of the group speaking language j (at home) in the total population of workers of city c in year t. If all city residents are in the same linguistic group, the index takes on its minimum value of 1. The more equal is the distribution of citizens across groups, the larger is the index.

In order to check that our results do not depend too strongly on the particular form chosen for the diversity index, we also consider, however, a more standard measure of diversity, namely, the so called 'index of fractionalization.' This index, popularized in cross-country studies by Mauro [28] and widely used thereafter, captures the probability that two individuals, taken at random from a universe made of different groups, belong to the same group. The index of fractionalization is calculated as 1 minus the Herfindahl index of concentration across groups. Formally, we define the fractionalization index of linguistic diversity of city c in year t as:

$$frac(Lang_{c,t}) = 1 - \sum_j (l_j^c)_t^2. \tag{2}$$

This index is an increasing measure of both the cultural 'richness' of a city (i.e. the number of groups) and its cultural 'diversity' (i.e. the evenness of the groups' sizes). It reaches its minimum value 0 when all individuals speak the same language, and its maximum value 1 when there are no individuals speaking the same language. Intuitively, when all individuals share the same language, the probability that two randomly selected individuals belong to different linguistic groups is 0, whereas it equals 1 when all individuals speak different languages. On the other hand, for a given number of linguistic groups M (i.e. controlling for 'richness'), the index reaches its maximum at $(1 - 1/M)$ when individuals are uniformly distributed across groups.[6]

In addition to its usefulness for robustness checks, fractionalization also allows us to get a feeling of the extent of diversity in US cities by comparing their linguistic diversity with those calculated in cross-country studies. Note that the correlation between the two indices, $div Lang_{ct}$ and $frac(Lang_{c,t})$, across the 160 MSAs is about 0.85, which confirms that the two indices are indeed capturing the same features of linguistic diversity across cities.

2.2. Diversity in US cities

Table 1 reports the summary statistics on the shares of the five main linguistic groups after merging all other groups together. Columns 1 and 3 report the averages in 1970 and 1990 for each share across the 160 metropolitan areas, while columns 2 and 4 report the standard deviations in 1970 and 1990. A linguistic group is defined as those people prevalently speaking a particular language at home. For parsimony, the table includes very few

---

[6] See Maignan et al. [27] for details.

G.I.P. Ottaviano, G. Peri / Journal of Urban Economics 58 (2005) 304–337   311

Table 1
Main linguistic shares in 160 US metropolitan areas

Language shares	Average 1970	Std. Dev. 1970	Average 1990	Std. Dev. 1990
English	0.800	0.123	0.789	0.120
German	0.033	0.032	0.006	0.004
Italian	0.017	0.024	0.006	0.004
Spanish	0.039	0.091	0.132	0.110
Chinese	0.001	0.013	0.015	0.010
Other	0.129	0.071	0.052	0.020
Fractionalization Index of language	0.333	0.150	0.180	0.133

Source: Authors' calculations on Census PUMS Data 1970 and 1990.

Table 2
Linguistic shares in some metropolitan areas, 1990

City	English	German	Italian	Spanish	Chinese	Other	Fractionalization
Atlanta, GA	0.934	0.005	0.001	0.026	0.004	0.030	0.137
Chicago, IL	0.804	0.009	0.008	0.094	0.006	0.079	0.355
Cincinnati, OH-KY-IN	0.962	0.008	0.002	0.009	0.001	0.018	0.080
Dallas, TX	0.850	0.004	0.001	0.112	0.005	0.029	0.265
El Paso, TX	0.322	0.009	0.001	0.656	0.002	0.011	0.473
Indianapolis, IN	0.963	0.005	0.001	0.014	0.001	0.016	0.070
Los Angeles, CA	0.570	0.005	0.003	0.300	0.025	0.097	0.591
New York, NY	0.645	0.007	0.028	0.177	0.032	0.111	0.550
Philadelphia, PA-NJ	0.922	0.007	0.009	0.026	0.003	0.034	0.148
Pittsburgh, PA	0.958	0.005	0.008	0.008	0.002	0.020	0.080
San Francisco, CA	0.679	0.009	0.006	0.107	0.087	0.112	0.620
Washington, DC-MD-VA-WV	0.857	0.007	0.003	0.053	0.009	0.071	0.278

Source: Authors' calculations on Census PUMS Data, 1990.

specific linguistic groups, even though other groups are important in certain cities. The fractionalization index reported in the last row of the table is calculated, instead, using all 29 groups listed in Appendix A. Besides English speakers we report the average shares of German, Spanish, and Italian speakers (corresponding to the most largely represented European languages), as well as Chinese speakers. Table 1 displays a tendency for linguistic diversity to decrease between 1970 and 1990, for the index of fractionalization falls significantly. In particular, while the share of English speakers remains stable, other European languages become less relevant, while Spanish turns into the second most common linguistic group in the country. The share of Chinese speakers slightly increases as well. The diversity of European languages, still present to a certain extent in 1970, gives way to a single large Spanish speaking minority by 1990.

Table 2 reports the fractionalization index of some representative MSAs in 1990. The two largest metropolises, New York and Los Angeles, are the most diverse cities along the linguistic dimension. Both cities have very large Spanish speaking communities (in L.A. they represent 30% of the population, while in N.Y. they reach 17%) and a non negligible Chinese speaking group. The third most diverse city in our group is San Francisco. Cities in

312   *G.I.P. Ottaviano, G. Peri / Journal of Urban Economics 58 (2005) 304–337*

the Midwest such as Cincinnati and Indianapolis rank very low in diversity. The fact that in general larger cities are associated with more diversity implies that we will have to control for some measure of city size when analyzing the impact of diversity on productivity. To put into context the extent of diversity in US cities, their linguistic fractionalization can be compared with the cross-country values reported by the Atlas Narodov Mira and published in Taylor and Hudson [35] for the year 1960. Those values have been largely used in the growth literature (see, e.g., Easterly and Levine [19], and Collier [16]). A diversified city such as San Francisco has a linguistic fractionalization equal to 0.62, which is the level of Malawi or Pakistan. Afghanistan, well known for hosting many different ethnicities, reaches a value of 0.66 that is only slightly higher. More homogeneous cities such as Cincinnati and Pittsburgh have a level of fractionalization equal to 0.08, which is the same as that of very homogeneous Sweden. Between these extremes US cities span a range of linguistic diversity that is about two thirds of the range spanned by the countries of the world.[7]

Finally, Fig. 1 presents a partial scatter-plot of the average wage change for US-born workers during the period 1970–1990 against the change in the index of linguistic diversity, $div Lang_{c1990}$. Each variable is 'cleaned' of the effects of changing city demographics,

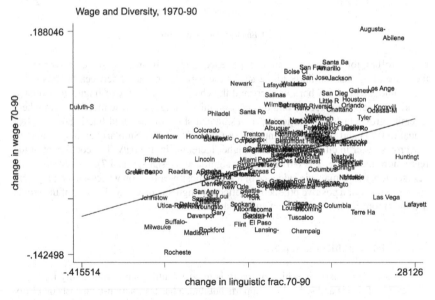

Fig. 1. Wage and diversity.

[7] Given the properties of the fractionalization index discussed above, this evidence shows that, when jointly measured, the linguistic richness and diversity of some US cities are very close to those of very rich and diverse countries. However, the comparison across different countries have to be taken with a grain of salt as the range spanned by the fractionalization index depends on the total number of groups.

G.I.P. Ottaviano, G. Peri / Journal of Urban Economics 58 (2005) 304–337　　　313

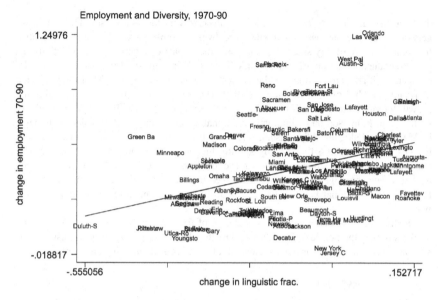

Fig. 2. Employment and diversity.

by controlling for average schooling, experience (and its square), the share of women and the share of blacks. Similarly Fig. 2 shows the partial correlation between the change in city employment of US-born workers and the change in the index of linguistic diversity. Figure 1 reveals the presence of a diversity premium: wages increase more in cities where diversity grows faster. In particular, the estimated slope of the fitted line is both positive (equal to 0.21) and very significant (with a t-statistic of 6.9). Similarly employment density grows faster in cities experiencing higher increases in diversity. The coefficient of the regression line in Fig. 2 is 0.6 and highly significant (t-statistic is 4.7). As argued in the next section, the prima facie evidence of a jointly positive effect on wages and employment speaks in favor of a positive productivity effect of linguistic diversity. The rest of the article qualifies more precisely this effect and checks its robustness.

3. A model of multicultural cities

We model a scenario in which diversity is good for utility and productivity thanks to the variety of goods and services it supports but it also has transaction-type costs on utility and productivity, so that its net effect may be ambiguous. Before illustrating these different effects in a formal model let us provide some intuition for each one of them. First, foreign-born workers and US-born ones provide differentiated services and skills to production. One reason is that, for given observable skills, US and foreign born workers tend to choose different "occupations" (see Card [15] for more detail). Among less educated, for instance, foreign born are highly over-represented in professions like tailors (54% were foreign-born in 1990) and plaster-stucco masons (44% were foreign-born in 1990) while US-born are over-represented, say, among crane operators (less than 1% were foreign-born) and sewer-pipe cleaners (less than 1% foreign-born). If those services are not perfect substitutes increased cultural diversity would imply increased variety of available services. Among highly educated the same is true. Foreign-born are, for instance, highly over-represented in scientific and technological fields (45% of medical scientists and 33% of computer engineers were foreign-born) while US-born are largely over-represented among lawyers (less than 4% are foreign-born) or museum curators and archivists (less than 3% are foreign-born). Even within the same occupation often US and foreign-born provide different services and benefit from complementing each other. Among less educated, for instance, a Chinese cook and a US-born cook or an Italian tailor and a US-born tailor do not provide the same services. Similarly, among highly educated professionals a German-trained physicist (more inclined to theory) is not perfectly substitutable with a US-trained one (more inclined to experimental approach). As long as the overall production benefits from larger diversity of skills and services, cultural diversity will have a positive impact on it. Diversity, however, can also have negative effects on production due to difficult interactions ('communication') between different cultures, incompatible behaviors, lack of shared values and norms or sheer antipathy. Similarly, on the consumption side, while variety in available foods, crafts, entertainment shows, styles of design (clearly correlated with cultural diversity) has a positive utility value, diversity may also generate various utility losses. Individuals may need a (costly) diversified cultural background to fully enjoy a variety of cultural goods and services and, more simply, diversity may generate fear of losing national identity and reactions against 'aliens' such as reciprocal distaste if not outright aversion and conflict. These costs and benefits depend on the number and relative sizes of cultural groups living in the city. Finally, the costs of interaction could also depend on the time of arrival of the different cohorts of immigrants: interactions are likely to be easier when groups have had enough time to assimilate a common set of norms and habits from the host society. We will come back to these points later in the empirical analysis.

3.1. Preferences and technologies

We consider an open system of a large number C of non-overlapping cities, indexed by $c = 1, \ldots, C$. There are two primary factors of production, labor and land. There are a total of L workers who are perfectly mobile between and within cities, while L^c is the number of workers located in city c. We assume that inter-city commuting costs are prohibitive, so that for each worker, their cities of work and residence coincide. We also ignore intra-city commuting costs, which allows us to focus on the inter-city allocations of workers. Workers are differentiated by 'culture' (language) across M groups, with L_i^c measuring the number of residents of city c belonging to group $i = 1, \ldots, M$. Land is owned by absentee landlords. We call K^c the land endowment of city c and K the total land available in the economy. Land is homogeneous across alternative uses (residential and productive). Workers demand two goods, Y (tradable and homogeneous) and D (non-tradable and differentiated), as well as land K for residential purposes. Utility is assumed to be Cobb–Douglas with expenditures shares η, γ, and $1 - \eta - \gamma$ going to Y, D and K respectively:

$$U_i^c = \left(K_{u,i}^c\right)^{1-\eta-\gamma} \left(Y_i^c\right)^{\eta} \left(D_i^c\right)^{\gamma}, \tag{3}$$

G.I.P. Ottaviano, G. Peri / Journal of Urban Economics 58 (2005) 304–337   315

where $K_{u,i}^c$ and Y_i^c denote individual consumptions of land and good Y by a typical member of group i in city c. In addition, D_i^c is a CES sub-utility defined on the set of different varieties of good D:

$$D_i^c = \left(1 - \tau^c\right) \left[\sum_{j=1}^M (D_{j,i}^c)^\alpha \right]^{1/\alpha}, \quad 0 < \alpha < 1 \tag{4}$$

with $D_{j,i}^c$ labeling the consumption of variety j. The sub-utility function (4) exhibits 'love for variety' in that for a given total amount of consumption it is preferable to distribute it across all available varieties than to concentrate it on a single variety. Thus, utility is higher the larger the number of available varieties and the more balanced their supply. The CES aggregator D_i^c is supposed to capture utility from those goods/services (such as restaurants, specialty food, entertainment, hair stylists) that are supplied in different varieties by people of different cultures (think of Chinese food, French hair-stylists or Italian Opera-singers) and are non tradable. Low values of α (determining low elasticity of substitution between different cultural groups, defined as $\varepsilon \equiv 1/(1 - \alpha)$) magnify the "love of variety" effect. The term τ^c measures the utility loss ('disamenity') of diversity: the larger τ^c the lower the utility derived from the differentiated good. We think of τ^c as an increasing function of diversity but we leave this dependence implicit to simplify notation.[8]

The production side is modeled by adapting the multi-regional trade model by Alesina et al. [4] to a multi-cultural set-up with freely mobile workers. Product and input markets are perfectly competitive. Land is homogeneous whereas labor is horizontally differentiated across groups. Each worker contributes one unit of her group-specific labor inelastically. Labor may be supplied only within the city of residence.

The differentiated good D is supplied using labor only with productivity equal to A. Such good is freely traded within cities but non-traded between them. Each variety is produced employing workers of a specific group, hence there is a one to one relation between groups and varieties. Accordingly, the output of variety i is $D_i^c = AL_{i,D}^c$, where $L_{i,D}^c$ is labor supply of group i to sector D.

The homogeneous good Y is produced using labor and land. It is freely traded both within and between cities. It is chosen as numeraire, hence its price equals one. While groups do not interact in supplying the varieties of good D, they do interact in the production of good Y. This interaction entails iceberg transaction costs: of one unit supplied by any worker only a fraction $(1 - \tau^c) \in (0, 1)$ is available for production. Specifically, aggregate production of good Y is given by:

$$Y^c = A\left(1 - \tau^c\right)^\alpha \left(K_Y^c\right)^{1-\alpha} \sum_{j=1}^M \left(L_{i,Y}^c\right)^\alpha \tag{5}$$

where A is total factor productivity, K_Y^c is land used by sector Y, and $L_{i,Y}^c$ is labor supplied by group i to that sector. Accordingly, $(1 - \tau^c)L_{i,Y}^c$ is the fraction available for production net of transaction costs. Notice that (5) exhibits a 'love for variety' in terms of

---

[8]   Using the notation introduced in Section 2.1 the parameter τ^c would be an increasing function of $div Lang_{ct}$, formally $\tau^c(\sum_j (l_j^c)_t^{0.66})$.

316   G.I.P. Ottaviano, G. Peri / Journal of Urban Economics 58 (2005) 304–337

labor inputs: given total amount of jobs it is more productive to distribute them across all available groups than to concentrate all of them on a single group. The CES aggregator captures the fact that different cultures provide different workers with different observable and unobservable skills choosing different occupations (as argued above) and, therefore, not perfectly substitutable for each other. Thus, productivity is higher the larger the number of available varieties and the more balanced their supply. The more so the smaller the elasticity of substitution between groups $\varepsilon \equiv 1/(1 - \alpha)$.[9]

3.2. Labor demand and supply

Since workers are freely mobile, in equilibrium they must be indifferent about location, which requires each of them to enjoy the same level of utility ('real wage') wherever located. On average this implies

$$\bar{u} = \left(\frac{K_u^c}{L^c}\right)^{1-\eta-\gamma} (\eta \bar{w}^c)^{\eta} \left(\frac{D^c}{L^c}\right)^{\gamma}, \quad \forall c = 1, \ldots, C \tag{6}$$

where K_u^c and D^c are aggregate consumptions of residential land and good D in city c respectively, whereas $\bar{w}^c = \sum_{i=1}^{M} w_i^c L_i^c / L^c$ is the average (nominal) wage in the city with w_i^c being the wage of group i.[10] With absentee landlords aggregate expenditures are equal to the total wage bill $\bar{w}^c L^c$, so $\eta \bar{w}^c$ represents average consumption of the numeraire good Y. Finally, $\bar{u}$ is the real average wage, which is the same in any city due to the mobility of workers. We assume that the number of cities C is large enough to make the reservation real wage $\bar{u}$ independent from city-level idiosyncrasies.

Under perfect competition, profit maximization and free entry imply that both factors are paid the value of their marginal productivity so that the value of production is split between them according to their cost shares. Moreover, for non-traded K and D, the values of production in city c equal the corresponding expenditures of local workers $\bar{w}^c L^c$. Therefore, remembering that good Y is the numeraire, we can write $\alpha Y^c = (1 - \gamma)\bar{w}^c L^c$ and $\alpha r^c K^c = (1 - \alpha \eta - \gamma)\bar{w}^c L^c$. This implies that the demands of group-specific labor L_i^c across sectors D and Y are linked by $L_{iX}/L_{iY} = \gamma/(1 - \gamma)$. Analogously, land demands satisfy $K_u^c/K_Y^c = \alpha[(1 - \eta - \gamma)]/[(1 - \gamma)(1 - \alpha)]$. These results can be inserted into the city resource constraints for labor and land to obtain the amounts of labor and land employed in the supply of good Y:

$$L_{i,Y}^c = (1 - \gamma)L_i^c, \qquad K_Y^c = \frac{(1-\alpha)(1-\gamma)}{1 - \alpha\eta - \gamma} K^c \tag{7}$$

---

[9] We have assumed that elasticity of substitution between different types of labor in production is the same as the elasticity of substitution between varieties in consumption. We have also assumed that the utility loss and the productivity loss due to diversity are both measured by the same function τ^c. These assumptions simplify the exposition of the model and have no bearing on our identification procedure.

[10] Mobility of workers of each type (L_i) between production of good Y and production of variety D_i implies that the wage for a type of worker (i) is equated between the two sectors.

with complementary shares of labor and land going to differentiated production and residential use respectively. Given (5), expressions (7) allows us to rewrite the free mobility condition (6) as:

$$\bar{w}^c = \frac{(\bar{u})^{1/\eta}}{\eta}\left(\frac{\alpha(1-\eta-\gamma)}{1-\alpha\eta-\gamma}\frac{L^c}{K^c}\right)^{\frac{1-\eta-\gamma}{\eta}}\left[(1-\tau^c)A\right]^{-\gamma/\eta}\left[\sum_{j=1}^{M}(\lambda_j^c)^{\alpha}\right]^{-\frac{\gamma}{\alpha\eta}} \tag{8}$$

where $\lambda_i^c \equiv L_i^c/L^c$ is the share of residents of city c belonging to group i. Equation (8) identifies an upward sloping labor-supply relation between employment L^c and the average wage in city c. It shows that, for a given wage, workers are willing to move to cities that have:

(i) a more balanced distribution across groups;
(ii) lower costs of interaction;
(iii) more abundant land.

The reason is that under all three counts utility ('quality of life') is higher. This, however, does not imply that workers are drawn to more diverse cities which have a richer set of varieties of good D but also higher "interaction" costs. The overall effect of diversity on labor supply depends on the relative effect of diversity on the term $(1 - \tau^c)$, that captures the dis-utility effect and the term $\sum_{j=1}^{M}(\lambda_j^c)^{\alpha}$ that captures the positive effect from love of variety.

Lastly, under our choice of numeraire, Eq. (7) also implies that the average profit-maximizing wage $\bar{w}^c$ satisfies:

$$\bar{w}^c = \alpha A(1-\gamma)\left(\frac{(1-\alpha)}{1-\alpha\eta-\gamma}\frac{K^c}{L^c}\right)^{1-\alpha}(1-\tau_Y^c)^{\alpha}\sum_{j=1}^{M}(\lambda_i^c)^{\alpha} \tag{9}$$

which identifies a downward sloping labor-demand relation between employment and the average wage in city c. Equation (9) shows that, for a given wage, firms are willing to hire more workers in cities that have:

(i) a more balanced distribution across groups;
(ii) lower costs of interaction;
(iii) more abundant land.

The reason is that under all three counts labor productivity is higher. Nevertheless, this does not imply that firms are drawn to more diverse cities. These, in fact, offer a richer set of labor types but also higher transaction costs. Again the relative impact of diversity on $(1 - \tau_Y^c)$ and on $\sum_{j=1}^{M}(\lambda_i^c)^{\alpha}$ will determine the net effect on the labor demand equation.

3.3. Identification: wage and employment

To prepare the model for empirical investigation, it is useful to evaluate wages and employment levels at the equilibrium allocation. This is achieved by solving labor demand (9) and labor supply (8) together, which yields, once we take logs on both sides, the following employment (density) equation:

$$\ln\left(\frac{L^c}{K^c}\right) = \text{constant}_L + \frac{\alpha\eta + \gamma}{1 - \alpha\eta - \gamma}\ln\left(1 - \tau^c\right) + \frac{\alpha\eta + \gamma}{\alpha(1 - \alpha\eta - \gamma)}\ln div^c \qquad (10)$$

and the following 'wage equation':

$$\ln\left(\overline{w}^c\right) = \text{constant}_w + \frac{\alpha(1 - \eta) - \gamma}{1 - \alpha\eta - \gamma}\ln\left(1 - \tau^c\right) + \frac{\alpha(1 - \eta) - \gamma}{\alpha(1 - \alpha\eta - \gamma)}\ln div^c \qquad (11)$$

where we defined, following (1) of Section 2.1, the diversity index as $div^c \equiv \sum_{j=1}^{M}(\lambda_j^c)^\alpha$. Recall that the "transaction cost" τ^c is itself an increasing function of diversity, $\tau^c(div^c)$. The model, therefore, yields ambiguous predictions on the impact of diversity on average wage and employment density, the reason being the opposing effects of diversity on both utility and productivity captured by the second and third term on the right hand sides of Eqs. (10) and (11). Depending on the relative importance of these effects in each equation we may have the four cases illustrated below.

Equations (9) and (8) can be used to identify the net impact of diversity shocks on urban performance. Those equations are depicted in Fig. 3. The vertical axis measures the logarithm of the average wage in a city (w) while the horizontal axis measures the logarithm of its employment density (l). The city index c is dropped for parsimony. The downward sloping lines are derived from Eq. (9) and depict labor demand. The upward sloping lines are derived from Eq. (8) and represent labor supply. The exact positions of demand and supply depend on city-specific characteristics. For example, suppose we observe two cities. In the first city labor demand and supply are represented by the solid lines, whose intersection identifies the local equilibrium wage and employment density (point A). Now suppose that we observe a second city with higher average wage ($w' > w$). Figure 3 shows that in principle this could be associated with either an upward shift of labor demand (point B) or an upward shift of labor supply (point C). In both cases the wage is higher but for very different reasons. The upward shift of labor demand implies that firms in this city are able to make zero profit even though they face higher wages and higher land rents due to a

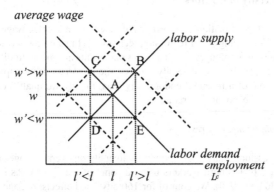

Fig. 3. Labor market equilibrium.

G.I.P. Ottaviano, G. Peri / Journal of Urban Economics 58 (2005) 304–337   319

higher population density. This is possible only if firms are more productive in the second city than in the first one. The upward shift of labor supply implies, instead, that in order for workers to be as happy in the second city as in the first one, a higher wage has to be associated with a lower land rent stemming from lower density. This reveals the presence of a real wage premium that compensates for a poorer quality of life.

To distinguish whether higher nominal wages signal higher productivity or a worse quality of life, additional information is therefore needed. We see in Fig. 3 that, as implied by the above argument, such information is provided by employment density: whereas higher productivity is associated with both a higher wage and a higher employment density (point B), a worsening of the quality of life is associated with a higher wage but a lower density (point C). By symmetry the foregoing arguments can be applied to downward shifts of labor demand and supply. This implies that only the parallel estimation of (9) and (8) allows one to establish which effect indeed dominates. Focussing on diversity as city-characteristic that may shift labor demand or labor supply, the analysis of Fig. 3 suggests the following four possibility.

$$\frac{\partial L^c}{\partial div^c} > 0 \text{ and } \frac{\partial \bar{w}^c}{\partial div^c} > 0 \quad \text{iff } there\ exists\ a\ dominant\ positive\ productivity\ effect,$$

$$\frac{\partial L^c}{\partial div^c} > 0 \text{ and } \frac{\partial \bar{w}_c}{\partial div_c} < 0 \quad \text{iff } there\ exists\ a\ dominant\ positive\ utility\ effect,$$

$$\frac{\partial L^c}{\partial div^c} < 0 \text{ and } \frac{\partial \bar{w}_c}{\partial div_c} < 0 \quad \text{iff } there\ exists\ a\ dominant\ negative\ productivity\ effect,$$

$$\frac{\partial L^c}{\partial div^c} < 0 \text{ and } \frac{\partial \bar{w}_c}{\partial div_c} > 0 \quad \text{iff } there\ exists\ a\ dominant\ negative\ utility\ effect.$$

This identification procedure, based on estimating the effect of diversity on average wage and employment density is 'dual' to the one based on wages and rents that Ottaviano and Peri [30] propose following Roback [32].

4. Effects of diversity in US cities

We now turn to the estimation of the effects of diversity on average wages and employment across US cities using panel regression techniques. In so doing, we address several econometric issues. In particular, we check that our results are robust to different specifications, we qualify the effects of diversity across some important demographic groups and we address the issue of a potential endogeneity bias. Finally we qualify our results and compare them with the existing literature.

4.1. Wage and employment regressions

Our basic regressions analyze the impact of diversity on average wages and aggregate employment levels of US-born workers using a panel of the 160 MSAs in three census years (1970, 1980 and 1990). We control for 160 city fixed effects, α_c, and for three year dummies, β_t. Therefore, we identify the effect of diversity on productivity by exploiting only the within-city variation over time. Based on the theoretical model presented in Section 3, our basic wage equation is:

$$\ln(\overline{w}_{c,t}) = \alpha_c + \beta_t + \underline{\gamma}_d(\underline{d}_{c,t}) + \gamma_w(Lang\_diversity_{c,t}) + e_{c,t}. \tag{12}$$

On the left hand side, the dependent variable $\ln(\overline{w}_{c,t})$ is the log of the average hourly wage of US-born workers (age 16–65). On the right hand side, along with our fixed effects, we include in the vector $\underline{d}_{c,t}$ several demographic controls, namely the average level of schooling of workers, their average experience and its square, the share of women, the share of blacks and the share of native Americans for each city. $Lang\_diversity_{c,t}$ is the index of linguistic diversity measured either using the index defined in (1) or the one defined in (2). The coefficient γ_w captures the effect of a variation in the linguistic diversity on the average wage of US-born workers and is our primary parameter of interest. The city fixed effects control for permanent differences across cities (such as size, location, weather and so on), while the time effects control for common national trends (such as improved technology and increased openness). The term $e_{c,t}$ is a random error with zero mean and no correlation with the regressors.

The basic employment equation, similarly, is:

$$\ln(Empl_{c,t}) = \alpha_c + \beta_t + \gamma_e(Lang\_diversity_{c,t}) + u_{c,t}. \tag{13}$$

As in the previous expression the parameters α_c and β_t denote a set of city-specific and time-specific dummies, $Lang\_diversity_{c,t}$ is the measure of linguistic diversity and $u_{c,t}$ is a zero mean random error uncorrelated with the regressors. The coefficient γ_e captures the impact of linguistic diversity on the density of employment in a city.

We estimate Eq. (12) for the average US-born city worker, as well as for the average worker in several sub-groups. The results are reported in Table 3. Column I contains the basic regression that uses all US-born workers in the calculation of the average city wage and controls for their demographic characteristics. Column II considers only the group of white male workers. Column III considers only black males and column IV considers only workers with more than two years of college (skilled workers). We also run a specification that includes only unskilled workers, but we do not report it for the sake of brevity. We will however refer to it in the text. Columns I–IV use the 'diversity index' $divLang_{ct}$ as the measure of linguistic diversity. Columns V to VIII reproduce specifications I–IV but instead use the fractionalization index $frac(Lang_{c,t})$ as the measure of diversity. Table 4 reports the coefficient estimates of Eq. (13) using groups and specifications that parallel those of Table 3. In Table 4 the dependent variable that measures employment for each group is calculated using data on aggregate employment (from the city databook) multiplied by the share of each group in total city employment obtained using the PUMS data. The joint analysis of Tables 3 and 4 conveys the basic message of this paper.

Before focussing on the coefficients of interest, namely those on linguistic diversity (first row of every table) let us briefly comment on the estimated effects of demographic controls. The effect of one extra year of schooling on average wages is close to 7% for the whole population. This is close to the estimates of private returns to schooling for the US (around 6.5–8.5% as reviewed in Card [14]). Average experience has a mild positive (and concave) effect on wage. This estimate is smaller than for individual wage estimates, but a city with lower average experience may be adopting newer technologies, reducing the aggregate

Table 3
Wage regressions

Adopted measure of linguistic diversity:	$div\,Lang_{ct} = \sum_j (l_c^j)_t^{0.66}$				$frac\,Lang_{c,t} = 1 - \sum_j (l_c^j)_t^2$			
Specification:	I All US-born	II White males	III Black males	IV More skilled	V All US-born	VI White males	VII Black males	VIII More skilled
Linguistic diversity	0.23* (0.04)	0.22* (0.04)	−0.05 (0.20)	0.31* (0.05)	0.27* (0.04)	0.28* (0.05)	−0.07 (0.30)	0.44* (0.06)
Average schooling	0.062* (0.01)	0.067* (0.01)	0.15* (0.03)	0.12* (0.04)	0.074* (0.01)	0.071* (0.01)	0.15* (0.03)	0.14* (0.04)
Average experience	0.006 (0.02)	0.027 (0.02)	0.025 (0.015)	0.06 (0.04)	0.01 (0.02)	0.03 (0.02)	0.023 (0.015)	0.03 (0.03)
Average experience, squared	−0.0004 (0.0003)	−0.001 (0.001)	−0.0001 (0.0002)	−0.002 (0.002)	−0.004 (0.006)	−0.001 (0.0007)	−0.0001 (0.0002)	−0.001 (0.001)
Share of women	−1.08* (0.21)			−0.52* (0.20)	−1.05* (0.21)			−0.46* (0.17)
Share of black	−0.16 (0.16)			−0.12* (0.42)	−0.15 (0.16)			−0.19* (0.35)
Share of native Americans	0.15 (0.70)			0.03 (0.10)	−0.03 (0.65)			0.10 (0.10)
City fixed effects	Yes	Yes	Yes	Yes	Yes	Yes	Yes	Yes
Year fixed effects	Yes	Yes	Yes	Yes	Yes	Yes	Yes	Yes
Partial R^2 (excluding fixed effects)	0.10	0.06	0.07	0.04	0.10	0.05	0.07	0.04
Observations	480	480	480	480	480	480	480	480

In parentheses, heteroskedasticity-robust standard errors.
Dependent variables:
specifications I and IV: Natural logarithm of average hourly wage in the SMSA expressed in 1990 US $, for all US-born workers aged 16–65;
specifications II and V: Natural logarithm of average hourly wage in the SMSA expressed in 1990 US $, for white male US-born workers aged 16–65;
specifications III and VI: Natural logarithm of average hourly wage in the SMSA expressed in 1990 US $, for black male US-born workers aged 16–65;
specifications IV and VIII: Natural logarithm of average hourly wage in the SMSA expressed in 1990 US $, for US-born workers aged 16–65 with at least two years of college education.
* Significant at the 1% level.

positive effect of experience on productivity. The share of women in the workforce reduces the average wage significantly (this is the aggregate counterpart of a significant negative wage premium for women) while the share of blacks and that of natives have smaller effects, respectively negative and positive, on average wages. When we consider only white

322 *G.I.P. Ottaviano, G. Peri / Journal of Urban Economics 58 (2005) 304–337*

Table 4
Employment regressions

Adopted measure of linguistic diversity:	$div Lang_{ct} = \sum_j (l_c^j)_t^{0.66}$				$frac Lang_{c,t} = 1 - \sum_j (l_c^j)_t^2$			
Specification:	I	II	III	IV	V	VI	VII	VIII
	All US-born	White males	Black males	More skilled	All US-born	White males	Black males	More skilled
Linguistic diversity	0.61*	0.45*	0.50	0.54*	0.77*	0.43*	0.55	0.53*
	(0.16)	(0.20)	(0.30)	(0.15)	(0.16)	(0.20)	(0.30)	(0.18)
City fixed effects	Yes	Yes	Yes	Yes	Yes	Yes	Yes	Yes
Year fixed effects	Yes	Yes	Yes	Yes	Yes	Yes	Yes	Yes
Partial R^2 (excluding fixed effects)	0.03	0.03	0.01	0.04	0.04	0.03	0.01	0.04
Observations	480	480	480	480	480	480	480	480

In parentheses, heteroskedasticity-robust standard errors.
Dependent variables:
specifications I and IV: Natural logarithm of employment of all US-born workers aged 16–65;
specifications II and V: Natural logarithm of employment of white male US-born workers aged 16–65. The employment is calculated by multiplying total employment figures by the share of white males in the SMSA obtained using the PUMS data;
specifications III and VI: Natural logarithm of employment of black male US-born workers aged 16–65. The employment is calculated by multiplying total employment figures by the share of black males in the SMSA, obtained using the PUMS data;
specifications IV and VIII: Natural logarithm of employment of US-born workers aged 16–65 with at least two years of college education. The employment is calculated by multiplying total employment figures by the share of workers with more than two years of college in the SMSA, obtained using the PUMS data.
* Significant at the 1% level.

males the effect of schooling is unchanged but average experience has a stronger positive and concave effect.

The estimates in the first columns of Tables 3 and 4 show that the overall effects of diversity on the wage and employment of US-native workers is positive and significant. Its magnitude is most decidedly relevant. A change in the diversity index of 0.60, comparable to the differences in diversity between Pittsburgh (a very homogeneous city) and Los Angeles (a very diverse one), is associated with a 13% increase in the average wage of US-born workers.[11] A very similar effect is obtained using the estimates of column V in Table 3, in which diversity is proxied by the index of linguistic fractionalization. The main message from the basic wage specification is that diversity is associated with a very large increase in productivity. By way of comparison, a city would need an average increase of

---

[11] The standard deviation of the two indices is around 0.16 so that an increase of one standard deviation implies an increase of average wages by 4% and an increase of employment by 8%.

G.I.P. Ottaviano, G. Peri / Journal of Urban Economics 58 (2005) 304–337   323

more than one year of schooling for each worker in order to achieve the same 13% increase in productivity.

This average effect is very significant and forms the main focus of our analysis. This may, however, conceal different effects for different demographic groups in the native population; thus the remaining columns of Tables 3 and 4 analyze the impact of diversity on narrower groups. The effects of linguistic diversity on the wage and employment of US-born white males (columns II and VI of Tables 3 and 4) is positive and significant and, quantitatively, rather similar to the overall effect. As this is the largest group among all workers, a large part of the total effect is likely driven by the effect on this group. To the contrary, the effect on the wages of black males is negative and not significant (while the effect on the employment of black males is positive and not significant). Potentially this may arise if non-native speakers compete with blacks more than with whites for similar occupations (low-skill jobs, personal services), so that diversity harms (or at least does not help) black workers. Alternatively we may think that the composition of black workers (in terms of skills and age) is such that they are the most adversely affected by competition from non-native speakers. Columns IV and VIII provide partial support for this explanation. The positive impact of linguistic diversity on the wages of skilled US-born workers is higher than its average impact on all workers (coefficient is 0.31, significantly larger than the average of 0.23). The effect of diversity on less skilled workers (i.e. workers with less than 2 years of college education), not reported, is equal to 0.23 (standard error 0.04) when measured using the diversity index and to 0.28 (0.04) when measured using linguistic fractionalization. Thus the estimated impact of diversity on the less educated, while smaller than for the highly educated, remains positive and significant. The explanation for the insignificant effect on black workers should then arise, at least in part, from the occupational composition of the black labor force, rather than simply from their schooling. Columns IV and VIII in Table 4 show how diversity is beneficial to the employment of high skilled workers, confirming the hypothesis of a positive productivity effect on this group.

If we believe that the variation in linguistic diversity across cities is exogenous (as it is driven by exogenous migration flows) we can interpret the results of the above regressions as evidence of a strong positive effect of diversity on the productivity of average US-born workers. Moreover, there is evidence of an even stronger positive effect on the productivity of highly educated native workers, a smaller but still positive effect on the productivity of less educated native workers, while no effect (or a small negative one) is found on the productivity of black native workers. This array of correlations is compatible with the idea that non-native speakers bring a diversity of abilities that is beneficial to native speakers. Complementarities in 'vertical skills' may also be part of the story, as aggregate schooling levels may in part influence the benefits received by US-born workers. However, a significant part of the positive effect seems to be due to 'horizontal differentiation' (in the provision of occupations and abilities) which benefits skilled and unskilled alike. White workers, in aggregate, receive a beneficial productivity effect from non-native speakers (and their diversity) while black workers apparently do not receive any such gains. In the effort to better characterize the features of linguistic diversity that enhance the productivity of natives, we run a series of robustness checks before addressing the crucial issue of the potential endogeneity of linguistic diversity.

324   *G.I.P. Ottaviano, G. Peri / Journal of Urban Economics 58 (2005) 304–337*

4.2. Robustness checks

The wage regressions in Table 5 (complemented by the corresponding employment regressions in Table 6) test the robustness of the effects of linguistic diversity on other measures of diversity, on characteristics of the non-native speakers and on different measures of productivity.

Our strategy consists of including sequentially a series of controls (in Tables 5 and 6) that could potentially act as relevant omitted variables and thereby generate a bias in the estimates of Tables 3 and 4. If an extra control added to a specification enters with a significant coefficient, it is maintained in the following specifications, otherwise it is dropped.

Table 5
Wage regressions: robustness checks

Specification:	I	II	III Large linguistic groups	IV	V	VI Yearly wage as dependent variable	VII Weighted regression
Linguistic diversity	0.91* (0.21)	0.28* (0.04)	0.36* (0.05)	0.91* (0.13)	0.27* (0.09)	0.20* (0.04)	0.35* (0.05)
Racial diversity	0.17 (0.21)						
State of birth diversity	0.02 (0.02)						
Ancestry diversity	0.01 (0.06)						
Diversity of schooling		0.27* (0.09)	0.30* (0.09)	0.57* (0.13)	0.28* (0.04)	0.25* (0.09)	0.29* (0.12)
percentage with good knowledge of English				0.07 (0.04)			
Average schooling of non-native speakers					0.02 (0.06)		
Demographic controls	Yes	Yes	Yes	Yes	Yes	Yes	Yes
City fixed effects	Yes	Yes	Yes	Yes	Yes	Yes	Yes
Year fixed effects	Yes	Yes	Yes	Yes	Yes	Yes	Yes
Observations	320	480	480	320	480	480	480

Dependent variable: natural logarithm of average hourly wage of US-born workers aged 16–65. Each regression includes also average schooling, average experience, average experience squared, share of women, share of black, share of native Americans in the SMSA. City- and year-fixed effects are also included.
Linguistic diversity is measured using the index $frac(Lang_{c,t})$.
* Significant at the 1% level.

Table 6
Employment regressions: robustness checks

Specification:	I	II	III Large linguistic groups	IV	V	VI Weighted regression
Linguistic	1.03*	0.79*	0.99*	0.91*	0.82*	0.76*
diversity	(0.43)	(0.10)	(0.12)	(0.31)	(0.10)	(0.16)
Racial	−0.07					
diversity	(0.35)					
State of birth	0.01					
diversity	(0.02)					
Ancestry	0.29					
diversity	(0.19)					
Diversity		0.83*	0.93*	0.97*	0.84*	0.37
of schooling		(0.27)	(0.27)	(0.39)	(0.27)	(0.27)
percentage with				0.14		
good knowledge				(0.18)		
of English						
Average					−0.04	
schooling of					(0.04)	
non-native						
speakers						
City fixed	Yes	Yes	Yes	Yes	Yes	Yes
effects						
Year fixed	Yes	Yes	Yes	Yes	Yes	Yes
effects						
Observations	320	480	480	320	480	480

Dependent variable: natural logarithm of total employment of US-born workers aged 16–65. Each regression includes city- and year-fixed effects.
Linguistic diversity is measured using the index $frac(Lang_{c,t})$.
* Significant at the 1% level.

The first columns of Tables 5 and 6 include alternative indices that may proxy for 'cultural' diversity. As we wrote in the introduction, our focus on linguistic diversity is driven by the clearness of the concept: people from different countries (and their immediate descendants) refer to their own sets of traditions and values, and are easy to identify through the language they speak at home. However, vaguer concepts such as ethnicity or ancestry could also help us define identity groups. To check whether linguistic diversity uniquely influences productivity, we include in our regression indices of fractionalization based on ethnic groupings, on groupings based on 'ancestry' (this variable is available only in census 1980 and 1990), and on groupings based on the state of birth (limited to people born in the US).[12] Notice that the other indices of diversity can be very different and little correlated with linguistic diversity. For instance African Americans (who are English speakers)

---

[12] The index of ethnic diversity is constructed including the following five 'ethnic groups,' identifiable across censuses: White, Black, Native-American, Asian, and Others.

heavily influence our measure of ethnic diversity, while Hispanics are not even included as a separate "ethnicity" (in line with what was done in the censuses of 1970 and 1990). Similarly the diversity of one's state of birth only refers to the fraction of population that is US-born, and therefore is utterly orthogonal to measures of linguistic diversity. To convince the reader that these variables have a large amount of independent variation, note that the correlation coefficient between linguistic diversity and ethnic fractionalization is 0.09, while between linguistic diversity and fractionalization of state of birth it is 0.11. To give a concrete example of a change in the diversity index that is not highly correlated with changes of ethnic diversity and state of origin but that nonetheless has large positive effects on productivity, consider the large increases in immigration of highly skilled Europeans (eastern and western) and of low skilled Latin Americans that have characterized the 1980s and 1990s. These shocks would not be captured by the other two indices since Europeans and Latin Americans are classified as mostly white (Hispanic is not a category), and the foreign born are excluded from the state of birth index.

Our prior is that, while ethnic diversity may capture the black-white divide and so help us apprehend potential productivity losses associated with racial 'fissures,' the concepts of 'ancestry' and 'state of birth' are simply too weak to define identity or capture significant differences in abilities and skills. Thus we expect no significant effect from them. The estimated coefficients confirm our prior: linguistic diversity is the only measure having a significantly positive effect on productivity. Specifically, ethnic diversity has a negative impact on employment and a positive impact on wages, but both are insignificant. The direction of the correlations, however, may suggest that workers mildly dislike ethnic diversity and ask for a wage premium. The other two measures have insignificant effects as well. Due to some collinearity with the other variables, and to the restriction of the sample to only 1980 and 1990, the coefficient estimates on linguistic diversity (captured throughout this table with $divLang_{ct}$) become much more imprecise in the wage and employment regressions. However the magnitude of the estimates increases, and this makes us confident that the variable is capturing the type of diversity relevant for productivity. Because their coefficients are highly insignificant, and because we wish to use the whole sample, we drop the other indices of diversity in the following specifications.

The main explanation, backed by our model, for the beneficial effect of linguistic diversity is that non-native speakers provide a variety of skills complementary to those of native speakers. If this is true, there may be a 'vertical' as well as an 'horizontal' components to this diversity. It is well known (see for instance Borjas et al. [12]) that the foreign born are over-represented both among workers without a high school degree and among those with college and higher education. On the other hand, they are under-represented in the intermediate group of high-school graduates. Therefore the beneficial effects of having a more polarized distribution of skills (through complementarities) for a given average schooling may be a source of the productive impact of the foreign-born on natives (vertical differentiation). On the other hand, even within a group with homogeneous schooling, non-native speakers may have abilities different from those of natives (horizontal differentiation).

Column II in Tables 5 and 6 include a measure of the vertical diversity of skills in a city. Controlling for average schooling (as we do in all the regressions), we include the

G.I.P. Ottaviano, G. Peri / Journal of Urban Economics 58 (2005) 304–337   327

total share of workers in the two 'extreme' education groups (high-school dropouts and college graduates). The variable is denoted as 'diversity of schooling' in the tables. We find that this variable enters very significantly in the wage and employment regressions, in accordance with a positive productivity effect of vertical skill diversity (due for instance to complementarity of skills). However, linguistic diversity maintains its significance and the magnitude of the coefficient does not much differ from the baseline estimate (column I in Tables 3 and 4) . This suggests that linguistic diversity is not simply a proxy for the complementarity of observable skills, but rather captures a relevant form of horizontal, (unobservable) diversity as well.

Column III uses broader linguistic groupings to construct the diversity index, as languages with common roots (Neo-Latin, Slavic, Anglo-Saxon, South-Asian, East-Asian, African, and Native languages) may indicate similar cultures. The objective is to capture the varying *degrees* of cultural differences: for example, Spanish and Chinese cultures are arguably more different than Spanish and Italian cultures. Thus, diversity between the former pair may bring higher benefits from diversity along with higher communication costs. The estimates of the effects of diversity, both in the wage and employment regressions, increase somewhat, suggesting that the differences between large cultural groups (rather than the nuisances within a group) might be most relevant for ability and skill complementarities.

In columns IV and V we look at some characteristics of non-native speakers that may affect their contribution to productivity. Using the results of a question available only in the 1980 and 1990 censuses we can calculate what percentage of non-native speakers speaks English 'well' or 'very well' (according to a self-evaluation). This percentage provides information on whether the communication barrier (transaction costs) is relevant for non-native speakers and whether it matters for the productivity of natives. Two interesting facts should be pointed out. First this percentage is highly *negatively* correlated with the index of diversity across cities. Clearly non-natives who predominantly live with other non-natives tend to speak worse English. Second, however, the overall percentage of non-native speakers who speak English well is very high (87% in 1980 and 90% in 1990). Once we include this measure (column IV) the coefficient on linguistic diversity becomes larger, and the coefficient on English proficiency is positive in both regressions and significant at the 10% level in the wage regression. We can conclude that the effect of cultural diversity is even stronger once we control for the ability of interacting with natives. Moreover if we consider proficiency in spoken English as inversely correlated with the cost of communication across groups, our results confirm that the benefits of diversity are stronger when barriers between groups are lower. Column V includes the average schooling of non-native speakers, which does not seem to matter much. This confirms that the skill-differentiation of non-natives, rather than their average schooling, may be the most beneficial feature of diversity's role in enhancing productivity.

Columns VI and VII in Table 5 confirm these results using average yearly wages (rather then hourly) as a measure of productivity, and weighting each city observation by its size. Column V in Table 6 also shows the weighted regression for employment. No relevant differences emerge, confirming the robustness of the effect of diversity on productivity.

4.3. Endogeneity and IV

The most problematic assumption made so far in the estimation of the wage and employment regressions is the exogeneity of linguistic diversity. A positive unobservable productivity shock to a city could in fact be the cause of higher wages and employment and may, in turn, attract a wider share and variety of foreign-born workers, thereby increasing the linguistic diversity of a city. If this 'reverse' channel of causation is active, the OLS estimates of the coefficients γ_w and γ_e are upward biased. Furthermore the inclusion of other controls, as done in Tables 5 and 6, would not solve this problem.

Short of performing a randomized experiment, it is hard to rule out this channel completely. One way to reduce the endogeneity bias, however, is to resort to instrumental variable estimation. Specifically, we consider the growth of wages (and employment) in the period 1970–1990 as our dependent variable and growth in linguistic diversity as our key explanatory variable. We then instrument the latter using two sets of instruments. Notice that our sets of instruments should be correlated with the changes in linguistic diversity (rather than with their levels) so we take the time differences of the data (1970–1990) and thus estimate a cross section without fixed effects. As the estimation in differences is completely equivalent to a panel with fixed effects the results of the IV estimation are fully comparable with the previous OLS estimates.

The first set of instruments we use is the distance of each city from the international border, from the coast, and from the closest main 'gateway' into the US (i.e. New York, Los Angeles or Miami, which in total admit each year about 30% of all inbound US travelers). The underlying idea is that, during the period 1970–1990, the US experienced a large increase in immigration for reasons exogenous to the events of any particular city. Thus, simply by geographic accident, cities closer to the coast, the border or the main gateways received a larger inflow of those immigrants. Presumably, these distances have less of a direct impact on productivity if productivity shocks during the period of observation did not depend on the position of a city. Worried that the distance from New York or Los Angeles could proxy for the access to a large market (which may be a cause for larger productivity) we also use "distance from the coast" and "distance from the border" only as instruments. Tests of over-identifying restrictions (more on this below) confirm that distance from the main gateways is the most problematic variable as an instrument. The full set of instruments explains about 40 percent of the variation in linguistic diversity, while the first two variables explain 20 percent of it (see Table 7).

The second instrument was used in a previous study of ours (Ottaviano and Peri [30]), building on a work by Card [14]. It is based on a 'shift-share' methodology. We construct the variation in diversity of foreign-born workers in a city using the initial share of each group in 1970. Then we impute to each linguistic city-group the growth in population that the group experienced nationally (due to immigration) in the 1970–1990 period. In so doing we construct the imputed change in linguistic diversity that does not depend on the actual flow of non-native speakers into a city. This construction only uses national trends and should be orthogonal to city-specific shocks. The idea is that the presence of a large linguistic group attracts newcomers from the same group. As long as this effect is due to the preferences of immigrants, it should be correlated with the actual increase in diversity but not with the productivity of the city. For instance, due to the large increases in Spanish

G.I.P. Ottaviano, G. Peri / Journal of Urban Economics 58 (2005) 304–337   329

Table 7
IV estimates, differences 1990–1970

Dependent variable	Δ Ln(Wage)				Δ Ln(Employment)			
Specification: Instruments:	I Distance from all gateways	II Distance from coast-border	III Shift-share	IV All	V Distance from all gateways	VI Distance from coast-border	VII Shift-share	VIII All
Δ(Linguistic diversity)	0.49* (0.06)	0.68* (0.11)	0.38* (0.17)	0.55* (0.08)	1.08* (0.21)	0.96* (0.32)	1.55* (0.71)	1.02* (0.21)
R^2	0.22	0.20	0.30	0.15	0.05	0.06	0.04	0.05
First stage								
Distance from coast	−0.079* (0.022)	−0.09* (0.02)		−0.079* (0.022)	−0.079* (0.022)	−0.09* (0.02)		−0.079* (0.022)
Distance from border	−0.015 (0.01)	−0.05* (0.01)		−0.015 (0.01)	−0.015 (0.01)	−0.05* (0.01)		−0.015 (0.01)
Distance from closest major gateway	−0.011* (0.001)			−0.011* (0.001)	−0.011* (0.001)			−0.011* (0.001)
Constructed diversity of foreign-born			0.31* (0.11)	0.11 (0.11)			0.31* (0.11)	0.11 (0.11)
p-value of the test of overid. restrictions	0.42	0.21	n.a.	0.22	0.94	0.32	n.a.	0.94
Partial R^2 of instruments	0.40	0.17	0.09	0.41	0.40	0.17	0.09	0.41
Observations	160	160	160	160	160	160	160	160

Wage regressions include the usual demographic controls: average schooling, average experience, average experience squared, share of women, share of black and share of native-American in the MSA.
The variable Δ(Linguistic diversity) is the change of the index of linguistic fractionalization between 1970 and 1990.
* Significant at the 1% level.

speaking communities, a city with a large initial Spanish speaking population would be assigned a larger share of this group in 1990 and, through this channel, a larger diversity, independently of how this city attracted the foreign born. This instrument appears to satisfy the requirement of exogeneity but is rather weak. Specifically it explains slightly less than 10% of the variation in the diversity index across cities. We also use the two instruments together to increase their power. Diagnostic tests cannot reject the exogeneity of these instruments in the wage regression at any standard confidence level, but in the employment regression the exogeneity of the distance from main gateways is rejected at the 10% level (but not at the 5 or 1%).

Table 7 shows the results of instrumental variables estimation of the wage and employment regressions using different combinations of the instruments. Columns I and V use all

330 G.I.P. Ottaviano, G. Peri / Journal of Urban Economics 58 (2005) 304–337

three distance variables, columns II and VI use only distance from the coast and from the border, columns III and VII use the imputed 'shift-share' instrument only, and columns IV and VIII use all instruments together. Reassuringly all of the instrumental variable estimates are positive, significant and close to our OLS estimates. If anything they are slightly larger than their OLS counterparts, implying that the upward endogeneity bias of the OLS estimates cannot be too severe. The estimate that only uses the 'imputed' diversity as an instrument has the largest standard error (due to the weakness of that instrument) but, being based on the most exogenous instrument, is also the one we regard with the most confidence. The coefficient estimate on diversity is positively significant and very close to (possibly higher than) the OLS estimates. Overall we are reassured by the IV estimation. It successfully confirms our view that the correlation between the diversity and productivity of cities is unlikely to be only the result of reverse causation.

5. Recent immigrants and public goods

The last section of this empirical analysis is devoted to qualifying our previous results. In particular, we first show that our findings are not incompatible with studies that identify a small *negative* impact of increased immigration on the wages of natives (see Card [15]). We then reconcile our findings of a positive effect of linguistic diversity on productivity with previous studies that find a negative association of ethnic diversity with the provision of public goods.

5.1. Recent immigrants

Our study reveals a positive effect of linguistic diversity on the average wage at the city level. Some influential existing studies on US immigration, however, find a moderately negative effect of immigrant inflows on the wages of natives (Borjas [8,9], Card [15]). These studies focus on low-skilled workers, whereas we consider the average wage of all US-born workers. Given that the inflow of foreign-born is larger among low educational groups and smaller among higher educational groups a pure "relative scarcity" effect may explain the different effect when considering low skilled workers rather than the whole population. Nevertheless, our positive result may seem at odds with this literature.

These apparently conflicting findings can be reconciled. First, our definition of linguistic diversity is based on the language people speak at home. That comprises not only new immigrants but also long-time foreign-born residents and that portion of the second generation that has maintained its linguistic identity (quite large for some groups). In this respect, our theoretical model can be used to explain the contrasting results one gets when only new immigrants are considered. In particular, as discussed in Section 3, interactions are likely to be easier when groups have had enough time to assimilate a common set of norms and habits from the host society. In the language of our theoretical model (Section 3) the costs of interactions between groups as well as the "distaste" for foreigners (τ_c) may decrease as foreign-born workers assimilate into the local culture. If such an 'assimilation effect' were indeed relevant, we should observe a decrease in the "cost" of diversity but no decrease in benefits (due to variety of skills-services provided) as immigrant spend time in the US.

Table 8
IV estimates including new immigrants, differences 1990–1970

Dependent variable	Δ Ln(Wage)		Δ Ln(Employment)	
Instruments:	Distance from coast-border	Shift-share + distance from coast-border	Distance from coast-border	Shift-share + distance from coast-border
Δ(Linguistic diversity)	0.52* (0.19)	0.41* (0.13)	0.79* (0.38)	0.93* (0.34)
Percentage of new immigrants	−2.21 (2.75)	−3.02 (2.21)	−0.78 (0.85)	−0.65 (0.83)
Observations	160	160	160	160
R^2	0.20	0.30	0.06	0.04

Wage regressions include the usual demographic controls: average schooling, average experience, average experience squared, share of women, share of black and share of native-American in the MSA.
The variable Δ(Linguistic diversity) is the change of the index of linguistic fractionalization between 1970 and 1990.
The variable "Percentage of new immigrants" measures the foreign-born workers, as percentage of initial employment, who immigrated into the city within the last 5 years.
* Significant at the 1% level.

As a consequence the positive effect of linguistic diversity should be associated with the presence of "old" immigrants more than with the presence of "new" immigrants.

In each year we define as 'new immigrants' the foreign-born that immigrated into the US within the previous five years; the reason for this is that the censuses in 1970 and 1990 report the place of residence of individuals five years earlier. The share of new immigrants in each city is then included in our regressions as additional controls, and we perform IV estimation using the same instruments as in Table 7, excluding the distance from major gateways (as it did not survive the most stringent tests of exogeneity in the employment regression). The corresponding results are reported in Table 8. While the estimates for the effects of overall linguistic diversity on wages and employment are still positive and significant, the effects of new immigrants turn out to be mostly insignificant, however negative in sign. The impact of new immigrants is therefore more controversial than the overall impact of linguistic diversity. Our estimates however imply that a city like Dallas, with an index of linguistic diversity 0.18 higher than Pittsburgh and with 2% more new immigrants, will benefit by a 5% higher wage, even when we combine the two effects. The effects of diversity are quantitatively larger and more significant than the effects of new immigration. Overall, these findings support the 'assimilation effect' hypothesis. Cities may face some initial costs in coping with cultural diversity: the effect of recent immigration on local wages is rather variable across cities and possibly slightly negative. However, once the initial costs of assimilation are incurred, the benefits of diversity for productivity materialize.

5.2. Public goods

A recently developed line of research analyzes the effects of racial heterogeneity on local policies, particularly policies that involve redistribution (see, e.g., Alesina and La Ferrara, [1], for a survey). The idea is that communities with a higher degree of ethnic

Table 9
Effects of ethnic and linguistic diversity on the provision of public goods

Specification:	I Total local spending per capita	II Local spending in education	III Local spending in police–security
Linguistic diversity	−0.14	−0.15	−0.11
	(0.10)	(0.08)	(0.10)
Racial diversity	−0.24*	−0.23*	0.27
	(0.12)	(0.11)	(0.16)
Time effects	Yes	Yes	Yes
City effects	Yes	Yes	Yes
Observations	480	480	480

Regressions include time dummies and city fixed effects. Each regression includes also the demographic controls: average schooling, average experience, average experience squared, share of black, share of women and share of native Americans in the city.
Specification I: Dependent variable is natural logarithm of real total public spending per capita of local administration in 1990 US $. Method of estimation is OLS with city and time fixed effects;
Specification II: Dependent variable is natural logarithm of real public spending per capita of local administration for School and Education in 1990 US $. Method of estimation is OLS with city and time fixed effects;
Specification III: Dependent variable is natural logarithm of real public spending per capita of local administration for Police and Security in 1990 US $. Method of estimation is OLS with city and time fixed effects.
* Significant at the 1% level.

fragmentation are less willing to pool their resources for public goods provision. Intuitively, in the presence of higher fragmentation each ethnic group cares less about the provisions granted to other ethnic groups. This causes the under-provision of public goods because individuals do not pay the marginal cost of a service. However, in the case of well defined markets, where people do pay the marginal costs of the services they use, there is no efficiency loss in having heterogeneous agents. This is why we did not consider such an effect in our model. Here, however, we want to make sure that our data are consistent with previous works showing ethnic fragmentation to be harmful for the local provision of public goods, especially education (see, Alesina et al. [2,3]).

Table 9 considers whether the racial and linguistic diversity of a city reduces its per capita spending for local public services after we control for local demographics and for city and time fixed effects. Column I shows the impacts of linguistic and racial diversity on overall local spending per capita. Consistent with the existing literature, racial diversity has a negative and significant impact on public spending. Linguistic diversity, however, has no significant impact (the point estimate of the effect is, however, negative). Columns II and III report the impact of diversity on the provision of local public goods. In particular, they show that racial diversity decreases expenditures in public education, thus confirming the findings of Alesina et al. [2]. Racial diversity also increases expenditures for police and security, which supports the idea that ethnic diversity may generate social unrest. As for linguistic diversity, its effect on both variables is not significant. This exercise shows that

G.I.P. Ottaviano, G. Peri / Journal of Urban Economics 58 (2005) 304–337   333

linguistic diversity is less harmful than ethnic diversity in fostering the under-provision of public goods. It seems that, while the costs of ethnic fragmentation are higher than those of linguistic fragmentation, the benefits to production from ethnic diversity are smaller than those from linguistic diversity. The reason for this difference may be found in the particularly disadvantaged and segregated position of the African American community.

6. Conclusions

We have investigated whether immigration into the US contributes to the economic prosperity of host cities by increasing cultural diversity. In particular, we have studied the effects of cultural diversity on the wages of the native population. We started with no obvious prior. On the production side, if different cultures contribute different skills and expertise in producing goods and services, cultural diversity may enhance productivity. However, difficulties in integration and communication across different groups of citizens may harm aggregate productivity. On the consumption side, cultural diversity may increase the variety of available goods and services. At the same time, however, heterogeneous preferences or distaste for different groups may decrease utility or trigger social conflicts.

By studying 160 US MSAs in the period 1970–1990, we find a significant and robust positive correlation between cultural diversity and the wages of white US-born workers. By comparing the distributions of wages and employment densities across US cities, we have argued that this correlation is compatible only with a dominant positive correlation between productivity and diversity. Moreover, instrumental variable estimation supports the idea of causation going from the latter to the former. These results match our previous findings in terms of wages and land rents (Ottaviano and Peri [30]).

Finally we qualify our findings in two respects. First, our analysis points out that the benefits from immigrants who have integrated (i.e. have been in the US for a longer period of time and speak English well) are larger than those from new immigrants. Second, our results agree with previous studies that find ethnic diversity to be bad for the provision of local public goods, as more diverse societies are less willing to pool resources for collective purposes. This suggests that integration and assimilation may be prerequisites for reaping the full gains of cultural diversity.

Acknowledgments

We are grateful to Jan K. Brueckner and two anonymous referees for useful comments and suggestions. Alberto Alesina, Ed Glaeser, Eliana LaFerrara, Dino Pinelli, Vernon Henderson, and workshop participants at FEEM Milan and UBC Vancouver also provided helpful discussions. We thank Elena Bellini for outstanding research assistance. A.S. Rahman provided extremely competent assistance in editing the paper. Ottaviano gratefully acknowledges financial support from Bocconi University, FEEM and MIUR. Peri gratefully acknowledges the UCLA International Institute for financial support. Errors are ours.

334   *G.I.P. Ottaviano, G. Peri / Journal of Urban Economics 58 (2005) 304–337*

Table A.1
Name and state of the cities used

Abilene, TX	Dayton-Springfield, OH	Lexington, KY	Rockford, IL
Akron, OH	Decatur, IL	Lima, OH	Sacramento, CA
Albany-Schenectady-Troy, NY	Denver, CO	Lincoln, NE	Saginaw-Bay City-Midland, MI
Albuquerque, NM	Des Moines, IA	Little Rock-North Little Rock, AR	St. Louis, MO-IL
Allentown-Bethlehem-Easton, PA	Detroit, MI	Los Angeles-Long Beach, CA	Salem, OR
Altoona, PA	Duluth-Superior, MN-WI	Louisville, KY-IN	Salinas, CA
Amarillo, TX	El Paso, TX	Lubbock, TX	Salt Lake City-Ogden, UT
Appleton-Oshkosh-Neenah, WI	Erie, PA	Macon, GA	San Antonio, TX
Atlanta, GA	Eugene-Springfield, OR	Madison, WI	San Diego, CA
Atlantic-Cape May, NJ	Fayetteville, NC	Mansfield, OH	San Francisco, CA
Augusta-Aiken, GA-SC	Flint, MI	Memphis, TN-AR-MS	San Jose, CA
Austin-San Marcos, TX	Fort Lauderdale, FL	Miami, FL	Santa Barbara-Santa Maria-Lompoc, CA
Bakersfield, CA	Fort Wayne, IN	Milwaukee-Waukesha, WI	Santa Rosa, CA
Baltimore, MD	Fresno, CA	Minneapolis-St. Paul, MN-WI	Seattle-Bellevue-Everett, WA
Baton Rouge, LA	Gainesville, FL	Modesto, CA	Shreveport-Bossier City, LA
Beaumont-Port Arthur, TX	Gary, IN	Monroe, LA	South Bend, IN
Billings, MT	Grand Rapids-Muskegon-Holland, MI	Montgomery, AL	Spokane, WA
Biloxi-Gulfport-Pascagoula, MS	Green Bay, WI	Muncie, IN	Springfield, MO
Binghamton, NY	Greensboro-Winston-Salem-High Point, NC	Nashville, TN	Stockton-Lodi, CA
Birmingham, AL	Greenville-Spartanburg-Anderson, SC	New Orleans, LA	Syracuse, NY
Bloomington-Normal, IL	Hamilton-Middletown, OH	New York, NY	Tacoma, WA
Boise City, ID	Harrisburg-Lebanon-Carlisle, PA	Newark, NJ	Tampa-St. Petersburg-Clearwater, FL
Brownsville-Harlingen-San Benito, TX	Honolulu, HI	Norfolk-Virginia Beach-Newport News, VA-NC	Terre Haute, IN
Buffalo-Niagara Falls, NY	Houston, TX	Odessa-Midland, TX	Toledo, OH
Canton-Massillon, OH	Huntington-Ashland, WV-KY-OH	Oklahoma City, OK	Trenton, NJ
Cedar Rapids, IA	Indianapolis, IN	Omaha, NE-IA	Tucson, AZ
Champaign-Urbana, IL	Jackson, MI	Orlando, FL	Tulsa, OK
Charleston-North Charleston, SC	Jackson, MS	Pensacola, FL	Tuscaloosa, AL
Charlotte-Gastonia-Rock Hill, NC-SC	Jacksonville, FL	Peoria-Pekin, IL	Tyler, TX
Chattanooga, TN-GA	Jersey City, NJ	Philadelphia, PA-NJ	Utica-Rome, NY

(continued on next page)

Table A.1 (*continued*)

Chicago, IL	Johnstown, PA	Phoenix-Mesa, AZ	Vallejo-Fairfield-Napa, CA
Cincinnati, OH-KY-IN	Kalamazoo-Battle Creek, MI	Pittsburgh, PA	Waco, TX
Cleveland-Lorain-Elyria, OH	Kansas City, MO-KS	Portland-Vancouver, OR-WA	Washington, DC-MD-VA-WV
Colorado Springs, CO	Kenosha, WI	Raleigh-Durham-Chapel Hill, NC	Waterloo-Cedar Falls, IA
Columbia, MO	Knoxville, TN	Reading, PA	West Palm Beach-Boca Raton, FL
Columbia, SC	Lafayette, LA	Reno, NV	Wichita, KS
Columbus, OH	Lafayette, IN	Richmond-Petersburg, VA	Wilmington-Newark, DE-MD
Corpus Christi, TX	Lancaster, PA	Riverside-San Bernardino, CA	Wilmington, NC
Dallas, TX	Lansing-East Lansing, MI	Roanoke, VA	York, PA
Davenport-Moline-Rock Island, IA-IL	Las Vegas, NV-AZ	Rochester, NY	Youngstown-Warren, OH

336   *G.I.P. Ottaviano, G. Peri / Journal of Urban Economics 58 (2005) 304–337*

Appendix A. Data appendix

The data on the ethnic and linguistic composition of cities have been obtained from the 1970–1990 Public Use Microdata Sample of the US Census. We select all people of working age (16–65) in each year and identify the city where they lived using the MSA code for 1980 and 1990, while in 1970 we use the county group code to identify the metropolitan area. We use the variable 'Language Spoken in the Home' in order to identify the linguistic category of the person. We construct groups that can be kept homogeneous across census years. The linguistic groups that we identify are the following: English, Scandinavian, Dutch, French, Celtic, German, Polish, Czech, Slovac, African language, Russian, Rumanian, Indo-European, Hungarian, Yiddish, Greek, Italian, Spanish, Portuguese, Chinese, Arabic, Albanian, Persian, Hindi, Hebrew, East-Southeast Asian, Filipino, American Indian, and Other languages. Once we have grouped people, we use the shares of each group within a city in our sample as a measure of the share of the population in that city belonging to that group. In Table 4 we use the following racial groups to construct racial fractionalization: white, black, native American, Japanese, Chinese, Filipino, Hawaiian, Korean, and others. In Table 5 we use the following 15 groups of Ancestry for white people: Dutch, English, French, German, Greek, Hungarian, Irish, Italian, Norwegian, Polish, Portuguese, Russian, Scottish, Swedish, and Ukrainian.

We use the variable 'Salary and Wage' to measure the yearly wage income, and we divide this by the number of weeks worked in a year and then by the number of hours worked in a week in order to obtain the hourly wage. We transform the wage in real terms by using the GDP deflator. The data on total city employment are from the 'County and City Databook' and measure the total non-farm employment in the metropolitan area. The list of metropolitan areas used in our study is reported in the following table.

References

[1] A. Alesina, E. La Ferrara, Ethnic diversity and economic performance, Mimeo, Harvard University, Department of Economics, 2003.
[2] A. Alesina, R. Baqir, W. Easterly, Public goods and ethnic divisions, Quarterly Journal of Economics 114 (1999) 1243–1284.
[3] A. Alesina, R. Baqir, C. Hoxby, Political jurisdictions in heterogeneous communities, Journal of Political Economy 112 (2004) 349–396.
[4] A. Alesina, E. Spolaore, R. Wacziarg, Economic integration and political disintegration, American Economic Review 90 (2000) 1276–1296.
[5] P. Bairoch, Cities and Economic Development: From the Dawn of History to the Present, Oxford Univ. Press, Oxford, 1988.
[6] M. Berliant, M. Fujita, Knowledge creation as a square dance on the Hilbert Cube, Mimeo, Washington University, Department of Economics, 2003.
[7] O. Blanchard, L. Katz, Regional evolutions, Brookings Papers on Economic Activity 1 (1992) 1–76.
[8] G. Borjas, The economics of immigration, Journal of Economic Literature 32 (1994) 1667–1717.
[9] G. Borjas, The economic benefits of immigration, Journal of Economic Perspectives 9 (1995) 3–22.
[10] G. Borjas, Heaven's Door, Princeton Univ. Press, Princeton and Oxford, 1999.
[11] G. Borjas, The labor demand curve is downward sloping: Reexamining the impact of immigration on the labor market, Quarterly Journal of Economics 118 (4) (2003) 1335–1374.
[12] G. Borjas, R. Freeman, L. Katz, How much do immigrants and trade affect labor market outcomes, Brookings Papers on Economic Activity 1 (1997) 1–90.

G.I.P. Ottaviano, G. Peri / Journal of Urban Economics 58 (2005) 304–337   337

[13] D. Card, The impact of the Mariel Boatlift on the Miami labor market, Industrial and Labor Relations Review 43 (1990) 245–257.

[14] D. Card, The causal effect of education on earnings, in: O. Ashenfelter, D. Card (Eds.), Handbook of Labor Economics, vol. 3A, North-Holland, Amsterdam, 1999, pp. 1801–1863.

[15] D. Card, Immigrant inflows, native outflows and the local labor market impacts of higher immigration, Journal of Labor Economics 19 (2001) 22–61.

[16] P. Collier, Implications of ethnic diversity, Economic Policy: A European Forum 1 (2001) 27–55.

[17] P. Collier, J. Gunning, Explaining African economic performance, Journal of Economic Literature 37 (1999) 64–111.

[18] W. Easterly, Can institutions resolve ethnic conflict? Economic Development and Cultural Change 49 (2001) 687–706.

[19] W. Easterly, R. Levine, Africa's growth tragedy: Policies and ethnic division, Quarterly Journal of Economics 112 (1997) 1203–1250.

[20] R. Florida, Bohemia and economic geography, Journal of Economic Geography 2 (2002) 55–71.

[21] R. Florida, The economic geography of talent, Annals of the Association of Economic Geographers 92 (2002) 743–755.

[22] E. Glaeser, J. Scheinkman, A. Shleifer, Economic growth in a cross section of cities, Journal of Monetary Economics 36 (1995) 117–143.

[23] E. Glaeser, J. Kolko, A. Saiz, Consumer city, Journal of Economic Geography 1 (2001) 27–50.

[24] J. Jacobs, The Economy of Cities, Random House, New York, 1969.

[25] E. Lazear, Globalization and the market for team-mates, Economic Journal 109 (1999) C15–C40.

[26] E. Lazear, Culture and language, Journal of Political Economy, Supplement (1999) 95–125.

[27] C. Maignan, G. Ottaviano, D. Pinelli, F. Rullani, Bio-ecological diversity vs. socio-economic diversity: A comparison of existing measures, Working paper No. 13, FEEM, 2003.

[28] P. Mauro, Corruption and growth, Quarterly Journal of Economics 110 (1995) 681–712.

[29] C. O'Reilly, K. Williams, S. Barsade, Group demography and innovation: Does diversity help? in: D. Gruenfeld, et al. (Eds.), Research on Managing Groups and Teams, JAI Press, 1998.

[30] G.I.P. Ottaviano, G. Peri, The value of cultural diversity: Evidence from US cities, Discussion paper 4233, Centre for Economic Policy Research, 2004.

[31] J. Quigley, Urban diversity and economic growth, Journal of Economic Perspectives 12 (1998) 127–138.

[32] J. Roback, Wages, rents and the quality of life, Journal of Political Economy 90 (1982) 1257–1278.

[33] S. Sassen, Cities in a World Economy, Pine Forge Press, Thousand Oaks, 1994.

[34] C. Sparber, Racial diversity and economic productivity: Industry level evidence, Manuscript, University of California, Davis, 2005.

[35] C. Taylor, M. Hudson, World Handbook of Political and Social Indicators, second ed., Yale Univ. Press, New Haven, 1972.

Chapter 7

The economic value of cultural diversity: evidence from US cities†

Gianmarco I.P. Ottaviano* and Giovanni Peri**

Abstract

What are the economic consequences to U.S. natives of the growing diversity of American cities? Is their productivity or utility affected by cultural diversity as measured by diversity of countries of birth of U.S. residents? We document in this paper a very robust correlation: US-born citizens living in metropolitan areas where the share of foreign-born increased between 1970 and 1990, experienced a significant increase in their wage and in the rental price of their housing. Such finding is economically significant and survives omitted variable bias and endogeneity bias. As people and firms are mobile across cities in the long run we argue that, in equilibrium, these correlations are consistent with a net positive effect of cultural diversity on the productivity of natives.

Keywords: cultural diversity, immigrants, productivity, local amenities, urban economics
JEL classifications: O4, R0, F1, O18
Date submitted: 7 September 2004 Date accepted: 20 April 2005

1. Introduction

Since the 1965 amendments to the Immigration and Nationality Act immigration into the United States has been on an upward surge. Indeed, immigration rates have been accelerating since the eighties. As a consequence, during the last thirty years foreign born residents in the United States have increased substantially as a share of both the total population and the labor force. In 1970 only 4.8% of the US residents were foreign-born; that percentage grew to 8% in 1990 and to 12.5% in the year 2000. Similarly, although to a lesser extent, other industrialized countries such as Europe and Australia have also recently experienced rising pressures from immigrants.[1] This phenomenon has spurred a heated policy debate and galvanized academic interest.

There is a large and growing body of empirical literature on the consequences of migration (see, among others Borjas 1994, 1995, 1999, 2003; Borjas et al., 1997; Boeri et al., 2002; Card 1990, 2001; Card and Di Nardo, 2000). This literature, however, has disproportionately focussed on one aspect of the subject: the impact of low-skilled immigrants on US wages. These studies typically treat labor markets for different skills as segmented, and focus on the consequences of wages for different skill-groups in the

* Department of Economics, University of Bologna, Strada Maggiore 45, 40125 Bologna, Italy, FEEM and CEPR.
email <ottavian@economia.unibo.it>
** Giovanni Peri, UCLA International Institute, 10266 Bunche Hall, UCLA, Los Angeles, CA 90024 USA, University of California, Davis and NBER.
email <gperi@international.ucla.edu>
1 See Peri (2005) for a comparison of immigration in the US and in the EU during the nineties.

†This article originally appeared in *Journal of Economic Geography*, **6** 9–44 © 2006 Oxford University Press.

10 • *Ottaviano and Peri*

short and medium run. Our work takes a different angle. Rather than study the short-run effects of new immigrants on the receiving country in a classic model of skill supply and demand, we consider a simple multi-city model of production and consumption in order to ask 'what is the economic value of "diversity" that the foreign born bring to each city'. The foreign born conceivably have different sets of skills and abilities than the US born, and therefore could serve as valuable factors in the production of differentiated goods and services. As different US cities attract very different shares of foreign-born we can learn about the value of such 'diversity' from the long-run equilibrium distribution of wages and prices across cities. For the rest of the paper, the term 'cultural diversity' will refer to the diversity of the workers' countries of birth (rather than ethnicity or ancestry characteristics) and will be measured by an index of 'plurality' of countries of origin.

Diversity over several dimensions has been considered by economists as valuable both in consumption and production. Jacobs (1969) attributes the prosperity of cities to their industrial diversity. Quigley (1998) and Glaeser et al. (2001) identify the diversity of available consumption goods and services as one of the attractive features of cities. Florida (2002a, 2002b) stresses the importance of the diversity of creative professions employed in research and development or high tech industries. More generally, Fujita et al. (1999) use the 'love of variety' in preferences and technology as the building block of their theory of spatial development: the production of a larger variety of goods and services in a particular location increases the productivity and utility of people living in that location.

Against this background, we conjecture that cultural diversity may very well be an important aspect of urban diversity, influencing local production and/or consumption.[2] The aim of this paper is to test this conjecture by quantifying the value of cultural diversity to US-born people. Who can deny that Italian restaurants, French beauty shops, German breweries, Belgian chocolate stores, Russian ballets, Chinese markets, and Indian tea houses all constitute valuable consumption amenities that would be inaccessible to Americans were it not for their foreign-born residents? Similarly the skills and abilities of foreign-born workers and thinkers may complement those of native workers and thus boost problem solving and efficiency in the workplace.[3] Cultural diversity, therefore, may increase consumption variety and improve the productivity of natives. On the other hand, natives may not enjoy living in a multi-cultural environment if they feel that their own cultural values are being endangered. Moreover, intercultural frictions may reduce productivity, particularly if natives associate increasing immigration with further job losses for the US born. Thus cultural diversity could possibly decrease both the utility and the productivity of natives.

We focus on 160 major metropolitan areas in the US, for which we can construct consistent data between 1970 and 1990. While these metropolitan areas do not cover

---

2 An economically oriented survey of the pros and cons of ethnic diversity is presented by Alesina and La Ferrara (2003).

3 The anedoctical evidence of the contribution of foreign born to 'big thinking' in the US is quite rich. One striking example is the following. In the last ten years, out of the 47 US-based Nobel laureates in Chemistry, Physics and Medicine, 25% (14 laureates) were not US-born. During the same time period the share of foreign-born in the general population was on average only 10%. From our perspective, such example is interesting because research in hard sciences is typically based on large team work.

The economic value of cultural diversity: evidence from US cities • **11**

the whole US urban population, they include the largest and most important cities. More importantly, they span the whole range of 'diversity', for they include the most diverse cities (New York, Los Angeles, San Francisco) along with some of the least diverse. We use the 'index of fractionalization' (by the country of birth of each city resident) in order to measure cultural diversity across these 160 cities.[4] This index measures the probability that, in any one city, two individuals chosen at random were born in different countries. Cities entirely populated by US-born individuals would have an index of fractionalization equal to 0. Going to the other extreme, if each individual within a city was born in a different country, the index would equal one. US cities vary wildly by this measure, ranging from 0.02 (Cleveland) to 0.58 (Los Angeles). Since US-born people are highly mobile across US cities, following Roback (1982) we develop a model of 'open cities' that allows us to use the observed variations of wages and rents of US-born workers to identify the production and consumption gains associated with cultural diversity. In particular, we estimate two regressions in which cultural diversity, measured as 'fractionalization' (or the share of foreign-born residents) affects the average wage received and the average rent paid by US-born workers. Our main finding is that, on average, *cultural diversity has a net positive effect on the productivity of US-born citizens* because it is positively correlated with both the average wage received and the average rent paid by US-born individuals. This partial correlation survives the inclusion of many variables that proxy for productivity and amenity shocks across cities.

Two fundamental concerns arise when we attempt to interpret these correlations as *causal* effects of diversity on the wages and rents of natives, namely a potential endogeneity bias and the possibility of spatial selection of natives. Endogeneity works as follows. Cities may experience an increase in the average wage from a positive economic shock, disproportionately attracting immigrants and thus witnessing an increase in diversity (this hypothesis is often referred to as 'boom cities'). If this were the true story, the measured impact of diversity on wages and rents would be upwardly biased. To tackle this problem, we use instrumental variable estimations, a method widely used among economists that requires an 'auxiliary' variable whose exogenous variation affects diversity in a city (but not its productivity). Such a variable allows us to isolate that portion of the correlation between diversity and wages that is due to the causal effect of diversity on wages.

The spatial selection of native workers, on the other hand, is harder to deal with. In fact, if the presence of foreign-born people attracts a particular type of US born worker (call this group 'tolerant') and these workers also happen to be more productive, then the correlation between diversity and productivity of natives may be the effect of this selection rather than of complementarities or externalities with foreign-born. The best we can do is to control for observable characteristics of US-born residents and assume that their 'tolerance' is not highly correlated with the residual (unobserved) productivity. This issue, however, is certainly not settled with this paper and needs more research. We will come back to it in the final part of the paper.

The rest of the paper is organized as follows. Section 2 reviews the literature on the economic consequences of immigration and cultural diversity. In particular we

---

4   As an alternative and perhaps more intuitive measure of diversity in a city we also use, in several parts of the analysis, the share of foreign-born residents.

differentiate our work from (and reconcile it with) the common findings in labor economics that immigrants have negative or zero effects on the wages of US-born workers. Section 3 introduces our dataset and surveys the main stylized facts. Section 4 develops the theoretical model that is used to design and interpret our estimation strategy. Section 5 presents the results from the basic estimation, checks their robustness and tackles the issue of endogeneity. Section 6 discusses the results and provides some important caveats and qualifications to our conclusions.

2. Literature on diversity

Cultural diversity is a broad concept that has attracted the attention of both economists and social scientists. The applied 'labor' literature has analyzed ethnic diversity and ethnic 'segregation' in the US, as well as their impact on economic discrimination and the achievements of minorities.[5] The present paper does not focus on this aspect of cultural diversity even though we control for black-white composition issues.

More closely related to our analysis is the literature concerning the impact of immigration on the US labor market. Several contributions by George Borjas (notably Borjas, 1994, 1995, 1999, 2001 and 2003) focus on the issue of US immigration as a whole, and its effect on native workers. Similarly, important contributions by David Card (notably, Card, 1990; Butcher and Card, 1991; Card and Di Nardo, 2000; Card, 2001) analyze the wages and reactions of domestic workers to inflows of new immigrants by exploiting the geographic variation of immigration rates and wages across US states or US cities. These contributions do not achieve a consensus view either on the effect of new immigrants on the wages of domestic workers (which seems small except, possibly, for low skill levels) or on the effect of new immigrants on the migration behavior of domestic workers. Let us emphasize, however, that the negative (significant or small) effect that is found in this literature is merely a 'relative' effect. Immigrants bring down the relative wages of low-skilled workers (but raise the wages of intermediately-skilled workers) due to their composition (abundant in low skills and scarce in intermediate skills). This, however, does not comment on the overall (average) effect on US workers. In the presence of complementarities between the skills of immigrants and the skills of natives, or of externalities from highly skilled workers (who are also abundant among immigrants), the impact of immigration on the average wage of US born workers may very well be positive. While the labor literature estimates the relative effect of immigration within labor markets segmented by skills (such an effect would be negative if different skills are imperfect substitutes), we focus on the average effect of immigration that results from aggregating those effects with the positive complementarity-effects and the positive externality-effects.[6] This is a novel approach, and while we do not deny that a shift of relative wages (between skills) takes place as a consequence of immigration, we focus on the average overall effect on wages of US-born workers

---

5   Notable examples are Card and Krueger (1992, 1993), Cutler and Glaeser (1997), Eckstein and Wolpin (1999), Mason (2000).

6   While in the present paper we simplify these effects into an overall effect of diversity on the TFP of US-born workers, in Ottaviano and Peri (2005) we separately model and analyze the effects of complementarieties across skills. We find that the (positive) empirical effects of migration on the average wage of US-born workers are very close to the theoretically calculated effects from the diversity of skills generated by immigrants.

and find it significantly positive. Recently, evidence of a positive effect of immigrant inflows on rents in cities has been provided by Saiz (2003a, 2003b), although he interprets this as a consequence of increased demand in housing rather than an increased value of houses due to higher diversity and higher wages. To our knowledge this is the first work that looks at a general equilibrium effect of immigration (diversity) on wages, employment and rents of US born residents.

In short, the standard labor literature assumes that immigrants and domestic workers within a particular skill group are homogeneous, so that immigration will shift the labor supply and change local wages in that skill group, the extent of which will depend on the mobility of domestic workers. Our approach takes a rather different stand. We believe that 'place of birth' can be a feature that differentiates individuals in terms of their attributes, and that this differentiation may have positive or negative effects on the productivity (through complementarities and externalities) and the utility (through taste for variety) of US-born residents. Moreover, we consider equilibrium variations of wages and rents in the long-run, relying on the assumption of mobility of native workers and firms across cities.

Relevant to our work, several researchers in the social sciences have related diversity with urban agglomeration. The functioning and thriving of urban clusters relies on the variety of people, factors, goods and services within them. Examples abound in the urban studies literature. Jacobs (1969) views economic diversity as the key factor of a city's success. Sassen (1994) studies 'global cities' (such as London, Paris, New York, and Tokyo) and their strategic role in the development of activities that are central to world economic growth and innovation. A key feature of these cities is the cultural diversity of their populations. Similarly, Bairoch (1988) sees cities and their diversity as the engines of economic growth. Such diversity, however, has been seen mainly in terms of the diversified provision of consumer goods and services, as well as productive inputs (see, e.g. Quigley, 1998; Glaeser et al., 2001). In his work within the nexus of sociology and economics, Richard Florida (2002a, 2002b) argues that 'diverse' and tolerant cities are more likely to be populated by creative people, thus attracting industries such as high tech and research that heavily rely on creativity and innovative ability. The positive 'production value' of diversity has also been stressed in the literature on the organization and management of teams. Here the standard assumption is that higher diversity can lead to more innovation and creativity by increasing the number of ways groups frame problems, thus producing a richer set of alternative solutions and consequently better decisions. Lazear (1999) provides an attempt to model team interactions. He defines the 'global firm' as a team whose members come from different cultures or countries. Combining workers whose countries of origin have different cultures, legal systems, and languages imposes costs on the firm that would not be present if all the workers had similar backgrounds. However, complementarity between workers, in terms of skills, can more than offset the costs of cross-cultural interaction.[7]

Finally, several studies in political economics have looked at the historical effects of cultural and ethnic diversity on the formation and quality of institutions.

---

7 Berliant and Fujita (2004) model 'assimilation' as a result of team work: the very process of cooperative knowledge creation reduces the heterogeneity of team members through the accumulation of knowledge in common. In this respect, a perpetual reallocation of members across different teams may be necessary to keep creativity alive.

The traditional wisdom (confirmed by Easterly and Levine, 1997) had been that more fragmented (i.e. diverse) societies promote more conflicts and predatory behavior, stifling economic growth. However, recent studies have questioned that logic by showing that higher ethnic diversity is not necessarily harmful to economic development (see, e.g., Lian and Oneal, 1997). Collier (2001) finds that, as long as institutions are democratic, fractionalized societies perform better in the private sector than more homogenous ones. Framed within efficient institutions, diversity may serve as a valuable asset for society.

3. Cultural diversity, wages and rents

The questions we are interested in are the following. How does cultural diversity affect the US-born? Do they benefit or loose from the presence of foreign-born? How do we measure such benefits or costs?

We are able to extract interesting insights into these questions by analyzing the wage and rent distributions across cities, assuming that such distributions are the equilibrium outcomes of economically motivated choices. We assume that workers and firms are mobile across cities, and so can change their location in the long run if a productivity shock or a price differential were to arise. Since people can respond to changes in the local working and living environment of cities, the wage and rent variations that we observe in the long run should reflect a spatial equilibrium: workers and firms are indifferent among alternative locations as they have eliminated any systematic difference in indirect utility and profits through migration. Before formalizing these ideas in Section 4, we put our theoretical analysis into context by introducing our measure of cultural diversity (Section 3.1) and by establishing the main stylized facts about wages, rents and diversity in US cities (Section 3.3).

3.1. Data and diversity index

Data at the Metropolitan Statistical Area (MSA) level for the United States are available from different sources. We use mostly the Census Public Use Microdata Sample (PUMS) for the years 1970 and 1990 in order to calculate wages and rents for specific groups of citizens in each MSA. We use the 1/100 sample from the 15% PUMS of 1970 and the 5% PUMS for 1990. We also use data from the 'County and City Data Book' from several years in order to obtain some aggregate variables, such as employment, income, population and spending on local public goods. We consider 160 Standard MSA's that could be consistently identified in each census year. Our dataset contains around 1,200,000 individual observations for 1990, and 500,000 for 1970. We use these to construct aggregate variables and indices at the MSA level. The reasons for focusing on metropolitan areas are two-fold. First, urban areas constitute closely connected economic units within which interactions are intense. Second, they exhibit a higher degree of diversity than non-urban areas because immigrants traditionally settle in large cities. While it is possible to construct data only on 160 metropolitan areas (using 1970 and 1990 PUMS of the US Bureau of Census) those areas include the most important US cities, spanning a wide range of variation in terms of cultural diversity. Adding all the other metropolitan areas would simply amount to adding more observations characterized by low and similar levels of diversity. This would certainly add some noise, but probably would not help much in the identification of the effect of diversity on wages and rents.

We measure the average wage of native workers in an MSA using the yearly wage of white US-born male residents between 40 and 50 years of age. We denote by $\bar{w}_{US,c,t}$ the resulting average wage for city c in year t. This value is neither affected by composition effects nor distorted by potential discrimination factors (across genders or ethnicity) or life-cycle considerations. It can therefore serve as a good proxy for the average wage of US-born workers in the city, comparable across census years. The correlation between $\bar{w}_{US,c,t}$ and the degree of diversity of a city comes only through the equilibrium effect of diversity on the labor demand and supply of native workers. As a measure of the average land rent in an MSA we use the average monthly rent paid per room (i.e. the monthly rent divided by the number of rooms) by white US-born male residents of working age (16–65 year).[8] We denote this measure (for city c in year t) as $\bar{r}_{US,c,t}$. While this measure does not control for housing quality (beyond the number of rooms), there is no reason to think that housing quality is related to the percentage of foreign-born in a city, so this measure should not induce any relevant bias in the relation.

Turning to our key explanatory variable, our measure of cultural diversity considers the country of birth of people as defining their cultural identity. Foreign born residents have always been an important part of the US population, and their share of the population has only grown larger in the past decades. In 1970, they constituted 4.8% of the total population, while in 1990 they reached 8%, still continuing to grow afterwards. Our measure of cultural diversity is the so called 'index of fractionalization' (henceforth, simply 'diversity index'), routinely used in the political economics literature. This index has been popularized by cross-country studies by Mauro (1995) and has been widely used since. The index is simply the probability that two randomly selected individuals in a community belong to different groups. It accounts for the two main dimensions of diversity, i.e. 'richness' (number of groups) and 'evenness' (balanced distribution of individuals across groups).[9] Specifically, we use the variable CoB (Country of Birth of a person) to define the cultural identity of each group. The diversity index is defined as:

$$div_{ct} = 1 - \sum_{i=1}^{M} (CoB_i^c)_t^2 \qquad (1)$$

where $\left(CoB_i^c\right)_t$ is the share of people born in country i among the residents of city c in year t. This index is an increasing measure of both the cultural 'richness' of a city (i.e. the number of groups) and its cultural 'diversity' (i.e. the evenness of groups' sizes). It reaches its minimum value 0 when all individuals are born in the same country, and its maximum value 1 when there are no individuals born in the same country. Intuitively, when all individuals belong to the same group, the probability that two randomly selected individuals belong to different groups is 0, whereas it equals 1 when all individuals belong to

---

8 The housing market is less segmented by skills than the labor market. Therefore we use a larger age-range in order to calculate average rents.

9 Despite differences that may seem notable at first sight, most statistical measures of diversity are either formally equivalent or at least highly correlated when run on the same data set. See Maignan et al. (2003) for details.

16 • *Ottaviano and Peri*

Table 1.   Foreign Born living in 160 U.S. metropolitan areas 15 Largest Groups 1970, 1990

Country of origin	Percentage of total foreign born 1970	Country of origin	Percentage of total foreign born 1990
Canada	9.0%	Mexico	20.0%
Italy	8.1%	Philippines	6.0%
Germany	7.8%	Cuba	4.2%
Mexico	7.3%	Germany	3.2%
Syria	7.0%	Canada	3.2%
Cuba	5.1%	China	2.8%
Poland	4.5%	India	2.8%
UK	4.4%	Viet-Nam	2.7%
Philippine	2.3%	El Salvador	2.6%
USSR	2.3%	Italy	2.4%
Ireland	2.3%	Korea	2.2%
China	2.3%	UK	2.2%
Yugoslavia	1.7%	Japan	1.8%
Greece	1.6%	Jamaica	1.7%
Hungary	1.6%	Colombia	1.6%
Foreign born as % of working age total population, 1970	8.0%	Foreign born as % of working age total population, 1990	11.9%

Source: Authors' elaborations on 1970 and 1990 PUMS census data.

different groups. On the other hand, for a given number of groups M (i.e. controlling for 'richness'), the index reaches its maximum at $(1 - 1/M)$ when individuals are uniformly distributed across groups.[10]

The 1970 and 1990 PUMS data report the country of birth of each individual. We count as separate groups the migrants of each country of origin contributing at least 0.5% of the total foreign-born population working in the US. Migrants from other countries of origin are gathered in a residual group. This choice implies that we consider 35 countries of origin both in 1970 and in 1990. These groups constitute 92% of all foreign-born immigrants; the remaining 8% are merged into a single group. The complete list of countries for each census year is reported in the data appendix, while the largest 15 of these groups are reported in Table 1. As the Table shows, between 1970 and 1990, the origin of immigrants has increasingly become Mexico; the share of foreign born, however, has increased as well, so that overall the diversity index has increased. As to the main countries of origin of immigrants, we note the well known shift from European countries towards Asian and Latin American countries.

3.2. Diversity across US cities

Table 2 shows the percentage of foreign-born and the diversity index for a representative group of metropolitan areas in the year 1990. To put into context the extent of

---

10   In our case as M, the number of groups, is 36 the maximum for the index is 0.972. See Maignan et al. (2003) for further details.

The economic value of cultural diversity: evidence from US cities • **17**

Table 2. Diversity in representative Metropolitan Areas, 1990

City	Share of foreign born	Country of origin of the five largest foreign groups	Diversity index
Atlanta, GA	5.8%	Germany, Mexico, India, England, Korea	0.11
Chicago, IL	15.2%	Mexico, Poland, Philippines, India, Germany	0.28
Cincinnati, OH-KY-IN	2.3%	Germany, England, India, Canada, Viet-Nam	0.057
Dallas, TX	10.6%	Mexico, Salvador, Viet-Nam, India, Germany	0.20
El Paso, TX	29%	Mexico, Japan, Korea, Canada, Panama	0.43
Indianapolis, IN	2.3%	Germany, England, Korea, Canada, Philippines	0.046
Las Vegas, NE	12%	Mexico, Philippines, Germany, Canada, Cuba	0.23
Los Angeles, CA	37%	Mexico, Salvador, Philippines, Guatemala, Korea	0.58
New York, NY	31%	Dominican Republic, China, Jamaica, Italy, Colombia	0.51
Oklahoma City, OK	4.1%	Mexico, Viet-Nam, Germany, England, Japan	0.08
Philadelphia, PA-NJ	5%	Germany, India, Italy, England, Philippines	0.10
Pittsburgh, PA	2.3%	Italy, Germany, India, England, Canada	0.04
Sacramento, CA	10.6%	Mexico, Philippines, Germany, China, Canada	0.19
San Francisco, CA	30.3%	Philippines, China, Mexico, Salvador, Hong Kong	0.50
Washington, DC-MD-VA-WV	14.8%	Salvador, Germany, India, Korea, Viet-Nam	0.27

Source: Authors' Elaborations on 1990 PUMS census data.

diversity across US cities, each diversity index can be compared with the cross-country value of the index of linguistic fractionalization reported by the Atlas Narodov Mira and published in Taylor and Hudson (1972) for the year 1960. These values have been largely used in the growth literature (see e.g. Easterly and Levine, 1997; Collier, 2001). Since foreign-born immigrants typically use their country's mother tongue at home, thus signalling their country's cultural identity, our diversity index captures cultural and linguistic fragmentation for different US cities much as that index does for different countries in the world. The comparison is instructive. Diversified cities, such as New York or Los Angeles, have diversity indices between 0.5 and 0.6, which are comparable to the values calculated for countries such as Rhodesia (0.54), which is often disrupted by ethnic wars, or Pakistan (0.62), which also features a problematic mix of conflicting cultures. More homogenous cities, such as Cincinnati and Pittsburgh, exhibit a degree of fractionalization of only 0.05, which is the same as that of very homogenous European countries, such as Norway or Denmark in the sixties. Between these two extremes, US cities span a range of diversity that is about two-thirds of the range spanned by the nations of the world.

Table 2 also shows that, even though people born in Mexico constitute an important group in many cities, the variety of countries of origin of residents of US cities is still remarkable. Finally we note that there is a very high correlation between the diversity index and the share of foreign born in a city. The main reason an American city is considered 'diverse' is because there is a large percentage of foreign born living there, not necessarily because there is a high degree of diversity within the foreign born.

3.3. Stylized facts

The key empirical finding of our paper is readily stated: *ceteris paribus, US-born workers living in cities with higher cultural diversity are paid, on average, higher wages, and pay higher rents, than those living in cities with lower cultural diversity.* In Section 5 we show that this correlation not only survives the inclusion of several other control variables, but it is likely to be the result of causation running from diversity to wages and rents.

We report in Figures 1 and 2, below, the correlation between the change of the diversity index for the 1970–1990 period, $\Delta(div_{c,t})$, and the percentage change in the wage of the US-born, $\Delta \ln(\bar{w}_{US,c})$, or the percentage change in rents paid by the US-born, $\Delta \ln(\bar{r}_{US,c})$ in 160 metropolitan areas. The effect of fixed city characteristics, such as location or geographic amenities, are eliminated by differencing. The figures show the scatter-plots of these partial correlations and report the OLS regression line. Cities whose diversity increased more than the average, during the 20 years considered (such as Jersey City, Los Angeles, San Francisco, and San Jose), have also experienced larger than average wage increases for their US-born residents. Similarly they also experienced a larger than average increase in rents. The OLS coefficient estimates imply that a city experiencing an increase of 0.09 in the diversity index (as Los Angeles did) would experience associated increases of 11 percentage points in the average wage and 17.7 percentage points in the average rent paid by US-born residents, relative to a city whose diversity index did not change at all (such as Cleveland).

4. Theoretical framework

4.1. The model

To structure and interpret our empirical investigation, we develop a stylized model in which 'diversity' affects both the productivity of firms and the satisfaction of consumers through a localized effect. Both the model and the identification procedure build on Roback (1982).[11]

We consider an open system of a large number N of non-overlapping cities, indexed by $c=1, \ldots, N$. There are two factors of production, labor and land. We assume that inter-city commuting costs are prohibitive, so that for all workers the city of work and residence coincides. We also ignore intra-city commuting costs, which allows us to focus on the inter-city allocation of workers.

The overall amount of labor available in the economy is equal to L. It is inelastically supplied by urban residents; without loss of generality, we choose units such that each resident supplies one unit of labor. Accordingly, we call L_c the number of workers who work and reside in city c. Workers are all identical in terms of attributes that are

---

11   Roback's (1982) framework has been extensively applied to measure the value of local amenities or local factors of production. Examples include Rauch (1993), Kahn (1995), and Dekle and Eaton (1999).

The economic value of cultural diversity: evidence from US cities • **19**

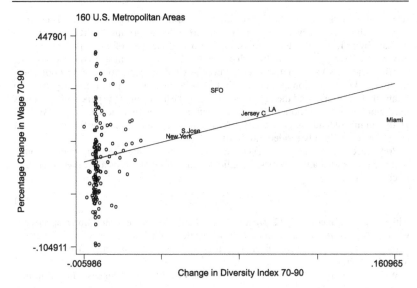

Figure 1.   Wages of US-born and diversity.

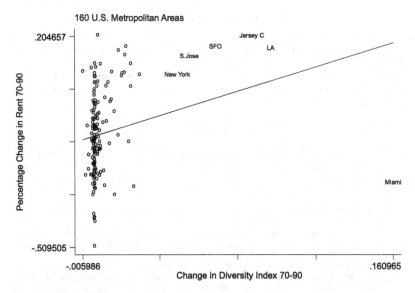

Figure 2.   Rents of US-born and diversity.

20 • *Ottaviano and Peri*

relevant for market interactions. However, they differ in terms of non-market attributes, which exogenously classifies them into M different groups ('cultural identities') indexed by $i=1, \ldots, M$. Hence, calling L_i the overall number of workers belonging to group i, we have $\sum_{i=1}^{M} L_i = L$. In each city cultural diversity d_c, measured in terms of the number ('richness') and relative size L_{ic} ('evenness') of resident groups, enters both production and consumption as an effect that, in principle, can be positive or negative. To establish the existence and the sign of such effect is the final aim of the paper. While land is fixed among cities, it is nonetheless mobile between uses within the same city.[12] We call H_c the amount of land available in city c. As to land ownership, we assume that the land of a city is owned by locally resident landlords.[13]

Preferences are defined over the consumption of land H and a homogeneous good Y that is freely traded among cities. Specifically, the utility of a typical worker of group i in city c is given by:

$$U_{ic} = A_U(d_c)H_{ic}^{1-\mu}Y_{ic}^{\mu} \tag{2}$$

with $0 < \mu < 1$. In equation (2) H_{ic} and Y_{ic} are land and good consumption respectively, while $A_u(d_c)$ captures the 'utility effect' associated with local diversity d_c. If the first derivative $A_u'(d_c)$ is positive, diversity can be seen as a local amenity; if negative as a local dis-amenity.

We assume that workers move to the city that offers them the highest indirect utility. Given equation (2), utility maximization yields:

$$r_c H_{ic} = (1 - \mu)E_{ic}, \quad p_c Y_{ic} = \mu E_{ic} \tag{3}$$

which implies that the indirect utility of the typical worker of group i in city c is:

$$V_{ic} = (1 - \mu)^{1-\mu}\mu^{\mu}A_u(d_c)\frac{E_{ic}}{r_c^{1-\mu}p_c^{\mu}} \tag{4}$$

where E_{ic} is her expenditures, while r_c and p_c are the local land rent and good price respectively.

As to production, good Y is supplied by perfectly competitive firms using both land and labor as inputs. The typical firm in city c produces according to the following technology:

$$Y_{jc} = A_Y(d_c)H_{jc}^{1-\alpha}L_{jc}^{\alpha} \tag{5}$$

with $0 < \alpha < 1$. In equation (5) H_{jc} and L_{jc} are land and labor inputs respectively. $A_Y(d_c)$ captures the 'productivity effect' associated with local diversity d_c. It is convenient to treat the effect of diversity as a shift in total factor productivity, $A_Y'(d_c)$, that is

---

12   The assumption of exogenous and constant land area of a city is harmless. The same implications would follow under the more realistic assumption that expanding the land area of a city comes at a cost because of internal commuting costs and lower quality of the marginal land.

13   This assumption is made only for analytical convenience. What is crucial for what follows is that the rental income of workers, if any, is independent of location, and thus does not affect migration choice. The alternative assumptions of absentee landlords or balanced ownership of land across all cities would also serve that purpose.

The economic value of cultural diversity: evidence from US cities • **21**

common to all firms in city c. This shift could be positive or negative.[14] We should notice at this point that assuming identical effects of diversity on utility, $A_U(d_c)$, and productivity, $A_Y(d_c)$, across agents (i) and firms (j) is critical in order to use the model by Roback (1982) to characterize the average equilibrium rent and wage as a function of only diversity. If diversity were to affect firms and agents in different ways (say because some people like diversity more than others and some firms need diversity of workers more than others) then in equilibrium US-born agents would sort themselves across cities (see e.g. Combes et al., 2004). In this case the equilibrium wages and rents across cities would reflect not only different levels of diversity but also different evaluations of diversity by US-born individuals and firms. Such an equilibrium with heterogeneous agents would complicate the use of average wages and rents to infer the impact of diversity on productivity. The analysis of diversity assuming heterogeneous effects on US born agents is certainly an interesting issue that we leave for future research.

Given equation (5) and perfect competition, profit maximization yields:

$$r_c H_{jc} = (1 - \alpha) p_c Y_{jc}, \quad \omega_c L_{jc} = \alpha p_c Y_{jc} \tag{6}$$

which implies marginal cost pricing:

$$p_c = \frac{r_c^{1-\alpha} \omega_c^\alpha}{(1-\alpha)^{1-\alpha} \alpha^\alpha A_Y(d_c)} \tag{7}$$

so that firms make no profits in equilibrium. Given our assumption on land ownership, this implies that aggregate expenditures in the city equal local factor incomes and that workers' expenditures consist of wages only: $E_{ic} = \omega_c$. Since good Y is freely traded, its price is the same everywhere. We choose this good as numeraire, which allow us to write $p_c = 1$.[15]

In a spatial equilibrium there exists a set of prices ($\omega_c, r_c, c = 1, \ldots, N$) such that in all cities workers and landlords maximize their utilities given their budget constraints, firms maximize profits given their technological constraints, and factor and product markets clear. Moreover, no firm has an incentive to exit or enter. This is granted by equation (7) that, given our choice of numeraire, can be rewritten as:

$$r_c^{1-\alpha} \omega_c^\alpha = (1-\alpha)^{1-\alpha} \alpha^\alpha A_Y(d_c) \tag{8}$$

We will refer to equation (8) as the 'free entry condition'. Finally, in a spatial equilibrium no worker has an incentive to migrate. For an interior equilibrium (i.e. $L_c > 0 \ \forall c = 1, \ldots, N$) this will be the case when workers are indifferent between alternative cities:

$$V_{ic} = V_{ik}, \quad \forall c, k = 0, \ldots, N \tag{9}$$

We will refer to equation (9) as the 'free migration conditions'.

---

14 The contribution of diversity to total factor productivity could stem from imperfect substitutability of different groups as well as from pecuniary or learning externalities. For instance, Ottaviano and Peri (2004a) derive a production function similar to equation (5) with non-tradable intermediates and taste for variety.

15 Anticipating the empirical implementation of the model, by setting $p_c = 1$ for all cities we are requiring the law-of-one-price to hold for tradable goods and non-tradable goods prices to be reasonably proxied by land rents. This is supported by the large positive correlation between local price indices and land rents at the SMSA level.

To complete the equilibrium analysis we have to determine the spatial allocation of workers L_{ic}. This is achieved by evaluating the implications of market clearing for factor prices. Specifically, given $L_c = \sum_j L_{jc}$ and $Y_c = \sum_j Y_{jc}$, equation (6) implies $\omega_c L_c = \alpha p_c Y_c$. Given $H_c = \sum_j H_{jc} + \sum_i H_{ic}$, equation (6) and (3) imply $\mu r_c H_c = (1-\alpha\,\mu)$ $p_c Y_c$. Together with $E_{ic} = \omega_c$ and $p_c = 1$, these results can be plugged into equation (4) to obtain:

$$V_{ic} = \mu \left(\frac{1-\mu}{1-\alpha\mu} \right)^{1-\mu} \left(\frac{H_c}{L_c} \right)^{1-\alpha\mu} A_U(d_c)[A_Y(d_c)]^{\mu} \tag{10}$$

Equation (10) shows that the indirect utility of a person is higher, *ceteris paribus*, in a city with low population density, L_c/H_c, (because of the lower price of housing) and is affected by diversity through its impact on productivity, $A_Y(d_c)$, which determines wages, and its direct effect on utility $A_U(d_c)$. Substituting equation (10) into equation (9) generates a system of equations that can be solved for the equilibrium spatial allocation of workers. In particular, substitution gives $M(N-1)$ free migration conditions that, together with the M group-wise full-employment conditions $\sum_{c=1}^{N} L_{ic} = L_i$, assign L_{ic} mobile workers of each group $i = 1, \ldots, M$ to each city $c = 1, \ldots, N$. Constant returns to scale and fixed land ensure that the spatial equilibrium is unique and has a positive number of workers in every city ('no ghost town'). Then, the composition of the urban community depends on the net impact of diversity on utility and productivity.

4.2. Identification: wage and rent equations

To prepare the model for empirical investigation, it is useful to evaluate wages and land rents at the equilibrium allocation. This is achieved by solving together the logarithmic versions of the free entry condition as in equation (8) and the free migration conditions in equation (9) that take equation (4) into account. Specifically, call v the equilibrium value of indirect utility. Due to the free mobility of US-born individuals, this value is common among cities and, due to the large number of cities, is unaffected by city-level idiosyncratic shocks. Then, solving equations (8) and (9) for factor prices gives the 'rent equation':

$$\ln r_c = \frac{\eta_Y + \alpha\eta_U}{1 - \alpha\mu} + \frac{1}{1 - \alpha\mu} \ln \left(A_Y(d_c)[A_U(d_c)]^{\alpha} \right) \tag{11}$$

and the 'wage equation':

$$\ln w_c = \frac{(1-\mu)\eta_Y - (1-\alpha)\eta_U}{1 - \alpha\mu} + \frac{1}{1 - \alpha\mu} \ln \left(\frac{[A_Y(d_c)]^{1-\mu}}{[A_U(d_c)]^{1-\alpha}} \right) \tag{12}$$

where $\eta_Y \equiv \ln(1-\alpha)^{1-\alpha}\,\alpha^{\alpha}$ and $\eta_U \equiv (1-\mu)^{1-\mu}\,\mu^{\mu}/v$.

Equations (11) and (12) constitute the theoretical foundation of our empirical analysis. They capture the equilibrium relationship between diversity and factor prices. In light of Roback (1982), the two equations must be estimated together in order to identify the effects of diversity on productivity and utility. Consider, for instance, equation (11) in isolation. A positive correlation between d_c and r_c is consistent either with a positive effect of diversity on utility ($A_U(d_c) > 0$) or a positive effect of diversity on productivity ($A_Y(d_c) > 0$). Analogously, if one considers equation (12) in isolation, a positive correlation between d_c and w_c is consistent either with a negative utility effect ($A'_U(d_c) < 0$) or a positive productivity effect ($A'_Y(d_c) > 0$) from diversity. Only the joint estimation of equations (11) and (12) allows one to establish which effect indeed dominates. Specifically:

$$\frac{\partial r_c}{\partial d_c} > 0 \text{ and } \frac{\partial w_c}{\partial d_c} > 0 \quad \text{iff } \textit{dominant positive productivity effect } (A'_Y(d_c) > 0)$$

$$\frac{\partial r_c}{\partial d_c} > 0 \text{ and } \frac{\partial w_c}{\partial d_c} < 0 \quad \text{iff } \textit{dominant positive utility effect } (A'_U(d_c) > 0)$$

$$\frac{\partial r_c}{\partial d_c} < 0 \text{ and } \frac{\partial w_c}{\partial d_c} < 0 \quad \text{iff } \textit{dominant negative productivity effect } (A'_Y(d_c) < 0)$$

$$\frac{\partial r_c}{\partial d_c} < 0 \text{ and } \frac{\partial w_c}{\partial d_c} > 0 \quad \text{iff } \textit{dominant negative utility effect } (A'_U(d_c) < 0)$$

$$(13)$$

Figure 3 provides a graphical intuition of the proposed identification. In the Figure w_c and r_c are measured along the horizontal and vertical axes respectively. Given the utility level v and diversity d_c, the free entry condition in equation (8) is met along the downward sloping curve, while the free migration condition in equation (9) holds along the upward sloping curve. The equilibrium factor prices for city c are found at the intersection of the two curves. Diversity d_c acts as a shift parameter on the two curves: any shock to diversity shifts both curves. An increase in d_c shifts equation (8) up (down) if diversity has a positive (negative) productivity effect and it shifts equation (9) up (down) if diversity has a positive (negative) utility effect. Thus, by looking at the impact of a diversity shock on the equilibrium wage and rent, we are able to identify the dominant effect of diversity. For example, consider the initial equilibrium A and the new equilibrium A' that prevails after a shock to diversity. In A' both w_c and r_c have risen. Our identification argument states that both factor prices rise if and only if an

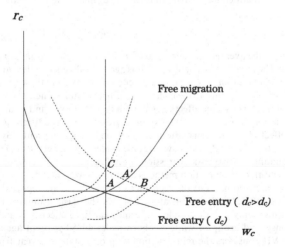

Figure 3. The spatial equilibrium.

upward shift of equation (8) dwarfs any shift of equation (9); i.e. the positive productivity effect dominates.

5. Wage and rent regressions

5.1. Basic specifications

The theoretical model above provides us with a consistent framework to structure our empirical analysis. In particular it suggests how to use wage and rent regressions to identify the effects of diversity, a characteristic particular to each city, on the productivity and utility of US natives. Our units of observation are the 160 Metropolitan Statistical Areas (MSA's) listed in the Appendix. The years of observation are 1970 and 1990. As an empirical implementation of the wage equation (12), we run the following basic regression:

$$\ln(\bar{w}_{US,c,t}) = \beta_1(Controls_{c,t}) + \beta_2(div_{c,t}) + e_c + e_t + e_{c,t} \tag{14}$$

The average wage of natives in city c in year t, $\bar{w}_{US,c,t}$, is defined as described in Section 3.1. The focal independent variable is $div_{c,t}$, which is the diversity index defined in equation (1). The other independent variable, $Controls_{c,t}$, capture other controls. Specifically we always include among the controls some measure of the average education of workers in city c at time t (either the average schooling or the share of education groups) while in Section 5.2 we include several other alternative variables which may potentially affect the productivity and the share of foreign-born in a city. We also include 160 city fixed effects e_c and common time-effects e_t. Finally, $e_{c,t}$ is a zero-mean random error term independent from the other regressors.

Under these assumptions, the coefficient β_2 captures the equilibrium effect of a change in cultural diversity on wages. However, as discussed in subsection 4.2, the sign of β_2 cannot be directly interpreted as evidence of any positive effect of diversity on production. Identification thus requires us to estimate the following parallel rent regression:

$$\ln(\bar{r}_{US,c,t}) = \gamma_1(Controls_{c,t}) + \gamma_2 div_{c,t} + \varepsilon_c + \varepsilon_t + \varepsilon_{ct} \tag{15}$$

Our definition of the average rent per room of natives $\bar{r}_{US,c,t}$ in city c in year t is described in Section 3.1. The focal independent variable is again the diversity index $div_{c,t}$. The other independent variables, $Controls_{c,t}$, capture other controls. We add these to check that the correlation of interest is robust to the inclusion of other variables, and thus is not spurious. Further we control for city fixed effects ε_c, include a year dummy ε_t, and assume that $\varepsilon_{c,t}$ is a zero-mean random error uncorrelated with the regressors. The coefficient γ_2 captures the equilibrium effect of a change in cultural diversity on average city rents. By merging the information on the signs of β_2 and γ_2, we are able to identify the net effect of diversity. We begin by estimating the two basic regressions using least squares, including further controls and using different estimation methods later on as we proceed.

The least squares estimates of the regressions (14) and (15) are reported in specifications I and VII of Table 3. Specification I shows the basic estimates for the wage equation, when we only include, besides state and year fixed effects, the average schooling of the considered group of white US-born males 40–50 years of age as a control. Specification VII considers the rent equation with only state and year fixed effects as controls. The estimated coefficients β_2 and γ_2 are both positive and statistically and

The economic value of cultural diversity: evidence from US cities • **25**

Table 3. Basic Wage and Rent Specifications

	Average log wage for US-born workers						Average log rent for US-born residents		
	I	II	III	IV	V	VI	VII	VIII	XI
Dependent variable	Base 1	4 school	Polynomial	Base 1, Pop.	Include	Base 2	Base 1	With	Base 2
Specification:	wage	groups	school	weighted	empl.	wage	rent	population and income	rent
Average schooling	0.11**			0.11*	0.11**	0.10**			
	(0.01)			(0.01)	(0.01)	(0.01)			
4 School groups		Yes							
Quartic in schooling			Yes						
ln(income per capita)								0.67**	
								(0.08)	
ln(employment)					0.02				
					(0.02)				
ln(population)								0.03	
								(0.04)	
Diversity index	1.27**	1.17**	1.29**	1.37**	1.29**		1.90*	0.95**	
	(0.30)	(0.36)	(0.30)	(0.23)	(0.29)		(0.60)	(0.50)	
Share of foreign born						0.57**			1.13**
						(0.11)			(0.24)
Diversity index among foreign born						0.14*			0.12
						(0.08)			(0.16)
City fixed effects	Yes	Yes	Yes	Yes	Yes	Yes	Yes	Yes	Yes
Time fixed effects	Yes	Yes	Yes	Yes	Yes	Yes	Yes	Yes	Yes
R^2 (excluding city and time fixed effects)	0.10	0.14	0.12	0.11	0.10	0.12	0.30	0.30	0.31
Observations	320	320	320	320	320	320	320	320	320

Specification 1–VI: Dependent variable is logged average yearly wage of white, US-born, males 40–50 years expressed in 1990 US$.
Specification VII–IX: Dependent variable is logged average monthly rent per room paid by white, US born 16–65 years of age, expressed in 1990 US$.
**Significant at 5%, * significant at 10%.
In parenthesis: heteroskedasticity-robust standard errors.

economically significant. An increase in the diversity index by 0.1 (roughly the increase experienced by Los Angeles during the 1970–1990 period) is associated with a 13% increase in the average real wage of US natives and with a 19% increase in real rents.

Similarly specifications VI and IX of Table 3 use the same controls as specification I and VII and decompose the effect of diversity (on wages and rents) into two parts. Specifically the diversity index can be expressed as the contribution of two factors. First, a city is more diverse if the overall group of foreign-born people is larger. Second, a city is more diverse if the foreign-born group is made up of a wider variety of groups. The diversity index can thus be written as a (non-linear) function of the share of foreign-born, or a diversity index can be calculated considering only the foreign born. We enter these two factors separately in specifications VI and IX in order to analyze their impact on wages and rents, respectively. Let us note that the share of foreign born is, by far, the most important component in determining the variation of the diversity index across cities. It explains, by itself, almost 90% of the index variation. It is not a surprise, therefore, to find that the share of foreigners is the most important contributor to the effect on wages and rents. An increase in the share of foreign born by 0.25 (experienced by Los Angeles during the considered period) is associated with a 14.5% increase in wages of US natives and a 28% increase in rents. The effect of the diversity of foreigners, on the other hand, has a positive but hardly significant impact.

The intermediate specifications (II to V for the wage equations and VIII for the rent equation) in Table 3 include alternative controls in order to check wether the correlation is robust to potential omitted variables. Specification II of the wage regression controls for the schooling of the group of US-born by including the shares of three groups (high school graduates, college dropouts and college graduates) among the total employed in each city, rather than simply the average years of schooling. Specification III includes a quartic polynomial in average schooling. While non-linear effects at different schooling levels may be relevant, here we see that the coefficient on diversity changes only marginally when we use different methods to control for education. We also run a specification (not reported) controlling for individual years of schooling in the construction of $\ln(\bar{w}_{US,c,t})$, rather than at the second stage. Doing this reduces the coefficient on diversity somewhat to 1.00 (standard error equal to 0.32). All in all how we control for education does not seem to have a relevant effect on the coefficient on diversity. Specification IV weighs each observation (city) by its population. This control allows us to under-emphasize the role of small cities. The effect of diversity does not change much with this amendment; in fact it increases a bit (the coefficient is now equal to 1.37), which is a consequence of the fact that cities in which diversity has the largest impact (as seen in Figure 1 and 2) are indeed the largest cities, such as Los Angeles and New York. Specification V includes the log of employment as an additional control. On the one hand, if there are effects of employment density on productivity (as suggested by Ciccone and Hall, 1996) it may be relevant to control for employment; on the other hand employment (along with wages and rents) is determined endogenously as an equilibrium outcome in our model. As a consequence, including an endogenous variable as a control may bias the estimates of all coefficients. Fortunately we find that employment is not significantly correlated to wages (coefficient equal to 0.02 with standard error equal to 0.02), and its inclusion does not change the coefficient on diversity much. Omitting employment, therefore, is theoretically justified and empirically sound. These specifications reassure us that our basic specification captures both the correct sign and magnitude of the correlation between diversity and wages.

As for the rent regression, column VIII includes the average log income and log population of each city as controls. In reality, these variables may depend on several exogenous factors and may affect the value of housing. They are, however, endogenously determined in the equilibrium described in Section (4). In fact wages are the main determinant of income, while population is affected by internal migration. The two channels through which diversity can affect rents, described by our model, are either by increasing productivity (which pushes up income and rents), or by increasing the desirability of a city. When controlling for income and population, a residual positive effect of diversity would imply that people do value diversity per se, and are willing to bid up rents more than what would be implied only by higher income and higher population. The problem, however, is that including these two endogenous variables may induce a bias in the estimates of the coefficients of regression in equation (15). The estimated coefficients in specification VIII show that including income and population reduces the effect of diversity by half. In particular income per capita is a main determinant of rents and enters the regression with a very significant coefficient. Even controlling for this effect through income, however, diversity still plays a very important role in determining rents (coefficient equal to 0.90). While we take this as a potential sign that diversity has a positive amenity value (it actually shifts the free migration condition in Figure 3 to the left) we are concerned with the endogeneity of the income and population variables, and so we omit them in the rest of the analysis. To summarize, diversity has *positive and highly significant correlations* with both wages ($\beta_2 > 0$) and land rents ($\gamma_2 > 0$). These positive correlations can be interpreted as consistent with a dominant and positive effect of diversity on productivity.

Finally, as we have mentioned that employment and population are endogenous variables in the equilibrium of our model, let us consider another correlation that reinforces our interpretation of a dominant positive effect of diversity on productivity. The theoretical model makes clear (see equation (6)) that, in the presence of a positive productivity effect, the increase of diversity in a certain city shifts the local labor demand up, thus raising not only local wages but also local total employment. In contrast, a negative utility effect would be associated with higher wages but lower native employment. Table 4 reports the correlation between changes in diversity and changes in employment as well as the population of US cities between 1970 and 1990. If the labor supply curve had shifted up and the labor demand curve remained fixed, we should observe an increase in wages but a decrease in total employment caused by the outflow of US-born workers. The Table rather shows positive effects of diversity on both employment and population, consistent with the idea that there was no outflow of natives counterbalancing immigration. This is consistent with a dominant upward shift of labor demand as expected in the presence of a dominant positive productivity effect.

5.2. Checks of robustness

Our basic specifications for the wage (I and VI in Table 3) and rent (VII and IX in Table 3) regressions omit several variables that, in principle, could simultaneously affect local diversity, wages, and rents, thus creating spurious correlation. In so far as they change over time, the impacts of such omitted variables are not captured by city fixed effects. We have already discussed the potential roles of employment, income and population in the previous section. This section is devoted to testing whether the estimated

Table 4. Correlation between growth in diversity and in employment/population

Dependent variable:	Index of diversity	City fixed effects	Time fixed effects	R^2	Observations
Ln (employment)	0.72 (1.12)	Yes	Yes	0.97	320
Ln (population)	1.70* (1.02)	Yes	Yes	0.97	320

**Significant at 5%, *significant at 10%.
Heteroskedasticity-robust standard errors are reported in parentheses.

effects of diversity are robust to the inclusion of other omitted exogenous variables. While our list of potential controls can not be considered exhaustive, we do include some important ones for which we can think of plausible stories that could generate spurious correlation. Table 5 reports the estimated effects of the diversity index (and its components) in the wage equation as we include additional controls. Table 6 presents analogous results for the rent regression. The coefficients in each row of Tables 5 and 6 arise from separate regressions. While it may be informative to discuss each regression in detail, we prefer simply to focus on the coefficients of interest; thus for the sake of brevity we comment only briefly on each specification. This section is meant to give the reader a general impression of the robustness of our estimates to a very ample range of controls, rather than to analyze in detail any one of the alternative specifications proposed.[16]

The positive effect of diversity on the wage of the US-born may simply be a result of the foreigners' measurable average education. Specifications (2) in Tables 5 and 6 include the average years of schooling of the foreign-born workers as an additional control variable in the wage and rent regressions respectively. While analyzing human capital externalities using average schooling has been a common practice (Rauch, 1993; Moretti, 2004), if workers with different schooling levels are imperfect substitutes, or if the distribution of their skills matters, then average schooling may not be a sufficient statistic to capture the presence of complementarity or externalities. The estimated effects of diversity on wages and rents remain significant and positive when we include this control. Interestingly, the effect of the average schooling of the foreign-born on the wages of the US-born (not reported) is not significant, while it is small and positive on the rents of the US-born. This result tells us that the simple average schooling of the foreign-born does not fully capture their true 'value.' Not only might the skill distribution of the foreign-born matter, but their abilities may be differentiated from (and complementary to) those of natives, even at the same schooling level. When we decompose the overall diversity (column 2 and 3 in the Tables) by including separately the share of foreign born and their diversity, we still find a significant and positive effect of the share of foreign born on both rents and wages, while the diversity of foreigners has a significant positive impact on wages but not on rents.

Another plausible (but spurious) reason for positive correlations between diversity and wages-rents may be that immigration responds to productivity and amenity shocks.

---

16 If the reader is interested in the details of each regression and in a more thorough discussion of each specification we suggest reading the working paper Ottaviano and Peri (2004b).

The economic value of cultural diversity: evidence from US cities • **29**

Table 5. Wage regression: robustness checks

Specification	1 Coefficient on the diversity index	2 Coefficient on the share of foreign born	3 Coefficient on diversity index among foreign born
Specification:			
(1) Basic	1.27**	0.57**	0.14*
	(0.30)	(0.11)	(0.08)
(2) Including schooling	1.26**	0.56**	0.14*
of foreign born	(0.38)	(0.16)	(0.09)
(3) Including share of out of	1.35**	0.58**	0.09
state born	(0.38)	(0.15)	(0.11)
(4) Including share of non whites	1.39**	0.66**	0.12
	(0.40)	(0.17)	(0.10)
(5) Including public spending	1.28**	0.63**	0.14*
on local services per capita	(0.38)	(0.17)	(0.09)
(6) Including public spending in	1.27**	0.65**	0.13
education per capita	(0.38)	(0.16)	(0.09)
(7) Including employment of	1.32**	0.67**	0.14
white-US born males 40–50.	(0.39)	(0.16)	(0.10)
(8) Including all of the above	1.43**	0.75**	0.10
	(0.40)	(0.18)	(0.08)
(9) Basic without CA, FL, NY	0.96**	0.23	0.21**
	(0.49)	(0.27)	(0.12)
(10) In changes 1990–1970 with	0.85**	0.64**	0.02
state-fixed effects	(0.31)	(0.17)	(0.12)
(11) Using wage of white-US born	1.20*	0.69*	0.04
males 30–40 as dep. variable	(0.37)	(0.14)	(0.10)

Dependent variable: ln average yearly wage to white, US born, males 40–50 years old expressed in 1990 US$. The coefficients in column 1 correspond to different regressions in each row. The coefficients in column 2 and 3 correspond to different regressions for each row.
(1) Basic: specification from Table 3 column I (for coefficient 1) and Column VI (for coefficients 2 and 3).
(2) Includes average years of schooling of foreign born.
(3) Includes the share of US-born outside the state in which they live.
(4) Includes the share of non-white people in working age.
(5) Include the spending per capita on local government services.
(6) Includes the spending in education per capita.
(7) Includes ln(Employment) of the group US-born, white males 40–50 years old.
(8) Includes all the variables in (1)–(7) together as controls.
(9) Excluding from the regression MSAs in the biggest immigrations states: CA, FL, NY.
(10) Regression in changes including 49-state fixed-effects.
(11) Uses the wage of the group white, US, born, males, 30–40 years old as dependent variable.
**Significant at 5%, *significant at 10%.
Heteroskedasticity-robust standard errors are reported in parentheses.s

In so far as we do not observe these shocks, we are potentially omitting the common underlying cause of changes in wages, rents and diversity. To address this issue we use two strategies. The first strategy, which we postpone implementing until Section 3, attempts to identify a variable correlated (or at least more correlated) with the share of foreign born and not otherwise correlated (or at least less correlated) with shocks to productivity or amenities. Then, it uses this variable as an instrument in the estimation. The second strategy, pursued here, exploits the fact that productivity shocks which attract workers into a city should attract the US-born and the

30 • *Ottaviano and Peri*

Table 6. Rent regression: robustness checks

Specification	1 Coefficient on the diversity index	2 Coefficient on the share of foreign born	3 Coefficient on diversity index among foreign born
Specification:			
(1) Basic	1.90**	1.13**	0.12
	(0.50)	(0.20)	(0.13)
(2) Including schooling of	2.00**	1.24**	0.14
foreign born	(0.59)	(0.23)	(0.15)
(3) Including share of out	1.98**	1.03*	0.22
of state born	(0.59)	(0.24)	(0.17)
(4) Including share of non	1.50**	0.96**	0.09
whites	(0.62)	(0.26)	(0.16)
(5) Including Public spending	1.93**	0.98**	0.22
on local services per capita	(0.59)	(0.25)	(0.16)
(6) Including public spending	1.92**	0.98**	0.22
in education per capita	(0.58)	(0.25)	(0.16)
(7) Including population of	1.50**	0.96**	0.08
white US-born males	(0.62)	(0.26)	(0.16)
(8) Including All of the above	1.69**	1.12**	0.07
	(0.60)	(0.27)	(0.16)
(9) Basic without CA, FL, NY	4.70*	1.23*	0.24*
	(1.20)	(0.27)	(0.16)
(10) 1990–1970	0.15	0.21	0.14
with state-fixed effects	(0.64)	(0.31)	(0.20)

Dependent variable: ln average monthly rent paid by white, US born, expressed in 1990 US$. The coefficients in column 1 correspond to different regressions in each row. The coefficients in column 2 and 3 correspond to different regressions for each row.
(1) Basic: specification from Table 4 column VII (for coefficient 1) and column IX (for coefficients 2 and 3).
(2) Includes average years of schooling of foreign born.
(3) Includes the share of US born outside the state in which they live.
(4) Includes the share of non-white people in working age.
(5) Include the Spending per capita on local government services.
(6) Includes the Spending in education per capita.
(7) Includes the ln(population) of white US-born males.
(8) Includes all the variables in (1)–(7) together as controls.
(9) Excluding from the regression MSAs in the biggest immigrations states (CA, FL, NY).
(10) Regression in changes including 49 state fixed-effects.
**Significant at 5%, *significant at 10%.
Heteroskedasticity-robust standard errors are reported in parentheses.

foreign-born by the same degree. Therefore, the share of US-born citizens in each city coming from out of state (i.e. born in a different state) is a variable that should be correlated with the same local productivity and amenities shocks that attract foreigners.[17] Accordingly, its inclusion in the wage and rent regressions should

---

17 It may be the case, however, as argued by Borjas (2001), that the US-born move away from cities in which immigrants go because they look for different amenities or better wages. However, both our results shown in Table 4 (population increases where diversity increases) as well as recent studies by Card (2001) and Card and Di Nardo (2000) do not find evidence of this 'displacement effect'.

significantly decrease the estimated coefficients β_2 and γ_2. Moreover, we should find a significant positive correlation between this share and the wage-rents of US-born citizens. Specification (3) in Tables 5 and 6 include the share of US-born citizens who were born out of state. Its coefficient (not reported) is not significant in either regression, while the effects of diversity and the share of foreign born on wages and rents are still significantly positive and virtually unchanged. These results suggest that the presence of the foreign born does not simply signal that cities have experienced an unobserved positive shock, since that would have attracted both foreign and US-born workers. Interestingly, they also imply that their presence does not simply reveal that boom cities have attracted more talented people, since people of similar talent should respond similarly to the same shock.

Some sociologists have advanced the hypothesis that environments which are tolerant towards diversity are more productive and more pleasant to live in. Along similar lines, Richard Florida (2002a, 2002b) has argued that cities with larger numbers of artists and bohemian professionals are more innovative in high tech sectors. It is likely that part of our correlations may actually depend on this positive attitude of cities towards diversity. However, to show that there is something specific to the presence of foreign-born, we include in specification (4) of Tables 5 and 6 the share of US-born people identifying themselves as 'non-white.' Since we consider only US-born people, this index essentially captures the white-black composition of a city. The coefficients on this variable (not reported) turn out to be positive in the wage regression (0.20) and negative in the rent regression (-0.22). We may interpret these results as (weak) evidence of the aversion white US-born individuals feel living close to large non-white (US-born) communities. The standard errors however (in both cases around 0.2), render the estimated coefficients insignificant. As to the coefficients of the diversity index, they are still positive, significant (except in one case for the rent regression), and similar to previous estimates. Thus, in spite of the more ambiguous effect of ethnic diversity, diversity in terms of the country of birth maintains its importance.

Several public services in US cities are supplied by local governments. Public schools, public health care, and public security are all desirable local services. Therefore, cities whose quality of public services has improved in our period of observation may have experienced both an increase in the share of foreign born (possibly because they are larger users of these services) and a rise in property values. From the County and City Databook we have gathered data on the spending of local government services per person in a city and on its breakdown across different categories, particularly in education. Specification (5) of Tables 5 and 6 includes overall spending by local government, whereas specification (6) includes spending on just education, a very important determinant of the quality of schools. The effect of public spending per person on rents (not reported) is positive in both specifications; however, its inclusion does not change the effects of diversity.

If different groups of workers are imperfect substitutes, then even among US natives the average wage of white males 40–50 years of age may be affected by their relative supply. While there is no clear reason to believe that the relative size of this group is correlated with the diversity of a city, it may be appropriate to control for the (log) employment of this group, and not just for total employment. The corresponding results are reported in specification (7) of Table 5, which shows that the coefficient of the diversity index is still equal to 1.32. Specification (7) of Table 6 considers instead the group of white US-born males as potentially competing for similar housing, and therefore includes the log of their population together with that of total population. This specification is very similar to specification (4), which includes the share of non-whites and produces similar estimates: 1.50 for the coefficient on diversity and 0.96 for the coefficient on the share of foreign born.

The most conservative check is specification (8), which includes together all the controls that are included separately in specifications (2) to (7). Reassuringly, the coefficient on the share of foreign-born is still positive, very stable, and significant in both regressions. The coefficient on the diversity index is also positive, very stable, and significant in the wage regression, while it turns out not significant in the rent regression.[18]

Specifications (9) and (10) of Tables 5 and 6 push our data as far as they can go. Specification (9) estimates the wage and rent regressions excluding the three states with the highest shares of foreign-born, namely California, New York and Florida. The aim is to check whether a few highly diverse cities in those states generate the correlations of diversity with wages and rents. This turns out not to be the case. In the wage regression the coefficient on diversity decreases somewhat but remains both positive and significant. In the rent equation the coefficient on diversity grows larger but also becomes less precisely estimated. In general, however, there is no evidence that in the long run the effect of diversity is different for high immigration states than low immigration states.

In Specification (10), rather than use city and year dummies, we use the differences of the basic variables between 1990 and 1970. We also include state fixed effects to control for differences in the state-specific growth rates of wages and rents. In so doing we identify the effects of diversity on wages and rents through the variation across cities within states. This is an extremely demanding specification as we are probably eliminating most of the variation needed to identify the results by estimating 48 dummies using 160 observations. Remarkably, the positive effect of diversity on productivity still stands, and its point estimate is similar to those of previous specifications. The effect of diversity on rents, however, while still positive, is no longer significant.

We perform one more check in specification (11) of Table 5 in order to verify that our results survive when we consider groups that are more mobile across cities than 40 to 50 year-old workers. We estimate the wage equation using the average wage of white US-born males between 30 and 40 years of age. The coefficients on diversity and the share of foreign born are still significantly positive, equal to 1.20 and 0.69, respectively.

Finally, since our theoretical model shows that in equilibrium wages and rents are simultaneously determined (see equations (11) and (12)), thus implying correlation between the unobservable idiosyncratic shocks to wages $\varepsilon_{c,t}$ and rents $e_{c,t}$, we can increase the efficiency of our estimates by explicitly accounting for such correlation, and estimate a seemingly unrelated regression (SUR). While OLS estimates are still consistent and unbiased even when $\varepsilon_{c,t}$ and $e_{c,t}$ are correlated, SUR estimates are more efficient. The estimated coefficients are virtually identical to those estimated in Table 5 and 6. For sake of brevity we do not report the results here.[19]

---

18   Some authors (see e.g. Sivitanidou and Wheaton, 1992) have argued that the institutional constraints on land use ('zoning') can affect land values. Thus, higher property values may be associated with more efficient institutional constraints in the presence of market failures. This effect, however, should be captured by our local public goods measures.

19   The results of SUR estimations are available in Ottaviano and Peri (2004b).

The economic value of cultural diversity: evidence from US cities • **33**

In summary, most wage and rent regressions yield positive and significant coefficients for both the diversity index and the share of foreign born. The diversity of the foreign born also has a positive effect but this effect is less often significant. We do not find any specification such that the coefficients on the diversity variable are simultaneously not significant in both the wage and the rent regressions. Moreover, each single estimate delivers positive estimates of diversity on wages and rents of natives. Therefore, our identification (13) allows us to conclude that *no specification contradicts the hypothesis of a positive productivity effect of diversity.*

5.3. Endogeneity and instrumental variables

Short of a randomized experiment in which diversity across cities is changed randomly, we cannot rest assured that our correlations reveal any causal link from diversity to wages and rents. Nonetheless, some steps towards tackling the endogeneity problem can be taken using instrumental variables (IV) estimation. Our instruments should be correlated with the change in the diversity of cities between 1970 and 1990, and not otherwise correlated with changes in wages and rents. We construct our main instrument building on the fact that foreigners tend to settle in 'enclaves' where other people from their country of origin already live (Winters et al., 2001; Munshi, 2003). Following Card (2002) and Saiz (2003b) we construct the 'predicted' change in the number of immigrants from each country in each city during the observed period. The predicted change is based on the actual shares of people from each country in each city at the beginning of the period, and the total immigration rate from each country of origin to the US during the whole period. By construction the 'predicted' change does not depend on any city-specific shock during the observed period. We then observe that the stocks and flows of immigrants tend to be larger in cities that are closer to important 'gateways' into the US. By contrast, the stocks of the native born and their changes over time are much less dependent on their proximity to these gateways. Therefore, as additional instruments, we also add the distance of a city from the main gateways into the US after having tested for the exogeneity of these instruments. The inclusion of more instruments, as long as they are exogenous, should improve our estimates while still correcting for the potential endogeneity bias. We now describe the instruments and the estimation results in the following two sections.

5.3.1. Shift-Share methodology

We construct our main instrument by adopting the 'shift-share methodology,' used by Card (2001) and more recently by Saiz (2003b), to migration in MSA's. Immigrants tend to settle, at least initially, where other immigrants from the same country already reside (immigration enclaves). Therefore, we can use the share of residents of an MSA in 1970 for each country of birth, and attribute to each group the growth rate of that group within the whole US population in the 1970–1990 time period. In so doing we compute the predicted composition of the city based on its 1970 composition and attribute to each group the average growth rate of its share in the US population. Once we have constructed these 'predicted' shares for 1990 we can calculate a 'predicted' diversity index for each city in 1990.

Let us use the notation introduced in Section 3.1, where $\left(CoB_i^c\right)_t$ denotes the share of people born in country i among the residents of city c in year t. Hence,

$(CoB_i)_t = \sum_c (CoB_i^c)_t$ is the share of people born in country i among US residents in year t. Between 1970 and 1990 its growth rate is:

$$(g_i)_{1970\text{-}90} = [(CoB_i)_{1990} - (CoB_i)_{1970}]/(CoB_i)_{1970} \tag{16}$$

This allows us to calculate the 'attributed' share of people born in country j and residing in city c in 1990 as:

$$(\widehat{CoB_i^c})_{1990} = (CoB_i^c)_{1970}[1 + (g_i)_{1970\text{-}90}] \tag{17}$$

The attributed share of foreign born and the attributed diversity index can be evaluated accordingly. In particular, the latter equals:

$$\widehat{div}_{c,1990} = 1 - \sum_i (\widehat{CoB_i^c})^2_{1990} \tag{18}$$

As the attributed diversity for each city in 1990 is built using the city's share in 1970 and the 1970–1990 national growth rates of each group, this value is independent from any city-specific shock during the period.

Tables 7 and 8 present the results of the IV estimation of the wage and rent regressions. Relative to previous regressions, some adjustments in the grouping of countries of birth are needed. This is because as we input the shares in 1990 based on the initial shares in 1970, we need to identify the same countries of origin across census years. This is achieved by allocating more than one country of birth to the same group, as some countries have disappeared or changed during the period. In so doing, we follow the classification adopted by Card (2001) and described in the data appendix.

In Tables 7 and 8, column 1 reports the OLS estimates of the basic specification in which we control for schooling using the change in average years of schooling in the city (Δ schooling). The point estimates of the OLS specification are very similar to our previous estimates (Table 3, columns I and VII), confirming that the reclassification

Table 7. Wage regression. IV estimation, instrument: shift-share imputed diversity

Dependent variable : $\Delta\ln$(wage)	1 OLS in differences	2 Controlling for initial average wage	3 IV	4 IV without CA-FL-NY
ΔSchooling	0.11**	0.11**	0.11**	0.10**
	(0.01)	(0.01)	(0.01)	(0.01)
Δ(diversity)	1.27**	1.43**	0.98**	0.99*
	(0.38)	(0.39)	(0.50)	(0.60)
R^2	0.34	0.36	0.35	0.33
Observations	160	160	160	145
		First stage regression		
Shift-share constructed diversity	n.a.	n.a.	0.51** (0.05)	0.21** (0.04)
Partial R^2	n.a.	n.a.	0.31	0.17

Dependent variable: change between 1970 and 1990 in ln average yearly wage of white, US born, males, 40–50 years, expressed in 1990 US $.
Instrumental variable: imputed change in diversity index and share of foreign born, using the shift-share method described in the text.
**Significant at 5%, *significant at 10%.
Heteroskedasticity-robust standard errors are reported in parentheses.

The economic value of cultural diversity: evidence from US cities • 35

Table 8. Rent regression. IV estimation, instrument: shift-share imputed diversity

Dependent variable : Δln(rent)	1 OLS in differences	2 Controlling for initial average rent	3 IV	4 IV, Without CA-FL-NY
Δ(diversity)	1.97**	2.07**	2.60**	3.29**
	(0.60)	(0.65)	(0.96)	(1.50)
R²	0.07	0.12	0.10	0.12
Observations	160	160	160	145
		First stage regression		
Shift-share constructed	n.a.	n.a.	0.51**	0.21**
diversity			(0.05)	(0.04)
Partial R²	n.a.	n.a.	0.23	0.11

Dependent variable: Change between 1970 and 1990 in logged average yearly rent of white, US-born, aged 16–65, expressed in 1990 US$.
Instrumental variable: imputed change in diversity index and share of foreign born, using the shift-share method, described in the text.
**Significant at 5%, *significant at 10%.
Heteroskedasticity-robust standard errors are reported in parentheses.

by country groups has only small effects. In column 2, as we are running the specifications in differences (rather than in levels with fixed effects), we also check that the
implicit treatment of long-run effects as equilibrium effects is appropriate. In particular
we include the initial values of average wages and rents (coefficients on those variables
are not reported), in order to control for the possibility that cities were not at a long-run
equilibrium at the beginning of the period (1970), so that their dynamic behavior exhibits 'conditional convergence'. The estimated effects of diversity do not change much,
and are statistically not different from the previous estimates.

As for the IV estimates of columns 3 and 4, we notice that the first stage regressions
(of the endogenous measure of diversity on the instrument) imply that the imputed
diversity indices are good predictors of the actual ones, explaining 31% of their variation (orthogonal to the other regressors) when all states are included. The exclusion of
large immigration states, however, reduces significantly the partial R^2 of the first stage
regression to 17%.

The estimated effect of diversity on wages is reported in column 3 of Table 7. Its
value (0.98) is close to the OLS estimate and significantly positive. When we exclude the
high-immigration states (column 4 of Table 7), the effect of diversity is estimated to be
positive but significant only at the 10% confidence level. However, the main problem
encountered when we exclude California, Florida and New York is that, as just mentioned, the instruments lose much of their explanatory power (the partial R^2 of the
excluded instruments drops to 0.17). Therefore, insignificance is mostly driven by
large standard errors, rather than by evidence of any endogeneity bias (i.e., changes
in point estimates).

Columns 3 and 4 in Table 8 show that the rent regression exhibits a similar qualitative pattern but sharper results. Using the shift-share instruments, the diversity index
has a positive and significant effect in each specification. Including all states, the IV
estimates are 30% higher than the OLS estimates (although, due to the large standard
error we cannot reject the hypothesis that they are equal). When we exclude California,
Florida, and New York (specification 4 of Table 8), both the estimate and the standard

error increase significantly. The point estimates of the effect of diversity are still firmly in the positive range. Somewhat surprising (possibly driven by the exclusion of some 'perverse' outliers such as Miami, see Figure 2) is the very large (and imprecisely estimated) effect of diversity on rents in this specification.

5.3.2. Gateways into the US

We can increase the set of instruments by noting the fact that immigrants tend to enter the US through a few 'gateways,' or through the border. As a consequence, the total number of foreign born in city c at time t, F_{ct}, as well as the total increase in foreign born in city c, ΔF_{ct}, depend negatively on the distance from the closest gateway. As long as the total number of US-born residents in a city, N_{ct}, does not depend (or depends to a lesser extent) on that distance, we have that both the share of foreign born, $F_{ct}/(F_{ct}+N_{ct})$, and its change are negatively correlated with the distance from the immigration gateways into the US.

Each year the US Office of Tourism publishes the percentage of inbound travellers by point of entry. Looking at this data for the eighties, we see that the three main gateways were New York, Miami, and Los Angeles. About 30% of foreign (immigrant and non-immigrant) travellers entered the US through the airports and ports of these cities. Moreover, due to the benefits of networks, the costs of travelling, and the costs of spreading information, immigrants were more likely to settle in cities closer to these gateways. A similar argument can be made for Canadian and Mexican immigrants. For them, it seems reasonable to assume that the US borders with their own countries constitute the natural place of entry into the US. Thus, as before, cities closer to these borders were more likely to receive Canadian or Mexican immigrants during the 1970–1990 period.

These considerations suggest the use of the overall distance of a city from the main gateways into the US (New York, Miami, Los Angeles, and the US borders with Canada and Mexico) to instrument for its diversity index (heavily dependent on the share of foreign-born). This distance should be negatively correlated with diversity but not with shocks to wages and rents.

This strategy is certainly open to criticism. If the three main gateways (New York, Miami, and Los Angeles) or the region of the US-Mexican border experienced above average growth during the time period considered, then positive spillover effects on nearby cities could attract foreigners. As a result, the distance of a city from these gateways would be negatively correlated with the increases in wages and rents because of a 'boom city' effect rather than a positive effect from diversity. This criticism, however, does not apply to the 'predicted diversity' constructed in the previous section. As we are confident of the 'exogeneity' of one instrument (the 'predicted diversity'), when using additional instruments (distance from gateways) we can test for their exogeneity[20]. We find that the variables that do not fail the exogeneity test jointly are 'predicted diversity', distance from NY, distance from LA and distance from Miami. We had to drop the distance from the border variable, as it failed this exogeneity test.

---

20   The exact form of our test of exogeneity can be find in Woolridge (2001), 124–125. Intuitively the test checks wether the restriction that excludes the extra-instruments from the second-stage regression is rejected or not by the data. If it is not rejected the assumption of exogeneity stands.

The economic value of cultural diversity: evidence from US cities • **37**

Table 9. Wage regression. IV estimation, instruments are distance from 'Gateways' and imputed diversity

Dependent variable : Δln(wage)	1 IV	2 IV with state effects	3 IV, without CA-FL-NY
ΔSchooling	0.11**	0.11**	0.11**
	(0.01)	(0.02)	(0.01)
Δ(Diversity)	1.50**	0.68**	1.91**
	(0.39)	(0.33)	(0.54)
State fixed effects	No	Yes	No
R²	0.35	0.63	0.30
Observations	160	160	144
	First stage regression		
Shift-share constructed	0.44**	0.44**	0.30**
diversity	(0.04)	(0.04)	(0.04)
Ln(distance from LA)	−0.01**	−0.01**	−0.01**
	(0.001)	(0.001)	(0.002)
Ln(distance from NY)	−0.005**	−0.005**	−0.006**
	(0.0008)	(0.0008)	(0.0007)
Ln(distance from Miami)	−0.01**	−0.01**	−0.004**
	(0.001)	(0.001)	(0.002)
Partial R²	0.71	0.51	0.46

Dependent variable: change between 1970 and 1990 in ln average yearly wage of white, US-born, males, 40–50 years, expressed in 1990 US$.
**Significant at 5%, *significant at 10%
Heteroskedasticity-robust standard errors are reported in parentheses.
Test of over-identifying restrictions, from Woolridge (2001) pp. 124–125, cannot reject the joint exogeneity of instruments at the 5% confidence level. The value of the test statistic is 3.2 for the first specification, 4.5 for the second and 3.7 for the third. The statistic is distributed as a chi-square with 3 degrees of freedom under the null hypothesis of no Instrument included in the second stage equation.

Tables 9 and 10 report the first and second stage estimates of the described IV regressions using wages and rents, respectively, as the dependent variable. Column 1 of Table 9 shows the basic specification of the wage regression; column 2 includes 48 state fixed-effects; column 3 excludes the biggest immigration states. Similarly column 1 of Table 10 includes the basic specification while column 2 and 3 exclude from the regression coastal cities and cities in California, Florida and New York as a check for potential outliers driving the results. The first stage regressions confirm that our excluded instruments are excellent: in the first stage they explain about 70% of the variation in diversity that is orthogonal to the other regressors. Even including state effects, more than 50% of the residual variation in diversity is still explained by the instruments. This increases the power of instrument, relative to Table 7 and 8 and may result in more precise estimates.

The estimates of specification 1 (Table 9 and 10) confirm that the effects of diversity on wages and rents are positive and large. The estimated coefficient is significant and very large for wages (1.50) as well as for rents (1.48). Moreover, the IV estimates of the effect on wages are somewhat higher than the OLS ones; hence we are reassured that no significant (endogeneity-driven) downward OLS bias exists. For the wage regressions we obtain a positive and significant effect of diversity when controlling for 48 state fixed effects (specification 2 of Table 9) and when eliminating coastal cities (specifications 3 of Table 9). The last specification has quite large standard errors, but it certainly

Table 10.   Rent regression. IV estimation, instruments are distance from 'Gateways' and imputed diversity.

Dependent variable : Δln (rent)	1 IV	2 IV non-coastal cities	3 IV, without CA-FL-NY
Δ(Diversity)	1.48**	5.50**	4.70**
	(0.61)	(2.31)	(1.04)
State fixed effects	No	No	No
R^2	0.13	0.10	0.12
Observations	160	160	144
	First stage regression		
Shift-share constructed diversity	0.44**	0.23**	0.30**
	(0.04)	(0.05)	(0.04)
Ln(distance from LA)	−0.01**	−0.005**	−0.01**
	(0.001)	(0.001)	(0.002)
Ln(distance from NY)	−0.005**	−0.004**	−0.006**
	(0.0008)	(0.0008)	(0.0007)
Ln(distance from Miami)	−0.01**	−0.01**	−0.004**
	(0.001)	(0.001)	(0.002)
Partial R^2	0.71	0.38	0.46

Dependent variable: change between 1970 and 1990 in ln average monthly rent paid by white, US-born, expressed in 1990 US$.
**Significant at 5%, *significant at 10%.
Heteroskedasticity-robust standard errors are reported in parentheses.
Test of over-identifying restrictions, from Woolridge (2001) pp. 124–125, cannot reject the joint exogeneity of instruments at the 5% confidence level. The value of the test statistic is 4.8 for the first specification, 7.2 for the second and 4.5 for the third. The statistic is distributed as a chi-square with 3 degrees of freedom under the null hypothesis of no instrument included in the second stage equation.

reinforces our thesis that the foreign-born have a positive effect in non-coastal cities as well. As for the rent regressions, the share of foreigners once again has a positive and significant effect in specifications 2 and 3 of Table 10 (excluding coastal cities and excluding the largest immigration states). Again, somewhat oddly, and probably due to the elimination of some outliers, the estimated effect on rents increases significantly in specifications 2 and 3.

All in all the results using shift-share instruments seem to confirm very strongly the positive effect of diversity on wages and rents of natives. In particular, considering all the IV regressions, we find no specification in which the coefficients of diversity are not significant in either the wage or rent equations. Moreover the point estimates are always robustly positive (although sometimes they are not very precise due to instrument weakness). Thus, on the basis of the discussion in subsection 2, we can conclude that our data support the hypothesis of a positive productivity effect of diversity with *causation running from diversity to productivity of US workers.*

6. Discussion and conclusions

We have looked at US metropolitan areas as a system of open cities in which cultural diversity can affect the productivity and utility of natives. In principle, the effects of diversity can be positive or negative. We have considered a simple model that handles all possible cases (i.e. positive or negative effects on productivity and utility),

The economic value of cultural diversity: evidence from US cities • **39**

and we have designed a simple identification procedure to figure out which case receives empirical support based on cross-city wage and rent variations. We have showed that higher wages and higher rents for US natives are significantly correlated with higher diversity. This result has survived several robustness checks against possible alternative explanations based on omitted variables and instrumental variables estimation.

Given our identification procedure, these findings are consistent with a dominant positive effect of diversity on productivity: *a more multicultural urban environment makes US-born citizens more productive.* To the best of our knowledge, in terms of both data and identification procedure, our results are new. We need to add two caveats, however, to these conclusions. First, while we are confident that the identified positive correlation between diversity and wage-rents is a robust feature of the data, our interpretation of a positive effect of diversity on productivity is not the only possible one. A plausible, and not less interesting one, is that spatial selection of US born residents in cities with high or low diversity may reflect some of their characteristics. For instance, people with higher education, higher international experience, and higher exposure to culture and news may be more appreciative of diversity. They may also be different from other US natives in several characteristics that are related to productivity. If this is true, 'tolerant' cities are more productive due to the characteristics of US-born residents rather than to the 'diversity' of these cities. Our current and future research is proceeding in the direction of analyzing this selection effect better and trying to determine which factor (diversity or tolerance) is more relevant for productivity (in fact both effects are likely to play important roles).

Secondly, even assuming the existence of a positive effect of foreign-born residents on the productivity of US natives, we have not yet opened the 'black box' to analyze theoretically and empirically what the channels are through which that effect works. The complementarity of skills between the US and foreign born seems a very promising avenue of research. Even at the same level of education, problem solving, creativity and adaptability may differ between native and foreign-born workers so that reciprocal learning may take place. Another promising avenue is that foreign-born workers may provide services that are not perfectly substitutable with those of natives. An Italian stylist, a Mexican cook and a Russian dancer simply provide different services that their US-born counterparts cannot. Because of a taste for variety, this may increase the value of total production. We need to analyze more closely the effects in different sectors and on different skill groups in order to gain a better understanding of these channels. Overall our findings look plausible and encouraging, leaving to future research the important goal of pursuing further the analysis of the mechanisms through which foreign-born residents affect the US economy.

Acknowledgements

We are grateful to Gilles Duranton, Michael Storper and two anonymous referees for very helpful comments and suggestions. We also thank Alberto Alesina, Richard Arnott, David Card, Masa Fujita, Ed Glaeser, Vernon Henderson, Eliana LaFerrara, David Levine, Doug Miller, Enrico Moretti, Dino Pinelli, Matt Turner as well as workshop participants at FEEM Milan, RSAI Philadelphia, UBC Vancouver, UC Berkeley and UCLA International Institute for helpful discussions and suggestions. We thank Elena Bellini for outstanding research

40 • *Ottaviano and Peri*

assistance. Ahmed Rahman provided extremely competent assistance with the editing of the article. Ottaviano gratefully acknowledges financial support from Bocconi University and FEEM. Peri gratefully acknowledge financial support form UCLA International Institute. Errors are ours.

References

Alesina, A., La Ferrara, E. (2003) Ethnic diversity and economic performance. Working Paper 10313, NBER, Cambridge, MA.

Bairoch, P. (1988) *Cities and Economic Development: from the Dawn of History to the Present.* Oxford: Oxford University Press.

Berliant, M., Fujita, M. (2004) Knowledge creation as a square dance on the Hilbert Cube. Working Paper Washington University at Saint Louis, Department of Economics.

Boeri, T., Hanson G., McCormick, B. (2002) *Immigration Policy and the Welfare System.* Oxford: Oxford University Press.

Borjas, G. (1994) The economics of immigration. *Journal of Economic Literature*, 32: 1667–1717.

Borjas, G. (1995) The economic benefits of immigration. *Journal of Economic Perspectives*, 9: 3–22.

Borjas, G. (1999) *Heaven's Doors.* Princeton: Princeton University Press.

Borjas, G. (2001) Does Immigration Grease the Wheels of the Labor Market? *Brookings Papers on Economic Activity*, 1: 69–119.

Borjas, G. (2003) The labor demand curve is downward sloping: Re-examining the impact of immigration on the labor market. *Quarterly Journal of Economics*, 118: 1335–1374.

Borjas, G., Freeman, R., Katz, L. (1997) How much do immigration and trade affect labor market outcomes? *Brookings Papers on Economic Activity*, 1: 1–90.

Butcher, K., Card, D. (1991) Immigration and wages, evidence from the 1980's. *American Economic Review*, 81, *Papers and Proceedings of the Hundred and Third Annual Meeting of the American Economic Association*, 292–296.

Card, D. (1990) The impact of the Mariel Boatlift on the Miami labor market. *Industrial and Labor Relations Review*, 43: 245–257.

Card, D. (2001) Immigrant inflows, native outflows and the local labor market impacts of higher immigration, *Journal of Labor Economics*, 19, 22–61.

Card, D., Di Nardo, J. (2000) Do immigrant inflows lead to native outflows? *American Economic Review*, 90: 360–367.

Card, D., Krueger, A. (1992) School quality and black-white relative earnings: A direct assessment. *Quarterly Journal of Economics*, 107: 151–200.

Card, D., Krueger, A. (1993) Trends in relative black-white earnings revisited. *American Economic Review, Papers and Proceedings*, 83: 85–91.

Ciccone, A, Hall, R. (1996) Productivity and the Density of Economic Activity. *American Economic Review*, 86: 54–70.

Collier, P. (2001) Implications of ethnic diversity, *Economic Policy: a European Forum*, 0: 127–55.

Combes, P. P., Duranton, G., Gobillon, L. (2004) Spatial wage disparities: Sorting matters!, Discussion Paper, 4240, CEPR, London UK.

Cutler, D., Glaeser, D. (1997) Are ghettos good or bad? *Quarterly Journal of Economics*, 112: 827–72.

Dekle, R., Eaton, J. (1999) Agglomeration and Land Rents: Evidence from the Prefectures. *Journal of Urban Economics*, 46(2): 200–214.

Easterly, W., Levine, R. (1997) Africa's growth tragedy: Policies and ethnic division. *Quarterly Journal of Economics*, 112: 1203–50.

Eckstein, Z., Wolpin, K. (1999) Estimating the effect of racial discrimination on first job wage offers. *Review of Economics and Statistics*, 81: 384–392.

Florida, R. (2002a) Bohemia and economic geography. *Journal of Economic Geography*, 2: 55–71.

Florida, R. (2002b) *The Rise of the Creative Class*. Basic Books, New York.

Fujita, M., Krugman, P., Venables, A. (1999) *The Spatial Economy. Cities, regions and international trade*. Cambridge MA: MIT Press.

Glaeser, E., Kolko, J., Saiz, A. (2001) Consumer city. *Journal of Economic Geography*, 1: 27–50.

Jacobs, J. (1969) *The Economy of Cities*. New York: Random House.

Kahn, M. E. (1995), A revealed preference approach to ranking city quality of life. *Journal of Urban Economics*, 38: 221–235.

Lazear, E. (1999) Globalization and the market for team-mates. *Economic Journal*, 109: C15–C40.

Lian, B., Oneal J. (1997) Cultural diversity and economic development: a cross-national study of 98 Countries. 1960–1985. *Economic Development and Cultural Change*, 46: 61–77.

Maignan, C., Ottaviano, G., Pinelli, D., Rullani, F. (2003) Bio-Ecological Diversity vs Socio-Economic Diversity: A Comparison of Existing Measures. Working Paper n.13 Fondazione Enrico Mattei, Venice.

Mason, P. (2000) Persistent discrimination: racial disparity in the United States, 1967–1998, *American Economic Review*, 90: 312–16.

Mauro, P. (1995) Corruption and growth. *Quarterly Journal of Economics*, 110: 681–712.

Moretti, E. (2004) Workers' education, spillovers and productivity: evidence from plant-level production functions. *American Economic Review*, 94: 656–690.

Munshi, K. (2003) Networks in the modern economy: Mexican migrants in the US labor market. *Quarterly Journal of Economics*, 118: 549–599.

Ottaviano, G., Peri, G. (2004a) Cities and Cultures. Discussion Paper, 4438 CEPR London, UK.

Ottaviano, G., Peri, G. (2004b) The economic value of cultural diversity: evidence from US Cities. CESifo Working Paper 1117, Munich, Germany.

Ottaviano, G., Peri, G. (2005) Gains from "Diversity": Theory and Evidence from Immigration in US Cities. Manuscript, Department of Economics UCLA, January 2005.

Park, J. (1994) Estimation of sheepskin effects and returns to schooling using the old and new CPS measures of educational attainment. Princeton University Industrial Relation Section, Working Paper No. 338.

Peri, G. (2005) Skills and Talent of Immigrants: A Comparison between the European Union and the United States, Institute of European Studies (UC Berkeley) Working Paper, March 2005.

Quigley, J. (1998) Urban diversity and economic growth. *Journal of Economic Perspectives*, 12: 127–138.

Rauch, J. (1993) Productivity gains from geographic concentration in cities. *Journal of Urban Economics*, 34: 380–400.

Roback, J. (1982) Wages, rents and the quality of life. *Journal of Political Economy*, 90: 1257–78.

Saiz, A. (2003a) Room in the kitchen for the melting pot: immigration and rental prices, *Review of Economics and Statistics*, 85(3): 502–521.

Saiz, A. (2003b) Immigration and housing rents in American cities. Working Paper No. 03–12, Federal Reserve Bank of Philadelphia.

Sassen, S. (1994) *Cities in a World Economy*. Thousand Oaks: Pine Forge Press.

Sivitanidou, R., Wheaton, S. (1992) Wage and rent capitalization in the commercial real estate market, *Journal of Urban Economics*, Vol, 31: 206–229.

Taylor, C., Hudson, M. (1972) *World Handbook of Political and Social Indicators*. Second edition, New Haven: Yale University Press.

Winters, P., de Janvry, A., Sadoulet, E. (2001) Family and community networks on Mexico-US migration. *Journal of Human Resources*, 36: 159–184.

Woolridge, J. L. (2001) Econometric Analysis of Cross Section and Panel Data, MIT Press, Boston MA.

A. Data Appendix

A.1 Data for MSA's

The data on cultural diversity and foreign-born are obtained from the 1970–1990 Public Use Microdata Sample (PUMS) of the US Census. We selected all people in working age (16–65 year) in each year and we identified the city where they lived using the SMSA code for 1990, while in 1970 we used the county group code to identify the metropolitan area. We used the variable 'Place of Birth' in order to identify the country of origin of the person. We considered only the countries of origin in which was born at least 0.5 % of the foreign-born working age population. We obtained 35 groups for 1970 as well as for 1990.

We used the Variable 'Salary and Wage' to measure the yearly wage income of each person. We transformed the wage in real 1990 US$ by deflating it with the national GDP deflator. The years of schooling for individuals are measured using the variable 'higrad' for the 1970 census, which indicates the highest grade attended, while for 1990 the variable 'grade completed' is converted into years of schooling using Park's (1994) correspondence Table 4. Average rents are calculated using gross monthly rent per room (i.e. rent divided by number of rooms) expressed in real 1990 US$ terms. The data on total city employment, total local public spending, and public spending in education are from the County and City Databook.

The list of metropolitan areas used in our study is reported in the following table.

A.2 Grouping by country of birth

In Tables from 1 to 8 we consider the diversity index constructed using 35 countries of origin of immigrants which top the list of all countries of origin plus a residual group called 'others'. These account for more than 90 % of all foreign-born, both in 1970 and 1990, and a country that is not in this list supplies at most 0.5 % of all foreign-born living in the US. Here is the list of the non-residual countries, in alphabetical order. For year 1970 the countries are: Argentina, Australia, Canada, Czechoslovakia, China, Colombia, Cuba, Dominican Republic, England, France, Germany, Greece, Hungary, India, Ireland, Italy, Jamaica, Japan, Korea, Latvia, Lithuania, Mexico, Netherlands, Norway, Philippines, Poland, Portugal, Romania, Scotland, Sweden, Syria, Ukraine, USSR, Yugoslavia, Others. For 1990 the countries are: Argentina, Canada, China, Colombia, Cuba, Dominican Republic, Ecuador, England, France, Germany, Greece, Guyana, Haiti, Honduras, Hong-Kong, India, Iran, Ireland, Italy, Jamaica, Japan, Korea, Mexico, Nicaragua, Panama, Peru, Philippines, Poland, Portugal, El Salvador, Taiwan, Trinidad and Tobago, USSR, Vietnam, Yugoslavia.

In Tables 9 and 10, in order to have the same groups in 1970 and 1990, we allocate more than one non-residual country to the same group based on geographical proximity. Our fifteen groups are almost the same as those defined and used in Card (2001). This is the list: Mexico, Caribbean Countries, Central America, China-Hong-Kong-Singapore, South America, South East Asia, Korea and Japan, Philippines, Australia-New Zealand-Canada-UK, India and Pakistan, Russia and Central Europe, Turkey, North Africa and Middle East, Northwestern Europe and Israel, South-western Europe, Sub-Saharan Africa, Cuba.

The economic value of cultural diversity: evidence from US cities • **43**

Table A1. Name and state of the cities used

Abilene, TX	Dayton-Springfield, OH	Lexington, KY	Rockford, IL
Akron, OH	Decatur, IL	Lima, OH	Sacramento, CA
Albany-Schenectady-Troy, NY	Denver, CO	Lincoln, NE	Saginaw-Bay City-Midland, MI
Albuquerque, NM	Des Moines, IA	Little Rock-North Little Rock, AR	St. Louis, MO-IL
Allentown-Bethlehem-Easton, PA	Detroit, MI	Los Angeles-Long Beach, CA	Salem, OR
Altoona, PA	Duluth-Superior, MN-WI	Louisville, KY-IN	Salinas, CA
Amarillo, TX	El Paso, TX	Lubbock, TX	Salt Lake City-Ogden, UT
Appleton-Oshkosh-Neenah, WI	Erie, PA	Macon, GA	San Antonio, TX
Atlanta, GA	Eugene-Springfield, OR	Madison, WI	San Diego, CA
Atlantic-Cape May, NJ	Fayetteville, NC	Mansfield, OH	San Francisco, CA
Augusta-Aiken, GA-SC	Flint, MI	Memphis, TN-AR-MS	San Jose, CA
Austin-San Marcos, TX	Fort Lauderdale, FL	Miami, FL	Santa Barbara-Santa Maria- Lompoc, CA
Bakersfield, CA	Fort Wayne, IN	Milwaukee-Waukesha, WI	Santa Rosa, CA
Baltimore, MD	Fresno, CA	Minneapolis-St. Paul, MN-WI	Seattle-Bellevue-Everett, WA
Baton Rouge, LA	Gainesville, FL	Modesto, CA	Shreveport-Bossier City, LA
Beaumont-Port Arthur, TX	Gary, IN	Monroe, LA	South Bend, IN
Billings, MT	Grand Rapids-Muskegon-Holland, MI	Montgomery, AL	Spokane, WA
Biloxi-Gulfport-Pascagoula, MS	Green Bay, WI	Muncie, IN	Springfield, MO
Binghamton, NY	Greensboro–Winston-Salem-High Point, NC	Nashville, TN	Stockton-Lodi, CA
Birmingham, AL	Greenville-Spartanburg-Anderson, SC	New Orleans, LA	Syracuse, NY
Bloomington-Normal, IL	Hamilton-Middletown, OH	New York, NY	Tacoma, WA
Boise City, ID	Harrisburg-Lebanon-Carlisle, PA	Newark, NJ	Tampa-St. Petersburg-Clearwater, FL
Brownsville-Harlingen-San Benito, TX	Honolulu, HI	Norfolk-Virginia Beach-Newport News, VA-NC	Terre Haute, IN
Buffalo-Niagara Falls, NY	Houston, TX	Odessa-Midland, TX	Toledo, OH
Canton-Massillon, OH	Huntington-Ashland, WV-KY-OH	Oklahoma City, OK	Trenton, NJ
Cedar Rapids, IA	Indianapolis, IN	Omaha, NE-IA	Tucson, AZ
Champaign-Urbana, IL	Jackson, MI	Orlando, FL	Tulsa, OK
Charleston-North Charleston, SC	Jackson, MS	Pensacola, FL	Tuscaloosa, AL
Charlotte-Gastonia-Rock Hill, NC-SC	Jacksonville, FL	Peoria-Pekin, IL	Tyler, TX
Chattanooga, TN-GA	Jersey City, NJ	Philadelphia, PA-NJ	Utica-Rome, NY
Chicago, IL	Johnstown, PA	Phoenix-Mesa, AZ	Vallejo-Fairfield-Napa, CA
Cincinnati, OH-KY-IN	Kalamazoo-Battle Creek, MI	Pittsburgh, PA	Waco, TX

44 • *Ottaviano and Peri*

Table A1. *Continued*

Cleveland-Lorain-Elyria, OH	Kansas City, MO-KS	Portland-Vancouver, OR-WA	Washington, DC-MD-VA-WV
Colorado Springs, CO	Kenosha, WI	Raleigh-Durham-Chapel Hill, NC	Waterloo-Cedar Falls, IA
Columbia, MO	Knoxville, TN	Reading, PA	West Palm Beach-Boca Raton, FL
Columbia, SC	Lafayette, LA	Reno, NV	Wichita, KS
Columbus, OH	Lafayette, IN	Richmond-Petersburg, VA	Wilmington-Newark, DE-MD
Corpus Christi, TX	Lancaster, PA	Riverside-San Bernardino, CA	Wilmington, NC
Dallas, TX	Lansing-East Lansing, MI	Roanoke, VA	York, PA
Davenport-Moline-Rock Island, IA-IL	Las Vegas, NV-AZ	Rochester, NY	Youngstown-Warren, OH

Chapter 8

The labor market impact of immigration in Western Germany in the 1990s[†]

Francesco D'Amuri[a], Gianmarco I.P. Ottaviano[b], Giovanni Peri[c,*]

[a] Bank of Italy and ISER, University of Essex, UK
[b] Bocconi University, FEEM and CEPR, Italy
[c] University of California, Davis and NBER, USA

ARTICLE INFO

Article history:
Received 25 February 2008
Accepted 20 October 2009
Available online 31 October 2009

JEL classification:
E24
F22
J61
J31

Keywords:
Immigration
Wages
Labor market rigidities
Employment

ABSTRACT

In this article we estimate the wage and employment effects of recent immigration in Western Germany. Using administrative data for the period 1987–2001 and a labor-market equilibrium model, we find that the substantial immigration of the 1990s had very little adverse effects on native wages and on their employment levels. Instead, it had a sizeable adverse employment effect on previous immigrants as well as a small adverse effect on their wages. These asymmetric results are partly driven by a higher degree of substitution between old and new immigrants in the labor market and in part by the rigidity of wages in less than flexible labor markets. In a simple counter-factual experiment we show that in a world of perfect wage flexibility and no unemployment insurance the wage-bill loss of old immigrants would be much smaller.
© 2009 Elsevier B.V. All rights reserved.

1. Introduction

Within Europe, Germany hosts the largest number of immigrants. Workers with foreign origin have represented more than 10% of the total German labor force since the late 1990s.[1] The socioeconomic worries produced by rising immigration led the German government to introduce selective immigration measures and stirred a lively public debate.[2]

The present paper investigates the interactions between immigration, employment and wages in Western Germany by adopting a structural labor market equilibrium approach recently employed, following Borjas (2003), in several national studies. This approach aims at providing a full picture of the adjustment of the labor market to immigration by modeling aggregate production through a multi-level constant elasticity of substitution (CES) production function in which workers with different observable characteristics are imperfect substitutes. Considering explicitly the production structure makes clear that the marginal productivity of workers with certain skills depends not only on the supply of workers with their same skills but also on the supply of other workers. Hence this structure produces a better identification of competition and complementarity effects of immigrants on natives. The assessment of the effects of immigration thus requires a careful

---

[*] Corresponding author. Tel.: +1 530 5542304
E-mail addresses: francesco.damuri@gmail.com (F. D'Amuri), gianmarco.ottaviano@unibocconi.it (G.I.P. Ottaviano), gperi@ucdavis.edu (G. Peri).
[1] Authors' calculation using the IAB data.
[2] See, e.g., Zimmermann et al. (2007) for an outline and an economic evaluation of the norms contained in the measured contained Immigration Act of 2004.

[†] This article originally appeared in *European Economic Review*, **54** 550–570 © 2009 Elsevier Science Publishers B.V.

F. D'Amuri et al. / European Economic Review 54 (2010) 550–570   551

estimation of all the elasticities of substitution between different groups of workers. The original framework proposed by Borjas (2003) and then enriched (adding imperfect native-immigrant substitutability) by Ottaviano and Peri (2008) and Manacorda et al. (2006) focuses only on wage adjustment. This is not enough in the case of Germany, where due to labor market rigidities, persistent changes in employment could be important effects of immigration.

This paper contributes to this recently revived literature in three respects. First, it produces new estimates of very important elasticity parameters: between new and old immigrants, between immigrants and natives and between workers of different age and education. These estimates can be interpreted as short-run elasticities as we use a yearly panel of German workers drawn from a large administrative dataset, representative of all employment spells subject to social security taxation (see Section 3 and the Data Appendix for details). Also new in the identification strategy is the use of the large inflow of Eastern Germans after the fall of the Berlin Wall as an exogenous shock. Second, the paper extends the labor market equilibrium approach to allow for employment as well as wage responses. This is very important especially when we consider short-run effects (as we do here) and when we move beyond the US data analyzing countries characterized by wage rigidities, as it is typical of the German labor market.[3] Third, having identified the actual employment and wage effect of immigration we can produce a counter-factual scenario in which, with perfect wage flexibility, all the inflow of immigrants is absorbed by wage changes (Walrasian markets). Comparing this case with the actual one we can compute the total difference in wage bill and welfare under each scenario and hence the loss in total wages from having the existing rigidities.

In the estimation of the elasticities of substitution, 'new' immigrants are defined as those who have worked in Germany for five years or less whereas 'old' immigrants are those who have worked in Germany for strictly more than five years. Then, for each year we stratify workers in cells defined according to their education, experience and nativity (native-immigrant; new/old immigrant). We allow the relative wage of natives and immigrants (or new/old immigrants) across cells to depend systematically on the year and on their education and experience. We interpret the remaining within-cell variation of immigrants over time as being supply driven. The results reveal stronger competition between new and old immigrants than between immigrants and native workers: while natives and new immigrants are imperfect substitutes, new and old immigrants are close to perfect substitutes. In particular, we estimate a significant elasticity of substitution between natives and immigrants of around 20 (close to what Ottaviano and Peri, 2008; Card, 2009, find between native and immigrants in the US and somewhat larger than what Manacorda et al., 2006, found for the UK) and an elasticity of substitution between new and old immigrants around 60 and not significantly different from the one implied by perfect substitutability.

Previous work by Ottaviano and Peri (2008) on the US and Manacorda et al. (2006) on the UK not only did not distinguish between new and old immigrants but only focussed on the effects of immigration on wages neglecting its effects on employment levels. The reason for this is that the US and the UK labor markets can be reasonably considered as fully flexible with wages adjusting to their market clearing level. In those countries the employment effects of immigration are negligible. This is not the case for Germany where labor market institutions are characterized by generous unemployment benefits and other sources of wage rigidities leaving room for possible employment effects (Angrist and Kugler, 2003; Schmidt et al., 1994).[4] To detect the presence of these effects, we regress the cell specific year-to-year variation in the number of immigrants (new immigrants) on the same measure calculated for the total workforce (total immigrant workforce). The corresponding results reveal the presence of significantly negative impacts of new immigrants on previous immigrants but not on native workers. In particular, our estimates suggest that, for any 10 new immigrants in the German labor market, three to four old immigrants are driven out of employment, whereas no native is affected.

Combining the estimated elasticities of substitution between different types of workers with data on immigration and with the related employment response in each cell, it is finally possible to recover the full impact of migration on wages. Our estimated elasticities imply that over the period 1992–2001 new immigrants to Western Germany reduced the average wages of old immigrants by 0.5%, with highly educated old immigrants losing around 1.1% of their wages. Approximately half of the negative wage effect on the highly educated was due to immigration from Eastern Germany. As for the effects of new immigration on natives, there is essentially a null average effect: negative on highly educated (−1%) and positive on the less educated (+1%).[5]

---

[3] See Dickens et al. (2007) for a recent cross-country comparison of wage rigidity levels. In this study, the fraction of workers potentially affected by real wage rigidity in Germany is estimated to be twice the United States' one.

[4] The importance of the employment effects of migration in Germany is stressed by Pischke and Velling (1997) who, using data on 167 German regions for the 1985–1989 period, show evidence of displacement of the native workforce by immigration. More recently, Glitz (2006), analyzing the specific issue of the impact of *ethnic German* immigration on the relative skill-specific employment and wage rates of the resident population, finds evidence of adverse employment effects but no detrimental effects on average wages.

[5] Bonin (2005) recently applied a skill-based analysis of immigration to the German labor market using IAB data for a different time period (1975–1997). His approach, however, is a reduced-form one. He identifies the partial effect of immigration on wages of each skill group but, since he does not specify a structure of labor demand and supply he cannot identify the total effect of immigration on wages and employment. Moreover, the analysis defines immigrants simply as foreign nationals in the IAB and therefore omits the very important inflow of Eastern Germans and Ethnic German immigrants. Nevertheless, his results do not systematically differ from ours: he finds small wage effects of migration on native workers and no effects on unemployment.

552 F. D'Amuri et al. / European Economic Review 54 (2010) 550–570

We conclude the paper with some simple calculations in which we use our estimated elasticities to discuss the aggregate wage effects of immigration in the presence of wage rigidities compared to the case of fully flexible wages and no negative employment effects. In particular, assuming that the negative employment effects are due to labor market frictions present in the German labor market, we calculate the sum of foregone production (equal to the wage bill of displaced workers) and unemployment benefits paid to displaced workers. We then simulate a counter-factual scenario in which wages are free to adjust to their market clearing level and no adverse employment effects arise and we calculate the total wage effect of immigrants. We find that the adverse effect of immigration on the total wage bill is much larger under the scenario with wage rigidity and unemployment benefits than under perfect wage flexibility.

Following the working paper version of the present work (D'Amuri et al., 2008), other studies have analyzed the impact of immigration on employment and wages of West German workers. Those studies have either used different data (such as the GSOEP used in Felbermayr et al., 2008) or focused on different policy experiments (as Brucker and Jahn, 2008). While generally confirming our results those studies provide interesting extensions, robustness checks and alternative policy analyses that complement the present work.

The rest of the paper is organized as follows. Section 2 describes the theoretical framework behind our evaluation of the wage and employment effects of immigration. Section 3 presents the data used for our econometric analysis and presents summary statistics. Results from the econometric analysis of the employment effects of immigration are presented in Section 4, which also discusses important empirical issues, estimates the relevant elasticities of substitution and uses these estimates to calculate the equilibrium effects of immigration on employment and wages. Section 5 discusses the implications of our findings in terms of the aggregate wage impact of immigration comparing the actual scenario with a counter-factual of perfect wage flexibility. Section 6 concludes.

2. Theoretical framework

2.1. Production

The production side of our economy is similar to Ottaviano and Peri (2008) and Borjas (2003). Firms employ labor and physical capital (K) to produce a homogeneous final product, which is sold in a perfectly competitive market and is taken as numeraire good. Technology is such that physical capital and a labor composite are combined in a Cobb–Douglas production function to produce output under constant returns to scale. The labor composite is itself a CES aggregator of employees with different work experience nested within educational groups. We allow for further degrees of imperfect substitutability between natives and immigrants and also between old and new immigrants to Western Germany. The aggregate production function is

$$Y_t = A_t L_t^\alpha K_t^{1-\alpha} \tag{1}$$

where the subscript t indicates the time period, Y_t is output, A_t is total factor productivity (TFP), K_t is physical capital, L_t is the CES aggregator of different types of employees and $\alpha \in (0, 1)$ is the income share of labor. The labor composite L_t is in turn defined as

$$L_t = \left[\sum_{k=1}^{3} \theta_{kt} L_{kt}^{(\delta-1)/\delta} \right]^{\delta/(\delta-1)} \tag{2}$$

where L_{kt} is itself a CES aggregator of employees with educational level k and θ_{kt} are education-specific productivity levels standardized such that $\sum_k \theta_{kt} = 1$. Workers are grouped in three educational levels, $k = 1, 2, 3$, corresponding to workers with no vocational degree, workers with vocational degree and workers with tertiary education. The parameter $\delta \geq 0$ measures the elasticity of substitution among the three educational groups.

As in Card and Lemieux (2001), workers with the same education but different work experience are also considered as imperfect substitutes, with L_{kt} defined as

$$L_{kt} = \left[\sum_{j=1}^{8} \theta_{kjt} L_{kjt}^{(\eta-1)/\eta} \right]^{\eta/(\eta-1)} \tag{3}$$

where $j = 1, 2, \ldots, 8$ is an index capturing five-year intervals of potential experience, spanning from a minimum of 0 to a maximum of 40 years. The term $\eta \geq 0$ measures the elasticity of substitution between workers with the same education but different potential experience and θ_{kjt} are their education–experience-specific productivity levels, standardized such that $\sum_j \theta_{kjt} = 1$. Following Ottaviano and Peri (2008), native and immigrant workers are allowed to be imperfect substitutes in production since the two groups may have different abilities and skills which affect their comparative advantages and hence their choices of occupation (Peri and Sparber, 2009). Consequently, L_{kjt} is defined as

$$L_{kjt} = \left[\theta_{Hkjt} H_{kjt}^{(\sigma-1)/\sigma} + \theta_{Mkjt} M_{kjt}^{(\sigma-1)/\sigma} \right]^{\sigma/(\sigma-1)} \tag{4}$$

where H_{kjt} and M_{kjt} denote, respectively, native ('Home') and immigrant ('Migrant') workers; $\sigma \geq 0$ is their elasticities of substitution; θ_{Hkjt} and θ_{Mkjt} are their specific productivity levels, with $\theta_{Hkjt} + \theta_{Mkjt} = 1$. Finally, we also allow M_{kjt} to be a CES

F. D'Amuri et al. / European Economic Review 54 (2010) 550–570   553

aggregator of old and new immigrants:

$$M_{kjt} = [\theta_{kjt}^{OLD}(M_{kjt}^{OLD})^{(\lambda-1)/\lambda} + \theta_{kjt}^{NEW}(M_{kjt}^{NEW})^{(\lambda-1)/\lambda}]^{\lambda/(\lambda-1)} \tag{5}$$

where M_{kjt}^{OLD} (M_{kjt}^{NEW}) denotes migrants with education k and experience j who are observed working in Western Germany for five years or less (strictly more than five years). In (5) the parameter $\lambda \geq 0$ denotes their elasticity of substitution while θ_{kjt}^{OLD} and θ_{kjt}^{NEW} represent their specific productivity levels standardized so that $\theta_{kjt}^{OLD} + \theta_{kjt}^{NEW} = 1$.

In all expressions, the relative efficiency parameters, θ, and the total factor productivity, A_t, depend on technological factors only and are thus independent of the supply of migrant workers.

2.2. Wage rigidity and employment effects

We account for wage rigidities by assuming that the wage of natives with education k and experience j has to satisfy the following reduced-form constraint:

$$H_{kjt} = [w_{Hkjt}(1 - r)]^{\xi_H}\overline{H}_{kjt} \tag{6}$$

where $\overline{H}_{kjt}$ is the native labor force, w_{Hkjt} is the native wage rate, $\xi_H \geq 0$ measures the elasticity of native employment with respect to wages, and $0 \leq r \leq 1$ is the unemployment insurance replacement rate.

Expression (6) captures the fact that native employment and the uninsured portion of the wage they receive are linked. Hence a change in wages (produced by a change in the supply of some type of labor) may induce an employment response for natives. An analogous expression holds for old immigrants:

$$M_{kjt}^{OLD} = [w_{Mkjt}^{OLD}(1 - r)]^{\xi_M}\overline{M}_{kjt}^{OLD} \tag{7}$$

where $\xi_M \geq 0$ measures the elasticity of immigrant employment with respect to their wage. The elasticities ξ_H and ξ_M are allowed to be different for natives and immigrants.

The theoretical underpinnings of (6) and (7) are simply stated. If there was unemployment in a perfect labor market, unemployed workers would bid the wage down until labor demand meets labor supply. In (6) and (7) that happens when $\xi = 0$. Different theories of unemployment suggest reasons why this mechanism fails to operate.[6]

In presence of the positive relation between native and old immigrant workers' wages and employment levels captured by (6) and (7), wage changes due to immigration may give rise to employment effects:

$$\left(\frac{\Delta H_{kjt}}{H_{kjt}}\right)_{response} = \xi^H\frac{\Delta w_{Hkjt}}{w_{Hkjt}}$$

$$\left(\frac{\Delta M_{kjt}^{OLD}}{M_{kjt}^{OLD}}\right)_{response} = \xi^M\frac{\Delta w_{Hkjt}^{OLD}}{w_{Hkjt}^{OLD}}$$

$$\frac{\Delta M_{kjt}}{M_{kjt}} = \frac{\Delta M_{kjt}^{OLD} + \Delta M_{kjt}^{NEW}}{M_{kjt}^{OLD} + M_{kjt}^{NEW}} \tag{8}$$

where $(\Delta H_{kjt}/H_{kjt})_{response}$ and $(\Delta M_{kjt}^{OLD}/M_{kjt}^{OLD})_{response}$ represent the changes in labor supply of native and old immigrant workers.

The population of new immigrants is subject to exogenous shocks. In particular, since new immigrants appear in our dataset only upon finding their first job in Germany, we assume that the employment of new immigrants M_{kjt}^{NEW} coincides with their level in the labor force $\overline{M}_{kjt}^{NEW}$. Accordingly, M_{kjt}^{NEW} is exogenous whereas H_{kjt} and M_{kjt}^{OLD} are determined as wages adjust to the inflow of M_{kjt}^{NEW}. Then, since we observe $\Delta H_{kjt}/H_{kjt}$ and $\Delta M_{kjt}^{OLD}/M_{kjt}^{OLD}$, we can estimate their responses to the exogenous changes $\Delta M_{kjt}^{NEW}/M_{kjt}^{NEW}$. In particular, (as in Card, 2007), we can assess the possible employment effects of new immigrants on old immigrants by implementing the following regression:

$$\frac{\Delta M_{kjt}}{M_{kjt-1}} = D_k + D_j + D_t + \gamma\frac{\Delta M_{kjt}^{NEW}}{M_{kjt-1}} + u_{kjt} \tag{9}$$

where D_k, D_j and D_t are, respectively, education, experience and year fixed effects included in order to control for systematic differences in employment growth across education groups, experience groups and years and u_{kjt} a zero-mean cell-specific random shock in employment of immigrants. Eq. (9) is the basis for the empirical analysis implemented in Section 4.2.1. Similarly, in order to assess the effect of immigrant on native employment, we can implement

$$\frac{\Delta EMPL_{kjt}}{EMPL_{kjt-1}} = D_k + D_j + D_t + \rho\frac{\Delta M_{kjt}}{EMPL_{kjt-1}} + u_{kjt} \tag{10}$$

---

[6] Three main reasons have been highlighted in the literature (see, e.g., Romer, 2001, for a survey): efficiency wages, contracting, search and matching.

Using the notation from the model, the variable $EMPL_{kjt-1} = M_{kjt-1} + H_{kjt-1}$ is total employment (immigrants plus natives) with education k and experience j at time $t - 1$ and $\Delta EMPL_{kjt} = [(M_{kjt} + H_{kjt}) - (M_{kjt-1} + H_{kjt-1})]$ is its variation from $t - 1$ to t. The variables D_k, D_j and D_t are the usual education, experience and time dummies and u_{kjt} is a zero mean cell-specific random shock. The parameter ρ captures the impact of immigration on total employment. Eq. (10) is estimated in Section 4.2.2.

An estimated coefficient γ (ρ) equal to one entails the absence of any employment effects on natives, since the increase in immigrant workers (new immigrants) adds to total employment (immigrant) without crowding out existing workers, while values below (above) one would entail negative (positive) employment effects of migration on natives.

Once we have identified the employment effect of new immigrants on old immigrants and natives we plug those effects into the demand condition for each skill group to find the wage effects.

2.3. Labor market equilibrium

In equilibrium wages and employment levels are such that firms maximize profits (i.e., they are on their labor demand curves) and the two constraints (6) and (7) bind. The production function (1) can be used to calculate the demand for each type of labor at a given period t. Specifically, profit maximization requires that the natural logarithm of the wage of native workers with education k and experience j equals the natural logarithm of their marginal productivity in units of output:

$$\ln(w_{Hkjt}) = \ln(\alpha A_t \kappa_t^{1-\alpha}) + \frac{1}{\delta}\ln(L_t) + \ln(\theta_{kt}) - \left(\frac{1}{\delta} - \frac{1}{\eta}\right)\ln(L_{kt}) + \ln(\theta_{kjt}) - \left(\frac{1}{\eta} - \frac{1}{\sigma}\right)\ln(L_{kjt}) + \ln(\theta_{Hkjt}) - \frac{1}{\sigma}\ln(H_{kjt}) \qquad (11)$$

where $\kappa_t = K_t/L_t$ is the capital–labor ratio. Taking the ratio between Eq. (11) and the similar expression for the wage of immigrant workers yields Eq. (12) below that we use in Section 4.3.2 to estimate the inverse elasticity of substitution $1/\sigma$ by considering the variation of M_{kjt} and H_{kjt} as exogenous, once we control for education, experience and time fixed effects:

$$\ln\left(\frac{w_{Hkjt}}{w_{Mkjt}}\right) = \ln\left(\frac{\theta_{Hkjt}}{\theta_{Mkjt}}\right) - \frac{1}{\sigma}\ln\left(\frac{M_{kjt}}{H_{kjt}}\right) \qquad (12)$$

Similarly, the natural logarithm of the wage of old immigrants with education k and experience j is

$$\ln(w_{Mkjt}^{OLD}) = \ln(\alpha A_t \kappa_t^{1-\alpha}) + \frac{1}{\delta}\ln(L_t) + \ln(\theta_{kt}) - \left(\frac{1}{\delta} - \frac{1}{\eta}\right)\ln(L_{kt}) + \ln(\theta_{kjt}) - \left(\frac{1}{\eta} - \frac{1}{\sigma}\right)\ln(L_{kjt}) + \ln(\theta_{Mkjt})$$
$$- \left(\frac{1}{\sigma} - \frac{1}{\lambda}\right)\ln(M_{kjt}) + \ln(\theta_{kjt}^{OLD}) - \frac{1}{\lambda}\ln(M_{kjt}^{OLD}) \qquad (13)$$

By taking the ratio between (13) and the analogous expression for w_{Mkjt}^{NEW}, we recover Eq. (14) that we use in Section 4.3.1 to estimate the inverse elasticity of substitution $1/\lambda$ by considering the variation of M_{kjt}^{OLD} and M_{kjt}^{NEW} as exogenous, once we control for education, experience and time fixed effects:

$$\ln\left(\frac{w_{Mkjt}^{OLD}}{w_{Mkjt}^{NEW}}\right) = \ln\left(\frac{\theta_{kjt}^{OLD}}{\theta_{kjt}^{NEW}}\right) - \frac{1}{\lambda}\ln\left(\frac{M_{kjt}^{OLD}}{M_{kjt}^{NEW}}\right) \qquad (14)$$

Aggregating the marginal pricing conditions for each education–experience group implies the following relationship between the compensation going to the composite labor input L_{kjt} and its supply:

$$\ln(\overline{W}_{kjt}) = \ln\left(\alpha A_t^{1/\alpha} \kappa_t^{(1-\alpha)/\alpha}\right) + \frac{1}{\delta}\ln(L_t) + \ln\theta_{kt} - \left(\frac{1}{\delta} - \frac{1}{\eta}\right)\ln(L_{kt}) + \ln\theta_{kj} - \frac{1}{\eta}\ln(L_{kjt}) \qquad (15)$$

where $\overline{W}_{kjt} = w_{Mkjt}(M_{kjt}/L_{kjt}) + w_{Hkjt}(H_{kjt}/L_{kjt})$ is the average wage paid to workers in the education–experience group k,j and can be considered as the compensation to one unit of the composite input L_{kjt}. Aggregating the production function one level further, together with marginal cost pricing, implies that the compensation going to the labor input L_{kt} satisfies the following expression:

$$\ln(\overline{W}_{kt}) = \ln\left(\alpha A_t^{1/\alpha} \kappa_t^{(1-\alpha)/\alpha}\right) + \frac{1}{\delta}\ln(L_t) + \ln\theta_{kt} - \frac{1}{\delta}\ln(L_{kt}) \qquad (16)$$

where $\overline{W}_{kt} = \sum_j (L_{kjt}/L_{kt})\overline{W}_{kjt}$ is the average wage in education group k.[7] The two equations (15) and (16) are the basis for the empirical estimation of the elasticity $1/\eta$ and $1/\delta$ once we absorb with education by year and year fixed effects the variation of the aggregate indices and productivity and we consider the remaining variation of supply (L_{kjt} and L_{kj}) as exogenous.

2.3.1. Wage effects
Finally, when calculating the effects of new immigration on wages, we will take into account that physical capital adjusts to changes in the labor supply so as to keep its real rate of return constant. This is a reasonable assumption since

---

[7] The weight for the wage of each group equals the size of the composite input for that education–experience cell, L_{kjt}, relative to the size of the composite input for the whole education group L_{kt}. This is measured by the share of group k,j in educational group k.

F. D'Amuri et al. / European Economic Review 54 (2010) 550–570   555

Ortega and Peri (2009) recently found that within OECD countries physical capital fully adjusts to immigration within one year, in order to maintain constant returns to capital. This implies that in expressions (11) and (13), the capital–labor ratio κ_t follows a trend determined only by the growth of total factor productivity A_t so that the overall impact of new immigration on native and old immigrant wages can be obtained by computing the total changes of (11) and (13) with respect to the changes in the labor aggregates (L_t, L_{kt}, L_{kjt}) induced by new immigrants:

$$
\left(\frac{\Delta w_{Hkjt}}{w_{Hkjt}}\right)^{Total} = \frac{1}{\delta}\sum_m\sum_i\left[s_{Mmit}\frac{\Delta M_{mit}}{M_{mit}}+s_{Hmit}\left(\frac{\Delta H_{mit}}{H_{mit}}\right)_{response}\right] + \left(\frac{1}{\eta}-\frac{1}{\delta}\right)\frac{1}{s_{kt}}\sum_i\left[s_{Mkit}\frac{\Delta M_{kit}}{M_{kit}}+s_{Hkit}\left(\frac{\Delta H_{kit}}{H_{kit}}\right)_{response}\right]
$$
$$
+\left(\frac{1}{\sigma}-\frac{1}{\eta}\right)\frac{1}{s_{kjt}}\left[s_{Mkjt}\frac{\Delta M_{kjt}}{M_{kjt}}+s_{Hkjt}\left(\frac{\Delta H_{kjt}}{H_{kjt}}\right)_{response}\right]-\frac{1}{\sigma}\left(\frac{\Delta H_{kjt}}{H_{kjt}}\right)_{response} \qquad (17)
$$

where the variable $s_{Mkjt}=w_{Mkjt}M_{kjt}/\sum_j\sum_i(w_{Mmit}M_{mit}+w_{Hmit}H_{mit})$ is the share of total wage income paid to migrant workers of education k and experience j in year t and s_{Hkjt} is the share of wage income paid to native workers in the same education–experience group. Similarly, $s_{kjt}=(w_{Mkjt}M_{kjt}+w_{Hkjt}H_{kjt})/\sum_m\sum_i(w_{Mmit}H_{mit}+w_{Hmit}M_{mit})$ is the share of wage income paid to all workers of education k and experience j in year t, s_{kt} is the wage share paid to all workers with education k in year t, and so on. The first double summation captures the cross-effects of immigration in groups of any education-experience level, the second double summation captures the effects of immigration in groups with the same education at all experience levels, and the third and fourth summations capture the effects of immigrants within the same education-experience group. The term $\Delta M_{kjt}/M_{kjt}=(M_{kjt+1}-M_{kjt})/M_{kjt}$ represents the change in the supply of immigrant workers with education k and experience j between t and $t+1$. The term $(\Delta H_{kjt}/H_{kjt})_{response}$ represents the change in labor supply of native workers in the same group caused by immigration and estimated by Eq. (10).

Similarly, we can express the long run effect of new immigrants on old immigrants' wages as

$$
\left(\frac{\Delta w_{Mkjt}^{OLD}}{w_{Mkjt}^{OLD}}\right)^{Total} = \frac{1}{\delta}\sum_m\sum_i\left[s_{mit}^{NEW}\frac{\Delta M_{mit}^{NEW}}{M_{mit}^{NEW}}+s_{mit}^{OLD}\left(\frac{\Delta M_{mit}^{OLD}}{M_{mit}^{OLD}}\right)_{response}+s_{Hmit}\left(\frac{\Delta H_{mit}}{H_{mit}}\right)_{response}\right]
$$
$$
+\left(\frac{1}{\eta}-\frac{1}{\delta}\right)\frac{1}{s_{kt}}\sum_i\left[s_{kit}^{NEW}\frac{\Delta M_{kit}^{NEW}}{M_{kit}^{NEW}}+s_{kit}^{OLD}\left(\frac{\Delta M_{kit}^{OLD}}{M_{kit}^{OLD}}\right)_{response}+s_{Hkit}\left(\frac{\Delta H_{kit}}{H_{kit}}\right)_{response}\right]
$$
$$
+\left(\frac{1}{\sigma}-\frac{1}{\eta}\right)\frac{1}{s_{kjt}}\left[s_{kjt}^{NEW}\frac{\Delta M_{kjt}^{NEW}}{M_{kjt}^{NEW}}+s_{kjt}^{OLD}\left(\frac{\Delta M_{kjt}^{OLD}}{M_{kjt}^{OLD}}\right)_{response}+s_{Hkjt}\left(\frac{\Delta H_{kjt}}{H_{kjt}}\right)_{response}\right]
$$
$$
+\left(\frac{1}{\lambda}-\frac{1}{\sigma}\right)\frac{1}{s_{Mkjt}}\left[s_{kjt}^{NEW}\frac{\Delta M_{kjt}^{NEW}}{M_{kjt}^{NEW}}+s_{kit}^{OLD}\left(\frac{\Delta M_{kjt}^{OLD}}{M_{kjt}^{OLD}}\right)_{response}\right]-\frac{1}{\lambda}\left(\frac{\Delta M_{kjt}^{OLD}}{M_{kjt}^{OLD}}\right)_{response} \qquad (18)
$$

Hence, once the parameters δ, η, σ and λ are estimated and once we know the employment responses of old immigrants and native workers to new immigrants, we will be able to plug in those terms and calculate the wage effect of immigration for each group.

3. Data and empirical implementation

3.1. The IAB employment sub-sample

The data we employ are from the German Institute for Employment Research (IAB).[8] The administrative dataset spans the period 1975–2001 and covers all employment spells subject to social security taxation and the unemployment spells during which the individual received unemployment benefits. We limit our analysis to the 1987–2001 period that experienced a steep rise in the number of immigrants. The population includes workers and trainees liable to make social security contributions. The self-employed, civil servants and students enrolled in higher education are not included in the dataset. The IAB dataset is well suited for the analysis of labor market outcomes in the German labor market, especially for people with high attachment to the labor market such as male heads of households. One major advantage of these data is the very large, consistent and continuous coverage over time and the method of collection that guarantees minimum reporting errors. The sample is representative of total (social-security-paying) employment each year. In the Data Appendix we describe in greater detail these data and the refinements that we introduced to identify immigrants, inclusive of Ethnic Germans and Eastern Germans.[9] We also provide a systematic comparison of these data with those from the German Socioeconomic Panel Study (GSOEP, see Haisken-DeNew and Frick, 2005, for a description). While that panel study

---

[8] The interested reader can also refer to Bender et al. (2000) for a description of the data.

[9] Since country of birth is not available in this dataset, we use nationality as a proxy for migration status. This introduces measurement error since the focus of this paper is on immigration rather than nationality. The problem might be made more severe by the presence of a large pool of second generation immigrants with non-German nationality and of a large group of *Ethnic Germans*. As discussed at length in the Data Appendix, we perform many robustness checks in order to test the robustness of our results to bias arising from this aspect. We think it is important for future analysis of German data to relate more carefully measures of nationality and foreign-born status.

F. D'Amuri et al. / European Economic Review 54 (2010) 550–570

Table 1
Comparison between IAB and GSOEP, Year 1987, 1991 and 2001.

	1987				1991				2001			
	GSOEP		IAB		GSOEP		IAB		GSOEP		IAB	
	Mean	S.D.	Mean	S.D.	Mean	S.D.	Mean	S.D.	Mean	S.D.	Mean	S.D.
Natives												
Share females	0.40		0.42		0.40		0.43		0.46		0.44	
No vocational education	0.21		0.26		0.25		0.22		0.16		0.18	
Vocational education	0.66		0.68		0.65		0.71		0.64		0.71	
Higher education	0.12		0.06		0.10		0.07		0.20		0.11	
Years of experience	17.73	11.77	16.90	11.28	17.69	11.40	17.67	11.10	19.58	10.60	19.52	10.72
Less than 20 years of pot. exp.	0.59		0.62		0.60		0.60		0.53		0.53	
Daily wage	69.69	42.41	68.87	33.25	70.60	45.58	75.09	33.56	81.80	52.08	79.15	39.37
Immigrants												
Share of total	0.07		0.09		0.12		0.10		0.13		0.14	
Share females	0.30		0.31		0.33		0.33		0.40		0.37	
No vocational education	0.61		0.62		0.66		0.59		0.29		0.38	
Vocational education	0.36		0.34		0.31		0.37		0.46		0.54	
Higher education	0.03		0.04		0.02		0.04		0.25		0.08	
Years of experience	20.59	10.75	18.64	10.15	20.37	11.98	18.22	10.69	17.88	11.09	18.68	10.56
Less than 20 years of pot. exp.	0.46		0.54		0.47		0.56		0.61		0.58	
Daily wage	62.42	23.36	68.54	26.75	61.27	25.10	70.83	29.10	76.86	52.54	71.85	32.87

Note: The German Socio-Economic Panel GSOEP is a panel of individuals started in 1984 with refreshments (i.e. inclusion of new waves of people) in 1994/1995, 1998 and 2000 over the considered period. The IAB is an administrative dataset including workers of the private sector contributing to social security. Immigrants are defined as foreign-born plus those living in East Germany in 1989 in the GSOEP and as foreign-nationals plus those who report having started to work in East Germany in the IAB. We follow the same selection rules for both datasets (see Section 3). In particular, we include only private sector, not self-employed workers, aged 17–64 and living in West Germany. For GSOEP data we use the cross-sectional weights; as daily wages are not recorded in the GSOEP, we recover them from gross monthly wages assuming that the average individual works a fraction of the month which is equal to the fraction of the days worked in the year as calculated from the IAB sample on a migration status and year basis.

has some desirable features, such as the identification of country of birth (which is better than nationality in identifying immigrants) it also has two serious problems. The first is that it is based on a much smaller sample so that in many education–experience cells (according to our definition) it contains very few observations or none at all, especially for immigrants. Second, it is a panel dataset started in 1984 with infrequent refreshments (1994, 1998 and 2000). During the intermediate years only the sample weights are adjusted to reflect the changing population but no new information on flows and wages is used. Therefore we decided to use the IAB dataset and to address a series of issues by refining and cleaning the data (as described in the Data Appendix). The interested reader can see in Table 1 how some summary statistics compare between the two datasets and read in the Data Appendix a detailed account of the comparison between IAB and GSOEP and of the refinement and robustness checks that we performed.

The supply of labor for each education–experience and nativity cell in a year is calculated as the sum of employees in the cell weighted by their yearly working days. Nominal gross wages are all converted to 2000 Euros using the CPI-based deflator across years before calculating the cell averages. While we do not impose further restrictions on the sector of activity and on work arrangements, we do not include marginal employees, that is workers earning a wage below a really low threshold (approximately 330 euros per month in 1999, according to Wagner, 1999) that are in the IAB sample after 1999.

Fig. 1 reports the share of immigrants on total employment as obtained from the refined IAB dataset (including Ethnic and East–West moving Germans), showing that it climbed from about 9% in 1987 to 14% in 2001. The time period analyzed is particularly interesting for the analysis of the labor market impact of immigration: the inflow of immigrant workers was very large and mostly supply-driven (due to the fall of the Iron Curtain and the uncertainty following the aftermath of the end of socialism in the countries of origin). Indeed, the large and sudden rise in the share of immigrant workers, mostly due to push factors, makes this somewhat of a 'natural experiment'—one which is well suited to assessing the impact of immigration on incumbent workers.[10]

3.2. Stylized facts and descriptive statistics

Let us first describe simple aggregate evidence that points to the existence of significant differences in the labor market performances between immigrants and natives. Fig. 2 shows the evolution of the share of individuals receiving

---

[10] Bauer et al. (2005, p. 217) provide descriptive evidence on the independence between the growth of foreign employment and the business cycle after the fall of the Iron Curtain.

F. D'Amuri et al. / European Economic Review 54 (2010) 550–570   557

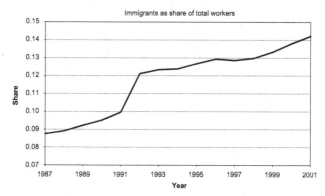

Fig. 1. Immigrants as share of total workers. *Source:* Authors' calculations based on IAB data. Immigrants are the sum of foreign nationals plus workers who immigrated from Eastern Germany plus ethnic Germans who immigrated from abroad.

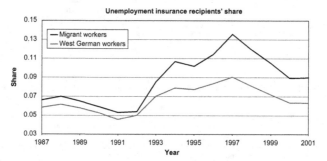

Fig. 2. Unemployment insurance recipients' share. *Source:* Authors' calculations based on IAB data. The 'unemployment insurance recipients' share' is equal to the share of individuals receiving unemployment benefits relative to the sum of workers and individuals receiving unemployment benefits.

unemployment benefits relative to the total workforce, calculated separately for native Germans and immigrant workers for the period 1987–2001 from the IAB dataset. Two tendencies emerge. First, the rates for native German and immigrant workers are quite stable and fairly similar over the period 1987–1991, a period of relatively small inflows of immigrants. Second, beginning in 1991 the unemployment rate for immigrants increases significantly. For native Germans it increases much less, opening a gap that is quite persistent, though it narrows toward the end of the 1990s.

Table 2 reports, for selected years, the shares of immigrants in each of the education–experience cells used in the regressions. Ethnic Germans are classified, as usual, as immigrants following the procedure described in the Data Appendix. In Table 2 we show the percentage of non-Western Germans both from foreign countries and from Eastern Germany. The share of non-native workers in total employment more than doubles in many cells between 1987 and 2001. Large inflows of immigrants took place in all education groups. Interestingly, while Eastern German immigrants were over-represented among those of intermediate and high levels of educations, immigrants from foreign countries were proportionally more numerous among the less educated group. Merging the two groups we obtain a group of immigrants which is fairly balanced among the three education groups.

To summarize, a preliminary look at the data suggests that the substantial increase in the number of immigrant workers over the period of observation has been evenly distributed across educational levels. The performance of migrants has been worse than that of natives in terms of unemployment rates, suggesting stronger competition of new immigrants with existing foreign-born workers.

Table 2
Share of foreign immigrants/Eastern German immigrants in total workers by education and potential experience.

Education	Potential experience	1987		2001	
		Overall share of migrants (%)	Overall share of migrants (%)	Share Eastern Germans (%)	Share foreign immigrants (%)
No vocational education	Up to 4	7.2	8.8	1.0	7.8
	5–9	20.6	22.9	2.9	20.0
	10–14	20.1	42.5	3.7	38.8
	15–19	24.7	39.3	3.4	35.9
	20–24	32.4	35.7	2.5	33.2
	25–29	38.1	27.9	3.0	24.9
	30–34	23.3	26.1	2.4	23.8
	35–40	16.4	33.7	1.5	32.2
Vocational education	Up to 4	4.9	15.4	5.0	10.4
	5–9	4.0	18.2	5.5	12.7
	10–14	4.2	14.1	4.9	9.2
	15–19	5.5	11.1	3.8	7.3
	20–24	7.7	9.6	3.8	5.8
	25–29	4.9	8.4	3.3	5.1
	30–34	3.4	9.1	2.7	6.5
	35–40	2.8	8.7	1.9	6.8
Higher education	Up to 4	4.8	13.7	3.8	10.0
	5–9	4.3	8.9	3.0	5.8
	10–14	5.7	7.9	2.9	5.0
	15–19	7.5	7.7	2.8	4.9
	20–24	6.4	8.2	2.9	5.4
	25–29	4.3	9.4	2.8	6.5
	30–34	4.2	10.1	3.3	6.8
	35–40	0.0	10.0	2.9	7.1

Note: The percentages are calculated from IAB data refined as described in the main text. Immigrants are defined as foreign-nationals and foreign-born ethnic Germans. Eastern Germans are those workers who report having started to work in East Germany.

4. Employment and wage effects

The aim of the present section is to estimate the employment and wage responses of old immigrants and natives to the arrival of new immigrants. We calculate average employment and wage levels for each of the education–experience-year cell. We have considered three educational levels (No Vocational Education, Vocational Education and Higher Education), 8 experience levels (5 year intervals for individuals with a 0–40 year potential experience levels) and 15 years (1987–2001) for a total of 360 cells. The average cell-size in the sample is equal to 7571 for natives and 1006 for migrants (678 and 328, respectively, for *NEW* and *OLD* migrants). The percentage of empty cells, therefore not used for estimation, ranges between zero for natives to a maximum of 3.1% for *NEW* immigrants.

In our empirical analysis we proceed in three steps. First, we estimate the effects of new immigration on the employment levels of native and old immigrant workers in the same skill group implementing Eqs. (9) and (10). Second, implementing empirically Eqs. (12) and (14) we estimate the elasticity of substitution between natives and immigrants for given education and experience (σ) as well as the elasticity between new and long-term immigrants for given education and experience (λ). We then estimate the elasticity of substitution between educational levels (δ) as well as between experience levels for a given educational level (η) by implementing empirically Eqs. (15) and (16). Finally, once we have the estimated employment effects and elasticities of substitution, we use expressions (17) and (18) to compute the impact of the inflow of new immigrants on the wages of natives and old immigrants with different levels of education.

4.1. Empirical issues: demand shocks and estimation bias

Before implementing the empirical specifications let us note that a common feature throughout the estimation procedure is that we consider changes in the employment of new immigrants as a supply shock. In particular, when we estimate either the employment response of previous immigrants and natives, or the response of wages, we rely on the assumption that the inflow of new immigrants is an exogenous supply shock. Therefore, (i) we can consider the employment response of natives as actually caused by the immigrant inflow and (ii) we can consider the wage responses as identifying the relative wage elasticity (elasticity of substitution) of labor demand. This may look like a strong assumption. After all we are essentially regressing (total) employment and wages on immigration and we may be identifying a

F. D'Amuri et al. / European Economic Review 54 (2010) 550–570   559

parameter that mixes demand and supply changes. We think, however, that considering the estimated parameters in Section 4.2 as genuine measures of the employment response, and those in Section 4.3 as demand elasticities, is reasonable in light of the following three facts.

First, and least important, the entire literature which analyzes the national effects of immigration using this framework makes the same simple assumption that immigrants are an exogenous shock to the national labor supply (e.g., Borjas, 2003; Borjas and Katz, 2007; Ottaviano and Peri, 2008). Second, while the overall flow of immigrants can be driven by demand pull, since we use variations and control for year, education and experience fixed effects we rely on the differential change of immigrant flows within an education–experience cell. This is likely to be driven mostly by demographic factors in the sending country (i.e., the size of a cohort relative to the others). Moreover, in estimating native-immigrant elasticity we use relative native-immigrant wages and relative native-immigrant employment so that any demand shock common to immigrants and natives within education and experience groups would be canceled when taking the ratio. Hence many demand shocks simply affecting highly educated or younger workers would not affect the estimate of that elasticity. Third, and most important, in our estimates we also rely on an IV strategy based on a quasi-natural experiment: the German reunification. In the aftermath of the reunification (1991) a large increase in Eastern German immigrants was observed which was simply due to the fact that migrating became a possibility. Hence, treating the inflow of Eastern Germans as a pure supply shock, post-1991, we perform several 2SLS estimations using that flow as an instrument for all new immigrants. Notice, finally, that if some demand shock, not controlled for, were still driving part of the correlation (between relative wages and relative supply of new immigrants) that would likely bias our estimates of the inverse elasticity of substitution towards 0. Hence, particularly for the elasticity of substitution between native and immigrants, our estimates (around 0.04–0.05) could be a lower bound of the actual inverse elasticity, which would imply even lower substitutability between native and immigrants and certainly less than perfect substitutability.

4.2. Employment effects

We first estimate the response of old (i.e., long-term) immigrants' and natives' employment levels to the inflow of new immigrants in the same education–experience cells. Such an adjustment in employment likely depends on wage rigidities and frictions that prevent full wage adjustment.

4.2.1. New and old immigrants

To estimate the impact of immigrants on the employment of native workers, we estimate the empirical specification (9) described in Section 2.2. Since the data used are yearly data, the coefficient γ captures the short-run employment effect of recent immigration on the employment of previous immigrants. A value of $\gamma = 1$ implies that an inflow of new immigrants with education k and experience j equal to 1% of the initial employment in that cell is associated with an increase in total immigrant employment within the same education–experience cell of 1%. In this case, new immigrants add to previous employment without crowding out any old immigrants so there is no response of employment of old immigrants to inflows of new immigrants. In contrast, an estimated value of $\gamma < 1$ implies that new immigrants crowd out the employment of old immigrants inducing a decrease in their employment.

Table 3 reports the estimates of the coefficient γ from estimating Eq. (9). Different columns show estimates from different specifications. Column (1) reports the basic specification: Least Squares estimates, weighting each cell by the total employment in it, spanning the period 1987–2001, including males only in the sample and considering the sum of Eastern Germans, foreign nationals and ethnic Germans born abroad as immigrants. Specification (2) omits the ethnic German imputation, specification (3) includes both men and women in the sample. In specification (4) we assign workers to education cells according to their imputed education (computed as described in the Data Appendix). Specifications (5) and (6) restrict data to subsamples that omit the very early years (pre-unification) or recent years. Finally the last two columns (7) and (8) estimate the coefficient γ using 2SLS with the flow of Eastern Germans as an instrument for total immigrants. Most of the point-estimates of γ are between 0.6 and 0.7, and in all cases the hypothesis $\gamma = 1$ can be rejected at standard confidence levels against the alternative $\gamma < 1$. This constitutes evidence that new immigrants are crowding out old immigrants. The estimates of γ are the lowest when using the 2SLS method, implying the largest crowding out. Notice that the first stage reveals that the inflow of Eastern Germans is a powerful instrument.[11] In the post-1991 period, the inflow of Eastern Germans represented a very sizeable group among new immigrants. A formal test cannot reject the hypothesis that WLS and 2SLS estimates are identical. This suggests that, if we believe that the inflow of Eastern Germans was mainly a supply shock, the largest part of the immigration fluctuations are supply-driven once we control for year and cell fixed effects. Our estimates for γ imply that, on average, when 10 new immigrants find employment in Germany, 3–4 old immigrants lose their jobs.

4.2.2. Immigrants and natives

To analyze the impact of immigration on native employment we estimate Eq. (10) described in Section 2.2. The parameter ρ in (10) captures the impact of immigration on total employment. If it is smaller than 1, it implies that

---

[11] The F-test is above 200, much larger than the lower bound of 10 suggested by the literature on weak instruments (Bound et al., 1995; Stock and Yogo, 2002).

Table 3
Estimates of γ: the effect of new immigrants on total immigrant employment.

Column	(1) Basic	(2) No ethnic imputation	(3) Males and female	(4) Imputed education	(5) 1992–2001 subsample	(6) 1987–1999 subsample	(7) 2SLS, basic	(8) 2SLS, no ethnic imputation
Estimate of γ	0.6860***	0.668***	0.623***	0.727***	0.658***	0.640***	0.580***	0.590***
	(0.097)	(0.105)	(0.094)	(0.077)	(0.093)	(0.094)	(0.11)	(0.11)
P-value: H_0: $\gamma = 1$	0.004	0.005	0.001	0.002	0.002	0.002	0.00	0.00
Period	1987–2001	1987–2001	1987–2001	1987–2001	1992–2001	1987–1999	1992–2001	1992–2001
Group	Males	Males	Males and females	Males	Males	Males	Males	Males
Ethnics' imputation	Yes	No	Yes	Yes	Yes	Yes	Yes	No
Equivalent education	No	No	No	Yes	No	No	No	No
Observations	313	313	313	313	210	271	210	210
First stage								
East–West migrants							1.01	1.00
Standard error							0.04	0.07
T statistic							25.42	14.47
F-test of exclusion							163.40	209.42

Note: Dependent variable is the yearly change in total immigrant employment in an education–experience cell as a percentage of initial immigrant employment in the cell; the explanatory variable is the change in new immigrant employment as a percentage of the initial immigrant employment. New immigrants are those who have been in the country five years or less. Each regression, weighted by the number of workers in the education–experience-period cell, includes education, experience and year fixed effects. Each observation point is an education–experience cell in a year. In parenthesis we report the heteroskedasticity-robust standard errors, clustered by education–experience group.
***, **, * different from 0 at the 1%, 5%, 10% significance level.

Table 4
Estimates of ρ the effects of immigrants on total employment.

Column	(1) Basic	(2) No ethnic imputation	(3) Males and female	(4) Imputed education	(5) 1992–2001 subsample	(6) 1987–1999 subsample	(7) 2SLS, basic	(8) 2SLS, no ethnic imputation
Estimates of ρ	1.272***	1.327***	1.023***	1.358***	1.280***	1.207***	2.683***	2.819***
	(0.384)	(0.391)	(0.520)	(0.431)	(0.530)	(0.324)	(1.015)	(1.069)
T statistic	3.310	3.393	1.967	3.151	2.416	3.728	2.640	2.640
P-value: H_0: $\rho = 1$	0.487	0.412	0.965	0.415	0.603	0.529	0.097	0.089
Period	1987–2001	1987–2001	1987–2001	1987–2001	1992–2001	1987–1999	1992–2001	1992–2001
Group	Males	Males	Males and females	Males	Males	Males	Males	Males
Ethnics' imputation	Yes	No	Yes	Yes	Yes	Yes	Yes	No
Equivalent education	No	No	No	Yes	No	No	No	No
Observations	359	359	359	359	240	311	238	238
First stage								
East–West migrants							1.29	1.23
Standard error							0.17	0.17
T statistic							7.58	7.34
F-test of exclusion							57.38	53.91

Note: Dependent variable is the yearly change in total employment in an education–experience cell as a percentage of the initial employment in the cell; the explanatory variable is the change in immigrant employment in the same cell as a percentage of the initial employment. Each regression, weighted by the number of workers in the education–experience-period cell, includes education, experience and year fixed effects. In parenthesis we report the heteroskedasticity-robust standard errors, clustered by education–experience group.
***,**,* different from 0 at the 1%, 5%, 10% significance level.

immigrants crowd natives out. If it equals 1, new immigrants have no impact on native employment. Table 4 presents the estimates of the coefficient ρ. The different specifications across columns of Table 4 mirror those of Table 3. In this case, while the estimates are less precise, they are all above one. We can never reject the hypothesis of $\rho = 1$ at any significance level and even the point estimates seem to rule out the possibility of crowding out. The 2SLS estimates, while they are very imprecise in part because the inflow of Eastern Germans is not as good an instrument for the change in employment of total immigrants as it was for new immigrants, confirm this result. All in all, the estimates in Table 4 do not provide any support for the idea that changes in immigrant employment crowd out employment of native Germans. These results seem to preclude the presence of adverse employment effects of new immigrants on natives even in the short run (as we use yearly observations). To further check this result, we run another regression (not in the table) in which we stratify native

F. D'Amuri et al. / European Economic Review 54 (2010) 550–570   561

and migrant workers according to their education only, instead of using the finer stratification of education–experience cells. If Western German employers valued differently the work experience acquired inside and outside Western Germany, our labor market segmentation along education and experience levels could fail to appropriately identify groups of workers competing for the same jobs. Also, if there are employment effects spilling across experience groups one would not capture them with the above regression. Hence, we group workers according to their education level only and we run the following regression:

$$\frac{\Delta EMPL_{kt}}{EMPL_{kt-1}} = D_k + Trend_k + \rho_{EDU}\frac{\Delta M_{kt}}{M_{kt-1}} + u_{kt}$$

where $EMPL_{kt-1} = \sum_j EMPL_{kjt-1}$, $M_{kt} = \sum_j M_{kjt-1}$ and u_{kt} is a zero mean education-specific shock. This regression controls for education fixed effects (D_k) as well as education-specific trends ($Trend_k$) and is estimated with the usual samples. The point estimate of ρ_{EDU} in the basic specification is 1.48 (standard error 0.51) so that we cannot reject $\rho_{EDU} = 1$. The limit of this regression is that it is run on 45 observations only.

The results from employment regressions imply that *there is no evidence of adverse effects of new immigration on the employment levels of native workers, while long-term immigrants seem negatively affected by newcomers.*

4.3. Elasticities of substitution

4.3.1. New and old immigrants

In order to estimate the elasticity of substitution between immigrants, we estimate Eq. (12) obtained from the labor demand conditions and we capture the relative demand term $\ln(\theta_{kjt}^{OLD}/\theta_{kjt}^{NEW})$ using fixed education (D_k), experience (D_j) and year (D_t) effects. Hence we implement the following specification:

$$\ln\left(\frac{w_{Mkjt}^{OLD}}{w_{Mkjt}^{NEW}}\right) = D_k + D_j + D_t - \frac{1}{\lambda}\ln\left(\frac{M_{kjt}^{OLD}}{M_{kjt}^{NEW}}\right) + u_{kjt} \tag{19}$$

Essentially we allow the relative new/old immigrant productivity to depend systematically on their education, age and on the year. We interpret the remaining within-cell variation of migrants over time as being supply driven. The response of relative wages identifies the inverse elasticity of substitution between new and old immigrants. The corresponding estimates are reported in Table 5. Different specifications check the robustness of results to different definitions of the sample, of immigrants, and of the education groups. Specification (1) adopts the basic specification described above, specification (2) does not include the imputed ethnic Germans among immigrants. Specification (3) includes men and women in the sample, specification (4) includes only people who worked full time during the year (meaning for at least 40 weeks) and specification (5) groups workers according to their occupation-industry imputed schooling. Finally, specifications (6) and (7) consider two sub-samples and (8) and (9) adopt 2SLS as the estimation method using Eastern German immigrants as an instrument for total immigrants. The estimates are quite precise and consistent across specifications. The point estimates of the inverse elasticity are around 0.01 with a standard error also close to 0.01. In most cases we can reject a value for the inverse elasticity larger than 0.03. Hence no evidence of imperfect substitutability between new and old immigrants is found. Thus, new and old immigrants are perfectly substitutable, $\lambda = \infty$ and all immigrants belonging to each education–experience group can be considered as an homogeneous group of workers, which is what we assume in the remainder of the analysis ($M_{kjt} = M_{kjt}^{OLD} + M_{kjt}^{NEW}$).

4.3.2. Natives and immigrants

Following the same strategy we estimate the degree of substitutability between native and immigrant workers within education–experience cells. Specifically, we implement Eq. (12) with education, experience and year fixed effects to control for relative productivity levels. Table 6 reports the values of $1/\sigma$ from estimating the equation below:

$$\ln\left(\frac{w_{Mkjt}}{w_{Hkjt}}\right) = D_k + D_j + D_t - \frac{1}{\sigma}\ln\left(\frac{M_{kjt}}{H_{kjt}}\right) + u_{kjt} \tag{20}$$

Following the same type of specifications as in Table 5 we obtain a range of estimates of $1/\sigma$. All columns show significant values between 0.03 and 0.06 with standard errors around 0.01 and never larger than 0.02. While the values are not too large, they systematically indicate some degree of imperfect substitutability. Moreover, these estimates are perfectly in line with what Ottaviano and Peri (2008) and Card (2009) find for the US (a value around 0.05), and are somewhat smaller than the values estimated for the UK by Manacorda et al. (2006), which range between 0.1 and 0.2. While small, these elasticity values, coupled with the large increase in immigrants relative to natives in most groups, deliver significant effects on the relative native-immigrant wage ratio. In particular, consider that the percentage of immigrants in Germany went from 9% to 14% between 1987 and 2001, implying an increase in the M_t/H_t ratio for the aggregate economy of 64%. This would imply, using the median estimate of 0.045 as the inverse elasticity, an increase in the wage of natives relative to immigrants of $0.045 * 0.64 = 2.8\%$.

562   F. D'Amuri et al. / European Economic Review 54 (2010) 550–570

Table 5
Estimates of $1/\lambda$, the inverse elasticity of substitution between new and old immigrants.

Column	(1) Basic	(2) No ethnic imputation	(3) Males and female	(4) Full time workers only	(5) Imputed equivalent education	(6) 1992–2001 subsample	(7) 1987–1999 subsample	(8) 2SLS, basic	(9) 2SLS, no ethnic imputation
Estimation method	OLS	OLS	OLS	OLS	OLS	OLS	OLS	2SLS	2SLS
Estimate of $1/\lambda$	0.017	0.014	0.000	0.022	0.004	0.017	0.010	0.02	0.02
	(0.011)	(0.010)	(0.009)	(0.012)	(0.010)	(0.010)	(0.010)	(0.01)	(0.01)
Period	1987–2001	1987–2001	1987–2001	1987–2001	1987–2001	1992–2001	1987–1999	1992–2001	1992–2001
Group	Males	Males	Males and females	Males	Males	Males	Males	Males	Males
Ethnics' imputation	Yes	No	Yes	Yes	Yes	Yes	Yes	Yes	No
Equivalent education	No	No	No	No	Yes	No	No	No	No
Wages of FY work. only	No	No	No	Yes	Yes	No	No	No	No
Observations	313	313	313	313	313	210	313	210	210
First stage									
East-West migrants								0.66	0.67
Standard error								0.05	0.05
T statistic								12.10	13.85
F-test of exclusion								146.74	191.91

Note: Dependent variable is the relative new/old immigrant wages in an experience–education cell, explanatory variable is the relative new/old immigrant employment in the cell. Each regression, weighted by the number of workers in the education–experience–period cell, includes education, experience and year fixed effects. In parenthesis we report the heteroskedasticity-robust standard errors, clustered by education–experience group. ***,**,* different from 0 at the 1%, 5%, 10% significance level.

Table 6
Estimates of $1/\sigma$, the inverse elasticity of substitution between immigrants and natives.

Column	(1) Basic	(2) No ethnic imputation	(3) Males and females	(4) Full time workers only	(5) Imputed education	(6) 1992–2001 subsample	(7) 1987–1999 subsample	(8) 2SLS, basic	(9) 2SLS, no ethnic imputation
Estimation method	OLS	OLS	OLS	OLS	OLS	OLS	OLS	IV	IV
Estimates of $1/\sigma$	0.046***	0.046***	0.038***	0.035***	0.037*	0.029**	0.060***	0.030**	0.030**
	(0.011)	(0.011)	(0.011)	(0.011)	(0.020)	(0.013)	(0.013)	(0.016)	(0.013)
Period	1987–2001	1987–2001	1987–2001	1987–2001	1987–2001	1992–2001	1987–1999	1992–2001	1992–2001
Group	Males	Males	Males and females	Males	Males	Males	Males	Males	Males
Ethnics' imputation	Yes	No	Yes	Yes	Yes	Yes	Yes	Yes	No
Equivalent education	No	No	No	No	Yes	No	No	No	No
Wages of FY work. only*	No	No	No	Yes	Yes	No	No	No	No
Observations	359	359	359	359	359	240	359	238	238
First stage									
East-West migrants								0.80	0.80
Standard error								0.05	0.05
T statistic								16.24	17.29
F-test of exclusion								263.67	298.86

Note: The dependent variable is the relative native/immigrant wages in an experience–education cell; the explanatory variable is the relative native/immigrant employment in the cell. Each regression, weighted by the number of workers in the education–experience–period cell, includes education, experience and year fixed effects. In parenthesis we report the heteroskedasticity-robust standard errors, clustered by education–experience group. ***,**,* different from 0 at the 1%, 5%, 10% significance level.

4.3.3. Across experience and education groups

Following the implications of the model in Section 2 we can use the expressions (15) and (16) to estimate $1/\eta$ and $1/\delta$, the inverse elasticity of substitution between experience and education groups. In particular, following Ottaviano and Peri (2008) we implement regressions (21) and (22) below:

$$\ln(\overline{W}_{kjt}) = D_t + D_j + Time\ Trend_k - \frac{1}{\eta}\ln(\hat{L}_{kjt}) + u_{kjt} \tag{21}$$

$$\ln(\overline{W}_{kt}) = D_t + Time\ Trend_k - \frac{1}{\delta}\ln(\hat{L}_{kt}) + u_{kt} \tag{22}$$

F. D'Amuri et al. / European Economic Review 54 (2010) 550–570　　　563

Table 7
Estimates of the inverse elasticity of substitution between workers with different potential experience $(1/\eta)$ and education $(1/\delta)$.

Estimated parameter	$1/\eta$		$1/\delta$	
Column	(1)	(2)	(3)	(4)
	Using the model to calculate (L_{kj}) as a CES composite	L_{kj} calculated as simple employment count	Using the model to calculate L_k as a CES composite	L_k calculated as simple employment count
Coefficient	0.31***	0.33***	0.34***	0.37***
Standard error	(0.11)	(0.13)	(0.14)	(0.16)
Education trend	Yes	Yes	Yes	Yes
Experience dummies	Yes	Yes	–	–
Year dummies	Yes	Yes	Yes	Yes
Observations	359	359	45	45

Note: In columns 1 and 2 the dependent variable is the average daily wage in real terms for the education–experience group. In column (1) the explanatory variable is log of L_{kj} obtained as a CES composite of natives and immigrants for a value of $1/\sigma = 0.046$. In column (2) the explanatory variable is the log of the L_{kj} obtained as the simple sum of native and immigrant employment. The method of estimation used is 2SLS using as instrumental variable for $\ln(L_{kj})$ the variable $\ln(M_{kj})$, that is the log of immigrant employment in the cell. In columns 3 and 4 the dependent variable is the average daily wage in real terms for the education group. In column (3) the explanatory variable is log of L_k obtained as a CES composite of different experience groups for a value of $1/\eta = 0.31$. In column (4) the explanatory variable is the log of the L_k obtained as the simple sum of employment across experience groups. The method of estimation is 2SLS using as instrumental variable for $\ln(L_k)$ the variable $\ln(M_k)$, that is the log of immigrant employment in the education cell. Standard errors are heteroskedasticity-robust clustered at the education–experience level. Regressions are weighted with the number of workers in each cell.
***,**,* different from 0 at the 1%, 5%, 10% significance level.

The dependent variable is the log average wage in the education–experience group ($\overline{W}_{kjt}$) or in the education ($\overline{W}_{kt}$) group. In (21) we control for an education-specific time trend (*Time Trend$_k$*) and for year (D_t) and experience (D_j) fixed effects, while in (22) we use time dummies and education-specific time trends (*Time Trend$_k$*) to control for the change in cell-specific productivity. In both regressions we allow for a zero-mean disturbance. Instrumenting for the change in the cell labor-composites, $\hat{L}_{kjt}$ and $\hat{L}_{kt}$, with the inflow of immigrants (assumed to be supply-driven once we control for the fixed effects), we can obtain consistent estimates of the coefficients $1/\eta$ and $1/\delta$.

Table 7 reports the estimates of $1/\eta$, which are between 0.31 and 0.33. In column (1), the supply index $\hat{L}_{kjt}$ is constructed using a CES aggregator of native and immigrant employment with $1/\sigma = 0.046$. In column (2) the supply index is the simple sum of native and immigrant employment. Similarly, columns 3 and 4 present the estimates of $1/\delta$ which range, respectively, between 0.34 when the supply index is constructed as a CES aggregate and 0.37 when the supply index is constructed as the sum of employment across education cells. These estimates imply an elasticity of substitution between education groups of around 2.9 and across experience groups of 3.3. The first is a bit larger than the corresponding estimates for the US (usually ranging between 1.5 and 2.5) and the second is smaller than its US counterpart, usually estimated between 5 and 10 (see, e.g., Card and Lemieux, 2001). On the other hand, using a comparable sample Brucker and Jahn (2008) report estimated values for the parameter $1/\delta$ close to 0.3. While this is similar to ours, they estimate a lower value of $1/\eta$ around 0.06. The elasticity across age groups, however, does not play much of a role in our simulations in which we aim at characterizing the wage effect across education groups and between natives and immigrants. Hence, we use our estimated elasticity $1/\eta$ in simulating the wage effects of immigration and reassure the reader that using the Brucker and Jahn (2008) elasticity estimates of $1/\eta$ would give essentially identical results.

4.4. Wage effects

Based on the expressions (17) and (18) of Section 2 we are now able to evaluate the total impact of immigration on the wages of native and old migrant workers. In so doing, we rely on the employment effects estimated in Section 4.2 and the elasticities of substitution σ, λ, η and δ estimated in Section 4.3. Section 4.4.1 analyzes the impact of the inflow of new immigrants between 1992 and 2001 on average wages and the total wage income of old (pre-1992) immigrants.[12] Then Section 4.4.2 focuses on the impact of the same flow of immigrants on wages of native workers.

4.4.1. Wage effects on long-term immigrants, 1992–2001

The effects of new immigration on the wages of long-term immigrants are given by expression (18). Following Ottaviano and Peri (2008) and Ortega and Peri (2009) we also assume adjustment of capital to keep return to capital constant. This is an appropriate long-run assumption and Ortega and Peri (2009) show that this seems to be the case also for yearly inflow of immigrants into European countries.[13]

---

[12] We define as post-1992 (pre-1992) immigrants who appear in our dataset 1992 or later (strictly before 1992).
[13] A slower short-run adjustment of capital would imply a negative short-run additional impact for all wages.

564   F. D'Amuri et al. / European Economic Review 54 (2010) 550–570

Table 8
Simulated long-run effects of immigration, 1992–2001.

Educational level		No vocational edu.	Vocational edu.	Higher edu.	Average edu.
Long term immigrants					
Percentage changes in real wages					
Due to east–west movers	Direct immigration effect (A)	0.17	−0.54	−1.08	−0.22
	Response effect (B)	−0.04	0.37	0.59	0.18
	Total effect (A+B)	0.14	−0.17	−0.49	−0.04
Due to foreigners	Direct immigration effect (A)	−1.63	−0.34	−1.57	−1.07
	Response effect (B)	0.79	0.32	0.95	0.60
	Total effect (A+B)	−0.84	−0.02	−0.62	−0.47
Total	Direct immigration effect (A)	−1.46	−0.88	−2.65	−1.29
	Response effect (B)	0.76	0.69	1.54	0.78
	Total effect (A+B)	−0.70	−0.19	−1.11	−0.51
Percentage changes in real wage bill					
Due to east–west movers		−0.93	−9.74	−14.37	−5.71
Due to foreigners		−10.11	−11.86	−25.12	−11.93
Total		−11.04	−21.60	−39.49	−17.64
Native workers					
Percentage changes in real wages					
$\sigma = 21.5$		1.68	−0.14	−1.01	−0.02
$\sigma = $ Infinite		1.85	−0.25	−1.26	−0.11

Note: Long-run simulations, assuming that capital adjusts over the period to keep the real return constant. The columns labeled 'direct immigration effects' show the real wage impact of a change in supply due to new immigrants, while those labeled 'indirect effect' show the wage impact of the reduction in labor supply of old immigrants in response to new immigration. The reported values express changes in share of initial wages so that 1 means a change of 1% of the initial wage. Parameters used for the simulation: $\delta = 2.9$, $\eta = 3.3$; $\sigma = 21.5$ (unless differently specified); $\lambda = 58.1$; $\gamma = 0.69$.

Table 8 reports the simulated wage effects of immigration obtained using the average point estimates for the elasticity parameters, namely $\delta = 2.9$, $\eta = 3.3$, $\sigma = 21.5$, $\lambda = 58.1$ and $\gamma = 0.69$. The terms on the right-hand side of formula (18) can be sorted into three groups, contained in each square bracket. The first terms (containing the expressions $\Delta M^{NEW}_{kjt} / M^{NEW}_{kjt}$) capture the *direct* effect of the change in the supply of new immigrants on wages. The second and third terms, containing the expressions $(\Delta M^{OLD}_{kjt} / M^{OLD}_{kjt})_{response}$ and $(\Delta H_{kjt} / H_{kjt})_{response}$ capture the indirect wage effects, due to the change in supply of old immigrants and natives triggered by the inflow of new immigrants. In light of the estimates of Tables 3 and 4 the terms $(\Delta H_{kjt} / H_{kjt})_{response}$ are essentially 0 while $(\Delta M^{OLD}_{kjt} / M^{OLD}_{kjt})_{response}$ is around −0.4% for an increase in new immigrants equal to 1% of the cell employment. In Table 8 the direct and indirect effects of new immigrants are reported and denoted by A and B, respectively. The table shows the direct, indirect and total wage effects of new immigration from Eastern Germany, from the rest of the world including Ethnic Germans and the total effects, obtained by adding the two flows. Notice, intuitively, that the indirect effects, driven by the reduced employment of old immigrants, attenuate the negative wage impact of new immigrants on previous immigrants. This is because the reduction in old immigrants' employment is a partial offset of the increased supply of new immigrants. Table 8 shows that the overall effects of 10 years worth of new immigration on the wages of old immigrants are negative, implying an average loss for the pre-1992 immigrant workers of 0.5% of their real wage. This is not a particularly large number for two reasons: first, the inflow of new immigrants between 1992 and 2001 increased the share of foreign-born in employment by only 2.2 percentage points, which is a 20% increase in the initial level; second, the elasticity of substitution between natives and immigrants, while not infinite, is fairly large so that the effect of new immigrants on wages spreads in part to natives too. Old immigrant workers with a high level of education suffer the largest wage losses (−1.11%), which is explained by the fact that post-1992 immigration to Western Germany is relatively high-skilled, mainly due to Eastern Germans (see in column 1 the direct effect of Eastern German immigration on wages of the highly educated). The reduction in the employment levels of old immigrants, in response to immigration, attenuates the negative impact of immigration on the wages of those who keep their job by 0.78% on average, and by 1.5% for the highly educated.

Eastern German immigrants account for almost half of the negative wage effect on highly educated workers while they account for none of the negative effect on less educated workers. This is due to the fact that Eastern German immigrants are on average more educated than immigrants from the rest of the world.

Overall, Table 8 shows that the wage response of old immigrants to new immigrants is not too large. This leads us to inquire more carefully into the employment effect and to quantify it in terms of aggregate wage income lost. One way of doing this is to consider the effect of immigration on the wage bill of old immigrants: while the average wage of old immigrants is not much affected, their employment is and this would show in the wage bill. Table 8 reports the simulated effect of immigration 1992–2001 on the total wage bill of old immigrants. Such effect combines the decrease in employment and the decrease in the average wages of each worker who keeps her job. Combining employment and wage losses, immigration from Eastern Germany reduced the total wage bill of old immigrants by 5.7% while immigration from

F. D'Amuri et al. / European Economic Review 54 (2010) 550–570   565

the rest of the world added a further negative effect of 11.9%. Immigration from Eastern Germany penalized only the highly educated, while immigration from the rest of the world had a more balanced effect. Overall, the wage bill of old immigrants was reduced by a substantial 17.6%, and this loss was mainly driven by lost employment. These simulations already suggest that the loss in employment for long-term immigrants was the most costly consequence of immigration. In particular, such an employment response, combined with generous unemployment benefits (as we will illustrate below) constituted a large burden on the German welfare system. The question is whether the aggregate cost of employment losses (lost production) and unemployment benefits was larger than the cost in terms of wage losses that old immigrants would have experienced in a flexible labor market in which wages would have adjusted to absorb the full inflow of immigrants without a reduction in the employment of old immigrants. These counter-factual calculations will be performed in Section 5.

In summary, we can say that *new immigrants penalized old immigrants primarily in terms of employment, and only a small amount by decreasing their wages.* In terms of wages, old immigrants with high education and old immigrants with no vocational education were the groups hurt the most.

4.4.2. Wage effects on natives, 1992–2001

Turning to the effects of immigration on native wages, we use expression (17) with no employment effects for natives ($\mu = 1$) and imperfect substitutability between native and immigrant workers. The lower panel of Table 8 reports the simulated wage effect for natives with three different educational attainments over the period 1992–2001. We report the results when we consider imperfect substitutability between natives and immigrants and, for reference, those obtained assuming perfect substitutability between natives and immigrants. With imperfect substitutability, no average impact of immigration on native wages is found over the period 1992–2001. Across educational levels, relatively low educated workers experience a moderate improvement in their wage levels ($+1.68$%), while highly educated ones suffer a small loss (-1%). This is again due to the fact that, during the period of observation, immigration to Germany (mostly from Eastern Germany) was relatively skilled. These small wage effects are consistent with the absence of negative employment effects found in Section 4.2.2. Moreover, even when we impose perfect substitutability ($\sigma = \infty$) between natives and immigrants, the overall effect on wages is negative but still very close to zero, with the same distributional pattern across educational groups as in the case of $\sigma = 21.5$. Hence, *new immigrants did not penalize native workers much either in terms of employment or in terms of wages.* Indeed, native workers with low education experienced a rise in their wages.

5. Comparison with the scenario of full wage flexibility

The main finding of the previous section is that new immigrants did not affect native workers much in terms of either employment or wages, while they did have a negative impact on old immigrants, mostly in terms of employment and only a little in terms of wages. In this section we propose a simple calculation whose aim is to compare the loss in the wage-bill of native and old immigrants between the actual scenario and one in which all the adjustment takes place only through wage changes. First, we calculate the impact of immigrants on natives and old immigrants in terms of foregone wage income and unemployment insurance, assuming that all old immigrants displaced by new immigrants are indeed covered by insurance. Second, we calculate the changes that natives' and immigrants' wages would undergo if wages adjusted to completely eliminate the employment effects on old immigrants. Then we compare the two aggregate amounts.

Our calculations focus on the year 2001. The results of the first calculation are shown at the bottom of Table 9 where all values are expressed in constant Euros at year 2000 prices. Column (1) shows that, based on an estimate of $\gamma = 0.69$, approximately 25,600 old immigrants were displaced by the inflow of new immigrants in 2001. This number of displaced workers can be multiplied by the average yearly wage of old immigrants (equal to 25,996 as shown in column (3)) to obtain the 665 million Euros of foregone wage income reported in column (5). On top of this, the total yearly cost sustained to fund the unemployment insurance is shown in column (4), which multiplies the number of displaced old immigrant workers by unemployment insurance payments. Following Adema et al. (2003), these payments are set at 14,449 Euros per displaced worker, leading to the total value of 370 million Euros.[14] Thus, in the presence of employment effects associated with wage rigidity, in 2001 the overall yearly cost of new immigration in foregone wages and unemployment benefits was around 1 billion Euros.

Table 10 reports what would have happened to the wages of natives and old immigrants if they had been allowed to fall to preserve full employment. Based on (17), (18) and parameter estimates, column (3) shows that the employment effects on old immigrants would have disappeared if their average wage had fallen by 0.15% relative to its actual level, with a corresponding rise of 0.016% in native wages.[15] These percentage variations are first multiplied by the average yearly wages in column (2), then by the employment levels in column (1) to obtain the overall changes in the wage bills paid to native and old immigrant workers.[16] These are reported in column (5) where old immigrants suffer in aggregate a wage

---

[14] This is just a lower bound estimate of the overall cost borne by taxpayers because the full cost should also include unemployment assistance (for the long-term unemployed), housing benefits, active labor market policies, etc.

[15] The wages of natives rise thanks to the imperfect substitutability between natives and immigrants.

[16] Average yearly wages are computed from our sample by multiplying the average daily wages by the average number of days worked in a year.

566 F. D'Amuri et al. / European Economic Review 54 (2010) 550–570

Table 9
Estimated effects of new immigrants on natives and old immigrants with displacement.

Column	(1) Number of displaced old immigrants	(2) Cost for unemployed worker	(3) Average yearly wage	(4) = (1 * 2) Absolute yearly cost of unemployment insurance	(5) = (1 * 3) Absolute yearly wage loss from displacement
Unemployment insurance for displaced workers	25,586	14,449		369,694,682	
Foregone production	25,586		25,996		665,129,807

Note: Parameter used for the simulation of the employment effect: $\gamma = 0.69$.

Table 10
Policy experiment: redistributive effects.

Column	(1) Number of employed workers	(2) Average yearly wage	(3) Percentage wage variation	(4) = (2 * 3) Absolute variation in yearly wage	(5) = 1 * 4 Total yearly variation	(6) Average yearly cost per worker[a]	(7) = (1 * 6) Total yearly cost[a]
			Wage losses under wage flexibility			Unemployment insurance cost[a] in wage-rigid markets	
Total natives	8,519,550	30,917	0.016	5.0	42,758,744	38.0	324,023,685
No vocational education	1,448,750	18,993	−0.006	−1.2	−1,708,739	23.4	33,849,305
Vocational education	5,972,550	31,619	0.031	9.8	58,333,987	38.9	232,310,814
Higher education	1,098,250	42,829	−0.029	−12.6	−13,866,505	52.7	57,863,566
Total old immigrants	1,428,150	25,996	−0.153	−39.7	−56,633,145	32.0	45,670,997
No vocational education	573,700	22,310	−0.117	−26.1	−14,951,133	27.4	15,745,620
Vocational education	747,150	26,818	−0.124	−33.1	−24,756,151	33.0	24,649,383
Higher education	107,300	39,979	−0.395	−157.7	−16,925,860	49.2	5,275,994
Total	9,947,700	30,210	−0.005	−1.4	−13,874,401	37.2	369,694,682

Note: Parameters used for the simulations: $\delta = 2.9$, $\eta = 3.3$; $\sigma = 21.5$; $\lambda = 58.1$; $\gamma = 0.69$. Employment is calculated as the total count of workers employed as of 1 July of year 2000. Average yearly wages are expressed in 2000 Euros.
[a] The average yearly cost sustained by each type of worker to finance the unemployment insurance scheme assumed to be proportional to her wage.

decrease of 57 million Euros whereas natives enjoy a wage increase of slightly less than 43 million Euros. Hence, the immigration of 2001, with no employment response and full wage adjustment would have implied a decrease in the total wage bill of natives and old immigrants equal to 14 million Euros (last row of column (5)). Table 10 column (4) shows also the wage effect for each education group in the presence of no employment effects. The group receiving the biggest loss is that of highly educated old immigrants who still would only experience a decrease of 158 Euros per year. Column 5 shows the total wage losses by education and nativity group under the scenario of no employment effect (and full wage adjustment). Column 7 shows, by comparison, the overall costs sustained to finance unemployment benefits for displaced immigrants (in the case of wage rigidities) if those were funded by a tax proportional to the wage level of each worker, thus penalizing the relatively better educated. The cost of immigration on the employed old immigrants and on natives is much (20 times) larger under the scenario of wage rigidity and unemployment insurance than in the scenario with full wage flexibility and no effect on employment (from the comparison of the last row of column (5) and column (7) of Table 10).

To sum up, immigration seems to be much more costly when labor market adjustment happens mostly via the employment margin rather than through the wage margin. The institutional characteristics of the German labor market, such as the very generous unemployment benefits scheme (virtually open-ended, long-term unemployment assistance, 'Arbeitslosenhilfe', was abolished only in 2005), hurt the efficient absorption of the migration supply shock occurred in that period. This result is in line with Angrist and Kugler (2003), who argue that the reaction of a country's labor market to immigration depends on its institutional features and, in particular, that more 'flexible' labor markets are more effective in absorbing the supply shocks arising from migrant inflows. In recent times, a series of reforms have increased the flexibility of the German labor market. In 2002, the Job-Aqtiv Act increased the sanctions on the unemployed for refusing a job offer. Starting in 2003, the so-called Hartz reforms reduced the level, as well as the duration, of unemployment benefits, rationalized the overall social assistance scheme in order to increase the incentives to work, further restricted the acceptable reasons for rejecting a job offer without losing benefits, and liberalized employment services (Ebbinghas and Eichhorst, 2009; Eichhorst and Kaiser, 2006). In general, the aim of these reforms was to accelerate labor market flows (Fahr and Sunde, 2006)

F. D'Amuri et al. / European Economic Review 54 (2010) 550–570   567

and to increase the incentives to work. Coupled with the diffusion of opening clauses from collective contracts (OECD, 2006), these reforms have increased the flexibility of the German labor market and thus the capacity to deal efficiently with labor supply shocks due to migration. Interestingly, in our context, among the beneficiaries of such flexibility are the long-term immigrants: with more flexibility they can retain their jobs (not be displaced), although at a lower wage. The benefit to other citizens is in the form of lower taxes, under the assumption that unemployment insurance is funded by a general tax.

6. Conclusion

This paper contributes to the recently revived literature analyzing the impact of immigration within a labor market equilibrium framework fully accounting for the interactions between production factors (Aydemir and Borjas, 2007; Borjas, 2003; Manacorda et al., 2006; Ottaviano and Peri, 2008; Peri, 2007). With respect to this literature, we have three novel contributions. First we produced new estimates of the elasticity parameters necessary to disentangle the wage effects of immigration on natives and old immigrants exploiting a large yearly panel of German workers, using yearly variations and relying on the (exogenous) large inflow of Eastern Germans after the fall of the Berlin Wall. Second, in order to better estimate the impact of new immigrants on old ones, we have extended the labor market equilibrium approach to allow for employment responses driven by wage rigidities. Taking these responses into account, we have been able to distinguish between the 'direct effect' of immigration, which refers to the change in wages taking place for given employment levels of natives and old immigrants, and the 'indirect effect', which refers to the change in wages due to changes in those employment levels. Third, using this model we have compared the aggregate wage-bill and unemployment insurance costs of the actual scenario, compared with a counter-factual scenario of full wage flexibility that preserves full employment.

Looking at the employment effects of immigration, we have found that new immigration had a negative impact on the employment of old immigrants and no impact on the employment of natives, suggesting closer competition between new and old immigrants than between immigrants and natives as well as different insider–outsider status of natives and immigrants. The estimated wage effects of new immigrants are on average very small for natives and small and negative for old immigrants. The most statistically and economically significant impact of new immigration is the negative employment effect on old immigrants driven by wage rigidities.

Acknowledgments

We thank Zvi Eckstein and two anonymous referees for their helpful and constructive comments. Mark Bryan, Andreas Damelang, Joan Esteban, Marco Francesconi, Anette Haas, Tim Hatton, David Jaeger, Arianna Miglietta, Cheti Nicoletti, Chiara Pronzato, Alfonso Rosolia, Thomas Siedler, Max Steinhardt and Silvia Stiller also provided helpful comments. D'Amuri is grateful for support from the Economic and Social Research Council. Ottaviano acknowledges the financial support from the European Commission and the Volkswagen Foundation as part of the Study Group 'Diversity, Integration and the Economy'. Peri gratefully acknowledges the John D. and Catherine T. MacArthur Foundation. The opinions expressed in this paper do not necessarily reflect those of the Bank of Italy.

Appendix A. Data appendix

A.1. Data refinements and comparison with the GSOEP

The IAB dataset is well suited for the analysis of labor market outcomes in the German labor market, especially for people with high attachment to the labor market such as male heads of households. One major advantage of these data is the very large, consistent and continuous coverage over time. For each employment spell, all the relevant information regarding the employees is collected by the employer and reported directly to the social security agencies. Measurement error is therefore kept to a minimum. The transmission of all the relevant information to the employment agency is mandatory, so that there are no issues arising from non-response. At the same time the sample is representative of total (social-security-paying) employment each year in the sample.

To obtain a representative sample of days worked in a year in the economy, in each relevant year we include men aged 17–64 who were working and receiving salary income on the 1st of July. Apart from seasonal fluctuations in employment, the probability of working that day (and hence being in the sample) is proportional to the number of days worked in a year. Hence the probability works as a weight for each worker by days worked. The number of hours worked per day is another possible dimension to look at. Unfortunately, daily hours worked are not reported in this dataset. Nevertheless, National Accounts data (available at http://www.sourceoecd.org.) show little year-to-year variations in hours worked per dependent worker for the period 1991–2001, controlled for by the year dummies which we employ in our regressions.

The IAB dataset has some limitations. We try to carefully address each one of them to produce a dataset that is as good and as representative as possible for our purposes. In Table 1 we compare systematically some summary statistics obtained from our refined dataset with summary statistics from a subsample of GSOEP for years 1987, 1991 and 2001 (the initial, an

568   *F. D'Amuri et al. / European Economic Review 54 (2010) 550–570*

intermediate and the final year for our empirical analysis), accurately selected in order to have an underlying population consistent with the IAB one.[17]

A first limitation of the IAB data is that there are no recall questions on the working history of each worker prior to the date of entry in the dataset. Hence we impute experience as potential experience that is equal to the worker's age minus the typical age at which she is expected to have completed her education (Borjas, 2003). The age of entry in the labor force is assumed to be 16 for individuals without A-level (in the German system, A-level corresponds with the completion of the second phase of the secondary school, see Carey, 2008) and without vocational education, 19 those without A-levels with vocational education or with A-levels without vocational education, 21 for A-levels with vocational education, 24 for those who completed non-university higher education and 25 for workers who hold a university degree. While this method can introduce some error, Table 1 shows the comparison of population mean and standard deviation of imputed experience (IAB) with actual experience from the GSOEP (worker history is available in these data). There is usually less than one year difference in the averages and standard deviations for both natives and immigrants.

A second and, for our purposes, more severe limitation of the IAB data is that for immigrants neither the place of birth, nor the year of arrival in Western Germany are recorded. What is available for each individual is the exact nationality at the country level. Since the focus of this paper is on immigration rather than nationality, this requires further assumptions about the link between the former and the latter. In particular, we assume that workers that declare *at least once* to be foreign nationals are immigrants. Hence, people who naturalize during the period under consideration (notice that since 2000 the naturalization laws have become less strict) are still considered immigrants. Also, there are very few people naturalized before 1975. On the other hand, the presence of a large second generation of immigrants with foreign nationality may produce an over-count of the number of immigrants. However, our main results are unaffected when we instrument total immigrants' shares using only Germans who moved from the East to the West after reunification, a recent flow of migrants for which the second generation group does not exist. Besides workers with *foreign nationality* we also identify two other groups as immigrants: German workers who migrated *from the East* to the West after reunification (and are recorded as Eastern German by the IAB); and *Ethnic German* workers, who primarily immigrated from Eastern Europe and who constitute a large share of recent immigrant inflows. The imputation of 'Ethnic German' workers has been done using external data sources and is described in detail in the Section A.2 below.

After these imputations we compare the share and characteristics of immigrants (including ethnic and Eastern Germans) in the IAB and in a subsample of the GSOEP (see Table 1). Notice again that their share in total employment is similar (in the IAB we have if anything a slight over-count) and their gender, experience and educational distribution are very close, except for a much larger share of highly educated immigrants in 2001 according to the GSOEP. The surge in the share of highly educated workers in GSOEP in 2001 is not due to a change in the definition of the relevant variable. As a robustness check we calculated the same statistic using the German data of the EU-LFS (EUROSTAT, 2008) on a sample selected approximately as the ones used in this comparison (data refer to 2002, we could not exclude the public sector and some Eastern regions) and found a slightly lower share of highly educated workers compared to the IAB. As this over-representation of the highly educated in the GSOEP is also present for natives it may be worth inquiring as to the cause, but it should not affect the procedures by which we impute immigrants nor should it affect much the measure of immigrants as percentage of the group among highly educated.

A third refinement on the data is that we impute the daily wage data which are right censored by the upper limit of the social insurance contribution in the IAB. Right censoring occurs in around 2% of the spells. Censored wages are imputed using the estimated wage values obtained from a Tobit regression model. This is run separately for each year and includes the following independent variables: experience, experience squared, educational attainment, nationality, 17 sector dummies and 131 occupational dummies. Table 1 shows that the average wages in IAB are 10–15% higher for all groups relative to those in GSOEP, and their standard deviation is similar in the two groups. As daily wages are not recorded in the GSOEP we recover them from gross monthly wages assuming that the average individual works a fraction of the month which is equal to the fraction of the days worked in the year as calculated from the IAB sample on a migration status and year basis. These fractions are equal to 0.98, 0.98 and 0.90 (natives) and 0.91, 0.89 and 0.85 (migrants) for the years 1987, 1991 and 2001, respectively.

A fourth refinement that we use in some regressions is to allow for educational downgrading. Immigrants, in fact, may accept jobs requiring a lower level of qualification than they have (Dustmann et al., 2007). In this case the reported level of education can be a poor indicator of the labor market position of immigrants, decreasing the precision of our stratification of workers across education–experience cells. In order to address this problem, we group native and immigrant workers according to reported education as well as according to 'adjusted' educational levels. In particular, similar to Card (2001, 2007), for each available year we run an ordered Probit regression for the native population with the reported level of education as the dependent variable and 17 sector plus 131 occupational dummies as independent variables. This regression estimates, for each worker, the probability of having each of the possible educational levels, given his position in the labor market. Out of sample predictions are obtained for all immigrant workers and for those natives who failed to report their educational level and should otherwise have been dropped from the sample. The corresponding densities,

---

[17] In particular, we select only non-marginal, private sector employees residing in the West, aged 17–64 and earning a positive wage. We use the cross-sectional weights to calculate all the reported statistics.

F. D'Amuri et al. / European Economic Review 54 (2010) 550–570   569

averaged across individuals in each year, are then used to calculate weighted employment and wage levels for our education–experience cells. While this correction should improve the homogeneity of workers' skills within the group, it is more subject to endogeneity bias as immigrants may adjust their occupation in Germany according to sector demand. For this reason, we only use it as a robustness check.

A.2. The Ethnic Germans' imputation

A worker is considered as Western German if her nationality is German and if she has always been working in Western Germany. All the others are considered as immigrants. Eastern Germans are considered as immigrants. They are identified as individuals with German nationality who started working in the East and then moved to the West within the considered period. Foreign migrants are individuals without German nationality at least in one observation or are *ethnic Germans* coming from abroad. Particular attention is devoted to identifying the consistent *ethnic German* group of immigrants,[18] not distinguishable from Western German nationals in the dataset since their nationality is German. These are foreign born immigrants mostly from Eastern European countries. The perception is that "Ethnic Germans are basically facing the same difficulties with social and economic integration as foreigners" (Zimmermann, 1999) and, therefore, they should be considered as foreign immigrants in our context. However, they are.

We estimate the total inflow of *ethnic Germans* in each education–experience-year group merging different sources of information. First, we obtain E_{xt}, the total yearly inflow of *ethnic Germans* by year of arrival t and country of origin x from Bundesverwaltungsamt (2003) and Statistisches-Bundesamt-Deutschland (2006), respectively. Then, from the IAB data we retrieve the exact information on the characteristics and labor market performance of foreign immigrants coming from the same set of countries in the same year of arrival as *ethnic Germans*.[19] Finally, we assume that, for country of origin x and year of arrival t, the educational and age composition of *ethnic Germans* is identical to that of foreign immigrants and that, within education–experience cells, *ethnic Germans* and foreign immigrants from the same country of origin have exactly the same labor market performance in terms of employment levels and wages. For example, we consider *ethnic Germans* who migrated to Western Germany from the Czech Republic in 1994 as exactly mirroring the observed and unobserved characteristics of the group of Czech citizens migrating to Western Germany in the same year.

Specifically, as a first step, for each of the major *ethnic Germans'* countries of origin x and each year t, we construct $f_{xkjt} = M_{xkjt}/M_{xt}$ as the share of immigrant workers with education k and experience j in the total immigrant flow. Notice that the total inflow of immigrants from country x and year t, M_{xt} is obtained from Bundesverwaltungsamt (2003) and Statistisches-Bundesamt-Deutschland (2006) while the number in each education-specific group M_{xkjt} is taken from the IAB. Hence the share f_{xkjt} corrects for the employment/population ratio and allows us to impute employment in each group from the total population of immigrants. We then calculate the imputed number of immigrant *ethnic German* workers from country x with education k and experience j in year t as $E_{xtkj} = E_{xt}f_{xtkj}$.

Since the inflows of *ethnic Germans* and foreign immigrants from a specific country x can be highly volatile, our second step is to smooth the imputed values by taking averages over two consecutive years. We then attribute to each group E_{xtkj} the average wage of foreign immigrants coming from the same country x in the same year t and with the same education and age. After those two steps, we obtain a complete education–experience distribution of employment and wages for the *ethnic German* immigrants by country of origin x and year of arrival t. Summing across different years of arrival (starting with 1987) and countries of origin, we finally obtain the employment levels within education–experience cells for each year. Similarly, the cell-specific wages are reconstructed using a weighted average of average wages by country of origin and year of arrival. As a final step, we subtract the imputed employment levels by cell from the analogous cells of the native Western German population and we add them to the immigrant population.

The procedure may systematically alter the education structure of ethnic immigrants if for each country of origin regular immigrants have a systematically different education than ethnic Germans. We confirm in two different ways that this potential mis-classification does not alter our findings. First, we run some regressions using the 'imputed' education of immigrants obtained from their occupation-industry rather than from their schooling. If ethnic Germans have a systematically different educational level they would choose appropriate occupations and the imputing of education should address this problem. Second, we specify some regressions omitting the ethnic Germans' imputation to see if it drives the results. While certainly imperfect, we think that our procedure uses the available data in its most efficient way and does not seem to introduce a systematic bias in the results.

References

Adema, W., Gray, D., Kahl, S., 2003. Social assistance in Germany. OECD Labour Market and Social Policy Occasional Papers 58.
Angrist, J., Kugler, A., 2003. Protective or counter-productive? Labour market institutions and the effect of immigration on EU natives. Economic Journal 113, 302–331.

---

[18] With the end of the Cold War a large number of *ethnic Germans* (slightly less than 3 million over the period 1989–2001, according to Bundesverwaltungsamt, 2003) previously living in Eastern Europe moved to Western Germany, settling there permanently.
[19] The countries are: Czech Republic, Slovakia, former Soviet Union, former Yugoslavia, Hungary, Poland, Romania.

Aydemir, A., Borjas, G., 2007. Cross-country variation in the impact of international migration: Canada, Mexico, and the United States. Journal of the European Economic Association 5, 663–708.

Bauer, T., Dietz, B., Zimmermann, K.F., Zwintz, E., 2005. German migration: development assimilation and labour market effects. In: Zimmermann, K.F. (Ed.), European Migration: What Do We Know?. Oxford University Press, Oxford, pp. 197–261.

Bender, S., Haas, A., Klose, C., 2000. IAB employment subsample 1975–1995. Opportunities for Analysis Provided by the Anonymised Subsample. IZA Discussion Paper (117).

Bonin, H., 2005. Wage and employment effects of immigration in Germany: evidence from a skill group approach. IZA Discussion Paper (1875).

Borjas, G., 2003. The labor demand curve is downward sloping: reexamining the impact of immigration on the labor market. Quarterly Journal of Economics 118, 1335–1374.

Borjas, G., Katz, L.F., 2007. The evolution of the Mexican-Born workforce in the United States. In: Borjas, G. (Ed.), Mexican Immigration to the United States. National Bureau of Economic Research.

Bound, J., Jaeger, D.A., Baker, R.M., 1995. Problems with instrumental variables estimation when the correlation between the instruments and the endogenous explanatory variable is weak. Journal of the American Statistical Association 90, 443–450.

Brucker, H., Jahn, E.J., 2008. Migration and the wage curve: a structural approach to measure the wage and employment effects of migration. IZA Discussion Paper (3423).

Bundesverwaltungsamt, 2003. Jahresstatistik Aussiedler.

Card, D., 2001. Immigrant inflows, native outflows, and the local labor market impacts of immigration. Journal of Labor Economics 19, 22–64.

Card, D., 2007. How immigration affects U.S. cities. CREAM Discussion Papers Series (11).

Card, D., 2009. Immigration and inequality. NBER Working Paper (14683).

Card, D., Lemieux, T., 2001. Can falling supply explain the rising returns to college for younger men? A cohort based analysis. Quarterly Journal of Economics 116, 705–746.

Carey, D., 2008. Improving education outcomes in Germany. OECD, Economics Department Working Paper (611).

D'Amuri, F., Ottaviano, G., Peri, G., 2008. The labor market impact of immigration in Western Germany in the 1990s. NBER Working Paper (13851).

Dickens, W.T., Goette, L., Groshen, E.L., Holden, S., Messina, J., Schweitzer, M.E., Turunen, J., Ward, M.E., 2007. How wages change: micro evidence from the international wage flexibility project. Journal of Economic Perspectives 21, 195–214.

Dustmann, C., Frattini, T., Preston, I., 2007. Immigration and wages: new evidence for Britain. University College of London, mimeo.

Ebbinghas, B., Eichhorst, W., 2009. Employment regulation and labor market policy in Germany, 1991–2005. In: deBeer, P., Schils, T. (Eds.), Social Policy and the Labour Market: Achieving an Optimal Policy Mix. Cheltenham, Edward Elgar, pp. 1991–2005.

Eichhorst, W., Kaiser, L.C., 2006. The German labor market: still adjusting badly? IZA Discussion Paper (2215).

EUROSTAT, 2008. EU Labour Force Survey Database—User Guide.

Fahr, R., Sunde, U., 2006. Did the Hartz reforms speed-up job creation? A macro-evaluation using empirical matching functions. IZA Discussion Paper (2470).

Felbermayr, G.J., Geis, W., Kohler, W., 2008. Restrictive immigration policy in Germany: pains and gains foregone? CESifo Working Paper (2316).

Glitz, A., 2006. The labour market impact of immigration: quasi-experimental evidence. CREAM Discussion Paper (12/06).

Haisken-DeNew, J.P., Frick, J.R., 2005. Desktop companion to the German socio-economic panel (SOEP).

Manacorda, M., Manning, A., Wadsworth, J., 2006. The impact of immigration on the structure of male wages: theory and evidence from Britain. CEP Discussion Paper, London School of Economics (754).

OECD, 2006. Labour market reforms should go on. Economic Surveys: Germany.

Ortega, F., Peri, G., 2009. The causes and effects of international migrations: evidence from OECD countries 1980–2005. NBER Working Paper (14883).

Ottaviano, G., Peri, G., 2008. Immigration and the national wages: clarifying the theory and the empirics. NBER Working Paper (14188).

Peri, G., 2007. Immigrants' complementarities and native wages: evidence from California. NBER Working Paper (12956).

Peri, G., Sparber, C., 2009. Task specialization, immigration, and wages. American Economic Journal: Empirical Economics 1 (3), 135–169.

Pischke, J.S., Velling, J., 1997. Employment effects of immigration to Germany: an analysis based on local labor markets. Review of Economics and Statistics 79, 594–604.

Romer, D., 2001. Advanced Macroeconomics. McGraw-Hill, New York.

Schmidt, C.M., Stiltz, A., Zimmermann, K.F., 1994. Mass migration, unions, and Government intervention. Journal of Public Economics 55, 185–201.

Statistisches-Bundesamt-Deutschland, 2006. Information zur OstWest Wanderung.

Stock, J.H., Yogo, M., 2002. Testing for weak instruments in linear IV regression. NBER Technical Working Papers (0284).

Wagner, G.G., 1999. Reform of the regulations on marginal employment lacks cohesion. Economic Bulletin 36, 13–16.

Zimmermann, K.F., 1999. Ethnic German migration since 1989—results and perspectives. IZA Discussion Paper (50).

Zimmermann, K.F., Bonin, H., Fahr, R., Hinte, H., 2007. Immigration Policy and the Labor Market. Springer, Berlin.

Chapter 9

RETHINKING THE EFFECT OF IMMIGRATION ON WAGES[†]

Gianmarco I. P. Ottaviano
London School of Economics and
Bocconi University

Giovanni Peri
University of California, Davis

Abstract
This paper calculates the effects of immigration on the wages of native US workers of various skill levels in two steps. In the first step we use labor demand functions to estimate the elasticity of substitution across different groups of workers. Second, we use the underlying production structure and the estimated elasticities to calculate the total wage effects of immigration in the long run. We emphasize that a production function framework is needed to combine own-group effects with cross-group effects in order to obtain the total wage effects for each native group. In order to obtain a parsimonious representation of elasticities that can be estimated with available data, we adopt alternative nested-CES models and let the data select the preferred specification. New to this paper is the estimate of the substitutability between natives and immigrants of similar education and experience levels. In the data-preferred model, there is a small but significant degree of imperfect substitutability between natives and immigrants which, when combined with the other estimated elasticities, implies that in the period from 1990 to 2006 immigration had a small effect on the wages of native workers with no high school degree (between 0.6% and +1.7%). It also had a small positive effect on average native wages (+0.6%) and a substantial negative effect (−6.7%) on wages of previous immigrants in the long run. (JEL: F22, J61, J31)

1. Introduction

The empirical analysis of cross-city and cross-state evidence in the United States has consistently found small and often insignificant effects of immigration on the wages of native workers.[1] However, two recent influential contributions by Borjas (2003) and Borjas and Katz (2007) have emphasized the importance of estimating the effects of immigration using national level data and have found a significant negative effect of immigration on the wages of natives with no high school

The editor in charge of this paper was Orazio Attanasio.

Acknowledgments: We thank the editor in charge and three anonymous referees for very useful and constructive comments. We thank David Card, Steve Raphael, Chad Sparber and participants to several seminars and presentations for very helpful discussions and comments on previous drafts of this paper. Ottaviano gratefully acknowledges funding from the European Commission and MIUR. Peri gratefully acknowledges funding from the John D. and Catherine T. MacArthur Foundation.

E-mail addresses: g.i.ottaviano@lse.ac.uk (Ottaviano); gperi@ucdavis.edu (Peri)

1. See the influential review by Friedberg and Hunt (1995) and, since then, National Research Council (1997), Card (2001), Friedberg (2001), Lewis (2005), Card and Lewis (2007) and Card (2007).

[†] This article originally appeared in *Journal of the European Economic Association*, **10** 152–197 © 2012 Oxford University Press.

diploma.[2] These studies have argued that wages across local labor markets are subject to the equalizing pressure that arises from the spatial arbitrage of mobile workers. As a result, the wage effects of immigration are better detected at the national level since one can exploit variation in wages and immigrants across groups of workers with different skills (as captured by education and experience) over time.

The underlying logic is that while it may be relatively easy for a US worker to react to local immigration by changing their residence within the United States it is much harder for her to do so by relocating across the US border or by changing her own skill mix. Accordingly, the estimation of the substitutability among workers with different skills should play a key role in the analysis of the wage effects of immigration. Our aim is to contribute to this approach at the national level in two ways: through an improved estimation of the substitutability among workers with different characteristics and through the clarification of a crucial distinction between the partial and the total wage effects of immigration, a distinction not fully appreciated in the existing literature.

First, in terms of substitutability and in contrast to Borjas (2003) and Borjas and Katz (2007), we estimate the elasticity of substitution between immigrant and native workers within the same education and experience group without assuming ex ante that they are perfectly substitutable. Given that natives and immigrants of similar education and age have different skills, often work in different jobs and perform different productive tasks, their substitutability is an empirical question, the answer to which has important implications since the degree of imperfect substitutability affects the impact that immigrants have on the wage of natives with similar skills.

Some recent papers have also estimated the native–immigrant elasticity of substitution. Card (2007), using US city data for year 2000, Raphael and Smolensky (2008), using US data over 1970–2005, and D'Amuri et al. (2010), using German data, all find small but significant values for the inverse of the native–immigrant elasticity implying less than perfect substitutability between these groups of workers (with an elasticity between 20 and 30).[3] While our estimates are in the same ballpark, a closely related work by Manacorda, Manning, and Wadsworth (this issue) using UK data finds an even smaller substitutability between natives and immigrants (with elasticity between 5 and 10). This may be due to their use of yearly net inflows (rather than the ten-year flows we use) implying that the elasticity of substitution is identified on very recent immigrants, who are likely to be the most different from natives. On the other hand, Borjas, Grogger, and Hanson (2008) show that one can get small and

---

2. See, also, Borjas, Freeman, and Katz 1997.

3. In the older literature, indirect evidence of imperfect substitution between natives and immigrants was found in the form of small wage effects of immigrants on natives and larger negative effects on the wages of previous immigrants (see Longhi, Nijkamp, and Poot, 2005, pp. 468–469, for a discussion of this issue). Until very recently, however, only a very few studies have directly estimated the elasticity of substitution between natives and immigrants. Jaeger (1996) covers metropolitan areas only over 1980–1990, obtaining estimates that may be susceptible to attenuation bias and endogeneity problems related to the use of local data. Cortes (2008) considers low-skilled workers and uses metropolitan area data, finding a rather low elasticity of substitution between US- and foreign-born workers.

insignificant estimates for the inverse of the native–immigrant elasticity, and therefore little evidence of imperfect substitutability, in specifications that are highly saturated with fixed effects.[4]

We also reconsider the substitutability between workers of different schooling and experience levels. We produce new estimates and compare them with those found in the existing literature. In particular, since the inflow of immigrants to the United States in recent decades has been much larger among workers with no high school degree than among high school graduates, we emphasize the importance of distinguishing the substitutability between workers with no high school degree and workers with a high school diploma from the substitutability between those two groups taken together and workers with at least some college education. This distinction has a long tradition since Katz and Murphy (1992) argued that in order to understand the impact of changes in labor supply and demand on the wages of workers with different education levels it is important to consider highly educated and less-educated workers as imperfectly substitutable.[5] This has been motivated by the observation that the wage time series of workers with and without high school degrees move together much more than do the wages of high school dropouts and college educated workers.[6] The substitutability across alternative experience groups has been similarly investigated.[7]

Our second contribution concerns the distinction between partial and total wage effects. While the former refers to the direct impact of immigration on native wages within a skill group given fixed supplies in other skill groups, the latter accounts for the indirect impacts of immigration in all other skill groups. Accordingly, the total wage effects on natives across skill groups depend on the relative sizes of the different skill groups, the relative strength of own- and cross-skill impacts and the pattern of immigration across skill groups.

To clarify the distinction between partial and total wage effects, we introduce an aggregate production function that produces marginal productivity equations that can be used to compute both sorts of effects of immigration on the wage of natives in each skill group. Because we consider a rich set of skills, a large number of cross-skill effects need to be estimated. Doing this with minimal structure is impossible given available data. For example, the 32 education-by-experience groups proposed in Borjas (2003) and Borjas and Katz (2007) imply 992 cross-skill effects. But US Census data only consists of 192 skill-by-year observations on employment and wages. Adding structure, like the nested-CES labor composite we introduce in what follows, allows the

---

4. A more detailed discussion of the results by Borjas, Grogger, and Hanson (2008) is presented in Section 4.1.

5. See also Murphy and Welch 1992; Angrist 1995; Autor, Katz, and Krueger 1998; Johnson 1997; Krusell et al. 2000; Acemoglu 2002.

6. See, for instance, Katz and Murphy (1992), p. 68, and Goldin and Katz (2008) and also Figures 7 and 8 in this paper.

7. Katz and Murphy (1992) consider a simple structure with two groups (young and old) and find an elasticity of substitution between them of around 3.3. Welch (1979) as well as Card and Lemieux (2001) use a symmetric CES structure with several age groups and estimate elasticities between 5 and 10.

plethora of cross-skill effects to be expressed in terms of a limited number of structural parameters that can, in turn, be estimated with available data. In other words, the aggregate production function provides a structural foundation to the wage regressions used to assess workers' substitutability and provides parametric interpretations of the estimated coefficients. That said, economic interpretation of estimates from any reduced-form equation requires assumptions on the form of the cross-skill interactions. So, by explicitly introducing the aggregate production function we are able to get the required estimates and we can discuss the pros and cons of the underlying assumptions.

While the nested-CES approach imposes restrictions on the form of the cross-elasticities, it is still flexible enough to allow for the exploration of alternative nesting structures in terms of number of cells, order of nesting and skill grouping. In particular, we explore four different nesting models, which together span most of the structures used to estimate the substitutability among skill groups in the existing literature. Model A augments the structure proposed by Borjas (2003, Section VII) by allowing for imperfect substitutability between US- and foreign-born workers of equal education and experience. This model assumes the same substitutability between any pair of education groups and between any pair of experience groups with identical education. While the latter assumption is standard in the labor literature, the former is rather unusual as it is more common to divide workers into two broad education groups of workers, those with high education (some college education and more) and those with low education (high school education or less).[8] This alternative partition is considered in model B. Models C and D cover plausible alternatives that are not much used by the existing literature. Model C considers the possibility that some experience groups may be closer substitutes than others by allowing for the elasticity across broad experience groups to differ from the elasticity across narrow experience groups. Finally, in model D the nesting order of education and experience in Borjas (2003, Section VII) is inverted with respect to model A.

We estimate the relevant elasticities of substitution for the four models using data from the Census in 1960, 1970, 1980, 1990, and 2000, and from the American Community Survey (ACS) 2006 downloaded from IPUMS (Ruggles et al. 2009). As this set of data generates only six time-series observations, in order to better estimate the elasticities of substitution between large aggregate groups we also use Current Population Survey (CPS) yearly data for the period 1962–2006 (downloaded from IPUMS-CPS, King et al. 2009). We then use the different nested-CES models to compute the effects of immigration on the wages of natives and previous immigrants in the period 1990–2006 based on the corresponding estimated elasticities.[9]

While overall the elasticity estimates and, therefore, the computed wage effects are somewhat sensitive to model specification, some results are robust across

---

8. See, for example, Welch (1979) as well as Card and Lemieux (2001) on experience groups; Katz and Murphy (1992), Angrist (1995), Krusell et al. (2000), Goldin and Katz (2008) on education groups.

9. In so doing, we focus on the wage effects that materialize in the long run, that is, after capital has fully adjusted to the labor supply shock caused by the inflow of foreign-born workers. See Ottaviano and Peri (2008) for the evaluation of the short-run effects.

specifications. First, we find a small but significant degree of imperfect substitutability between natives and immigrants within the same education and experience group. When we constrain the native–immigrant elasticity to be the same for all education groups, our preferred estimate is 20. It becomes much lower (around 12.5) for less educated workers once we remove that constraint. Using model A, such large but finite elasticities imply that the negative wage impact of immigration on less-educated natives is −1.1% to −2.0% over the period 1990–2006. This model would imply a wage loss of less educated natives of −3.1% when the elasticity of substitution between natives and immigrants is infinite, as in Borjas (2003) and Borjas and Katz (2007). Hence, allowing for imperfect substitutability reduces the impact of immigration on native wages by no less than a third. This imperfect substitutability also implies that, on average, immigrants already in the United States suffer much larger wage losses than natives as a consequence of inflows of new immigrants. Based on model A, their average wage losses due to immigration are calculated to be around 6.7% for the period 1990–2006.

Second, while model A is a useful tool to assess the effects of introducing imperfect native–immigrant substitutability in the framework proposed by Borjas (2003), the data suggest that model B should be preferred instead. The key evidence for this is gathered when the different models are estimated on CPS data. That sample is large enough to allow for the separate estimation of the elasticity of substitution between broad education groups and between narrow education groups. These elasticities are indeed estimated to be quite different from each other, with the first evaluated around 2 and the second evaluated above 10. Using these estimates in model B generates wage effects that are rather different from those obtained from model A. In particular, the effect of immigration on the wages of natives with low education is now a small positive effect (between 0.6% and 1.7%). This result is due to the balanced inflow of immigrants between the broad high-education and low-education groups together with the imperfect substitutability between natives and immigrants, especially those with low education levels.

Finally, there is not much support for model C as the elasticity across broad experience groups is not very different from the elasticity across narrow experience groups (both being estimated around 5). There is no reason to favor model D either, as this leads to similar parameter estimates as model A. Indeed, for given parameter estimates, both models C and D generate wage effects that are very similar to those of model A.

The rest of the paper is organized as follows. In Section 2 we introduce the aggregate production function and the alternative nested-CES models. We also derive the equations used to estimate workers' substitutability as well as those needed to calculate the partial and total effects of immigration on wages. Section 3 presents the data and describes how we compute the relevant variables. Section 4 details the empirical estimation of the relevant elasticities of substitution among different groups of workers. Section 5 uses the estimated elasticities in the alternative models to compute the wage effects of immigration. Section 6 concludes.

2. Theoretical Framework

We treat immigration as a labor supply shock, omitting any productivity impact that it may produce (due, for example, to improved efficiency, choice of better technologies, or scale externalities). We may therefore miss part of its positive impact on wages, often identified as a positive average wage effect on natives in cross-city or cross-state analyses such as Card (2007) and Ottaviano and Peri (2005, 2006b).[10] Moreover, we focus on the effects of immigration on wages in the long run, that is, after capital has fully adjusted to the labor supply shock caused by the inflow of foreign-born workers.[11]

In order to evaluate the effects of immigrants on wages, we need a model of how the marginal productivity of a given type of worker reacts to changes in the supply of other types. The model we adopt is based on the nested-CES approach that has become the workhorse for the evaluation of the wage response to labor supply and demand shocks at the national level (see, for example, Katz and Murphy 1992; Card and Lemieux 2001; Borjas 2003; Borjas and Katz 2007). This is based on an aggregate production function that parameterizes the elasticity of substitution between different types of workers together with a simple theory of capital adjustment.

2.1. Aggregate Production and Capital Accumulation

Aggregate production takes place according to the following constant-returns-to-scale Cobb–Douglas function:

$$Y = AL^{\alpha}K^{1-\alpha}, \tag{1}$$

where Y is aggregate output, A is exogenous total factor productivity (TFP), K is physical capital, L is a CES aggregate of different types of labor (more on this in Section 2.2), and $\alpha \in (0, 1)$ is the income share of labor. All variables are relative to time t but their time dependence is left implicit to alleviate the notational burden. The functional form (1) has been widely used in the macro-growth literature (recently, for instance, by Jones 2005; Caselli and Coleman 2006) and is supported by the empirical observation that the share of income going to labor is rather constant in the long run and across countries (Kaldor 1961; Gollin 2002).[12] Profit maximization under perfect competition implies that the effect of physical capital on wages operates through its effect on the marginal productivity of L whose remuneration absorbs $\alpha A(K/L)^{1-\alpha}$ units of aggregate output.

---

10. Our method may also miss any potential aggregate negative productivity effect of immigration.

11. See Ottaviano and Peri (2008) for a discussion of short-run effects.

12. The Cobb–Douglas functional form implies that physical capital has the same degree of substitutability with each type of worker. Some influential studies (for example, Krusell et al. 2000) have argued that physical capital complements highly educated workers and substitutes for less educated workers. This assumption, however, implies that the income share of capital should have risen over time following the large increase in the supply and the income share of highly educated workers. This has not happened in the United States over the period considered.

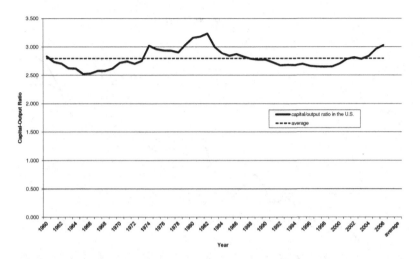

FIGURE 1. US capital–output ratio 1960–2006. Source: Authors' calculations using BEA data on the stock of physical capital and GDP.

When nested into standard Ramsey (1928) or Solow (1956) models, the production function (1) also implies that in the long run the economy follows a balanced growth path, along which the real interest rate and the aggregate capital–output ratio are both constant while the capital–labor ratio K/L grows at a constant rate equal to $1/\alpha$ times the growth rate of TFP. The intuition behind this result is that a rise in labor supply makes capital relatively scarce. This boosts its marginal productivity and depresses the marginal productivity of labor. As a reaction, capital accumulation increases until the capital–labor ratio is brought back to its balanced growth path. This implication is also supported by the data, as the real return to capital and the capital–output ratio in the United States do not exhibit any trend over the long run, while the capital–labor ratio grows at a constant rate. This is shown in Figures 1 and 2 for the period 1960–2004: both the capital–output ratio and the detrended log capital–labor ratio exhibit cyclical movements but also a remarkable mean reversion in the long run. Hence, at the aggregate level the average wage does not depend on labor supply and, therefore, on immigration in the long run. This implication of the model will be maintained throughout the paper.

2.2. Worker Heterogeneity in a Flexible Nested-CES Model

As workers are heterogeneous, the zero effect of immigration on the average wage may hide asymmetric effects at more disaggregated levels. In qualitative terms, immigrants should put downward pressure on the wages of workers with similar characteristics and upward pressure on the wages of workers with different characteristics. In quantitative

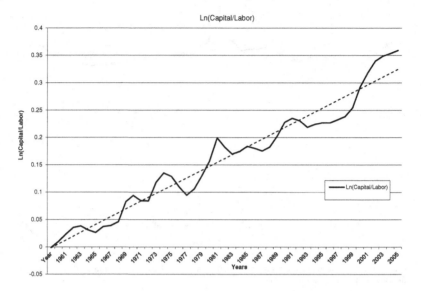

FIGURE 2. Log capital–labor ratio and trend 1960–2006. Source: Authors' calculations using BEA data on the stock of physical capital and BLS data on total nonfarm employment.

terms, these effects on wages should depend on how substitutable workers of different types are and how large the inflow of workers of each type is.

We propose a flexible nested-CES structure that embeds various alternative models studied in the literature as special cases. Though slightly demanding, the chosen notation has the advantage of allowing for recursive expressions of general results. Consider $N + 1$ characteristics numbered $n = 0, \ldots, N$. Characteristic 0 is common to all workers and defines them as such. We first partition workers into groups $i_1 = 1, \ldots, M_1$ that differ according to characteristic 1. Then, each of these groups is itself partitioned into groups $i_2 = 1, \ldots, M_2$ that differ according to characteristic 2, and so on up to characteristic N. This sequential partitioning and its relative notation is illustrated in Figure 3. The index $n = 0, \ldots, N$ identifies the characteristic used to partition workers into the corresponding groups. The figure shows how groups i_{n+1} are *nested* in groups i_n so that we can use n to also index the nesting level along the depicted partitioning structure.

Let us call $i(n)$ a group (*type*) of workers defined by common characteristics up to n, and define as $L_{i(n)}$ the corresponding labor supply. The CES aggregator at the generic level n is then defined:

$$L_{i(n)} = \left[\sum_{i(n+1) \in i(n)} \theta_{i(n+1)} \left(L_{i(n+1)} \right)^{\frac{\sigma_{n+1}-1}{\sigma_{n+1}}} \right]^{\frac{\sigma_{n+1}}{\sigma_{n+1}-1}}, \quad n = 0, \ldots, N, \qquad (2)$$

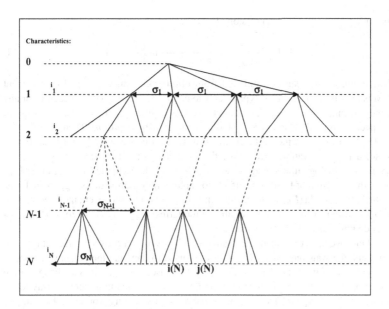

FIGURE 3. Scheme of the CES nests and relative notation.

where $\theta_{i(n)}$ is the relative productivity level of type $i(n)$ standardized so that $\sum_{i(n) \in i(n-1)} \theta_{i(n)} = 1$ and any common multiplying factor is absorbed in the TFP parameter A of (1). Both A and $\theta_{i(n)}$ depend on exogenous technological factors only. The parameter $\sigma_n > 0$ is the elasticity of substitution between types $i(n)$. The fact that the sequential partitioning of workers leads to fewer and fewer heterogeneous groups $i(n)$ as n increases is captured by assuming that $\sigma_{n+1} > \sigma_n$. Since type $i(0)$ includes all workers, we can embed the nested structure defined by (2) in (1) by imposing $L = L_{i(0)}$.

Using this structure and notation, we can calculate the profit-maximizing wage of a worker of type $i(N)$ as the value of her marginal productivity:

$$\ln(w_{i(N)}) = \ln(\alpha A \kappa^{1-\alpha}) + \frac{1}{\sigma_1}\ln(L) + \sum_{n=1}^{N} \ln\theta_{i(n)}$$

$$- \sum_{n=1}^{N-1}\left(\frac{1}{\sigma_n} - \frac{1}{\sigma_{n+1}}\right)\ln(L_{i(n)}) - \frac{1}{\sigma_N}\ln(L_{i(N)}). \qquad (3)$$

This expression holds for $N > 2$ and can be used as the empirical basis for estimating the substitutability parameters σ_n with $n = 1, \ldots, N$. First, focusing on the last level of nesting N and considering two different groups $i(N)$ and $j(N)$ with all characteristics up to $N - 1$ in common, expression (3) implies

$$\ln \left(\frac{w_{i(N)}}{w_{j(N)}} \right) = \ln \frac{\theta_{i(n)}}{\theta_{j(n)}} - \frac{1}{\sigma_N} \ln \left(\frac{L_{i(N)}}{L_{j(N)}} \right). \qquad (4)$$

Therefore, $-1/\sigma_N$ can be estimated from observations on wages and employment levels over time, using fixed-type effects to control for $\ln (\theta_{i(n)}/\theta_{j(n)})$. Second, for any other nesting level $m = 1, \ldots, N - 1$, we can define $w_{i(m)}$ as the average wage of a specific group of workers $i(m)$ sharing characteristics up to m. Then, substituting m for N in (3) gives the profit maximizing relation between $w_{i(m)}$ and $L_{i(m)}$. In this case, using observations over time, the estimation of $-1/\sigma_m$ can be achieved by regressing the logarithmic wage of group $i(m)$ on the logarithmic CES aggregate $L_{i(m)}$ with the inclusion of fixed-time effects to capture the variation of the aggregate terms $\ln (\alpha A \kappa^{1-\alpha})$ and $\ln (L)$, and group-specific effects varying only over characteristics up to $m - 1$ and by year in order to absorb the terms $\sum_{n=1}^{m-1} (1/\sigma_n - 1/\sigma_{n+1}) \ln \left(L_{i(n)} \right)$ that do not change with characteristic m.

Once we have estimated the elasticities of substitution between different types of workers, the wage equation (3) can also be used to compute the percentage change in the wage of workers of a certain type $j(N)$ caused by a percentage change in the labor supply of workers of another type $i(N)$. To show this in a compact way let us denote by $s_{i(N)}^n$ type $i(N)$'s share of the labor income among workers exhibiting the same characteristics up to n as that type. Hence, $s_{i(N)}^{n-1} \le s_{i(N)}^n$ and $s_{i(N)}^N = 1$. Then, we can write the percentage impact of a change in labor supplied by workers of type $i(N)$ on the wage of a worker of type $j(N)$ with the same characteristics up to m as

$$\frac{\Delta w_{j(N)}^0 / w_{j(N)}^0}{\Delta L_{i(N)} / L_{i(N)}} = \frac{s_{i(N)}^0}{\sigma_1} > 0, \quad m = 0 \qquad (5)$$

and

$$\frac{\Delta w_{j(N)}^m / w_{j(N)}^m}{\Delta L_{i(N)} / L_{i(N)}} = - \sum_{n=0}^{m-1} \frac{s_{i(N)}^{n+1} - s_{i(N)}^n}{\sigma_{n+1}} < 0, \quad m = 1, \ldots, N. \qquad (6)$$

Two remarks on equations (5) and (6) are in order. First, an increase in the labor supply of a certain type $i(N)$ causes an increase in the wage of another type $j(N)$ only if the two types differ in terms of characteristic 1. Second, if the two types share at least characteristic 1, then a rise in the labor supply of $i(N)$ always depresses the wage of $j(N)$. This effect is stronger the larger the number of differentiating characteristics $j(N)$ has in common with $i(N)$. Both results rely on the characteristics having been nested, so that $\sigma_{n+1} > \sigma_n$.

2.3. Alternative CES Nesting Structures

The traditional characteristics used in the literature to partition heterogeneous workers are education and experience (see, for example, Borjas 2003; Borjas and Katz 2007).

We consider birthplace ("US-born", "foreign-born") as an additional characteristic differentiating workers in the same education and experience categories.

There are several reasons for adding this new source of heterogeneity since, even when considering workers with equivalent education and experience, natives and immigrants differ in several respects that are relevant to the labor market. First, people who migrate are different from those that do not. Immigrants have skills, motivations and tastes that may set them apart from natives. Second, in manual and intellectual work they have culture-specific skills (for example, cooking, crafting, opera singing, soccer playing) and limits (for example, limited knowledge of the language or culture of the host country), which create comparative advantages in some tasks and comparative disadvantages in others.[13] Third, due to comparative advantages, migration networks, or historical accidents, immigrants tend to choose different occupations with respect to natives, even for given education and experience levels. In particular, new immigrants tend to work disproportionately in those occupations where foreign-born workers are already over-represented.[14] Finally, there is no need to impose perfect substitutability between natives and immigrants ex ante as this elasticity can be estimated. Hence, while exploring alternative nesting structures for education and experience, we always consider the birthplace of the worker as her Nth differentiating characteristic. This allows us to partition each education by experience cell into US-born workers (labeled D, for domestic) and foreign-born workers (labeled F).

In combining education and experience, we borrow different nesting models from the literature and, where possible, we test one against the other to allow the data to identify a preferred one. These alternative models are depicted in Figure 4 as specific cases of the flexible nested-CES model presented in Section 2.2. Model A builds on Borjas (2003) and Borjas and Katz (2007). In this model we have $N = 3$; education is characteristic 1 partitioned into four categories:

$$i_1 = \text{(No Degree, High School Degree, Some College Education, College Degree)};$$

experience is characteristic 2 partitioned into eight experience categories over a working life of 40 years:

$$i_2 = (0\text{--}5, 6\text{--}10, 11\text{--}15, 16\text{--}20, 21\text{--}25, 26\text{--}30, 31\text{--}35, 36\text{--}40);$$

birthplace is characteristic 3 partitioned, as already mentioned, into two categories $i_3 = (D, F)$.

An alternative partitioning of education is more frequently used in the labor literature.[15] Accordingly, in model B workers are first partitioned in terms of two

---

13. See Peri and Sparber (2009) for evidence supporting the existence of different comparative advantages in production tasks between US- and foreign-born workers.

14. Ottaviano and Peri (2006a) find a positive and very significant correlation between the initial share of immigrants in an occupation and the inflow of new immigrants in that occupation over the subsequent decade.

15. See among others Goldin and Katz 2008; Katz and Murphy 1992; Autor, Katz, and Krueger 1997; Krusell et al. 2000; Card and Lemieux 2001; Acemoglu 2002; Caselli and Coleman 2006.

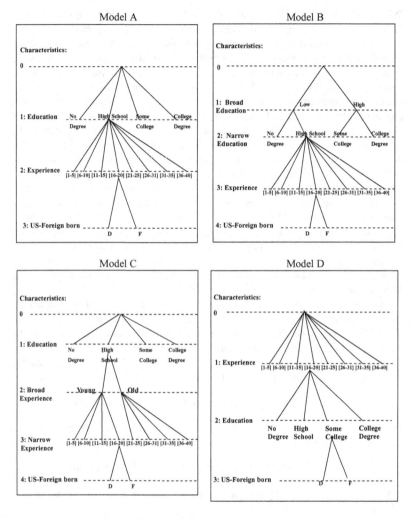

FIGURE 4.   Alternative nesting models.

broad educational characteristics, each of which comprises two narrower educational categories. In this case, we have $N = 4$ with broadly defined education being characteristic 1 so that $i_1 =$ (High education, Low education). Narrowly defined education is characteristic 2, with $i_2 =$ (No degree, High school degree) partitioning Low education and $i_2 =$ (Some college education, College degree) partitioning High education. Experience is characteristic 3, still partitioned into the same eight categories as before, and place of birth is characteristic 4.

Model C is based instead on the mirror idea that substitutability may differ across pairs of experience rather than education categories, and will be smaller for groups that are closer in terms of experience. We again have $N = 4$ but there is only one level of educational characteristics, again with four categories as in model A. Broad experience is characteristic 2 with $i_2 =$ (Young, Old) and narrow experience is characteristic 3 with $i_3 =$ (0–5, 6–10, 11–15, 16–20) within the group Young and $i_3 =$ (21–25, 26–30, 31–35, 36–40) within the group Old.

These three models all proceed from the idea that characteristics are chosen to sequentially nest groups that are increasingly substitutable ($\sigma_{n+1} > \sigma_n$). As we will see, this is consistent with our estimates implying that the elasticity of substitution across education groups is generally smaller than across experience groups. If, however, workers of different education levels were more substitutable with each other than workers of different experience levels, an inverted order of nesting would be more appropriate. Hence, we also consider model D, which reverses the nesting order between education and experience. This is a natural check, though we are not aware of previous studies that adopt it. Specifically, model D maintains the same categories as model A for both education and experience but defines experience as characteristic 1 and education as characteristic 2. The structure is completed by the place of birth as a last category so that $N = 3$.

2.4. Partial and Total Wage effects of Immigration

The flexible nested-CES model from Section 2.2 allows us to clarify a crucial distinction between partial and total wage effects. While the former refer to the direct impact of immigration within a given group of workers, the latter also account for the indirect impact of immigration on all other groups of workers. This implies that the total wage effect on natives across groups depends on the relative sizes of the different groups, the relative strength of own- and cross-group impacts, and the actual pattern of immigration across all groups.

Specifically, recall that birthplace is the Nth characteristic in all our nesting structures so that σ_N always represents the elasticity of substitution between native and immigrant workers with similar education and experience. We call the *direct partial wage effect* of immigration the wage impact on native workers due to a change in the supply of immigrants with the same $N - 1$ characteristics, while keeping constant the labor supplies of all other workers. This effect has been the main or only coefficient of interest in most *reduced-form* approaches that regress native wages on the employment of immigrants in the same skill-groups.[16] The direct partial wage effect has been

---

16. For instance, in Borjas (2003, sections II to VI) or in Borjas (2006) and in the studies inspired by these seminal papers, the *direct partial wage effect* of immigration is the main estimated wage effect. Even the recent meta-study by Longhi, Nijkamp, and Poot (2005) considers this partial effect as the relevant estimate across studies.

estimated by panel regressions of $\ln w_{j(N)}^{N-1}$ on $\ln L_{i(N)}$, where the former is the wage of group $j(N)$ of native workers sharing $N - 1$ characteristics (i.e., all but the birthplace) with the group $i(N)$ of immigrants and the latter is the employment of group $i(N)$ of immigrants. Careful econometric specifications (such as Borjas 2003) control for year-specific effects (to absorb the variation of $L = L_{i(0)}$) and characteristic-by-year specific effects (to absorb the variation of $L_{i(n)}$ for $n = 1, \ldots, N - 1$). In terms of our flexible model, the resulting partial elasticity can be written as

$$\varepsilon_{i(N)}^{N-1} = -\left(\frac{1}{\sigma_{N-1}} - \frac{1}{\sigma_N} \right) s_{i(N)}^{N-1}. \tag{7}$$

Note, however, that the direct partial wage effect (7) coincides only with the last among the several terms composing the summation in (6) as this includes both direct and indirect wage effects. This happens because, by construction, the elasticity $\varepsilon_{i(N)}^{N-1}$ captures only the wage effect of a change in labor supply operating through the term $-(1/\sigma_{N-1} - 1/\sigma_N)\ln (L_{i(N-1)})$ in (3).

Hence, two important observations on (7) are in order. First, $\varepsilon_{i(N)}^{N-1}$ is negative whenever the chosen nesting structure is such that the substitutability between immigrants and natives sharing $N - 1$ characteristics is larger than the substitutability between workers sharing only $N - 2$ characteristics (that is, $\sigma_N > \sigma_{N-1}$). Second, the value and the sign of $\varepsilon_{i(N)}^{N-1}$ give incomplete information about the overall effect of immigrant supply changes on the wages of domestic workers. Indeed, (7) includes only the last term of (6), which itself is only one of the terms entering the *total wage effect* for domestic workers of type $j(N)$. In order to evaluate the total wage effect, one has to combine the impacts generated by (6) across all the $i(N)$ that include foreign-born workers for which $L_{i(N)}$ changes due to immigration.

This definition of the total wage effect implies that it cannot be directly estimated from a regression.[17] In particular, one can directly estimate the elasticities σ_1 to σ_N as well as $\varepsilon_{i(N)}^{N-1}$. However, in order to compute the total wage effect of immigration, one needs to combine the estimated elasticities σ_n with the income shares $s_{i(N)}^n$ in equation (6) and aggregate across all groups for which $L_{i(N)}$ changes due to immigrants. Intuitively, this depends on the fact that the total wage effect can only be computed by combining *own*-group effects with the set of *cross*-group effects.

To see how misleading it can be to use the direct partial wage effects to infer the total wage effects of immigration consider, for instance, model A with an elasticity of substitution between experience categories equal to 0.20 and an elasticity of

---

17. Dustmann, Frattini, and Preston (2008) propose an estimate of the *total wage effect* of immigrants on natives in a specific portion (cell) of the native wage distribution by regressing the wage of natives in that cell on the total inflow of immigrants (plus several controls). Such an approach, however, assumes the same wage effect of immigrants in any other group on natives. This is consistent with a one-level CES (which they assume) but not with a nested CES. A nested CES implies different effects depending not only on total immigration but also on the distribution of immigrants across skill groups. Moreover, to obtain enough observations for their estimates, they consider UK provinces as separate labor markets. Considering one national labor market, as we do here, would not provide enough observations (only one per year) to estimate the *total wage effect*.

substitution between natives and immigrants equal to 0.05, which we will use as reasonable estimates for the United States over our observation period 1990–2006. Assume further that the share of immigrant employment in an education group is similar to its share in the wage bill of the group. Then, (7) implies that an inflow of immigrants increasing labor supply in an education–experience group by 1% would produce a −0.15% change in the real wage of native workers in that group. If one failed to realize the partial nature of the above elasticity, one could be tempted to generalize these findings by arguing that, over the period 1990–2006, the increase of 11.4% in total hours worked in the United States due to immigration caused a decrease of −1.7% = (−0.15 ∗ 11.4%) in the average wages of natives; or that groups, such as high school dropouts, for which the inflow of immigrants was as high as 23% of initial hours worked, lost −3.4% of their wages. Such generalization would, however, be incorrect since expression (7) only accounts for the effect on wages of immigrants in the same skill group and omits all the cross-group effects. In fact, as we will detail in Section 5, while sharing the same negative partial elasticity, the wage effects on natives were very different across skill groups, depending on the relative size of the groups, the relative strength of cross-group effects, and the actual pattern of immigration across groups. As a result, the values of −1.7% or −3.4% calculated earlier do not bear any resemblance to the total wage effects.

3. Data, Variables and Sample Description

The definitions of variables, their construction and the sample selection coincide exactly with those in Borjas, Grogger, and Hanson (2008).[18] The data we use are downloaded from the integrated public use microdata samples (IPUMS) where the original sources are the US Decennial Census 1960–2000 and the 2006 American Community Survey (Ruggles et al. 2009). Following the Katz and Murphy (1992) tradition we construct two somewhat different samples to produce measures of hours worked (or employment) by cell and average wages by cell. The employment sample is more inclusive as it aims at measuring the hours worked in each education–experience–birthplace cell. The wage sample is more restrictive as it aims at producing a representative average wage (price of labor) in the cell.

To construct the measure of hours worked in each cell and year we consider people aged 18 and older in the Census year not living in group quarters, who worked at least one week in the previous year. We then group them into four schooling groups, eight potential experience groups and two birthplace (US- and foreign-born) groups. Four schooling groups are identified: individuals with no high school degree, high school graduates, individuals with some college education, and college graduates. Years of potential experience are calculated under the assumption that people without

---

18. For further details see Appendix B and the companion technical appendices available online (called Online Appendix). Together with exhaustive information on data, variable definitions and sample selection, the online appendices also provide the files and code needed to reproduce all the results in this paper.

a high school degree enter the labor force at age 17, people with a high school degree enter at 19, people with some college enter at 21, and people with a college degree enter at 23. We group workers into eight five-year experience intervals beginning with those with one to five years of experience and ending with those with 36 to 40 years of experience.[19] The status of *foreign-born* is given to those workers who are noncitizens or are naturalized citizens. We calculate the hours of labor supplied by each worker and then multiply them by the individual weight (PERWT) and aggregate within each education–experience group. This measure of hours worked by cell is the basic measure of labor supply. As an alternative measure of supply, we calculate the employment level (that is, count of employed people) by cell summing up the person weights for all people in the cell.

To construct the average wage in each cell we use a more selective sample. The basic wage sample is a subset of the employment sample where workers who do not report wages (or report 0 wages) and those who are self-employed are eliminated. In a more restrictive wage sample we only include full-time workers, defined as those working at least 40 weeks in the year and at least 35 hours in the usual workweek.[20] The average weekly wage in a cell is constructed by calculating the real weekly wages of individuals (equal to annual salary and income, INCWAGE, deflated using the CPI and adjusted for top-coding, divided by weeks worked in a year) and then taking their weighted average where the weights are the hours worked by the individual times her person weight.

The procedure just described allows us to construct the variables *hours worked* or *employment* and *average weekly wages* for all groups defined by their education, experience, and nativity characteristics in each year t (1960, 1970, 1980, 1990, 2000, 2006). The data also allow us to construct the wage bill share of each group and subgroup. When estimating the elasticity parameters, we always use the entire panel of data, 1960–2006. When we compute the effects of immigration on real wages based on those estimates, we focus on the most recent period, 1990–2006.

Table 1 reports the percentage increase in hours worked due to immigrants (column 3) and the percentage change in weekly wages of natives (column 4) for each education–experience group over the period 1990–2006, pooling men and women together. This period is the one on which we focus for our assessment of the total wage effects of immigration. Even a cursory look at the values in column 3 of Table 1 reveals that the inflow of immigrants has been uneven across groups. Focusing on the rows marked All Experience Groups, in each of the four narrow educational groups we notice that the group of workers with no high school degree experienced the largest percentage increase in hours worked due to immigrants over the 1990–2006 period (equal to +23.6%) followed by the group of college graduates (+14.6%), while high

---

19. Workers with 0 years of potential experience or less and with more than 40 years of potential experience are dropped from the sample.

20. This sample excludes workers with low *labor market attachment* who could be different from full-time workers and whose average weekly wage can introduce nonclassical measurement error, as argued by Borjas, Grogger, and Hanson 2008.

TABLE 1. Immigration and changes in native wages: education-experience groups, 1990–2006.

Column 1: Education	Column 2: Experience	Column 3: Percentage change in hours worked in the group due to new immigrants 1990–2006	Column 4: Percentage change in weekly wages, Natives, 1990–2006
No High School Degree (ND)	1 to 5 years	8.5%	0.7%
	6 to 10 years	21.0%	−1.5%
	11 to 15 years	25.9%	0.6%
	16 to 20 years	31.0%	1.6%
	21 to 25 years	35.7%	1.3%
	26 to 30 years	28.9%	−1.6%
	31 to 35 years	21.9%	−8.8%
	36 to 40 years	14.3%	−10.1%
	All Experience groups	**23.6%**	**−3.1%**
High School Degree (HSD)	1 to 5 years	6.7%	−5.3%
	6 to 10 years	7.7%	−1.6%
	11 to 15 years	8.7%	−1.4%
	16 to 20 years	12.1%	1.8%
	21 to 25 years	13.0%	0.6%
	26 to 30 years	11.8%	−0.9%
	31 to 35 years	11.0%	−2.0%
	36 to 40 years	9.3%	−4.0%
	All Experience groups	**10.0%**	**−1.2%**
<u>Low Education</u> (ND+HSD)	**All Experience groups**	**13.2%**	**−1.5%**
Some College Education (SCO)	1 to 5 years	2.6%	−5.4%
	6 to 10 years	2.6%	−2.0%
	11 to 15 years	3.9%	0.1%
	16 to 20 years	6.2%	0.6%
	21 to 25 years	8.4%	−2.5%
	26 to 30 years	12.0%	−3.1%
	31 to 35 years	12.3%	−3.8%
	36 to 40 years	12.7%	−3.0%
	All Experience groups	**6.0%**	**−1.9%**
College Degree (COD)	1 to 5 years	6.8%	0.4%
	6 to 10 years	12.2%	6.5%
	11 to 15 years	13.7%	14.2%
	16 to 20 years	12.2%	17.3%
	21 to 25 years	17.5%	9.1%
	26 to 30 years	24.4%	4.3%
	31 to 35 years	26.1%	1.7%
	36 to 40 years		
	All Experience groups	**14.6%**	**9.3%**
<u>High Education</u> (SCO+COD)	**All Experience groups**	**10.0%**	**4.5%**

school graduates and the group of workers with some college education experienced only a 10% and a 6% increases, respectively. Interestingly, however, such imbalances are drastically reduced if we consider the broad educational categories corresponding to High Education and Low Education as defined in Section 2.3. When we merge workers with a high school degree and those with no degree (see the row in the middle of Table 1) immigrant labor represents a 13.2% increase in hours worked (1990–2006). This is because the group of high school graduates received few immigrants and the group of workers with no degree constitutes only a very small share of the total labor. supply.[21] In comparison, merging workers with some college education and those with a college degree implies that immigration represented a 10% increase in hours worked by the High Education group (last row of Table 1). Therefore, it is already clear from these numbers that the substitutability between the group of workers with no degree and those with a high school degree will be very important in determining how much of the downward pressure of immigrants on wages remains localized in the group of workers with no degree and how much is instead diffused to the group of workers with at most a high school degree. This suggests that the extra degree of flexibility allowed by model B in Figure 1 may be very important to correctly evaluate the total wage effects of immigration.

Column 4 of Table 1 shows the percentage change of real weekly wages in each education–experience group between 1990 and 2006. A cursory comparison of columns 3 and 4 of Table 1 suggests that it would be hard to find a strong negative correlation between increases in the share of immigrants and the real wage changes of natives across the narrow education groups. We are now ready to use our model to check whether this obviously superficial and possibly wrong prima facie impression survives deeper scrutiny.

4. Elasticity Estimates

4.1. Place of Birth

We begin with the estimation of the elasticity of substitution between natives and immigrants sharing all education and experience characteristics. As discussed in Section 2.3, in all our nesting models the place of birth is the Nth characteristic and σ_N is the corresponding elasticity of substitution (hence, intuitively N can be seen also as a mnemonic for *nativity*). Moreover, in all our nesting models we have the same 32 skill groups at level $N - 1$ (4 narrow education categories times 8 narrow experience categories). This allows us to implement equation (4) for all models through the following common empirical specification:

$$\ln\left(\frac{w_{Fkt}}{w_{Dkt}}\right) = \varphi_k + \varphi_t - \frac{1}{\sigma_N}\ln\left(\frac{L_{Fkt}}{L_{Dkt}}\right) + u_{it}, \tag{8}$$

---

21. Only 8% of total hours worked in 2006 are supplied by workers with no degree versus 30% by workers with a high school degree.

where w_{Dkt} and w_{Fkt} are the average wages of natives and immigrants in group k with k spanning all the 32 skill (education by experience) groups in Census year t. L_{Dkt} and L_{Fkt} are the corresponding hours worked (or employment). Expression (8) assumes that relative productivity $\ln(\theta_{Fkt}/\theta_{Dkt})$ in skill group k can be represented as $\varphi_k + \varphi_t + u_{it}$ where φ_k is a set of 32 education–experience effects, φ_t is a set of six year effects, and u_{it} are zero-mean random variables uncorrelated with relative labor supply $\ln(L_{Fkt}/L_{Dkt})$ (more on this in what follows). Accordingly, φ_k captures the relative productivity of foreign-born versus natives workers of similar education and experience. We allow relative productivity to have a common component of variation over time φ_t across groups, due for instance to changes in immigration policies. We also assume that the remaining time variation u_{it} is independent of relative labor supply. While imposing specific restrictions on the behavior of relative productivity, these assumptions seem reasonable. First, since we use *ratios* of wages and labor supply within education–experience groups, any variation of group specific efficiency in a Census decade would cancel out. In particular, any biased technological change affecting the productivity of more educated (experienced) workers relative to less educated (experienced) workers would be washed out in the ratios. Second, our assumptions are still less restrictive than those made in the existing literature to similarly estimate the elasticity of substitution between skill groups.[22]

Before commenting on the regression results reported in Table 2, it is useful to have a preliminary look at the data. Figure 5 shows the scatterplot of $\ln(w_{Fkt}/w_{Dkt})$ versus $\ln(L_{Fkt}/L_{Dkt})$ and the corresponding regression line from a simple OLS estimation including all 32 education–experience groups in all the years considered. The negative and significant correlation between relative wages and relative labor supplies provides prima facie evidence of imperfect substitutability. The elasticity σ_N implied by the OLS coefficient is around 20 and precisely estimated. Figure 6 shows the scatterplot restricted to the groups of workers with no degree, which have experienced the largest percentage immigrant inflows over the period. In this case the negative correlation is even stronger and more significant with the OLS coefficient, implying an elasticity of substitution σ_N of about 14.

This first impression of imperfect substitutability between natives and immigrants is confirmed in Table 2 which reports the values of $-1/\sigma_N$ estimated using specification (8). Each entry in the table corresponds to a point estimate from a different regression and the standard errors, reported in parentheses below the estimates, are heteroskedasticity robust and clustered by education–experience group to allow error correlation within group. The method of estimation is Least Squares. In specifications 1, 2, 4, and 5 we weight each cell by its employment in order to down-weight those cells with large sampling errors (due to their small size). Specifically, columns (1) and

---

22. For instance, in estimating the elasticity of substitution between experience groups, Borjas (2003, Section VII.A) and Borjas and Katz (2007, Section 1.4) assume that, within each education category, the experience-specific productivity terms are constant over time. This would correspond to including only φ_k in our regression. In Katz and Murphy (1992) the elasticity of substitution between education groups is estimated by assuming that the evolution of their relative productivity follows a time trend. This would correspond to restricting our φ_t to follow a time trend.

TABLE 2. Estimates of the coefficient $(-1/\sigma_N)$.

Specification	(1) No Fixed Effects	(2) With FE	(3) Not weighted with FE	(4) No Fixed Effects	(5) With FE	(6) Not weighted with FE
Wage Sample:	All workers, weighted by hours			Full time workers only		
	PANEL A Estimates of $(-1/\sigma_N)$.					
Men	-0.053*** (0.008)	-0.033** (0.013)	-0.045*** (0.013)	-0.063** (0.005)	-0.048** (0.010)	-0.059*** (0.012)
Women	-0.037*** (0.009)	-0.058*** (0.017)	-0.067*** (0.016)	-0.050*** (0.007)	-0.066*** (0.014)	-0.071*** (0.012)
Pooled Men and Women	-0.032*** (0.008)	-0.024* (0.015)	-0.026** (0.015)	-0.044*** (0.006)	-0.037*** (0.012)	-0.038** (0.013)
Men, Labor supply measured as employment	-0.057** (0.007)	-0.027** (0.014)	-0.030* (0.015)	-0.066*** (0.006)	-0.040** (0.012)	-0.041** (0.014)
	PANEL B Separate estimates of $(-1/\sigma_N)$ by education group.					
Men, No degree	-0.073*** (0.007)	-0.070*** (0.010)	-0.070*** (0.009)	-0.085*** (0.004)	-0.084** (0.006)	-0.081** (0.007)
Men, High School Graduates	-0.089*** (0.016)	-0.090*** (0.020)	-0.093*** (0.018)	-0.097*** (0.013)	-0.099*** (0.015)	-0.100*** (0.015)
Men, Some College education	-0.071** (0.024)	-0.060 (0.035)	-0.070* (0.034)	-0.077** (0.023)	-0.068* (0.033)	-0.075** (0.034)
Men; College Graduates	-0.017 (0.026)	0.006 (0.042)	0.019 (0.030)	-0.024 (0.027)	-0.009 (0.041)	-0.0150 (0.029)

TABLE 2. Continued.

Specification	(1) No Fixed Effects	(2) With FE	(3) Not weighted with FE	(4) No Fixed Effects	(5) With FE	(6) Not weighted with FE
Wage Sample:	All workers, weighted by hours			Full time workers only		

PANEL C
Separate estimates of $(-1/\sigma_N)$ by experience group

	(1)	(2)	(3)	(4)	(5)	(6)
Men, 0–10 years of experience	−0.012 (0.018)	−0.14*** (0.028)	−0.15** (0.030)	−0.037** (0.014)	−0.151*** (0.020)	−0.157*** (0.031)
Men, 11–20 years of experience	−0.044** (0.011)	−0.061*** (0.014)	−0.066** (0.013)	−0.050*** (0.011)	−0.068*** (0.014)	−0.073*** (0.014)
Men, 21–30 years of experience	−0.073** (0.008)	−0.052** (0.022)	−0.058** (0.017)	−0.077*** (0.007)	−0.059** (0.022)	−0.066*** (0.018)
Men, 31–40 years of experience	−0.094** (0.013)	−0.065** (0.014)	−0.063** (0.016)	−0.096*** (0.013)	−0.064*** (0.015)	0.060** (0.018)

Note: National Census and ACS, U.S. data 1960–2006. Each cell reports the estimate of the parameter $-1/\sigma_N$ from specification (8) in the text. Method of estimation is Least Squares. In parentheses we report the heteroskedasticity-robust standard errors, clustered over the 32 education-experience groups. In specifications 1, 2, 4 and 5 we weight each cell by its employment. FE (fixed Effects) include Education by Experience plus time effects in rows one to four; Experience fixed effects are included in rows 5 to 8 and Education fixed effects are in rows 9–12. *** = significant at 1% level; ** = significant at 5% level; * = significant at 10% level.

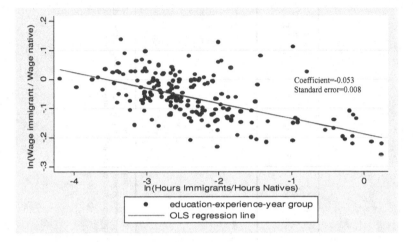

FIGURE 5. Correlation between relative wages and hours worked, immigrant-natives. Cells are education–experience–year groups. Men, 1960–2006.
Note: Each observation corresponds to one of the 32 education–experience group in one of the considered years (1960, 1970, 1980, 1990, 2000, 2006). The horizontal axis measures the logarithm of the relative hours worked in the group by male immigrants relative to natives and the vertical axis measure the logarithm of the weekly wage paid to male immigrants relative to natives.

(4) report the estimates obtained without including the fixed effects φ_k and φ_t in the regression, while other columns always include them. In columns (3) and (6), instead, we use OLS without weighting the cells. Moreover, in columns (1) to (3) all (non-self-employed) workers are used to construct the wage sample while in columns (4) to (6) only full time workers are used. Turning to rows, the top four rows show the coefficient estimates obtained for the whole sample (192 observations), assuming that σ_N is the same for each group. The subsequent rows explore the possibility that σ_N varies across education groups (Rows 5 to 8) or across different experience groups (Rows 9 to 12). In addition, the top four rows show the coefficients obtained by focusing alternatively on male relative wages (Row 1), female relative wages (Row 2) or pooled relative wages (Row 3). Finally, the fourth row uses employment, rather than hours worked, as the measure of the relative labor supply.

Two clear results emerge from the estimates reported in Panel A of Table 2. First, in each case the estimated coefficient $-1/\sigma_N$ is significantly negative at the 5% level, and in most cases at the 1% level. Second, the estimated values range between -0.024 and -0.071. Most of them are around -0.05 implying estimates of σ_N in the neighborhood of 20. Somewhat larger estimates of $-1/\sigma_N$ in absolute value are obtained when using the sample of full-time workers and of women, but these differences are not significant. To test robustness along other dimensions, we have also performed additional estimates (not reported but available upon request): excluding the early period of data (1960s) or the most recent period (2000–2006), clustering the standard errors over education

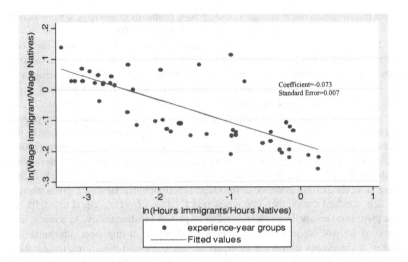

FIGURE 6. Correlation between relative wages and hours worked, Immigrant–natives with no degree; cells are experience–year groups, male with no degree only, 1960–2006
Note: Each observation corresponds to one of the 32 education–experience group in one of the considered years (1960, 1970, 1980, 1990, 2000, 2006). The horizontal axis measures the logarithm of the hours worked in the group by male immigrants relative to natives and the vertical axis measure the logarithm of the weekly wage paid to male immigrants relative to natives.

groups (or experience groups) only, or weighting the cells by hours rather than total employment. None of the resulting estimates is much different in size and statistical significance from those reported in Table 2.

For the estimates of $-1/\sigma_N$ to be consistent, relative productivity have to be uncorrelated with relative labor supplies after controlling for the fixed effects. Our structural model only calls for education–experience fixed effects.[23] Immigrant-biased productivity shocks concentrated in some cells, however, may attract more immigrants to those cells, thus inducing a positive correlation between relative productivity and labor supply. This would cause OLS to be upward biased and the bias would be more severe the larger the correlation. In this case, our estimates would represent an upper bound for the true value of $-1/\sigma_N$ so that the actual elasticity σ_N would be even smaller than what is implied by our estimates.

To control for some systematic types of correlation of the error with the explanatory variables over time and across groups, one can include additional specific effects. Borjas, Grogger, and Hanson (2008) in a specification otherwise similar to (8) include education-by-time and experience-by-time effects. Accordingly, they estimate 102 fixed effects with 192 observations and a very large part of the panel variation is absorbed by the fixed effects. This increases the standard errors, which become mostly

---

23.   As in the estimation of the other elasticities, we only include the effects required by the model.

larger than 0.03 and often as large as 0.04, posing problems in identifying a coefficient $-1/\sigma_N$ that is mostly estimated in the neighborhood of -0.05.

Specifically, let us consider their preferred specifications (for pooled men and women) which include all workers, weighted by hours worked, or full time workers only. These are reported in columns (2) and (3) of their Table 4, which show estimates of $-1/\sigma_N$ equal to 0.005 and -0.034 respectively, with associated standard errors of 0.024 and 0.036. Our corresponding estimates can be found in columns (2) and (5) of Panel A of Table 2 and are equal to -0.024 and -0.037 respectively, with associated standard errors of 0.015 and 0.012. An important difference lies in the standard errors, which are significantly larger in Borjas, Grogger, and Hanson (2008), implying that both of our point estimates are well within two standard deviations of theirs. Based on these results, Borjas, Grogger, and Hanson (2008) conclude that there is no compelling evidence of imperfect substitutability. However, given the size of their standard errors, they can rarely reject values of $-1/\sigma_N$ equal to -0.05, so that there is no compelling evidence either of perfect substitutability. As a result, and since, as we will see in Section 5, even a small degree of imperfect substitutability makes a significant difference in terms of the computed effects of immigration on native wages, we prefer our point estimates and standard errors as reported in Table 2.[24]

Imperfect substitutability between immigrants and natives of similar observable characteristics may derive from somewhat different skills among these groups leading to different choices of occupations. Peri and Sparber (2009) suggests that this is particularly true for low levels of education since these immigrants tend to have less English language skill. Since they do have similar physical and manual skills as natives they tend to specialize in manual-intensive tasks. This does not happen at high levels of education because the skills of college-educated workers are more similar between native and immigrants. Moreover, since the difference in skills tends to decrease the longer immigrants stay in the United States, imperfect substitutability could be particularly acute among young workers. For both reasons the estimated elasticity of substitution should be smaller for young and less-educated workers. In Table 2, Panel B shows the estimates of $-1/\sigma_N$ when we restrict the sample to cells including, alternatively, workers with no degree (first row of Panel B), a high school degree (second row), some college education (third row), or a college degree (fourth row). Each of the estimates is based on 48 observations (8 experience groups times 6 years) and controls for experience fixed effects (except specifications in columns (1) and (4)). Interestingly, the estimates of $-1/\sigma_N$ for the groups up to "Some college

---

24. Two recent studies have estimated $-1/\sigma_N$ for countries different from the United States using specifications similar to (8) but relying on even fewer dummies as controls. D'Amuri, Ottaviano, and Peri (2010) for Germany and Manacorda, Manning, and Wadsworth (this issue) for the UK both include only education, experience and time effects. As for their estimated values, while the results in D'Amuri, Ottaviano, and Peri are similar to ours, Manacorda, Manning, and Wadsworth find lower native–immigrant substitutability. This is possibly due to the fact that they identify the native–immigrant elasticity of substitution on yearly data, thus including among immigrants only the newest arrivals, who are likely to be the most different in skills and abilities from natives.

education" are very significant and between -0.06 and -0.10, with an average value around -0.08. They imply an average elasticity of substitution of 12.5. For college educated workers, on the other hand, there is no evidence of imperfect substitutability. Although not very precise, the estimate of $-1/\sigma_N$ for this group is very close to 0. Panel C of Table 2 shows the estimates when pooling education groups and separating cells for workers with potential experience up to 10 years (Row 9), 11 to 20 years (Row 10), 21 to 30 years (Row 11), or 31 to 40 years (Row 12). Each coefficient is estimated using 48 observations (4 education times 2 experience groups times 6 years). The estimates are in this case mostly significant. When we control for education fixed effects we also observe the predicted pattern according to which $-1/\sigma_N$ is larger in absolute value for the youngest group (-0.15 with corresponding elasticity of substitution 6.6) than for the others (-0.06 with corresponding elasticity of substitution 16.6).

To sum up, when the substitutability between natives and immigrants is constrained to be the same across education and experience groups, the estimated elasticity of substitution σ_N is about 20. When we allow for differences across education and experience groups, we find that natives and immigrants have a particularly low substitutability among low educated workers ($\sigma_N = 12.5$) and among young workers ($\sigma_N = 6.6$).

4.2. Education and Experience

We have used equation (8) to estimate $-1/\sigma_N$. From the same regression we also obtain estimates of the fixed effects φ_k. These can be translated into estimates of the systematic (time-invariant) component of immigrant and native productivities, $\hat{\theta}_{F,k} = \exp(\varphi_k)/(1 + \exp(\varphi_k))$ and $\hat{\theta}_{D,k} = 1/(1 + \exp(\varphi_k))$ respectively, which can be used to construct the labor composite $L_{i(N-1)}$ for group $i(N-1)$ using formula (2) for $n = N - 1$.[25] We can then calculate the corresponding average wage $w_{i(N-1)}$ and estimate $-1/\sigma_{N-1}$ by implementing equation (3). In so doing, we include two types of fixed effects. The first controls for the variation of the common aggregate term $\ln(\alpha A \kappa^{1-\alpha})$ + $(1/\sigma_1)\ln(L)$ and group-specific aggregates $\sum_{n=1}^{N-2}(1/\sigma_n - 1/\sigma_{n+1})\ln(L_{i(n)})$. The second controls for the systematic variation of group-specific productivities $\ln\theta_{i(N-1)}$.

The first type of fixed effect is dictated by the nested-CES structure and, therefore, depends on the chosen nesting model.[26] The second type is, instead, required by the fact that the variation of $\ln\theta_{i(N-1)}$ may be correlated with $L_{i(N-1)}$, which would affect the consistency of the estimates. As the theoretical framework has no implication as to which specific effects to include in order to control for such a correlation, we simply assume that while $\ln\theta_{i(N-1)}$ may have a systematic component across groups

---

25. In the derivation of the expressions for $\hat{\theta}_{F,k}$ and $\hat{\theta}_{D,k}$ we have used the standardization $\hat{\theta}_{F,k} + \hat{\theta}_{D,k} = 1$.

26. For instance, in model A the common aggregate term can be controlled for by time effects whereas $\ln L_{i(N-2)}$ can be captured by education-by-time effects.

potentially correlated with the distribution of $L_{i(N-1)}$, the remaining variation over time is a zero-average random variable uncorrelated with changes in $L_{i(N-1)}$, and we add some structure over time (such as time trends). This method can be iterated upward so that, once we have the estimates of σ_n and $\ln \theta_{i(n)}$, we can construct $L_{i(n-1)}$ and $w_{i(n-1)}$ and proceed to estimate σ_{n-1} by applying (3) to level $n - 1$.

Let us emphasize that while we estimate the elasticity σ_{N-1} (and higher level elasticities σ_n with $n = 1, \ldots, N - 2$) by implementing (3), the interpretation of the elasticity σ_{N-1} and the type of fixed effects included depend on the nesting structure chosen. While so far our recursive notation has proved useful in order to embed the alternative nesting models in a single flexible nested-CES framework, the comparative discussion of estimated elasticities across models will benefit from a more intuitive notation. Say, for example, that we want to compare the estimated substitutability between narrow experience groups. Depending on the model, the corresponding elasticity would be σ_{N-1} (models A, B and C) or σ_{N-2} (model D). Hence, from now on we prefer to label the various elasticities by the name of the relevant characteristics rather than by their order in the nesting structure. Of course each elasticity coming from the different nesting models is estimated using the appropriate specification of (3) and includes the appropriate set of fixed effects prescribed by the corresponding structure. Henceforth, σ_{EXP} will denote the elasticity of substitution between five-year experience groups and will be estimated for all models; σ_{Y-O} will denote the elasticity of substitution between twenty-year experience groups and, therefore, will be estimated only for model C; σ_{EDU} will denote the elasticity of substitution between narrow education groups and, therefore, will be estimated for all models; and σ_{H-L} will denote the elasticity of substitution between high- and low-education workers and, therefore, will be estimated only for specification B.

Before presenting our estimates, two comments are in order. First, in the existing literature there are estimates of all these elasticities. In particular, σ_{Y-O} and σ_{EXP} have been estimated by Welch (1979), Katz and Murphy (1992) and Card and Lemieux (2001) while σ_{H-L} and σ_{EDU} have been estimated by Katz and Murphy (1992) and Goldin and Katz (2008). This means that our estimates and those in the literature can be used to inform the choice of parameters for the computation of total wage effects in Section 5. Second, as we estimate elasticities at higher levels of the nesting structure (especially σ_{H-L}), we end up using only a few large labor aggregates for which the Census data provide very few observations over time (six year points only). For this reason, we complement the estimates that use Census data with estimates obtained on data from the Current Population Survey (CPS) 1963–2006, which provides 44 yearly observations.

4.2.1. Census Data.   First, let us discuss our estimates of the elasticities of substitution for experience groups using Census data. Table 3 reports the estimates of the parameters $-1/\sigma_{\mathrm{EXP}}$ and $-1/\sigma_{Y-O}$ obtained for the different nesting structures by implementing the appropriate version of equation (3). All regressions are estimated using 2SLS and immigrant labor supply to instrument total labor supply (measured as

TABLE 3. Estimates of $(-1/\sigma_{EXP})$.

Structure of the nest	Model A and B		Model C	Model D
Estimated coefficient:	(1) $(-1/\sigma_{EXP})$	(2) $(-1/\sigma_{EXP})$	(3) $(-1/\sigma_{Y-O})$	(4) $(-1/\sigma_{EXP})$
Men	−0.16***	−0.19**	−0.31*	−0.30***
Labor Supply is Hours worked	(0.05)	(0.08)	(0.15)	(0.06)
Women	−0.05	−0.08*	−0.14	−0.01
Labor Supply is Hours worked	(0.05)	(0.045)	(0.12)	(0.06)
Pooled Men and Women	−0.14***	−0.17**	−0.28**	−0.23***
Labor Supply is Hours worked	(0.04)	(0.06)	(0.12)	(0.05)
Men	−0.13***	−0.18**	−0.26*	−0.22***
Labor Supply is Employment	(0.05)	(0.08)	(0.12)	(0.06)
Cells:	Education-experience-year	Education-experience-year	Education-Young/Old-year	Experience-year
Effects Included	Education by Year and Education by Experience	Education-Young-Year, Education-Old-Year and Education by Experience	Education-Year and Education-Young/Old	Experience effects and year effects
Observations	192	192	96	48

Note: National Census and ACS U.S. data 1960–2006. Each cell reports the estimates from a different regression that implements equation (3) in the text for the appropriate characteristics and using the appropriate aggregate and fixed effects. The method of estimation is 2SLS using immigrant workers' hours as an instrument for total workers' hours. Cells are weighted by their employment. Standard errors are heteroskedasticity robust and clustered at the education-experience level for columns (1) and (2), at the education-young/old level for column (3) and at the experience level for column (4).
*, **, *** = significant at the 10, 5 and 1% level.

hours worked or employment) in the relevant labor composite[27]. As in Section 4.1, we are assuming that, after controlling for the fixed effects, the variation of immigrants by cell is random and orthogonal to relative productivity changes. As before, rows 1 to 3 report the estimates obtained using men, women, or both in the wage sample whereas row 4 uses employment rather than hours worked as measure of labor supply. The other rows report the cells, the fixed effects, and the number of observations included in the various specifications. In estimating $-1/\sigma_{\text{EXP}}$, models A and B generate exactly the same regression equation, for which estimates are reported in column (1). Model C produces estimates of $-1/\sigma_{\text{EXP}}$ at level $N-1$ and of $-1/\sigma_{Y-O}$ at level $N-2$. These are in columns (2) and (3), respectively. Model D generates estimates of $-1/\sigma_{\text{EXP}}$ at level $N-2$, which are reported in column (4).

There is some variation in the estimates depending on the sample and the model. In particular, estimates using the wage sample of women are never significant. The estimates for men and for the pooled sample are, however, remarkably consistent, always significantly different from 0 and averaging around -0.20. The wage sample of women may have a significant amount of error. Women often have a more discontinuous working career than men, so potential experience may be a noisy proxy of actual experience. For this reason most studies (see, for example, Card and Lemieux 2001) focus on men only and, when considering women, one should expect an attenuation bias. The other estimates vary between -0.13 and -0.31, which is exactly the range previously estimated in the literature for this parameter. In a setup similar to ours with five-year experience categories within education categories, Welch (1979, Tables 7 and 8) finds a value of $-1/\sigma_{\text{EXP}}$ between -0.080 and -0.218. Katz and Murphy (1992, footnote 23) estimate a value of -0.342 using only two experience groups (*young*, equivalent to 1–5 years of experience and *old*, equivalent to 26–35 years of experience). Finally, in the most influential contribution, Card and Lemieux (2001, Table V) use the supply variation due to the baby boomers' cohorts to estimate a value between -0.107 and -0.237. Hence, an estimate of -0.20, which is around the middle of our range, would be also in the middle of the combined ranges of previous estimates. We take this as a reasonable reference value, implying $\sigma_{\text{EXP}} = 5$.

Another overall implication of the estimates in Table 3 is that there is no strong evidence that the elasticity of substitution between broad experience groups (*young* and *old*) is lower than the elasticity between narrow five-year experience groups. The coefficient $-1/\sigma_{\text{EXP}}$ is estimated in the pooled sample at -0.17 with a standard deviation of 0.06 while $-1/\sigma_{Y-O}$ for the same sample is -0.28 with a standard error of 0.12. A formal test does not reject the hypothesis of them being equal at the 10% level.[28] Thus, given that for $1/\sigma_{Y-O} = 1/\sigma_{\text{EXP}}$ model C reduces to model A and no

---

27.   This reflects the idea that changes in immigrants' employment in each skill group, once we control for fixed effects, is mainly driven by supply shocks such as demographic factors and migration costs. Such an assumption is the common one in the literature on the national wage effect of immigrants.

28.   We have also estimated $-1/\sigma_{Y-O}$ and $-1/\sigma_{\text{EXP}}$ on yearly CPS data, using a method similar to Katz and Murphy (1992). This is reported in our online appendices. Doing so, we do not find evidence that those elasticities are statistically different either. Also in this case the point estimates of $-1/\sigma_{Y-O}$ and $-1/\sigma_{\text{EXP}}$ are mostly between -0.1 and -0.2.

previous study has found $1/\sigma_{Y-O}$ different from $1/\sigma_{EXP}$. We interpret these results as suggesting that *model C can be reasonably absorbed into model A*.

Second, let us discuss our estimates of elasticity of substitution for education groups using Census data. Table 4 shows the estimates of $-1/\sigma_{EDU}$, reporting the estimates obtained from the appropriate versions of (3) for model A in columns (1) and (2) and those for model D in columns (3) and (4). The estimates for model C (not reported) are essentially identical to those obtained for model A, further confirming the coincidence between these two models. The estimates in Table 4 are very sensitive to the nesting structure adopted and to the fixed effects included. Model A prescribes the inclusion of time effects, so we either include education effects and education-specific time trends (to capture relative changes in education demand) or only education-specific time trends. Model D dictates the inclusion of experience by year effects (column (3)) but we also include education–experience and education–year effects to control for heterogeneous productivity (column (4)). We have also tried several other combinations of fixed effects and trends obtaining mostly negative, non-significant estimates. The specifications that produce significant estimates (column (2) and (3)) show values ranging between -0.22 and -0.43. The literature provides scant guidance for this parameter. The only clear comparisons we can make are with Borjas (2003), whose estimate is -0.759 (with standard error equal to 0.582), and with Borjas and Katz (2007), whose estimate is -0.412 (with standard error equal to 0.312) due to the fact that both papers use the same nesting structure as model A. The estimate in Borjas and Katz (2007) is indeed very close to those reported in column (2) of our Table 4, which uses exactly the same set of dummies and trends that they use.

Most of the literature, however, has assumed a split between two imperfectly substitutable education groups (High and Low) and has produced several estimates of the corresponding elasticity $-1/\sigma_{H-L}$. This is also assumed by our model B. Unfortunately, however, $-1/\sigma_{H-L}$ cannot be estimated with available Census data since by considering high school graduates or less as low-education workers and college-educated or more as high-education workers we are left with only twelve observations to work with. Hence, in order to obtain estimates of $-1/\sigma_{H-L}$, we revert to CPS data.

4.2.2. CPS Data. Writing (3) for model B at the highest level of nesting ($n = 1$) for $i(1) = $ High and $i(1) = $ Low and taking the ratio between the resulting expressions, we obtain

$$\ln\left(\frac{w_{Ht}}{w_{Lt}}\right) = \ln\frac{\theta_{Ht}}{\theta_{Lt}} - \frac{1}{\sigma_{H-L}}\ln\left(\frac{L_{Ht}}{L_{Lt}}\right), \qquad (9)$$

where w_{Ht} is the average weekly wage of workers with a college degree or more (calculated as an hours-weighted average) and w_{Lt} is the hours-weighted average weekly wage of high school graduates or less. The parameters θ_{Ht} and θ_{Lt} capture the productivities of the two groups and L_{Ht} and L_{Lt} measure their labor supplies. Note that equation (9) is identical to the one estimated by Katz and Murphy (1992) (henceforth, simply KM).

TABLE 4. Estimates of $(-1/\sigma_{EDU})$.

Specification:	Model A		Model D	
	(1) With education-specific FE and trends	(2) With education-specific trends only	(3) With experience-year FE	(4) With experience-year, education-experience and education-year FE
Men Labor Supply is Hours worked	-0.16 (0.12)	-0.28** (0.10)	-0.22* (0.12)	-0.04 (0.03)
Women Labor Supply is Hours worked	-0.16 (0.15)	-0.34** (0.14)	-0.25** (0.11)	-0.02 (0.04)
Pooled Men and Women Labor Supply is Hours worked	-0.15 (0.10)	-0.30** (0.11)	-0.23** (0.11)	-0.02 (0.03)
Men Labor Supply is employment	-0.17 (0.10)	-0.43** (0.16)	-0.28** (0.09)	-0.03 (0.03)
Cells	Education-Year	Education-Year	Education-Experience-years	Education-Experience-years
Fixed Effects Included:	Education-specific effects, Education-specific trends and Year effects	Education-specific trends and Year effects	Experience by year only	Experience by year, Education by year and education by Experience
Number of observations	24	24	192	192

Note: National Census and ACS, U.S. data 1960–2006. Each cell reports the estimates from a different regression that implements (3) in the text using the appropriate wage as dependent variable and labor aggregate as explanatory variable and the appropriate fixed effects. The method of estimation is 2SLS using immigrant workers as instrument for total workers in the relative skill group. Cells are weighted by their employment. Standard errors are heteroskedasticity robust and clustered at the education level for columns (1) and (2), and at the education-experience level for columns (3) and (4).
*, **, *** = significant at the 10, 5 and 1% level.

We implement (9) on the yearly IPUMS–CPS data from King et al. (2008) with the sample and variable definitions generally identical to those used for the Census data in the previous section.[29] The data cover the period 1963–2006, so we have 44 yearly observations to estimate each elasticity. Assuming that the relative productivity $\ln(\theta_{Ht}/\theta_{Lt})$ can be decomposed into a systematic time trend and a random variable u_t uncorrelated with relative labor supply, we can estimate $-1/\sigma_{H-L}$ using OLS. There are only two small differences between our procedure and the KM one. First, our measures of labor supply L_{Ht} and L_{Lt} are CES labor composites rather than simple sums of hours. The two measures of labor supply, however, turn out to be very highly correlated so that the distinction does not matter much. Second, in KM workers with some college education contribute their hours of work partly to L_{Ht} and partly to L_{Lt} according to some regression weights. In our case all workers with some college education are included in L_{Ht}.

The estimates of $-1/\sigma_{H-L}$ based on (9) are reported in column (1) of Table 5. As in KM, we use the pooled sample of men and women and show both the heteroskedasticity-robust and the Newey–West autocorrelation-robust standard errors (as the time-series data may contain some autocorrelation). Rows 1 and 2 differ in terms of the allocation of hours worked by workers with some college education. Row 1 splits them between the high-education and the low-education groups as in KM whereas row 2 includes all workers in the former group, as implied by our model. In addition, row 3 uses employment rather than hours worked as the measure of labor supply while row 4 omits the 1960s. Finally, parentheses highlight the OLS standard errors while square brackets highlight the Newey–West autocorrelation-robust standard errors.

According to column (1), all estimates of $-1/\sigma_{H-L}$ are between -0.32 and -0.66, with standard errors between 0.06 and 0.09, hence very significantly different from 0. These estimates are close to the value estimated by KM at -0.709 with a standard error of 0.15 and confirm the imperfect substitutability between high- and low-education workers with an elasticity of substitution ranging between 1.5 and 1.8. When workers with some college education are included only in the High Education group (row 2), the estimated $-1/\sigma_{H-L}$ is -0.32, thus somewhat smaller in absolute value and compatible with an elasticity of substitution of 3. All in all, these results suggest that an elasticity around 2 (as frequently used in the literature) represents indeed a reasonable estimate of σ_{H-L}.

The KM method embedded in specification (9) is also useful to estimate the elasticities of substitution $\sigma_{EDU,H}$ and $\sigma_{EDU,L}$ between narrow education categories within the high- and low-education groups. In particular, in model B the ratios of equations (3) at the nesting stage $n = 2$ within the two broad groups produce the two equations that allow estimation of the inverse of those elasticities by regressing the within-group wage ratios on the corresponding within-group employment ratios,

---

29. The IPUMS (Integrated Public Use Microdata Samples) produces comparable variable definitions and names between the CENSUS data (that we used in the previous sections) and CPS data. Additional information on the construction of sample and variables using CPS data can be found in Appendix B and, in greater detail, in the online appendix to this paper.

TABLE 5. Elasticity of substitution between broad and narrow education groups.

	Model B			
	(1) $-1/\sigma_{H\text{-}L}$	(2) $-1/\sigma_{EDU,L}$	(3) $-1/\sigma_{EDU,H}$	Observations
"Some College" split between L_H and L_L	−0.54*** (0.06) [0.07]	−0.029 (0.018) [0.021]	−0.16* (0.08) [0.10]	44
"Some College" in L_H	−0.32*** (0.06) [0.08]	−0.029 (0.018) [0.021]	−0.16* (0.08) [0.10]	44
Employment as a Measure of Labor Supply	−0.66*** (0.07) [0.09]	−0.039 (0.020) [0.024]	−0.08 (0.09) [0.11]	44
1970–2006	−0.52*** (0.06) [0.08]	0.021 (0.028) [0.025]	−0.13 (0.08) [0.09]	36

Note: CPS data 1962–2006, Pooled Men and Women. Each cell is the estimate from a separate regression using yearly CPS data. In the first column we estimate the relative wage elasticity of the group of workers with a high school degree or less relative to those with some college or more. Method and construction of the relative supply (hours worked) and relative average weekly wages are described in the text in Section 4.2.2. In the first row we split workers with some college education between H and L. In the second row we include them in group H, following the CES nesting in our model. In the second column we consider only the groups of workers with no degree and those with a high school degree (the dependent variable is relative wages and the explanatory is relative hours worked). In the third column we consider only workers with some college education and workers with a college degree or more (the dependent variable is relative wages and the explanatory is relative hours worked). In brackets are the standard errors and in square brackets the Newey-West autocorrelation-robust standard errors. *** = significant at 1% level; ** = significant at 5% level; * = significant at 10% level.

assuming that relative productivities follow a time trend plus a random term uncorrelated with relative supplies. Columns (2) and (3) of Table 5 report the estimates of $-1/\sigma_{EDU,L}$ and $-1/\sigma_{EDU,H}$.[30] Both estimates, and particularly the former, are much smaller in absolute value than $-1/\sigma_{H-L}$. In the majority of cases they are not significantly different from 0. The estimates of $-1/\sigma_{EDU,L}$ are at most equal to −0.039 and a one-sided test can exclude at any confidence level that the estimate is larger than 0.10 in absolute value. The F-test statistic for $-1/\sigma_{EDU,L} = -0.32$ (a value that corresponds to the lowest estimate of $-1/\sigma_{H-L}$) is 258, thus rejecting the null hypothesis of $-1/\sigma_{EDU,L} = -1/\sigma_{H-L}$ at an overwhelming level of confidence. The estimate of $-1/\sigma_{EDU,H}$ is around −0.10. Again, the hypotheses $-1/\sigma_{EDU,H} = -0.32$ and $-1/\sigma_{EDU,H} = -1/\sigma_{H-L}$ are rejected.

Hence, three important results emerge from Table 5. First, the restriction $-1/\sigma_{EDU,H} = -1/\sigma_{EDU,L} = -1/\sigma_{H-L}$ is overwhelmingly rejected by the data. This provides evidence that model *B* better fits the time-series CPS data than model A.

---

30. The corresponding estimates using wages calculated on the male sample only are available in the Table G.5 of the online appendix.

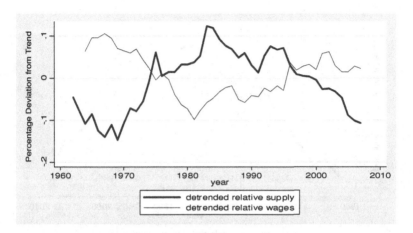

FIGURE 7. Relative supply and relative wages: (college and more)/(high school or less)
1963–2006.

Second, the estimates of $-1/\sigma_{H-L}$ are between -0.32 and -0.66 with an average of -0.50. This implies $\sigma_{H-L} = 2$, which is perfectly in line with the estimates of Katz and Murphy (1992), Angrist (1995), Johnson (1997), and Krusell et al. (2000) which range between 1.5 and 2.5. Third, the estimated value of $-1/\sigma_{\text{EDU},L}$ is between -0.039 and 0, implying an elasticity of substitution between workers with a high school degree and those with no high school degree of 25 or above.

The reason for the extremely different estimates of $-1/\sigma_{\text{EDU},L}$ and $-1/\sigma_{H-L}$ is clear from the detrended time series of relative supplies (thick line) versus relative wages (thin line) of college graduates and more versus high school graduates and less (Figure 7) and of high school graduates versus high school dropouts (Figure 8). In particular, Figure 7 shows clear and strong mirror movements of the relative (detrended) wages and supplies, a clear sign of negative correlation resulting in negative and significant $-1/\sigma_{\text{EDU},H}$. In contrast, Figure 8 shows no movement at all of relative wages vis à vis the very large fluctuations of the relative detrended relative supplies, which are similar in direction and larger in magnitude than those in Figure 7. This results in a value of $-1/\sigma_{\text{EDU},L}$ close to 0.

To sum up, CPS data suggest that reasonable estimates are in the neighborhood of -0.5 for $-1/\sigma_{\text{EDU},H}$ and between -0.10 and 0 for $-1/\sigma_{\text{EDU},L}$ and $-1/\sigma_{\text{EDU},H}$ with the first coefficient closer to 0 and the second closer to -0.10. Accordingly, while one should be cautious in interpreting these values given the sensitivity of the estimates to specifications and nesting structures, the pattern that emerges seems to suggest that model B is preferred by the data to model A, with σ_{H-L} around 2 and $\sigma_{\text{EDU},H}$ and $\sigma_{\text{EDU},L}$ both larger than or equal to 10.

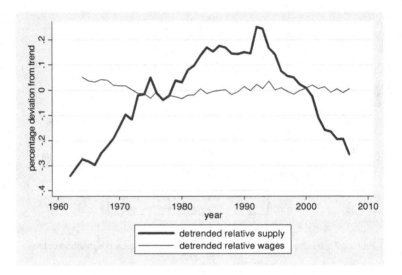

FIGURE 8.   Relative supply and relative wages: (college and more)/(high school or less)
1963–2006.

5. Wage Effects of US Immigration

In Section 4 we have presented a new set of estimated elasticities of substitution
between workers with different education, experience, and place of birth. In particular,
we have argued in favor of a common elasticity of substitution σ_{EXP} (in the range
of 5.5 to 6.25) between any pair of experience groups, and for an elasticity of
substitution σ_N around 20 between natives and immigrants with the same education
and experience, with some evidence that if one allows σ_N to vary between more and
less educated, the corresponding elasticities become 33 and 11.1 respectively. The
support for a common σ_{EXP} has led us to subsume model C in model A. Moreover,
the findings against a common elasticity of substitution σ_{EDU} between different pairs
of education groups have led us to prefer model B to both model A and model D
with an elasticity of substitution σ_{H-L} around 2 between broad education groups, and
elasticities of substitution $\sigma_{\text{EDU},H}$ and $\sigma_{\text{EDU},L}$ around 6.25 and 33.3 respectively. On
the other hand, if one still wanted to use models A and D as a robustness check,
it would be reasonable to adopt an estimate of σ_{EDU} from column (2) of Table 4 of
around 3.3.

Whereas, as discussed in Section 2.4, the previous literature has often focused
on generally uninformative *partial* wage effects, we provide here an assessment of
the *total* wage effects of immigration to the United States in the period 1990–2006
by comparing the implications of models A, B, and D based on the corresponding
estimated elasticities. Specifically, we use the estimated elasticities from Tables 2 to

5 and the data on actual immigrant flows by skill group reported in column 3 of Table 1 (together with the appropriate wage shares) to calculate the percentage impact of immigration in any skill group on the wages of each skill group as implied by expressions (5) and (6). We then aggregate all these impacts to obtain averages for specific sets of workers.[31]

Table 6 reports the simulations of the total long-run wage effects of immigration over the 1990–2006 period, separating US-born workers in panel A and foreign-born workers in panel B. The term *long-run* implies that the simulated effects assume full adjustment of the capital stock of the economy in order to restore the capital–labor ratio as it was before the inflow. We focus on 1990–2006 as this was the period of fastest immigration growth in recent US history.[32] As highlighted in the top row of the table, we consider models A, B, and D due to the fact that, according to the data, model C can be absorbed into model A (see Section 4.2.1). The values of the elasticities used in each simulation are reported in the first six rows of the table. The elasticities are the estimated parameters. They are asymptotically normal and their point estimates and standard deviations are reported in the first rows of Table 6. We consider 1,000 draws from the joint normal parameter distribution with the specified average and standard deviation. Then, using the formulas for the appropriate model, we calculate the total wage effect for each education–experience group for each draw of the parameters. This produces 1,000 simulated effects for each skill group and each parameter configuration. From those simulated realizations we obtain the simulated average total wage effect for the group and its simulated standard error. The reported wage change (and standard error) in each education group for foreign- and US-born workers are obtained by weighting the percentage total wage change (and standard errors) of each experience-education group by its wage share in the education group.[33] This provides the entries in the rows labeled "less than HS", "HS graduates", "Some CO", and "CO graduates", which show the simulated total effects, averaging by education group and their simulated standard error. We also average the changes across education groups for US- and foreign-born workers separately, again weighting the effect in each group (and its standard error) by their wage shares. The resulting values are reported in the rows labeled "Average US-born" and "Average Foreign-Born". Finally, we average the changes for the two groups of US- and foreign-born workers, still using wage share weights, to obtain the overall wage change (and its standard deviation) reported in the last row labeled "Overall Average".

Recall that Table 6 reports the "long-run" effects, after capital has fully adjusted to the labor supply shock caused by immigration. Consistent with our theoretical framework the overall average wage effect is always zero in the long run (as the average wage depends only on the capital–labor ratio and this does not change in

---

31. The detailed formulas relative to model B are described in Appendix A.2. The formulas for the other models are analogous. The STATA code to implement the formulas for all models are available in the online appendix.

32. Net immigration decreased in 2007 and 2008 and it was negative in 2009.

33. Weighting by wage shares is dictated by the nested-CES structure.

TABLE 6. Calculated long-run wage effects of immigration, 1990–2006. (with simulated standard errors)

Nesting Structures:		Model A/C			Model D		Model B		
Parameter values (std. errors in parentheses):	(1) $1/\sigma_N = 0$	(2) Estimated $1/\sigma_N$	(3) Education specific $1/\sigma_N$	(4) Estimated $1/\sigma_N$	(5) Education specific $1/\sigma_N$	(6) Estimated $1/\sigma_N$	(7) Education specific $1/\sigma_N$	(8) Katz-Murphy $1/\sigma_{HIGH-LOW}$	(9) $1/\sigma_{EXP} = 0.13$
$1/\sigma_{H-L}$	0.30 (0.11)	0.30 (0.11)	0.30 (0.11)	0.28 (0.09)	0.28 (0.09)	0.54 (0.06)	0.54 (0.06)	0.71 (0.15)	0.54 (0.06)
$1/\sigma_{EDU.H}$	0.30 (0.11)	0.30 (0.11)	0.30 (0.11)	0.28 (0.09)	0.28 (0.09)	0.16 (0.08)	0.16 (0.08)	0	0.16 (0.08)
$1/\sigma_{EDU.L}$	0.30 (0.11)	0.30 (0.11)	0.30 (0.11)	0.28 (0.09)	0.28 (0.09)	0.03 (0.02)	0.03 (0.02)	0	0.03 (0.02)
$1/\sigma_{EXP}$	0.16 (0.05)	0.16 (0.05)	0.16 (0.05)	0.30 (0.05)	0.30 (0.05)	0.16 (0.05)	0.16 (0.05)	0.16 (0.05)	0.13 (0.05)
$1/(\sigma_N)_H$	0	0.05 (0.01)	0.03 (0.03)	0.05 (0.01)	0.03 (0.03)	0.05 (0.01)	0.03 (0.03)	0.03 (0.03)	0.03 (0.03)
$1/(\sigma_N)_L$	0	0.05 (0.01)	0.09 (0.01)	0.05 (0.01)	0.09 (0.01)	0.05 (0.01)	0.09 (0.01)	0.09 (0.01)	0.09 (0.01)

PANEL A

Real percentage change of the wage of us-born workers due to immigration, 1990–2006.
(simulated standard errors in parentheses)

Less than HS	−3.1 (1.0)	−2.0 (1.0)	−1.1 (1.0)	−1.8 (1.0)	−1.0 (1.0)	0.6 (0.4)	1.5 (0.4)	1.7 (0.4)	1.5 (0.5)
HS graduates	0.7 (0.3)	1.1 (0.3)	1.5 (0.3)	1.1 (0.4)	1.5 (0.4)	0.3 (0.1)	0.7 (0.1)	0.6 (0.2)	0.7 (0.1)
Some CO	1.6 (0.5)	1.9 (0.6)	1.8 (0.6)	1.8 (0.5)	1.7 (0.6)	1.3 (0.3)	1.2 (0.4)	0.3 (0.3)	1.1 (0.5)
CO graduates	−1.1 (0.5)	−0.3 (0.5)	−0.6 (0.6)	−0.2 (0.4)	0.5 (0.6)	0.3 (0.4)	0.0 (0.6)	0.6 (0.5)	0.0 (0.6)
Average US-born	**0.0 (0.5)**	**0.6 (0.6)**	**0.6 (0.6)**	**0.6 (0.5)**	**0.6 (0.6)**	**0.6 (0.3)**	**0.6 (0.4)**	**0.6 (0.4)**	**0.6 (0.5)**

TABLE 6. Continued

Nesting Structures:		Model A/C		Model D		Model B			
Parameter values (std. errors in parentheses):	(1) $1/\sigma_N = 0$	(2) Estimated $1/\sigma_N$	(3) Education specific $1/\sigma_N$	(4) Estimated $1/\sigma_N$	(5) Education specific $1/\sigma_N$	(6) Estimated $1/\sigma_N$	(7) Education specific $1/\sigma_N$	(8) Katz-Murphy $1/\sigma_{HIGH-LOW}$	(9) $1/\sigma_{EXP} = 0.13$
					PANEL B				

Real percentage change of the wage of foreign-born workers due to immigration, 1990–2006.
(simulated standard errors in parenthesis)

	(1)	(2)	(3)	(4)	(5)	(6)	(7)	(8)	(9)
Less than HS	-3.1 (1.0)	-7.4 (1.4)	-10.6 (1.3)	-7.3 (1.3)	-10.5 (1.4)	-4.8 (0.9)	-8.1 (0.9)	-7.8 (0.9)	-8.1 (0.9)
HS graduates	0.7 (0.3)	-6.3 (1.4)	-11.7 (1.4)	-6.3 (1.5)	-11.8 (1.4)	-7.1 (1.4)	-12.6 (1.4)	-12.8 (1.4)	-12.6 (1.4)
Some CO	1.6 (0.5)	-2.9 (1.1)	-1.1 (2.8)	-3.1 (1.1)	-1.1 (2.7)	-3.6 (1.0)	-2.2 (2.7)	-2.6 (2.8)	-1.8 (2.9)
CO graduates	-1.1 (0.5)	-8.8 (1.6)	-5.7 (4.6)	-8.8 (1.6)	-5.6 (4.5)	-8.2 (1.6)	-5.5 (4.4)	-4.6 (4.8)	-5.3 (4.8)
Average Foreign-born	0.0 (0.5)	-6.8 (1.4)	-6.7 (3.0)	-6.8 (1.4)	-6.7 (3.0)	-6.4 (1.3)	-6.7 (2.8)	-6.3 (3.0)	-6.4 (3.0)
Overall average	0.0 (0.4)	0.0 (0.6)	0.0 (0.8)	0.0 (0.6)	0.0 (0.8)	0.0 (0.4)	0.0 (0.6)	0.0 (0.6)	0.0 (0.7)

Note: The percentage wage changes for each education group are obtained averaging the wage change of each education-experience group weighting by the wage share in the education group. The wage change for each group is calculated using the formulas for the appropriate nesting structure. Since the parameters used (listed in the first 6 rows) are normally distributed random variables we proceed as follows. We first generate 1000 extractions per each configuration of the parameters (described in the top of the column) from a joint normal distribution. We then calculate the wage effect for each education-experience group and then we take the average and the std. deviation of the 1000 values. The US-born and foreign-born average changes and their standard errors are obtained by weighting changes (and standard errors) of each education group by its share in the 1990 wage bill of the group. The overall average wage change adds the change of US- and foreign-born weighted for the relative wage shares in 1990 and it is always equal to 0 due to the long-run assumption that the capital-labor ratio adjusts to maintain constant returns to capital.

the long run). However the imperfect substitutability between natives and immigrants implies that there may be a permanent effect of immigration on the average wage of each group (as shown in the last row of panels A and B) which is, in this case, positive for natives (whose relative supply decreases) and negative for immigrants (whose relative supply increases).

Turning to the columns, column (1) shows the simulated wage effects using model A and the parameter combination estimated on Census data using model A (namely the estimates in the third row of column (2) in Table 4 and in the first row of column (1) in Table 3) except for $1/\sigma_N$, which is taken to be 0. Such a combination of parameters is close to that adopted by Borjas (2003) and Borjas and Katz (2007). Columns (2) and (3) present simulations using the same nesting model and parameter combination as column (1), except for $1/\sigma_N$ whose value is estimated. We either impose that $1/\sigma_N$ is equal for all groups, and specifically equal to 0.05 (which is roughly the average estimate in Table 2, panel A), or we allow it to differ across education groups using $1/\sigma_N = 0.09$ for those with a high school degree or less and $1/\sigma_N = 0.03$ for those with some college education or more (column (3)). These are the average estimates from Table 2, panel B. In columns (4) and (5) we use the parameter configuration estimated using model D (first row of specification 4 in Table 3 and fourth row of specification 3 in Table 4) and the formulas from model D to produce the simulated values. Columns (6), (7), and (9) show the results obtained using the parameter configuration estimated with model B when, as estimated in Section 4.2.2, substitutability is significantly lower between broad education groups than between narrow education groups within the same broad group. Specifications 6 and 7 use the estimates from the first row of Table 5 and differ only in their treatment of $1/\sigma_N$ as equal across all groups or as education-specific. Specification 9 uses an alternative, smaller estimate of $1/\sigma_{EXP}$. Finally, column (8) uses the elasticity between education groups from Katz and Murphy (1992) and the other parameters from our model B estimates. Those authors estimate a value of $1/\sigma_{H-L}$ equal to 0.71 and perfect substitution within broad education groups.

Let us first compare the results reported in column (1), in which natives and immigrants are perfect substitutes, with those in columns (2) or (3), in which they are instead imperfect substitutes. Three main differences emerge. First, the wage loss of the least-educated native workers is reduced by 1.1 or 2 percentage points. Given that in column (1) the negative wage impact is estimated at −3.1 percentage points, that loss is reduced between one- and two-thirds of its absolute value. Accounting for the uncertainty of the effects, captured by the simulated standard errors, the wage loss of less-educated natives is not significant in column (3) and marginally significant in column (2). Second, on average, all the other native groups gain a bit more (or lose a bit less) in columns (2) and (3) relative to column (1). In fact, natives as a whole gain 0.6% of their average wage in columns (2) and (3) (although the gain is not significantly different from 0 if we account for the standard error). Third, the gains of natives in columns (2) and (3) relative to column (1) happen at the expense of previous immigrants as these bear most of the competitive pressure from new immigrants due to their perfect substitutability. This is the relevant distributional shift due to immigration and imperfect substitutability: on average, natives gain 0.6 to 0.7% of their wages whereas previous immigrants lose 6.6 to 7% of their wages. The losses of immigrants are statistically significant at a 1% confidence level if we use the simulated standard error and a normal two-sided test.

The results for model D in columns (4) and (5) are quite similar to those of model A. This is because the estimated elasticities across education and nativity groups are similar. Moreover, for given elasticities, the order of nesting between education and experience has little bearing on the wage effects. In particular, the losses of natives with low or intermediate education seem a bit attenuated but the gaps are small. Otherwise, the three main differences with respect to column (1) apply to these cases too.

Finally, columns (6)–(9) report the wage effects in model B, which Section 4.2.2 has shown to be preferred by the data. In light of the estimates in that section, columns (6), (7), and (9) set $1/\sigma_{H-L} = 0.54$, $1/\sigma_{EDU,H} = 0.16$ and $1/\sigma_{EDU,LOW} = 0.03$, assuming imperfect substitutability between natives and immigrants to be either equal across groups (column (6)) or education-specific (columns (7) to (9)). Column (8) uses $1/\sigma_{H-L} = 0.71$, which is the exact estimate from Katz and Murphy (1992), and in column (9) we test how sensitive the results are to changing $1/\sigma_{EXP}$ to 0.13. The wage effects are not too different across all columns. Interestingly, the wage effects on less-educated natives are usually small but are positive and sometimes significant, especially when one allows the lower substitutability between natives and immigrants among less educated workers (columns (7) to (9)). Natives still gain as a group (0.6% of their average wages) and immigrants still lose (-6.1%). The main difference with columns (2) or (3) is that the relative wage changes of more and less educated natives are now much smaller, with the two groups experiencing more homogeneous (usually positive but not very significant) effects. This is because, while from 1990 to 2006 immigration led to rather unbalanced increases in labor supplies between workers with no high school degree (23.6%) and high school graduates (10%), increases were rather balanced between workers with high school or less (13%) and those with some college or more (10%). Hence, the value of $1/\sigma_{EDU,L}$ plays a fundamental role in determining the relative wage effects, and a value as large as 0.3 (column (1)) produces much larger effects relative to the preferred value of 0.03 used in columns (6)–(9). Indeed, in these specifications the negative effect on the least educated natives, due to the fact that the distribution of immigrants is tilted towards lower educational levels, is balanced, or more than balanced, by the positive effects, due to their imperfect substitutability. That is why even the least-educated natives face a small long-run positive effect of immigration. The wage loss of less-educated previous immigrants is between 4.8 and 8.1%. Increasing the value of $\sigma_{EDU,L}$ to infinity (which is never rejected in the estimates of Section 4.2.2) would only marginally change the estimated effect of immigrants on less educated natives.[34]

---

34. The corresponding results are not reported but are available on request.

6. Conclusions

The present paper has extended the *national approach* to the analysis of the effect of immigration on wages in the tradition of Borjas (2003) and Borjas and Katz (2007). In particular, it has argued that a structural model of production, combining workers of different skills with capital, is necessary to assess the effect of immigration on the wages of native workers of different skills in the long run. Estimating a reduced-form or a partial elasticity does not give complete information about the total wage effect of immigration as these estimate only the effect of direct competition, whereas the total wage effect is also determined by indirect complementarities among different types of immigrants and natives. Using a nested-CES framework seems to be a promising way to make progress in understanding the total wage effect of immigration. And while such a framework imposes restrictions on cross-elasticities, it is flexible enough to allow for different nesting structures and, therefore, for testing alternative restrictions.

In this framework we found a small but significant degree of imperfect substitutability between natives and immigrants within education and experience groups. A substitution elasticity of around 20 is supported by our estimates. Allowing this elasticity to vary across education groups results in significantly lower estimates among less educated workers (around 11.1). In the long run, these estimates imply an overall average positive effect of immigration on native wages of about 0.6% and an overall average negative effect on the wages of previous immigrants of about −6%.

We have also argued that the elasticity of substitution between workers with no degree and workers with a high school degree is an important parameter in determining the wage effects of immigration. The established tradition in labor economics of assuming that this elasticity is large (around 33) is strongly supported by the data. Also consistent with the labor literature, we found that the elasticity of substitution between workers with some college education or more and those with a high school education or less is much smaller (around 2). The relatively balanced inflow of immigrants belonging to these two groups from 1990 to 2006 implies very small relative wage effects due to immigration. Varying the nesting or other elasticity assumptions (for example, by inverting education and experience in the nest, or allowing different elasticities of substitution between young and old workers) matter much less in determining the total wage effect of immigration on natives of different educational levels.

All in all, one finding seems robust: once imperfect substitutability between natives and immigrants is allowed for, over the period 1990–2006 immigration to the United States had at most a modest negative long-run effect on the real wages of the least educated natives. This effect is between −2.1% and +1.7% depending on the chosen nesting structure, with the positive results coming from the nesting structure preferred by the data. Our finding at the national level of a small wage effect of immigration on less-educated natives is in line with the findings identified at the city level.

192   Journal of the European Economic Association

Appendix A: Theory Appendix

A.1. Income Shares in the Nested CES

For parsimony it is useful to consider a situation in which workers' diversity is defined in terms of only one characteristic. This characteristic identifies groups that are numbered $d = 1, \ldots, D$. In this case, the CES labor aggregate in (1) can be defined as follows:

$$L = \left[\sum_{d=1}^{D} \theta_d (L_d)^{\frac{\sigma_D - 1}{\sigma_D}} \right]^{\frac{\sigma_D}{\sigma_D - 1}}, \qquad (A.1)$$

where L_d is the number of workers in group d, θ_d is the relative productivity level of that group, and $\sigma_D > 0$ is the elasticity of substitution between any two groups. Productivity levels are standardized so that $\sum_d \theta_d = 1$.

Given (A.1), the labor demand for workers in category d is

$$L_d = \frac{(w_d / \theta_d)^{-\sigma_D}}{\sum_d (w_d / \theta_d)^{1 - \sigma_D}} \sum_d w_d L_d, \qquad (A.2)$$

so that the labor income share of workers with education d can be written as

$$s_d \equiv \frac{w_d L_d}{\sum_d w_d L_d} = \theta_d \frac{(w_d / \theta_d)^{1 - \sigma_D}}{\sum_d (w_d / \theta_d)^{1 - \sigma_D}}. \qquad (A.3)$$

On the other hand, differentiation of (A.1) yields

$$\frac{dL}{dL_d} = \theta_d \left(\frac{L}{L_d} \right)^{\frac{1}{\sigma_D}}. \qquad (A.4)$$

Then, (A.2), (A.3) and (A.4) together imply

$$\frac{d \ln L}{d \ln L_d} = \frac{dL}{dL_d} \frac{L_d}{L} = s_d.$$

A.2. Total Wage Effects of Immigration in Model B

We denote the change in the supply of foreign-born due to immigration between two Censuses in group $j(N)$ as $\Delta L_{F,j(N)} = L_{F,j(N),t+10} - L_{F,j(N),t}$. Then, we can use the demand functions (3) and take the total differential with respect to variation in all groups $j(N - 1)$ to derive the total effect of immigration on native and immigrant wages. The resulting expressions are

$$
\left(\frac{\Delta w_{i(N-1)}^{D}}{w_{i(N-1)}^{D}}\right)^{\text{Total}} = \frac{1}{\sigma_{H-L}} \sum_{H-L}\sum_{\text{EDU}}\sum_{\text{EXP}}\left(s_{j(N-1),F}^{0}\frac{\Delta L_{F,j(N-1)}}{L_{F,j(N-1)}}\right)
$$
$$
+ \left(\frac{1}{\sigma_{\text{EDU},i}} - \frac{1}{\sigma_{H-L}}\right)\sum_{\text{EDU}}\sum_{\text{EXP}}\left(s_{j(N-1),F}^{1}\frac{\Delta L_{F,j(N-1)}}{L_{F,j(N-1)}}\right)
$$
$$
+ \left(\frac{1}{\sigma_{\text{EXP}}} - \frac{1}{\sigma_{\text{EDU},i}}\right)\sum_{\text{EXP}}\left(s_{j(N-1),F}^{2}\frac{\Delta L_{F,j(N-1)}}{L_{F,j(N-1)}}\right)
$$
$$
+ \left(\frac{1}{\sigma_{N}} - \frac{1}{\sigma_{\text{EXP}}}\right)\left(s_{j(N-1),F}^{3}\frac{\Delta L_{F,j(N-1)}}{L_{F,j(N-1)}}\right) \tag{A.5}
$$

and

$$
\left(\frac{\Delta w_{i(N-1)}^{F}}{w_{i(N-1)}^{F}}\right)^{\text{Total}} = \frac{1}{\sigma_{H-L}} \sum_{H-L}\sum_{\text{EDU}}\sum_{\text{EXP}}\left(s_{j(N-1),F}^{0}\frac{\Delta L_{F,j(N-1)}}{L_{F,j(N-1)}}\right)
$$
$$
+ \left(\frac{1}{\sigma_{\text{EDU},i}} - \frac{1}{\sigma_{H-L}}\right)\sum_{\text{EDU}}\sum_{\text{EXP}}\left(s_{j(N-1),F}^{1}\frac{\Delta L_{F,j(N-1)}}{L_{F,j(N-1)}}\right)
$$
$$
+ \left(\frac{1}{\sigma_{\text{EXP}}} - \frac{1}{\sigma_{\text{EDU},i}}\right)\sum_{\text{EXP}}\left(s_{j(N-1),F}^{2}\frac{\Delta L_{F,j(N-1)}}{L_{F,j(N-1)}}\right)
$$
$$
+ \left(\frac{1}{\sigma_{N}} - \frac{1}{\sigma_{\text{EXP}}}\right)\left(s_{j(N-1),F}^{3}\frac{\Delta L_{F,j(N-1)}}{L_{F,j(N-1)}}\right) - \frac{1}{\sigma_{N}}\frac{\Delta L_{F,i(N-1)}}{L_{F,i(N-1)}},
$$
$$
\tag{A.6}
$$

where $w_{i(N-1)}^{D}$ is the wage of domestic workers in group $i(N-1)$, $s_{j(N-1),F}^{m}$ is the share of labor income of foreign workers with characteristics $j(N-1)$ among all workers exhibiting the same characteristics up to m.

Using the percentage change in wages for each skill group, we can then aggregate and find the effect of immigration on several representative wages. The average wage for the whole economy in year t, inclusive of natives and immigrants, is given by

$$
\bar{w}_{t} = \sum_{H-L}\sum_{\text{EDU}}\sum_{\text{EXP}}\left(w_{i(N-1)}^{F}\varkappa_{i(N-1),F} + w_{i(N-1)}^{D}\varkappa_{i(N-1),D}\right),
$$

where $\varkappa_{i(N-1),F}$ ($\varkappa_{i(N-1),D}$) are the hours worked by immigrants (natives) in group $i(N-1)$ as a share of total hours worked in the economy. Similarly, the average wages of immigrants and natives can be expressed as weighted averages of individual group wages:

$$
\bar{w}_{Ft} = \frac{\sum_{H-L}\sum_{\text{EDU}}\sum_{\text{EXP}}\left(w_{i(N-1)}^{F}\varkappa_{i(N-1),F}\right)}{\sum_{H-L}\sum_{\text{EDU}}\sum_{\text{EXP}}\varkappa_{i(N-1),F}}
$$

and

$$\bar{w}_{Dt} = \frac{\sum\limits_{H-L} \sum\limits_{\text{EDU}} \sum\limits_{\text{EXP}} \left(w_{i(N-1)}^{D} \varkappa_{i(N-1),D} \right)}{\sum\limits_{H-L} \sum\limits_{\text{EDU}} \sum\limits_{\text{EXP}} \varkappa_{i(N-1),D}}.$$

The percentage change in the average wage of natives as a consequence of changes in each group's wage due to immigration is given by

$$\frac{\Delta \bar{w}_{Dt}}{\bar{w}_{Dt}} = \frac{\sum\limits_{H-L} \sum\limits_{\text{EDU}} \sum\limits_{\text{EXP}} \left(\frac{\Delta w_{i(N-1)}^{D}}{w_{i(N-1)}^{D}} \frac{w_{i(N-1)}^{D}}{\bar{w}_{Dt}} \varkappa_{i(N-1),D} \right)}{\sum\limits_{H-L} \sum\limits_{\text{EDU}} \sum\limits_{\text{EXP}} \varkappa_{i(N-1),D}}$$

$$= \frac{\sum\limits_{H-L} \sum\limits_{\text{EDU}} \sum\limits_{\text{EXP}} \left(\frac{\Delta w_{i(N-1)}^{D}}{w_{i(N-1)}^{D}} \right) s_{j(N-1),D}^{0}}{\sum\limits_{H-L} \sum\limits_{\text{EDU}} \sum\limits_{\text{EXP}} s_{j(N-1),D}^{0}}, \tag{A.7}$$

where $\Delta w_{i(N-1)}^{D}/w_{i(N-1)}^{D}$ represents the percentage change in the wage of US-born in group $i(N-1)$ due to immigration, and its expression is given in (A5). Similarly, the percentage change in the average wage of foreign-born workers is

$$\frac{\Delta \bar{w}_{Ft}}{\bar{w}_{Ft}} = \frac{\sum\limits_{H-L} \sum\limits_{\text{EDU}} \sum\limits_{\text{EXP}} \left(\frac{\Delta w_{i(N-1)}^{F}}{w_{i(N-1)}^{F}} \frac{w_{i(N-1)}^{F}}{\bar{w}_{Ft}} \varkappa_{i(N-1),F} \right)}{\sum\limits_{H-L} \sum\limits_{\text{EDU}} \sum\limits_{\text{EXP}} \varkappa_{i(N-1),F}}$$

$$= \frac{\sum\limits_{H-L} \sum\limits_{\text{EDU}} \sum\limits_{\text{EXP}} \left(\frac{\Delta w_{i(N-1)}^{F}}{w_{i(N-1)}^{F}} \right) s_{j(N-1),F}^{0}}{\sum\limits_{H-L} \sum\limits_{\text{EDU}} \sum\limits_{\text{EXP}} s_{j(N-1),F}^{0}}, \tag{A.8}$$

where $\Delta w_{i(N-1)}^{F}/w_{i(N-1)}^{F}$ represents the percentage change in the wage of foreign-born workers in group $i(N-1)$ due to immigration, and its expression is given in (A.6). Finally, by aggregating the total effect of immigration on the wages of all groups, native and foreign, we can obtain the effect of immigration on average wages:

$$\frac{\Delta \bar{w}_t}{\bar{w}_t} = \sum\limits_{H-L} \sum\limits_{\text{EDU}} \sum\limits_{\text{EXP}} \left(\frac{\Delta w_{i(N-1)}^{F}}{w_{i(N-1)}^{F}} s_{j(N-1),F}^{0} + \frac{\Delta w_{i(N-1)}^{D}}{w_{i(N-1)}^{D}} s_{j(N-1),D}^{0} \right). \tag{A.9}$$

Recall that the variables $s_{j(N-1),F}^{0}$ and $s_{j(N-1),D}^{0}$ represent the group's share in total wages and, as shown in Section A.1, in the nested-CES framework the correct weights in order to obtain the percentage change in average wages are the shares in the wage bill and not the shares in employment. We adopt the same averaging procedure (weighting percentage changes by wage shares) in calculating the effects of immigration on specific groups of US- and foreign-born workers.

Appendix B: Data Appendix

B.1. IPUMS Census Data

We downloaded the IPUMS data on 1 June 2008. The data originate from these samples: 1960, 1% sample of the Census; 1970, 1% sample of the Census; 1980, 5% sample of the Census; 1990, 5% sample of the Census; 2000, 5% sample of the Census; 2006, 1% sample of the ACS. We constructed two datasets that cover slightly different samples. The first aggregates the employment and hours worked by US- and foreign-born males and females in 32 education–experience groups in each Census year. This is called the *employment sample*. The second is called the *wage sample* and is used to calculate the average weekly and hourly wages for US- and foreign-born males and females in the same 32 education–experience groups in each Census year. The first sample is slightly more inclusive than the second.

B.2. IPUMS–CPS Data

We downloaded the IPUMS–CPS data on 28 April 2008, including the years 1963 to 2006 in the extraction. As for the Census data, we constructed an *employment sample* and a *wage sample*. We used the first sample to calculate measures of hours worked and employment, and the second sample to calculate the average weekly wages for US- and foreign-born males and females in each skill group and in each Census year. The first sample is more inclusive than the second. We constructed hours worked, employment and the average wage for each of 4 education groups (workers with no high school, high school graduates, workers with some college, college graduates), following as closely as possible the procedure described in Katz and Murphy (1992), pp. 67–68.

Further details on the definitions of samples and variables that allow the exact reproduction of the sample and results of this paper can be found in the online appendix to the present paper.

Appendices C–G are available online.

References

Acemoglu, Daron (2002). "Directed Technical Change." *Review of Economic Studies*, 69, 781–810.
Angrist, Joshua (1995). "The Economic Returns to Schooling in the West Bank and Gaza Strip." *American Economic Review*, 85, 1065–1087.
Autor, David, Lawrence Katz, and Alan Krueger (1998). "Computing Inequality: Have Computers Changed The Labor Market?" *The Quarterly Journal of Economics*, 113, 1169–1213.
Borjas, George, Richard Freeman, and Larry Katz (1997). "How Much Do Immigration and Trade Affect Labor Market Outcomes?" *Brookings Papers on Economic Activity*, 1997(1), 1–90.
Borjas, George (2003). "The Labor Demand Curve is Downward Sloping: Reexamining the Impact of Immigration on the Labor Market" *Quarterly Journal of Economics*, 118, 1335–1374.

Borjas, George (2006). "Native Internal Migration and the Labor Market Impact of Immigration." *Journal of Human Resources*, 41, 221–258.

Borjas, George, and Lawrence Katz (2007). "The Evolution of the Mexican-Born Workforce in the United States." In *Mexican Immigration to the United States*, edited by George Borjas .National Bureau of Economic Research Conference Report, Cambridge, MA.

Borjas, George, Jeffrey Grogger, and Gordon Hanson (2008). "Imperfect Substitution between Immigrants and Natives: A Reappraisal." National Bureau of Economic Research, Working Paper # 13887, Cambridge, MA.

Card, David, and Thomas Lemieux (2001). "Can Falling Supply Explain the Rising Returns to College for Younger Men? A Cohort Based Analysis." *Quarterly Journal of Economics*, 116, 705–746.

Card, David (2001). "Immigrant Inflows, Native Outflows, and the Local Labor Market Impacts of Higher Immigration." *Journal of Labor Economics*, 19, 22–64.

Card, David (2007). "How Immigration Affects U.S. Cities." CReAM Discussion Paper, no. 11/07, University College London.

Card, David, and Ethan Lewis (2007). "The Diffusion of Mexican Immigrants During the 1990s: Explanations and Impacts." In *Mexican Immigration to the United States*, edited by George Borjas. National Bureau of Economic Research Conference Report, Cambridge, MA.

Caselli, Francesco and Wilbur Coleman (2006). "The World Technology Frontier." *American Economic Review*, 96, 499–522.

Cortes, Patricia (2008). "The Effect of Low-skilled Immigration on US Prices: Evidence from CPI Data." *Journal of Political Economy*, 116, 381–422.

D'Amuri, Francesco, Gianmarco Ottaviano, and Giovanni Peri (2010) "The Labor Market Impact of Immigration in Western Germany in the 1990s." *European Economic Review*, 54, 550–570.

Dustamnn Christian, Tommaso Frattini and Ian Preston (2008) "The Effect of Immigration along the Distribution of Wages." CReAM Discussion Paper 0803, University College London.

Friedberg, Rachel, and Jennifer Hunt (1995). "The Impact of Immigrants on Host Country Wages, Employment and Growth." *Journal of Economic Perspectives*, 9, 23–44.

Friedberg, Rachel (2001). "The Impact of Mass Migration on the Israeli Labor Market." *Quarterly Journal of Economics*, 116, 1373–1408.

Goldin, Claudia and Larry Katz (2008). "The Race Between Education and Technology." Harvard University Press, Cambridge, MA.

Gollin, Douglas (2002). "Getting Income Shares Right." *Journal of Political Economy*, 100, 458–474.

Jaeger, David (1996). "Skill Differences and the Effect of Immigrants on the Wages of Natives." U.S. Bureau of Labor Statistics, Economic Working Paper #273. Washington, DC.

Johnson, George E., (1997). "Changes in Earnings Inequality: The Role of Demand Shifts." *The Journal of Economic Perspectives*, 11, 41–54.

Jones, Charles (2005). "The Shape of Production Functions and the Direction of Technical Change." *Quarterly Journal of Economics*, 120, 517–549.

Kaldor, Nicholas (1961). "Capital Accumulation and Economic Growth." In *The Theory of Capital*, edited by F. A. Lutz and D. C. Hague. St. Martins, New York.

Katz, Larry and Kevin Murphy (1992). "Changes in Relative Wages 1963–1987: Supply and Demand Factors." *Quarterly Journal of Economics*, 107, 35–78.

King, Miriam, Steven Ruggles, Trent Alexander, Donna Leicach, and Matthew Sobek (2009). Integrated Public Use Microdata Series, Current Population Survey: Version 2.0. [Machine-readable database]. Minneapolis, MN: Minnesota Population Center [producer and distributor], http://www.ipums.org.

Krusell, Per, Lee Ohanian, Victor Rios-Rull, and Giovanni Violante (2000). Capital–Skill Complementarity and Inequality: A Macroeconomic Analysis. *Econometrica*, 68, 1029–1053.

Lewis, Ethan (2005). "Immigration, Skill Mix, and the Choice of Technique." Federal Reserve Bank of Philadelphia Working Paper no. 05-08.

Longhi, Simonetta, Peter Nijkamp, and Jacques Poot (2005). "A Meta-Analytic Assessment of the Effect of Immigration on Wages." *Journal of Economic Surveys*, 86, 451–477.

Manacorda Marco, Alan Manning, and John Wadsworth (Forthcoming). "The Impact of Immigration on the Structure of Wages: Theory and Evidence from Britain." *Journal of European Economic Association*, this issue.

Murphy, Kevin and Finis Welch (1992). "The Structure of Wages." *The Quarterly Journal of Economics*, 107, 285–326.

National Research Council (1997). "The New Americans: Economic, Demographic, and Fiscal Effects of Immigration." National Academy Press, Washington, DC.

Ottaviano, Gianmarco, and Giovanni Peri (2005). "Cities and Cultures." *Journal of Urban Economics*, 58, 304–307.

Ottaviano, Gianmarco, and Giovanni Peri (2006a) "Rethinking the Effect of Immigration on Wages" National Bureau of Economic Research, Working Paper # 12496, Cambridge, MA.

Ottaviano, Gianmarco, and Giovanni Peri (2006b). "The Economic Value of Cultural Diversity: Evidence from U.S. Cities." *Journal of Economic Geography*, 6, 9–44.

Ottaviano, Gianmarco, and Giovanni Peri (2008). "Immigration and National Wages: Clarifying the Theory and the Empirics." National Bureau of Economic Research Working Papers # 14188, Cambridge, MA.

Peri, Giovanni and Chad Sparber (2009). "Task Specialization, Immigration, and Wages." *American Economic Journal: Applied Economics, American Economic Association*, 1, 135–169.

Ramsey, Frank (1928). "A Mathematical Theory of Saving." *Economic Journal*, 38, 543–559.

Raphael Steven and Ed Smolensky (2008). "Immigration and Poverty in the Unites States." Working paper, UC Berkeley, April 2008.

Ruggles, Steven, Matthew Sobek, Trent Alexander, Catherine A. Fitch, Ronald Goeken, Patricia Kelly Hall, Miriam King, and Chad Ronnander (2009) Integrated Public Use Microdata Series: Version 4.0 [Machine-readable database]. Minneapolis, MN: Minnesota Population Center [producer and distributor], http://www.ipums.org.

Solow, Robert (1956). "A Contribution to the Theory of Economic Growth." *Quarterly Journal of Economics*, 70, 65–94.

Welch, Finis (1979). "Effects of Cohort Size on Earnings: The Baby Boom Babies Financial Boost." *Journal of Political Economy*, 87, 65–97.

Chapter 10

Immigration, Offshoring, and American Jobs[†,§]

By Gianmarco I. P. Ottaviano, Giovanni Peri, and Greg C. Wright*

The relocation of jobs abroad by multinationals and the increased labor market competition due to immigrant workers are often credited with the demise of many manufacturing jobs once held by American citizens. While it is certainly true that manufacturing production and employment, as a percentage of the total economy, have declined over recent decades in the United States, measuring the impact of those two aspects of globalization on jobs has been difficult. This is due to the possible presence of two opposing effects. On the one hand, there is a direct "displacement effect": offshoring some production processes or hiring immigrants to perform them directly reduces the demand for native workers. On the other hand, there is an indirect "productivity effect": the cost savings associated with employing immigrant and offshore labor increases the efficiency of the production process, thus raising the demand for native workers—if not in the same tasks that are offshored or given to immigrant workers, then certainly in tasks that are complementary to them.

Several recent papers have emphasized the potential productivity effect of offshoring, arguing that this effect could offset or even reverse the displacement effect and thereby generate an overall non-negative effect on the wage or employment of native workers (Grossman and Rossi-Hansberg 2008; Costinot and Vogel 2010; Harrison and McMillan 2011; Wright 2012). These papers focus on the patterns of substitutability between native and offshore workers. Other papers have suggested that immigrants may generate an analogous productivity effect by increasing the demand for native workers, especially in production tasks that are complementary to those performed by immigrants (Ottaviano and Peri 2012; Peri 2012; Peri and Sparber 2009). These papers look at the patterns of substitutability between native and immigrant workers. Little attention has been paid so far to the simultaneous patterns of substitutability between native, immigrant and offshore workers.

In this paper we argue that the joint investigation of the interactions among these three groups of workers is useful in order to improve our understanding of the impact of globalization on the US labor market and, in particular, to answer two hotly debated questions. First, how do declines in offshoring and immigration costs affect the employment of native workers? Second, what kinds of jobs suffer, or benefit, the most from the competition created by offshore and immigrant workers?

*Ottaviano: Department of Economics, London School of Economics and Political Science, Houghton Street, London, WC2A 2AE, UK and Bocconi University (e-mail: g.i.ottaviano@lse.ac.uk); Peri: Department of Economics, UC Davis, One Shields Avenue, Davis, CA 95616 (e-mail: gperi@ucdavis.edu); Wright: Department of Economics, University of Essex, Wivenhoe Park, Colchester CO4 3SQ (e-mail: gcwright@essex.ac.uk). This paper was written as part of the project "Mobility of People and Mobility of Firms" coordinated by the Centro Studi Luca d'Agliano (LdA) and funded by the Fondazione CRT. We thank Daron Acemoglu, Giorgio Barba-Navaretti, Rosario Crinò, Gordon Hanson, Rob Feenstra, Gene Grossman, Alan Manning, John McLaren, Peter Neary, Esteban Rossi-Hansberg, Dan Trefler, and participants in several seminars and conferences for useful comments and suggestions.
† Go to http://dx.doi.org/10.1257/aer.103.5.1925 to visit the article page for additional materials and author disclosure statement(s).

§This article originally appeared in *American Economic Review*, **103** 1925–1959 © 2013 American Economic Association.

1926   THE AMERICAN ECONOMIC REVIEW   AUGUST 2013

At the core of our argument are two observations: first, that jobs ("tasks") vary in terms of the relative intensity of use of complex tasks and, second, that native, immigrant and offshore groups differ in their efficiency in performing complex tasks. Throughout the paper we consider the complexity of a task to be increasing in the intensity of use of communication and cognitive skills and decreasing in the manual content of the task. Communication skills may be important because the execution of complex tasks often requires a sophisticated dialogue between workers whereas, in contrast, manual tasks are much easier to describe and carry out in the absence of these skills. It is therefore natural to think that the cost of performing tasks in other countries (offshoring) or assigning these tasks to people with limited knowledge of the local language and culture (immigrants) increases with the complexity of the task. Efficiency gains can then be reaped by hiring these workers to perform tasks in which they have a comparative advantage, that is, in which they generate a lower cost per efficiency unit of labor,[1] while also giving native workers the opportunity to specialize in the tasks in which they exhibit their own comparative advantage. If strong enough, the productivity effect associated with this efficient pattern of task specialization may offset the displacement effect of immigration and offshoring on native workers' employment.

We develop this argument in three steps. First, we present some new facts on 58 industries, which together comprise the US manufacturing sector, from 2000 to 2007. We argue that these facts are consistent with a scenario in which: (i) there is stronger substitutability between immigrants and offshore workers than between immigrants and natives; (ii) immigrant, native and offshore workers are relatively specialized in tasks of different skill complexity; and, in particular, (iii) immigrants are relatively specialized in low complexity tasks, natives in high complexity tasks, and offshore workers in medium complexity tasks.[2] Unfortunately, the complexity of the tasks performed by offshore workers is not directly observable.

In the second step we build on Grossman and Rossi-Hansberg (2008) to design a partial equilibrium model of task assignment among heterogeneous native, immigrant and offshore workers within an industry that is consistent with the observed facts. We then use the model to draw systematic predictions of the effects of falling barriers to immigration and offshoring on the tasks, the employment share, and the employment level of native workers. An important assumption of the model, consistent with a series of facts that we present, is that offshore workers specialize in tasks of intermediate "complexity" between those of immigrants and natives. The model generates two main sets of predictions. First, borrowing the terminology of Costinot and Vogel (2010), a decline in immigration costs leads to "task upgrading" of immigrants as these workers are assigned some medium complexity tasks that were previously performed by offshore workers. Second, lower immigration costs have little impact on the task complexity of native workers, who are located at

---

[1] See Costinot and Vogel (2010) for the equivalence of the trade concept of "comparative advantage" and the matching concept of "log-supermodularity."

[2] The choice to focus on manufacturing and not include services reflects the research questions we have chosen to address. It is also forced on us by data availability as there is limited data on services offshoring. Moreover, the production function approach at the core of our analysis is much better understood in the context of manufacturing than in the context of services. Lastly, the range of skills spanned by tasks is richer in manufacturing than in services, leaving more room for gains due to their reallocation.

the high end of the task complexity spectrum. On the other hand, a decline in off-shoring costs simultaneously leads to task upgrading of natives and task downgrad-ing of immigrants: offshore workers are assigned the most complex among the low complexity tasks previously performed by immigrants, as well as the least complex among the high complexity tasks previously performed by natives. In this case, the result is increased task polarization between immigrants and natives in the domestic labor market.

The other set of predictions concerns the response of industry employment fol-lowing the reallocation of tasks described above. Employment shares move as dic-tated by the "displacement effect": a group of workers from which tasks are taken away sees its employment share fall; a group of workers to which new tasks are assigned sees its employment share increase. If the "productivity effect" is weak, employment levels move in the same direction as employment shares. On the other hand, when the efficiency gains from immigration or offshoring are strong enough, employment levels may increase for all groups of workers and not only for those whose employment shares go up. Intuitively, the changes in employment *shares* are determined by movements along the relative labor demand curves of the different groups of workers, as dictated by changes in their relative efficiency. The changes in employment *levels*, however, are also affected by the outward shifts in labor demand produced by the increase in the overall efficiency of the production process.

In the end, whether the employment of natives rises or falls when immigration and offshoring become easier, and whether the observed change is consistent with our story, is an empirical issue. By using employment data on immigrants and natives from the American Community Survey (ACS) and on offshore workers by US mul-tinational affiliates from the Bureau of Economic Analysis (BEA), we indeed find that easier offshoring reduces the employment shares of both native and immigrant workers while easier immigration reduces the employment share of offshore work-ers only, with no impact on the employment share of natives. Nonetheless, when we look at employment levels (rather than shares), we find that easier offshoring does not have any significant effect whereas easier immigration has a positive and mildly significant impact on natives. This is consistent with the existence of positive pro-ductivity effects due to immigration and offshoring.

By matching occupation data from the ACS with the manual, communication and cognitive skill content of tasks performed in each occupation (from the US Department of Labor's O*NET abilities survey), we then assess the response of the "complexity" of those tasks to immigration and offshoring. Here we find that easier offshoring raises the average complexity of native tasks, increasing the gap between native and immigrant task complexity. In contrast, easier immigration has no effect on the average complexity of native tasks. Overall, our findings imply that immi-grants do not compete directly with natives. We suggest that the reason for this is that immigrants and natives are concentrated at opposite ends of the task complexity spectrum. Offshore workers, instead, are specialized in tasks of intermediate com-plexity (though we do not directly observe this) generating some competition with both immigrants and natives, as revealed by the effect on employment shares and on task intensities of those two groups.

The rest of the paper is organized as follows. The next section describes the novel contributions of this paper in the context of the existing literature. Section II presents the data, highlighting some key facts that inform the subsequent analysis. Section III presents a theoretical model consistent with those facts, deriving predictions to be brought under econometric scrutiny. Section IV produces the econometric evidence on the predictions of the theoretical model. Section V concludes.

I. Related Literature

Several recent papers have analyzed the effect of offshoring on the demand for domestic labor and are relevant to the present analysis. On the theoretical front, Grossman and Rossi-Hansberg (2008) provide a simple model of trade in production tasks. This model will serve as the framework for our analysis, though we will focus on employment rather than on wage effects.[3] Recent and relevant empirical work includes Crinò (2010); Hummels et al. (2010); Harrison and McMillan (2011); and Wright (2012), each of which have tested some of the implications of existing theories with respect to the wage and employment effects of offshoring. Crinò (2010), who focuses on services offshoring, and Hummels et al. (2010), who focus on Denmark, both find positive wage and employment effects of offshoring for relatively skilled workers, especially for those performing more complex production tasks, but find that less skilled workers may suffer displacement. Wright (2012) finds a positive productivity effect of offshoring for domestic firms but, on net, an aggregate decline in low-skill employment. Harrison and McMillan (2011) find that a crucial distinction is between "horizontal" and "vertical" offshoring (the first aimed at locally serving foreign markets and the second aimed at producing intermediates that the multinational then re-imports to its domestic market), with the first hurting and the second stimulating domestic employment.

The present paper combines the above literature with the literature on the labor market effects of immigrants (e.g., Card 2001; Card 2009; Borjas 2003), proposing a common structure to think about offshoring and immigration within manufacturing industries. To do this, we extend the offshoring model by Grossman and Rossi-Hansberg (2008) to allow for immigration, which provides a simple, though still rich, way of thinking about these two phenomena within a unified framework. While the immigration literature has also analyzed the impact of immigrants on task allocation and productivity (e.g., Peri and Sparber 2009; Peri 2012; Chassamboulli and Palivos 2010), we expand on it by considering a multi-sector environment and an open economy.[4] What we find is that the joint analysis of immigration and offshoring indeed generates novel insights that get overlooked when considering each of those two phenomena in isolation.

---

[3] It is worth mentioning that this theory owes much to previous work on trade in intermediates, including seminal work by Jones and Kierzkowski (1990) and Feenstra and Hanson (1996, 1999), who present models in which trade in intermediate goods has consequences for labor demand much like those described in Grossman and Rossi-Hansberg (2008).

[4] Blinder (2007); Jensen and Kletzer (2007); Levy and Murnane (2006); and Becker, Ekholm, and Muendler (2009) find that tasks that intensively use cognitive-communication and non-routine skills are harder to offshore. Peri and Sparber (2009) find that immigrants have a comparative disadvantage (lower productivity) in performing communication-intensive tasks. None of these contributions, however, tackles the issue of the joint effects of offshoring and immigration on the employment shares, the employment levels and the task assignment of native, immigrant, and offshore workers as we do.

VOL. 103 NO. 5   *OTTAVIANO ET AL.: IMMIGRATION, OFFSHORING, AND AMERICAN JOBS*   *1929*

The only other papers we are aware of that tackle the analysis of immigration and offshoring in a joint framework are Olney (2012) and Barba Navaretti, Bertola, and Sembenelli (2008). The first paper assumes that immigrants are identical to natives and that their variation across US states and industries is exogenous. Moreover, native workers are assumed to be immobile across states and industries so that the impacts of immigration or offshoring manifest themselves entirely through wages. We think our model and its derived empirical implementation constitute a step forward from the reduced form approach of that study. The second paper presents a model of immigration and offshoring and tests its implications on firm-level data for Italy. It does not look, however, at the skill endowments of workers and the skill intensity of tasks nor at industry-level employment effects.

The importance of assortative matching between the skill requirements of tasks and the skill endowments of workers has been recently stressed by Costinot and Vogel (2010). By focusing on a Roy-like assignment model, in which a continuum of factors ("workers") are employed to produce a continuum of goods ("tasks"), they show that the comparative advantage of high skill workers in high complexity tasks provides sufficient conditions for rich comparative static predictions on the effects of various shocks to labor demand and supply. They explicitly analyze the consequences of easier offshoring, which they model as an increase in offshore labor productivity. Assuming that offshore workers have a comparative advantage in low complexity tasks, they conclude that easier offshoring induces task upgrading of all workers and rising wage inequality due to the increase in the effective supply of poorer low-skill workers. They do not consider immigration explicitly, but they discuss the effects of changes in the composition of labor supply. If one assumes that immigrants are relatively less skilled than natives, the impact of immigration is then similar to the impact of offshoring: task upgrading for all workers and increasing wage inequality. Since our model also features a Roy-like assignment problem, their tools and techniques can be used to generalize our theoretical results, with two important differences. First, our focus is on the employment effects rather than on the wage effects. Second, our joint consideration of immigration and offshoring uncovers a differential response of native employment to shocks to the cost of immigrating or offshoring workers.[5]

Finally, also related to our paper is work on the determinants of "job polarization," defined as rising employment shares in the highest and the lowest wage occupations (Autor, Katz, and Kearney 2006; Goos and Manning 2007). Three main explanations of job polarization have been put forth: the technological substitution of non-manual, routine jobs in the middle of the wage distribution (Katz and Autor 1999; Autor, Levy, and Murnane 2003); the offshoring of these jobs (Blinder 2007); or the "butlerization" or demand-driven explanation, whereby a rising income share at the top of the distribution leads to increased demand for low-skill services (Manning 2004). In summarizing the findings of this literature, Goos, Manning, and Salomons (2009) conclude that technical substitution of non-manual, routine jobs

---

[5] Costinot and Vogel (2010) are not the first to deal with assignment models in an international context. Applications to trade can be found, for instance, in Grossman and Maggi (2000); Grossman (2004); Yeaple (2005); Ohnsorge and Trefler (2007); Blanchard and Willmann (2011); Costinot (2009); Monte (2011); and Sly (2012). Examples of applications to offshoring are Kremer and Maskin (2006); Antràs, Garicano, and Rossi-Hansberg (2006); and Nocke and Yeaple (2008). None of these papers, however, deals jointly with offshoring and immigration.

1930 THE AMERICAN ECONOMIC REVIEW *AUGUST 2013*

seems to be a better explanation of job polarization than offshoring and butlerization because of the pervasive effect of technology across sectors and countries. The present paper focuses on manufacturing jobs only, while also bringing immigration into the picture. We provide a somewhat different characterization of polarization in the US labor market, defined as the increasing difference in the types of jobs performed by immigrants relative to those performed by natives.

II. Data and Descriptive Statistics

In this section we present simple statistical evidence on US manufacturing industries that is consistent with a story of task specialization among native, immigrant, and offshore workers according to a specific pattern of comparative advantages. In particular, the data show that natives and immigrants have revealed comparative advantages in high and low complexity jobs, respectively. The revealed comparative advantage of offshore workers is not directly observable. However two related facts are observed. First, the cognitive and communication intensities of native jobs are higher (and the manual intensity lower) in manufacturing industries in which offshoring is relatively important. Second, within manufacturing the cognitive, communication and manual intensities of native jobs are not related to the relative importance of immigration. Third, a positive and significant relationship between immigration and the cognitive and communication intensities of native jobs exists in non-manufacturing industries where offshoring is negligible. These facts suggest that, in manufacturing industries, immigrants specialize in low complexity tasks, natives specialize in high complexity tasks and offshore workers specialize in intermediate complexity tasks. Specialization according to comparative advantages implies not only that immigration has a weaker "displacement effect" on natives relative to offshoring, but also that immigration and offshoring may generate a positive "productivity effect."[6] Again, it is important to note that throughout the paper we consider the complexity of a task to be increasing in the intensity of use of communication and cognitive skills and decreasing in the manual content of the task. We formalize this story in Section III through a simple theoretical model. Section IV then brings these predictions to the data. It should be noted that, while the theoretical model is designed to be consistent with the descriptive evidence that we present, the econometric scrutiny will involve a more rigorous methodology and will test moments of the data different from those on which the assumptions of the model are based.

A. *Employment*

To measure the employment of native, immigrant, and offshore workers in each industry-year using a consistent and comparable industry classification, we merge data on multinational employment from the Bureau of Economic Analysis (BEA) with data on native and foreign-born workers from the IPUMS samples (Ruggles et al. 2008) of the Census and the American Community Survey (ACS). The only

---

[6] In non-manufacturing sectors offshoring tasks is relatively costly. Thus tasks are assigned primarily to natives or immigrants with a higher likelihood of substitution between them. The productivity effect may still exist, however.

VOL. 103 NO. 5   OTTAVIANO ET AL.: IMMIGRATION, OFFSHORING, AND AMERICAN JOBS   1931

years in which this merger can be consistently and reliably done are those from 2000 to 2007. We therefore take these eight years as our period of observation.

Information on offshore employment is obtained from the BEA US Direct Investment Abroad dataset, which collects data on the operations of US parent companies and their affiliates. From this dataset we obtain the total number of employees working abroad in foreign affiliates of US parent companies, by industry of the US parent.[7] These are jobs directly generated abroad by multinationals.[8] Data on native and immigrant workers come from the ACS and Census IPUMS samples for the period 2000–2007.[9] We add up all workers not living in group quarters, who worked at least one week during the year, weighting them by the sample weights assigned by the ACS in order to make the sample nationally representative. "Immigrants" are all foreign-born workers who were not citizens at birth. "Natives" are all other US workers. The relevant industry classification in the Census-ACS data 2000–2007 is the INDNAICS classification, which is based on the North American Industry Classification System (NAICS). Since the BEA industries are also associated with unique 4-digit NAICS industries, we are able to develop a straightforward concordance between the two datasets.

The 58 industries on which we have data and their BEA codes are reported in Table A1 in the online Appendix, while Figure A1 (also in the online Appendix) reports the evolution of the employment shares of immigrant and offshore workers across industries in each year with the connecting lines showing averages over time. From 2000 to 2007 there was only a fairly modest increase in the overall share of immigrant and offshore employment in total manufacturing (the former increased from 12.8 percent to 14 percent and the latter from 22.3 percent to 29.3 percent). The figure shows both that all industries hired some immigrant and offshore workers and, further, that the differences across industries are potentially large enough to allow for the identification of the differential effects of immigration and offshoring over the period.

While the employment shares of the different groups of workers vary across industries, there are interesting patterns of covariation. Panel A of Figure 1 depicts the correlations between native and immigrant employment shares over the period of observation. Panel B provides the same type of information for native and offshore workers and panel C shows employment shares for immigrant and offshore workers.

---

[7] As is standard in this literature, here we do not include in the definition of offshoring jobs that are subcontracted abroad by purely national firms.

[8] Jobs created by US multinational firms outsourcing production to unaffiliated foreign subcontractors, so-called *arm's length* offshoring (see, e.g. Antràs 2003) were not included in our analysis. We constructed a proxy for this variable, however. Assuming that a large part of the production output of these offshored jobs is subsequently imported as intermediate inputs by the US parent company, we calculated the ratio of imports of intermediates by the US parent coming from affiliates and employment in those affiliates. We then scaled the imports of the US parent coming from *non-affiliates* (data that are also available from the BEA) by this ratio to impute the employment in subcontracting companies. This procedure assumes that the labor content per unit of production of subcontracted intermediate inputs is the same as for production in US affiliates in the same industry. Adding the imputed employment increases offshore employment by 60–80 percent in most industries, confirming the importance of arm's length offshoring. The regression results using this measure of offshore employment are very similar to those presented in IV and we do not report them here. They can be found in a previous version of this paper (Ottaviano, Peri, and Wright 2010).

[9] For year 2000 we use the 5 percent Census sample. For 2001 we use the 1-in-232 national random sample. For 2002, we use the 1-in-261 national random sample. For 2003 we use the 1-in-236 national random sample. For 2004 we use the 1-in-239 national random sample. For 2005, 2006, and 2007 the 1-in-100 national random samples are used.

1932   *THE AMERICAN ECONOMIC REVIEW*   *AUGUST 2013*

Panel A. Native and immigrant employment shares; Slope of the regression line: 0.05, standard error: 0.10

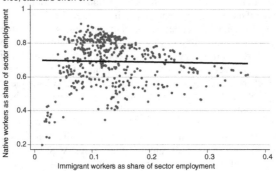

Panel B. Native and offshore employment shares; Slope of the regression line: −0.80, standard error: 0.02

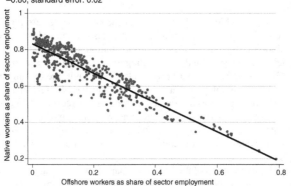

Panel C. Immigrants and offshore employment shares; Slope of the regression line: −0.19, standard error: 0.02

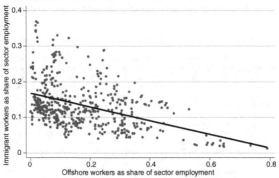

FIGURE 1. SHARES OF IMMIGRANT, NATIVE, AND OFFSHORE WORKERS
(58 *manufacturing sectors, 2000–2007*)

Panel A. Slope of the regression line: 0.13, standard error: 0.03

Panel B. Slope of the regression line: 0.01, standard error: 0.01

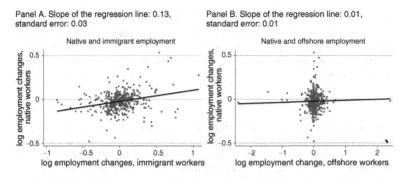

Panel C. Slope of the regression line: –0.02, standard error: 0.02

Panel D. Slope of the regression line 0.014, standard error: 0.012

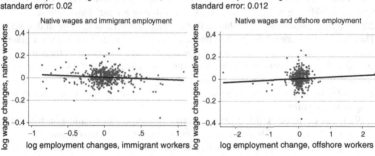

FIGURE 2. GROWTH RATES OF EMPLOYMENT AND WAGES (*58 manufacturing sectors, yearly growth 2000–2007*)

The figure reveals a lack of correlation between the shares of immigrant and native workers. In contrast, it highlights a strong negative correlation between the shares of offshore and native workers, and a significant (but less strong) negative correlation between the share of immigrants and offshore workers. These correlations suggest that competition for jobs may be strongest between natives and offshore workers, intermediate between immigrant and offshore workers and weakest between natives and immigrants.

Figure 2 looks at yearly employment- and wage-growth rates across 58 manufacturing industries over eight years. Panel A reveals a positive correlation between the growth rates of employment of natives and immigrants whereas panel B shows no correlation between the growth of native and offshore workers. This is consistent with weaker native-immigrant employment competition relative to native-offshore worker competition in the presence of positive productivity effects due to both immigration and offshoring. Panels C and D look at the correlations between changes in native wages and changes in immigrant and offshore employment.[10] The two panels

---

[10] The wages of natives are constructed as follows. From the Census-ACS data we consider only US-born individuals who are employed (i.e., who have worked at least one week in the year and at least one hour in the week) and who have non-zero wage income, excluding the self-employed. We take yearly wage income deflated by the

do not suggest any significant correlation between changes in native wages and changes in immigrant and offshore employment across sectors. We interpret this as consistent with the equalization of native wages across manufacturing industries due to worker mobility between them, with the effect that the wage variation across sectors is random.[11]

B. *Tasks*

Data on the tasks performed by immigrants and natives is constructed using the US Department of Labor's (2012) O*NET abilities survey, which provides information on the characteristics of each occupation. Based on the Standard Occupation Classification (SOC), the dataset assigns numerical values to describe the importance of distinct abilities ("skills") required by different occupations ("tasks"). Each numerical value measures the intensity of a skill in a given task. Following Peri and Sparber (2009), we merge these task-specific values with individual workers in the 2000 Census, re-scaling each value so that it equals the percentile score in that year. This gives a measure of the relative importance of a given skill among US workers ranging between zero and one. For instance, a task with a score of 0.02 for some skill indicates that only 2 percent of workers in the United States in 2000 were supplying that skill less intensively. We then assign these O*NET percentile scores to individuals from 2000 to 2007 using the ACS variable *occ1990*, which provides an occupational crosswalk over time.

We focus on three skill indices: Cognitive Intensity, Communication Intensity, and Manual Intensity. These are constructed by averaging the relevant skill variables. Specifically, Cognitive Intensity includes ten variables classified as "cognitive and analytical" in O*NET. Communication Intensity includes four variables capturing written and oral expression and understanding. Manual Intensity includes nineteen variables capturing dexterity, strength, and coordination.[12] We have also calculated a synthetic Complexity index summarizing the intensity of a task in cognitive-communication skills *relative* to manual skills. This index is defined as: Complexity $= \ln((\text{Cognitive Intensity} + \text{Communication Intensity})/\text{Manual Intensity})$. It ranges between $-\infty$ and $+\infty$.

Overall, our sample consists of 295 occupations ("tasks") in the manufacturing sector over eight years, 2000–2007. This type of information is available for immigrants and natives but not for offshore workers. Absent direct information on the specific occupations of offshore workers, a crucial challenge for us is to indirectly assess the average complexity of offshore tasks. The four panels of Figure 3 plot the share of hours worked by immigrants relative to the total number of hours worked by immigrant and native workers as a function of Cognitive Intensity, Communication

---

consumption price index to constant 2005 dollars and average it at the industry level, weighting each individual by the corresponding sample weight in the Census.

[11] We also provide a more formal analysis of the correlation between offshore/immigrant employment and native wages in the online Appendix. Table A3 shows the estimated effects of log offshore employment and log immigrant employment on (log) native wages. The effects are estimated using 2SLS with tariffs as an instrument for offshoring and imputed immigration as an instrument for actual immigration (as described in Section IVA below). In all cases we obtain small and insignificant coefficients.

[12] The exact definition and list of the variables used for each index can be found in the online Appendix of this paper.

Panel A. Slope of the regression line: −0.13, standard error: 0.01

Panel B. Slope of the regression line: −0.14, standard error: 0.01

Panel C. Slope of the regression line: 0.087, standard error: 0.01

Panel D. Slope of the regression line: −0.034, standard error: 0.002

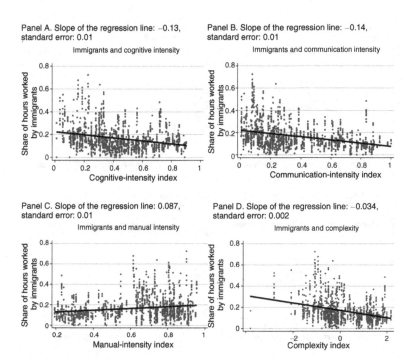

FIGURE 3. IMMIGRANTS AND TASK COMPLEXITY (*across occupations*)

Notes: Sample is 295 occupations over 2000–2007. Only occupations with over 5,000 workers are reported.

Intensity, Manual Intensity, and Complexity across occupation-years.[13] The figure clearly shows that immigrants are disproportionately represented in occupations characterized by low Cognitive Intensity, low Communication Intensity, high Manual Intensity, and low overall Complexity.[14]

While the complexity of offshored tasks is unobservable (because we do not observe offshore occupations), we can nonetheless gauge some indirect evidence from the way offshoring affects the complexity of native and immigrant tasks. Figure 4 reports this type of information in the case of all immigrants and natives. It plots the change in the Complexity of tasks performed by natives and immigrants against the change in the shares of offshore and immigrant employment, across manufacturing industries over the period 2000–2007. The figure conveys a clear

[13] A very similar picture would be obtained if we only considered workers with low educational attainment (i.e., workers with a high school diploma or less) This was shown in Ottaviano, Peri, and Wright (2010). Even within the low educated, immigrants are relatively specialized in tasks with low cognitive and communication content, low complexity and high manual content.

[14] This finding concurs with existing evidence. Peri and Sparber (2009) show that, due to their imperfect knowledge of language and local norms, immigrants have a relative advantage in tasks with high manual intensity and a relative disadvantage in tasks with high communication intensity.

1936   THE AMERICAN ECONOMIC REVIEW   *AUGUST 2013*

Panel A. Slope of the regression line: 0.35,
standard error: 0.14

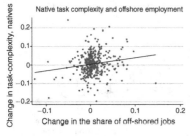

Panel B. Slope of the regression line: −0.77,
standard error: 0.40

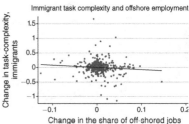

Panel C. Slope of the regression line: −0.05,
standard error: 0.14

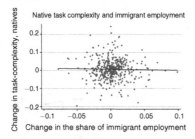

Panel D. Slope of the regression line: 0.65,
standard error: 0.58

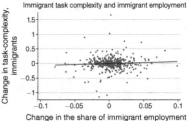

FIGURE 4. NATIVE COMPLEXITY, IMMIGRATION, AND OFFSHORING (*all workers*)

Notes: Sample from 58 manufacturing sectors of 295 occupations over 2000–2007. Only occupations with over 5,000 workers are reported.

message: increases in the share of offshore workers are associated with significant increases in the complexity of tasks performed by natives as well as decreases in the complexity of tasks performed by immigrants. In contrast, increases in the share of immigrants are not associated with any significant change in the complexity of native or immigrant tasks. Hence, a stronger presence of offshore workers is associated with a larger polarization in task complexity between natives and immigrants. Similar patterns arise when we focus on Cognitive Intensity, Communication Intensity, and Manual Intensity separately but we do not report them for conciseness.

The finding that changes in native complexity are not significantly correlated with changes in the share of immigrants may surprise readers familiar with Peri and Sparber (2009), as these authors find that native task complexity is sensitive to the share of immigrants. This can easily be explained in a manner that is consistent with our theory. In this study we focus on (mostly-tradable) manufacturing industries whereas Peri and Sparber (2009) consider all employment, most of which is in (non-tradable) services. Since offshoring was still negligible outside the manufacturing sector during our period of observation, we interpret this discrepancy as a signal that, when viable, offshore workers play an important role in weakening the

VOL. 103 NO. 5   OTTAVIANO ET AL.: IMMIGRATION, OFFSHORING, AND AMERICAN JOBS   1937

TABLE 1—COMPLEXITY OF NATIVE AND IMMIGRANT SHARE IN TRADABLE
VERSUS NON-TRADABLE INDUSTRIES

Dependent variable is the complexity index for natives	Complexity $= \ln[(\text{Cognitive} + \text{Communication})/\text{Manual}]$	
	Tradable sectors, 2000–2007 (1)	Non-tradable sectors, 2000–2007 (2)
Complexity index for the foreign-born	0.04** (0.02)	0.07** (0.01)
Share of foreign-born	−0.01 (0.09)	0.15** (0.07)
Industry effects	Yes	Yes
Observations	647	1,456

Notes: The estimation method is ordinary least squares including industry and time effects. Heteroskedasticity robust standard errors, clustered at the sector level are reported.
***Significant at the 1 percent level.
**Significant at the 5 percent level.
*Significant at the 10 percent level.

competition between immigrants and natives. Table 1 explores this interpretation by regressing native complexity on immigrants' complexity and employment share across industries and over time, distinguishing between manufacturing ("tradable") and non-manufacturing ("non-tradable") industries. All workers are included. The table shows significant positive correlation between native complexity and immigrant employment share within non-tradable industries (column 2), but no correlation is detected between native complexity and immigrant employment share in tradable industries (column 1).[15] This supports the idea that in non-tradable industries the competition between natives and immigrants is more direct and immigration pushes native workers to "upgrade" their jobs. In tradable industries this does not happen because offshore workers perform a large part of the intermediate-complex tasks and are therefore in direct competition with immigrants. While the results shown are not direct evidence of this, they are consistent with this explanation.

Our overall interpretation of the descriptive evidence presented in this section is that natives compete more directly with offshore workers relative to immigrant workers. This can be explained by a specific pattern of comparative advantages across the three groups of workers, with immigrants specializing in low complexity tasks, natives in high complexity tasks and offshore workers in intermediate complexity tasks.

III. A Labor Market Model of Task Allocation

A simple partial equilibrium model consistent with the descriptive evidence reported in the previous section can be designed following Grossman and Rossi-Hansberg (2008). Consider a small open economy that is active in several perfectly competitive sectors, indexed $s = 1, \dots, S$. We focus on one of these sectors

---

[15] In the regressions in Table 1 we also control for time and industry fixed effects.

1938   THE AMERICAN ECONOMIC REVIEW   AUGUST 2013

and leave both the sector index s and the time dependence of variables t implicit for ease of notation. We will make them explicit when we get to the empirics.

The sector employs two primary factors, workers with employment level N_L and a sector-specific factor with endowment H. To match the descriptive evidence on wages in Section II, the sector is small enough to face infinitely elastic labor supply at given wages.[16] All workers are endowed with one unit of labor each but differ in terms of productivity. They are employed in the production of intermediates ("tasks"), which are then assembled in a composite labor input L. This, in turn, is transformed into final output Y according to the following Cobb-Douglas production function:

$$(1) \qquad\qquad Y = AL^{\alpha}\,H^{1-\alpha},$$

where $A \in (0, \infty)$ and $\alpha \in (0, 1)$ are technological parameters. The price of final output p_Y is set in the international market.

Specifically, the composite labor input L is produced by assembling a fixed measure of differentiated tasks, indexed $i \in [0, 1]$ in increasing order of complexity, through the following CES technology:

$$(2) \qquad\qquad L = \left[\int_0^1 L(i)^{\frac{\sigma-1}{\sigma}}\, di \right]^{\frac{\sigma}{\sigma-1}},$$

where $L(i)$ is the input of task i and $\sigma > 0$ is the elasticity of substitution between tasks.[17]

A. Task Assignment

Each task can be managed in three modes: domestic production by native workers (D), domestic production by immigrant workers (M), and production abroad by offshore workers (O). The three groups of workers are perfect substitutes in the production of any task but differ in terms of their productivity as well as in terms of their wages, which we call w, $\tilde{w}$, and w^*, respectively. To allow for a "productivity effect" to arise from both immigration and offshoring, we assume that employers can discriminate between the three groups of workers so that w, $\tilde{w}$, and w^* may not be equal. We assume, however, that immigrant and offshore wages are linked, with a fixed gap between them determined by a differential "cost of hardship" that immigrants face with respect to their fellow countrymen who stay at home. In particular, if a foreign worker immigrates, she incurs a frictional cost $\delta \geq 1$ in terms of foregone productivity. In other words, an immigrant endowed with one unit of labor in her country of origin is able to provide only $1/\delta$ units of labor in the country of

---

[16]This leads to a crucial difference between our model and those by Grossman and Rossi-Hansberg (2008) and by Costinot and Vogel (2010). Both these models consider the general equilibrium effects of offshoring on wages under economy-wide full employment constraints. In the online Appendix we propose an extension of our model in which the assumption of perfectly elastic labor supply at given wages does not hold. There we show that, when the native wage is endogenous, immigration and offshoring generate wage effects, however the corresponding employment effects discussed in Section IIIB remain qualitatively the same.

[17]In Grossman and Rossi-Hansberg (2008) tasks are not substitutable. This corresponds to the limit case of $\sigma = 0$ where (2) becomes a Leontief production function.

destination. The migration decision therefore entails a choice between earning w^* in the country of origin or $\tilde{w}/\delta$ in the country of destination.[18] Positive supply of both immigrant and offshore workers then requires the migration indifference condition $\tilde{w} = w^*\delta$ to hold.[19]

In light of the descriptive evidence reported in Section II, we now introduce assumptions that ensure that immigrant, offshore, and native workers specialize in low, medium, and high complexity tasks, respectively. In so doing, we follow Grossman and Rossi-Hansberg (2008) and define tasks so that they all require the same unit labor requirement a_L when performed by native workers. Accordingly, the marginal cost of producing task i employing native workers is $c_D(i) = wa_L$. If task i is instead offshored, its unit input requirement is $\beta t(i)a_L$ with $\beta t(i) \geq 1$. This implies a marginal cost of producing task i employing offshore workers equal to $c_O(i) = w^*\beta t(i)a_L$. Lastly, if task i is assigned to immigrants, its unit input requirement is $\tau(i)a_L$ with $\tau(i) \geq 1$ so that the marginal cost of producing task i employing immigrants is $c_M(i) = \tilde{w}\tau(i)a_L = w^*\delta\tau(i)a_L$. Hence, in all tasks natives are more productive but, due to wage differences, not necessarily cheaper than immigrant and offshore workers. We interpret a lower value of the frictional parameter β as "easier offshoring" and a lower value of the frictional parameter δ as "easier immigration."

Since native, immigrant and offshore workers are perfectly substitutable, in equilibrium any task will be performed by only one type of worker: the one that entails the lowest marginal cost for that task.[20] Hence, a set of sufficient conditions for immigrant, offshore and native workers to specialize in low, medium and high complexity tasks can be stated as:

PROPOSITION 1: *Suppose*

$$(3) \qquad \frac{dt(i)}{di} > 0, \qquad \frac{w}{w^*t(1)} < \beta < \frac{w}{w^*t(0)}.$$

Then there exists a unique "marginal offshore task" $I_{NO} \in (0, 1)$ such that $c_O(I_{NO}) = c_D(I_{NO})$, $c_O(i) < c_D(i)$ for all $i \in [0, I_{NO})$ and $c_O(i) > c_D(i)$ for all $i \in (I_{NO}, 1]$. This task is implicitly defined by $w = w^*\beta t(I_{NO})$. Suppose in addition that

$$(4) \qquad \delta\frac{d\tau(i)}{di} > \beta\frac{dt(i)}{di}, \qquad \frac{\tau(0)}{t(0)} < \frac{\beta}{\delta} < \frac{\tau(I_{NO})}{t(I_{NO})}.$$

---

[18] For simplicity, in the theoretical model we consider only one country of origin for all immigrants.

[19] There is much empirical evidence that, for similar observable characteristics, immigrants are paid a lower wage than natives. Using data from the 2000 Census, Antecol, Cobb-Clark, and Trejo (2001); Butcher and DiNardo (2002); and Chiswick, Lee, and Miller (2005) all show that recent immigrants from non-English speaking countries earn on average 17 to 20 percent less than natives with identical observable characteristics. Our data provide estimates in the same ball park. Hendricks (2002) also shows that the immigrant-native wage differential, controlling for observable characteristics, is highly correlated with the wage differential between the United States and their country of origin. See, however, Section IIIB and the online Appendix for a detailed discussion of how the predictions of the model would change were firms assumed to be unable to discriminate between native and immigrant workers.

[20] If native, immigrant and offshore workers were imperfectly substitutable, each task could be performed by "teams" consisting of the three types of workers. Then, rather than full specialization of workers' types in different tasks, one would observe partial specialization, with the shares of the three types in each task inversely related to the corresponding marginal costs. In reality several tasks are indeed performed by a combination of different types of workers, nonetheless the intuition behind the key results of the model is better served by assuming perfect substitutability.

1940   THE AMERICAN ECONOMIC REVIEW   *AUGUST 2013*

Then there exists a unique "marginal immigrant task" $I_{MO} \in (0, I_{NO})$ such that $c_M(I_{MO}) = c_O(I_{MO})$, $c_M(i) < c_O(i)$ for all $i \in [0, I_{MO})$ and $c_M(i) > c_O(i)$ for all $i \in (I_{MO}, 1]$. This task is implicitly defined by $\beta t(I_{MO}) = \delta\tau(I_{MO})$.

See the Appendix for the proof. Intuitively, the first condition in (3) implies that the productivity of offshore workers relative to natives decreases with the complexity of tasks. The second condition in (3) requires offshoring frictions to be neither too large nor too small in order to generate a trade-off in the assignment of tasks between native and offshore workers. The first condition in (4) also implies that the productivity of immigrants falls with the complexity of tasks, and falls faster than in the case of offshore workers. The second condition in (4) requires offshoring frictions to be neither too large nor too small relative to migration frictions such that there is a trade-off in the assignment of tasks between immigrant and offshore workers. Conditions (3) and (4) together thus imply that tasks of complexity $0 \le i \le I_{MO}$ are assigned to immigrants, tasks of complexity $I_{MO} < i \le I_{NO}$ to offshore workers and tasks of complexity $I_{NO} < i \le 1$ to natives, where marginal tasks have been arbitrarily assigned to break the tie.[21]

The allocation of tasks among the three groups of workers is portrayed in Figure 5, where the task index i is measured along the horizontal axis and the production costs along the vertical axis. The flat line corresponds to c_D and the upward sloping curves correspond to $c_M(i)$ and $c_O(i)$, with the former starting from below but steeper than the latter. Since each task employs only the type of workers yielding the lowest marginal cost, tasks from 0 to I_{MO} are assigned to immigrants, tasks from I_{MO} to I_{NO} are offshored, and tasks from I_{NO} to 1 are assigned to natives.

B. Comparative Statics

We are interested in how tasks, employment shares, and employment levels, vary across the three types of workers when offshoring and migration costs change. The solution of our task assignment problem summarized in Proposition 1 implies that marginal tasks exhibit the following properties:

$$\frac{\partial I_{NO}}{\partial \beta} < 0, \qquad \frac{\partial I_{MO}}{\partial \beta} > 0$$

$$\frac{\partial I_{NO}}{\partial \delta} = 0, \qquad \frac{\partial I_{MO}}{\partial \delta} < 0.$$

---

[21] Readers familiar with Costinot and Vogel (2010) will recognize the log-supermodularity of this assignment problem in which, due to their different skills, native, immigrant, and offshore workers have a relative advantage in high, medium, and low skill intensity tasks. Indeed, the approach of Costinot and Vogel (2010) could be used to go beyond the stark view expressed in our theory by introducing skill heterogeneity among the three groups of workers. This could be achieved by matching the assumption that higher skill workers have a comparative advantage in more skill intensive tasks (see Costinot and Vogel 2010, Section IIIA) with the assumption that natives are more skilled relative to offshore and immigrant workers (see Costinot and Vogel 2010, Section VIIB).

VOL. 103 NO. 5   OTTAVIANO ET AL.: IMMIGRATION, OFFSHORING, AND AMERICAN JOBS   1941

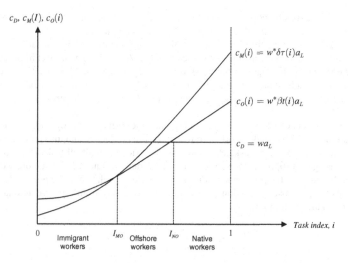

FIGURE 5. TASK ASSIGNMENT

These highlight the adjustments in employment occurring in terms of the number of tasks allocated to the three groups of workers. They can be readily understood using Figure 5. For example, a reduction in offshoring costs (lower β) shifts $c_O(i)$ downward, thus increasing the number of offshored tasks through a reduction in both the number of tasks assigned to immigrants ($\partial I_{MO}/\partial\beta > 0$) and the number of tasks assigned to natives ($\partial I_{NO}/\partial\beta < 0$). Analogously, a reduction in the migration costs (lower δ) shifts $c_M(i)$ downward, thus increasing the number of tasks assigned to immigrants through a decrease in the number of offshored tasks (higher I_{MO}).

While the theoretical model identifies the marginal tasks as cutoffs between tasks performed by different groups of workers, the distinction is not so stark in reality as workers are also heterogeneous within groups and some overlap among individuals belonging to different groups is possible along the complexity spectrum.[22] For the empirical analysis it is, therefore, also useful to characterize the "average task," I_M, I_O, or I_D, performed by each group, defined as the employment-weighted average across the corresponding is.[23] Average tasks exhibit the following properties:

$$(5) \qquad \frac{\partial I_D}{\partial\beta} < 0, \qquad \frac{\partial I_M}{\partial\beta} > 0$$

$$\frac{\partial I_D}{\partial\delta} = 0, \qquad \frac{\partial I_M}{\partial\delta} < 0.$$

---

[22] See the previous footnote on how the model could be extended to the case of within-group heterogeneity.
[23] See the Appendix for a formal definition of average tasks.

1942   THE AMERICAN ECONOMIC REVIEW   *AUGUST 2013*

These are driven by compositional changes due to adjustments both in the number of tasks allocated to the three groups and in the employment shares of the different tasks allocated to the three groups. Note that changes in migration costs also have a negative impact on the average offshored task $(\partial I_O / \partial \delta < 0)$. The impact of offshoring costs on the average offshore task $(\partial I_O / \partial \beta)$ is, instead, ambiguous. This is due to opposing adjustments in the allocation of tasks given that, when β falls, some of the additional offshore tasks have low i (i.e., I_{MO} falls) while others have high i (i.e., I_{NO} rises).

The impacts of declining β and δ on employment shares, s_M, s_O, and s_D, are all unambiguous.[24] By making offshore workers more productive and thus reducing the price index of offshore tasks P_O relative to the price index of all tasks P_L, a lower offshoring cost, β, reallocates tasks from immigrants and natives to offshore workers. By reducing the price index of immigrant tasks P_M relative to the price index of all tasks P_L, a lower migration cost, δ, moves tasks away from offshore and native workers toward immigrants:

$$(6) \qquad \frac{\partial s_M}{\partial \beta} > 0, \qquad \frac{\partial s_O}{\partial \beta} < 0, \qquad \frac{\partial s_D}{\partial \beta} > 0$$

$$\frac{\partial s_M}{\partial \delta} < 0, \qquad \frac{\partial s_O}{\partial \delta} > 0, \qquad \frac{\partial s_D}{\partial \delta} > 0.$$

These results capture the signs of the "displacement effects" for the three groups of workers.

Turning to the impact of declining β and δ on the employment levels N_M, N_O, and N_D, there is an additional effect beyond the substitution among groups of workers in terms of employment shares.[25] This is due to the fact that lower β and δ ultimately cause a fall in the price index of the labor composite P_L because, as a whole, workers become more productive. This is the "productivity effect" of offshoring and immigration. Specifically, a fall in the price index P_L of the labor composite has a positive impact on sectoral employment (due to the productivity effect), which is then distributed across groups depending on how the relative price indices of the three groups of workers P_M / P_L, P_O / P_L, and P_D / P_L vary (due to the displacement effects).

The impact of declining β and δ on employment levels can be signed only when the productivity effect and the displacement effects go in the same direction. In particular, since $\partial P_L / \partial \beta > 0$ and $\partial P_L / \partial \delta > 0$, we have

$$(7) \qquad \frac{\partial N_O}{\partial \beta} < 0, \qquad \frac{\partial N_M}{\partial \delta} < 0,$$

while the signs of $\partial N_M / \partial \beta$, $\partial N_D / \partial \beta$, $\partial N_O / \partial \delta$, and $\partial N_D / \partial \delta$ are generally ambiguous. In other words, whether the productivity effect is strong enough to offset the displacement effect for all groups of workers is an empirical question that we will

---

[24] See the Appendix for the expressions of employment shares and price indices.
[25] See the Appendix for the expressions of employment levels.

address in the next section. Lower β and δ certainly raise total sector employment $N_L = N_M + N_O + N_D$, as long as there is a non-zero productivity effect.

Results (5), (6), and (7) are the reduced form implications of the model that we will bring to the data in the next sections.[26]

IV. Empirical Specifications and Econometric Results

In this section we bring the predictions of our model to the data. We target the three sets of predictions highlighted in the previous section regarding the effects of easier immigration and easier offshoring on the employment shares, the employment levels and the average task assignments of natives and of the other groups of workers, as highlighted in (5), (6), and (7), respectively. The empirical specifications are derived from the theory but can be justified in a very general way. First, the impact of immigration or offshoring on the share of native employment allows us to infer the degree of direct competition (substitutability) between types of workers. Second, estimating the impact of immigration or offshoring on total employment allows us to quantify the productivity effects of those activities. Finally, the impact of immigration or offshoring on native task assignment tests whether the distribution of tasks across worker types according to task complexity is consistent with our hypothesis and with the estimated pattern of cross-substitution.

The predictions of the model have been derived for a single industry leaving industry and time indices implicit for notational convenience. Hence, in order to implement (5), (6), and (7) empirically we begin by identifying the parameters that vary across industries (to be indexed by s) and over time (to be indexed by t) and those that do not (and carry no index). First, the offshoring and immigration cost parameters vary across industries and over time, and thus we label them β_{st} and δ_{st}. We motivate this in Section IVA in which we present our empirical measures. Second, we consider the specific factor endowment H_s to be industry-specific but not time-varying. The same holds for the baseline sector-specific total factor productivity A_s. We allow, however, for random productivity shocks through a possibly serially correlated error term ε_{st}. Both H_s and A_s will be captured by an industry fixed effect. Finally, as wages have been assumed to be equalized across industries, we allow them to vary only over time, writing w_t and w_t^*, which calls for a time effect.

In sum, we will exploit differences in immigration and offshoring costs within industries over time in order to identify the impact on native and immigrant employment as well as on native and immigrant task specialization.

A. Costs of Immigration and Offshoring

Driving the shifts in β_{st} and δ_{st} are changes in the accessibility of offshore and immigrant workers. Since we do not observe industry-specific offshoring and

---

[26] Employers' ability to discriminate between natives and immigrants is crucial for the productivity effects of immigration to materialize. If employers were unable to discriminate, immigrants would always be paid native wages w earning rents $w - w'\delta$. Thus, any reduction in δ would simply increase immigrants' rents with no impact on firms' costs. Note, however, that our assumption of perfect discrimination is not crucial to generate the productivity effect due to immigration since even partial discrimination generates rents for the firm. See the online Appendix for additional details.

immigration costs, we begin by using direct measures of the employment share of immigrant and offshore workers across industries and over time as explanatory variables. If the variation in costs, once we control for industry and time effects, were the main source of variation in immigration and offshoring within an industry, then the OLS regression would identify the effect on native outcomes of changes in the cost of immigration and offshoring. As we are aware that this is an heroic assumption, we instrument the share of immigrants and offshore workers with variables proxying their cross-industry costs and availability.

The assumption that offshoring costs vary across industries departs from Grossman and Rossi-Hansberg (2008), who suggest that this cost is more or less the same across industries. This is probably true if one wants to stress, as they do, the technological dimension of offshoring costs, which implies very little variation across similar tasks in different industries. Our focus is, instead, on the trade cost dimension of offshoring, which hampers the re-import of the output generated by offshored tasks and is affected by industry-specific characteristics. In this respect, in order to capture exogenous variation in offshoring costs and generate an instrument for offshore employment in an industry-year, we collect two types of US tariff data, each by year and product: Most Favored Nation (MFN) tariffs and Information Technology Agreement (ITA) tariffs.[27] These are then aggregated up to the BEA industry level for each year, weighting the tariffs by the value of imports in each detailed industry, where we obtain US imports from Feenstra, Romalis, and Schott (2002).[28] We call this variable $(Tariffs)_{st}$.

The instrument we use to proxy cost-driven immigration by industry and year extends the method first proposed by Altonji and Card (1991) and Card (2001) to identify cost-driven local shifts in immigrants. We exploit the fact that foreigners from different countries have increased or decreased their relative presence in the United States according to changes in the cost of migrating and to domestic conditions that are specific to their countries of origin. Differences in the initial presence of immigrants from different countries in an industry make that industry more or less subject to those shifts in origin-specific cost- and push-factors. Using these two facts we impute the population of each of 10 main groups of immigrants across industries over time.[29] Specifically, we use the share of immigrant workers, by origin-group, in each industry in year 2000 and we augment it by the aggregate growth rate of the specific immigrant group's population in the United States relative to the total US population. Then summing over origin-groups within an industry we obtain the imputed share of foreign-born in total employment. We call this measure $(Imputed\_s_M)_{st}$ and note that it varies across industries and over time.[30]

---

[27] These data come primarily from UNCTAD's TRAINS dataset, but were extended somewhat by Yingying Xu (2006) as part of her dissertation at UC Davis. The ITA data was added by the authors. ITA data is available via http://www.wto.org

[28] The MFN tariffs are mandated for all WTO signatories, while the ITA tariffs had been adopted by 43 countries at the end of our period (2007), covering 97 percent of world trade in technology products. The ITA covers a range of manufactured technology products (see the online Appendix for a full list of products and adopters) and, for our purposes, is an important source of time-series variation, as MFN tariffs do not change much within industries over our period.

[29] The ten countries/regions of origin are: Mexico, Rest of Latin America, Canada-Australia-New Zealand, Western Europe, Eastern Europe, China, India, Rest of Asia, Africa, and Other.

[30] This index is similar to the constructed shift-share instrument often used in studies of immigration in local labor markets (e.g., Card 2001; Card and DiNardo 2000; Peri and Sparber 2009), except that it exploits differences

VOL. 103 NO. 5   *OTTAVIANO ET AL.: IMMIGRATION, OFFSHORING, AND AMERICAN JOBS*   1945

Our identification approach is valid as long as industries, like localities, are important conduits for immigrant networks. This is likely to be more true for industries that are geographically concentrated. In Section IVE we focus exclusively on industries that are highly concentrated geographically. Because of localized ethnic networks (Bartel 1989), we would expect that the initial distribution of immigrants in such industries would be an even stronger predictor of future immigration flows.

B. *Effects on Employment Shares*

We begin by estimating the impact of variation in immigration and offshoring costs on the *shares* of native, immigrant, and offshore workers, thereby exploring the relative substitutability of these worker types through the extent to which they displace one another. In Section IVC we will then analyze the impact on the employment *levels* of these groups, which includes the productivity impact of the changing costs of immigration and offshoring. Finally, in Section IVD, we will explore the impact on the *task specialization* of natives and immigrants. Using the same notation as we used in the theoretical model but making industry and time indices explicit as discussed above, we implement (B4) empirically by estimating the following three regressions:

$$(8) \qquad s_{Dst} = \phi_s^D + \phi_t^D + b_{DO}(s_{Ost}) + b_{DM}(s_{Mst}) + \varepsilon_{st}^D$$

$$(9) \qquad s_{Mst} = \phi_s^M + \phi_t^M + b_{MO}(s_{Ost}) + \varepsilon_{st}^M$$

$$(10) \qquad s_{Ost} = \phi_s^O + \phi_t^O + b_{OM}(s_{Mst}) + \varepsilon_{st}^O,$$

where s_{Dst}, s_{Ost}, and s_{Mst} are the employment shares of domestic (native), offshore and immigrant workers in industry s at time t, the ϕ_ss are industry fixed effects, the ϕ_ts are time effects, and the ε_{st}s are (potentially) serially correlated errors. Estimation is based on 2SLS using the instruments $(Tariffs)_{st}$ for s_{Ost} and $(Imputed\_s_M)_{st}$ for s_{Mst} as described in Section IVA.

Equation (8) estimates the impact of variation in the offshoring and immigration share, driven by push and cost factors as captured by $(Tariffs)_{st}$ and $(Imputed\_s_M)_{st}$, on native workers' share of employment. By including industry effects we only exploit variation within industries over time. We also control for common-year effects and, as a result, any time-invariant difference in offshoring costs across industries and any common trend in offshoring costs over time will not contribute to the identification of the effect. Equation (9) estimates the effect of variation in offshoring costs on the immigrant share of employment and, conversely, equation (10) estimates the effect on the share of offshore workers due to a decrease in immigration costs.

Specifications (8) to (10) combine two desirable features. First, the coefficients can be easily interpreted as the percentage variation in native (immigrant/offshore)

---

in the presence of immigrant groups (from different countries) across industries, rather than across localities. There are some recent papers that document the existence of industry- and occupation-specific immigrant networks (e.g., Patel and Vella 2007), arising in part due to the geographic concentration of industries.

1946   THE AMERICAN ECONOMIC REVIEW   AUGUST 2013

TABLE 2—EFFECTS OF OFFSHORING AND IMMIGRATION ON EMPLOYMENT SHARES

	Native share of employment				Immigrant share of employment		Offshore share of employment	
	2SLS		OLS		2SLS	OLS	2SLS	OLS
Specifications	IV, One instrument (1)	IV, One instrument (2)	Direct OLS regression (3)	Direct OLS regression (4)	IV, One instrument (5)	Direct OLS regression (6)	IV, One instrument (7)	Direct OLS regression (8)
Immigrant share of employment		−0.46 (0.39)					−0.53 (0.39)	
Offshore share of employment	−0.79** (0.07)				−0.21** (0.07)			
Industry fixed effects	Yes	Yes	Yes	Yes	Yes	Yes	Yes	Yes
Year fixed effects	Yes	Yes	Yes	Yes	Yes	Yes	Yes	Yes
First stage:	Offshore share of employment	Immigrant share of employment			Offshore share of employment		Immigrant share of employment	
Imputed sector-specific share of immigrants		1.95** (0.55)		−0.91 (1.16)			1.90** (0.48)	−1.03 (0.94)
Sector-specific tariffs	−0.06** (0.01)		0.036* (0.022)		−0.06** (0.01)	0.01* (0.005)		
Observations	464	464	464	464	464	464	464	464
Wald F-stat of first stage	16.6	12.5	NA	NA	16.6	NA	12.5	NA

Notes: The dependent variable in each regression is specified at the top of the relative columns. The units of observations are industry by year. All regressions include industry and year effects. Heteroskedasticity-robust standard errors are reported in parenthesis. In the OLS regressions the standard errors are also clustered by industry.

***Significant at the 1 percent level.
**Significant at the 5 percent level.
*Significant at the 10 percent level.

employment in response to a 1 percent change in immigrant/offshore employment. In addition, since we use $(Tariffs)_{st}$ and $(Imputed\_s_M)_{st}$ as instruments we only rely on variation driven by changes in the costs of immigration and offshoring. These will be our main specifications. Alternatively, we could regress employment shares directly on the constructed measures of offshoring costs $(Tariffs)_{st}$ and ease of immigration $(Imputed\_s_M)_{st}$. This is more consistent with the model, as we can interpret $(Tariffs)_{st}$ as a measure of β_{st} (cost of offshoring) and $(Imputed\_s_M)_{st}$ as an inverse measure of δ_{st} (cost of migration). However the quantitative interpretation of the coefficient will be less straightforward (because the constructed variables have a somewhat arbitrary scale). The significance and sign of the estimates, however, should be consistent. We will use this more direct regression as an alternative specification.

From Section IIIB the predictions of the model are as follows: $b_{DO} < 0$, $b_{DM} \approx 0$, $b_{MO} < 0$, and $b_{OM} < 0$. Table 2 reports the estimated effects. First, columns 1 and 2 show the 2SLS effects of increasing shares of immigrant and offshore workers on the share of native workers. Because the shares must sum to 1, the immigrant and offshore worker shares are collinear, and so we must estimate their effects separately (as the sole regressors in separate regressions). We therefore estimate each effect, with instrumental variables. In column 1 we use the tariff measure as an instrument for the offshore share of employment while in column 2 we use the imputed

VOL. 103 NO. 5   OTTAVIANO ET AL.: IMMIGRATION, OFFSHORING, AND AMERICAN JOBS   1947

immigration shares to instrument actual immigration.[31] The impact of the cost of offshoring (tariffs) and ease of immigration (imputed immigrants) on the explanatory variables, displayed in the first stage of the regressions, is quite significant and has the expected sign. Furthermore, the measures of ease of offshoring and migration are strong instruments, with a Wald F-statistic that is above the Stock and Yogo critical value (15 percent maximal IV size) equal to 8.96 (see last row of Table 2). Columns 3 and 4 show the coefficients from the corresponding "direct regressions." The native share of employment is regressed directly on the sector-specific tariff (column 3) and on the imputed immigration (specification 4). Columns 5 and 6 report the effects of variation in offshoring costs on the share of immigrants, first using the 2SLS specification and then the direct regression with tariffs as a measure of offshoring costs. Columns 7 and 8 show the effect of variation in immigration costs on the share of offshore workers either directly (specification 8) or using imputed migration as an instrument for the share of immigrants (specification 7). The standard errors reported in each regression are heteroskedasticity robust and, in the case of the OLS regressions, they are clustered at the industry level to account for potential serial correlation of errors.

The results are encouraging as the four predictions of the model are mostly matched by the estimates and the 2SLS and the direct OLS regressions provide the same qualitative evidence. Focussing on the 2SLS coefficients, and looking along the first row, we see that increased immigration in an industry has a non-significant effect on the share of native employment in that industry and a negative (but marginally non-significant, with a p-value of 0.18) effect on the share of offshore employment (recall that the model predicted no effect on natives and a negative effect on immigrants, respectively). Stronger results are obtained in the second row, which shows that there is a negative effect of offshore employment on the share of both native and immigrant workers in an industry, exactly as predicted in (6). Each of the estimates is significantly different from zero. Similarly, the direct regression coefficients show that an increase in the cost of offshoring (tariffs) has a positive and significant effect on the native and immigrant share of employment, while an increase in the ease of immigration has a negative (but non-significant) effect on the offshore share and a non-significant effect on the native share of employment.

These findings are in line with our model. More generally, they suggest that immigrants and natives compete more with offshore workers than with one another. This is consistent with a large part of the labor literature (e.g., Card 2001; or Ottaviano and Peri 2012) that does not find a significant negative impact of immigrants on native employment. Moreover, the decline in offshoring costs is shown to have a significant impact on the employment share of natives and immigrants, but one that is quantitatively larger for the first group. This suggests that over the eight years considered (2000–2007) the tasks that were offshored were more likely to be at the high end of the task spectrum for offshore workers.

---

[31] Using the definition of offshore employment that is inclusive of arm's length offshoring we obtain an effect of off-shoring on native share—in a specification as that in column 1—equal to −0.71, (with a standard error of 0.18). The estimated effect on the immigrant share—in a specification as that in column 5—is −0.29, (with a standard error of 0.18).

1948   THE AMERICAN ECONOMIC REVIEW   AUGUST 2013

TABLE 3—EFFECTS OF OFFSHORING AND IMMIGRATION ON EMPLOYMENT LEVELS

	ln(native employment)				ln(immigrant employment)		ln(offshore employment)	
	2SLS		OLS		2SLS	OLS	2SLS	OLS
Specifications	IV, One instrument (1)	IV, One instrument (2)	Direct OLS regression (3)	Direct OLS regression (4)	IV, One instrument (5)	Direct OLS regression (6)	IV, One instrument (7)	Direct OLS regression (8)
ln(Immigrant employment)		0.41* (0.22)					0.15 (0.43)	
ln(Offshore employment)	−0.12 (0.12)				−0.23 (0.21)			
Industry fixed effects	Yes	Yes	Yes	Yes	Yes	Yes	Yes	Yes
Year fixed effects	Yes	Yes	Yes	Yes	Yes	Yes	Yes	Yes
First stage:	ln(Offshore employment)	ln(Immigrant employment)			ln(Offshore employment)		ln(Immigrant employment)	
Imputed sector-specific share of immigrants		14.07** (4.76)		5.83 (3.69)			14.07** (4.76)	2.07 (9.15)
Sector-specific tariffs	−0.032** (0.008)		0.004 (0.008)		−0.032** (0.007)	0.007 (0.010)		
Observations	464	464	464	464	464	464	464	464
Wald F-stat of first stage	17.2	8.7	NA	NA	17.2	NA	8.70	NA

Notes: The dependent variable in each regression is specified at the top of the relative columns. The units of observations are industry by year. All regressions include industry and year effects. Heteroskedasticity-robust standard errors are reported in parenthesis. In the OLS regressions the standard errors are also clustered by industry.
  *** Significant at the 1 percent level.
   ** Significant at the 5 percent level.
    * Significant at the 10 percent level.

C. Effects on Employment Levels

Another important implication of our model, highlighted in Section IIIB, is the existence of a "productivity effect" that results from the cost decline associated with hiring immigrant and offshore workers. Such an effect leads to an increase in the aggregate demand for all worker types. This productivity effect, if significant, combined with the effect on shares described in the previous section, should imply a mitigated, or perhaps even positive effect of offshoring on native employment. Additionally, immigration should have a positive effect on native employment.

Table 3, which replicates the structure of Table 2, presents the estimated coefficients from the following four regressions:

$$(11) \qquad N_{Dst} = \phi_s^D + \phi_t^D + B_{DO}(N_{Ost}) + B_{DM}(N_{Mst}) + \varepsilon_{st}^D$$

$$(12) \qquad N_{Mst} = \phi_s^M + \phi_t^M + B_{MO}(N_{Ost}) + \varepsilon_{st}^M$$

$$(13) \qquad N_{Ost} = \phi_s^O + \phi_t^O + B_{OM}(N_{Mst}) + \varepsilon_{st}^O,$$

TABLE 4—EFFECTS OF OFFSHORING AND IMMIGRATION ON TOTAL EMPLOYMENT: THE PRODUCTIVITY EFFECT

	ln(total employment)			
	Method of estimation: 2SLS		Method of estimation: OLS	
Specifications	IV, one instrument (1)	IV, one instrument (2)	Direct OLS regression (3)	Direct OLS regression (4)
Immigrant share of employment		3.87** (1.87)		
Offshore share of employment	1.71** (0.57)			
Industry fixed effects	Yes	Yes	Yes	Yes
Year fixed effects	Yes	Yes	Yes	Yes
Observations	464	464	464	464
First stage:	Offshore share of employment	Immigrant share of employment		
Imputed sector-specific share of immigrants		1.94** (0.55)		7.53** (2.85)
Sector-specific tariffs	−0.06** (0.01)		−0.08 (0.05)	
F-test	16.6	12.5	NA	NA

Notes: The dependent variable in each regression is the logarithm of total (native+immigrant+offshore) employment in the sector. The units of observations are industry by year. All regressions include industry and year effects. Heteroskedasticity-robust standard errors are reported in parenthesis. In the OLS regressions the standard errors are also clustered by industry.

  ***Significant at the 1 percent level.
  **Significant at the 5 percent level.
  *Significant at the 10 percent level.

where N_{Dst}, N_{Mst}, and N_{Ost} are the logarithm of the employment levels of native, immigrant and offshore workers, respectively. Similar to Table 2, columns 1 and 2 show the 2SLS estimates using the cost-driven offshoring and immigration instruments $(Tariffs)_{st}$ and $(Imputed\_s_M)_{st}$. In columns 3 and 4 we show the direct regressions. Similarly, columns 5 and 6 report the effect of offshoring costs on immigrant employment and columns 7 and 8 show the effect of ease of immigration on offshore employment. In Table 4 we then present the estimates for the aggregate employment regression:

$$(14) \qquad N_{Lst} = \phi_s^L + \phi_t^L + B_{LO}(s_{Ost}) + B_{LM}(s_{Mst}) + \varepsilon_{st}^L,$$

where N_{Lst} is the logarithm of aggregate employment in industry s and year t. Again we report the 2SLS estimates (columns 1 and 2) and then the direct regression results (columns 3 and 4). In all specifications the ϕ_ss are industry fixed effects, the ϕ_ts are time effects, and ε_{st}s are (possibly) serially correlated errors. The effects estimated in Table 3 combine the productivity effects with the displacement effects. Regression (14), instead, captures the pure productivity effects of offshoring and immigration at the industry level. A positive estimate of B_{LO} and B_{LM} would imply a positive overall productivity effect of a drop in offshoring and immigration costs. Heteroskedasticity-robust standard errors are reported and in the direct regression estimates we also cluster them by industry.

The results presented in Table 3 are in line with the predictions of the model. Firstly, it is important to note that the first-stage Wald F-Statistics are always above or close to the Stock and Yogo test critical value for weak instruments, equal to 8.96 (15 percent maximum IV size). They are slightly different from those in Table 2 because the explanatory variables are now employment levels (rather than employment shares) but their strength is similar. The employment estimates seem to reveal a positive and significant productivity effect of immigration, and an implied positive productivity effect of offshoring, on native-born workers. A decline of the costs of immigration associated with a 1 percent increase in immigrants produces a significant increase in the employment of natives equal to 0.42 percent (Table 3, column 2) and has no significant effect on the total employment of offshore workers (Table 3, column 7). The productivity effect of offshoring is revealed by the fact that, whereas offshoring unambiguously reduced the share of natives and immigrants in an industry (Table 2, columns 1 and 5), it has no significant effect on the aggregate employment of natives or immigrants (Table 3, columns 1 and 5). Thus, while offshore workers compete with natives and immigrants, their employment seems to generate productivity gains that increase the size of the pie, leading to an overall neutral impact on native and immigrant employment.

Table 4 shows the results from specification (14) which are informative on the size and significance of the productivity effects. The coefficients represent the impact of decreasing costs of offshoring and immigration on the overall size of the "employment pie" to be distributed across workers. As evidenced by the 2SLS results, both offshoring and immigration have positive productivity effects on an industry. The effect is quantitatively larger in the case of immigration.[32] Columns 1 and 2 in Table 4 show that an increase in the immigrant share equal to 1 percent increases aggregate employment by 3.9 percent, implying a significant expansion, again driven by the productivity effect. This is a substantial effect, particularly if we keep in mind that manufacturing employment actually declined over this period. At the same time an increase in the share of offshore employment by 1 percent is associated with an increase in aggregate employment of 1.7 percent. Columns 3 and 4 of Table 4 show the direct OLS regression of aggregate employment on the imputed share of immigrants and on sector-specific tariffs. The regression confirms that an increase in cost-driven availability of immigrants increases the employment of the sector. A decrease in offshoring costs, on the other hand, has a positive, but not significant, effect on employment. The presence of productivity effects due to immigration and offshoring implies that, even taken together, these two forms of globalization of labor have not harmed native employment in the industries most exposed to them. To the contrary, the cost savings obtained from the tasks performed by immigrants and offshore workers have promoted an expansion of these industries relative to others and have ultimately led to increased demand for native workers relative to a scenario in which all tasks were performed by natives.

---

[32]The results on offshoring are broadly consistent with Amiti and Wei (2005), who also find evidence of productivity effects by estimating conditional and unconditional labor demand functions.

D. Effects on Tasks

Finally, we test the model's predictions regarding the effects of offshoring and immigration costs on the complexity of the tasks performed by the three groups of workers. To see whether these predictions find support in the data, we focus on the average rather than the marginal task. Since in the data there is significant idio-syncratic heterogeneity across workers, there is, of course, a region of task overlap between workers of different types (native/offshore and immigrants). It is therefore impossible to define a marginal task in the clear and deterministic way suggested by the model. However, the predictions on average tasks also hold in a probabi-listic environment where individual heterogeneity produces a less sharp and more continuous transition between the tasks performed by native, offshore, and immi-grant workers. Therefore, we test the model's predictions in terms of average tasks. Formally, we compute the average task for each group by weighting the individual indices of complexity described in Section II by hours worked.

Given that complexity measures are only available for natives and immigrants, we implement (B5) empirically for these two groups by estimating the following two regressions:

$$(15) \qquad I_{Dst} = \phi_s^D + d_{DO}(s_{Ost}) + d_{DI}(s_{Mst}) + \varepsilon_{st}^D$$

$$(16) \qquad I_{Mst} = \phi_s^M + d_{MO}(s_{Ost}) + d_{MI}(s_{Mst}) + \varepsilon_{st}^M,$$

where the variables I_{Dst} and I_{Mst} in (15) and (16) are the average skill intensities of tasks assigned to natives and immigrants, respectively; s_{Ost} and s_{Mst} are the employ-ment shares of offshore and immigrant workers in industry s at time t; and the ϕ_ss rep-resent industry fixed effects. Finally the ε_{st}s are (possibly) serially correlated errors.

Table 5 shows the results from the 2SLS specifications (upper part of the Table) where we use, as always, the instruments $(Tariffs)_{st}$ and $(Imputed\_s_M)_{st}$ and from the direct OLS regressions (lower part of the table). We present the effects on the summary indices of Complexity, I_D and I_M (in columns 1 and 5, respectively), as well as the effect on Cognitive Intensity (column 2), Communication Intensity (col-umn 3), and Non-Manual Intensity (the inverse of the Manual index, in column 4) separately. We focus on the 2SLS results, reported in the first and second row. The direct regression confirms those estimates. In this case the coefficients on offshor-ing and immigration are estimated in the same regression (since now we do not face the issue of collinearity of shares). The first stage F-Statistics are well above the critical value for the Stock and Yogo test (15 percent maximal IV size) which in the case of two endogenous variables and two instruments is 4.58. The first column of the upper part of Table 5 shows a positive and significant effect of offshoring and no effect of immigration on the Complexity of native tasks. The same holds true for their Communication Intensity, Cognitive Intensity, and Non-Manual Intensity. Again this is consistent with the predictions of the theoretical model. [33] Columns 5

---

[33] The lower part of Table 5 shows the corresponding direct regression coefficients. We see a significant effect of decreasing tariffs on native task complexity and no significant effect of migration. The magnitudes of the coef-ficients cannot be interpreted as the instruments have somewhat arbitrary scale.

1952   THE AMERICAN ECONOMIC REVIEW   *AUGUST 2013*

TABLE 5—EFFECTS OF OFFSHORING AND IMMIGRATION ON THE SKILL INTENSITY OF NATIVE AND IMMIGRANT TASKS

Specification	Complexity index, natives (1)	Cognitive index, natives (2)	Communication index, natives (3)	Non-manual index, natives (4)	Complexity index, foreign-born (5)	Difference in complexity natives-foreign born (6)
Panel A. 2SLS estimates						
Immigrant share	0.04	0.04	0.12	0.01		
of employment	(0.66)	(0.43)	(0.510)	(0.22)		
Offshore share of	0.64*	0.38**	0.41*	0.26*	−0.10	0.75**
employment	(0.33)	(0.19)	(0.22)	(0.15)	(0.52)	(0.31)
First stage						
F-statistics	5.10	5.10	5.10	5.10	8.45	8.45
Panel B. Direct OLS estimate						
Imputed sector-	−0.73	−0.41	−0.37	−0.31		
specific share	(0.72)	(0.45)	(0.55)	(0.32)		
of immigrants						
Sector-specific	−0.028**	−0.017**	−0.019**	−0.011**	0.04	0.033
tariffs	(0.012)	(0.007)	(0.008)	(0.005)	(0.20)	(0.020)
Observations	464	464	464	464	464	464

Notes: Panel A shows the coefficients from the 2SLS estimation using imputed sector-specific share of immigrants and sector-specific tariffs as instrument. Panel B shows the results of a direct regression of the dependent variables on the instruments. The units of observations are industry by year. All regressions include industry fixed effects. Standard errors are heteroskedasticity robust and clustered at the sector level.

** Significant at the 5 percent level.

* Significant at the 10 percent level.

and 6 indicate that offshoring has little effect on the complexity of immigrant tasks but, at the same time, has a large positive impact on the gap between immigrant and native tasks $(I_D - I_M)$. This suggests that offshore workers affect native workers mainly by pushing them into more complex tasks, effectively hollowing out the task spectrum. This is consistent with the results found on employment shares (of natives and immigrants) in Table 2. These results are also consistent with Hummels et al. (2010) who find a positive effect of offshoring on the productivity of highly educated workers and with Harrison and McMillan (2011) who find that "vertical" offshoring has positive employment effects, mainly for the highly skilled. In summary we can say that offshoring leads to increased polarization in native and immigrant specialization, mainly by pushing natives toward more complex jobs. This effect is not negligible. Since the standard deviation across sectors in the share of offshore workers during the period is around 14 percent, when multiplied by the coefficient on the complexity index estimated in column 1 we find a difference in task complexity relative to natives of 9 percent. This is about half of the standard deviation of complexity across sectors, and also half of the average difference in complexity of tasks performed by immigrants and natives.

E. *Extensions and Checks*

Before concluding we briefly discuss the implications of three key assumptions of our theoretical framework. A more detailed discussion of these issues and details on the empirical results can be found in the online Appendix of the paper.

First, ours is a model of "vertical" offshoring. Namely, offshoring takes place in order to reduce costs and the intermediate tasks performed by offshore workers are combined to produce a good sold at home. Hence our implications on the impact of offshoring on native tasks should work better in industries that are engaged primarily in vertical offshoring. This is confirmed when we split the sample between industries that re-import a large share of their offshore production (vertical-offshoring) versus those that sell a larger share abroad (horizontal-offshoring). When running a specification as in (1) in Table 5, and focusing only on sectors doing vertical-offshoring, the impact of offshore employment on native complexity is large and significant (1.10 with standard error of 0.59). In contrast, the same regression run using the sample of sectors doing horizontal offshoring produces non-significant estimates (0.17 with standard error of 0.23).[34]

Second, whereas we assumed perfect mobility of workers, in the presence of imperfect mobility or barriers to transferring skills from one industry to another a portion of the industry-specific effects of immigration and offshoring could be captured by wage rather than employment differentials. In particular, while the US labor force is mobile geographically, as well as across industries, in the short run wages may not be perfectly equalized. We check directly whether industry wages are affected by offshoring and immigration by running a specification like (11), except using the average wage of natives instead of their employment as the dependent variable. The estimates (reported and described in online Appendix, Table A3) do not show any significant effect of offshoring and immigration on wages.

Finally, as discussed in Section IVA, imputed immigration, an instrument routinely used in the immigration literature, is usually constructed using variation across localities rather than industries. As a further check that industry-specific network effects are also driven, in part, by the geographic concentration of an industry, we re-run regression (11) focusing on industries that are particularly concentrated in space. Since our 2SLS approach relies on a strong relationship between the flow of immigrants from a particular country into an industry and the share of US immigrants from the same country already working in that industry, the first-stage regression should show increased power when we consider only highly geographically concentrated industries. Again, this is because new immigrants tend to favor destinations where there are ethnic networks created by previous immigrants (Card 2001; Card and DiNardo 2000; Peri and Sparber 2009). A recent paper by Patel and Vella (2007) also shows a concentration of immigrants by location and type of occupation.

In order to capture the degree to which an industry is concentrated within the United States, we calculate a geographic Gini coefficient for each industry using data on state and industry employment in 2000.[35] Interestingly, the manufacturing sector as a whole is significantly more concentrated than non-manufacturing, with an average Gini of 0.75 compared to 0.72, which bodes well for the validity of the instrument overall. In other words, an immigrant's decision regarding which industry to work in may overlap with their choice of location, strengthening the network effects underlying our IV approach. We therefore take the manufacturing average as our threshold and reproduce the first-stage regression using only

---

[34]The details of the empirical analysis and the exact definition of the variables are in the online Appendix.
[35]These employment data are available for download from the US Bureau of Labor Statistics website.

1954 THE AMERICAN ECONOMIC REVIEW *AUGUST 2013*

TABLE 6—EMPLOYMENT REGRESSIONS FOR GEOGRAPHICALLY CONCENTRATED INDUSTRIES

	ln(native employment)			
	Method of estimation: 2SLS		Method of estimation: OLS	
Specifications	IV, one instrument (1)	IV, one instrument (2)	Direct OLS regression (3)	Direct OLS regression (4)
ln(Immigrant employment)		0.49** (0.22)		
ln(Offshore employment)	−0.12 (0.08)			
Industry fixed effects	Yes	Yes	Yes	Yes
Year fixed effects	Yes	Yes	Yes	Yes
First stage:	ln(Offshore employment)	ln(Immigrant employment)		
Imputed sector-specific share of immigrants		20.96** (8.43)		10.37* (5.46)
Sector-specific tariffs	−0.06** (0.01)		0.08 (0.05)	
Observations	200	200	200	200
F-test of first stage	33.2	6.80	NA	NA

Notes: The dependent variable in each regression is the logarithm of native employment. We only include the manufacturing sectors with Gini coefficient of geographic concentration across states larger than 0.75, which is the average for the Gini in manufacturing. Heteroskedasticity-robust standard errors are reported. In specification (3) and (4) standard errors are also clustered at the industry level.
   ***Significant at the 1 percent level.
   **Significant at the 5 percent level.
   *Significant at the 10 percent level.

those industries with a Gini larger than 0.75, a value that is near the median and so selects nearly 50 percent of the sample.

The corresponding findings are depicted in Table 6. Comparing the 2SLS results in columns 1 and 2 with the results for the entire sample (in columns 1 and 2 of Table 3), we see that restricting the sample to more concentrated industries increases the estimated, average impact of immigrants on native employment (from 0.42 to 0.50). This, combined with the relatively larger first-stage coefficient shown in column 2 (to be compared with column 2 in Table 3) constitutes evidence that our immigration instrument is somewhat stronger for spatially concentrated industries and, for these industries, the productivity effect of immigration is also somewhat stronger.

V. Concluding Remarks

We have analyzed the effects of easier offshoring and immigration on the employment share, employment level, and task specialization of native workers within the US manufacturing sector from 2000 to 2007. There are very few attempts to combine analyses of immigration and offshoring on labor markets. Analyzing each in isolation ignores the possibility that hiring immigrants or offshoring productive tasks are alternatives that are simultaneously available to producers and, in fact, may compete with one another or with hiring a native worker.

VOL. 103 NO. 5   *OTTAVIANO ET AL.: IMMIGRATION, OFFSHORING, AND AMERICAN JOBS*   *1955*

We have modeled and found empirical support for a scenario in which jobs ("tasks") vary in terms of their relative intensity of use of workers' complex skills, while native, immigrant and offshore workers differ systematically in their relative endowments of these skills. When only natives are available, producers will only employ them. When immigrant and offshore workers become increasingly employable, efficiency gains can be reaped by hiring them to perform tasks in which they have a comparative advantage, giving native workers the opportunity to specialize in the tasks in which they exhibit their own comparative advantage. If strong enough, the productivity effect associated with this improved task assignment may offset the displacement effect of immigration and offshoring on native workers' employment.

Despite the widely held belief that immigration and offshoring are reducing the job opportunities of US natives, we have found instead that, during our period of observation, manufacturing industries with a larger increase in global exposure (through offshoring and immigration) fared better than those with lagging exposure in terms of native employment growth.

APPENDIX A. PROOF OF PROPOSITION 1

Sufficient conditions for the existence of $I_{NO} \in (0, 1)$ and $I_{MO} \in (0, I_{NO})$ such that

$$\min[c_D(i), c_M(i), c_O(i)] = \begin{cases} c_M(i), & 0 \le i < I_{MO} \\ c_O(i), & I_{MO} < i < I_{NO} \\ c_D(i), & I_{NO} < i \le 1 \end{cases}$$

are that, as i increases from 0 to 1, $c_O(i)$ crosses $c_D(i)$ once and only once and from below in the interval $i \in (0, 1)$ and $c_M(i)$ crosses $c_O(i)$ once and only once and from below in the interval $i \in (0, I_{NO})$. The first single-crossing condition holds if $c_O(0) < c_D(0)$, $c_O(1) > c_D(1)$, and $dc_O(i)/di > dc_D(i)/di = 0$. The "marginal offshore task" is then implicitly defined by $c_O(I_{NO}) = c_D(I_{NO})$. Substituting for $c_O(i) = w^*\beta t(i)a_L$ and $c_D(i) = wa_L$ gives (3) and $w = w^*\beta t(I_{NO})$. The second single-crossing condition holds if $c_M(0) < c_O(0), c_M(I_{NO}) > c_O(I_{NO})$ and $dc_M(i)/di > dc_O(i)/di$. The "marginal immigrant task" is then implicitly defined by $c_M(I_{MO}) = c_O(I_{MO})$. Substituting for $c_M(i) = w^*\delta\tau(i)a_L$ and $c_O(i) = w^*\beta t(i)a_L$ gives (4) and $\beta t(I_{MO}) = \delta\tau(I_{MO})$.

APPENDIX B.
EMPLOYMENT LEVELS, EMPLOYMENT SHARES, AND AVERAGE TASKS

Given the allocation of tasks in Proposition 1, marginal cost pricing under perfect competition implies that tasks are priced as follows

$$p(i) = \begin{cases} c_M(i) = w^*\delta\tau(i)a_L & 0 \le i < I_{MO} \\ c_O(i) = w^*\beta t(i)a_L & I_{MO} \le i < I_{NO}. \\ c_D = wa_L & I_{NO} < i \le 1 \end{cases}$$

1956   THE AMERICAN ECONOMIC REVIEW   AUGUST 2013

Then, by (1) and (2), the demand for task i is

$$L(i) = \left[\frac{p(i)}{P_L}\right]^{-\sigma} (P_L)^{-\frac{1}{1-\alpha}} (\alpha p_Y A)^{\frac{1}{1-\alpha}} H,$$

where P_L is the exact price index of the labor composite, defined as

$$P_L = a_L \left\{ \int_0^{I_{MO}} [\delta\tau(i)w^*]^{1-\sigma} \, di + \int_{I_{MO}}^{I_{NO}} [\beta t(i)w^*]^{1-\sigma} \, di + (1 - I_{NO})w^{1-\sigma} \right\}^{\frac{1}{1-\sigma}}.$$

Since $i \in [0, 1]$, P_L is also the average price (and average marginal cost) of tasks. Given Proposition 1, we can rewrite this as $P_L = wa_L\Omega(I_{MO}, I_{NO})$ with

$$(\text{B1}) \quad \Omega(I_{MO}, I_{NO}) = \left\{ \int_0^{I_{MO}} \left[\frac{\delta\tau(i)}{\beta t(I_{NO})}\right]^{1-\sigma} \, di + \int_{I_{MO}}^{I_{NO}} \left[\frac{t(i)}{t(I_{NO})}\right]^{1-\sigma} \, di + (1 - I_{NO}) \right\}^{\frac{1}{1-\sigma}}.$$

This highlights the relationship between P_L and the bundling parameter Ω in Grossman and Rossi-Hansberg (2008), which we encompass as a limit case when σ goes to zero and δ goes to infinity—that is, when tasks are not substitutable and migration is prohibitively difficult. Expression (B1) shows that changes in the migration friction δ and the offshoring friction β that decrease $\Omega(I_{MO}, I_{NO})$ imply improved efficiency in labor usage. This is the source of the productivity effects of immigration and offshoring discussed in Section IIIB.

Taking into account the different marginal productivity of the three groups of workers, the amount of labor demanded to perform task i is

$$N(i) = \begin{cases} a_L\delta\tau(i)L(i) & 0 \le i < I_{MO} \\ a_L\beta t(i)L(i) & I_{MO} \le i < I_{NO}, \\ a_L L(i) & I_{NO} < i \le 1 \end{cases}$$

so that immigrant, offshore, and native employment levels are given by

$$(\text{B2}) \qquad N_M = \int_0^{I_{MO}} N(i) \, di = \frac{1}{w^*}\left(\frac{P_M}{P_L}\right)^{1-\sigma} (P_L)^{-\frac{\alpha}{1-\alpha}} B$$

$$N_O = \int_{I_{MO}}^{I_{NO}} N(i) \, di = \frac{1}{w^*}\left(\frac{P_O}{P_L}\right)^{1-\sigma} (P_L)^{-\frac{\alpha}{1-\alpha}} B$$

$$N_D = \int_{I_{NO}}^{1} N(i) \, di = \frac{1}{w}\left(\frac{P_D}{P_L}\right)^{1-\sigma} (P_L)^{-\frac{\alpha}{1-\alpha}} B,$$

VOL. 103 NO. 5   *OTTAVIANO ET AL.: IMMIGRATION, OFFSHORING, AND AMERICAN JOBS*   1957

where $B = (\alpha p_Y A)^{\frac{1}{1-\alpha}} H > 0$ is a combination of parameters and exogenous variables, and the exact price indices of immigrant, offshore, and native tasks are given by

$$(B3) \quad P_M = a_L \left\{ \int_0^{I_{MO}} [\delta \tau(i) w^*]^{1-\sigma} \, di \right\}^{\frac{1}{1-\sigma}}, \quad P_O = a_L \left\{ \int_{I_{MO}}^{I_{NO}} [\beta t(i) w^*]^{1-\sigma} \, di \right\}^{\frac{1}{1-\sigma}},$$

$$P_D = a_L \{ (1 - I_{NO}) \, w^{1-\sigma} \}^{\frac{1}{1-\sigma}}.$$

Note that N_M is the number of immigrants employed whereas, due to the frictional migration cost, the corresponding number of units of immigrant labor is N_M/δ. Hence, sector employment is $N_L = N_M + N_O + N_D$. The shares of the three groups of workers in sectoral employment are thus

$$(B4) \qquad s_M = \frac{(P_M)^{1-\sigma}}{(P_M)^{1-\sigma} + (P_O)^{1-\sigma} + (P_D)^{1-\sigma}(w^*/w)}$$

$$s_O = \frac{(P_O)^{1-\sigma}}{(P_M)^{1-\sigma} + (P_O)^{1-\sigma} + (P_D)^{1-\sigma}(w^*/w)}$$

$$s_D = \frac{(w^*/w)(P_D)^{1-\sigma}}{(P_M)^{1-\sigma} + (P_O)^{1-\sigma} + (P_D)^{1-\sigma}(w^*/w)}.$$

Finally, the "average task" performed by each group is defined as the employment-weighted average across the corresponding is:

$$(B5) \qquad I_M = \frac{\int_0^{I_{MO}} i N(i) \, di}{N_M} = \frac{\int_0^{I_{MO}} i \tau(i)^{1-\sigma} \, di}{\int_0^{I_{MO}} \tau(i)^{1-\sigma} \, di}$$

$$I_O = I_{MO} + \frac{\int_{I_{MO}}^{I_{NO}} i N(i) \, di}{N_O} = I_{MO} + \frac{\int_{I_{MO}}^{I_{NO}} it(i)^{1-\sigma} \, di}{\int_{I_{MO}}^{I_{NO}} t(i)^{1-\sigma} \, di}$$

$$I_D = I_{NO} + \frac{\int_{I_{NO}}^{1} i N(i) \, di}{N_D} = \frac{I_{NO} + 1}{2}.$$

REFERENCES

Altonji, Joseph G., and David Card. 1991. "The Effects of Immigration on the Labor Market Outcomes of Less-Skilled Natives." In *Immigration, Trade, and the Labor Market,* edited by John M. Abowd and Richard B. Freeman, 201–34. Chicago: University of Chicago Press.

►**Amiti, Mary, and Shang-Jin Wei.** 2005. "Fear of Service Outsourcing: Is It Justified?" *Economic Policy* 20 (42): 307–39.

Antecol, Heather, Deborah A. Cobb-Clark, and Stephen J. Trejo. 2001. "Immigration Policy and the Skills of Immigrants to Australia, Canada, and the United States." Claremont Colleges Working Paper 2001-26.

►**Antràs, Pol.** 2003. "Firms, Contracts, and Trade Structure." *Quarterly Journal of Economics* 118 (4): 1375–1418.

►**Antràs, Pol, Luis Garicano, and Esteban Rossi-Hansberg.** 2006. "Offshoring in a Knowledge Economy." *Quarterly Journal of Economics* 121 (1): 31–77.

►**Autor, David H., Lawrence F. Katz, and Melissa S. Kearney.** 2006. "The Polarization of the US Labor Market." *American Economic Review* 96 (2): 189–94.

►**Autor, David H., Frank Levy, and Richard J. Murnane.** 2003. "The Skill Content of Recent Technological Change: An Empirical Exploration." *Quarterly Journal of Economics* 118 (4): 1279–1333.

Barba Navaretti, Giorgio, Giuseppe Bertola, and Alessandro Sembenelli. 2008. "Offshoring and Immigrant Employment: Firm-Level Theory and Evidence." Centro Studi Luca d'Agliano Development Studies Working Paper 245.

►**Bartel, Ann P.** 1989. "Where Do the New US Immigrants Live?" *Journal of Labor Economics* 7 (4): 371–91.

Becker, Sascha O., Karolina Ekholm, and Marc-Andreas Muendler. 2009. "Offshoring and the Onshore Composition of Tasks and Skills." Centre for Economic Policy Research Discussion Paper 7391.

Blanchard, Emily, and Gerald Willmann. 2011. "Trade, Education, and the Shrinking Middle Class." http://old-hha.asb.dk/nat/philipp/iei/2010/willmann.pdf.

Blinder, Alan S. 2007. "How many US Jobs might Be Offshorable?" Princeton University Center for Economic Policy Studies Working Paper 142.

►**Borjas, George J.** 2003. "The Labor Demand Curve Is Downward Sloping: Reexamining the Impact of Immigration on the Labor Market." *Quarterly Journal of Economics* 118 (4): 1335–74.

Bureau of Economic Analysis. 2000–2007. "U.S. Direct Investment Abroad, Majority-Owned Nonbank Foreign Affiliates." http://www.bea.gov/ (accessed February 10, 2010).

►**Butcher, Kristin F., and John DiNardo.** 2002. "The Immigrant and Native-Born Wage Distributions: Evidence from United States Censuses." *Industrial and Labor Relations Review* 56 (1): 97–121.

►**Card, David.** 2001. "Immigrant Inflows, Native Outflows, and the Local Labor Market Impacts of Higher Immigration." *Journal of Labor Economics* 19 (1): 22–64.

►**Card, David.** 2009. "Richard T. Ely Lecture: Immigration and Inequality." *American Economic Review* 99 (2): 1–21.

►**Card, David, and John DiNardo.** 2000. "Do Immigrant Inflows Lead to Native Outflows?" *American Economic Review* 90 (2): 360–67.

Chassamboulli, Andri, and Theodore Palivos. 2010. "'Give Me Your Tired, Your Poor,' so I Can Prosper: Immigration in Search Equilibrium." http://mpra.ub.uni-muenchen.de/32379/1/12-10.pdf.

►**Chiswick, Barry R., Yew Liang Lee, and Paul W. Miller.** 2005. "Immigrant Earnings: A Longitudinal Analysis." *Review of Income and Wealth* 51 (4): 485–503.

►**Costinot, Arnaud.** 2009. "An Elementary Theory of Comparative Advantage." *Econometrica* 77 (4): 1165–92.

►**Costinot, Arnaud, and Jonathan Vogel.** 2010. "Matching and Inequality in the World Economy." *Journal of Political Economy* 118 (4): 747–86.

►**Crinò, Rosario.** 2010. "Service Offshoring and White-Collar Employment." *Review of Economic Studies* 77 (2): 595–632.

Feenstra, Robert C., and Gordon H. Hanson. 1996. "Foreign Investment, Outsourcing and Relative Wages." In *The Political Economy of Trade Policy: Papers in Honor of Jagdish Bhagwati,* edited by Robert Feenstra, Gene Grossman, and Douglas Irwin, 89–128. Cambridge, MA: MIT Press.

Feenstra, Robert C., and Gordon H. Hanson. 1999. "The Impact of Outsourcing and High-Technology Capital on Wages: Estimates for the United States, 1979–1990." *Quarterly Journal of Economics* 114 (3): 907–40.

Feenstra, Robert C., John Romalis, and Peter K. Schott. 2002. "US Imports, Exports and Tariff Data." Unpublished.

►**Goos, Maarten, and Alan Manning.** 2007. "Lousy and Lovely Jobs: The Rising Polarization of Work in Britain." *Review of Economics and Statistics* 89 (1): 118–33.

►**Goos, Maarten, Alan Manning, and Anna Salomons.** 2009. "Job Polarization in Europe." *American Economic Review* 99 (2): 58–63.

►**Grossman, Gene M.** 2004. "The Distribution of Talent and the Pattern and Consequences of International Trade." *Journal of Political Economy* 112 (1): 209–39.

▶Grossman, Gene M., and Giovanni Maggi. 2000. "Diversity and Trade." *American Economic Review* 90 (5): 1255–75.

▶Grossman, Gene M., and Esteban Rossi-Hansberg. 2008. "Trading Tasks: A Simple Theory of Offshoring." *American Economic Review* 98 (5): 1978–97.

▶Harrison, Ann, and Margaret McMillan. 2011. "Offshoring Jobs? Multinationals and US Manufacturing Employment." *Review of Economics and Statistics* 93 (3): 857–75.

▶Hendricks, Lutz. 2002. "How Important Is Human Capital for Development? Evidence from Immigrant Earnings." *American Economic Review* 92 (1): 198–219.

Hummels, David, Rasmus Jorgenson, Jakob Munch, and Chong Xiang. 2011. "Wage and Employment Effects of Outsourcing: Evidence from Danish Matched Worker-Firm Data." National Bureau of Economic Research Working Paper 17496.

Jensen, Bradford J., and Lori G. Kletzer. 2007. "Measuring Tradable Services and the Task Content of Offshorable Services Jobs." http://www.irle-demo.berkeley.edu/events/fall08/kletzer/Kletzer_Job_task_content_080408.pdf (accessed February 14, 2010).

Jones, Ronald W., and Henryk Kierzkowski. 1990. "The Role of Services in Production and International Trade: A Theoretical Framework." In *The Political Economy of International Trade, Essays in Honor of Robert E. Baldwin*, edited by Ronald W. Jones and Anne O. Krueger, 31–48. New York: Basil Blackwell.

Katz, Lawrence F., and David H. Autor. 1999. "Changes in the Wage Structure and Earnings Inequality." In *Handbook of Labor Economics*, Vol. 3, Part A, edited by Orley C. Ashenfelter and David Card, 1463–1555. New York: Elsevier.

Kremer, Michael, and Eric Maskin. 2006. "Globalization and Inequality." Harvard University, Weatherhead Center for International Affairs Working Paper 2008-0087.

Levy, Frank, and Richard J. Murnane. 2006. "How Computerized Work and Globalization Shape Human Skill Demands." http://web.mit.edu/ipc/publications/pdf/05-006.pdf.

▶Manning, Alan. 2004. "We Can Work It Out: The Impact of Technological Change on the Demand for Low-Skill Workers." *Scottish Journal of Political Economy* 51 (5): 581–608.

▶Monte, Ferdinando. 2011. "Skill Bias, Trade, and Wage Dispersion." *Journal of International Economics* 83 (2): 202–18.

▶Nocke, Volker, and Stephen Yeaple. 2008. "An Assignment Theory of Foreign Direct Investment." *Review of Economic Studies* 75 (2): 529–57.

▶Ohnsorge, Franziska, and Daniel Trefler. 2007. "Sorting It Out: International Trade with Heterogeneous Workers." *Journal of Political Economy* 115 (5): 868–92.

▶Olney, William W. 2012. "Offshoring, Immigration, and the Native Wage Distribution." *Canadian Journal of Economics* 45 (3): 830–56.

▶Ottaviano, Gianmarco I. P., and Giovanni Peri. 2012. "Rethinking the Effect of Immigration on Wages." *Journal of the European Economic Association* 10 (1): 152–97.

Ottaviano, Gianmarco I. P., Giovanni Peri, and Greg C. Wright. 2010. "Immigration, Offshoring and American Jobs." National Bureau of Economic Research Working Paper 16439.

▶Ottaviano, Gianmarco I. P., Giovanni Peri, and Greg C. Wright. 2013. "Immigration, Offshoring, and American Jobs: Dataset." *American Economic Review.* http://dx.doi.org/10.1257/aer.103.5.1925.

Patel, Krishna, and Francis Vella. 2007. "Immigrant Networks and Their Implications for Occupational Choice and Wages." Institute for the Study of Labor Discussion Paper 3217.

▶Peri, Giovanni. 2012. "The Effect of Immigration on Productivity: Evidence from US States." *Review of Economics and Statistics* 94 (1): 348–58.

▶Peri, Giovanni, and Chad Sparber. 2009. "Task Specialization, Immigration, and Wages." *American Economic Journal: Applied Economics* 1 (3): 135–69.

Ruggles, Steven, Matthew Sobek, Trent Alexander, Catherine A. Fitch, Ronald Goeken, Patricia Kelly Hall, Miriam King, and Chad Ronnander. 2008. Integrated Public Use Microdata Series: Version 3.0 [Machine-readable database]. Minneapolis: MN: Minnesota Population Center [producer and distributor]. http://www.ipums.org.

▶Sly, Nicholas. 2012. "International Productivity Differences, Trade and the Distributions of Factor Endowments." *Review of International Economics* 20 (4): 740–57.

US Department of Labor. 2012. O*NET survey, version 11.0, http://www.onetcenter.org/ (accessed August 27, 2012).

Wright, Greg C. 2012. "Revisiting the Employment and Wage Impacts of Offshoring." http://gregcwright.weebly.com/uploads/8/2/7/5/8275912/wright_offemp_june.pdf (accessed July 18, 2009).

Xu, YingYing. 2006. "Global Tariff Database." PhD diss. University of California, Davis.

▶Yeaple, Stephen Ross. 2005. "A Simple Model of Firm Heterogeneity, International Trade, and Wages." *Journal of International Economics* 65 (1): 1–20.

This article has been cited by:

1. David Hummels, Rasmus Jørgensen, Jakob Munch, Chong Xiang. 2014. The Wage Effects of Offshoring: Evidence from Danish Matched Worker-Firm Data. *American Economic Review* **104**:6, 1597-1629. [Abstract] [View PDF article] [PDF with links]

Printed in the United States
by Baker & Taylor Publisher Services